ECONOMETRICS

Second Edition

Ronald J. Wonnacott
Department of Economics
University of Western Ontario

Thomas H. Wonnacott
Department of Mathematics
University of Western Ontario

JOHN WILEY & SONS
New York • Chichester • Brisbane • Toronto • Singapore

Library of Congress Cataloging in Publication Data:

Wonnacott, Ronald J
Econometrics.

(Wiley series in probability and mathematical statistics)
Includes bibliographical references and index.
1. Econometries. I. Wonnacott, Thomas H., 1935– joint author. II. Title.
HB139.W66 1979 330′.01′8 78-31257
ISBN 0-471-95981-2

Printed in the United States of America

10 9 8 7 6 5

To our great friend and colleague,
the late T. Merritt Brown

PREFACE

This book is written in two parts—elementary and more advanced. Thus, it is designed for an introductory course, followed by a more advanced treatment for the student with better mathematical preparation.

Part 1 can be used for either undergraduate or graduate students; the only prerequisite is a course in elementary statistics covering at least confidence interval estimation for a mean (prior background in regression is not required). The objective here is to provide a very simple presentation of the important statistical concepts used in econometrics—without involving the student in heavy mathematics at this early stage. Hence matrix algebra is never used; in fact, students may take Part 1 without a knowledge of calculus, although those with calculus will have an advantage. Students who cover this material will not become qualified in econometric theory, but they should get a good appreciation of the main problems that econometricians face; also, they will have covered a number of fairly demanding topics, such as Almon lags, Box-Jenkins techniques, two-stage least squares, and structurally ordered instrumental variables (SOIV).

The text in Part 1 is kept simple, with more difficult interpretations and developments reserved for footnotes, starred sections, and the corresponding chapters of Part 2. In all instances, these are optional; a special effort has been made to allow the more elementary student to skip these completely without losing continuity. Moreover, some of the more subtle issues (along with solutions to all problems) are provided in the Students' Manual. Thus, the instructor is allowed, at least to some degree, to tailor the course to the students' background.

Problems are starred (*) if they are more difficult, or set with an arrow (⇒) if they introduce important ideas examined later in the text, or bracketed ( ) if they duplicate previous problems, thereby providing optional exercise only. Answers to odd-numbered problems, along with a glossary of symbols, is provided in the back of the book.

Part 2 is a generalization of Part 1, with the 10 chapters in Part 2 roughly corresponding to the 10 chapters in Part 1; thus, Chapter 16 is a generalization of Chapter 6, and so on. In designing this book, our objective has been to provide maximum flexibility. Therefore, those who wish to teach the whole book can cover Part 1, followed by Part 2, or they can teach the corresponding chapters (e.g., 6 and 16) together.

The prerequisites for Part 2 are calculus and matrix algebra. Vector geometry is also used extensively, and our experience has been that this is a valuable aid to understanding; however, it is developed in this book from first principles, and no previous training is necessary. In Chapter 13, there is a self-contained discussion of statistical distributions—the relation of the normal, t, chi-square, and F; this provides the necessary background for students who may not have taken a previous course in mathematical statistics.

Since Part 2 relies heavily on matrix algebra and vector geometry, it can be used in a first course in econometrics for graduate students with the necessary background in mathematics and statistics; nevertheless, we have been surprised to discover that even students with a reasonably sophisticated mathematical background find the very simple treatment in Part 1 a useful reference. Our experience has been that graduate students in econometrics have a tendency to miss the forest for the trees; they often miss the statistical issues in mastering the matrix manipulations. Hence, many find it very useful, before disappearing into the matrix underbrush, to fully master the basic ideas of Part 1.

Special Note for the Second Edition

In addition to the revision of much of the material in the first edition (including new examples, problems, and bibliography) this edition includes a number of new topics. To cite a few: an entirely new introductory chapter; logit models and estimation of elasticity (Chapter 4); more time series material, including Almon lags, Box-Jenkins methods, and the treatment of serial correlation in both the error and the dependent variable (Chapter 6); principal components, and additional material on specification error (Chapter 15); new material on seasonal adjustment (Chapter 16); more on Monte Carlo (Chapters 6 and 20); and some recent simultaneous equation techniques, including SOIV, LIVE, and FIVE (Chapters 9 and 20).

In this revision, we have made a conscious effort to present the material in a simpler form, subject to the restriction that it not be intellectually diluted. Although we claim no spectacular success in this regard, we nonetheless hope that this edition may be a bit easier to read than its predecessor. A contributing factor is that econometric techniques (especially for estimating simultaneous equations) seem to be defying the academic law that the more advanced a subject, the more complex it must become.

In fact, these techniques seem to be getting somewhat simpler, both in concept and detail, and this should provide a note of encouragement to the student about to embark on a demanding voyage.

It is unfortunate that the English language does not have a sex-neutral pronoun. We find that "he or she" is just too awkward. (Econometrics is hard enough without carrying a burden like that.) So we use "they" when it is possible to pluralize, and where it is not, we use "he" sometimes and "she" other times. We welcome your suggestions for improving this makeshift solution, and look forward to the day when our language arrives at a really satisfactory solution: a new sexless pronoun perhaps?

So many have contributed to this book in its present and previous edition that it is impossible to thank them all individually. However, a special vote of thanks should go, without implication, to the following for their thoughtful reviews: D. A. Belsley, R. G. Bodkin, F. M. Fisher, A. S. Goldberger, W. Haessel, L. Hexter, D. Jorgenson, K. R. Kadiyala, I. B. MacNeill, I. A. McLeod, A. Ullah, G. S. Watson, and T. A. Yancey, and especially our two close colleagues, Robin Carter and the late T. M. Brown. We are also indebted to our students at the University of Western Ontario who have suggested many improvements. Finally, we should like to extend special thanks to three editors: Gerald Papke, for his help in the original development of this book, and P. J. Wilkinson and R. Esposito for their assistance in the production of this second edition.

Ronald J. Wonnacott
Thomas H. Wonnacott

London, Ontario, Canada, 1978

CONTENTS

PART 1 ELEMENTARY ECONOMETRICS

PART 2 MORE ADVANCED ECONOMETRICS

GLOSSARY OF IMPORTANT SYMBOLS

Symbol	*Meaning*	*Important Reference*
I SYMBOLS INTRODUCED IN PART I		
(a) English Symbols		
ANOVA	analysis of variance	p. 111
BLUE	best linear unbiased estimator	p. 28
d.f.	degrees of freedom	p. 32, p. 58, p. 361
e	error term in regression model	(2-23)
$E(\ )$	expected value $= \mu$	(2-21)
$F_{r,\, n-k}$	F statistic on r and $(n - k)$ d.f.	(5-21), (13-37)
H_0	null hypothesis	(2-57)
H_1	alternative hypothesis	(2-58)
iff	if and only if	p. 63
ILS	indirect least squares	p. 263
IV	instrumental variable(s)	p. 255, p. 456
k	number of regressors	(3-13)
$L(\ )$	likelihood function	(2-79), (10-16)
MLE	maximum likelihood estimate(tion)	p. 46
n	sample size	p. 33, p. 333
$N(\ ,\ )$	normal distribution	(10-27)
OLS	ordinary least squares	(2-3)
$p(y)$	probability function of y	(10-5)
$p(y, z)$	joint probability function of y and z	(10-5)
$p(y/z)$	conditional probability function of y, given z	(10-5)

Symbol	*Meaning*	*Important Reference*
$\Pr(a \leq y \leq b)$	probability that y will fall between two specified values a and b	(2-49)
r	simple correlation coefficient, or	(5-5), (5-14)
	number of regressors simultaneously tested	p. 184
r^2	coefficient of determination	(5-29)
$r_{XY/Z}$	partial correlation of X and Y, if Z were held constant	(5-46), (5-47)
R	multiple correlation coefficient	(5-50)
R^2	multiple determination	(5-51), (5-60)
$\bar{R}^2$	R^2 corrected for d.f.	(5-52)
s^2	sample residual variance about regression line, including	(2-44), (12-25)
	sample variance as a special case	(2-91)
s_{XY}	sample covariance of X and Y	p. 251
s_{XX}	sample variance of $X = s_X^2$	p. 253
2SLS	two-stage least squares	p. 292
t_{n-k}	Student's t variable on $(n-k)$ d.f. $= \pm\sqrt{F_{1,n-k}}$	p. 32, p. 368 (5-22), (13-44)
T	time	(6-13)
u	error term	(8-3b)
v	error term, especially in reduced form, or	(8-4b), (18-3)
	perturbation in autocorrelation	(6-15), (6-66)
var	variance	(2-28)
WLS	weighted least squares	(6-5), (16-25)
$X, Y, Z, \ldots$	variables in original form	(2-4)
$x, y, z, \ldots$	variables expressed as deviations from mean	(2-5)
$\bar{Y}$	sample mean of Y	(2-42)
$\hat{Y}$	fitted value of Y	(2-24)
Z	standard normal variable	(2-43)

(b) GREEK SYMBOLS are generally reserved for population parameters, as follows:

α	population regression intercept	(2-23)
β	population regression slope	(2-23)
$\gamma, \delta, \ldots$	population regression coefficients	(3-2)
θ	any population parameter	p. 55
$\hat{\theta}$	sample estimator of θ	p. 55

Symbol	Meaning	Important Reference
λ	Lagrange multiplier, or	p. 68, (19-75)
	variance ratio of errors in two variables	(7-50)
μ	population mean	p. 39, p. 318
$\prod$	product of	p. 49
ρ	population correlation, or	p. 159
	serial correlation of time series error	(6-15)
σ^2	population variance (about regression line, usually)	(2-22), (12-11)
σ_X	population standard deviation of X	(5-9), (7-14)
σ_{XY}	population covariance of X and Y	(7-14), (8-24)
$\sum$	sum of	(2-1)
τ	generalized differencing operator	(6-32), (16-53)
χ^2	chi-square	(13-1)
(c) OTHER MATHEMATICAL SYMBOLS		
$\equiv$	equals by definition	(1-2), (2-5)
$\approx$, $\simeq$	equals approximately	p. 91
$\triangleq$	equals in the limit	(7-21), (7-37)
$\rightarrow$	has a limit of	(2-107)
$\xrightarrow{p}$	has a probability limit of, i.e., is a consistent estimator of, (similar to $\triangleq$ above)	(2-108)
$\sim N(\mu,\sigma^2)$	is normally distributed, with mean μ and variance σ^2	(10-27)

II SYMBOLS INTRODUCED IN PART II

In Part II the symbolism of Part I is retained, but extended and modified as follows: A boldface capital letter such as **B** or **X** represents a matrix; a boldface small letter such as $\boldsymbol{\beta}$ or **x** represents a vector; to avoid too many transpose signs, a vector may be either row or column, depending on the context in which it is introduced. (Usually a set of observations on one variable is introduced as a column, while a set of variables is introduced as a row.) A single entry in a matrix or vector is an ordinary small letter. In Part II the variables x and y may refer either to their actual observed values or deviations from their mean; but as in Chapters 2 and 3 it is recommended that, unless otherwise specified, the y's be regarded as actual observed values and the x's as deviations from the mean.

The superscript hat (as in $\hat{\boldsymbol{\beta}}$) still means "estimated or fitted value (of $\boldsymbol{\beta}$)."

The "first" equation is the one being estimated (or identified).

We do not attempt to explain all the subscripted uses.

Symbol	Meaning	Important Reference
(a) English Matrix Symbols		
$\mathbf{B}$	matrix of coefficients of all exogenous variables in all equations in the system	(18-1), (20-45)
$\mathbf{C}$	linear transformation of $\boldsymbol{\beta}$	(12-36)
$\mathbf{D}$	transformation matrix; after use on GLS model, OLS becomes valid	(16-27), (16-45)
	or diagonal matrix	p.354
$\mathbf{e}$	vector of error terms in regression model	(12-9)
$\mathbf{M}$	transformation matrix; e.g., after use on GLS model, OLS becomes valid	(16-54)
$\mathbf{S}_1$	(Chapter 20 only) observations on all right-hand variables in first equation	(20-7), (20-27)
$\mathbf{U}$	covariance matrix of errors in GLS	(16-3)
$\mathbf{v}_1$	errors in reduced form equation; hence	(19-4)
$\mathbf{V}_1$	matrix of errors in reduced form	(19-17)
$\mathbf{V}$	covariance matrix of $\hat{\beta}$ (except for σ^2)	(12-34)
$\mathbf{x}$	a vector of observations on one exogenous variable, or	(19-13)
	vector of all exogenous variables in the model; hence	(18-7)
$\mathbf{X}$	matrix of observations on all exogenous variables in the model, being comprised of	(12-9), (19-14)
$\mathbf{X}_1$	matrix of observations on all exogenous variables included in the first equation, and	(19-14)
$\mathbf{X}_1^*$	matrix of observations on all exogenous variables excluded from the first equation	(19-14)
$\mathbf{Y}$	matrix of observations on all endogenous variables of first equation, being comprised of	(19-54), (20-45)
$\mathbf{Y}_1$	matrix of observations on all endogenous variables on right side of first equation, and	(19-14)
$\mathbf{y}$	vector of observations on single endogenous variable on left side, determined by first equation, or	(12-9), (19-14)
	(in Chapter 18 only) vector of all endogenous variables in the system	(18-1)

Symbol	*Meaning*	*Important Reference*
$\mathbf{z}$	vector of observations on one instrumental variable; hence	(17-8)
$\mathbf{Z}$	matrix of observations on several instrumental variables	(17-18)
(b) GREEK MATRIX SYMBOLS		
$\boldsymbol{\alpha}_1$	vector of coefficients of all right-hand variables in first equation; hence	(20-7)
$\boldsymbol{\alpha}$	vector of coefficients of all right-hand variables in all equations	(20-29)
$\boldsymbol{\beta}$	(with or without subscript) vector of coefficients of exogeneous variables in regression equation	(12-9), (19-15)
$\boldsymbol{\gamma}$	any linear combination, or	(12-36)
	vector of coefficients of all endogenous variables in first equation	(18-7), (19-54)
$\boldsymbol{\gamma}_1$	vector of coefficients of endogenous variables on right side of first equation	(19-15)
$\boldsymbol{\Gamma}$	matrix of coefficients of all endogenous variables in all equations in the system	(18-7), (20-45)
$\boldsymbol{\Pi}$	matrix of reduced form coefficients	(18-3)
$\boldsymbol{\Omega}$	covariance matrix of $\mathbf{v}$, the errors in the reduced form	(19-52)
(c) DIMENSIONS OF MATRICES		
k	number of regressors in first equation	(12-9)
M	number of exogenous variables in model (usually equal to number of instrumental variables), being the sum of	(18-7), (20-45)
m	number of exogenous variables in first equation, and	(18-7), (20-44)
m_0	number of exogenous variables excluded from first equation	(18-7), (20-44)
n	number of observations in sample	(12-9)
Q	number of endogenous variables in the system, being the sum of	(18-7), (20-45)
q	number of endogenous variables in first equation, and	(18-7), (20-44)
q_0	number of endogenous variables excluded from first equation	(18-7), (20-44)

Symbol	*Meaning*	*Important Reference*
r	number of regressors being simultaneously tested (note also its use as sample correlation coefficient as in Part I)	(20-36), (12-41)
(d) OTHER ENGLISH SYMBOLS		
C_r^2	modified chi-square statistic on r d.f.	(13-24), p. 374
FI/LGV, FI/ML	full information	p. 521
GLS	generalized least squares	p. 427
LI/LGV, LI/LVR, LI/ML	limited information	p. 491
LWV	least weighted variance	(19-50)
PC	principal components	p. 419
3SLS	three-stage least squares	p. 503
(e) OTHER MATHEMATICAL SYMBOLS		
$\|\mathbf{x}\|$	length (norm) of $\mathbf{x}$	(14-11)
$\mathbf{x} \cdot \mathbf{y}$	dot product of $\mathbf{x}$ and $\mathbf{y}$	(14-3)
$\perp$	perpendicular (orthogonal)	(14-13)
$\mathbf{\Pi}_0$ or $\mathbf{\Pi}_*$ (or $\mathbf{B}_0$, etc.)	selected submatrix of $\mathbf{\Pi}$ (or $\mathbf{B}$, etc.)	(18-9), (18-12)
*	(as a matrix element) any nonzero value	(18-22)
$._5371$	.00000371	p. 336
28_4	280000	p. 336
[ ]	a partitioned matrix	(19-16)

III GREEK ALPHABET

Letter	*Name*	*English Equivalent*	*Letter*	*Name*	*English Equivalent*
$A\alpha$	Alpha	a	$N\nu$	Nu	n
$B\beta$	Beta	b	$\Xi\xi$	Xi	x
$\Gamma\gamma$	Gamma	g	$O o$	Omicron	o
$\Delta\delta$	Delta	d	$\Pi\pi$	Pi	p
$E\varepsilon$	Epsilon	e	$P\rho$	Rho	r
$Z\zeta$	Zeta	z	$\Sigma\sigma$	Sigma	s
$H\eta$	Eta	—	$T\tau$	Tau	t
$\Theta\theta$	Theta	—	$\Upsilon\upsilon$	Upsilon	u or y
$I\iota$	Iota	i	$\Phi\phi$	Phi	—
$K\kappa$	Kappa	k	$X\chi$	Chi	—
$\Lambda\lambda$	Lambda	l	$\Psi\psi$	Psi	—
$M\mu$	Mu	m	$\Omega\omega$	Omega	—

PART 1

ELEMENTARY ECONOMETRICS

1

INTRODUCTION

Economics is the study of how and why variables in the economy are related. Econometrics involves measuring these relationships, and using them to predict.

1-1 ECONOMETRICS AND ECONOMIC THEORY

Economists are typically less interested in describing a single variable—like wheat sales—than in describing how two variables are related. For example, how does the interest rate influence investment? Econometrics is the measurement of such causal relationships, either to show how the economy operates, or to make predictions about the future. Thus an econometric estimate of how investment depends on the interest rate will throw light on the effectiveness of monetary policy. Similarly, an estimate of how consumption expenditures depend on income is necessary in order to predict the success of a tax reduction in stimulating employment.

In economics, as in any social science, everything tends—to some degree—to depend on everything else. Thus if we try to explain an economic variable such as consumption (C), we have to recognize that it depends on income (Y), asset holdings (A), and a large number of other variables; that is,

$$C = \alpha + \beta Y + \gamma A + \cdots + e \tag{1-1}$$

where the dots represent the other variables, and e is what is left unexplained, the error term. If for the moment the other variables may be ignored, then the statistical problem is to use observations of C, Y, and A to estimate the structure of this equation, that is, to estimate the parameters α, β, and γ.

But before collecting data on C, Y, and A for statistical analysis, we might well ask: Should not this equation be filled in with a whole list of the other variables that have some effect on consumption? The answer is: Not necessarily. There are two good reasons for simplifying by keeping the list fairly short. First, the more variables that are included, the larger the equation becomes; as a result, there may be an insufficient number of observations to estimate the equation. But even if this estimation problem is not serious, a strong case can be made for keeping relations simple in order to keep them mathematically manageable and avoid a hopeless confusion of detail (similar to the problem we would encounter in driving from New York to Chicago if we used a road map that included every street in every town en route).

Prior to statistical estimation, economic theory plays an important role in simplifying equations, that is, in the specification of which variables (like Y and A) are the most important in determining C, and which are less important. As an analogy, consider the problem facing an astronomer who must explain the orbit of the moon. Since gravity is a universal phenomenon, everything in the solar system, as in economics, depends on everything else—at least to some slight degree. Hence the moon is affected not only by the sun and the earth but also by the other planets. But since the other planets are too small or far away to exert an important influence, for most purposes they may be disregarded, and the orbit of the moon may be explained by reference to the sun and earth only. The gains from mathematical simplification more than outweigh the slight losses in accuracy.

Nevertheless, the inaccuracies in such simplification should not be forgotten, and in some cases they may be very important indeed. For example, some of the outlying planets in the solar system were discovered because the path of other planets could not be explained by the planets already known. A small error remained, which could only be explained by the existence of other unknown planets; these were consequently found by searching the appropriate area determined by the laws of gravity and motion. Examining the error in an economic relationship may be important for this same reason. If it is substantial, then the obvious questions are: How is this error to be explained? Has something important been missed?

In some cases economic theory provides a clearer specification than in others. On the one hand, in explaining the U.S. demand for automobiles, economic theory clearly indicates that a price variable should be included. But should a variable representing the advertising expenditure of the industry be included? Here the theoretical guidelines are far less clear. Is advertising important in influencing the total sales of autos, or does it just reallocate sales between competing firms?

Since many theoretical issues in economics have not yet been resolved (and others perhaps, by their nature, can never be completely resolved), economic theory can seldom give us as firm and clear a specification of variables as we would like. Consequently, econometrics is useful not only in measuring known relationships [i.e., in estimating β in equation (1-1)] but also in determining whether certain relationships even exist. For example, does the asset variable in (1-1) really affect consumption? (Technically, can one reject the hypothesis that γ is zero?) Another role of econometrics is to confirm or reject a relationship that may have been suggested, not by theoretical reasoning, but instead by observing data. For example, an economist working on the U.S. Census of Manufactures may find that for no immediately apparent reason two variables tend to rise or fall together (just as doctors many years ago observed that smoking and lung cancer tended to occur together). Statistical techniques can then be used to confirm this association; then theoretical questions such as "Why?" and "Does it mean anything?" can be addressed.

Since theory and estimation are so closely intertwined, every economist must have a good background in both. In this book we concentrate primarily on estimation.

1-2 SPECIAL STATISTICAL PROBLEMS IN ECONOMICS AND OTHER SOCIAL SCIENCES

In economics, business, or any of the social sciences, a variable such as consumption is often determined by a system of equations, rather than by a single equation. In other words, equation (1-1) alone is not sufficient to explain how consumption and income are related. It is true that (1-1) tells us how consumption depends on income. But we also know that income depends on consumption, according to the familiar relation:

$$Y \equiv C + I \tag{1-2}$$

This simply states that income is, by definition, the sum of consumption and investment expenditures. (For simplicity, we assume a closed economy with no government sector.) Together, (1-1) and (1-2) provide the simplest example of a simultaneous system of equations, or *economic model.*

The equations in an economic model fall into two categories—those that must be estimated, and those that need not.

Equations That Need Not Be Estimated

Equation (1-2) does not need to be estimated because it is an *identity*, true by definition: Income is defined as $C + I$. Accordingly, the usual equality sign is replaced by $\equiv$ which simply means "equals, by definition." Also, because (1-2) is always and exactly true, it includes no error term [such as (1-1) has].

As an example of another kind of equation that need not be estimated, suppose a country levies a 50% tax (T) on all corporate profits (P). Then we may write

$$T = .5P \tag{1-3}$$

Similarly, production engineers in the oil industry may be able to tell us precisely how many gallons of gasoline are produced from 1 barrel of crude oil.

Equations That Must Be Estimated

Equation (1-1) is an example of a *behavioral equation.* Since it reflects the partially unpredictable behavior of consumers, there is no way to exactly nail down this relationship; therefore, it must include an error term, and the unknown parameters must be estimated. As another example, if oil engineers tell us our problem is a complicated one—that Standard Oil uses one refining process, Sun Oil another, Gulf another, and so on, and that each involves a different ratio of gasoline to oil—then the overall ratio can no longer be immediately pinned down, and must be estimated.

Since many of the equations in any economic model must be estimated, econometrics has become a very important tool for the economist. Thus statistics is more important for the economist than for many physical scientists. For example, the physicist may initially be able to write down the required equations, ignoring the stochastic (or chance) error because it is small enough to disregard. To use our earlier example, knowledge of the law of gravity allows a physicist to write down how the orbit of the moon depends on the earth, just as the economist was able to write down (1-2).[1]

Therefore, the first reason for the rapid development of econometrics is that economists have had a pressing requirement for it. Falling objects follow a physical law, but consumers do not; accordingly, their behavior must be estimated by examining how large numbers of consumers have reacted in the past. Since other social scientists also look for patterns in human behavior, there is a growing requirement for statistics in their disciplines as well. It is no surprise, therefore, to observe the development of sociometrics, cliometrics, and similar applications of statistics to other social sciences.

But why have they developed less rapidly than econometrics? One of the most important explanations is the lack of numerical data: While economic and business concepts like inflation and unemployment have numerical

[1] It is not suggested that the task of physicists is easier. Although they may need to estimate less, the equations they must deal with are usually more difficult mathematically.

values, concepts like social class and political power do not. But as numerical information (e.g., voting and questionnaire data) becomes increasingly available to other social scientists, it is likely that they will use statistical techniques more and more. Fortunately, since their objective is also to explain human behavior, the statistical techniques used by other social scientists are often similar—though not identical—to those used by economists.

Psychometrics should be specially noted because, like econometrics, it has developed very rapidly. In fact, there is a very special reason that psychologists have become heavily dependent on statistical methods: They are in the favored position of being able to design and run experiments; thus they are able to collect a rich lode of data. Moreover, because their data may be acquired in this predesigned way, the statistical requirements of psychologists sometimes differ from those of economists and other social scientists who cannot experiment. For example, economists cannot experiment with the economy, doubling the interest rate in order to examine the effect on investment. (Nor can political scientists "try out" a different political or social system on a country in order to compare it to the present system.) Consequently, all the econometrician has to work with is a limited number of historical observations on interest and investment and, if the interest rate has not changed much over the period of observation, then even this information may be of little use. This serious limitation is inherent in most of the social sciences, but it may become less serious in the future. For the first time economists have recently begun to experiment—in particular, to test the effects of various tax systems. In New Jersey, Manitoba, and elsewhere, experiments have been designed to put large groups of people on a negative income tax system in order to examine their reactions.

In conclusion, it is probable that the social sciences will converge somewhat in their use of statistics—for two reasons. First, there is likely to be a weakening in the traditional distinction between the social sciences such as economics and psychology that "have numbers" and those that do not. This follows not only because other social scientists are acquiring more numbers, but also because it is becoming statistically easier to analyze nonnumerical information that can only be ranked (e.g., upper middle class versus lower middle class). Second, experimentation of the sort traditionally undertaken by psychologists is now being introduced in other social sciences like economics.

1-3 A BRIEF OUTLINE

Although we would like to begin by estimating an apparently simple equation like (1-1), this in fact is a very difficult and complicated task. The reason has already been noted: Like most economic relationships, this equation does not stand alone, but is instead embedded in the system of equations (1-1) and (1-2). When this "simultaneous equation problem" was first recognized, it raised statistical problems that could not be solved, even with the most advanced techniques then used by mathematical statisticians. So econometricians, for the most part, had to develop their own theory. While our eventual objective will be to develop this theory of simultaneous equations, we shall begin with a simpler problem—that of estimating one equation that stands alone and is not embedded in a system. In economics such single equations tend to be the exception rather than the rule, and are not too easy to find. We take an example from agricultural economics, which examines how wheat yield depends on fertilizer. The traditional regression theory originally developed by mathematical statisticians is appropriate for estimating such a single equation, and our first task (in Chapters 1 to 3) is to present that classical regression model.

Chapter 4 involves more complicated problems where it seems at first that this simple model cannot be applied. But with an imaginative twist (or transformation), these problems can still be made to fit the classical regression model. Finally, in Chapters 6 to 9, problems are eventually encountered that cannot be dealt with by the classical regression model; accordingly it must be appropriately redesigned.

In Chapter 10 we discuss Bayesian theory, a topic of increasing interest for the social sciences, since it has very important implications for decision making.

Chapters 11 to 20 in Part II are, by and large, a generalization of Chapters 1 to 10 in Part I. While a course can be based on Part I alone, Part II provides a more complete mathematical treatment and hence requires a background in calculus and matrix algebra. (The limited requirements of vector differentiation and vector geometry are taught en route through these chapters.) We have tried to maintain as close a correspondence as possible between the topics in Parts I and II; thus for example, Chapter 12 is a generalization of Chapters 1, 2, and 3; Chapter 16 is a generalization of 6; and Chapter 18 is a generalization of 8.

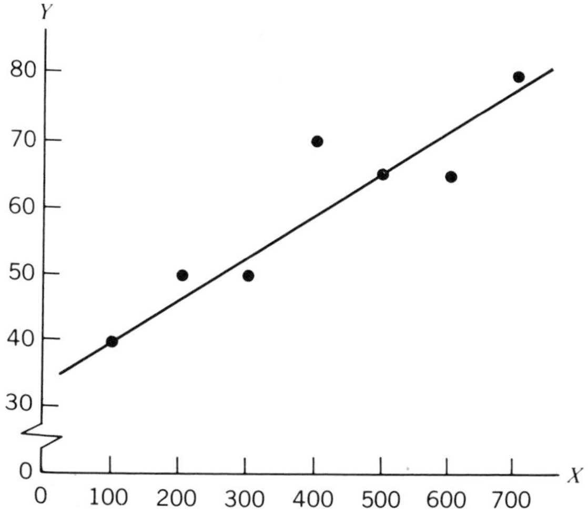

FIGURE 2-2 Yields at various levels of fertilizer application (data from Table 2-1).

how the slope (and other characteristics of this line) can be used in tests and confidence intervals for the underlying population parameters.

Since yield depends on fertilizer, yield is called the *dependent variable* or *response* Y. Since fertilizer application is not dependent on yield, but instead is determined independently by the experimenter, we call it a *factor*, or *independent variable*, or *regressor* X. Suppose funds are available for only seven experimental observations, so that the experimenter sets X at seven different values, taking only one observation Y in each case (see Figure 2-2 and Table 2-1).

TABLE 2-1 Seven Observations of Fertilizer and Yield

X *Fertilizer* (*Pound/Acre*)	Y *Yield* (*Bushel/Acre*)
100	40
200	50
300	50
400	70
500	65
600	65
700	80

2

SIMPLE REGRESSION

2-1 AN EXAMPLE

A simple illustration of regression is the problem an agricultural economist might face: How does fertilizer affect crop yield? As a first step, she[1] might plot the observed yield Y that follows from various fertilizer applications X; the result might be the hypothetical scatter of observations in Figure 2-1. From this scatter it seems clear that fertilizer does affect yield. Moreover, it should be possible to describe *how*, by a straight line relating Y to X. This is called the regression of Y on X; as a simple mathematical model, it provides a brief and precise description or a means of predicting the yield Y for a given amount of fertilizer X.

In the first three sections of this chapter we examine how a straight line is best fitted to a sample of points. Only then do we turn to the question of

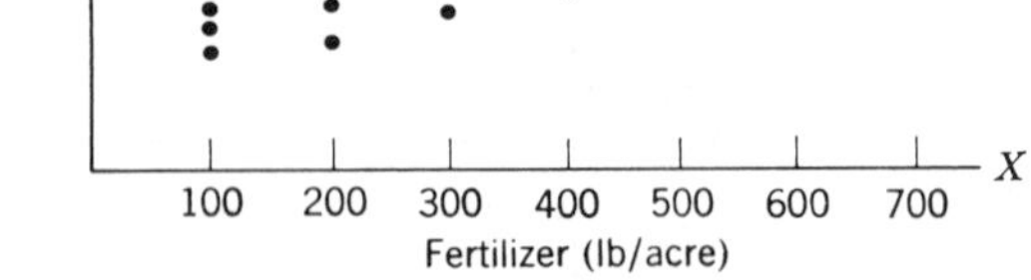

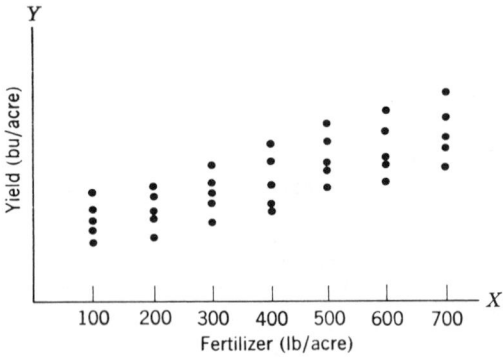

FIGURE 2-1 Observed relation of wheat yield to fertilizer application.

[1] As we mentioned in the Preface, to avoid sexism we have used "he" sometimes and "she" a other times. We avoided writing "he or she" explicitly, simply because we wanted to keep th text flowing smoothly.

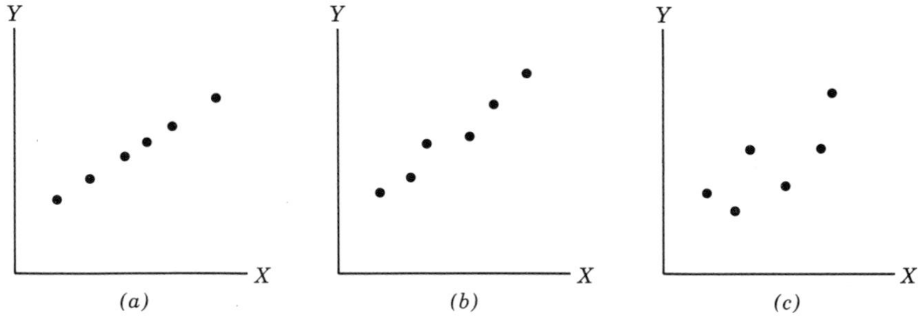

FIGURE 2-3 Various degrees of scatter.

First, notice that if all the points were exactly in a line, as in Figure 2-3*a*, then the fitted line could be drawn in with a ruler "by eye" perfectly accurately. Even if the points were *nearly* in a line, as in Figure 2-3*b*, fitting by eye would be reasonably satisfactory. But in the highly scattered case, as in Figure 2-3*c*, fitting by eye is too subjective and too inaccurate. We need to find a method that is objective, that is easily computerized, and that can easily be extended to handle more dimensions where fitting by eye is out of the question. The following sections, therefore, set forth algebraic methods for fitting a line.

2-2 POSSIBLE CRITERIA FOR FITTING A LINE

It is time to ask more precisely, "What is a good fit?" The answer surely is, "A fit that makes the total error small." One typical error (deviation) is shown in Figure 2-4. It is defined as the vertical distance[2] from the observed Y_i to the fitted value $\hat{Y}_i$ on the line, that is, $Y_i - \hat{Y}_i$. We note that this error is positive when the observed Y_i is above the line and negative when the observed Y_i is below the line. To minimize the total error, consider the following criteria:

1. As our first tentative criterion, consider a fitted line that minimizes the sum of all these errors:

$$\sum_{i=1}^{n} (Y_i - \hat{Y}_i) \tag{2-1}$$

   Unfortunately, this works badly. Using this criterion, the two lines shown in Figure 2-5 fit the observations equally well, even though the

[2] Vertical distance is used as the measure of error because our objective is to minimize the error in explaining Y, and Y is measured vertically.

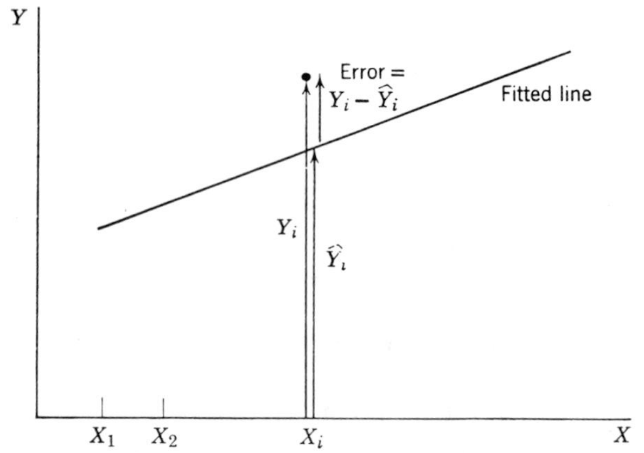

FIGURE 2-4 Typical error in fitting points with a line.

fit in panel (*a*) is intuitively a good one and the fit in panel (*b*) is a very bad one. The problem is one of sign; in both cases, positive errors just offset negative errors, leaving their sum equal to zero. This criterion must be rejected, since it provides no distinction between bad fits and good ones.

2. There are two ways of overcoming the sign problem. The first is to minimize the sum of the *absolute* values of the errors:

$$\sum |Y_i - \hat{Y}_i| \tag{2-2}$$

This method is sometimes referred to as MAD, since it Minimizes the Absolute Deviations; (or as the *least lines* criterion, since it minimizes the

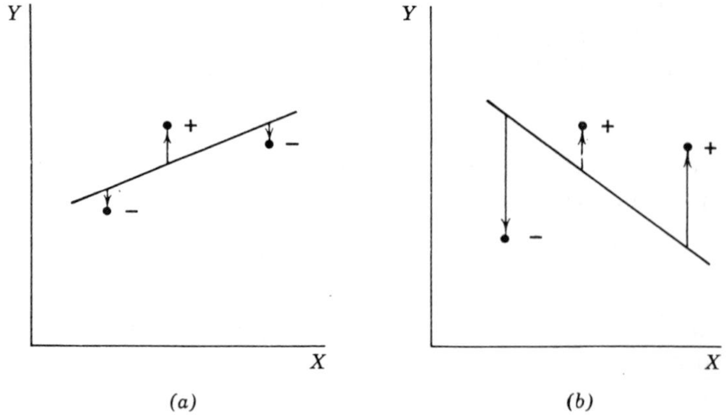

FIGURE 2-5 The weakness of using $\sum(Y_i - \hat{Y}_i)$ to fit a line.

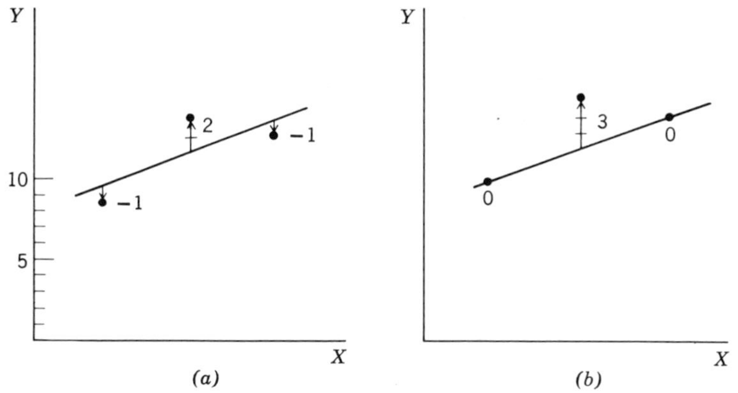

FIGURE 2-6 The weakness of using $\sum |Y_i - \hat{Y}_i|$ to fit a line.

total length of all the deviation lines). Since large positive errors are not allowed to offset large negative ones, this criterion would rule out bad fits like Figure 2-5*b*. However, it still has a drawback. In Figure 2-6 the fit in panel (*b*) satisfies this criterion better than the fit in panel (*a*) (since $\sum |Y_i - \hat{Y}_i|$ is 3, rather than 4). In fact, you can satisfy yourself that the line in panel (*b*) joining the two end points satisfies this criterion better than *any* other line. But it is perhaps not the best solution to the problem, because it pays no attention whatever to the middle point. The fit in panel (*a*) may be preferable because it takes account of all points.

3. As a second way to overcome the sign problem, we finally propose to minimize the sum of the squares of the errors:

$$\sum (Y_i - \hat{Y}_i)^2 \tag{2-3}$$

This criterion is called *least squares*, or *ordinary least squares* (OLS). Its advantages include the following:

(a) In overcoming the sign problem by squaring the errors, least squares produces very manageable algebra and some beautiful analogies to the geometric theorem of Pythagoras.

(b) There are two theoretical justifications for least squares, which will be discussed later: the Gauss-Markov theorem, and the maximum likelihood criterion for a normal regression model.

With these impressive advantages, least squares is the most basic and common technique. We will therefore concentrate on it until the end of Chapter 5.

2-3 THE LEAST SQUARES SOLUTION

The scatter of observed X and Y values from Table 2-1 is graphed again in Figure 2-7*a*. Our objective is to fit a line:

$$Y = a_0 + bX \tag{2-4}$$

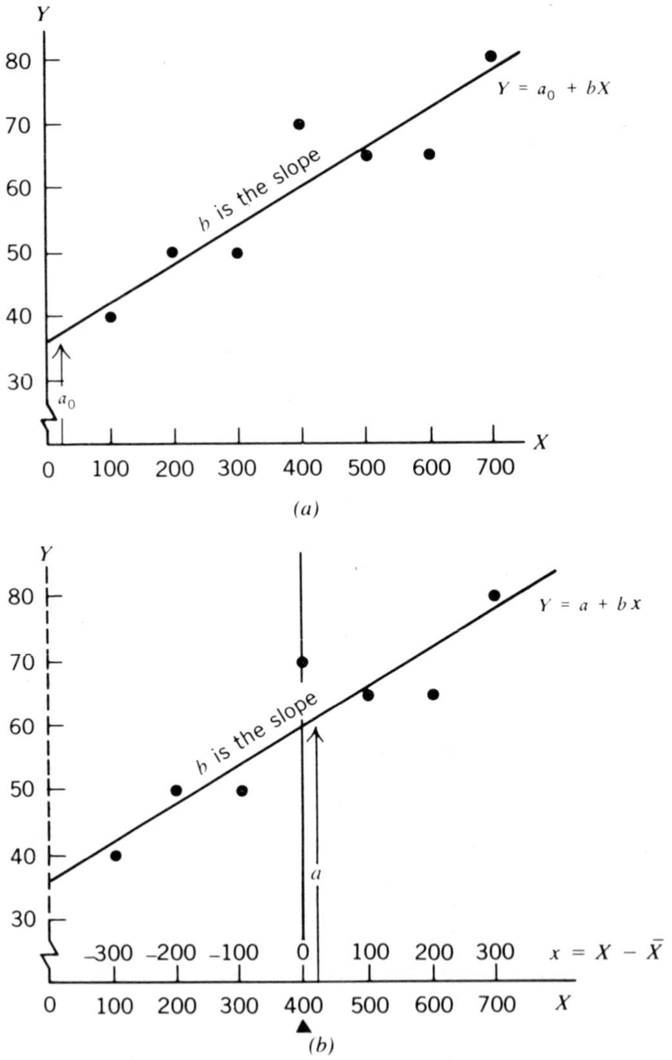

FIGURE 2-7 Translation of axis. (*a*) Regression using original variables. (*b*) Regression after translating X.

This involves three steps:

Step 1. Translate X into deviations from its mean; that is, define[2] a new variable x:

$$x \equiv X - \bar{X} \tag{2-5}$$

This is equivalent to a geometric translation of axis, as shown in Figure 2-7*b*; the Y axis has been shifted right from 0 to $\bar{X}$. The new x value becomes positive or negative, depending on whether X was greater than or less than $\bar{X}$. There is no change in the Y values. The intercept a differs from the original a_0, but the slope b remains the same.

Measuring X as a deviation from $\bar{X}$ will simplify the mathematics because the sum of the new x values equals zero; that is,[3]

$$\sum x_i = 0 \tag{2-6}$$

Step 2. Fit the line in Figure 2-7*b*; that is, the line

$$Y = a + bx \tag{2-7}$$

Fit it to the scatter by selecting the values for a and b that satisfy the least squares criterion; that is, select those values of a and b that

$$\text{minimize} \sum (Y_i - \hat{Y}_i)^2 \tag{2-8}$$

(2-3) repeated

Since each fitted value $\hat{Y}_i$ is on the estimated line (2-7),

$$\hat{Y}_i = a + bx_i \tag{2-9}$$

When this is substituted into (2-8), the problem becomes one of selecting a and b to minimize the sum of squares, that is,

$$\text{minimize } S(a, b) = \sum (Y_i - a - bx_i)^2 \tag{2-10}$$

The notation $S(a, b)$ is used to emphasize that this expression depends on a and b. As a and b vary (as various lines are tried), $S(a, b)$ will vary too, and we ask at what value of a and b it will be a minimum. This will give us our optimum (least squares) line.

---

[2] The symbol $\equiv$ in (2-5) means *equals, by definition.*

[3] Proof:

$$\sum x_i = \sum (X_i - \bar{X})$$
$$= \sum X_i - n\bar{X}$$

Noting that $\bar{X}$ is defined as $\sum X_i/n$, it follows that $\sum X_i = n\bar{X}$ and

$$\sum x_i = n\bar{X} - n\bar{X} = 0 \qquad \text{(2-6) proved}$$

The simplest minimization technique is calculus, and it will be used in the next paragraph. [Readers without calculus can skip this discussion and rejoin us where the resulting theorems (2-13) and (2-16) are set out in the box below.]

Minimizing $S(a, b)$ requires setting its partial derivatives equal to zero. So we first set the partial derivative with respect to a equal to zero.

$$\frac{\partial}{\partial a} \sum (Y_i - a - bx_i)^2 = \sum 2(-1)(Y_i - a - bx_i)^1 = 0 \tag{2-11}$$

Dividing through by -2 and rearranging,

$$\sum Y_i - na - b \sum x_i = 0 \tag{2-12}$$

Noting that $\sum x_i = 0$ by (2-6), we can solve for a:

$$a = \frac{\sum Y_i}{n} \quad \text{or} \quad a = \bar{Y} \tag{2-13}$$

Thus, the least squares estimate of a is simply the average value of Y. Referring back to Figure 2-7, we see that this ensures that the fitted regression line must pass through the point $(\bar{X}, \bar{Y})$, which may be interpreted as the center of gravity of the sample of n points.

It is also necessary in (2-10) to set the partial derivative with respect to b equal to zero:

$$\frac{\partial}{\partial b} \sum (Y_i - a - bx_i)^2 = \sum 2(-x_i)(Y_i - a - bx_i)^1 = 0 \tag{2-14}$$

Dividing by -2,

$$\sum x_i(Y_i - a - bx_i) = 0 \tag{2-15}$$

Rearranging,

$$\sum x_i Y_i - a \sum x_i - b \sum x_i^2 = 0$$

Noting that $\sum x_i = 0$, we can solve for b:

$$b = \frac{\sum x_i Y_i}{\sum x_i^2} \tag{2-16}$$

Our results[4] in (2-13) and (2-16) are important enough to restate;

[4] To be rigorous, it can be proved with second partial derivatives that we actually do have a minimum sum of squares—rather than a maximum or saddle point.

With x values measured as deviations from their mean, the least squares values of a and b are

$$a = \bar{Y} \tag{2-13}$$

$$b = \frac{\sum x_i Y_i}{\sum x_i^2} \tag{2-16}$$

For the data in Table 2-1, a and b are calculated in the first five columns in Table 2-2; (the last three columns may be ignored until Section 2-8). It follows that the least squares equation is

$$\hat{Y} = 60 + .059x \tag{2-17}$$

This fitted line is graphed in Figure 2-7*b*.

Step 3. If desired, this regression can now be retranslated back into our original frame of reference in Figure 2-7*a*. Express (2-17) in terms of the original X values:

$$\begin{aligned} Y &= 60 + .059(X - \bar{X}) \\ &= 60 + .059(X - 400) \\ &= 60 + .059X - 23.6 \end{aligned}$$

$$Y = 36.4 + .059X \tag{2-18}$$

This fitted line is graphed in Figure 2-7*a*.

A comparison of (2-17) and (2-18) confirms that the slope of our fitted regression ($b = .059$) remains the same; the only difference is in the intercept. Moreover, we note how easily the original intercept ($a_0 = 36.4$) was recovered.

An estimate of yield for any given fertilizer application is now easily derived from our least squares equation (2-18). For example, if 350 lb of fertilizer is to be applied,

$$\hat{Y} = 36.4 + .059(350) = 57$$

The alternative least squares equation (2-17) yields exactly the same result. When $X = 350$, then $x = -50$, and

$$\hat{Y} = 60 + .059(-50) = 57$$

TABLE 2-2 Fitting a Least Squares Line (Data from Table 2-1).

(a) Calculations for the Slope b and Intercept a (b) Calculations for the Residual Variance s^2

X	Y	$x = X - \bar{X}$ $= X - 400$	xY	x^2	$\hat{Y} = a + bx$ $= 60 + .059x$	$(Y - \hat{Y})$	$(Y - \hat{Y})^2$
100	40	−300	−12,000	90,000	42.3	−2.3	5.29
200	50	−200	−10,000	40,000	48.2	1.8	3.24
300	50	−100	−5,000	10,000	54.1	−4.1	16.81
400	70	0	0	0	60.0	10.0	100.00
500	65	100	6,500	10,000	65.9	−0.9	.81
600	65	200	13,000	40,000	71.8	−6.8	46.24
700	80	300	24,000	90,000	77.7	2.3	5.29

$\sum X = 2800$ $\sum Y = 420$ $\sum x = 0\surd$ $\sum xY = 16{,}500$ $\sum x^2 = 280{,}000$ $\sum (Y - \hat{Y})^2 = 177.68$

$$\bar{X} = \frac{1}{n}\sum X = \frac{2800}{7} = 400$$

$$\bar{Y} = \frac{1}{n}\sum Y = \frac{420}{7} = 60$$

$$\boxed{a = 60}$$

$$b = \frac{\sum xY}{\sum x^2} = \frac{16{,}500}{280{,}000}$$

$$\boxed{b = .059}$$

$$s^2 = \frac{1}{n-2}\sum (Y - \hat{Y})^2 = \frac{177.68}{5} = 35.5$$

and $s = 5.96$

PROBLEMS

(Save your work in the next three chapters for future reference.)

2-1 Suppose that four randomly chosen plots were treated with various levels of fertilizer, resulting in the following yields of corn:

Fertilizer X (Pounds/Acre)	*Yield Y (Bushels/Acre)*
100	70
200	70
400	80
500	100

(a) Calculate the regression line of yield on fertilizer.
(b) Plot the four points and the regression line. Check that the line fits the data reasonably well.
(c) Explain what the intercepts a and a_0 represent.
(d) Estimate how much the yield is increased for every pound of fertilizer applied—that is, what is the marginal physical product of fertilizer?
(e) If the value of the crop is \$2 per bushel, estimate how much revenue is increased for every pound of fertilizer applied—that is, what is the marginal *revenue* product of fertilizer? If fertilizer costs \$.10 per pound, would it be economical to apply?

2-2 Suppose that a random sample of five families had the following annual income and saving (in thousands of dollars):

Family	*Income X*	*Saving S*
A	8	.6
B	11	1.2
C	9	1.0
D	6	.7
E	6	.3

(a) Plot S on X for each of the families.
(b) Calculate and graph the regression line of saving S on income.
(c) Interpret the intercepts a and a_0.

2-3 Use the data of Problem 2-2 to regress consumption C on income X, where $C = X - S$. Then compare this slope with the slope of S on X in Problem 2-2.

2-4 Suppose that four firms had the following profits and research expenditures:

Profit, P (*Thousands of Dollars*)	*Research Expenditure, R* (*Thousands of Dollars*)
50	40
60	40
40	30
50	50

(a) Fit a regression line of P on R.
(b) Graph the data and the fitted line.
(c) Does this regression line show how research generates profits?

⇒ 2-5 (This problem is designated with an arrow because of its importance to the text that follows.) Suppose that we translate Y as well as X into deviation form (so that $y = Y - \bar{Y}$ and $x = X - \bar{X}$).

(a) Prove that $\sum x_i y_i = \sum x_i Y_i$. Hence, instead of (2-16), we may alternatively calculate b as:

$$b = \frac{\sum x_i y_i}{\sum x_i^2} \tag{2-19}$$

(b) Use (2-19) to calculate b in Problem 2-1. Check that it agrees with the value calculated previously using (2-16).
(c) Draw a figure similar to Figure 2-7 to show the translation of the y-axis as well as the x-axis. What is the new y-intercept? The new slope? Does this mean that the equation of the fitted line is simply

$$y = bx \tag{2-20}$$

*2-6 (Requires calculus.) Suppose that both X and Y are left in their original form, rather than being translated into deviation form.

(a) Write out the sum of squared deviations as in (2-10), in terms of a_0 and b.
(b) Set equal to zero the partial derivatives with respect to a_0 and b, thereby obtaining two so-called "normal equations."
(c) Write out these two normal equations using the data in Problem 2-1, and solve for a_0 and b.
(d) Does the regression line calculated in (c) correspond to the regression previously obtained in Problem 2-1? Which method do you think is easier?

2-4 THE MATHEMATICAL REGRESSION MODEL

So far, our treatment of regression has only involved mechanically fitting a line. Now we wish to make inferences about the parent population from which this sample was drawn. Specifically, we must consider the mathematical model that allows us to construct confidence intervals and test hypotheses.

(a) Simplifying Assumptions

Consider again the fertilizer-yield example. Suppose that the experiment could be repeated many times at a fixed level of fertilizer x. Even though fertilizer application is fixed from experiment to experiment, we would not observe exactly the same yield each time. Instead, there would be some statistical fluctuation of the Y values, clustered about a central value. We can think of the many possible values of Y forming a population; the probability distribution of Y for a given x we will call $p(Y/x)$. Moreover, there will be a similar probability distribution for Y at any other experimental level of x. One possible sequence of Y populations is shown in Figure 2-8*a*. There would obviously be great problems in analyzing populations as peculiar as these. To keep the problem manageable, therefore, we make several assumptions about the regularity of the populations; as shown in Figure 2-8*b*, we assume:

1. The probability distributions $p(Y_i \mid x_i)$ have the same variance σ^2 for all x_i.
2. The means $E(Y_i)$ lie on a straight line, known as the true (population) regression line
$$E(Y_i) = \mu_i = \alpha + \beta x_i \tag{2-21}$$
The population parameters α and β specify the line; they are to be estimated from sample information.
3. The random variables Y_i are statistically independent. For example, a large value of Y_1 does not tend to make Y_2 large; that is, Y_2 is "unaffected" by Y_1.

These assumptions may be written more concisely as:

> The random variables Y_i are statistically independent, with
> $$\text{mean} = \alpha + \beta x_i$$
> and
> $$\text{variance} = \sigma^2$$

(2-22)

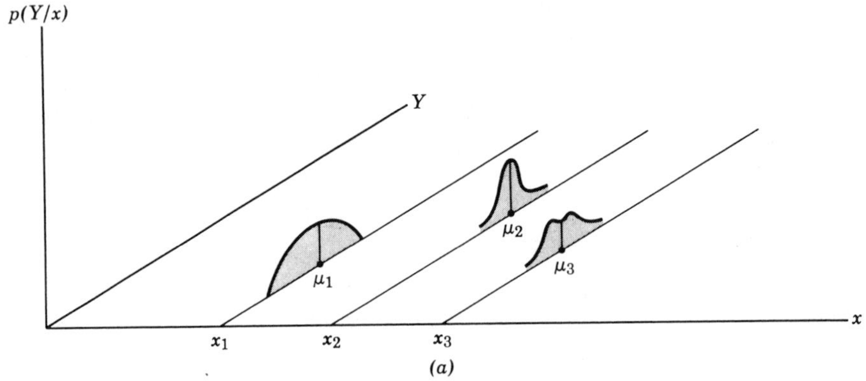

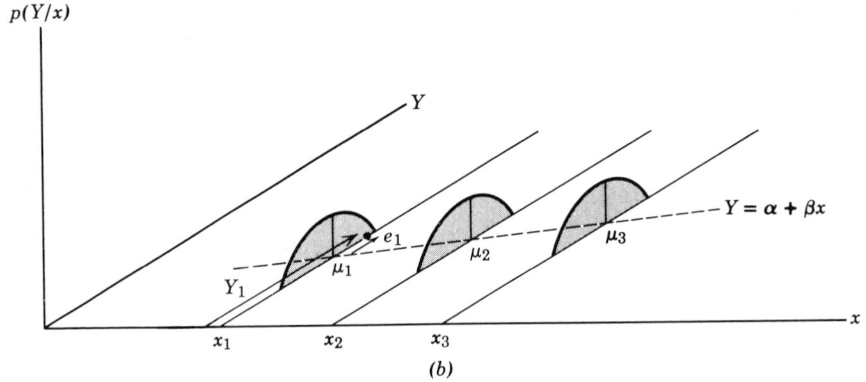

FIGURE 2-8 (*a*) General populations of *Y*, given *x*. (*b*) The special form of the populations of *Y* assumed in simple linear regression.

On occasion, it is useful to describe the deviation of Y_i from its expected value as the error or disturbance term e_i, so that the model may alternatively be written:

$$Y_i = \alpha + \beta x_i + e_i$$

where the e_i are independent random variables, with

$$\text{mean} = 0 \qquad (2\text{-}23)$$

and

$$\text{variance} = \sigma^2$$

We note that the distributions of *Y* and *e* are identical, except that their means differ. In fact, the distribution of *e* is just the distribution of *Y* translated onto a zero mean. To emphasize this, one observed value of Y_1 is shown in Figure 2-8*b*, along with the corresponding value of the error term e_1.

No assumption is yet made about the *shape* of the distribution of e (normal or otherwise), provided it has a finite variance. We therefore refer to assumptions (2-23) as the *weak set*. We will derive as many results as possible from these, before adding a more restrictive normality assumption later.

(b) The Nature of the Error Term

Now let us consider in more detail the "purely random" part of Y_i, the error or disturbance term e_i. Why does it exist? Or, why doesn't a precise and exact value of Y_i follow, once the value of x_i is given? The error may be regarded as the sum of two components:

1. *Measurement error*. There are various reasons why Y may be measured incorrectly. In measuring crop yield, there may be an error resulting from sloppy harvesting or inaccurate weighing. If the example is a study of the consumption of families at various income levels, the measurement error in consumption might consist of budget and reporting inaccuracies.
2. *Stochastic error* occurs because of the inherent irreproducibility of biological and social phenomena. Even if there were no measurement error, continuous repetition of an experiment using exactly the same amount of fertilizer would result in different yields; these differences are unpredictable and are called *random* or *stochastic*. They may be reduced by tighter experimental control—for example, by holding constant soil conditions, amount of water, etc. But *complete* control is impossible—for example, seeds cannot be duplicated. Stochastic error may be regarded as the influence on Y of many omitted variables, each with an individually small effect.

In the social sciences, controlled experiments are usually not possible. For example, an economist cannot hold U.S. national income constant for several years while examining the effect of interest rate on investment. Since the economist cannot neutralize extraneous influences by holding them constant, the best alternative is to take them explicitly into account, by regressing Y on x *and* the extraneous factors. This is a useful technique for reducing stochastic error; it is called multiple regression and is discussed fully in the next chapter.

(c) Estimating α and β

Suppose the true regression $E(Y) = \alpha + \beta x$ is the dotted line shown in Figure 2-9. This is unknown to the statistician, who must estimate it as accurately as possible by observing x and Y. At the first level x_1, if the random error e_1 takes on a negative value, as shown in the diagram, the statistician will observe Y_1 on the low side. Similarly, suppose he has two more observations, Y_2 and Y_3, resulting from positive values of e. The statistician would estimate the true line by applying the least squares method to the only information available—the sample values Y_1, Y_2, and Y_3. He

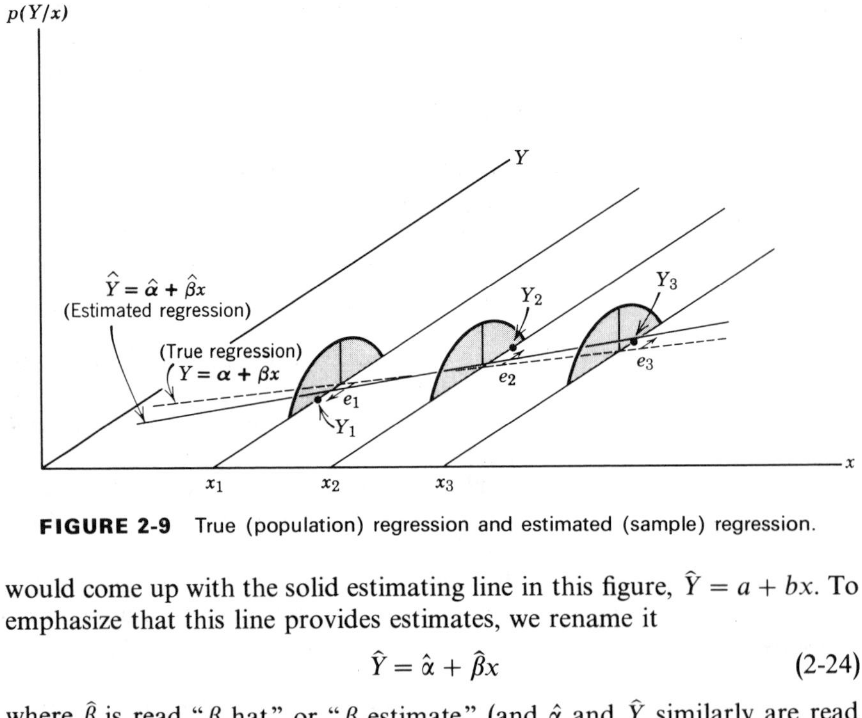

FIGURE 2-9 True (population) regression and estimated (sample) regression.

would come up with the solid estimating line in this figure, $\hat{Y} = a + bx$. To emphasize that this line provides estimates, we rename it

$$\hat{Y} = \hat{\alpha} + \hat{\beta}x \tag{2-24}$$

where $\hat{\beta}$ is read "β hat" or "β estimate" (and $\hat{\alpha}$ and $\hat{Y}$ similarly are read "α hat" and "Y hat").

Figure 2-9 is a critical diagram. Before proceeding, you should be sure that you can clearly distinguish between: (1) the true regression line and its surrounding e-distribution, which the statistician cannot observe and hence is indicated by a dotted line; and (2) the Y observations that the statistician does observe and the estimated regression line he fits to them, indicated by a solid line.

Unless the statistician is very lucky indeed, it is obvious that his estimated line will not exactly coincide with the true population line. The best the statistician can hope for is that it will be reasonably close to the target.

2-5 THE MEAN AND VARIANCE OF $\hat{\alpha}$ AND $\hat{\beta}$

How close does the estimated line come to the true population line? Specifically, how is the estimator $\hat{\alpha}$ distributed around its target α, and $\hat{\beta}$ around its target β? We will show that $\hat{\alpha}$ and $\hat{\beta}$ have the following moments:

$$E(\hat{\alpha}) = \alpha \tag{2-25}$$

$$\text{var}(\hat{\alpha}) = \frac{\sigma^2}{n} \tag{2-26}$$

$$E(\hat{\beta}) = \beta \tag{2-27}$$

$$\text{var}(\hat{\beta}) = \frac{\sigma^2}{\sum x_i^2} \tag{2-28}$$

where σ^2 is the variance of the error e (the variance of Y around the regression line).

Because of its greater importance, we will concentrate on the slope estimator $\hat{\beta}$, rather than $\hat{\alpha}$, for the rest of the chapter.

***Proof of* (2-27) *and* (2-28).** The formula for $\hat{\beta}$ in (2-16) may be rewritten as

$$\hat{\beta} = \sum \left\{\frac{x_i}{k}\right\} Y_i \tag{2-29}$$

where

$$k = \sum x_i^2 \tag{2-30}$$

Thus

$$\hat{\beta} = \sum w_i Y_i = w_1 Y_1 + w_2 Y_2 \cdots + w_n Y_n \tag{2-31}$$

where

$$w_i = \frac{x_i}{k} \tag{2-32}$$

Thus from (2-31) we establish the important conclusion:

$\hat{\beta}$ is a weighted sum (i.e., a linear combination) of the random variables Y_i. (2-33)

From the theory of linear transformations, reviewed in Appendix 2-A, it follows that

$$E(\hat{\beta}) = w_1 E(Y_1) + w_2 E(Y_2) \cdots + w_n E(Y_n) = \sum w_i E(Y_i) \qquad (2\text{-}34)$$

Also, noting that the variables Y_i were assumed independent, it follows[5] that

$$\text{var}(\hat{\beta}) = w_1^2 \text{ var } Y_1 + \cdots + w_n^2 \text{ var } Y_n = \sum w_i^2 \text{ var } Y_i \qquad (2\text{-}35)$$

For the mean, substitute (2-21) into (2-34):

$$E(\hat{\beta}) = \sum w_i[\alpha + \beta x_i] \qquad (2\text{-}36)$$

$$= \alpha \sum w_i + \beta \sum w_i x_i \qquad (2\text{-}37)$$

and noting (2-32),

$$E(\hat{\beta}) = \frac{\alpha}{k} \sum x_i + \frac{\beta}{k} \sum (x_i) x_i \qquad (2\text{-}38)$$

but $\sum x_i$ is zero, according to (2-6). Thus

$$E(\hat{\beta}) = 0 + \frac{\beta}{k} \sum x_i^2$$

Finally, from (2-30),

$$E(\hat{\beta}) = \beta \qquad (2\text{-}27) \text{ proved}$$

Hence $\hat{\beta}$ is an unbiased estimator of β. (Unbiasedness and other attractive characteristics of an estimator—efficiency and consistency—are reviewed in Appendix 2-B).

For the variance, substitute (2-22) into (2-35):

$$\text{var}(\hat{\beta}) = \sum w_i^2 \sigma^2 \qquad (2\text{-}39)$$

and noting (2-32),

$$= \sum \frac{x_i^2}{k^2} \sigma^2 \qquad (2\text{-}40)$$

$$= \frac{\sigma^2}{k^2} \sum x_i^2$$

From (2-30) again, we finally obtain

$$\text{var}(\hat{\beta}) = \frac{\sigma^2}{\sum x_i^2} \qquad (2\text{-}28) \text{ proved}$$

A similar derivation of the mean and variance of $\hat{\alpha}$ is left as an exercise.

---

[5] Since the Y_i are independent, their covariance is zero, and so there are no covariance terms in (2-35).

We observe from (2-32) that in calculating $\hat{\beta}$, the weight w_i attached to the Y_i observation is proportional to the deviation x_i. Hence, outlying observations exert a relatively heavy influence in the calculation of $\hat{\beta}$.

2-6 THE GAUSS-MARKOV THEOREM

A major justification for using the least squares method to estimate a linear regression is the following:

Gauss-Markov Theorem

> Within the class of linear unbiased estimators of β, the least squares estimator $\hat{\beta}$ has minimum variance (is most efficient). Similarly, $\hat{\alpha}$ is the minimum variance estimator of α.

(2-41)

This theorem is important because it follows even from the weak set of assumptions (2-23) and hence requires no assumption about the shape of the distribution of the error term. A proof is given in Appendix 2-C.

To interpret this important theorem, consider $\hat{\beta}$, the least squares estimator of β. We have already seen in (2-33) that it is a linear estimator, and we restrict ourselves to linear estimators because they are easy to compute and analyze. We restrict ourselves even further, as shown in Figure 2-10; within this set of linear estimators we consider only the limited class that is unbiased. The least squares estimator not only is in this class, according to (2-27), but also, of all the estimators in this class, it has the minimum

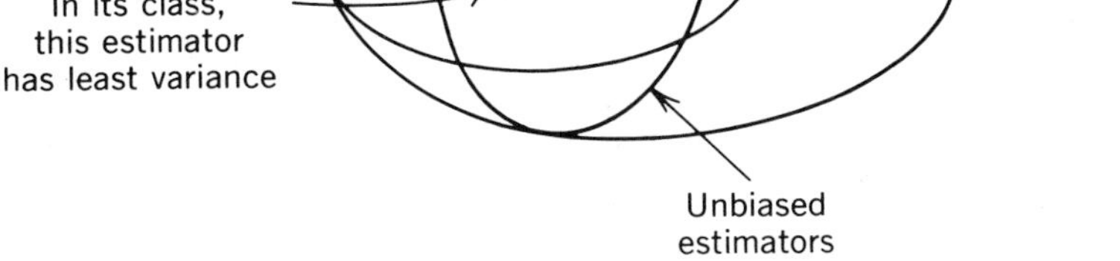

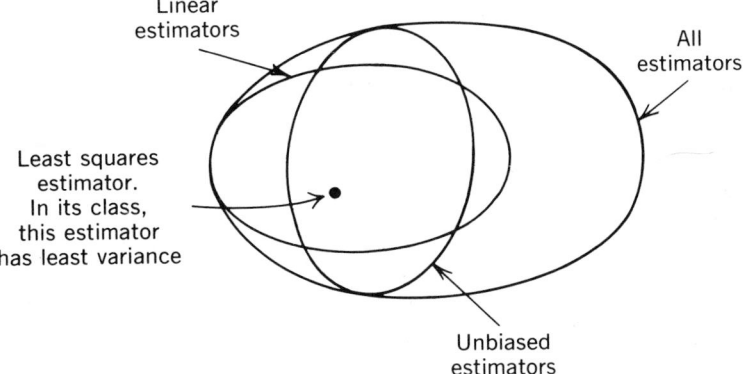

FIGURE 2-10 Diagram of the restricted class of estimators considered in the Gauss-Markov theorem.

variance. Therefore, it is often referred to as BLUE, the *best linear unbiased estimator.*

The Gauss-Markov theorem has an interesting corollary. As a special case of regression, we might ask what happens if we are explaining Y, but $\beta = 0$ in (2-21), so that no independent variable x comes into play. Then α is the mean μ of the Y population. Moreover, from (2-13), its least squares estimator is $\bar{Y}$. Thus:

Gauss-Markov Corollary

Within the class of linear unbiased estimators of a population mean μ, the sample mean $\bar{Y}$ has minimum variance.	(2-42)

It must be emphasized that the Gauss-Markov theorem is restricted, applying only to estimators that are both linear and unbiased. It follows that there may be a biased or nonlinear estimator that is better (i.e., has a smaller variance) than the least squares estimator. For example, to estimate a population mean, the sample median is a *nonlinear* estimator.[6] It is better than the sample mean for certain kinds of nonnormal populations.[7] (The sample median is just one example of a whole collection of estimators known as distribution-free or nonparametric statistics. These are expressly designed for inference when the population cannot be assumed to be normally distributed.)

PROBLEMS

2-7 Suppose the experimenter was in a hurry to analyze the data in Figure 2-2, and so drew a line joining the first and last points. We denote the slope of this line by $\tilde{\beta}$.

(a) Calculate $\tilde{\beta}$ for the data in Table 2-1.
(b) Write out a formula for $\tilde{\beta}$ in terms of X_1, Y_1, X_7, Y_7.

---

[6] The sample median also happens to be the MAD estimator.

[7] Populations with thick tails may give rise to a few extreme observations. The sample median "weights" these extreme observations less than does the sample mean, and is therefore more reliable. The classic example of such a thick-tailed distribution is the Cauchy distribution, $p(x) = [\pi(1 + x^2)]^{-1}$. Although it looks roughly bell-shaped (in fact it is student's t distribution with 1 degree of freedom), nevertheless it has such thick tails that the variance is infinite, and even the mean does not exist in a mathematical sense. The mean of a sample from the Cauchy distribution does not obey the Central Limit theorem and is very unstable. In fact, it is no more stable than a single observation, no matter how large a sample is taken. In this situation, the sample median is obviously better than the sample mean.

(c) Is $\tilde{\beta}$ a linear estimator?
(d) Is $\tilde{\beta}$ an unbiased estimator of β?
(e) Without doing any calculations, can you say how the variance of $\tilde{\beta}$ compares to the variance of the least squares estimator $\hat{\beta}$?
(f) Verify your answer in (e) by actually calculating the variance of $\tilde{\beta}$ and $\hat{\beta}$ for the data of Table 2-1. (Express your answer in terms of the unknown error variance σ^2.)

2-8 In Problem 2-7 we considered the two extreme values, X_1 and X_7. Now let us consider an alternative pair of less extreme values—say X_2 and X_6. We denote the slope of this line by $\hat{\beta}$. Like $\tilde{\beta}$, it can easily be shown to be linear and unbiased.

(a) Calculate the variance of $\hat{\beta}$. How does it compare with the variance of $\tilde{\beta}$?
(b) Answer true or false; if false, correct it:
$\tilde{\beta}$ has less variance than $\hat{\beta}$, which illustrates a general principle: The more a pair of observations are spread out, the more statistical leverage they exert, and hence the more efficient they are.

2-9 A statistician wishes to estimate the mean μ of a population from which only two sample observations Y_1 and Y_2 can be drawn. Consider the following two estimators:

$$\text{(i)} \quad \hat{\mu} = \tfrac{1}{2}Y_1 + \tfrac{1}{2}Y_2$$

$$\text{(ii)} \quad \hat{\hat{\mu}} = \tfrac{1}{3}Y_1 + \tfrac{2}{3}Y_2$$

(a) Are these both unbiased? Linear?
(b) What is the variance of each (expressed in terms of σ^2, the variance of each Y observation)?
(c) How does this illustrate the Gauss-Markov theorem?

2-7 THE DISTRIBUTION OF $\hat{\beta}$

Now that we have established the mean and variance of $\hat{\beta}$ in (2-27) and (2-28), we ask about the shape of the distribution of $\hat{\beta}$. Let us add (for the first time) the strong assumption that the Y_i are normal. Since $\hat{\beta}$ is a linear combination of the Y_i, it follows (from Appendix 2-A) that $\hat{\beta}$ will also be normal. But even without assuming the Y_i are normal, as sample size in-

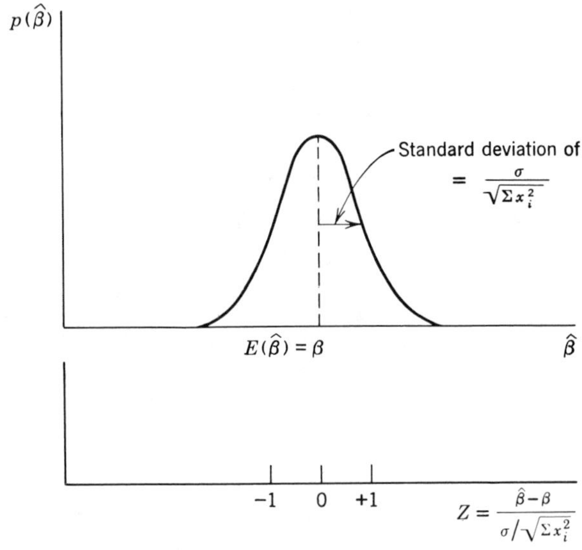

FIGURE 2-11 The probability distribution of the estimator $\hat{\beta}$.

creases, the distribution of $\hat{\beta}$ will usually approach normality; this can be justified by a generalized form of the central limit theorem.[8]

We are now in a position to graph the distribution of $\hat{\beta}$ in Figure 2-11 (for the time being, the bottom line in this diagram may be disregarded). Our objective is to develop a clear intuitive idea of how this estimator varies from sample to sample. First, of course, we note that (2-27) established that the distribution of $\hat{\beta}$ is centered on its target, so that $\hat{\beta}$ is unbiased.

The interpretation of its variance (2-28) is more subtle, with some interesting implications for experimental design. Suppose that the experiment has been badly designed with the X_i's close together. This makes the deviations x_i small, hence $\sum x_i^2$ small. Therefore the variance of $\hat{\beta}$ in (2-28) is large, and $\hat{\beta}$ is a comparatively unreliable estimator. To check the intuitive validity of this assertion, consider the scatter diagram in Figure 2-12*a*. The bunching of the X's means that the small part of the line being investigated is obscured by the error e, making the slope estimate $\hat{\beta}$ very unreliable. In this specific instance, our estimate has been pulled badly out of line by the errors—in particular, by the one indicated by the arrow.

By contrast, in Figure 2-12*b* we show the case where the X's are rea-

[8] Sometimes called the "normal approximation theorem," the central limit theorem proves the large-sample normality of the sample mean $\bar{X}$. It applies also to a *weighted* sum of random variables such as $\hat{\beta}$ in (2-33), under most conditions. Similarly, the normality of $\hat{\alpha}$ is justified.

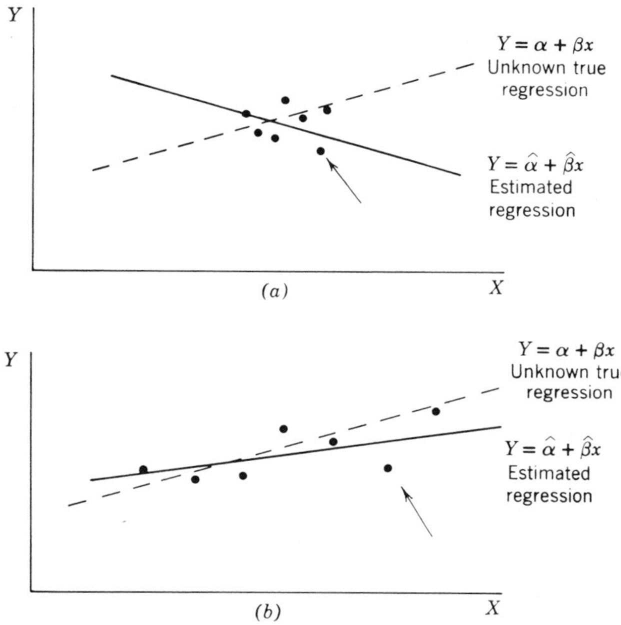

FIGURE 2-12 (*a*) Unreliable fit when X_i are very close. (*b*) More reliable fit when X_i are spread out.

sonably spread out. Even though the errors e remain the same, the estimate $\hat{\beta}$ is much more reliable, because errors no longer exert the same leverage.

As a concrete example, suppose we wish to examine how sensitive Canadian imports (Y) are to the international value of the Canadian dollar (x). A much more reliable estimate should be possible using the periods when the Canadian dollar was floating (and took on a range of values) than in the periods when this dollar was fixed (and only allowed to fluctuate within very narrow limits).

2-8 CONFIDENCE INTERVALS AND TESTS FOR β

(a) *t* Statistic

With the mean, variance, and normality of the estimator $\hat{\beta}$ established, statistical inferences about the population slope β are now in order. First we standardize $\hat{\beta}$, by subtracting its mean and dividing by its standard deviation:

$$Z = \frac{\hat{\beta} - \beta}{\sigma/\sqrt{\sum x_i^2}} \tag{2-43}$$

Z then is standard normal (with mean 0 and variance 1), as shown in Figure 2-11. We cannot use (2-43) in its present form, however, because we do not know σ^2, the variance of Y about the true line. A natural estimator is to use the deviations about the *fitted* line:

$$s^2 = \frac{1}{n-2} \sum (Y_i - \hat{Y}_i)^2 \tag{2-44}$$

compare with (2-3)

where $\hat{Y}_i$ is the fitted value of Y on the fitted line:

$$\hat{Y}_i = \hat{\alpha} + \hat{\beta} x_i \tag{2-45}$$

The divisor $(n - 2)$ is used in (2-44) rather than n in order to make s^2 an unbiased estimator[9] of σ^2. When s^2 is substituted for σ^2 in (2-43), the standardized $\hat{\beta}$ is no longer normal, but instead has the slightly more spread-out t-distribution[10]:

$$t = \frac{\hat{\beta} - \beta}{s/\sqrt{\sum x_i^2}} \tag{2-46}$$

The estimated standard deviation in the denominator of (2-46) is commonly called the *standard error* of $\hat{\beta}$, and is denoted by $s_{\hat{\beta}}$:

$$s_{\hat{\beta}} = \frac{s}{\sqrt{\sum x_i^2}} \tag{2-47}$$

Using this, (2-46) can be written:

$$\boxed{t = \frac{\hat{\beta} - \beta}{s_{\hat{\beta}}}} \tag{2-48}$$

We may now proceed to construct a confidence interval or test an hypothesis.

---

[9] Unbiasedness is discussed in Appendix 2-B. Meanwhile, an intuitive viewpoint may be helpful: If there were only $n = 2$ points in the data, the least squares line could be fitted. It would turn out to be a perfect fit (through any two given points, a line can always be drawn that goes through them exactly). Thus, although $\hat{\alpha}$ and $\hat{\beta}$ would be determined easily enough, there would be no information at all about the variance of the observations about the line, σ^2. Only to the extent that n exceeds 2 can we get information about σ^2. Thus it is customary to say, "Two degrees of freedom are used up in calculating the estimators for the line, $\hat{\alpha}$ and $\hat{\beta}$, leaving the remaining $(n - 2)$ degrees of freedom for the estimate of the variance about the line, s^2."

[10] For strict validity, use of the t-distribution requires the strong assumption that the distribution of Y_i is normal; but even when it is not, t often remains a good approximation.

(b) Confidence Intervals

Let $t_{.025}$ denote the t value that leaves $2\frac{1}{2}\%$ of the distribution in the upper tail, that is,

$$\Pr(-t_{.025} < t < t_{.025}) = .95$$

Substituting t from (2-48),

$$\Pr\left(-t_{.025} < \frac{\hat{\beta} - \beta}{s_{\hat{\beta}}} < t_{.025}\right) = .95 \tag{2-49}$$

The inequalities within the bracket may be reexpressed:

$$\Pr(\hat{\beta} - t_{.025}\, s_{\hat{\beta}} < \beta < \hat{\beta} + t_{.025}\, s_{\hat{\beta}}) = .95$$

which may then be written more briefly:

> 95% confidence interval for β:
>
> $$\beta = \hat{\beta} \pm t_{.025}\, s_{\hat{\beta}} \tag{2-50}$$

Substituting $s_{\hat{\beta}}$ from (2-47) yields the alternative form:

> 95% confidence interval for the slope:
>
> $$\beta = \hat{\beta} \pm t_{.025} \frac{s}{\sqrt{\sum x_i^2}} \tag{2-51}$$

where the degrees of freedom (d.f.) for t are, as always, the same as the divisor in s^2:

$$\text{d.f.} = n - 2 \tag{2-52}$$

Using a similar argument, and noting (2-26), we could easily derive:

> 95% confidence interval for the intercept:[11]
>
> $$\alpha = \hat{\alpha} \pm t_{.025} \frac{s}{\sqrt{n}} \tag{2-53}$$

---

[11] α is the intercept only if the y-axis is placed over the center of the data (as in Figure 2-7*b*). If the y-axis is left in its original position (as in Figure 2-7*a*), the intercept is denoted α_0; in Problem 2-20 we show that its 95% confidence interval is

$$\alpha_0 = (\bar{Y} - \hat{\beta}\bar{X}) \pm t_{.025}\, s\sqrt{\frac{1}{n} + \frac{\bar{X}^2}{\sum x_i^2}} \tag{2-54}$$

Before we illustrate these formulas with an example, we repeat the warning that we gave in the preface: Every numbered example in this text is an exercise that you should actively work out yourself, rather than passively read. We therefore put each example in the form of a question for you to answer; if you get stuck, then you may read the solution.

Example 2-1

Find the 95% confidence interval for the slope in (2-17) that relates wheat yield to fertilizer.

Solution

To evaluate (2-51), first s^2 is calculated according to (2-44), in the last three columns of Table 2-2, on page 18. The critical t value then has $n - 2 = 7 - 2 = 5$ d.f. (the same as the divisor in s^2); from Table V, in the Appendix at the end of the book, $t_{.025}$ is found to be 2.571. Finally, note that $\hat{\beta}$ and $\sum x_i^2$ were already calculated in Table 2-2. When these values are all substituted into (2-51),

$$\beta = .059 \pm 2.571 \frac{5.96}{\sqrt{280{,}000}}$$

$$= .059 \pm 2.571(.0113) \tag{2-55}$$

$$= .059 \pm .029$$

$$.030 < \beta < .088 \tag{2-56}$$

(c) Testing Hypotheses

The hypothesis typically tested is the null hypothesis:

$$H_0 : \beta = 0 \tag{2-57}$$

Should this be a one-tailed or a two-tailed test? This question must be answered on the basis of prior theoretical reasoning. To illustrate, suppose we wish to investigate the effect of wages W on the national price level P, using the simple relationship

$$P = \alpha + \beta W$$

On theoretical grounds, it may be concluded a priori that if wages affect prices at all, this relation will be a positive one. In this case H_0 is tested against the one-sided alternative

$$H_1 : \beta > 0 \tag{2-58}$$

On the other hand, as an example of a case in which such clear prior guidelines do not exist, consider an equation explaining saving. How does it depend on the interest rate? It is not clear, on theoretical grounds, whether this effect is a positive or a negative one. Since interest is the reward for saving, a high interest rate should provide an incentive, leading us to expect interest to positively affect saving. But if individuals save in order to accumulate some target sum (perhaps for their retirement, or to buy a house), then the higher the interest rate, the more rapidly any saving will accumulate, and hence the less they need to save to reach this target. In this case, interest affects saving negatively, and so it is appropriate to test H_0 against the two-sided alternative:[12]

$$H_1 : \beta \neq 0$$

In such a two-tailed test,

> H_0 can be rejected if it is excluded from the corresponding confidence interval for β.

(2-59)

Example 2-2

Run a two-sided test of the null hypothesis H_0 that wheat yield is not affected by fertilizer. (Suppose you select a two-sided test because the harmful properties of this fertilizer are not known and may offset, or more than offset, its stimulus to growth).

Solution

The null hypothesis $\beta = 0$ falls outside the 95% confidence interval for β, given in (2-56). It therefore may be rejected at the 5% level[13] in favor of the alternative hypothesis that fertilizer does affect yield.

---

[12] This may be viewed as testing H_0 (that the two effects cancel out) against H_1 (that one or the other dominates).

[13] We abbreviate the common term "5% level of significance" to "5% level". It is just the complement of the confidence level of 95%.

Now suppose it is known that this fertilizer cannot burn or otherwise harm the crop, and consequently any effect will be a positive one. Then it is appropriate to test (2-57) against the one-sided alternative (2-58). Assuming the null hypothesis ($\beta = 0$) is true, t in (2-48) reduces to

$$t = \frac{\hat{\beta}}{s_{\hat{\beta}}} \tag{2-60}$$

with the distribution shown in Figure 2-13. The rejection region appropriate for the one-sided alternative (2-58) is defined by the critical value $t_{.05}$ leaving 5% of the distribution in the upper tail. Next the observed t value is calculated; if it falls in the rejection range above $t_{.05}$, then there are two possible explanations: Either H_0 is true and we have been extremely unlucky in observing a sample that is atypical, or the world is not like this after all—that is, H_0 is not true. The implausibility of the first explanation allows us to choose the second, and we reject the hypothesis. But we cannot be certain that the first explanation is not the true one; all we know is that if H_0 is true, there is only a 5% probability that we will make the mistake of rejecting it.

Example 2-3

Again, using the wheat-yield example, run a one-sided test of the null hypothesis that yield is not affected by fertilizer.

Solution

Evaluate (2-60) using the calculations for $\hat{\beta}$ and $s_{\hat{\beta}}$ that already appeared in (2-55):

$$t = \frac{.059}{.0113} = 5.2 \tag{2-61}$$

Since the observed value exceeds the critical $t_{.05}$ value of 2.015, H_0 is rejected in favor of the alternative hypothesis that fertilizer favorably affects yield.

In a case such as this or the previous example, where we have established that there is some relation of yield to fertilizer, $\hat{\beta}$ or t is customarily called *statistically significant* at the 5% level. Although we usually bow to this custom, we would prefer the term *statistically discernible* to emphasize that t depends as much on sample size as on the size of the slope.[14]

[14] For a detailed discussion, see Wonnacott and Wonnacott, 1977, chapter 9.

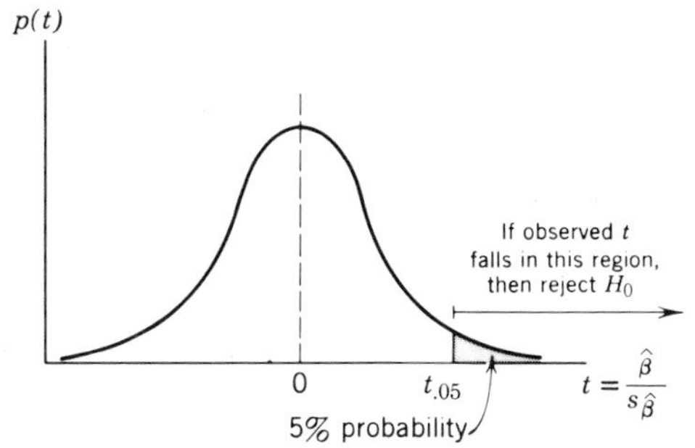

FIGURE 2-13 A one-tailed test of the null hypothesis.

PROBLEMS

2-10 (a) For each of Problems 2-1 to 2-4, construct a 95% confidence interval for the true slope β.

(b) For Problem 2-2, construct a 95% confidence interval for α.

2-11 Suppose that a random sample of 4 families had the following annual income and saving:

Family	Income X (Thousands of \$)	Saving S (Thousands of \$)
A	12	1.0
B	8	1.0
C	7	.6
D	17	2.2

(a) Estimate the regression line $S = \alpha + \beta x$.

(b) Construct a 95% confidence interval for the slope β.

(c) Graph the 4 points and the fitted line, and then graph as well as you can the acceptable slopes given by the confidence interval in (b).

(d) Construct a 95% confidence interval for α.

2-12 Which of the following hypotheses do the data of Problem 2-11 reject at the 5% level? Use a two-sided test.

(i) $\beta = 0$
(ii) $\beta = .05$
(iii) $\beta = .10$
(iv) $\beta = .50$

2-9 INTERPOLATION

In the previous section we considered the broad aspects of the model, namely, the position of the whole line (determined by α and β). In this section, we will consider two narrower problems:

(a) For a given value x_0, what is the interval that will predict the corresponding *mean* value of Y_0 [i.e., the confidence interval for $E(Y_0)$ or μ_0]? For example, in our fertilizer problem, we may want an interval estimate of the mean yield resulting from the application of 550 lb of fertilizer. (Note that we are not deriving an interval estimate of mean yield by observing repeated applications of 550 lb of fertilizer; in that case, we could apply the simpler technique of estimating a population mean with the sample mean. Instead we are observing only seven *different* applications of fertilizer. This is clearly a more difficult problem.)

(b) What is the interval that will predict a *single observed* value of Y_0 (referred to as the prediction interval for an individual Y_0). Again using our example, what would we predict a single yield to be from an application of 550 lb of fertilizer? This individual value is clearly less predictable than the mean value in (a). We now consider both in detail.

(a) The Confidence Interval for the Mean μ_0

First we find the point estimator $\hat{\mu}_0$, then construct an interval estimate around it. The appropriate estimator $\hat{\mu}_0$ is just the point on the estimated regression line above x_0:

$$\hat{\mu}_0 = \hat{\alpha} + \hat{\beta}x_0 \tag{2-62}$$

But as a point estimate, this will almost certainly involve some error, because of errors made in the estimates $\hat{\alpha}$ and $\hat{\beta}$. Figure 2-14 illustrates the effect of these errors. In panel (a), the true regression is shown, along with an estimated regression. Note how $\hat{\mu}_0$ overestimates in this case. In panel (b) the true regression is again shown, but now with several estimated regressions fitted from several possible sets of sample data. The fitted dot is sometimes too low, sometimes too high, but on average, it seems just right. To verify this, we note that $\hat{\mu}_0$ in (2-62) is a linear combination of the random variables $\hat{\alpha}$ and $\hat{\beta}$. Thus, from Appendix 2-A (and noting that x_0 is fixed),

$$E(\hat{\mu}_0) = E(\hat{\alpha}) + x_0 E(\hat{\beta})$$

From (2-25) and (2-27),

$$E(\hat{\mu}_0) = \alpha + x_0\beta = \mu_0$$

$$\boxed{E(\hat{\mu}_0) = \mu_0} \qquad (2\text{-}63)$$

Thus $\hat{\mu}_0$ is indeed an unbiased estimator of μ_0.

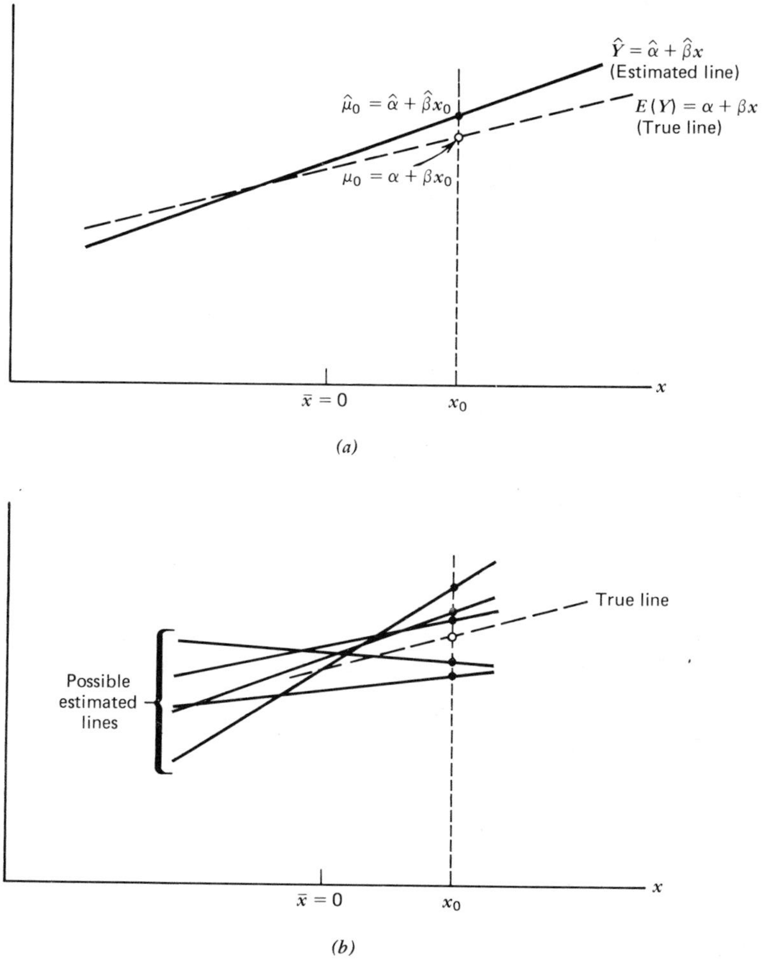

FIGURE 2-14 How the estimator $\hat{\mu}_0$ is related to the target μ_0 (hollow dot). (*a*) One single $\hat{\mu}_0$. (*b*) A whole series of possible $\hat{\mu}_0$.

Consider next its variance. Because $\hat{\alpha}$ and $\hat{\beta}$ are uncorrelated,[15] it follows from Appendix 2-A that

$$\text{var}(\hat{\mu}_0) = \text{var}\ \hat{\alpha} + x_0^2\ \text{var}\ \hat{\beta}$$

From (2-26) and (2-28),

$$\text{var}(\hat{\mu}_0) = \frac{\sigma^2}{n} + x_0^2 \frac{\sigma^2}{\sum x_i^2}$$

$$\boxed{\text{var}(\hat{\mu}_0) = \sigma^2\left(\frac{1}{n} + \frac{x_0^2}{\sum x_i^2}\right)} \tag{2-64}$$

where, of course, x_0 is the new specified x value, while the x_i are the originally observed x values. To interpret (2-64), we note that this variance (uncertainty) of $\hat{\mu}_0$ has two components, due to the variance (uncertainty) of $\hat{\alpha}$ and of $\hat{\beta}$, respectively. The uncertainty term resulting from $\hat{\beta}$ increases as x_0^2 increases, that is, the further x_0 is from the central value 0. This also can be seen from Figure 2-14*b*: if x_0 were further to the right, then the estimates $\hat{\mu}_0$ would be spread out over an even wider range.

Finally, we note that $\hat{\alpha}$ and $\hat{\beta}$ are normal (as established at the beginning of Section 2-7). It follows from Appendix 2-A that $\hat{\mu}_0$ is also normal. Thus from (2-64) the 95% confidence interval for μ_0 is

95% confidence interval:

$$\mu_0 = \hat{\mu}_0 \pm t_{.025}\, s\sqrt{\frac{1}{n} + \frac{x_0^2}{\sum x_i^2}} \tag{2-65}$$

where, of course, s has been substituted for the unknown σ, and the t-distribution (with d.f. $= n - 2$) has been used correspondingly. When x_0 is set at its central value of 0, note how this confidence interval reduces simply to the confidence interval for α in (2-53). In this case there is no uncertainty introduced by estimating β.

(b) The Prediction Interval for an Individual Y_0

In predicting a single, observed Y_0, once again the best estimate is the point on the estimated regression line above x_0. In other words, the best *point*

---

[15] One reason for redefining the X variable as a deviation from the mean was to make the covariance of $\hat{\alpha}$ and $\hat{\beta}$ zero. The proof, straightforward but tedious, is omitted.

prediction for Y_0 is

$$\hat{Y}_0 = \hat{\alpha} + \hat{\beta}x_0 = \hat{\mu}_0 \tag{2-66}$$

When we try to find the *interval* estimate for Y_0, we will face all the problems involved in the interval for the mean, μ_0. And we have an additional problem because we are trying to estimate only one observed Y, rather than the more stable mean of all the possible Y. Hence, to our previous variance (2-64), we must now add the inherent variance σ^2 of an individual Y observation, obtaining

$$\sigma^2\left(\frac{1}{n} + \frac{x_0^2}{\sum x_i^2}\right) + \sigma^2 = \sigma^2\left(\frac{1}{n} + \frac{x_0^2}{\sum x_i^2} + 1\right) \tag{2-67}$$

Except for this larger variance, the prediction interval for Y_0 is the same as the confidence interval for μ_0:

95% prediction interval for an individual Y observation:

$$Y_0 = \hat{\mu}_0 \pm t_{.025}\, s\sqrt{\frac{1}{n} + \frac{x_0^2}{\sum x_i^2} + 1} \tag{2-68}$$

with the t-distribution again having $(n - 2)$ d.f.

Example 2-4

If 550 pounds of fertilizer are applied in the wheat example (2-17), find a 95% confidence interval for:

(a) μ_0, the mean wheat yield that we would obtain if we planted many, many plots.

(b) Y_0, the wheat yield on just one plot.

Solution

The point estimate is the same in both cases. We simply calculate

$$\begin{aligned} x_0 &= X_0 - \bar{X} \\ &= 550 - 400 = 150 \end{aligned} \tag{2-69}$$

and substitute it into the equation of the estimated line (2-17):

$$\hat{\mu}_0 = \hat{Y}_0 = 60 + .059(150)$$
$$= 68.8 \tag{2-70}$$

(a) For an interval estimate for μ_0, substitute (2-69) and (2-70) into (2-65), along with s^2 and $\sum x_i^2$ from Table 2-2:

$$\mu_0 = 68.8 \pm 2.571(5.96)\sqrt{\frac{1}{7} + \frac{150^2}{280{,}000}}$$
$$= 68.8 \pm 7.2 \tag{2-71}$$

(b) For an interval estimate for Y_0, (2-68) yields the same calculation except for an extra one under the square root sign:

$$Y_0 = 68.8 \pm 2.571(5.96)\sqrt{\frac{1}{7} + \frac{150^2}{280{,}000} + 1}$$
$$= 68.8 \pm 16.9$$

This interval is more than twice as wide as (2-71), which shows how much more difficult it is to predict an *individual* observation than a *mean*.

The relationship of prediction and confidence intervals is shown in Figure 2-15. The two potential sources of error in a confidence interval for the mean are shown in panels (a) and (b); these are combined to form the dark band in panel (c).[16] The wider, lighter band in (c) gives the prediction intervals for individual Y observations. Note how both bands expand as x_0 moves farther away from its central value of zero; this reflects the fact that x_0^2 appears in both variances.

---

[16] We should be careful in interpretating the dark band: If we cut it in any vertical slice, there is a 95% chance this slice will contain the true mean. What is the chance that, for *all* vertical slices, the dark band always contains the true mean? Since this is a stronger requirement, its probability is clearly less than 95%. If we wanted a band that was 95% certain to contain the entire line of true means, we would need to broaden (2-65). We could show that this requires $t_{.025}$ in (2-65) to be replaced by $\sqrt{2F_{.05}}$, where $F_{.05}$ is the critical F point with 2 and $(n-2)$ d.f. Thus

95% confidence band for the *entire* true regression line:

$$E(Y) = (\hat{\alpha} + \hat{\beta}x) \pm \sqrt{2F_{.05}}\, s\sqrt{\frac{1}{n} + \frac{x^2}{\sum x_i^2}} \tag{2-72}$$

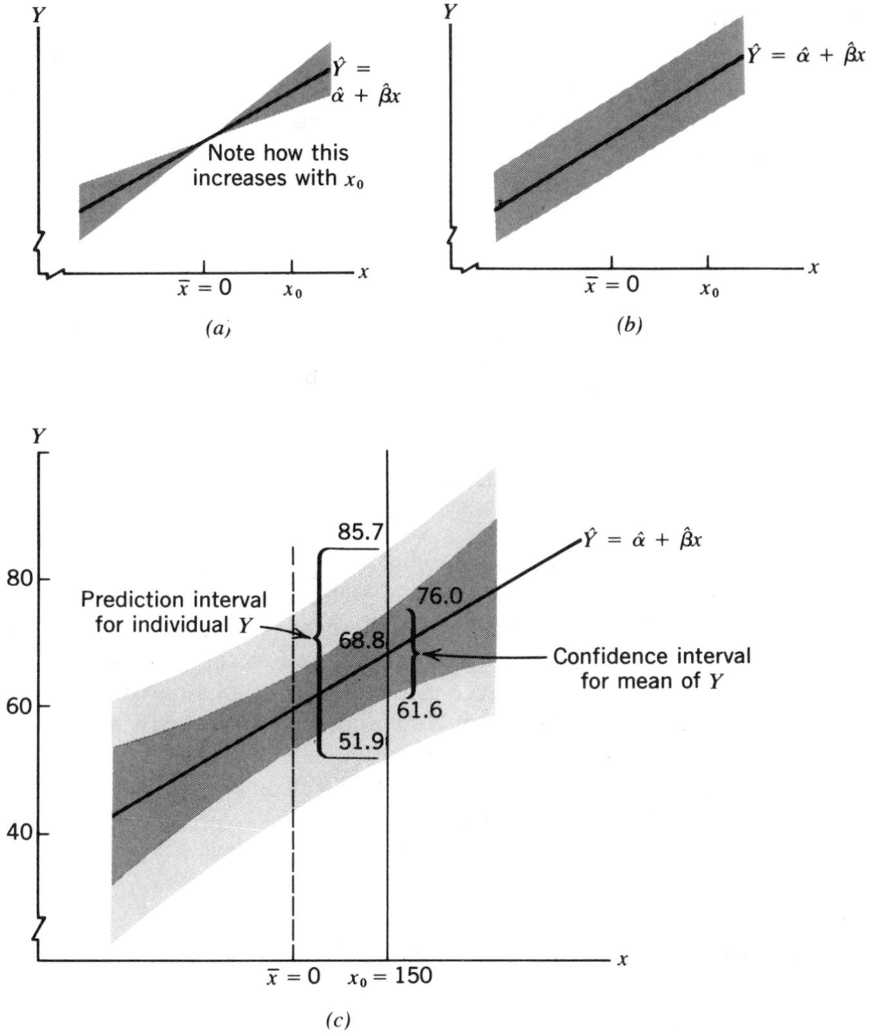

FIGURE 2-15 (*a*) Interval estimate of the mean of Y, if there were error only in estimating β. (*b*) Interval estimate of the mean of Y, if there were error only in estimating α. (*c*) Interval estimate for mean of Y, and prediction interval for individual Y, when there is error in estimating both α and β.

PROBLEMS

2-13 Using the data of Problem 2-2, what is the 95% prediction interval for the saving of a family with the following income (in thousands of dollars):

(a) 6?
(b) 8?
(c) 10?
(d) 12?
(e) Which of these four intervals is least precise? Most precise? Why?
(f) How is the answer in (b) related to the confidence interval for α found in Problem 2-10(b)?

2-14 Repeat Problem 2-13, calculating instead a 95% confidence interval for the *average* saving of all families at each given income level.

2-15 (a) Suppose that you are trying to explain how the interest rate affects investment. Would you prefer to take observations over a period in which the Federal Reserve is trying to stabilize the rate, or a period in which it is allowed to vary widely?
(b) Suppose that you have estimated the regression of saving on income using data from families in the \$8,000 to \$16,000 income range. Would you feel more confident predicting the future saving of a family with a \$16,000 income, or a family with a \$10,000 income? Why?

2-10 DANGERS OF EXTRAPOLATION

We emphasize that in formulas (2-65) and (2-68), x_0 may be *any* value of x. If x_0 lies *among* the values $x_1 \cdots x_n$, the process is called interpolation. (If x_0 *is* one of the values $x_1 \cdots x_n$, the process might be called, "using also the other values of x to sharpen our knowledge of this one population at x_0.") If x_0 is out beyond the observed x's, then the process is called extrapolation. The techniques developed in Section 2-9 may be used for extrapolation, but only with great caution.

There is no sharp division between safe interpolation and dangerous extrapolation. Instead, there is *continually* increasing danger of misinterpretation as x_0 gets further and further from its central value.

(a) Statistical Risk

It was emphasized in Figure 2-15 that interval estimates get larger as x_0 moves away from $\bar{x}$. This is true, even if all the assumptions underlying our mathematical model hold exactly.

(b) Risk of Invalid Model

In practice it must be recognized that a mathematical model is never absolutely correct. Instead, it is a useful approximation. In particular, one cannot take seriously the assumption that the population means are strung out in an *exactly* straight line. If we consider the fertilizer example, it is likely that the true relation increases initially, but then bends down eventually as a "burning point" is approached, and the crop is overdosed. This is illustrated in Figure 2-16, which is an extension of Figure 2-2, with the scale appro-

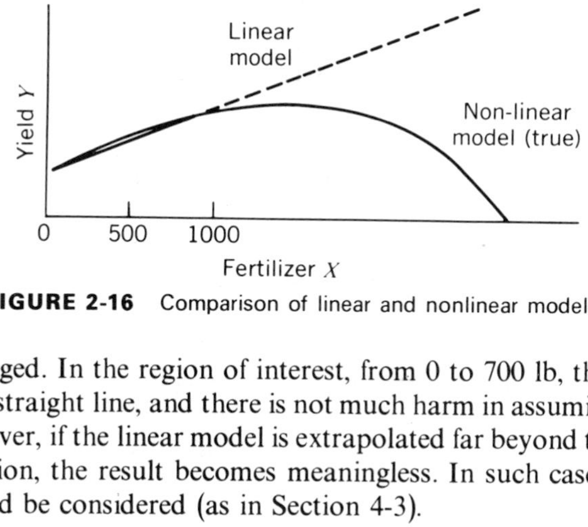

FIGURE 2-16 Comparison of linear and nonlinear models.

priately changed. In the region of interest, from 0 to 700 lb, the relation is practically a straight line, and there is not much harm in assuming the linear model. However, if the linear model is extrapolated far beyond this region of experimentation, the result becomes meaningless. In such cases, nonlinear models should be considered (as in Section 4-3).

2-11 LEAST SQUARES WHEN X IS RANDOM

Thus far it has been assumed that the independent variable x takes on a given set of fixed values (e.g., fertilizer application was set at certain specified levels). But in many cases x cannot be controlled in this way. For example, if we are examining the effect of rainfall on yield, it must be recognized that x (rainfall) is a random variable, completely outside our control. The surprising thing is that with some reinterpretation, most of this chapter is still valid whether x is fixed *or* a random variable, provided we assume, as well as (2-23), that:

$$\boxed{\text{The error } e \text{ is statistically independent of } x} \tag{2-73}$$

(As we shall see later in Chapter 7, if x and e are correlated, the least squares estimator $\hat{\beta}$ is biased and inconsistent.) When these assumptions are valid, we will prove that:

1. $\hat{\beta}$ is still an unbiased estimator of β.
2. The confidence interval for β is still valid.
3. Assuming a normal error, $\hat{\beta}$ is still the maximum likelihood estimate (MLE) of β.

Proofs

1. Consider one single set of specific values that the random variable x may take, say $x_1, x_2, \ldots, x_n$. The assumptions (2-23) and (2-73) imply that e will have zero mean at every one of these values $x_1, x_2, \ldots, x_n$. Thus the previous derivation of $E(\hat{\beta})$ in Section 2-5 remains the same:

$$E(\hat{\beta}/x_1, x_2, \ldots, x_n) = \beta \qquad \text{like (2-27)}$$

where this notation is used to emphasize that this expectation is conditional on the values of x. Since this is true for every configuration of x_1, $x_2, \ldots, x_n$, however, it remains true when we average over all possible configurations,[16] obtaining the unconditional expectation:

$$E(\hat{\beta}) = \beta \tag{2-74}$$

2. In the same way, if we consider a given configuration of x values, the confidence interval for β has a 95% probability of being right (i.e., including the true β). Since this is true for *every* possible set of x values, the probability of being right remains 95% regardless.
3. The proof that $\hat{\beta}$ is the MLE of β is given in Section 2-12 below.

*2-12 MAXIMUM LIKELIHOOD ESTIMATION (MLE)

(This section is starred because it is slightly more difficult; but, like other starred sections, it may be detoured without loss of continuity. For an elementary introduction to MLE, see Wonnacott and Wonnacott, 1977).

[16] Perhaps an analogy will help. If I played a game of dice where my expected reward was \$5 no matter how the dice turned up, what would my overall expected reward be? The same \$5, of course.

Sections 2-1 to 2-6, including the Gauss-Markov justification of least squares, required no assumption of the normality of the error term (i.e., normality of Y). In Sections 2-7 to 2-9, the normality assumption was required only for small sample estimation—and this because of a quite general principle that small sample estimation requires a normally distributed parent population to strictly validate the t-distribution. Throughout this next section, we make the strong assumption of a normally distributed error, in order to derive the maximum likelihood estimates (MLE) of α and β, that is, those hypothetical population values of α and β that generate the greatest probability for the sample values we observed. These MLE of α and β turn out to be the least squares estimates; thus, maximum likelihood provides another justification for using least squares.

Before examining the algebraic derivation, it is best to clarify what is going on with a bit of geometry. Specifically, why should the maximum likelihood line fit the data well? To simplify, assume for now a set of only three fixed x values (x_1, x_2, x_3), which have generated a sample of three observations (Y_1, Y_2, Y_3).

First, let us try out the line shown in Figure 2-17*a*. (Before examining it carefully, we note that it seems to be a pretty bad fit for our three observed points). Temporarily, suppose this were the true regression line; then the distribution of errors would be centered around it as shown. The likelihood that such a population would give rise to the sample we observed is the joint probability density of the particular set of three e values shown in this diagram. The individual probability densities of the three e values are shown as the ordinates above the points Y_1, Y_2, and Y_3. Because the three observations are by assumption statistically independent, the joint probability density (i.e., of getting the sample we observe), is the product of these three ordinates. This likelihood seems relatively small, mostly because the very small ordinate of Y_1 reduces the product value. Our intuition that this is a bad estimate is confirmed; such a hypothetical population is not very likely to generate our sample values. We should be able to do better.

In Figure 2-17*b* it is evident that we can do much better. This hypothetical population is more likely to give rise to the sample we observed. The disturbance terms are collectively smaller, with their probability density being greater as a consequence.

The MLE technique is seen to involve speculating on various possible populations. How likely is each to give rise to the sample we observed? Geometrically, our problem would be to try them all out, by moving the population through all its possible values—that is, *by moving the regression line and its surrounding e distribution through all possible positions in space.* Each position involves a different set of trial values for α and β. In each case the likelihood of observing Y_1, Y_2, Y_3 would be evaluated. For our MLE, we

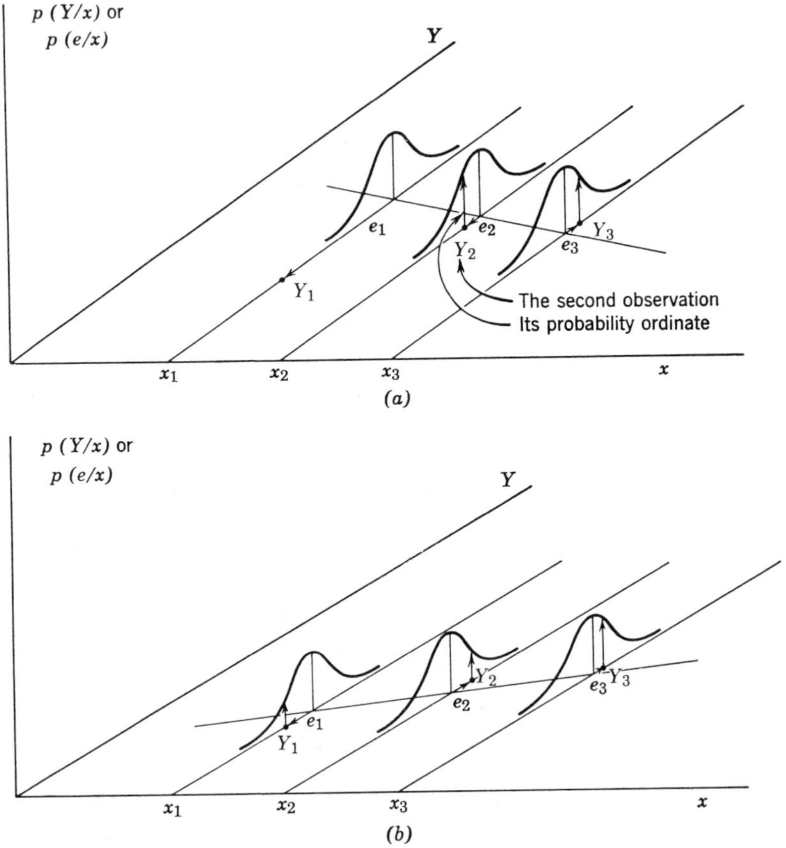

FIGURE 2-17 Maximum likelihood estimation. (*a*) This is *not* the true population; it is only a hypothetical population that the statistician is considering. But it is not very likely to generate the observed Y_1, Y_2, Y_3. (*b*) Another hypothetical population; this is more likely to generate Y_1, Y_2, Y_3.

choose that hypothetical population that maximizes this likelihood.[17] It is evident that little further adjustment is required in Figure 2-17*b* to arrive at the MLE. This procedure seems to result, intuitively, in a good fit; moreover, since it seems similar to the least squares fit, it is no surprise that we can now show that the two coincide.

[17] The likelihood of any population yielding our sample depends not only on the size of the *e* terms involved but also on σ^2, the variance of *e*. However, it can be shown that the maximum likelihood *line* does not depend on σ^2. In other words, if we assume σ^2 is larger, the geometry will look different, because *e* will have a flatter distribution; but the end result will be the same maximum likelihood line.

Although geometry has clarified the method, it has not provided a precise means of arriving at the specific MLE. This must be done algebraically. For generality, suppose that we have a sample of size n, rather than just 3. We wish to know

$$p(Y_1, Y_2 \cdots Y_n) \tag{2-75}$$

the likelihood or probability density of the sample we observed—expressed as a function of the possible population values of α, β, and σ^2. First, consider the probability density of the first value of Y, which is

$$p(Y_1) = \frac{1}{\sqrt{2\pi\sigma^2}} e^{-(1/2\sigma^2)[Y_1 - (\alpha + \beta x_1)]^2} \tag{2-76}$$

This is simply the normal distribution of Y_1, with its mean $\alpha + \beta x_1$ and variance σ^2 substituted into the appropriate positions. [In terms of the geometry of Figure 2-17, $p(Y_1)$ is the ordinate above Y_1.] The probability density of the second Y value is similar to (2-76), except that the subscript 2 replaces 1 throughout; and so on, for all the other observed Y values.

The independence of the Y values justifies multiplying all these probability densities together to find the joint probability density:

$$\begin{aligned} p(Y_1, Y_2, \ldots, Y_n) &= \left[\frac{1}{\sqrt{2\pi\sigma^2}} e^{-(1/2\sigma^2)[Y_1 - (\alpha + \beta x_1)]^2}\right]\left[\frac{1}{\sqrt{2\pi\sigma^2}} e^{-(1/2\sigma^2)[Y_2 - (\alpha + \beta x_2)]^2}\right] \cdots \\ &= \prod_{i=1}^{n} \left[\frac{1}{\sqrt{2\pi\sigma^2}} e^{-(1/2\sigma^2)[Y_i - (\alpha + \beta x_i)]^2}\right] \end{aligned} \tag{2-77}$$

where $\prod_{i=1}^{n}$ represents the product of n factors. Using the familiar rule for exponentials,[18] the product in (2-77) can be reexpressed by summing exponents:

$$p(Y_1, Y_2, \ldots, Y_n) = \left(\frac{1}{\sqrt{2\pi\sigma^2}}\right)^n e^{\Sigma(-1/2\sigma^2)[Y_i - (\alpha + \beta x_i)]^2} \tag{2-78}$$

Recall that the observed Y's are given. We are speculating on various values of α, β, and σ^2. To emphasize this, we rename (2-78) the likelihood function:

$$L(\alpha, \beta, \sigma^2) = \frac{1}{(2\pi\sigma^2)^{n/2}} e^{-(1/2\sigma^2)\Sigma[Y_i - \alpha - \beta x_i]^2} \tag{2-79}$$

[18] $e^a \cdot e^b = e^{a+b}$ for any a and b.

We now ask, which values of α and β make L largest? The only place α and β appear is in the exponent; moreover, maximizing a function with a negative exponent involves minimizing the magnitude of the exponent. Hence the MLEs are obtained by choosing the α and β that

$$\text{minimize} \sum [Y_i - \hat{\alpha} - \hat{\beta}x_i]^2 \tag{2-80}$$

Since the selection of maximum likelihood estimates of α and β to minimize (2-80) is identical to the selection of least squares estimates a and b to minimize (2-10),

In a normal regression model, the maximum likelihood estimates of α and β are identical to the least squares estimates.[19]	(2-81)

This establishes another important theoretical justification of the least squares method: It is the estimate that follows from applying maximum-likelihood techniques to a model with normally distributed error.

The final question is: Does the theorem (2-81) still hold up if x is a random variable, rather than a given set of fixed values? So long as we assume (2-73), the answer is yes. With x random, the likelihood of our sample now involves the probability of observing both x and Y. Therefore, the likelihood function is

$$L = p(x_1, x_2, \ldots, x_n)p(Y_1/x_1)p(Y_2/x_2)\cdots \tag{2-82}$$

Because of the normality assumption,

$$L = p(x_1, x_2, \ldots, x_n)\frac{1}{\sqrt{2\pi\sigma^2}}e^{-(1/2\sigma^2)(Y_1-\alpha-\beta x_1)^2} \tag{2-83}$$

$$\times \frac{1}{\sqrt{2\pi\sigma^2}}e^{-(1/2\sigma^2)(Y_2-\alpha-\beta x_2)^2}\ldots$$

Collecting the exponents,

$$L = p(x_1, x_2, \ldots, x_n)\frac{1}{(2\pi\sigma^2)^{n/2}}e^{-(1/2\sigma^2)\sum(Y_i-\alpha-\beta x_i)^2} \tag{2-84}$$

Assuming that $p(x_1, x_2, \ldots, x_n)$ does not depend on the parameters α, β, and σ^2, the problem of maximizing this likelihood function reduces to the minimization of the same exponent as before.

We conclude that MLE and least squares coincide and may be applied regardless of whether the independent variable x is fixed, or a random

[19] The MLE is more difficult to derive for σ^2 than for α and β, and is left to Appendix 2-D.

variable—provided x is independent of the error and parameters in the equation being estimated. This greatly generalizes the application of the regression model.

REVIEW PROBLEMS

2-16 When is the assumption of population normality required in the linear regression model, and when is it not? Explain.

2-17 (a) Let us define the variance of the X values as

$$\sigma_X^2 \equiv \frac{1}{n} \sum x^2$$

Then show that the standard error of $\hat{\beta}$ can be written as

$$\frac{\sigma/\sigma_X}{\sqrt{n}}$$

This formula has the advantage of showing explicitly how the reliability of $\hat{\beta}$ depends upon the following three components:

(i) σ^2, the residual variance about the line.
(ii) σ_X^2, the variance of the X values.
(iii) n, the sample size.

(b) Suppose that an agricultural economist cannot change the inherent inaccuracy of the individual observation (σ^2), but she does have a chance to change her experimental design. State how much the standard error of β will change if she takes:

(i) Four times as many observations, spread over the same X range.
(ii) The same number of observations, spread over four times the former X range.
(iii) Half as many observations, spread over twice the former X range.

2-18 A class of 150 registered students wrote two tests, for which the grades were denoted X_1 and X_2. The instructor calculated the following summary statistics:

$$\bar{X}_1 = 60 \qquad \bar{X}_2 = 70$$

$$\sum (X_1 - \bar{X}_1)^2 = 36{,}000 \qquad \sum (X_2 - \bar{X}_2)^2 = 24{,}000$$

$$\sum (X_1 - \bar{X}_1)(X_2 - \bar{X}_2) = 15{,}000$$

and residual variances about the fitted lines (X_1 on X_2, and X_2 on X_1):

$$s^2_{X_1/X_2} = 180 \qquad s^2_{X_2/X_1} = 120$$

The instructor then discovered that there was one more student, who was unregistered; worse yet, one of this student's grades (X_1) was lost, although the other grade was discovered ($X_2 = 55$). The dean told the instructor to estimate the missing grade X_1 as closely as possible.

(a) Calculate the best estimate you can. [*Hint*. Use (2-19).]
(b) Calculate an interval about your estimate in (a) that you have 95% confidence will contain the true grade.
(c) What assumptions did you have to make implicitly in (a) and (b)?

*2-19 In order to estimate this year's inventory, a tire company sampled 6 dealers, in each case getting inventory figures for both this year and last:

X = *Inventory Last Year*	Y = *Inventory This Year*
70	60
260	320
150	230
100	120
20	50
60	60

Summary statistics are $\bar{X} = 110$, $\bar{Y} = 140$.

$$\sum x^2 = 36{,}400 \qquad \sum y^2 = 61{,}800 \qquad \sum xy = 46{,}100$$

Residual variances about the fitted lines (X on Y, and Y on X):

$$s^2_{X/Y} = 500 \qquad s^2_{Y/X} = 850$$

(a) Calculate the least squares line showing how this year's inventory Y is related to last year's X. [*Hint*. Use (2-19).]
(b) Suppose that a complete inventory of all dealers is available for last year (but not for this year). Suppose also that the mean inventory for last year was found to be $\mu_X = 180$ tires per dealer. On the graph below, we show this population mean μ_X and sketch the population scatter (although this scatter remains unknown to the company, because Y values are not available yet).

On this graph, plot the six observed points, along with $\bar{X}$, $\bar{Y}$, and the estimated regression line.

(c) Indicate on the graph how μ_Y should be estimated. Construct a 95% confidence interval for μ_Y.

(d) If last year's data X had been unavailable or ignored (and you can therefore only use Y values) how then should μ_Y be estimated?

(e) Comparing (c) to (d), state in words the value of exploiting prior knowledge about last year's inventory.

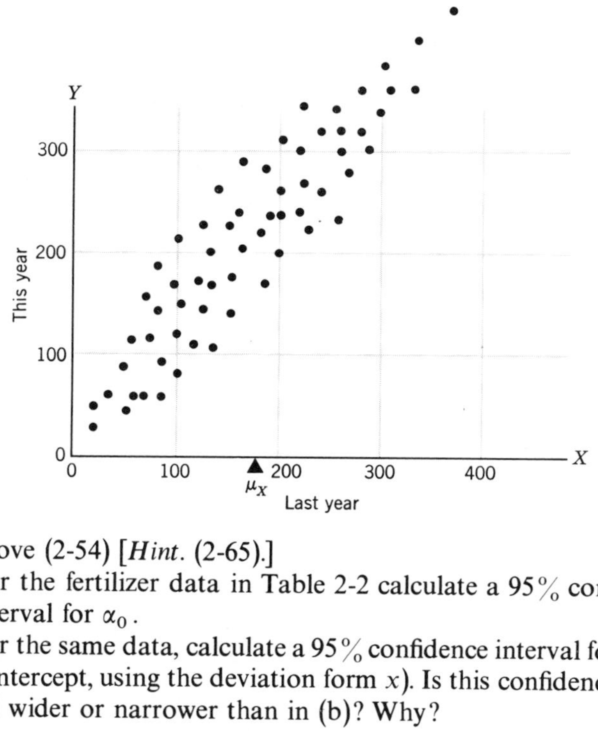

2-20 (a) Prove (2-54) [*Hint*. (2-65).]

(b) For the fertilizer data in Table 2-2 calculate a 95% confidence interval for α_0.

(c) For the same data, calculate a 95% confidence interval for α (the Y-intercept, using the deviation form x). Is this confidence interval wider or narrower than in (b)? Why?

2-21 Answer true or false; if false, correct it.

(a) In simple regression, it is assumed that

$$Y_i = \alpha + \beta x_i + e_i$$

where the e_i are independent errors, with positive means and decreasing variances.

(b) The least squares estimators $\hat{\alpha}$ and $\hat{\beta}$ are biased, consistent estimators of α and β.

(c) The more distant X_0 is from $\bar{X}$, the greater is the error in predicting Y, given X_0.

2-22 (a) In a random sample of $n = 24$ workers drawn from an assembly line, performance scores Y had a mean $\bar{Y} = 70$ and standard deviation $s_Y = 10$. When another (25th) worker is drawn from the same population, we may predict his score with 95% certainty by means of a formula analogous to (2-68):

$$Y_0 = \bar{Y} \pm t_{.025}s_Y\sqrt{\frac{1}{n} + 1}$$

where t has $(n - 1)$ d.f. With this formula, calculate the actual 95% prediction interval.

(b) In order to predict better, it was decided to exploit a variable Z for marital status, defined as follows: $Z = -1$ for divorced or separated, $Z = 0$ for single or widowed, $Z = 1$ for married. In the sample of 24 workers, the regression of Y on Z was $\hat{Y} = 70 + 13.3z$, leaving a residual variance of $s^2 = 38$. And Z itself had a mean of .20 and variance of .36.

If the 25th worker was married, what would you predict is the worker's score Y, with 95% certainty?

(c) Briefly express in simple words how the interval in (b) is better than the one in (a).

2-23 Suppose that the regression model (2-23) is changed slightly, as follows: e_i has variance σ_i^2 (no longer a constant σ^2). The least squares estimator:

$$\hat{\beta} = \frac{\sum x_i Y_i}{\sum x_i^2}$$

may still be calculated, although it no longer may have the optimal properties that it enjoyed formerly. What are the mean and variance of $\hat{\beta}$? (Incidentally, this sometimes is called the heteroscedastic model.).

APPENDIX 2-A

TABLE 2-3 Linear Transformations and Their Distributions[a]

	Variable	*Mean*	*Variance*	*Distribution*
(a) *Univariate case*				
Original variable	y	μ	σ^2	
Its transformation	$z = my$	$m\mu$	$m^2\sigma^2$	Normal if y is normal
(b) *Bivariate case*				
Original variables	y_1 y_2	μ_1 μ_2	σ_1^2 σ_2^2 and covariance σ_{12}	
Transformation	$z = m_1 y_1 + m_2 y_2$	$m_1 \mu_1 + m_2 \mu_2$	$m_1^2 \sigma_1^2 + m_2^2 \sigma_2^2 + 2m_1 m_2 \sigma_{12}$	Normal if y_1 and y_2 are normal

[a] For a detailed development of this theory, see, for example, Wonnacott and Wonnacott, 1977, Chapter 5.

APPENDIX 2-B DESIRABLE PROPERTIES OF ESTIMATORS

To be perfectly general, we consider any population parameter θ and denote an estimator for it by $\hat{\theta}$. We would like the random variable $\hat{\theta}$ to vary within only a narrow range around its fixed target θ. For example, we should like the distribution of $\hat{\beta}$ to be concentrated around β, as close to β as possible. We develop this notion of closeness in several ways.

(a) No Bias

An unbiased estimator is one that is, *on the average*, right on target, as shown in Figure 2-18*a*. $\hat{\beta}$ is an unbiased estimator of β, because its expected value is β, as in (2-27). In general, we may state:

Definition.

$$\hat{\theta} \text{ is an unbiased estimator of } \theta \text{ if } \quad E(\hat{\theta}) = \theta \tag{2-85}$$

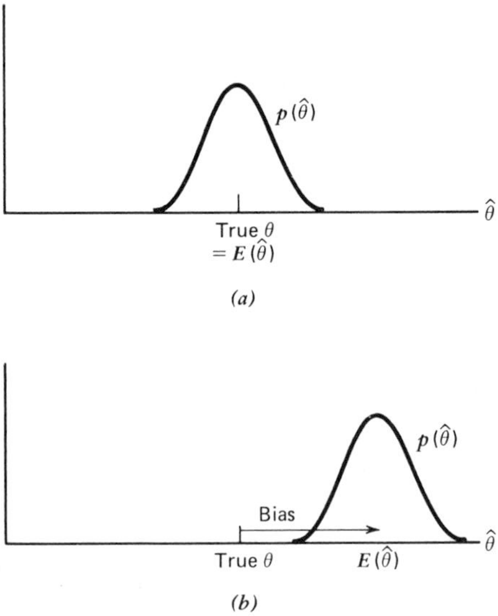

FIGURE 2-18 Probability distribution of an unbiased and a biased estimator. (*a*) Unbiased. (*b*) Biased.

Of course, an estimator $\hat{\theta}$ is called biased if $E(\hat{\theta})$ is different from θ; in fact, bias is defined as this difference:

Definition.

$$\boxed{\text{Bias } B \equiv E(\hat{\theta}) - \theta} \tag{2-86}$$

Bias is illustrated in Figure 2-18*b*. The distribution of $\hat{\theta}$ is "off target"; since $E(\hat{\theta})$ exceeds θ, there will be a tendency for $\hat{\theta}$ to overestimate.

Some examples of unbiased estimators are:

1. Given two sample observations Y_1 and Y_2 from a population, then the sample mean

$$\bar{Y} = \tfrac{1}{2}Y_1 + \tfrac{1}{2}Y_2 \tag{2-87}$$

is easily proved[20] to be an unbiased estimator of the population mean μ. It can similarly be shown that

$$\tfrac{1}{3}Y_1 + \tfrac{2}{3}Y_2 \tag{2-88}$$

[20] ***Proof.*** From Appendix 2-A,

$$E(\bar{Y}) = \tfrac{1}{2}E(Y_1) + \tfrac{1}{2}E(Y_2) \tag{2-90}$$
$$= \tfrac{1}{2}\mu + \tfrac{1}{2}\mu = \mu$$

or, in general,

$$cY_1 + (1 - c)Y_2$$

is an unbiased estimator of μ. Analogous results hold for a sample of any size n: $\bar{Y}$ is an unbiased estimator of μ and so also is

$$c_1 Y_1 + c_2 Y_2 + \cdots + c_n Y_n$$

provided $c_1 + c_2 + \cdots + c_n = 1$.

2. The natural intuitive concept of sample variance

$$s_*^2 = \frac{1}{n} \sum_{i=1}^{n} (Y_i - \bar{Y})^2 \tag{2-89}$$

will on average underestimate σ^2, the population variance.[21] But if we inflate it just a little, by dividing by $(n - 1)$ instead of n, it has been proved that the result is an unbiased estimator

$$s^2 = \frac{1}{(n-1)} \sum_{i=1}^{n} (Y_i - \bar{Y})^2 \tag{2-91}$$

---

[21] In fact, the estimator

$$\frac{1}{n} \sum (Y_i - \mu)^2 \tag{2-92}$$

would have just the right expectation σ^2. This follows because

$$E\left[\frac{1}{n} \sum (Y_i - \mu)^2\right] = \frac{1}{n} \sum E(Y_i - \mu)^2 \tag{2-93}$$

$$= \frac{1}{n} \sum \sigma^2 \tag{2-94}$$

$$= \sigma^2 \tag{2-95}$$

(A simpler but more abstract proof, would be to recognize (2-92) as simply a peculiar example of a sample mean, from the population of $(Y - \mu)^2$. Then, according to general sampling theory, the expectation of (2-92) is just the population expectation σ^2.)

Although we have proved that (2-92) is an unbiased estimator of σ^2, it cannot be calculated because μ is unknown. The best the statistician can do is to substitute the observed $\bar{Y}$ for μ, obtaining

$$s_*^2 = \frac{1}{n} \sum (Y_i - \bar{Y})^2 < \frac{1}{n} \sum (Y_i - \mu)^2 \tag{2-96}$$

This inequality follows because the sum of squares $\sum (Y_i - a)^2$ is a minimum when $a = \bar{Y}$ (recall from Section 2-6 that $\bar{Y}$ is the least squares estimator). Since $\bar{Y}$ and μ typically do not precisely coincide, $\sum (Y_i - a)^2$ will be smaller when $a = \bar{Y}$, than when $a = \mu$.

We conclude that since s_*^2 is less than the unbiased estimator (2-92), it tends to underestimate the population variance σ^2, and hence has a negative bias.

with $(n-1)$ degrees of freedom.[22] (When we say, "has been proved," we mean that it has been proved in advanced texts. If it has been proved in this text, we will usually say, "we have proved.") If you have been puzzled in an introductory course by this division by $(n-1)$, you can now see why sample variance is defined this way: We want an unbiased estimator of the population variance.

(b) Minimum Variance: Efficiency of Unbiased Estimators

In estimating μ, both (2-87) and (2-88) are unbiased. In judging which is preferable, we must look to their other characteristics. Specifically, we should also like the distribution of an estimator $\hat{\theta}$ to be highly concentrated, that is, to have a small variance. This is the notion of efficiency, shown in Figure 2-19. We describe $\hat{\theta}$ as more efficient because it has a smaller variance. Formally:

For unbiased estimators,

$$\text{relative efficiency of } \hat{\theta} \text{ compared to } \hat{\hat{\theta}} \equiv \frac{\operatorname{var} \hat{\hat{\theta}}}{\operatorname{var} \hat{\theta}} \tag{2-97}$$

An estimator that is more efficient than any other is called absolutely efficient, or simply efficient.

Now we are in a position to pass judgement on how the sample mean (2-87) and another weighted average (2-88) compare as estimators of μ. The variance of the sample mean is equal[23] to

$$(\tfrac{1}{2})^2 \operatorname{var}(Y_1) + (\tfrac{1}{2})^2 \operatorname{var}(Y_2) \tag{2-99}$$

Since each observation Y_i has the distribution of the parent population, $\operatorname{var}(Y_1) = \operatorname{var}(Y_2) =$ the population variance σ^2. Thus the variance of the

---

[22] Although there are originally n degrees of freedom in a sample of n observations, 1 d.f. is used up in calculating $\bar{Y}$, leaving only $(n-1)$ d.f. for the residuals $(Y_i - \bar{Y})$ to calculate s^2.

To illustrate, consider a sample of two Y observations, 21 and 15. Since $\bar{Y} = 18$, the residuals are $+3$ and -3, the second residual necessarily being just the negative of the first. While the first residual is "free," the second is strictly determined; hence, there is only 1 d.f. in the residuals. In general, for a sample size n, it may be shown that if the first $(n-1)$ residuals are specified, then the last residual is automatically determined.

[23] Since Y_1 and Y_2 are independent sample observations,

$$\operatorname{cov}(Y_1, Y_2) = 0 \tag{2-98}$$

When this is substituted into the last line of Appendix 2-A, (2-99) follows.

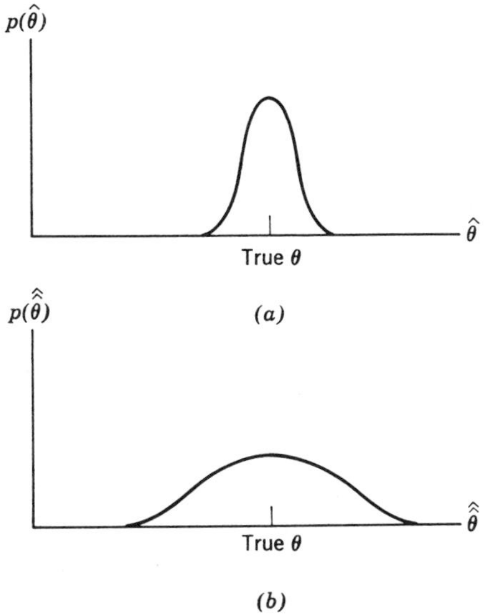

FIGURE 2-19 A comparison of an efficient ($\hat{\theta}$) and inefficient ($\hat{\hat{\theta}}$) estimator. Both are unbiased. (*a*) Efficient. (*b*) Inefficient.

sample mean reduces to

$$\left(\tfrac{1}{2}\right)^2\sigma^2 + \left(\tfrac{1}{2}\right)^2\sigma^2 = \tfrac{1}{2}\sigma^2$$

which is recognized as a special case of the general formula σ^2/n. On the other hand, the variance of the other estimator (2-88) is equal to

$$\left(\tfrac{1}{3}\right)^2 \operatorname{var}(Y_1) + \left(\tfrac{2}{3}\right)^2 \operatorname{var}(Y_2) = \tfrac{5}{9}\sigma^2 \tag{2-100}$$

Hence, the sample mean is more efficient. Specifically, from (2-97) its relative efficiency in this case is

$$\frac{(5/9)\sigma^2}{(1/2)\sigma^2} = \frac{10}{9} \tag{2-101}$$

Of course, by the Gauss-Markov corollary (2-42), $\bar{Y}$ must be more efficient than every other linear unbiased estimator as well.

For a final comparison, suppose the center of a normal distribution is to be estimated by the sample median. In any symmetric distribution, the sample median is, like the sample mean, unbiased. But, in a normal distribution, the sample median has larger variance, which is approximately

$$\frac{\pi}{2n}\sigma^2 \tag{2-102}$$

At the same time, it is well known that the variance of the sample mean is

$$\frac{1}{n}\sigma^2 \tag{2-103}$$

Thus, again using (2-97), the relative efficiency of the sample mean compared to the median is approximately

$$\frac{(\pi/2n)\sigma^2}{(1/n)\sigma^2} = 1.57$$

Because it is 57% more efficient, $\bar{Y}$ is preferred. It will give us a point estimate that will tend to be closer to the target μ. And it will give a more precise interval estimate.

Of course, by increasing sample size n we can reduce the variance of either estimator. Therefore, an alternative way of looking at the greater efficiency of the sample mean is to recognize that the sample median will yield as accurate an estimate only if we take a larger sample (specifically, 57% larger). Hence, in a normal population the sample mean is more efficient, because it costs less to sample. Notice how the economic and statistical definitions of efficiency coincide.

In summary, we have seen that $\bar{Y}$ is more efficient than every other linear estimator and even more efficient than one nonlinear estimator (the median) *when the population is normal.* In fact, it has been proved that for normal populations, $\bar{Y}$ is more efficient than every other possible estimator, that is, $\bar{Y}$ is *absolutely* efficient.

(c) Minimum Mean Squared Error: Efficiency of Any Estimator

So far we have concluded that, in comparing unbiased estimators, we choose the one with minimum variance. But suppose we are comparing several estimators—some biased, some unbiased, as in Figure 2-20.

Now it is no longer necessarily appropriate to select the estimator with minimum variance; $\hat{\theta}_3$ qualifies on that score, but it is unsatisfactory because it is so badly biased. Nor do we have to pick the estimator with least bias; $\hat{\theta}_1$ has zero bias, but it seems unsatisfactory because of its high variance. Instead the estimator that seems to perform best overall is $\hat{\theta}_2$, because it has the optimum combination of small bias and small variance.

This intuitive argument suggests using a criterion that appropriately takes into account both bias and variance. Alternatively we could say that we are not interested just in the variance of an estimator, since this only

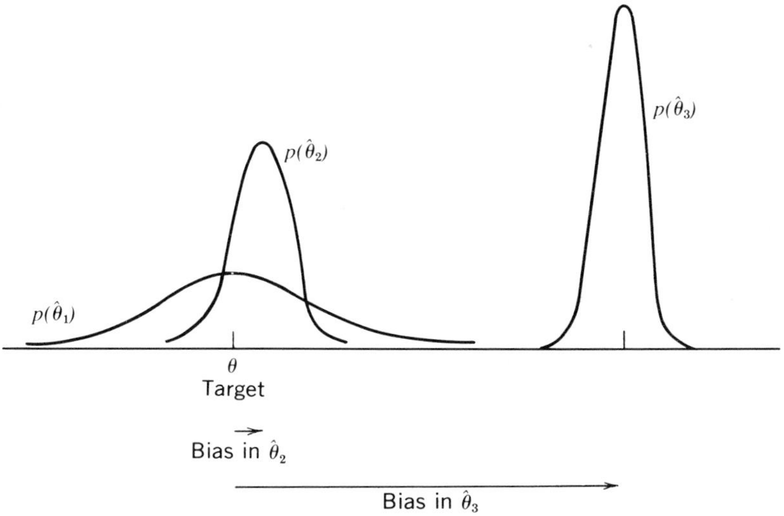

FIGURE 2-20 $\hat{\theta}_2$ as the estimator with the best combination of small bias and variance.

measures how it is spread around its (possibly biased) mean; instead we are interested in how it is spread around its *true target* θ. The most common measure of this kind is

$$\boxed{\text{Mean squared error (MSE)} \equiv E(\hat{\theta} - \theta)^2} \tag{2-104}$$

We reemphasize that this is exactly the same as the variance, except that it is measured around the target θ, rather than the mean of the estimator.

Finally, it can be proved that MSE is a measure of both variance and bias:[24]

$$\boxed{\text{MSE} = \sigma^2 + \text{bias}^2} \tag{2-105}$$

---

[24] ***Proof of (2-105).*** Letting $\mu = E(\hat{\theta})$, we may write the MSE in (2-104) as

$$\begin{aligned} E(\hat{\theta} - \theta)^2 &= E[(\hat{\theta} - \mu) + (\mu - \theta)]^2 \\ &= E(\hat{\theta} - \mu)^2 + 2(\mu - \theta)\underbrace{E(\hat{\theta} - \mu)}_{=0} + (\mu - \theta)^2 \\ &= \text{var } \hat{\theta} + 0 + (\mu - \theta)^2 \end{aligned}$$

$$\text{MSE} = \text{var } \hat{\theta} + (\text{bias } \hat{\theta})^2 \qquad \text{(2-105) proved}$$

This equation confirms two earlier conclusions: If two estimators with equal variance are compared (as in Figure 2-18) the one with less bias is preferred; and if two unbiased (or equally biased) estimators are compared (as in Figure 2-19) the one with smaller variance is preferred. In fact, if two estimators are unbiased, it is evident from either (2-104) or (2-105) that the MSE reduces to the variance. Thus MSE may be regarded as a generalization of the variance concept. Using MSE therefore leads to a generalized definition of the relative efficiency of two estimators:

For any two estimators, whether biased or unbiased,

$$\text{relative efficiency of } \hat{\theta} \text{ compared to } \hat{\hat{\theta}} \equiv \frac{\text{MSE}(\hat{\hat{\theta}})}{\text{MSE}(\hat{\theta})} \tag{2-106}$$

with (2-97) being recognized as just a special case of this concept.

Finally, to sum up, because it combines the two attractive properties of small bias and small variance, the concept of efficiency as defined in (2-106) becomes the single most important criterion for judging estimators.

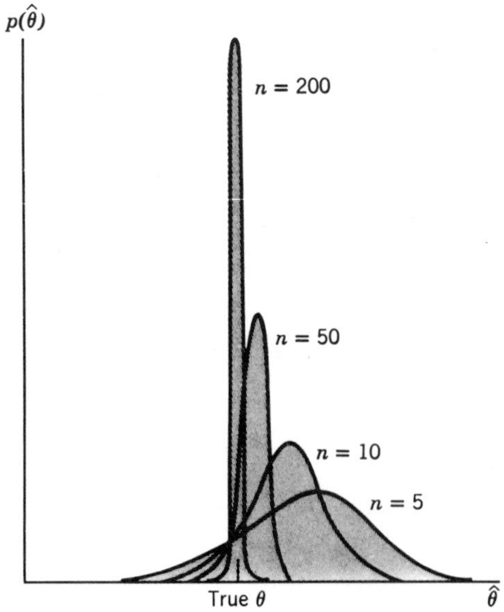

FIGURE 2-21 A consistent estimator, showing how the distribution of $\hat{\theta}$ concentrates on its target θ as n increases.

(d) Consistency

Roughly speaking, a consistent estimator is one that concentrates in a narrower and narrower band around its target as sample size increases indefinitely (Figure 2-21). The precise definition of consistency involves a limit statement: $\hat{\theta}$ is defined to be a consistent estimator of θ iff,[25] for any positive δ (no matter how small),

$$\Pr(|\hat{\theta} - \theta| < \delta) \to 1 \quad \text{as } n \to \infty \tag{2-107}$$

This is just a formal way of stating that it eventually becomes certain that $\hat{\theta}$ will draw as close to θ as we please (within δ). Accordingly, (2-107) is often abbreviated to

$$\hat{\theta} \xrightarrow{p} \theta \tag{2-108}$$

or

$$p \lim \hat{\theta} = \theta$$

where p means probability.

To be concrete, in the example below, we show that the sample mean $\bar{Y}$ is a consistent estimator of the population mean μ; for this case, (2-107) therefore becomes

$$\Pr(|\bar{Y} - \mu| < \delta) \to 1 \quad \text{as } n \to \infty$$

Stated informally, this means that, with increased sample size, it eventually becomes certain that $\bar{Y}$ will get as close to μ as we please (within δ).

An estimator $\hat{\theta}$ will be consistent if its MSE approaches zero.[26] According to (2-105), this may be reexpressed as

> $\hat{\theta}$ is a consistent estimator if its bias and variance *both* approach zero, as $n \to \infty$. (2-109)

[25] Iff is an abbreviation for *if and only if*. Although this is customarily taken for granted in definitions, we will make it explicit.

[26] The proof may be found in mathematical statistics texts such as Lindgren, 1968. Incidentally, we cannot make the implication the other way. That is, there exist consistent estimators where the MSE does not approach zero; consider, for example, an estimator $\hat{\theta}$ whose sampling distribution is shown in the following figure:

(*footnote continued*)

Example 2-5

Is the sample mean $\bar{Y}$ a consistent estimator of the population mean μ?

Solution

In view of (2-109), it will be adequate to prove that the bias and variance of $\bar{Y}$ both approach zero. Since $E(\bar{Y}) = \mu$,

$$\text{bias} = 0 \quad \text{for all } n$$

(*footnote* 26 *continued*)

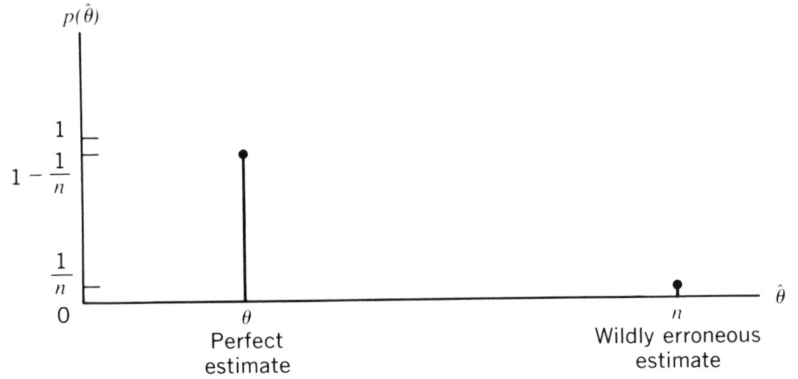

As n increases, note how the distribution of $\hat{\theta}$ becomes increasingly concentrated on its target θ, while the probability of getting an erroneous estimate becomes smaller and smaller (as $1/n$ decreases). Thus $\hat{\theta}$ is a consistent estimator according to the definition (2-107).

But now let us consider the MSE of $\hat{\theta}$:

$$\begin{aligned} \text{MSE} = E(\hat{\theta} - \theta)^2 &= \sum (\hat{\theta} - \theta)^2 p(\hat{\theta}) \\ &= 0^2\left(1 - \frac{1}{n}\right) + (n - \theta)^2\left(\frac{1}{n}\right) \\ &= n - 2\theta + \frac{\theta^2}{n} \end{aligned}$$

As $n \to \infty$, this MSE does *not* approach zero (in fact, it behaves much worse—it approaches infinity!) Accordingly, we conclude that a sufficient (but not necessary) condition for consistency is that MSE approaches zero.

At the same time,

$$\text{variance}^{27} = \frac{\sigma^2}{n} \to 0 \quad \text{as } n \to \infty$$

Thus $\bar{Y}$ is indeed a consistent estimator of μ.

Example 2-6

Is s_*^2 in (2-89) a consistent estimator of σ^2?

Solution

First, recall that we have already shown that it is biased; but as $n \to \infty$, this bias disappears; that is, it is asymptotically unbiased.[28] Since it can also be proved that its variance tends to zero, the conditions of (2-109) are satisfied. Thus s_*^2 is a consistent estimator of σ^2.

Consistency does not guarantee that an estimator is a good one. For example, as an estimator of μ in a normal population, the sample median has been proved to be consistent. Or, to take a more drastic example, if we throw away half our observations and average the remaining half, we still obtain a consistent estimator. But neither of these consistent estimators is very good; the sample mean is preferred because it is both consistent *and* efficient.

These examples show that there are many consistent estimators, and the criterion of consistency may not necessarily help us choose the best one, or even a sensible one. Why is this? It is because consistency is a limiting property, defined in very abstract mathematical terms that say nothing about how *fast* the approach to the limit is. To know that an estimator will eventually come close (though it may take a billion billion observations) is cold comfort to an applied statistician who has only a dozen observations in hand.

Why then should we put any effort into studying consistency? The answer is that in many difficult situations (especially simultaneous equation

[27] This is the same well-known formula quoted in (2-103). Incidentally, since we use the population variance σ^2 in this solution, we assume the population variance does exist.

[28] To establish this, we note that

$$s_*^2 = \left(\frac{n-1}{n}\right)s^2 \tag{2-110}$$

Thus $s_*^2 \to s^2$ as $n \to \infty$. Since s^2 is unbiased (for any n), it follows that s_*^2 is unbiased as $n \to \infty$.

estimation) estimators cannot easily be analyzed according to the really important criterion of efficiency. But the weaker property of consistency often can be established,[29] and this is better than nothing. In other words, when a statistician proposes a new estimator, nobody will cheer if it is proved to be consistent. But everybody will criticize if it turns out to be inconsistent.

PROBLEMS

2-24 In sampling from a normal population, the sample median and sample mean are both efficient estimators of μ. The difference is that the sample median is biased, whereas the sample mean is unbiased. Do you agree? If not, why?

2-25 Each of three guns is being tested by firing 12 shots at a target from a clamped position. Gun A was not clamped down hard enough, and wobbled. Gun B was clamped down in a position that pointed slightly to the left, due to a misaligned sight. Gun C was clamped down just right.

(a) Which of the following patterns of shots belongs to gun A? Gun B? Gun C?

(b) Which guns are biased? Which gun has minimum variance? Which has the largest MSE? Which is most efficient? Which is least efficient?

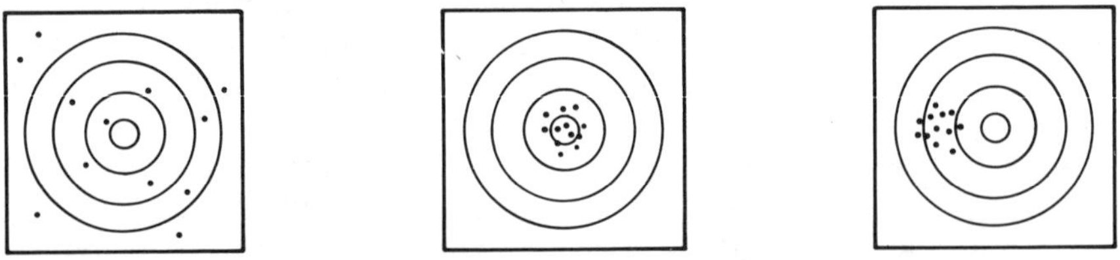

[29] This is primarily because the p lim operator is much easier to manipulate than the expectation operator E (which is used to define efficiency). For example, if $p \lim \hat{\theta}$ exists and f is any continuous function,

$$\boxed{p \lim f(\hat{\theta}) = f(p \lim \hat{\theta})} \qquad (2\text{-}111)$$

For example, if $\hat{\theta}$ is the estimator $\bar{Y}$, and f is the squaring function, (2-111) becomes

$$p \lim \bar{Y}^2 = (p \lim \bar{Y})^2$$

which is true, because both sides equal μ^2.

*APPENDIX 2-C PROOF OF THE GAUSS-MARKOV THEOREM

We shall prove this theorem in the case of simple linear regression for the estimator $\hat{\beta}$. The proof for $\hat{\alpha}$ is left to the reader.

First, we ask what it means for an estimator to be linear. By definition, it must be of the form

$$\hat{\beta} = \sum_{i=1}^{n} c_i Y_i \tag{2-112}$$

where the c_i are constants.[30] In addition, we insist that our estimator be unbiased, that is,

$$E(\hat{\beta}) = \beta \tag{2-113}$$

From (2-112)

$$\begin{aligned} E(\hat{\beta}) &= E\left(\sum c_i Y_i\right) \\ &= \sum c_i E(Y_i) \\ &= \sum c_i(\alpha + \beta x_i) \\ &= \alpha \sum c_i + \beta \sum c_i x_i \\ &= \beta \text{ iff} \end{aligned}$$

$$\sum c_i = 0 \tag{2-114}$$

and

$$\sum c_i x_i = 1 \tag{2-115}$$

In other words, the c_i must satisfy conditions (2-114) and (2-115) for $\sum c_i Y_i$ to be an unbiased estimator of β.

Now we turn to the condition that our estimator have minimum variance. The variance of $\hat{\beta}$ is given as

$$\operatorname{var}(\hat{\beta}) = \operatorname{var}\left(\sum c_i Y_i\right)$$

On the other hand, the analogue of (2-111) does not hold for the expectation operator E (unless f is a linear function). For example,

$$E(\bar{Y}^2) \neq [E(\bar{Y})]^2$$

because the left side is $\mu^2 + \sigma^2/n$, while the right side is μ^2.

[30] In this development, we regard the x_i as fixed, so that the c_i could depend on them. In fact, note in (2-124) that this is exactly what happens.

and, because the Y_i are independent,

$$= \sum c_i^2 \text{ var } Y_i$$

$$= (\sum c_i^2)\sigma^2 \tag{2-116}$$

Since σ^2 is fixed, it is only necessary to minimize

$$\sum c_i^2 \tag{2-117}$$

The problem of minimizing $\sum c_i^2$ subject to the two constraints (2-114) and (2-115) is best handled by Lagrangian multipliers. This involves setting up the Lagrangian function:

$$g(c_1 \cdots c_n, \lambda_1, \lambda_2) = \sum c_i^2 - \lambda_1(\sum c_i) - \lambda_2(\sum c_i x_i - 1)$$

and setting equal to zero its partial derivatives with respect to all the c_i, λ_1, and λ_2.

First, setting $\partial g/\partial c_i = 0$, we obtain

$$2c_i - \lambda_1 - \lambda_2 x_i = 0 \qquad (i = 1, 2, \ldots, n) \tag{2-118}$$

That is,

$$c_i = \frac{\lambda_1}{2} + \frac{\lambda_2}{2} x_i \tag{2-119}$$

Then, setting $\partial g/\partial \lambda_i = 0$, we obtain

$$\sum c_i = 0 \qquad \text{(2-114) repeated}$$

$$\sum c_i x_i = 1 \qquad \text{(2-115) repeated}$$

which are a restatement of our two side conditions.

Conditions (2-119), (2-114), and (2-115) must be satisfied for a minimization of the variance subject to the two constraints. Substitute (2-119) into (2-114):

$$\sum \left(\frac{\lambda_1}{2} + \frac{\lambda_2}{2} x_i \right) = 0 \tag{2-120}$$

$$n\frac{\lambda_1}{2} + \frac{\lambda_2}{2} \sum x_i = 0 \tag{2-121}$$

Since

$$\sum x_i = 0,$$

$$n\frac{\lambda_1}{2} = 0$$

$$\lambda_1 = 0 \tag{2-122}$$

To solve for λ_2, we substitute (2-119) into (2-115), and note that $\lambda_1 = 0$:

$$\sum \left(\frac{\lambda_2}{2} x_i\right) x_i = 1$$

$$\frac{\lambda_2}{2} \sum x_i^2 = 1$$

$$\lambda_2 = \frac{2}{\sum x_i^2} \tag{2-123}$$

Substituting (2-122) and (2-123) into (2-119) finally yields a solution for c_i:

$$c_i = \frac{1}{2} \cdot \frac{2}{\sum x_i^2} \cdot x_i = \frac{x_i}{\sum x_i^2} \tag{2-124}$$

This then is the c_i we require for our estimator in (2-112); thus $\hat{\beta} = \sum x_i Y_i / \sum x_i^2$ is the minimum variance estimator. But this is precisely the least squares estimator, as promised.

*APPENDIX 2-D THE MAXIMUM LIKELIHOOD ESTIMATE OF σ^2

To avoid confusion, we rename the variance v instead of σ^2, so that the likelihood function (2-79) may be written as

$$L(\alpha, \beta, v) = \frac{1}{(2\pi v)^{n/2}} e^{(-1/2v)\sum [Y_i - (\alpha + \beta x_i)]^2}$$

Since L and $\log L$ will be maximized at the same value of v, we select the value of v to maximize the easier function $\log L$ (which we rename Q):

$$Q = \log L = -\frac{n}{2} \log 2\pi - \frac{n}{2} \log v - \frac{1}{2v} \sum [Y_i - (\alpha + \beta x_i)]^2 \tag{2-125}$$

To find the maximum, we set $\partial Q/\partial v = 0$:

$$\frac{\partial Q}{\partial v} = -\frac{n}{2} \cdot \frac{1}{v} + \frac{1}{2v^2} \sum [Y_i - (\alpha + \beta x_i)]^2 = 0 \tag{2-126}$$

Recall that estimating v is part of the larger problem of simultaneously estimating α, β, and v. Hence, we should also set

$$\frac{\partial Q}{\partial \alpha} = 0 \tag{2-127}$$

$$\frac{\partial Q}{\partial \beta} = 0 \tag{2-128}$$

Now (2-126), (2-127), and (2-128) may be solved simultaneously for the MLE of v, α, and β. But (2-127) and (2-128) alone may be solved for $\hat{\alpha}$ and $\hat{\beta}$. (You are invited to confirm this; your solution of (2-127) and (2-128) for $\hat{\alpha}$ and $\hat{\beta}$ should be the least squares solution.) The only remaining step is to plug $\hat{\alpha}$ and $\hat{\beta}$ into (2-126), and solve for $\hat{v}$:

$$\boxed{\hat{v} = \frac{1}{n} \sum [Y_i - (\hat{\alpha} + \hat{\beta} x_i)]^2} \tag{2-129}$$

In the special case in which $\beta = 0$ (i.e., Y does not depend on x), $\hat{\alpha}$ becomes $\bar{Y}$, the last term disappears, and $\hat{v}$ becomes s_*^2. As a special case of (2-129), s_*^2 is, of course, the MLE; but it has been shown (in Appendix 2-B) to be biased. Using a similar argument, the MLE $\hat{v}$ in (2-129) can be shown to be biased; for this reason it is adjusted by division by $(n - 2)$ rather than n to provide the unbiased estimator:

$$\boxed{s^2 = \frac{1}{n-2} \sum [Y_i - (\hat{\alpha} + \hat{\beta} x_i)]^2} \tag{2-130}$$

with $(n - 2)$ d.f.[31]

This also illustrates a major limitation of maximum likelihood estimation. It is true that MLE provides an estimate with the very attractive large sample property of consistency; see, for example, how the consistency of the MLE s_*^2 was shown in Appendix 2-B. However, in small sample estimation, it must be used with great caution, since it may be biased; again s_*^2 provides an example.

---

[31] Just as the calculation of $\bar{Y}$ results in the loss of 1 d.f. in (2-91), the calculation of the *two* estimates $\hat{\alpha}$ and $\hat{\beta}$ used to evaluate (2-130) results in the loss of 2 d.f.

3

MULTIPLE REGRESSION

3-1 INTRODUCTION

Multiple regression is the extension of simple regression, to take account of more than one independent variable X. It is obviously the appropriate technique when we want to investigate the effects on Y of several variables simultaneously. Yet, even if we are interested in the effect of only one variable, it usually is wise to include the other variables influencing Y in a multiple regression analysis, for two reasons:

1. To reduce stochastic error (as we discussed in Section 2-4), and hence reduce the residual variance s^2. This makes confidence intervals more precise.
2. Even more important, to eliminate bias that might result if we just ignored a variable that substantially affects Y.

Example 3-1

In Figure 2-2, we might ask whether part of the fluctuation in Y (i.e., the disturbance term e) can be explained by varying levels of rainfall in different areas. A better prediction of yield may be possible if *both* fertilizer and rainfall are examined. The observed levels of rainfall are therefore given in Table 3-1, along with the original observations of yield and fertilizer from Table 2-1.

(a) On Figure 2-2, tag each point with its value of rainfall Z. Then, considering just those points with low rainfall ($Z = 10$), roughly fit a line by eye. Next, repeat for the points with moderate rainfall ($Z = 20$), and then for the points with high rainfall ($Z = 30$).

(b) Now, if rainfall were kept constant, roughly estimate what the slope of yield on fertilizer would be. That is, what would be the increase in yield per pound of fertilizer?

TABLE 3-1 Observed Yield, Fertilizer Application, and Rainfall

Y *Wheat Yield* *(Bushels/Acre)*	*X* *Fertilizer* *(Pounds/Acre)*	*Z* *Rainfall* *(Inches)*
40	100	10
50	200	20
50	300	10
70	400	30
65	500	20
65	600	20
80	700	30

(c) If fertilizer were kept constant, roughly estimate what would be the increase in yield per inch of rainfall.

(d) What would you estimate would be the yield if fertilizer were 400 pounds, and rainfall were 10 inches?

Solution

(a)

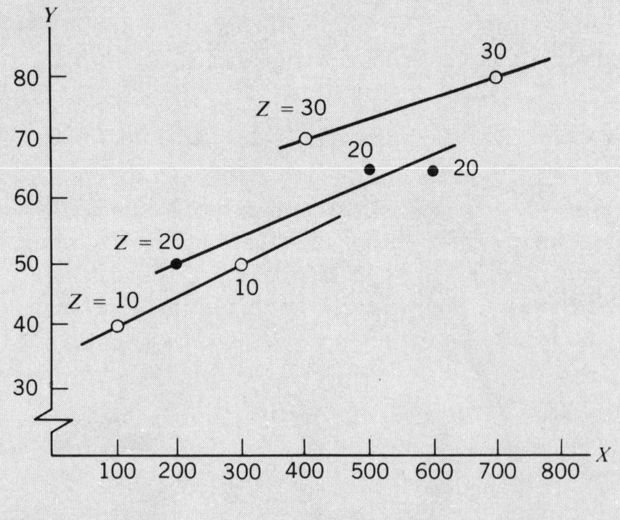

(b) The largest slope in the figure above is 10/200 = .05 for the line $Z = 10$, while the smallest slope is 10/300 = .033 for the line $Z = 30$; on the average, these slopes are about .04 bushels per pound of fertilizer.

(c) The vertical distance between the line where $Z = 10$ and the line where $Z = 30$ is about 15 bushels. Since this increase of 15 bushels comes from an increase of 20 inches of rain, this means that rain increases yield by about $15/20 = .75$ bushels per inch of rainfall.

(d) We use the line where $Z = 10$, at the point where $X = 400$, obtaining a yield of 55 bushels.

This example illustrates the two reasons why the additional variable Z improves our analysis:

1. We have a better fit of the data. Note how the fluctuations about the fitted lines are less than in Figure 2-2. This should allow us to make more precise statistical conclusions about how X affects Y.
2. This example shows the relationship of yield to fertilizer while rainfall is held constant. If rainfall is not held constant and is ignored, we obtain the slope in Figure 2-2; this slope is larger because high rainfall tends to accompany high fertilizer. Thus our estimate in Figure 2-2 was biased because we were erroneously attributing to fertilizer the effects of both fertilizer *and* rainfall.

Example 3-1 was vastly oversimplified. We need to develop a more objective, easily computerized method that will handle the more complicated cases where fitting by eye is out of the question.

3-2 THE MATHEMATICAL MODEL

Yield Y is now to be regressed on the two independent variables (regressors) fertilizer X and rainfall Z. Let us suppose the relationship is of the form:

$$E(Y_i) = \alpha + \beta x_i + \gamma z_i \qquad (3\text{-}1) \text{ like } (2\text{-}21)$$

where both regressors x and z are measured as deviations from their means. Geometrically this equation is a plane in the three-dimensional space shown in Figure 3-1. For any given combination of rainfall and fertilizer (x_i, z_i), the expected yield $E(Y_i)$ is the point on this plane directly above, shown as a hollow dot. Of course, the observed value of Y is very unlikely to fall precisely on this plane. For example, the particular observed Y_i at this fertilizer-rainfall combination is somewhat greater than its expected value and is shown as the solid dot lying directly above this plane.

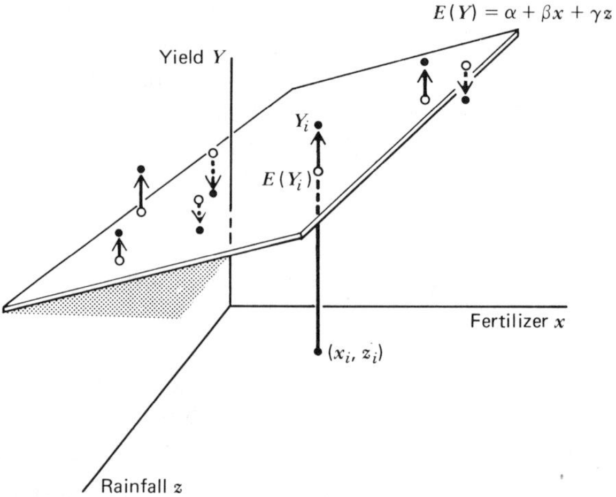

FIGURE 3-1 Scatter of observed points about the true regression plane.

The difference between the observed and expected value of Y_i is the stochastic or error term e_i. Thus, any observed value Y_i may be expressed as its expected value plus this disturbance term:

$$Y_i = \alpha + \beta x_i + \gamma z_i + e_i \tag{3-2}$$

with the assumptions about e_i the same as in Chapter 2 like (2-23)

β is geometrically interpreted as the slope of the plane as we move in the x-direction, keeping z constant. Thus β is the marginal effect of fertilizer x on yield Y. Similarly γ is the slope of the plane as we move in the z-direction, keeping x constant; thus γ is the marginal effect of z on Y. More generally,

β = the increase in Y if x is increased one unit, while all other regressors are held constant.[1] (3-3)

[1] ***Proof.*** Suppose that, in addition to x, there is only one other regressor z; then the true regression is the plane shown in Figure 3-1, that is,

$$Y = \alpha + \beta x + \gamma z$$

To establish (3-3), simply take the partial derivative of Y with respect to x in the equation above, i.e.,

$$\frac{\partial Y}{\partial x} = \beta$$

(*footnote continued*)

3-3 LEAST SQUARES (MAXIMUM LIKELIHOOD) ESTIMATION

As in simple regression, the problem is that the statistician does not know the true relationship [the true plane (3-1) shown in Figure 3-1]. The best she can do is fit an estimated plane of the form

$$Y_i = \hat{\alpha} + \hat{\beta}x_i + \hat{\gamma}z_i \tag{3-4}$$

using the least squares technique.[2] This involves selecting the estimates $\hat{\alpha}$, $\hat{\beta}$,

---

(*footnote* 1 *continued*)
You can easily confirm that this simple interpretation of β is valid because the regression is linear. If it is not, then $\partial Y/\partial x \neq \beta$. For example, if the regression is of the non-linear form

$$Y = \alpha + \beta x + \psi x^2 + \gamma z$$

then

$$\frac{\partial Y}{\partial x} = \beta + 2\psi x$$

To establish (3-3) without calculus, hold z constant at its initial value z_0, and increase x from its initial value x_0 to $(x_0 + 1)$. Substituting into the equation above, we may write

$$\begin{aligned} \text{Initial } Y &= \alpha + \beta x_0 + \gamma z_0 \\ \text{New } Y &= \alpha + \beta(x_0 + 1) + \gamma z_0 \\ \hline \text{Difference} &= \text{increase in } Y = \beta \end{aligned}$$

It is easy to confirm that this is still true if there are several z variables.

[2] Maximum likelihood estimates of α, β, and γ are derived the same way as in the simple regression case; again this coincides with least squares. Geometrically, this involves trying out all possible hypothetical regression planes in Figure 3-1, and selecting the one that is most likely to generate the solid-dot sample values we actually observed.

But first, note that Figure 3-1 involves three parameters (α, β, and γ), and three variables (Y, x, and z). However, there is one additional variable in our system—$p(Y/x, z)$—which has not yet been plotted. It may appear that there is no way of forcing four variables into a three-dimensional space, but this is not so. For example, economists often plot three variables (labor, capital, and output) in a two-dimensional labor-capital space by introducing the third output variable as a system of isoquants. Those for whom this is a familiar exercise should have little trouble in graphing four variables [Y, x, z, and $p(Y/x, z)$] in a three-dimensional (Y, x, and z) space by introducing the fourth variable, $p(Y/x, z)$, as a system of isoplanes. Each of these isoplanes represents Y, x, z combinations that are equiprobable (i.e., for which the probability density of Y is constant). Thus, the complete geometric model is the regression plane shown in Figure 3-1, with isoprobability planes stacked above and below it. Our assumptions about the error term (2-23) guarantee that the isoprobability planes will be parallel to the true regression plane.

For MLE, we introduce the additional assumption that the error configuration is normal. Then we shift around a hypothetical regression plane along with its associated set of parallel isoprobability planes. In each position the probability density of the observed sample of points is evaluated by examining the isoprobability plane on which each point lies, and multiplying these together. That hypothetical regression which maximizes this likelihood is chosen. The algebra resembles the simple case in Section 2-12; it is easy to show that this results in minimizing the sum of squares (3-5).

TABLE 3-2 Least Squares Multiple Regression of Y on X and Z.

Y	X	Z	$x = X - \bar{X}$	$z = Z - \bar{Z}$	xY	zY	x^2	z^2	xz
40	100	10	−300	−10	−12,000	−400	90,000	100	3,000
50	200	20	−200	0	−10,000	0	40,000	0	0
50	300	10	−100	−10	−5,000	−500	10,000	100	1,000
70	400	30	0	10	0	700	0	100	0
65	500	20	100	0	6,500	0	10,000	0	0
65	600	20	200	0	13,000	0	40,000	0	0
80	700	30	300	10	24,000	800	90,000	100	3,000
$\sum Y = 420$ $\bar{Y} = 60$	$\sum X = 2800$ $\bar{X} = 400$	$\sum Z = 140$ $\bar{Z} = 20$	0$\surd$	0$\surd$	$\sum xY = 16{,}500$	$\sum zY = 600$	$\sum x^2 = 280{,}000$	$\sum z^2 = 400$	$\sum xz = 7{,}000$

Estimating Equations (3-6)
$$\begin{cases} 16{,}500 = 280{,}000\hat{\beta} + 7{,}000\hat{\gamma} \\ 600 = 7{,}000\hat{\beta} + 400\hat{\gamma} \end{cases}$$

Solution
$$\begin{cases} \hat{\beta} = .0381 \\ \hat{\gamma} = .833 \end{cases}$$

and $\hat{\gamma}$ that minimize the sum of the squared deviations between the observed Y's and the fitted Y's; that is,

$$\text{minimize} \sum (Y_i - \hat{\alpha} - \hat{\beta}x_i - \hat{\gamma}z_i)^2 \tag{3-5}$$

like (2-10)

This is done with calculus by setting the partial derivatives with respect to $\hat{\alpha}$, $\hat{\beta}$, and $\hat{\gamma}$ equal to zero. The result is the following three estimating equations (sometimes called normal equations):

$$\left.\begin{aligned} \hat{\alpha} &= \bar{Y} \\ \sum x_i Y_i &= \hat{\beta} \sum x_i^2 + \hat{\gamma} \sum x_i z_i \\ \sum z_i Y_i &= \hat{\beta} \sum x_i z_i + \hat{\gamma} \sum z_i^2 \end{aligned}\right\} \tag{3-6}$$

Again, note that the intercept estimate $\hat{\alpha}$ is the average $\bar{Y}$. The second and third equations may be solved for $\hat{\beta}$ and $\hat{\gamma}$. These calculations are shown in Table 3-2, and yield the fitted multiple regression equation:

$$\begin{aligned} \hat{Y} &= 60 + .0381x + .833z \\ &= 60 + .0381(X - 400) + .833(Z - 20) \\ &= 28.1 + .0381X + .833Z \end{aligned} \tag{3-7}$$

Example 3-2

(a) Graph the relation of Y to X given by (3-7), when rainfall has the constant value:

(i) $Z = 10$
(ii) $Z = 20$
(iii) $Z = 30$

(b) Compare to the figure in Example 3-1.

Solution

(a) Substitute $Z = 10$ into (3-7):

$$\begin{aligned} Y &= 28.1 + .0381X + .833(10) \\ &= 36.4 + .0381X \end{aligned}$$

This is a line with slope .0381 and Y intercept 36.4. Similarly, when we substitute $Z = 20$ and then $Z = 30$ into (3-7), we obtain the lines

$$Y = 44.8 + .0381X$$

and

$$Y = 53.1 + .0381X$$

These are lines with the same slope .0381, but higher and higher intercepts.

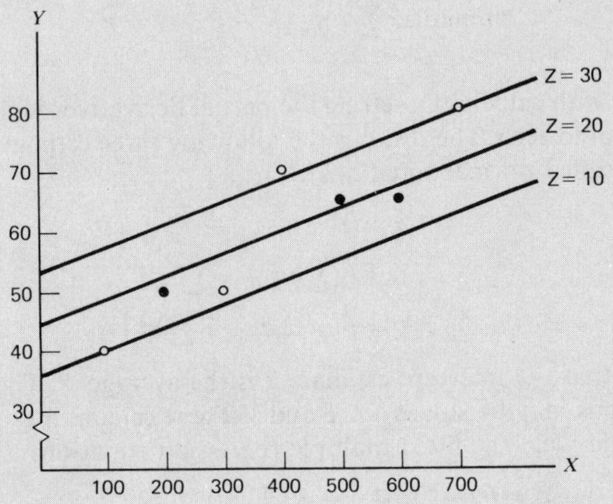

(b) The three lines given by the linear regression model (3-7) are evenly spaced because we selected evenly spaced values of Z in question (a). These three lines are also parallel, because they are drawn from a plane we have fitted to the scatter of observations.

In contrast, the three earlier lines fitted in Example 3-1 were not constrained to be parallel (in that case we were fitting three separate lines, rather than a plane). Therefore they fit the data a little better. However, they are harder to summarize: in Example 3-1(b), we calculated the average slope to be about .04; whereas in (3-7), we can immediately see the slope is .038. Similarly, in Example 3-1(c), we calculated the average effect of one inch of rain to be about .75; whereas in (3-7) we can immediately see that it is .83.

Another important difference is that in Example 3-1 we had only 2 or 3 observations to fit each line. However, in estimating the plane (3-7) we use all 7 observations. Thus we are in a much stronger position to test hypotheses or construct confidence intervals.

PROBLEMS

3-1 Suppose that a random sample of 5 families yielded the following data (an extension of Problem 2-2, where everything is measured in thousands of dollars):

Family	*Saving S*	*Income X*	*Assets W*
A	.6	8	12
B	1.2	11	6
C	1.0	9	6
D	.7	6	3
E	.3	6	18

(a) Estimate the multiple regression equation of S on X and W.
(b) Does the coefficient of X differ from the answer to Problem 2-2?
(c) For a family with assets of 5 thousand and income of 8 thousand dollars, what would you predict saving to be?
(d) If a family had a 2 thousand dollar increase in income, while assets remained constant, estimate by how much their saving would increase.
(e) If a family had a 1 thousand dollar increase in income, and a 3 thousand dollar increase in assets, estimate by how much their saving would increase.

(3-2) Suppose that a random sample of 5 families yielded the following data (another extension of Problem 2-2):

Family	*Saving S*	*Income X*	*Number of Children N*
A	.6	8	5
B	1.2	11	2
C	1.0	9	1
D	.7	6	3
E	.3	6	4

(a) Estimate the multiple regression of S on X and N.
(b) For a family with 5 children and income of 6 thousand dollars, what would you predict saving to be?

*3-3 Derive the estimating equations (3-6) from the least squares criterion (3-5) [*Hint*. See equations (2-11) to (2-16).]

*3-4 Suppose that the data in Problems 3-1 and 3-2 applies to exactly the same families. Then this information can be combined to obtain the following table:

Family	Saving S	Income X	Assets W	Number of Children N
A	.6	8	12	5
B	1.2	11	6	2
C	1.0	9	6	1
D	.7	6	3	3
E	.3	6	18	4

Measuring the independent variables as deviations from the mean, we want the estimated equation:

$$\hat{S} = \hat{\alpha} + \hat{\beta}x + \hat{\gamma}w + \hat{\psi}n$$

(a) Generalizing (3-6), use the least squares criterion to derive the system of 4 equations in the 4 unknown estimates, $\hat{\alpha}$, $\hat{\beta}$, $\hat{\gamma}$, and $\hat{\psi}$.
(b) Using a table such as Table 3-2, calculate the 4 estimates.

3-4 MULTICOLLINEARITY

(a) In Simple Regression

In Figure 2-12*a* it was shown how the estimate $\hat{\beta}$ became unreliable if the X_i were closely bunched, that is, if the regressor X had little variation. It will be instructive to consider the limiting case, where the X_i are concentrated on one single value $\bar{X}$, as in Figure 3-2. Then $\hat{\beta}$ is not determined at all. There are any number of differently sloped lines passing through $(\bar{X}, \bar{Y})$ that fit equally well: For each line in Figure 3-2, the sum of squared deviations is the

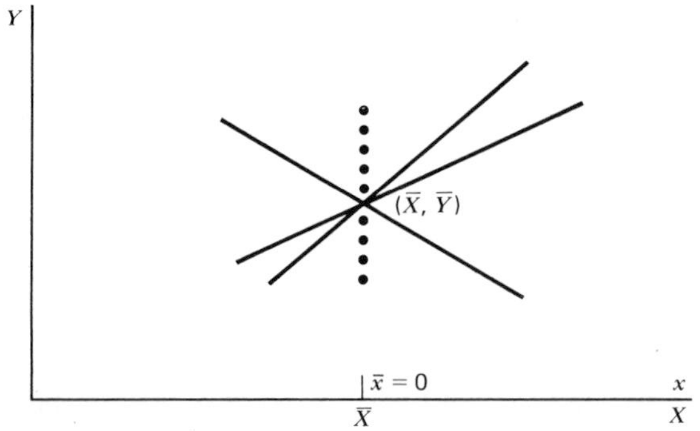

FIGURE 3-2 Degenerate regression, because of no spread (variation) in X.

same, since the deviations are measured vertically from $(\bar{X}, \bar{Y})$. This geometric fact has an algebraic counterpart. If all $X_i = \bar{X}$, then all $x_i = 0$, and the term involving $\hat{\beta}$ (or b) in (2-10) is zero; hence, the sum of squares does not depend on $\hat{\beta}$ at all. Consequently any $\hat{\beta}$ will do equally well in minimizing the sum of squares. Another way of looking at the same problem is that since all x_i are zero, $\sum x_i^2$ in the denominator of (2-16) is zero, and $\hat{\beta}$ is not defined.

In conclusion, when the values of X show little or no variation, then the effect of X on Y can no longer be sensibly investigated. But if the problem is *predicting* Y—rather than investigating Y's dependence on X—this bunching of the X values does not matter *provided* we limit our prediction to this same value of X. All the lines in Figure 3-2 predict Y equally well. The best prediction is $\bar{Y}$, and all these lines give us that result.

(b) In Multiple Regression

Again consider the limiting case: Suppose the values of the independent variables X and Z are completely bunched up on a line L, as in Figure 3-3. This means that all the observed points in our scatter lie in the vertical plane running up through L. You can think of the three-dimensional space as a room in a house; our observations are not scattered throughout this room, but instead lie embedded in an extremely thin pane of glass standing vertically on the floor.

In explaining Y, multicollinearity makes us lose one dimension. In the earlier case of simple regression, our best fit for Y was not a line, but rather a

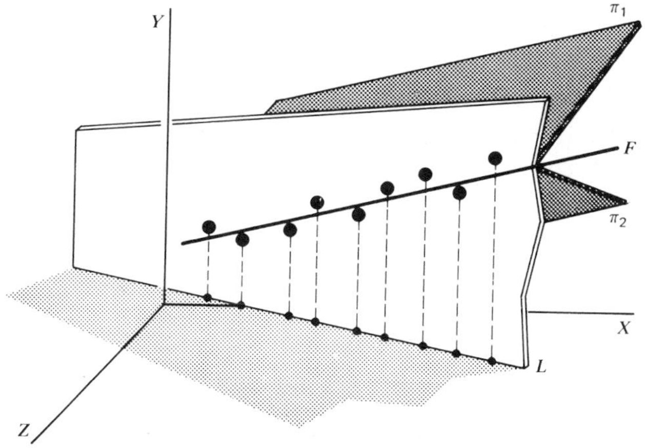

FIGURE 3-3 Multicollinearity.

point $(\bar{X}, \bar{Y})$; in this multiple regression case our best fit for Y is not a plane, but instead the line F. To get F, we just fit the least squares line through the points on the vertical pane of glass. The problem is identical to the one shown in Figure 2-2; in one case a line is fitted on a flat pane of glass; in the other case, on a flat piece of paper. This regression line F is, therefore, our best fit for Y. So long as we stick to the same *combination* of X and Z—that is, if we confine ourselves to predicting Y values on that pane of glass—no special problems arise. We can use the regression F on the glass to predict Y in exactly the same way as we did in the simple regression analysis of Chapter 2.

But there is no way to examine how X affects Y. Any attempt to define β, the marginal effect of X on Y (holding Z constant), involves moving off that pane of glass, and we have no sample information on what the world out there looks like. Or, to put it differently, if we try to explain Y with a plane—rather than a line F—we find there are any number of planes running through F (e.g., π_1 and π_2) that do an equally good job. Since each passes through F, each yields an identical sum of squared deviations; thus each provides an equally good fit. This is confirmed in the algebra in the estimating equations (3-6). When X is a linear function of Z (i.e., when x is a linear function of z), it may be shown that the last two equations are dependent, and cannot be solved uniquely[3] for $\hat{\beta}$ and $\hat{\gamma}$.

Now let's be less extreme in our assumptions and consider the near-limiting case, where Z and X are almost on a line (i.e., where all our observations in the room lie very close to a vertical pane of glass). In this case, a plane may be fitted to our observations, but the estimating procedure is very unstable; it becomes very sensitive to random errors, reflected in large variances of the estimators $\hat{\beta}$ and $\hat{\gamma}$. Thus, even though the relation of Y to X may be real, it may be indiscernible (insignificant) because the standard error of $\hat{\beta}$ is so large. This is analogous to the argument in the simple regression case in Figure 2-12(a).

When the independent variables X and Z are collinear, or nearly so (i.e., highly correlated), it is called the problem of multicollinearity.[4] As indicated earlier, this does not raise problems in predicting Y provided there is no

---

[3] Two linear equations can usually be solved for two unknowns, but not always. For example, suppose that John's age (X) is twice Harry's (Y). Then we can write

$$X = 2Y$$

$$5X = 10Y$$

These two equations tell us the same thing. We have two equations in two unknowns, but they don't generate a unique solution, because they don't provide independent information.

[4] Actually, it would be more accurate to call it the problem of *collinearity*, and reserve the term *multicollinearity* if there are many regressors $X, Z, \ldots$ that are highly correlated.

attempt to predict for values of X and Z removed from their line of collinearity. But structural questions cannot be answered—the influence of X alone (or Z alone) on Y cannot be sensibly investigated.

Example 3-3

Referring to equation (2-18), suppose that X is still the amount of fertilizer measured in pounds per acre. But now suppose the statistician makes the incredibly foolish error of also measuring fertilizer in ounces per acre, and using it as another regressor Z. Since any weight measured in ounces must be 16 times its measurement in pounds,

$$Z = 16X \tag{3-8}$$

Thus all combinations of X and Z must fall on this straight line, and we have an example of perfect collinearity. Now if we try to fit[5] a regression plane to the observations of yield and fertilizer given in Table 2-1, one possible answer would be the original regression given in (2-18):

$$\hat{Y} = 36.4 + .059X + 0Z \tag{3-9}$$

What other answers are possible?

Solution

An equally satisfactory solution would follow from substituting $X = \frac{1}{16}Z$ and $Z = 16X$ into (3-9):

$$\hat{Y} = 36.4 + 0X + .0037Z$$

Any number of solutions could be obtained by making a partial substitution for X into (3-9) with arbitrary weight λ:

$$\begin{aligned}\hat{Y} &= 36.4 + .059[\lambda X + (1-\lambda)X]\\ &= 36.4 + .059[\lambda X + (1-\lambda)\tfrac{1}{16}Z] \qquad (3\text{-}10)\\ \hat{Y} &= 36.4 + .059\lambda X + .0037(1-\lambda)Z\end{aligned}$$

By assigning successive values to λ, we could generate successive planes (such as π_1 and π_2 in Figure 3-3). But all these three-dimensional planes are just equivalent expressions for the simple two-dimensional relationship between fertilizer and yield. While all give the same correct prediction of Y, no meaning can be attached to whatever coefficients of X and Z we may come up with. Instead it should be viewed as a meaningless search for a 3-dimensional fit for a 2-dimensional relation.

---

[5] Since a computer program would probably break down, suppose the calculations are done by hand.

Although the previous extreme example may have clarified some of the theoretical issues, no statistician would make such a naive error in practice. Instead, more subtle difficulties arise. For example, suppose demand for a group of goods is being related to prices and income, with the overall price index being the first regressor. Suppose aggregate income measured in money terms is the second regressor. If this is real income multiplied by the same price index, the problem of multicollinearity may become a serious one. The solution is to use real income, rather than money income, as the second regressor. This is a special case of a more general warning: In any multiple regression in which price is one regressor, beware of other regressors measured in prices.

3-5 CONFIDENCE INTERVALS AND STATISTICAL TESTS

As in simple regression, the true relation of Y to X is measured by the unknown population parameter β; we estimate it with the sample estimator $\hat{\beta}$. Although the unknown β is fixed, our estimator $\hat{\beta}$ is a random variable, differing from sample to sample. The properties of $\hat{\beta}$ can be shown to be similar to those established in the simple regression of Chapter 2; $\hat{\beta}$ is normal—again provided the error term is normal or the sample is large. Also, $\hat{\beta}$ is unbiased, with mean equal to β. And the fluctuation of $\hat{\beta}$ is measured by its standard error (standard deviation) $s_{\hat{\beta}}$. Although the meaning of the standard error is quite analogous to the case of simple regression, its computation is complicated.[6] So it is customarily calculated by an electronic computer using a library program.

For example, in Table 3-3, we reproduce the computer output for the wheat-yield data of Table 3-2. In successive columns the computer prints, for each regressor:

1. The name.
2. The estimated coefficient.
3. The standard error.

From these basic quantities, we can easily go on to calculate confidence intervals and tests.

---

[6] With only two regressors X and Z, the standard error of $\hat{\beta}$ is

$$s_{\hat{\beta}} = \frac{s}{\sqrt{\sum x_i^2 - (\sum x_i z_i)^2 / \sum z_i^2}} \qquad \text{(3-11) like (2-47)}$$

where s^2, as usual, is the residual variance, the analogue of (2-44). With three regressors, the formula is three times as long, and at that point matrix notation becomes almost essential.

TABLE 3-3 Computer Output for Multiple Regression (Data in Table 3-1)

Multiple Regression Equation		
Variable	*Coefficient*	*Std Error*
Const.	28.09524	2.49148
Fert.	.03810	.00583
Rain	.83333	.15430

Residual Variance = 5.35714

(a) Confidence Intervals

The formula for the 95% confidence interval is of the standard form:

$$\beta = \hat{\beta} \pm t_{.025} s_{\hat{\beta}} \tag{3-12}$$

like (2-50)

With k regressors, the degrees of freedom for t are[7]:

$$\text{d.f.} = n - k - 1 \tag{3-13}$$

Example 3-4

A multiple regression was computed from 25 observations, as follows:

Variable	*Coefficient*	*Standard Error*
const.	10.6	2.1
X_1	28.4	11.2
X_2	4.0	1.5
X_3	12.7	14.1
X_4	.84	.76

Construct a 95% confidence interval for β_1. At the 5% level, can we reject the null hypothesis $\beta_1 = 0$ (Y is unrelated to X_1) in favor of the alternative hypothesis $\beta_1 \neq 0$ (Y is related to X_1)?

[7] Just as in (2-52), the degrees of freedom for t are always the same as the divisor in s^2. This is just the number of observations n reduced by the number of estimates ($\hat{\alpha}, \hat{\beta}_1, \hat{\beta}_2, \ldots, \hat{\beta}_k$). That is, d.f. $= n - (k + 1)$.

Solution

For d.f. $= n - k - 1 = 25 - 4 - 1 = 20$, we find $t_{.025} = 2.09$. Thus from (3-12),

$$\beta_1 = 28.4 \pm 2.09\,(11.2)$$
$$= 28.4 \pm 23.4 \tag{3-14}$$

Since $\beta_1 = 0$ is excluded from this confidence interval, it is rejected in favor of the alternative hypothesis.

In Example 3-4, since we have established that Y is related to X_1, we call $\hat{\beta}_1$ *statistically discernible* (*significant*) at the 5% level. And in general, any estimator is called statistically discernible:
(i) If the null hypothesis is rejected, or equivalently,
(ii) If the confidence interval for the population parameter (target) does not include the null hypothesis value.

(b) One-Sided Hypothesis Tests

A one-sided test is usually the more appropriate form, since a regressor is usually included in the equation because of a prior theoretical reason for expecting it to affect Y in a specific direction. For example, if the effect of X_1 on Y is expected to be positive, then it is appropriate to test

$$H_0\colon \beta_1 = 0 \tag{3-15}$$

against the alternative

$$H_1\colon \beta_1 > 0 \tag{3-16}$$

To test this hypothesis, it is natural to see how large is the estimate $\hat{\beta}_1$ relative to its standard error $s_{\hat{\beta}_1}$ (which, for simplicity, we refer to as s_1); that is, we form the ratio

$$t_1 = \frac{\hat{\beta}_1}{s_1} \tag{3-17}$$

like (2-60)

If this t ratio exceeds the critical value $t_{.05}$ in end-of-book Appendix Table V, we say that H_0 is rejected in favor of H_1 at a 5% level. (If H_0 is true, so that t_1 follows the t-distribution, there will be only a 5% chance that it will exceed the critical value $t_{.05}$ in Table V and erroneously result in the rejection of H_0.)

Example 3-5

For the multiple regression in Example 3-4, what are the t ratios? Which variables are statistically discernible (significant) at the 5% level in a one-sided test?

Solution

Substituting into (3-17),

$$t_1 = \frac{\hat{\beta}_1}{s_1} = \frac{28.4}{11.2} = 2.54 \tag{3-18}$$

Similarly, we can calculate the other t ratios, and summarize them in the following table:

Variable	*Coefficient*	*Standard Error*	*t ratio*
X_1	28.4	11.2	2.54*
X_2	4.0	1.5	2.67*
X_3	12.7	14.1	.90
X_4	.84	.76	1.11

For d.f. $= n - k - 1 = 25 - 4 - 1 = 20$, we find $t_{.05} = 1.72$. This critical value is exceeded only by t_1 and t_2. Therefore, only X_1 and X_2 are statistically discernible at the 5% level, and starred. To illustrate this, Figure 3-4 gives the analogue to Figure 2-13.

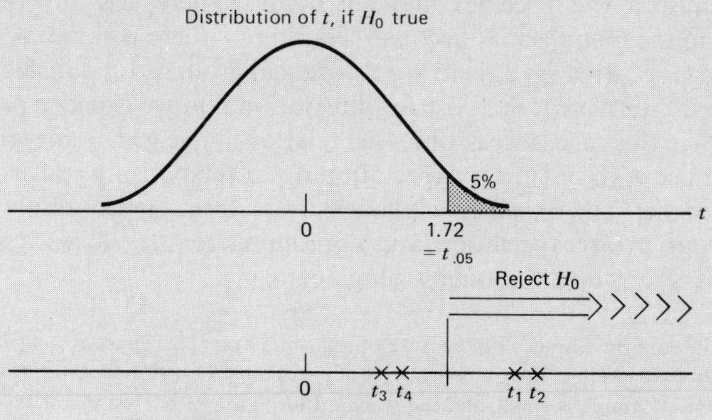

FIGURE 3-4 One-tailed t-test of four regressors.

3-6 HOW MANY REGRESSORS SHOULD BE RETAINED?

As long as we confine ourselves to rejecting hypotheses—as with β_1 and β_2 in the example above—we won't encounter too much difficulty. But if we *accept* the null hypothesis about β_3 and β_4, and consequently drop these regressors from the equation, we may run into trouble.

While it is true, for example, that our t coefficient for X_3 (.9) is not discernible, this does *not* prove there is no relationship between X_3 and Y. It is easy to see why. Suppose that we have strong theoretical grounds for believing that Y is positively related to X_3. In the table above this belief is confirmed: Y is related to X_3 by a positive coefficient. Thus our statistical evidence is consistent with our prior belief (even though it is not as strong a confirmation as we might like).[8] To accept the null hypothesis $\beta_3 = 0$ and conclude that X_3 doesn't affect Y would be in direct contradiction to both our prior belief and the statistical evidence. We would be reversing a prior belief, even though the statistical evidence weakly confirmed it. And this remains true for any positive t ratio although, as t becomes smaller, our statistical confirmation becomes weaker. Only if t is zero or negative do the statistical results clearly contradict our prior belief.

Consequently, if we had strong prior grounds for believing X_3 and X_4 to be positively related to Y, they should not be dropped from the regression equation, since they have the right sign; instead, they should be retained, with all the relevant information on their t ratios.

It must be emphasized that those who have accepted null hypotheses have not necessarily erred in this way. But that risk has been run by anyone who has mechanically accepted a null hypothesis because the t value was not statistically discernible. The difficulty is especially acute—as in the case we've cited—when the null hypothesis was introduced strictly for convenience (because it was specific), and not because there was any reason to believe it in the first place. It becomes less acute if there is some expectation that H_0 is true—that is, if there are theoretical grounds for concluding that Y and X are unrelated. Suppose for illustration that we expect *a priori* that H_0 is true; in this case, a weak observed relationship (e.g., $t = .6$) would be in some conflict with our prior expectation of no relationship. But it is not a serious conflict, and is easily explained by chance. Hence, resolving it in favor of our prior expectation and continuing to use H_0 as a working hypothesis might be a reasonable judgment.

[8] Perhaps the confirmation is weak because of too small a sample. Thus, $\hat{\beta}_3 = 12.7$ may be a very accurate description of how Y is related to X_3; but our t value is not statistically discernible because our sample is small, and the standard deviation of our estimator ($s_3 = 14.1$) is large as a consequence.

In the case of regression, there is another argument that may lead a statistician with very weak prior belief to accept H_0 when the test yields a statistically indiscernible result: It keeps the model simple and conserves degrees of freedom to strengthen tests on other regressors.[9] (When a regressor is dropped, the equation involving the fewer remaining regressors must be recalculated; then, since the number of regressors k is reduced, d.f. $= n - k - 1$ is increased.)

We conclude once again that classical statistical theory alone does not provide firm guidelines for accepting H_0; acceptance must be based also on an extrastatistical judgment. Thus, prior belief plays a key role, not only in the initial specification of which regressors should be in the equation, but also in the decision about which ones should be dropped in view of the statistical evidence, as well as the decision on how the model eventually will be used.

Prior belief plays a less critical role in the rejection of an hypothesis; but it is by no means irrelevant. Suppose, for example, that although you believed Y to be related to X_1, X_3, and X_4, you didn't really expect it to be related to X_2; someone had just suggested that you "try on" X_2 at the 5% level. This means that if H_0 (no relation) is true, there is a 5% chance of ringing a false alarm (and erroneously concluding that a relation does exist). If this is the only variable "tried on," then this is a risk you can live with. However, if many similar variables are included in a multiple regression by someone who is "bag-shaking" (i.e., trying on everything in sight),[10] then the chance of a false alarm increases dramatically.[11] Of course, this risk can be kept small by reducing the level for each t test from 5% to 1% or less. This

---

[9] A more sophisticated argument for accepting H_0 in these circumstances goes like this. Even though we know that $\beta = 0$ (i.e., accepting H_0 and dropping this regressor) must be somewhat wrong, we know that $\beta = \hat{\beta}$ (rejecting H_0 and retaining the regressor) is somewhat wrong too, but in a different way. Whereas the estimate 0 has some bias but no variance (it was arbitrarily prespecified), the estimate $\hat{\beta}$ has no bias but some variance. Which is more wrong? The best criterion, that combines bias and variance, is the mean squared error, which leads to accepting H_0:

(a) If we think the bias is small (if H_0 was considered near the truth, *a priori*).
(b) If $\hat{\beta}$ has a lot of variance, either because of a small sample, or multicollinearity problems.

These are recognized as the two conditions for accepting H_0 we have already encountered above.

[10] This procedure of trying on irrelevant variables is also referred to as the "kitchen sink" approach (i.e., tossing everything into the equation but the kitchen sink), or simply "garbage in, garbage out" (the fact that we can expect to eliminate 95% of the garbage that goes in is little consolation, since the 5% that comes out is still garbage).

[11] Suppose, for simplicity, that the t tests for the several variables (say k of them) were independent. Then the probability of no error at all is $.95^k$. For $k = 10$, for example, this is .60, which makes the probability of some error (some false alarm) as high as .40.

has led some statisticians to suggest a 1% level with the variables just being tried on and a 5% level with the other variables expected to affect Y.

To sum up, hypothesis testing should not be done mechanically. It requires:

1. Good judgment, and good prior theoretical understanding of the model being tested.
2. An understanding of the assumptions and limitations of the statistical techniques.

3-7 PROB-VALUE

The preceding discussion has introduced a number of difficulties that may be encountered if a hypothesis is tested in a mechanical or automatic way. There is another problem, illustrated in Figure 3-4. If an observed t value lies just slightly above the critical value of 1.72, H_0 is rejected; on the other hand, if it lies just slightly below 1.72, the opposite conclusion is reached—and H_0 is not rejected. The precise location of that critical value can be very important, and this in turn depends on the initial arbitrary selection of the level of the test (in this example, .05).

Another way of viewing the weakness of this arbitrary selection is to suppose that the observed t value for one regressor is 1.73 and for another is, say 9.62. Even though there is an overwhelming difference in the strength of this evidence, a mechanical hypothesis test will yield exactly the same conclusion in either case: Reject H_0. Thus an hypothesis test may be a very inefficient way of communicating the information provided by the sample data.

This leads naturally to the question: Instead of arbitrarily setting the level of the test at .05, why not take the observed t value and solve for the level of the test that would just *barely* allow us to reject H_0? For example, in the case of the regressor X_1, the observed t value [shown in Figure 3-4 and equation (3-18)] is $t_1 = 2.54$. From the t table we note that for 20 d.f., if we had arbitrarily set the test level $= .01$, we would have obtained $t_{.01} = 2.53$; then $t_1 = 2.54$ would just barely allow us to reject H_0. *This test level that would barely allow us to reject* H_0 is called the *prob-value, p-value,* or *observed level of significance.* Alternatively, prob-value is seen to be the probability of observing a sample value as large as the value we actually observed, assuming H_0 is true.

Example 3-6

Calculate the prob-values for all the coefficients in Example 3-5.

Solution

We have already calculated the prob-value for $\beta_1 = 0$; it was about .01. Similarly, we look in end-of-book Appendix Table V under 20 d.f. to roughly interpolate the remaining prob-values:[12]

$t_2 = 2.67$. For $\beta_2 = 0$, prob-value $\simeq .01$ (a little less)
$t_3 = .90$. For $\beta_3 = 0$, prob-value $\simeq .20$
$t_4 = 1.11$. For $\beta_4 = 0$, prob-value $\simeq .15$

As this example illustrates, the larger the observed t ratio, the smaller the prob-value and the less credible is the null hypothesis H_0. The prob-value is therefore an excellent way to *summarize what the data says*[13] *about the credibility of* H_0.

We have seen that a prob-value provides more information than simply accepting or rejecting at the 5% level. At the same time, it can easily be used to decide to accept or reject, if this is deemed desirable. To illustrate, consider again the first regressor in our example. If we wish to test H_0 at the 5% level, then our prob-value of .01 allows us to reject H_0; in other words,

---

[12] The prob-values calculated above may be referred to as one-sided, since they are appropriate if the alternative hypothesis H_1 is one-sided. On the other hand, if the alternative hypothesis is two-sided, then we are concerned not only with very large observed t values but also very small ones. The definition of a two-sided prob-value is, accordingly, the probability of observing a sample value as *extreme* as the value we actually observed, assuming H_0 is true.

In the case of X_1, we have already seen that the probability of observing a t value as large as 2.54 was about .01. Similarly, the probability of observing a t value as low as -2.54 is also about .01. Hence the two-sided prob-value (i.e., the probability of observing a t value as *extreme* as 2.54) is about .02. Thus the two-sided prob-value can always be calculated simply by doubling the one-sided prob-value.

[13] Of course, the data is not the only thing to be considered if we want to make a final judgment on the credibility of H_0; common sense, or what sometimes is more formally called "personal prior probability," must be considered too, especially when the sample is small and hence unreliable. For example, if a penny found on the street were flipped 10 times and showed 10 heads, the prob-value for H_0 (fair coin, i.e., no bias towards heads) would be only .001 (that is, $\frac{1}{2} \times \frac{1}{2} \times \cdots \times \frac{1}{2}$). But obviously it would be inappropriate to conclude from this that the coin was unfair. We know that a coin picked up on the street is almost certain to be fair; thus our common sense tells us that our sample result (of 10 heads) was just "the luck of the draw," and we discount it accordingly.

this very small prob-value is telling us that H_0 is just not credible enough, and must be rejected. This illustrates the general principle that:

$$\boxed{H_0 \text{ is rejected if the prob-value (credibility of } H_0\text{) is less than the specified level of the test.}} \tag{3-19}$$

To summarize, calculations of confidence intervals, t ratios, and prob-values are customarily laid out under the equation. For instance, for the regression of Example 3-4 to 3-6, we would have:

	$Y = 10.6$	$+ 28.4X_1$	$+ 4.0X_2$	$+ 12.7X_3$	$+ .84X_4$
standard error		11.2	1.5	14.1	.76
t ratio[14]		2.5	2.6	.9	1.1
95% confidence interval[15] (CI)		$\pm$ 23.4	$\pm$ 3.14	$\pm$ 29.5	$\pm$ 1.59
prob-value (one-sided)[16]		$\simeq$ .01	$\simeq$ .01	$\simeq$ .20	$\simeq$ .15

(3-20)

This equation also provides all the information necessary for either a one-tailed or two-tailed hypothesis test. On the one hand, for a two-tailed test (at a level = 5%), we can reject H_0 if it falls outside the 95% confidence interval shown above. On the other hand, for a one-tailed test, we can reject H_0 if its prob-value shown in the last line falls below whatever arbitrary test level is chosen.

PROBLEMS

3-5 Suppose that a multiple regression of Y on three independent variables yields the following estimates, based on a sample of $n = 30$:

	$\hat{Y} = 25.1$	$+ 1.2X_1$	$+ 1.0X_2$	$- .50X_3$
standard error	(2.1)	(1.5)	(1.3)	(.06)
t ratio	(11.9)	( )	( )	( )
95% CI	($\pm$4.3)	( )	( )	( )

---

[14] $t_i = \dfrac{\hat{\beta}_i}{s_i}$, as in (3-17).

[15] As calculated in (3-12).

[16] Interpolated value in Appendix Table V corresponding to t_i.

(a) Fill in the brackets.
(b) Answer true or false; if false, correct it.
   (i) If there were strong prior reasons for believing that X_1 is unrelated to Y, it is reasonable to reject the null hypothesis $\beta_1 = 0$ at the 5% level.
   (ii) If there were strong prior reasons for believing that X_2 is positively related to Y, it is reasonable to use the estimated coefficient 1.0 rather than accept the null hypothesis $\beta_2 = 0$.

3-6 A recent study of several hundred professors' salaries in a large American university in 1969[17] yielded the following multiple regression (in the interests of brevity, we omit many terms, some of which we will discuss later):

$$\hat{S} = 230B + 18A + 100E + 490D + 190Y + 50T + \cdots$$

	B	A	E	D	Y	T
standard error	(86)	(8)	(28)	(60)	(17)	(370)
t ratio	( )	( )	( )	( )	( )	( )
95% CI	( )	( )	( )	( )	( )	( )

where S = the professor's annual salary (dollars)
B = number of books he has written
A = number of ordinary articles
E = number of excellent articles
D = number of Ph.D.s supervised
Y = number of years' experience
T = teaching score as measured by student evaluations, severely rounded: The best half of the teachers were rounded up to 100% (i.e., 1); the worst half were rounded down to 0.

(a) Fill in the brackets below the equation.
(b) Answer true or false; where false, correct it. (Actually, since this is real data, you may find that certain points are controversial, rather than simply true or false. In such cases, clarify and support your own point of view as well as you can.)
   (i) The coefficient of B is estimated to be 230. Other social scientists might collect other samples from the same population and calculate other estimates. The distribution of these estimates would be centered around the true population value of 230. Therefore, the estimator is called unbiased.

[17] From Katz, 1973.

(ii) If there were no prior reason to believe that T affects S, it is reasonable to accept the null hypothesis that its coefficient is zero, thereby dropping it from the equation. This will, fortunately, make the equation briefer.

(iii) Repeat (ii), substituting Y for T.

(c) For someone who knows no statistics, briefly summarize the influences on professors' incomes, by indicating where strong evidence exists and where it does not.

3-7 Give an example of a multiple regression of Y on X_1 and X_2, in which you would retain X_1 in the equation but drop X_2, even though its coefficient had a higher t ratio.

3-8 Suggest possible additional regressors that might be used to improve the multiple regression analysis of wheat yield.

3-9 True or false? If false, correct it.

(a) Multicollinearity occurs when the regressors are linearly related, or nearly so.

(b) This means that some regression coefficients will have large standard errors.

(c) Some regressors therefore may be statistically indiscernible (insignificant); if these regressors also are regarded *a priori* as unimportant, they may be dropped from the model.

(d) Then, when the regression equation is recalculated, the multicollinearity problem will be reduced.

3-10 Suppose your roommate is a bright student, but she has studied no economics, and little statistics. (Specifically, she understands only simple—but not multiple—regression.) In trying to explain what influences the U.S. price level, she has regressed U.S. prices on 100 different economic variables, one at a time (i.e., in 100 simple regressions). Also, she apparently selected these variables in a completely haphazard way without any idea of potential cause-and-effect relations. She discovered 5 variables that were statistically discernible (significant) at the 5% test level, and concluded that each of these has an influence on U.S. prices.

(a) Explain to her in simple terms what reservations, if any, you have about her conclusion.

(b) If she had uncovered 20 statistically discernible variables, would your criticism remain the same? How would you suggest that she improve her analysis?

3-8 SIMPLE AND MULTIPLE REGRESSION COMPARED

In order to evaluate the benefits of a proposed irrigation scheme in a certain region, suppose the relation of yield Y to rainfall R is investigated over several years. From the data set out in the first 3 columns of Table 3-4, we could calculate the simple regression equation:

$$Y = 60 - 1.67r \qquad (s_{\hat{\beta}} = 4.0) \tag{3-21}$$

But the negative coefficient (implying that rainfall reduces yield!) strongly suggests that something in this analysis has gone very wrong. Actually, even before we calculated the regression (3-21) we should have known it might be wrong, because it only measures the simple relation of Y to R. What we really need to know is how yield is related to rainfall, *while all other important variables are held constant*. According to (3-3), therefore, we should carry out a multiple regression of yield on rainfall and any other important variables, such as temperature, obtaining:

$$Y = 60 + 5.71r + 2.95t \tag{3-22}$$

standard error $\qquad (2.68) \quad (.69)$

Introduced for this purpose, T is called a *control variable*.[18] It produces a much more reasonable conclusion. Rainfall R does have the expected effect

TABLE 3-4 Yield, Rainfall, and Temperature Observed Over Several Years

Year	*Yield, Y* (*bu/acre*)	*Total Spring Rainfall R* (*inches*)	*Average Spring Temperature T* (*° Fahr.*)
1963	60	8	56
1964	50	10	47
1965	70	11	53
1966	70	10	53
1967	80	9	56
1968	50	9	47
1969	60	12	44
1970	40	11	44

[18] Note that T couldn't be controlled, because this was an *observational* study (where the data was passively observed, rather than experimentally controlled). Nevertheless, in analyzing the data with multiple regression, we obtained the same rainfall coefficient we would have got if we *could* have controlled T and held it constant.

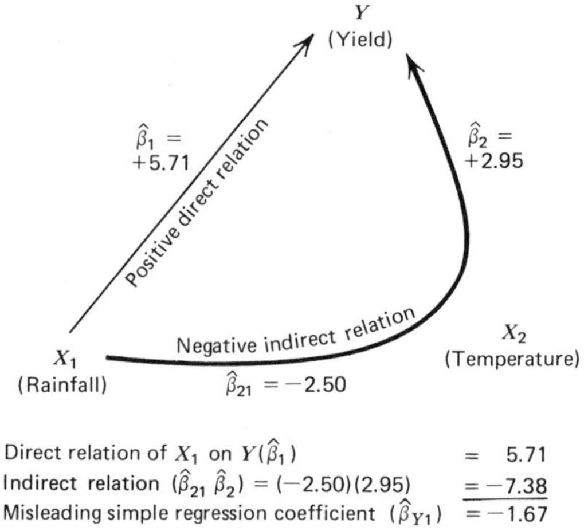

FIGURE 3-5 In applying simple regression to a multiple regression problem, the indirect relation causes bias.

of raising yield, other things being equal (i.e., when T is constant.)[19] This is the positive *direct relation*, shown in Figure 3-5.

To see why (3-21) yielded the wrong sign, we must realize that in the data from which it was calculated, T is *not* held constant. In fact, T and R are inversely related; for example, in 1970 high rainfall occurs with low temperature. Low temperature in turn results in low yields [because of the positive coefficient of t in (3-22)]. Thus high rainfall, by lowering temperature, *indirectly* lowers yield. This is the negative indirect relation, shown in Figure 3-5, and given by the following formula[20] (where the regressors R and T are renamed X_1 and X_2):

---

[19] The magnitude of the rainfall coefficient (5.71) is also important: It estimates the productivity of water, which can then be compared to the cost of water in order to determine whether irrigation is worthwhile.

[20] ***Proof of (3-23).*** We start with the middle estimating equation in (3-6) (renaming the regressors X_1 and X_2, of course):

$$\sum x_1 Y = \hat{\beta}_1 \sum x_1^2 + \hat{\beta}_2 \sum x_1 x_2 \tag{3-24}$$

Divide by $\sum x_1^2$:

$$\frac{\sum x_1 Y}{\sum x_1^2} = \hat{\beta}_1 + \hat{\beta}_2 \frac{\sum x_1 x_2}{\sum x_1^2} \tag{3-25}$$

We recognize the leftmost expression as the simple regression coefficient of Y on X_1 given in (2-16), and now called $\hat{\beta}_{Y1}$. Similarly, the rightmost expression is the simple regression

(footnote continued)

Simple regression coefficient = direct relation + indirect relation (bias)

$$\hat{\beta}_{Y1} = \hat{\beta}_1 + \hat{\beta}_2 \hat{\beta}_{21} \tag{3-23}$$

where

$\hat{\beta}_{Y1}$ = simple regression coefficient of Y on X_1

$\hat{\beta}_{21}$ = simple regression coefficient of X_2 on X_1

$\hat{\beta}_1$ = multiple regression coefficient of Y on X_1 (holding X_2 fixed)

$\hat{\beta}_2$ = multiple regression coefficient of Y on X_2 (holding X_1 fixed)

Whereas multiple regression sorts out and isolates the direct relation, simple regression does not; instead, the simple regression coefficient reflects both direct and indirect effects (in our example, positive direct effect of rainfall on yield, and its negative indirect effect). When the indirect relation predominates, it will determine the sign of the simple regression coefficient. But even in situations less spectacular than this, the simple regression coefficient will still be biased to some extent by the indirect effect of an omitted regressor.[21] This is the great advantage of multiple regression—to avoid bias.[22]

Another advantage of multiple regression is to reduce the residual variance; this reduces the standard error of the coefficient of r, from 4.0 in

---

(*footnote* 20 *continued*)
coefficient of X_2 on X_1, now called $\hat{\beta}_{21}$. Thus (3-25) may be written

$$\hat{\beta}_{Y1} = \hat{\beta}_1 + \hat{\beta}_2 \hat{\beta}_{21} \qquad \text{(3-23) proved}$$

A corresponding relation is true for the parameters β as well as the estimates $\hat{\beta}$.

[21] Unless, of course, the omitted regressor is totally unrelated to the other regressors or to the dependent variable (i.e., unless the indirect relationship in Figure 3-5 is totally broken at some point).

It may seem that we are giving contradictory advice about related regressors. Didn't we imply earlier that highly related regressors should be avoided because they may cause a problem of multicollinearity? Here is how we resolve the paradox:

To keep multicollinearity to a minimum one should design an experiment or collect data that has as little relation as possible among the regressors (e.g., as suggested at the end of Section 3-4, if one regressor is price, the second regressor should be real income rather than money income). In other words, we try to get our regressors as unrelated as possible; but having done this, we must then live with them. We should not simply omit a regressor we believe to be important because of multicollinearity, since this omission will introduce bias.

[22] To illustrate this issue geometrically, it would be interesting to graph the data of Table 3-4. We would plot Y against R, and label each point according to its value of T—just like Example 3-1. If you carry this out, you will see why the simple regression coefficient (ignoring T) was negative in (3-21), although the multiple regression coefficients were positive in (3-22).

(3-21) to 2.68 in (3-22). Hence statistical tests and confidence intervals are strengthened. Of course, the addition of other regressors (as well as R and T) might further reduce bias and residual variance.

PROBLEMS

3-11 (a) Should your previous answer to Problem 3-9(c) and (d) be changed, if the regressors are regarded *a priori* as important? If so, how?

(b) What further criticism do you now have of your roommate's analysis in Problem 3-10(a)?

3-12 Cigarette smokers have a life expectancy of about 5 years less than nonsmokers. Is all this necessarily caused by their smoking? Which way do you think the bias is (if any)?

3-13 Answer true or false; if false, correct it.

(a) The simple regression equation (3-21) occasionally can be useful. For example, in the absence of any information on temperature, it would correctly lead us to hope for a year with low rainfall, if we want high yield.

(b) In view of the positive multiple regression coefficients in (3-22), however, it would be even better to hope for a year with low rainfall, and then irrigate.

3-14 Referring to Table 3-4, suppose that we wished to know the relation of Y to R (other things being equal). Would there be a bias in the simple regression of Y on R:

(a) If R and T were positively related (i.e., $\hat{\beta}_{TR} > 0$)?

(b) If R and T had no relation (i.e., $\hat{\beta}_{TR} = 0$)?

(c) Now answer true or false; if false, correct it.
Applying simple regression to a multiple regression problem will introduce bias if the independent variables are unrelated.

*3-15 (a) From Table 3-1, calculate the regression coefficient of Z on X.

(b) Using also the regression coefficients calculated in (3-7) and (2-18), verify (3-23).

REVIEW PROBLEMS

3-16 Suppose that a psychologist computed the following multiple regression on the basis of a random sample of 60 people from a large population:

	$\hat{Y} =$	$64 +$	$16X_1 -$	$1.2X_2$
standard error		1.06	3.0	1.7
95% CI		± 2.1	± 6.0	± 3.4

Select the statement that is most appropriate for the coefficient $\hat{\beta}_1 = 16$ (and criticize the other statements):

(a) The null hypothesis $\hat{\beta}_1 = 0$ should be accepted at the 5% level.

(b) $\hat{\beta}_1$ estimates the total increase in Y that would be caused by a unit increase in X_1 (while X_1 simultaneously caused an estimated decrease of 1.2 units in X_2).

(c) $\hat{\beta}_1$ estimates the increase in Y that would accompany a unit increase in X_1, if X_2 were held constant.

(d) $\hat{\beta}_1$ is a fixed parameter that estimates the sample coefficient β_1, with a mean of 16 and variance of 3.

3-17 In Problem 3-6 recall that the salary regression was

$$\hat{S} = 230B + 18A + 100E + 490D + 190Y + 50T + \cdots$$

(a) Answer true or false; if false, correct it.

(i) Other things being equal, we estimate that a professor who has written one or more books earns \$230 more annually.

(ii) Or, to draw an analogy with the fertilizer-yield relation of Problem 2-1(d), we might say that \$230 estimates the salary increase from writing one or more books.

(iii) Other things being equal, we estimate that a professor who is one year older earns \$190 more annually. In other words, the annual salary increase averages \$190.

(b) Similarly, interpret all the other coefficients for someone who knows no statistics.

4

MULTIPLE REGRESSION EXTENSIONS

In this chapter we will see how versatile a tool multiple regression can be, when it is outfitted with several accessories.

4-1 DUMMY (0-1) VARIABLES

(a) Including a Dummy Variable

Suppose that we wish to investigate how the public purchase of government bonds (B) is related to national income (Y). A hypothetical scatter of annual observations of these two variables is shown for Canada in Figure 4-1 and in Table 4-1. It immediately is evident that the relationship of bonds to income

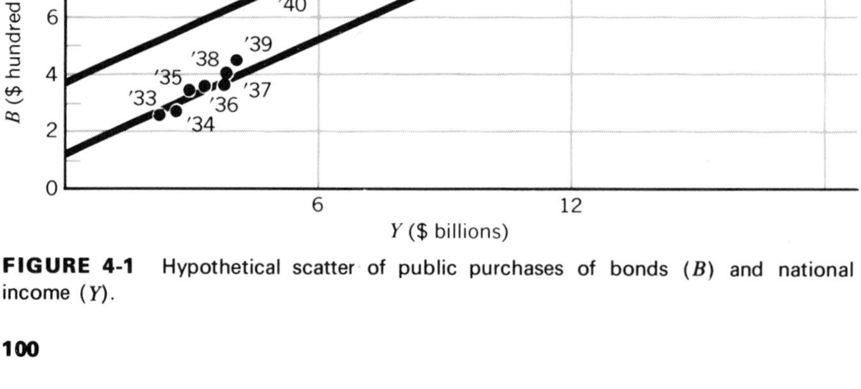

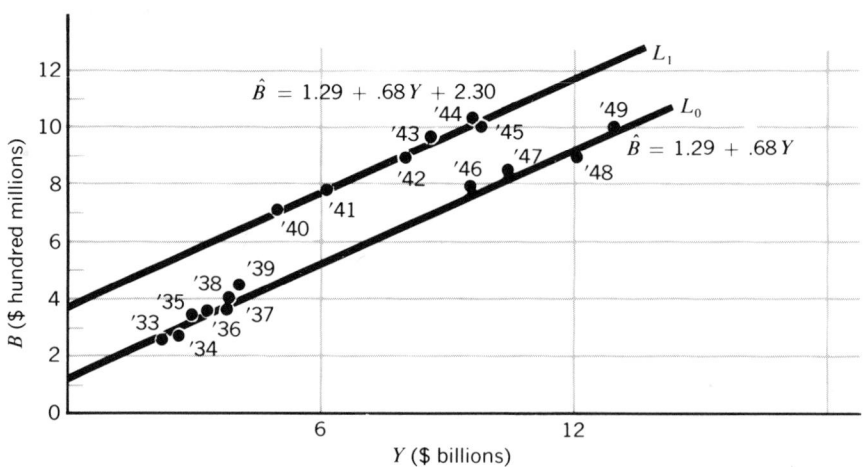

FIGURE 4-1 Hypothetical scatter of public purchases of bonds (B) and national income (Y).

TABLE 4-1 Calculations for Regression of B on Y and W, where W is a Dummy Variable.

	Year	B	Y	W	$y = Y - \bar{Y}$	$w = W - \bar{W}$	yw	By	Bw	y^2	w^2
	1933	2.6	2.4	0	−4.44	−.35	1.55	−11.54	−.91	19.71	.12
	1934	3.0	2.8	0	−4.04	−.35	1.41	−12.12	−1.05	16.32	.12
	1935	3.6	3.1	0	−3.74	−.35	1.31	−13.46	−1.26	13.99	.12
	1936	3.7	3.4	0	−3.44	−.35	1.20	−12.73	−1.29	11.83	.12
	1937	3.8	3.9	0	−2.94	−.35	1.03	−11.17	−1.33	8.64	.12
	1938	4.1	4.0	0	−2.84	−.35	0.99	−11.64	−1.43	8.07	.12
	1939	4.4	4.2	0	−2.64	−.35	0.92	−11.62	−1.54	6.97	.12
War years	1940	7.1	5.1	1	−1.74	.65	−1.13	−12.35	4.62	3.03	.42
War years	1941	8.0	6.3	1	−.54	.65	−.35	−4.32	5.20	.29	.42
War years	1942	8.9	8.1	1	1.26	.65	.82	11.21	5.78	1.59	.42
War years	1943	9.7	8.8	1	1.96	.65	1.27	19.01	6.30	3.84	.42
War years	1944	10.2	9.6	1	2.76	.65	1.79	28.15	6.63	7.62	.42
War years	1945	10.1	9.7	1	2.86	.65	1.86	28.89	6.56	8.18	.42
	1946	7.9	9.6	0	2.76	−.35	−.97	21.80	−2.77	7.62	.12
	1947	8.7	10.4	0	3.56	−.35	−1.25	30.97	−3.05	12.67	.12
	1948	9.1	12.0	0	5.16	−.35	−1.81	46.96	−3.19	26.63	.12
	1949	10.1	12.9	0	6.06	−.35	−2.12	61.21	−3.53	36.72	.12
		$\sum B = 115$	$\sum Y = 116.3$	$\sum W = 6$			$\sum yw$	$\sum By$	$\sum Bw$	$\sum y^2$	$\sum w^2$
		$\bar{B} = \frac{115}{17}$	$\bar{Y} = \frac{116.3}{17}$	$\bar{W} = \frac{6}{17}$			$= 6.55$	$= 147.2$	$= 13.74$	$= 193.7$	$= 3.88$
		$= 6.76$	$= 6.84$	$= .35$							

Estimating equations (like 3–6)

$$\begin{cases} \sum By = \hat{\beta} \sum y^2 + \hat{\gamma} \sum yw \\ \sum Bw = \hat{\beta} \sum yw + \hat{\gamma} \sum w^2 \end{cases}$$

or

$$\begin{cases} 147.2 = 193.7\hat{\beta} + 6.55\hat{\gamma} \\ 13.74 = 6.55\hat{\beta} + 3.88\hat{\gamma} \end{cases}$$

Solution:

$$\begin{cases} \hat{\beta} = .681 \simeq .68 \\ \hat{\gamma} = 2.30 \end{cases}$$

Thus our estimated regression is: $B = 6.76 + .68y + 2.30w$

Or, in terms of the original variables: $B = 6.76 + .68(Y - \bar{Y}) + 2.30(W - \bar{W})$

$$= 6.76 + .68(Y - 6.84) + 2.30(W - .35)$$

$$B = 1.29 + .68Y + 2.30W$$

follows two distinct patterns—one for wartime (1940–1945), the other for peacetime.

The normal relation of B to Y (shown as the line L_0) is subject to an upward shift (to L_1) during wartime; heavy bond purchases in those years is explained not by Y alone, but also by selling campaigns whose appeal was based on patriotism. B therefore should be related to Y *and* another variable—war W. W does not have a whole range of values, but only two: We set its value at 1 for all wartime years and 0 for all peacetime years.[1] W is called a *dummy*, or *counter*, or *0–1 variable*. With W included, the regression model is[2]

$$E(B) = \alpha_0 + \beta Y + \gamma W \tag{4-2}$$

where

$$\left.\begin{aligned} W &= 0 \text{ for peacetime years} \\ &= 1 \text{ for wartime years} \end{aligned}\right\} \tag{4-3}$$

By substituting (4-3) into (4-2), we obtain the following equivalent pair of equations:

$$E(B) = \alpha_0 + \beta Y \qquad \text{for peacetime} \tag{4-4}$$

$$E(B) = \alpha_0 + \beta Y + \gamma \qquad \text{for wartime} \tag{4-5}$$

We note that γ represents the effect of wartime on bond sales, and that β represents the effect of income changes. (The latter is assumed to remain the same in war or peace.) The important point is that one multiple regression of B on Y and W, as in (4-2), will yield the *two* estimated lines shown in Figure 4-1; L_0 is the estimate of the peacetime function (4-4), and L_1 is the estimate of the wartime function (4-5).

Complete calculations for this example are set out in Table 4-1, and the procedure is interpreted in Figure 4-2. Since all observations are at $W = 0$ or $W = 1$, the scatter is confined to the two vertical planes π_0 and π_1. The

[1] This 0–1 coding is not entirely arbitrary; it allows an easy verbal interpretation of W:

$$W = \text{the number of wars Canada was fighting in the given year} \tag{4-1}$$

This 0–1 definition also is motivated by the simplicity that it brings to the multiple regression analysis. In particular, when the coefficient of W is given the customary interpretation (3-3), it gives the increase in response (bond sales) if W is increased one unit (as we go from peace 0 to war 1), if the other variable (income) is held constant. This is just the distance between lines L_0 and L_1 in Figure 4-1.

[2] In equation (4-2), since Y and W are measured as original values (rather than deviations), we call the constant α_0 instead of α. This issue, which we first raised in Figure 2-7, is relatively trivial and will not occur again.

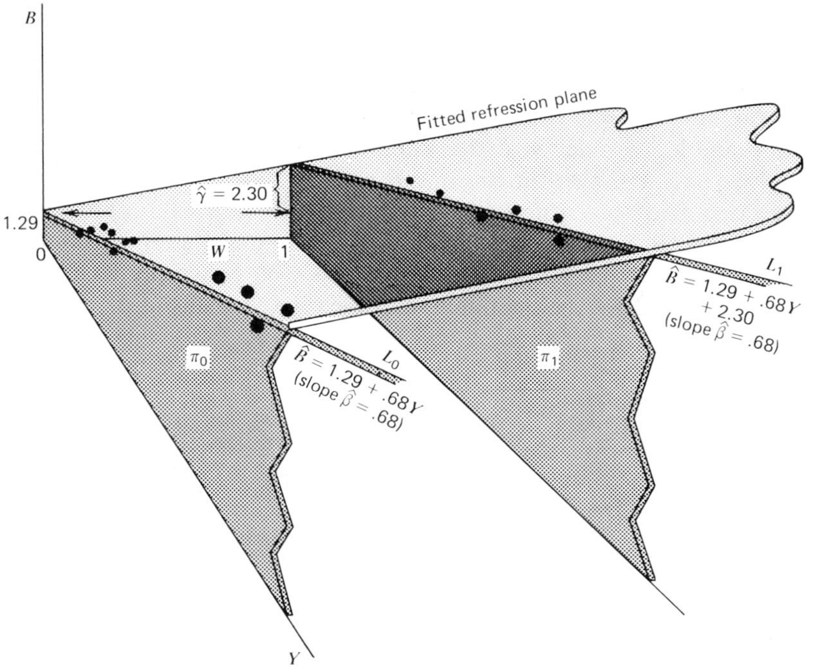

FIGURE 4-2 Multiple regression with a dummy variable (W).

estimated regression plane:

$$\hat{B} = \hat{\alpha}_0 + \hat{\beta}Y + \hat{\gamma}W \tag{4-6}$$

may be viewed as a plane resting on two supporting buttresses π_0 and π_1; some of the observed dots, of course, lie above this fitted plane, and others below it. The slopes of L_0 and L_1 are (by assumption) equal to the common[3] value $\hat{\beta}$, and the estimated wartime shift is $\hat{\gamma}$.

[3] This means that L_0 and L_1 are not fitted independently. In other words, the least squares plane (4-6) has a slope $\hat{\beta}$ that tries to fit *all* the data as well as possible. Thus, $\hat{\beta}$ cannot be the best possible least squares fit to the peacetime data alone, nor to the wartime data alone; instead, $\hat{\beta}$ is a compromise. (This same issue occurred in Example 3-2.)

By contrast, the uncompromising model that fits L_0 and L_1 independently, is

$$E(B) = \alpha_1 + \beta_1 Y \quad \text{for peacetime} \tag{4-7}$$

$$E(B) = \alpha_2 + \beta_2 Y \quad \text{for wartime} \tag{4-8}$$

where the slopes β_1 and β_2 are not constrained to be equal. So four parameters are required for this model, rather than the three parameters in the dummy variable model (4-2).

In this model, to independently estimate the wartime slope with only 5 observations may yield a very unreliable estimator $\hat{\beta}_2$. This was a good reason for our pooling the peacetime and wartime observations to obtain just one slope estimator $\hat{\beta}$ in (4-6).

(b) Bias Caused by Excluding the Dummy Variable

In this dummy variable model—as in any regression model—we can see how ignoring one variable would invite bias, as well as increase residual variance. For example, consider what happens if *W* is ignored, so that the scatter involves only the two dimensions *B* and *Y*. Geometrically, this involves projecting the three-dimensional scatter in Figure 4-2 onto the two-dimensional *B*–*Y* plane, as in Figure 4-3*a*. This immediately is recognized as the same scatter that we plotted in Figure 4-1. We also reproduce from that diagram L_0 and L_1, the estimated multiple regression, using *W* as a dummy

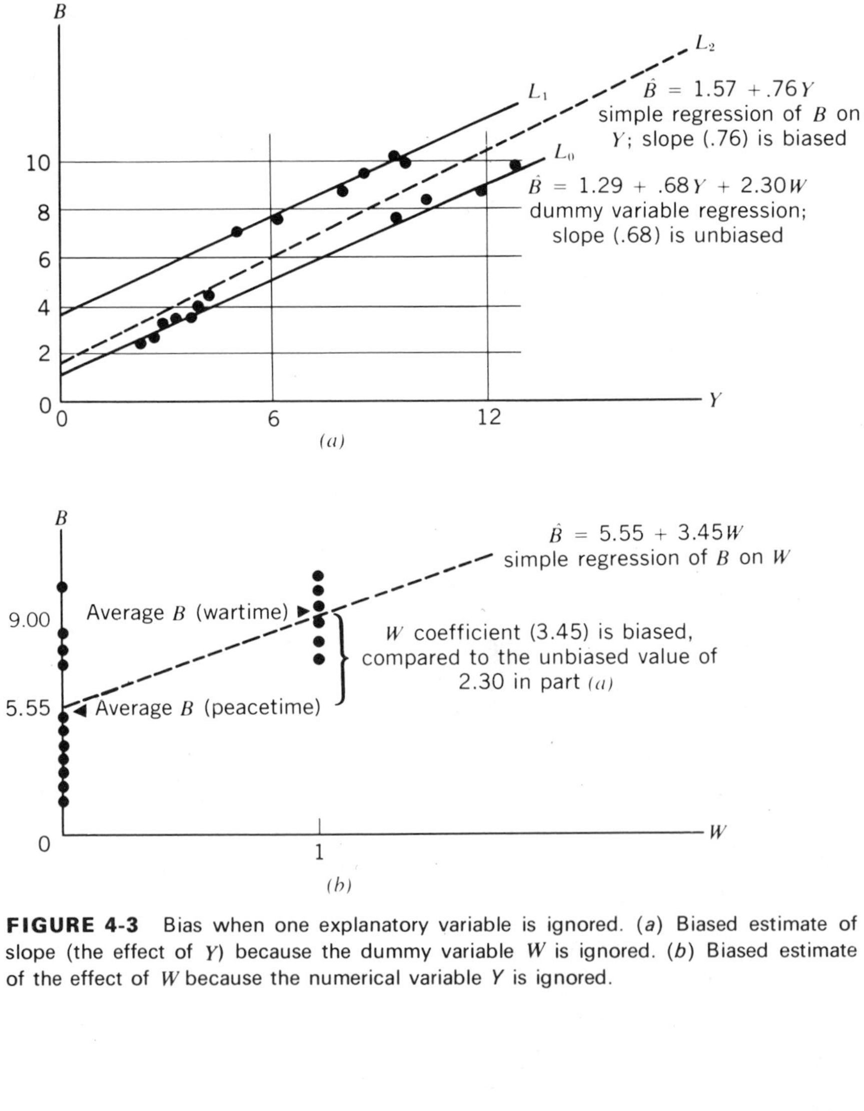

FIGURE 4-3 Bias when one explanatory variable is ignored. (*a*) Biased estimate of slope (the effect of *Y*) because the dummy variable *W* is ignored. (*b*) Biased estimate of the effect of *W* because the numerical variable *Y* is ignored.

variable. Now if we erroneously calculate the simple regression of B on Y (L_2 say), it clearly has too great a slope. This upward bias results from the fact that the war years had a slight tendency to be high-income years: thus, on the right-middle side of this scatter, higher bond sales that should be attributed in part to wartime would be attributed erroneously to income alone.

A similar bias occurs if Y is ignored in a regression of B on W. With no Y dimension, the scatter in Figure 4-2 would be projected into the B–W plane, as in Figure 4-3*b*. In this diagram, the slope of the best fit also happens to be the difference in means.[4] It is $9.00 - 5.55 = 3.45$, which is too large, compared with the unbiased estimate of wartime (2.30) obtained from the multiple regression. This upward bias comes from the same cause: higher bond sales that should be attributed in part to higher income would be attributed erroneously to wartime alone.

(c) Different Slopes as well as Intercepts

It is easy to extend (4-2) to give a model with different *slopes* as well as different intercepts,[5] by introducing one more term called the interaction:

$$E(B) = \alpha_0 + \beta Y + \gamma W + \delta YW \tag{4-9}$$

which is equivalent to the pair of equations:

$$E(B) = \alpha_0 + \beta Y \qquad \text{for peacetime} \tag{4-10}$$

$$E(B) = \alpha_0 + \beta Y + \gamma + \delta Y \qquad \text{for wartime} \tag{4-11}$$

$$= (\alpha_0 + \gamma) + (\beta + \delta) Y$$

Note that wartime has an intercept that is greater by the amount γ, and also a slope that is greater by the amount δ. Of course, this more complicated model (with the extra interaction parameter δ) requires more data to meaningfully estimate.[6]

---

[4] This is because the range of W is exactly 1, and the mean of a set of points is the position of best fit, according to the Gauss-Markov corollary (2-42). This same point will be illustrated again in Problem 4-3.

[5] In (4-9), Y and W are multiplied together to give a new regressor YW. Of course, since W is 0 or 1, YW becomes 0 in peacetime, and becomes Y in wartime. (For other examples of new regressors concocted from old, see Section 4-3.)

[6] Note that equations (4-10) and (4-11) are equivalent to (4-7) and (4-8), which we already suggested may be too complicated a model for the limited data.

(d) r Categories Handled with $r-1$ Dummies

Thus far we have considered a factor that had only two categories—war and peace. The dummy variable W measured the effect of wartime ($W = 1$) relative to the reference state peace ($W = 0$).

What happens if a factor has several categories? For example, in order to clinically test two drugs A and B against a control C, suppose a pharmaceutical company tests 30 persons. For each person, as well as measuring the response Y and other variables $X_1 \cdots X_k$ (such as age, bloodpressure, etc.), we would measure the drug by means of two dummy variables:

$$D_A = 1 \text{ if drug } A \text{ given; 0 otherwise} \tag{4-12}$$

$$D_B = 1 \text{ if drug } B \text{ given; 0 otherwise} \tag{4-13}$$

Notice that for individuals given control drug C, both D_A and D_B are zero. Thus, for example, typical data for the first three persons would be recorded as follows:

Person	*Comments*	Y	D_A	D_B	$X_1 \ldots X_k$
1	On drug A	60	1	0	. . . . .
2	On drug B	92	0	1	. . . . .
3	On drug C	81	0	0	. . . . .
.	.	.	.	.	. . . . .
.	.	.	.	.	. . . . .
.	.	.	.	.	. . . . .
30	.	.	.	.	. . . . .

(4-14)

Suppose that such data yielded the multiple regression equation:

$$\hat{Y} = 5 + 30D_A + 20D_B - 13X_1 + \cdots \tag{4-15}$$

standard errors	4	4	7
95% CI	±8	±8	±14

This means that the estimated effect of drug A (relative to the reference drug[7] C) is to raise Y by 30 ± 8, with 95% confidence.

Similarly, the estimated effect of drug B (relative to the reference drug C) is to raise Y by 20 ± 8, with 95% confidence. We could then deduce that

[7] While this is intuitively correct, it is reassuring to verify it precisely: According to (3-3), 30 represents the effect of changing D_A by one unit, while all other regressors are constant—in particular, keeping D_B constant. This entails changing a person from drug C onto drug A.

the estimated effect of drug A relative to B is $30 - 20 = 10$. (But we cannot so easily get a 95% *confidence interval* for this difference.[8])

To generalize, a factor with r categories requires only $r - 1$ dummies, because one category is left as the reference category. (In our example—where the factor was drug treatment—there were $r = 3$ categories of drugs, and we required only $r - 1 = 2$ dummies, D_A and D_B; drug C was the reference category.)

PROBLEMS

4-1 Referring to the bond sales in Figure 4-3*a*:

(a) Estimate what the bond sales would have been in 1946 if the war had lasted until then and if national income had still been only $9.6 billion.

(b) Suppose that the data in Table 4-1 and Figure 4-3*a* had not included the last 4 years. In a simple regression of B on Y, roughly estimate the slope by eye. Then what would be the bias caused by using simple regression instead of multiple regression?

(c) Repeat (b), assuming instead that the *first* 7 years were missing.

4-2 The following is the result of a test of gas consumption on a sample of 6 cars:

	M *Miles Per Gallon*	H *Engine Horsepower*
Make A	21	210
	18	240
	15	310
Make B	20	220
	18	260
	15	320

[8] If each of the three drugs were assigned at random to $n = 30/3 = 10$ persons, then *in this case* the confidence allowance for the difference between A and B would usually be about the same as between A and C, or between B and C. In other cases, we can get a confidence interval for the difference between A and B by computing a new regression equation that uses A or B as the reference category. For example, here is how we would use A as the reference category. Instead of (4-12) and (4-13), we would use the dummies:

$$\left.\begin{aligned} D_B &= 1 \text{ if drug } B \text{ given; 0 otherwise} \\ D_C &= 1 \text{ if drug } C \text{ given; 0 otherwise} \end{aligned}\right\} \quad (4\text{-}16)$$

(a) Code X as 0 or 1, depending on whether the car is make A or B. Then estimate the multiple regression equation of M as a function of H and X.
(b) Graph the data and the fitted pair of lines, as in Figure 4-1.

⇒ 4-3 A random sample of men and women in a large American university in 1969 gave the following annual salaries (in thousands of dollars, rounded):[9]

Men	12,	11,	19,	16,	22
Women	9,	12,	8,	10,	16

Denote income by Y and denote sex by a dummy variable X, having $X = 0$ for men and $X = 1$ for women. Then:

(a) Graph Y against X.
(b) Estimate by eye the regression line of Y on X. (*Hint*. Where will the line pass through the men's salaries? through the women's salaries?)
(c) Estimate by least squares the regression line of Y on X. How well does your eyeball estimate in (b) compare?
(d) Construct a 95% confidence interval for the coefficient of X. Explain what it means in simple language.
(e) Do you think that the answer to (d) is a measure of how much the university's sex discrimination affects women's salaries?

4-4 Now we can consider more precisely the regression equation for professors' salaries in Problem 3-6 by including some additional regressors:

$$\hat{S} = 230B + \cdots + 50T - 2400X + 1900P + \cdots$$

Standard error	(370)	(530)	(610)
t ratio	( )	( )	( )
95% CI	( )	( )	( )

where

S = the professor's annual salary (dollars)

$$T = \begin{cases} 0 \text{ if the professor received a student evaluation} \\ \quad \text{score below the median} \\ 1 \text{ if above the median} \end{cases}$$

[9] Same source as Problem 3-6 (Katz 1973).

$$X = \begin{cases} 0 \text{ if the professor is male} \\ 1 \text{ if the professor is female} \end{cases}$$

$$P = \begin{cases} 0 \text{ if the professor has no Ph.D.} \\ 1 \text{ if the professor has a Ph.D.} \end{cases}$$

(a) Fill in the brackets in the equation.
(b) Answer true or false; if false, correct it.

(i) A professor with a Ph.D. earns annually $1900 more than one without a Ph.D.
(ii) $1900 estimates the value (in terms of a professor's salary) of one more unit (in this case, a Ph.D.).

(c) Give an interpretation of the coefficient of X, and the coefficient of T.

4-5 For the raw data of Problem 4-4, the mean salaries for male and female professors were $16,100 and $11,200 respectively. By referring to the coefficient of X in Problem 4-4, answer true or false; if false, correct it.

After holding constant all other variables, women made $2,400 less than men. Therefore, $2,400 is a measure of the extent of sex discrimination and $2,500 (i.e., $16,100 – 11,200 – 2,400) is a measure of the salary differential due to other factors, for example, productivity and experience.[10]

4-6 Comparing Problems 3-6 and 4-4, note that the same variable T appears. In the form of Problem 3-6, it is apparent that it involves a severe degree of rounding. What are the advantages and disadvantages of such rounding?

4-7 A regression equation related personal income Y (annual, in $1000) to education E (in years) and geographical location, measured with dummies as follows:

$$D_S = 1 \text{ if in the south; 0 otherwise}$$

$$D_W = 1 \text{ if in the west; 0 otherwise}$$

The remaining region (north) is left as the reference region.

(a) Suppose the fitted regression was

$$\hat{Y} = 4.5 + 0.5E - 1.0D_S + 1.5D_W$$

Graph the estimated income $\hat{Y}$ as a function of E, for all 3 regions, with E running from 8 to 16.

---

[10] Quoted, with rounding, from the same source as Problem 3-6 and 4-4 (Katz, 1973).

(b) Redraw the graph in (a) according to the following interactive model:

$$\hat{Y} = 4.5 + 0.5E + 1.4D_S + 0.3D_W - 0.2D_SE + 0.1D_WE$$

4-8 A 1974 study[11] of 1072 subjects showed how lung function was related to several variables, including three hazardous occupations. The following abbreviations were used:

AIRCAP = air capacity (cubic centimeters) that the subject can expire in one second

BRONC = 1 if subject has bronchitis, 0 if not

AGE = age (years)

HEIT = height (inches)

PRSMOK = present smoking (cigarettes per day)

PASMOK = past smoking as measured by (cigarettes per day) × (years smoked)

CPSMOK = present cigar and pipe smoking: (cigars + pipes, per week)

CHEMW = 1 if subject is a chemical worker, 0 if not

FIREW = 1 if subject is a fire fighter, 0 if not

FARMW = 1 if subject is a farm worker, 0 if not

A fourth occupation, physician, served as the reference group, and so did not need a dummy. The following 2 regressions were computed, with standard errors in brackets. (All regressors are in deviation form.)

$$\begin{aligned}\text{AIRCAP} = 3605 &- \underset{(1.8)}{39}\ \text{AGE} + \underset{(7.5)}{98}\ \text{HEIT} - \underset{(2.2)}{9.0}\ \text{PRSMOK}\\ &- \underset{(.070)}{.0039}\ \text{PASMOK} - \underset{(1.1)}{2.6}\ \text{CPSMOK} - \underset{(46)}{350}\ \text{CHEMW}\\ &- \underset{(54)}{180}\ \text{FIREW} - \underset{(53)}{380}\ \text{FARMW}\end{aligned}$$

$$\begin{aligned}\text{BRONC} = .107 &+ \underset{(.0009)}{.0021}\ \text{AGE} + \underset{(.0038)}{.00037}\ \text{HEIT} + \underset{(.0011)}{.0047}\ \text{PRSMOK}\\ &+ \underset{(.000036)}{.000098}\ \text{PASMOK} + \underset{(.00054)}{.00063}\ \text{CPSMOK}\\ &+ \underset{(.024)}{.065}\ \text{CHEMW} - \underset{(.027)}{.032}\ \text{FIREW} + \underset{(.027)}{.002}\ \text{FARMW}\end{aligned}$$

[11] From Lefcoe and Wonnacott, 1974.

(a) Star the coefficients that are statistically discernible (significant) at the 5% level (one-sided).

Fill in the blanks:

(b) The average value of AIRCAP is ______ cc, while the average incidence of bronchitis is ______%.

(c) Other things (such as ______, ______, ______) being equal, chemical workers on average have AIRCAP values that are ______ cc lower than the physicians, and bronchitis rates that are ______ percentage points higher.

(d) Repeat (c), substituting "fire fighters" for "physicians."

(e) Other things being equal, on average a man who is 1 year older has an AIRCAP value that is ______ cc lower, and a bronchitis rate that is ______ percentage points higher.

(f) Repeat (e), substituting "presently smokes one more pack (20 cigarettes) per day" instead of "is 1 year older."

(g) As far as AIRCAP is concerned, we estimate that smoking one pack a day is roughly equivalent to aging ______ years. But this estimate may be biased because of ______.

4-2 ANALYSIS OF VARIANCE (ANOVA)

(a) One-Factor ANOVA

In Section 4-1, we saw how a factor (such as drug treatment) that had r categories (or levels, such as drugs A, B, and C) could be handled with $r - 1$ dummy variables. If the other factors can be omitted,[12] then the regression equation simplifies; for example, the drug study (4-15) reduces to a regression equation such as

$$Y = 5 + 30D_A + 20D_B \tag{4-17}$$

As an alternative to regression, the computations could be simplified with a scheme called *analysis of variance* (ANOVA), a technique introduced about

[12] ANOVA was developed to analyze *randomized experiments*, where the treatments are assigned at random (as opposed to an *observational* study, where the researcher has to take the treatments as they come—often chosen by the subjects themselves, for example). Randomization, being entirely impartial, will mean that individuals on any one treatment will, on average, have the same values of the omitted variables as the individuals on any other treatment. That is, the omitted variables will not change from treatment to treatment, and so there is no pressing need to introduce them in a long multiple regression, in order to reduce bias. [However, introducing one or two of the most important omitted variables will reduce variance, while keeping the computation still fairly simple, in a scheme called *analysis of covariance* (ANOCOVA).]

50 years ago when computations were done by hand. Although the computational savings are not so important today, ANOVA still provides certain conceptual advantages, especially in large models with many factors. In fact, ANOVA and experimental design is a topic so rich that it deserves a course of its own. For now, however, we must be satisfied with our very brief treatment, indicating only how traditional ANOVA may be equivalently done using a regression equation with dummies, such as (4-17).

(b) Two-Factor ANOVA

It is possible to use dummy variables to introduce another factor as well. For example, in the drug study, suppose we want to see the effect of a second factor, sex. Since it occurs at only two levels, we can take care of it with one dummy variable:

$$M = 1 \text{ if male; } 0 \text{ if female} \tag{4-18}$$

Then the fitted regression equation, instead of (4-17), would be something like

$$\hat{Y} = 5 + 15M + 30D_A + 20D_B \tag{4-19}$$

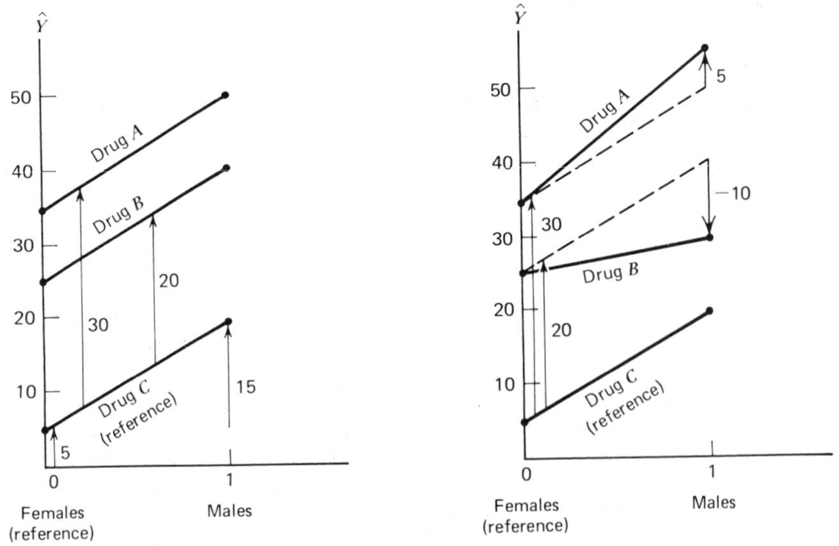

FIGURE 4-4 Graph of two-factor ANOVA. (*a*) Simple additive model (4-19). (*b*) Model with interaction (4-20).

TABLE 4-2 Typical tableau for recording 30 persons' response Y according to sex and drug (2-factor ANOVA)

Drug \ *Sex*	*Male*	*Female*
A	60 68 etc. — —	42 38 etc. — —
B	— — — — —	— — — — —
C	— — — — —	— — — — —

The equivalent traditional calculations would be called *2-factor ANOVA* (or *2-way ANOVA*, because the data is recorded in a 2-way table such as Table 4-2). One convenient way to graph (4-19) is like equation (4-6) was graphed in Figure 4-3—with M playing the former role of income Y, and D_A and D_B playing the former role of the wartime dummy W. This graph is shown in Figure 4-4*a*.

It is easy to extend (4-19) to give a model with different slopes as well as different intercepts, by introducing interaction terms. Then the estimated regression would be something like

$$\hat{Y} = 5 + 15M + 30D_A + 20D_B + 5MD_A - 10MD_B \qquad (4\text{-}20)$$

This relationship is graphed in Figure 4-4*b*.

To generalize two-factor ANOVA, suppose the first factor has r categories, while the second has c categories. Then we can analyze the data with multiple regression as follows:

(i) $r - 1$ dummies, $D_1 \cdots D_i \cdots D_{r-1}$ say, for the first factor.
(ii) $c - 1$ dummies, $M_1 \cdots M_j \cdots M_{c-1}$ say, for the second factor.
(iii) If a sophisticated interaction model is desired, it requires $(r - 1) \times (c - 1)$ interaction terms of the form $D_i M_j$.

(c) Conclusions

We can of course introduce into the model as many factors as desired, and as many interactions. Soon the model may grow so complex that the traditional ANOVA calculations may become a necessary simplification, even for a large-scale computer.

As well as simplifying calculations,[13] traditional ANOVA tends to emphasize *testing* whether or not a factor (like drug treatment) is statistically discernible (whereas the regression approach tends to emphasize *estimating* individual coefficients).

PROBLEMS

4-9 (a) Use equation (4-19) to fill in the fitted response $\hat{Y}$ in each cell of the following table:

Drug \ *Sex*	*Male*	*Female*
A		
B		
C		

Check that this table agrees with Figure 4-4.

(b) Repeat (a), using equation (4-20) instead of (4-19).

[13] Actually, traditional ANOVA simplifies the calculations when the data (such as Table 4-2) has *an equal number of observations* in each cell. This is an easy enough feature to incorporate into an experimental design; but it is an impossible feature to hope for in an observational study.

(c) Make the correct choice in each bracket:
In the [additive, interactive] model, the improvement of males over females is the same for all drugs. Then it is equally true that the improvement of drug A (or drug B) over drug C is the same for [both sexes, all treatments].

4-10 (a) In an additive 2-factor ANOVA model, the fitted response in some of the cells was as follows:

Drug \ Age-Group	*Infant*	*Child*	*Adolescent*	*Adult*
A	4	2	5	2
B	8			
C	9			

Fill in the blank cells.

(b) Make the correct choice in each bracket:
Consider now a *general* 2-way table, with $r \times c$ cells. Suppose the fitted response has been filled in the top row and left-hand column. To fill in the remaining [rc, $(r-1)(c-1)$] cells of the table, it is enough to additionally know either

(1) [$(r-1)(c-1)$, $rc-1$] interaction coefficients; or

(2) that all the interaction coefficients are zero, that is, the model is [additive, interactive].

4-11 Suppose three drugs (A, B, and control C) were given to two different age-groups (infant and adult). Let us define two dummies for drugs as in (4-12) and (4-13), and define one dummy for age:

$$I = 1 \text{ if infant; 0 otherwise}$$

Use a diagram such as Figure 4-4 to graph the response Y for each of the following equations:

(a) $\hat{Y} = 110 + 20I + 30A - 40B$

(b) $\hat{Y} = 110 + 20I + 30A - 40B - 40IA + 20IB$

(c) $\hat{Y} = 110 + 20I + 50T + 30A - 40B$ where a third age category (teenager) was introduced into the experiment and handled with the dummy variable T (where $T = 1$ if teenager; 0 otherwise).

4-3 SIMPLEST NONLINEAR REGRESSION

The regressions that we have studied so far have been of the linear form like (3-2)—linear in the variables (X, Y, Z) as well as in the parameters (α, β, γ). Now, if we closely examine the least squares method in Chapter 3, we note that as long as α, β, γ appear in a linear way, the estimating equations (3-6) will be linear in the estimates $\hat{\alpha}$, $\hat{\beta}$, $\hat{\gamma}$. Hence, no problems are involved in their solution.

For example, suppose a firm's marginal cost Y is a function of the total quantity of its output Q. If this function is U-shaped (initially falling, then rising), then an appropriate mathematical model may be a second-degree polynomial (parabola):

$$Y = \alpha + \beta Q + \gamma Q^2 + e \tag{4-21}$$

Although this model is nonlinear in the variable Q, it is nevertheless linear in the *parameters* α, β, γ; hence there should be no problem with ordinary least squares. To illustrate, we give some hypothetical data in Figure 4-5 and Table 4-3, columns (1) and (2). To find the least squares estimators, we simply *define our regressors appropriately*:

$$X \equiv Q \tag{4-22}$$

$$Z \equiv Q^2 \tag{4-23}$$

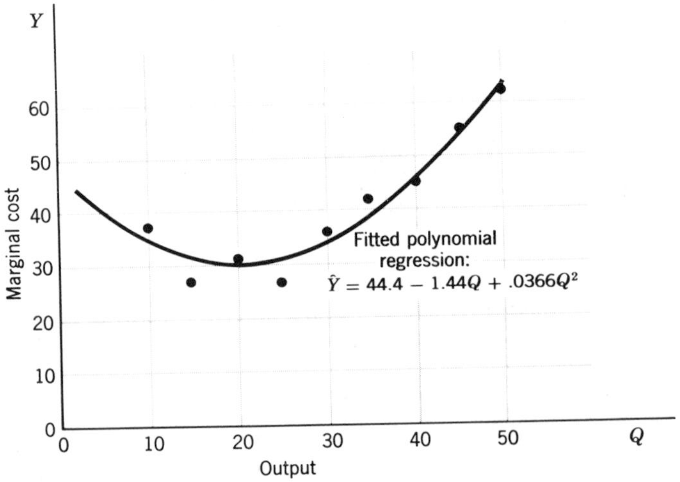

FIGURE 4-5 Fitted parabola relating marginal cost to output.

TABLE 4-3 Multiple Regression Fit of a Parabolic Marginal Cost Curve

Translation of Q and Q² into X and Z	*Regression of Y on X and Z*
Retranslation of X and Z back into Q and Q²	

(1) Y_i	(2) $X_i = Q_i$	(3) $Z_i = Q_i^2$	(4) $x_i = X_i - \bar{X}$	(5) $z_i = Z_i - \bar{Z}$	(6) $Y_i x_i$	(7) $Y_i z_i$	(8) x_i^2	(9) z_i^2	(10) $x_i z_i$	(11) $\hat{Y}_i = 40.2 - 1.44x_i + .0366z_i$
37	10	100	−20	−967	−740	−35,767	400	934,451	19,333	33.6
27	15	225	−15	−842	−405	−22,725	225	708,408	12,625	31.0
31	20	400	−10	−667	−310	−20,667	100	444,449	6,667	30.2
27	25	625	−5	−442	−135	−11,925	25	195,072	2,208	31.2
36	30	900	0	−167	0	−6,000	0	27,779	0	34.1
42	35	1,225	5	158	210	6,650	25	25,068	792	38.8
45	40	1,600	10	533	450	24,000	100	284,441	5,333	45.3
55	45	2,025	15	958	825	52,708	225	918,396	14,375	53.7
62	50	2,500	20	1,433	1,240	88,866	400	2,054,435	28,667	63.8
$\sum Y_i = 362$	$\sum X_i = 270$	$\sum Z_i = 9{,}600$	$\sum x_i = 0$	$\sum z_i = 0$	$\sum Y_i x_i = 1{,}135$	$\sum Y_i z_i = 75{,}140$	$\sum x_i^2 = 1{,}500$	$\sum z_i^2 = 5{,}592{,}500$	$\sum x_i z_i = 90{,}000$	
$\bar{Y} = 40.22$	$\bar{X} = 30$	$\bar{Z} = 1{,}067$								

$$\hat{Y} = 40.2 - 1.44(X - \bar{X}) + .0366(Z - \bar{Z})$$

or $\hat{Y} = 44.4 - 1.44X + .0366Z$

i.e., $\hat{Y} = 44.4 - 1.44Q + .0366Q^2$

When these are substituted into (4-21), we obtain the standard multiple regression equation:

$$Y = \alpha + \beta X + \gamma Z + e \tag{4-24}$$
like (3-2)

We note in passing that although Y is related to only one independent *variable* Q, our fit involves regressing Y on two *regressors*, Q and Q^2. This is the first time that we have had to distinguish between independent variables and regressors, but the distinction is important now. When one variable is used to obtain several regressors, as in this instance, we may wonder if multicollinearity becomes a problem.

Although Z_i and X_i are *functionally* dependent (i.e., one is the square of the other), they are not *linearly* dependent (i.e., one is not, say, three times the other). Geometrically, the points (X_i, Z_i) do lie on a curve, as shown in

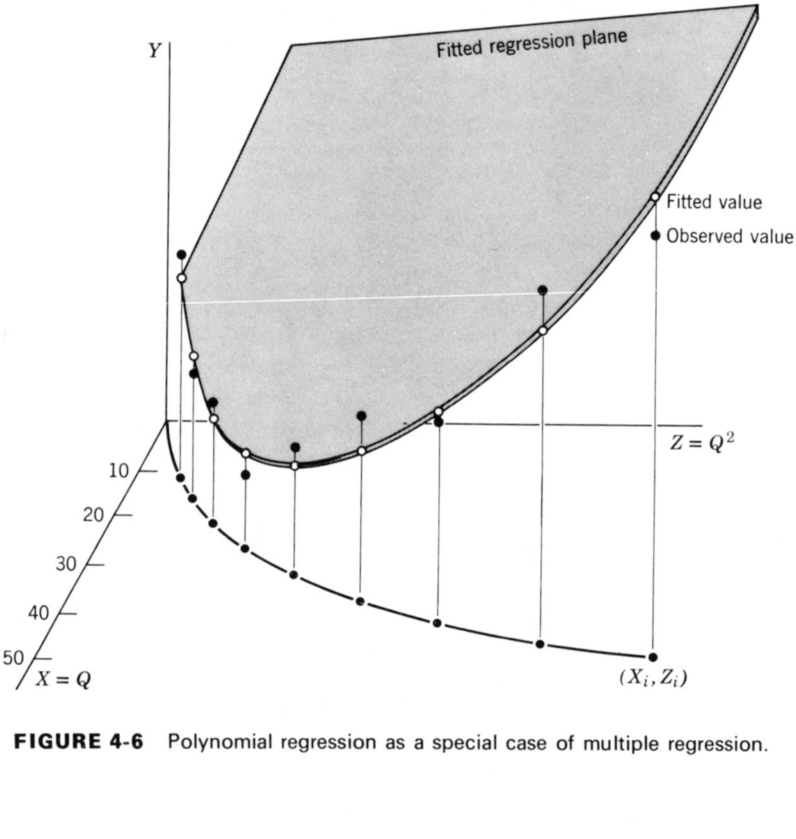

FIGURE 4-6 Polynomial regression as a special case of multiple regression.

Figure 4-6; however, the important point is that they do not lie on a line. Thus, we avoid the problem of complete multicollinearity. From a mathematical point of view, the physical or economic source of the X_i and Z_i values is irrelevant; just so long as X and Z are *linearly* independent, we can use the mathematical model of Chapter 3.

Therefore, we may compute the estimated coefficients $\hat{\alpha}$, $\hat{\beta}$, and $\hat{\gamma}$ using a standard computer program for multiple regression.[14] The results are:[15]

$$\hat{Y} = 44.4 - 1.44Q + .0366Q^2 \tag{4-26}$$

$$(t = -3.1) \quad (t = 4.9)$$

In conclusion, we have seen how a model that is linear in the *parameters* can be handled with ordinary least squares, even if the *variables* enter nonlinearly: We simply define the regressors appropriately.

---

[14] It is completely unnecessary nowadays to carry out the computations by hand; most computer programs not only wi!' run the regression but also will transform variables beforehand and retransform them afterward. Nevertheless, in order to explicitly show how this procedure works, we lay out the hand computations in Table 4-3.

Columns (2) and (3) set out the first step: the transformation of Q into X and Z. Columns (4) to (10) set out the second step: the standard regression of Y on X and Z. Our calculations are substituted into the last two estimating equations in (3-6), obtaining:

$$1{,}135 = \hat{\beta}(1{,}500) + \hat{\gamma}(90{,}000)$$

$$75{,}140 = \hat{\beta}(90{,}000) + \hat{\gamma}(5{,}592{,}500)$$

These two may be solved:

$$\hat{\beta} = -1.44 \tag{4-25}$$

$$\hat{\gamma} = .0366$$

In the last rows of Table 4-3, we then set out the third step: substituting (4-25) and retranslating X and Z back into Q. This yields (4-26).

In the last column of Table 4-3, we calculate the fitted points, which form the curve in Figures 4-5 and 4-6.

[15] When the regression (4-26) is plotted in Figure 4-5, it raises an interesting question: Is the parabolic model really necessary, or would a straight line suffice? The answer lies in prior knowledge and the statistical discernibility (significance) of the regressor Q^2, as we explained in Section 3-6. Since our prior expectation (that this was a parabolic relationship) is confirmed with a t value of 4.9 in equation (4-26), we retain Q^2.

PROBLEMS

4-12 (a) Fit Y with a second-degree polynomial in Q for the following data:

Output Q (Thousands)	*Marginal Cost Y*
1	32
2	20
3	20
4	28
5	50

(b) Graph the 5 points, and the fitted curve.
(c) What is the estimated Y when $Q = 2.5$?

4-13 (a) If a parabolic curve were fitted to the whole population in Problem 2-1, would you expect it to be concave up or down? What, then, would be the sign of the coefficient of X^2?
(b) Now fit a parabola to the data of Problem 2-1.
(c) Does the coefficient of X^2 have the sign that you expected *a priori*?
(d) Do you think that the straight line or the parabola is a better model to fit the data? Why?

4-4 NONLINEARITIES REQUIRING A TRANSFORMATION

(a) A Simple Growth Model

Figure 4-7a shows U.S. population P during a period of sustained growth, 1860–1900.[16] It curves up in a way that suggests a constant percentage growth (like compound interest, or unrestrained biological growth). The appropriate model is therefore the exponential:

$$P = Ae^{\beta T} \tag{4-27}$$

[16] From *The American Almanac*, 1974, Table 1.

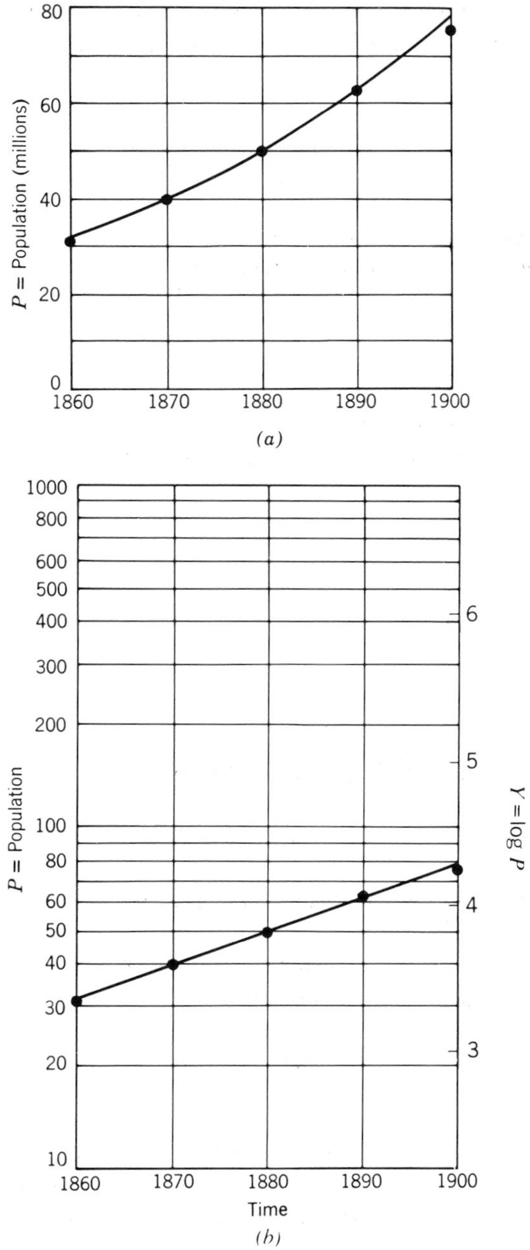

FIGURE 4-7 (*a*) U.S. population growth, 1860–1900, and its exponential fit. (*b*) Same curve plotted on semilog paper.

where $e \simeq 2.718$ is *Euler's constant*, which appears in the formula for the normal curve and is also the base for natural logs. The advantage of using this base is that, as we will prove in part (c),

$$\boxed{\beta \simeq \text{the growth rate}} \tag{4-28}$$

If it is reasonable to assume that large errors are associated with large values of the dependent variable P, then it is appropriate to treat the error term as multiplicative, rather than additive. Then the statistical model is

$$P = Ae^{\beta T} \cdot u \tag{4-29}$$

with the error assumed to have a distribution that fluctuates around 1. This model may be linearized by taking natural logarithms:

$$\log P = \log A + \beta T + \log u \tag{4-30}$$

If we now define

$$Y \equiv \log P \tag{4-31}$$

$$\alpha \equiv \log A$$

$$e \equiv \log u \tag{4-32}$$

then (4-30) can be written in the standard linear form:

$$Y = \alpha + \beta T + e \tag{4-33}$$

with the distribution of e fluctuating around zero (as illustrated in Figure 4-9).

For convenience, time T is measured in years since 1850. Then a standard computer program can be used to estimate (4-33). The result is

$$\begin{aligned} Y = 3.90 + &.0222t \\ &(t = 37) \end{aligned} \tag{4-34}$$

Again, for reference only, we also show the hand calculations in detail in Table 4-4. The transformed values $Y = \log P$ in column (3) are graphed in Figure 4-7*b*; (note the scale on the right of this diagram). This is seen to be equivalent to graphing the original values P on semilog graph paper. Notice how close the observed values are to the fitted regression (4-34); this provides further confirmation of our selection of the exponential model.

TABLE 4-4 Calculation of Exponential Growth Curve, U.S. Population 1860–1900.

(1) Year T (since 1850)	(2) Population P (million)	(3) $Y = \log P$	(4) $t = T - \bar{T}$	(5) Yt	(6) t^2
10	31.4	3.45	−20	−69.0	400
20	39.8	3.68	−10	−36.8	100
30	50.2	3.91	0	0	0
40	63.0	4.14	10	41.4	100
50	76.0	4.33	20	86.6	400
$\bar{T} = 30$		$\bar{Y} = 3.90$		$\sum Yt = 22.2$	$\sum t^2 = 1000$

$$\hat{\beta} = \frac{\sum tY}{\sum t^2} = \frac{22.2}{1000} \simeq .022$$

$$Y = 3.90 + .022t$$
$$\log P = 3.90 + .022t$$
$$P = e^{3.90}\, e^{.022t}$$
$$P = 49.5\, e^{.022t}$$

Transformation of Equation	Regression of Y on T
Retransformation	

To retransform (4-34) back into the exponential model, we substitute (4-31), obtaining

$$\log P = 3.90 + .022t \tag{4-35}$$

Taking antilogs (exponentials)

$$P = e^{3.90}\, e^{.022t} \tag{4-36}$$

that is,

$$P = 49.5\, e^{.022t} \tag{4-37}$$

For convenience we have left time t in deviation form. Thus the coefficient $\hat{A} = 49.5$ (million) may be interpreted as the estimate of the population in 1880 (when $t = 0$). The coefficient $\hat{\beta} = .022 = 2.2\%$ is the approximate annual growth rate.

Although a fitted equation like (4-37) may shed a good deal of light on past growth, there is an important final warning against using it for any short-term prediction of a time series such as population. In this sort of very simple growth model the error u is likely to be serially correlated (when population is unduly high in one period, it tends consequently to be high in the next period). Then (as we shall see in Chapter 6), any prediction should take account of this correlation.

The problems are even greater in a long-term projection. So many changes occur in the underlying process determining population growth (wars, recessions, the development and acceptance of birth control methods, etc.), that there is no single unchanging relationship that can be trusted for a long-term prediction. Hence, this sort of projection may be a futile exercise. It is far more to the point to try to discover what changes may be expected in the underlying growth process as the population adjusts to the pressure of increasing numbers.

(b) Some Other Models

To generalize our experience with the exponential growth model, we see that *any* model that consists of factors multiplied together, including a multiplicative error term u, can be simplified by taking logs. This is because logs transform the awkward multiplication into a convenient sum.

As another example, consider the Cobb-Douglas production function:

$$Q = \alpha K^{\beta} L^{\gamma} u \tag{4-38}$$

where K = capital, L = labor, and Q = quantity produced; the Greek letters α, β, and γ as usual represent parameters to be estimated, and u is the multiplicative error term. When we take logs of (4-38), we obtain

$$\log Q = (\log \alpha) + \beta(\log K) + \gamma(\log L) + (\log u) \tag{4-39}$$

which is of the standard form:

$$Y = \alpha' + \beta X + \gamma Z + e \qquad \text{(4-40) like (3-2)}$$

Yet another example is the demand function:

$$Q = \alpha P^{\beta} u \tag{4-41}$$

where $Q =$ quantity demanded and $P =$ price. When we take logs of (4-41), we obtain

$$\log Q = \log \alpha + \beta \log P + \log u \tag{4-42}$$

which is of the standard form:

$$Y = \alpha' + \beta X + e \qquad \text{(4-43) like (2-23)}$$

(c) Logs as Relative Changes

When we have estimated an equation like (4-42), it is often more useful to leave it in its log form than to translate it back into the exponential form. This is because logs have a very nice interpretation: For *small* changes in any variable x,[17]

$$\boxed{\text{Change in } \log x \simeq \textit{relative} \text{ change in } x \text{ itself}} \tag{4-44}$$

This theorem is so important that we illustrate it in Figure 4-8.

---

[17] The proof of (4-44) follows from an elementary differentiation formula:

$$\frac{d(\log x)}{dx} = \frac{1}{x}$$

or

$$d(\log x) = \frac{dx}{x}$$

That is, for infinitesimally small changes (differentials d),

$$\text{Change in } \log x = \text{relative change in } x \qquad \text{(4-44) proved}$$

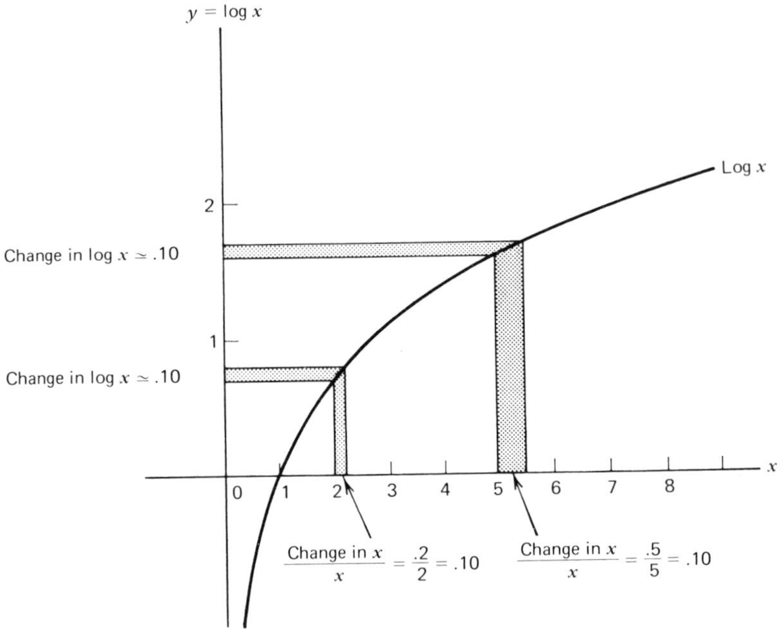

FIGURE 4-8 Change in log x = relative change in x itself.

Example 4-1

A demand function (4-42) was estimated to be

$$\log Q = 3 - 2 \log P \tag{4-45}$$

If price P increases by 1%, by how much does the quantity Q change?

Solution

The *relative* increase in P is given as $1\% = .01$. By (4-44), this is the increase in $\log P$, the regressor. Because the regression coefficient is -2, the increase in the response is -2 times as much:

$$-2(.01) = -.02$$

Since $\log Q$ decreases by .02, (4-44) assures us that Q itself has a relative decrease of $.02 = 2\%$.

In conclusion, a 1% increase in price results in a 2% fall in the quantity demanded. This factor 2 is called the *price elasticity* of demand. (This price elasticity is formally defined as the relative change in quantity demanded divided by the relative change in price).

To generalize this example, suppose we have a model where quantity Q depends on price P and income Y and other variables according to

$$\log Q = \alpha' + \beta \log P + \gamma \log Y \cdots \tag{4-46}$$

like (4-42)

Then

$$\left.\boxed{\begin{aligned} |\beta| &= \text{price elasticity} \\ |\gamma| &= \text{income elasticity} \end{aligned}}\right\} \tag{4-47}$$

Example 4-2

Suppose a population P (in millions) grows over time T (in years) according to

$$\log P = 4.1 + .03T \tag{4-48}$$

like (4-35)

(a) Approximately how much does the population grow in 1 year?
(b) Approximately how much in 5 years?
(c) Find the exact answer to (b).

Solution

(a) In 1 year the change in the regressor T is 1. Thus the change in the response is .03. Since $\log P$ increases by .03, (4-44) assures us that P itself has a relative change of $.03 = 3\%$. That is, P grows 3% in 1 year, and this is called the *growth rate*.

(b) In 5 years, the change in the regressor T is 5, and so the change in the response is

$$(.03)(5) = .15$$

Since $\log P$ increases by .15, (4-44) assures us that P itself has a relative increase of $.15 = 15\%$. That is, P grows 15%. However, this answer is only approximate, because (4-44) is only approximate, working best for small changes. This difficulty can be easily seen from another point of view: An increase of 3% a year over 5 years would give a total increase of 15% *if* there were no compounding. The difference that compounding makes will become evident when we answer this question more precisely in part (c).

(c) Suppose, for concreteness, we calculate the relative growth in the *first* 5 years (the relative growth would be the same in *any* 5 years). We begin by using the given equation (4-48) to find the exact value of P initially, and then after 5 years:

$$\text{at } T = 0, \log P = 4.1 + 0 = 4.10; \qquad \text{hence } P = e^{4.10} = 60.34$$

$$\text{at } T = 5, \log P = 4.1 + .03(5) = 4.25; \text{ hence } P = e^{4.25} = 70.10$$

$$\text{increase in } P = 9.76$$

$$\text{relative increase in } P = \frac{9.76}{60.34}$$

$$= .16 = 16\%$$

To generalize Example 4-2(a), we see that the growth rate is just the coefficient of T. Thus in the growth model (4-30) [or equivalently (4-29)], the growth rate will be β, and so (4-28) is proved.

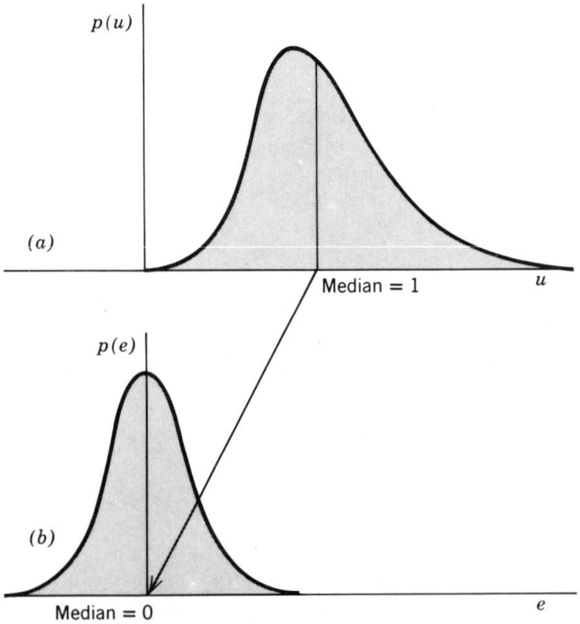

FIGURE 4-9 The error term in the multiplicative model. (*a*) Original skewed error. (*b*) The more symmetric error after the log transformation.

(d) A Closer Look At The Error Term

Taking logs in a model such as (4-29) or (4-38) not only makes the error term additive. It also may make the error term more normally distributed. This is shown in Figure 4-9: If the distribution of u is skewed to the right, the distribution of $\log u$ usually is more symmetric[18], and hence closer to normal. This provides certain advantages, such as more valid t tests.

As well, the log transformation often makes the error term follow the standard regression model (2-23) more closely—in particular, satisfy the assumption that the variance σ^2 of the error term does not change.

PROBLEMS

4-14 In the Cobb-Doublas production function, the model is sometimes assumed to have $\beta + \gamma = 1$, so that $\gamma = 1 - \beta$, and (4-38) becomes

$$Q = \alpha K^{\beta} L^{1-\beta} u \tag{1}$$

By taking logs and rearranging terms, show that this model is of the form

$$Y = \alpha' + \beta X + e$$

where

$$Y = \log Q - \log L$$

$$X = \log K - \log L$$

$$\alpha' = \log \alpha$$

$$e = \log u$$

4-15 In Problem 4-14, suppose a sample of 25 firms yielded the estimates $\hat{\beta} = .30$ and $\hat{\alpha}' = 1.40$. Thus the log form of (1) would be:

$$\widehat{\log Q} = 1.40 + .30 \log K + .70 \log L$$

(a) If K is increased by 10%, while L remains constant, estimate how much Q would increase.

(b) If all factors of production (both K and L) are each increased by 10%, estimate how much Q would increase.[19]

---

[18] In Figure 4-9, the old median ($u = 1$) is transformed into the new median ($e = 0$).

[19] A model such as this is said to have *constant* returns to scale, because when input is scaled up 10%, output is increased by 10% too. This happens whenever the capital and labor coefficients sum to 1 (in our example, $.30 + .70 = 1.00$).

By contrast, the model in Problem 4-16 is said to have *increasing* returns to scale: When input is scaled up 10%, output is increased by *more* than 10%. This happens whenever the capital and labor coefficients sum to more than 1 (in our example, $.50 + .70 = 1.20$).

4-16 Suppose the general Cobb-Douglas function (4-39) was estimated, and in log form turned out to be

$$\log Q = 1.10 + .50 \log K + .70 \log L$$

Answer the same questions as in Problem 4-15.

4-17 Suppose that a regression study of quantity demanded as a function of price yielded the following equation:

$$\log Q = 5.2 - 1.3 \log P$$

(a) What is the elasticity?
(b) If price increased by 3%, by how much would the quantity demanded fall?
(c) What price decrease would be required to increase the quantity demanded by 10%?

4-18 The population of the world since 1650 has been estimated as follows:

Year	*Population (Millions)*
1650	470
1750	690
1850	1090
1950	2510

(a) Graph. Join the dots by a rough curve, and extrapolate to the year 2000.
(b) Fit an exponential growth by least squares. Graph it. Extrapolate it to 2000. To predict population in the year 2000, how much better is this than (a)?
(c) What is the estimated growth rate?

4-19 Suppose that in 1950, a bank balance was left to accumulate at a constant interest rate i.

(a) Assuming no deposits or withdrawals, estimate the original balance B_0 in 1950, and the annual interest (growth) rate from the following observations:

Time	*Balance*
1952	\$106.09
1953	109.27
1954	112.55
1955	\$115.92

(b) If bank calculations are error-free (i.e., there is no random disturbance e), would you need all four observations to calculate i and B_0? How many observations are necessary?

4-20 Suppose we calculated the following multiple regression on the basis of a random sample of $n = 500$ persons:

$$\begin{array}{llll} \text{LOGIN} = .080\ \text{LOGFIN} + & .020\text{EDUC} + & .060\text{FEMALE} + \ldots \\ \text{(standard errors)} & (.005) & (.025) \end{array}$$

$$\begin{aligned} \text{LOGIN} &= \text{natural logarithm of the person's income} \\ \text{LOGFIN} &= \text{natural logarithm of the father's income} \\ \text{EDUC} &= \text{number of years education} \\ \text{FEMALE} &= 1 \text{ if female; } 0 \text{ if male.} \end{aligned}$$

(a) We estimate that, other things being equal, a man earns ______ % [more, less] income than a woman.
To allow for sampling error, however, we should hedge and say, "... earns between ______% and ______% [more, less] income than a woman, with 95% confidence."

(b) Peter and Paul are alike in all measured respects except income, and their fathers' income. Peter's father earns \$20,000, while Peter himself earns \$10,000. If Paul's father earns \$24,000, we estimate that Paul himself would make \$______.

*4-5 LOGITS TO REFINE A 0–1 RESPONSE

In studying bronchitis in Problem 4-8, we saw that a response Y as well as a regressor X could be a 0–1 variable. As another example, consider a simple regression where X = time invested in selling and $Y = 1$ or 0, depending on whether or not the customer buys. OLS applied to data such as in Figure 4-10 would produce a regression such as

$$\hat{Y} = -.20 + .06X$$

A unit increase in X would produce an increase of .06 in Y. This can be interpreted as an increase of .06 in the probability that a customer will buy, or equally well, an increase of 6 percentage points in sales. In view of this interpretation, we call the response P as well as Y.

The disadvantages of such a linear probability model are apparent in Figure 4-10: Constant increases in X produce constant increases in P. For example, an increase of $\Delta X = 5$ always produces an increase of $\Delta P = .30$, at every level of X. Thus the fitted values of P sometimes exceed 1 or fall below

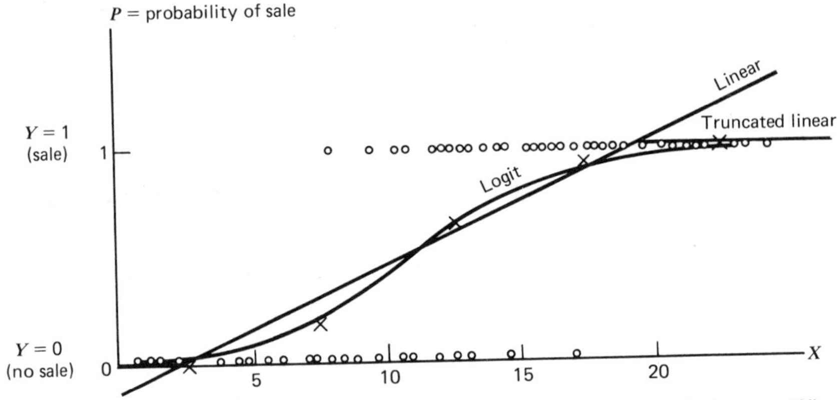

FIGURE 4-10 Linear and logit probability models. (Original data marked as o. When the data is partitioned into 5 cells, the proportion sold in each cell is marked as ×.)

0, which is obviously unrealistic—in fact, logically impossible. One solution is to truncate the linear model, bending the line horizontally when it reaches 0 or 1. Although this cures the most obvious defect, it still leaves the fundamental problem unsolved: In reality, constant increases in X do *not* produce constant increases in P. In fact, a given change in X generally produces a lot less change in P as P approaches[20] 0 or 1.

Let us first look at the low end of the scale. One way for P to approach 0 would be to halve, time and time again. That is, let a constant ΔX produce a constant *relative* change in P. It follows from (4-44) that this can be achieved by making log P depend linearly on X:

$$\log P = \alpha + \beta X$$

Similarly, at the high end of the scale where P approaches 1, we should

---

[20] For example, an increase of 10 percentage points in P is easiest to achieve in the middle of the range, where the customers are split .50–.50 (are most undecided). By contrast, when X is large and only a few of the customers remain unsold, to increase P by 10 percentage points will be very difficult to achieve—in fact impossible, if P is already at 95 percent.

Here is another way to see this same issue. The truncated linear model has a given ΔX produce a constant ΔP—up to the point of truncation. After that, ΔP drops suddenly to 0. Surely a more gradual decline in ΔP would be more reasonable. We will therefore develop a model that gradually tapers off: the *logit* model. (There also are other models that gradually taper off. The *probit* model, for example, uses the cumulative normal curve instead of the logistic curve in Figure 4-10.)

consider $\log(1-P)$. We can combine both ends of the scale with the model[21]

$$\log P - \log(1-P) = \alpha + \beta X \tag{4-49}$$

That is,

$$\log\left(\frac{P}{1-P}\right) = \alpha + \beta X \tag{4-50}$$

The ratio $P/(1-P)$ is called the *odds ratio*. Thus $\log[P/(1-P)]$ is called the *log odds* or *logit*. If desired, (4-50) can be solved for P, obtaining

$$P = \frac{1}{1 + e^{-(\alpha+\beta X)}} \tag{4-51}$$

which is called a *logistic* curve, and is graphed[22] in Figure 4-10.

To estimate (4-50) from the data, the easiest method is ordinary least squares (OLS) regression of $\log[P/(1-P)]$ on X. But OLS runs into difficulty. We cannot use the raw observations $Y = 0$ or 1 for P, because they make $\log[P/(1-P)]$ blow up. Instead, we have to partition the X-axis into cells, to capture enough observations in each cell to construct an observed proportion[23] P that is neither 0 nor 1. However, in grouping, we introduce an error in X that produces a bias (called errors-in-variable bias, discussed in Section 7-5). Furthermore, in the common case of multiple regression with several regressors X_i, the problems of partitioning become acute; for example, with 5 regressors each partitioned even crudely into 4 parts, the number of cells is huge: $4 \times 4 \times 4 \times 4 \times 4 = 1024$.

MLE provides a better way to estimate (4-50), which avoids any necessity for partitioning. To briefly describe how MLE works, suppose we are

---

[21] While P is near 0, the changes in $\log P$ dominate the changes in $\log(1-P)$. (For example, as P increases from .01 to .02, $\log P$ increases by .70 while $\log(1-P)$ changes by only .01.) Similarly, while P is near 1, the changes in $\log(1-P)$ dominate the changes in $\log P$. (For example, as P increases from .98 to .99, $\log(1-P)$ decreases by .70, while $\log P$ increases by only .01). The negative sign is introduced to make the change in $-\log(1-P)$ an *increase* of .70. Thus the function $\log(P) - \log(1-P)$ will be a consistently increasing function of P.

[22] This S-shaped curve is also commonly used in models for constrained growth, as well as constrained probability (Wonnacott, 1976).

[23] Even with $n = 5$ or 10 observations in each cell, the number of successes S may still be 0 or n, making the observed proportion $\hat{P} = S/n$ still 0 or 1. One solution for keeping the observed $\hat{P}$ away from 0 and 1 is to use the *modified* log odds:

$$\log\left[\frac{(S+\frac{1}{2})/n}{1-(S-\frac{1}{2})/n}\right] \tag{4-52}$$

which is what we had to use in fitting the logit curve in Figure 4-10. [In the first X cell (0 to 5) there are no successes (observed sales); and in the last X cell there are all successes.]

given a sample of n observations (X_i, Y_i) for the simple logit model (4-50). As we try different values of the parameters (α, β), the likelihood of getting our particular sample will vary. The parameter values that make this likelihood largest are the maximum likelihood estimates $(\hat{\alpha}, \hat{\beta})$. Since there are no explicit formulas[24] for $(\hat{\alpha}, \hat{\beta})$, the computer just has to go through a maximization search. [For a given sample, the computer tries out various alternative estimates $(\hat{\alpha}, \hat{\beta})$, selecting the one that generates the greatest likelihood.] Such computation would have been an impossible burden 25 years ago, but now it is quite feasible (at least for a small number of parameters). For a more detailed description of how MLE works, see Appendix 4-A.

PROBLEMS

4-21 In a study based on more than 10,000 students in 1966, the probability P that a student will live on campus was found by MLE to be[25]

$$\log\left(\frac{P}{1-P}\right) = 1.47R - .05F + \text{other variables}$$

$$\text{(std. error)} \quad (.16) \qquad (.11)$$

where R = 1 or 0, depending on whether or not the student would prefer to live on campus even if money were not a problem.

F = 1 or 0, depending on whether or not the student is female.

In a certain situation (e.g., male student with a preference for living on campus) the probability of the student living on campus is 60%. Other things remaining equal, estimate the probability of the student living on campus if the student were female instead of male. Is the difference statistically discernible (significant) at the 5% level?

4-6 INTRACTABLE NONLINEARITY

There are many models that cannot be transformed into linear functions and solved by well-established means. Consider a hypothetical example that an economic historian might face. Suppose he has uncovered a running annual asset statement (Y_t) over 20 years of a wealthy family (such as the Fuggers). Further suppose that additional fragmentary information becomes available: In the initial time period t_0 Jacob Fugger made a substantial loan α_1

---

[24] Contrast this with the simple regression model in Section 2-12, where MLE fortunately had an explicit formula: $\hat{\beta} = \sum x_i Y_i / \sum x_i^2$, as in least squares estimation.

[25] From Kohn et al., 1974.

to the Hapsburg monarch, none of which was repaid over the 20-year span; this sum was loaned at a "special" rate of interest i_1, while the balance of the family's assets α_2 was loaned out at the market rate of interest i_2. The historian might be very interested in knowing how much of this family's assets were tied up in loans α_2 to the monarchy. Furthermore, he might wish to establish whether or not the state loan carried a lower interest rate (perhaps in exchange for licenses, mineral concesssions, etc.); this would involve comparing estimates of i_1 and i_2.

The following model relating total assets to time would be appropriate:

$$Y_t = \alpha_1(1 + i_1)^t + \alpha_2(1 + i_2)^t + e \tag{4-53}$$

where t takes on values from 0 to 20, and Y_t represents the known total asset position at any time t; α_1, α_2, i_1, and i_2 are unknown. If there was also evidence that additions or withdrawals from this asset pool were negligible enough to be covered by the error term e, then the question is whether Y_t can be regressed on t in (4-53) to provide estimates of the parameters α_1, α_2, i_1, and i_2.

We have strong prior grounds for setting up the problem in the form (4-53); but this leaves us with several major difficulties in its estimation. First, there is no way of transforming (4-53) into a linear model. (For example, the log transformation used to fit the Cobb-Douglas function is quite out of the question.) This does not mean it is hopeless; least squares estimates can still be justified by maximum likelihood and a normally distributed error e in (4-53). The fitted value of Y is

$$\hat{Y} = \hat{\alpha}_1(1 + \hat{i}_1)^t + \hat{\alpha}_2(1 + \hat{i}_2)^t$$

So the sum of the squared residuals between the observed Y_t and the fitted $\hat{Y}_t$ is

$$S(\hat{\alpha}_1, \hat{\alpha}_2, \hat{i}_1, \hat{i}_2) = \sum [Y_t - \hat{\alpha}_1(1 + \hat{i}_1)^t - \hat{\alpha}_2(1 + \hat{i}_2)^t]^2 \tag{4-54}$$

Our procedure now is the same as was used to derive estimating equations (2-13) and (2-16). This sum of squares is minimized when the partial derivatives of S with respect to $\hat{\alpha}_1$, $\hat{\alpha}_2$, $\hat{i}_1$, and $\hat{i}_2$ are equal to zero:

$$\left.\begin{aligned}
\frac{\partial S}{\partial \alpha_1} &= \sum 2[-(1 + \hat{i}_1)^t][Y_t - \hat{\alpha}_1(1 + \hat{i}_1)^t - \hat{\alpha}_2(1 + \hat{i}_2)^t] = 0\\
\frac{\partial S}{\partial \alpha_2} &= \sum 2[-(1 + \hat{i}_2)^t][Y_t - \hat{\alpha}_1(1 + \hat{i}_1)^t - \hat{\alpha}_2(1 + \hat{i}_2)^t] = 0\\
\frac{\partial S}{\partial i_1} &= \sum 2[-\hat{\alpha}_1 t(1 + \hat{i}_1)^{t-1}][Y_t - \hat{\alpha}_1(1 + \hat{i}_1)^t - \hat{\alpha}_2(1 + \hat{i}_2)^t] = 0\\
\frac{\partial S}{\partial i_2} &= \sum 2[-\hat{\alpha}_2 t(1 + \hat{i}_2)^{t-1}][Y_t - \hat{\alpha}_1(1 + \hat{i}_1)^t - \hat{\alpha}_2(1 + \hat{i}_2)^t] = 0
\end{aligned}\right\} \tag{4-55}$$

Given observed values of Y_t and t, this is a system of four equations in the four parameters to be estimated. The problem is that they are nonlinear. Even a single nonlinear equation in a single unknown may be difficult to solve, and this system of four nonlinear equations poses even greater computational problems. Moreover, there may no longer be a unique solution to (4-55). If several solutions were found, each solution (set of parameter values) would have to be plugged into the sum of squares (4-54) to find which yields a minimum. So great are the difficulties, however, that in practice there is often no attempt made to derive and solve estimating equations (4-55). Instead it is customary to use a computer routine such as that described in Appendix 4-B.

Thus, major computational problems are involved in fitting any model that cannot be linearized by a redefinition of variables or a transformation. But the additional difficulty of multicollinearity is encountered in our particular model. Even if i_1 and i_2 were known, then there would be two regressors that are similar functions of t, namely $(1 + i_1)^t$ and $(1 + i_2)^t$; the collinearity problem is immediately evident, especially if i_1 and i_2 are roughly equal. Moreover, the problem is compounded because i_1 and i_2 are not known, but must be estimated.

PROBLEMS

4-22 For each of the following models, outline the method you would use to estimate the parameters (Greek letters).

(a) $Y = \alpha + \beta X + \gamma X^2 + \delta X^3$
(b) $Y = \alpha + \beta T + \gamma \sin(2\pi T/12)$ (Linear growth with cycle)
(c) $Y = \alpha + \beta X + \gamma Z + \delta X^2 + \varepsilon XZ + \zeta Z^2$ (Quadratic model)
(d) $Y = \alpha + \beta X^{\gamma}$
(e) $Y = \alpha(1 + \beta)^T$
(f) $Y = \alpha \beta^T \gamma^X$
(g) $Y = \alpha + \beta e^{\gamma X}$
(h) $Y = \alpha X^{\beta} Z^{\gamma}$

4-23 In each model in Problem 4-22, what form should the error term take in order for your transformation to work?

4-7 THE PHYSICAL AND SOCIAL SCIENCES CONTRASTED

Compared to social scientists, physical scientists have greater scope in designing experiments, and stronger theoretical justification for postulating models in a specific mathematical form. For example, an object dropping free of air resistance will fall distance Y in time t according to the quadratic function

$$Y = \tfrac{1}{2}gt^2 + vt \tag{4-56}$$

where g is the gravitational constant, and v is the initial velocity. This mathematical model (hypothesis) is called a law because its adequacy has been empirically verified innumerable times (Galileo discovered it around 1600, and it is still used today); furthermore, it is consistent with the other laws of physics (in fact, it can be theoretically derived from Newton's laws of motion). By contrast, in economics there are neither empirical nor theoretical reasons to justify, for example, always using a quadratic, rather than a linear, marginal cost function. The physical sciences, therefore, are often more exact than the social sciences because the *form* of the function to be fitted is known.

A second reason that the physical sciences are more exact is that observations are often more precise. Consequently, statistical considerations become secondary. This is illustrated with the same model. Suppose that g is very precisely estimated ("known") from previous experimental results, and that time t and distance Y can be observed very precisely too. Then the hypothesis $H_0: v = 0$ (i.e., the object was dropped from rest) can be tested quite adequately by taking only *one* observational pair (t, Y). When these values (along with g) are plugged into (4-56), they determine v. The problem is primarily a mathematical one of solving for a unique value of v, rather than a statistical problem of computing the best estimate using some criterion such as least squares.

While the physical sciences usually have precise observations, at the same time their mathematical models are often very complex. Thus, even though problems may theoretically involve a statistical dimension, it is often ignored because of the difficulties involved in just getting a mathematical solution; in our example, if the unique mathematical estimate of v is close enough to zero to be explained by a small observational error in t and Y, then H_0 might be accepted without much explicit reference to statistical guidelines. It is not that the world of economics is simpler than the world of physics (indeed, many economic problems call for general equilibrium models of great mathematical complexity). The point is that there is a different trade-off. Economists usually must use models with a statistical dimension, and this necessarily restricts the mathematical complexity of their model. On the other hand, because their error of observation is small, physicists may often drop the statistical dimension in favor of using a more complicated mathematical model.

The best summary is a paradox. Because social behavior is less predictable than physical phenomena, mathematical models are a less accurate approximation of reality in the social sciences; hence statistical methods are more necessary.

A mathematical model provides a useful structure with which an economist may perhaps better understand and predict economic phenomena; it can hardly be regarded as ultimate truth. In fact, in certain instances a mathematical model may be used even when it is known not to be exactly right, if it is "good enough." (See Figure 2-16, where a curve is approximated by a straight line in the region of interest.) At our present level of knowledge, it is often better to use a simple, more tractable model rather than a complicated one—even though the latter provides a somewhat better fit. This is especially true if there are no prior grounds for expecting that the complicated model better describes the real world.

REGRESSION REVIEW PROBLEMS

4-24 Consider a multiple regression model of personal income Y as a function of age A, number of years of education E, and sex S (where sex is coded 0 for male, 1 for female):

$$\hat{Y} = \hat{\alpha} + \hat{\beta}a + \hat{\gamma}e + \hat{\delta}s$$

Answer true or false; if false, correct it.

(a) The coefficient $\hat{\delta}$ may be interpreted as estimating the amount of income that the average man earns more than the average woman.

(b) Other things being equal, a person who is 1 year older earns $\hat{\beta}$ more income.

4-25 A sociologist collected a random sample of 1000 men to see how divorce rates are related to religion, income, region, and degree of urbanization. Outline how you would analyze the data.

4-26 A sociologist computed a regression of mobility M as a function of family income X_1:

$$M = b_0 + b_1 x_1$$

Then she realized that family size X_2 also was relevant, and so she calculated the multiple regression:

$$M = c_0 + c_1 x_1 + c_2 x_2$$

Under what conditions will the coefficients of x_1 in the two regressions be equal ($b_1 = c_1$)?

4-27 In a 1964 study[26] of how personal income was related to education, IQ, color, and other variables, the following multiple regression was estimated from a sample of 1400 U.S. veterans:

$$\begin{array}{lllll} LINC & = .046E & + .0010AFQT & + .17COLOR & + \text{other variables} \\ \text{(std error)} & (.007) & (.0004) & (.05) & \end{array}$$

where

$LINC$ = natural log of the veteran's weekly income

E = number of years of additional education (during and after military service)

$AFQT$ = the veteran's percentile rating on the Armed Forces Qualification Test Score, which roughly measures IQ

$COLOR$ = dummy variable for race, being 0 for blacks and 1 for whites

Other variables = age, amount of military service, amount of schooling before military service, father's education and occupational status, and degree of urbanization of his childhood home.

Other things being equal it is estimated that:

(a) A veteran with 1 more year's additional education earns ______% more income.
(b) A veteran who is white earns ______% more income than one who is black.
(c) A veteran who rates 1 point higher on the *AFQT* (e.g., by being in the 51st percentile instead of the 50th percentile) earns ______% more income.
(d) A black veteran who scores in the 80th percentile in the *AFQT* would earn ______% more than a white veteran who scores in the 50th percentile.

4-28 Assuming that the model in Problem 4-27 is specified correctly, by how much should you hedge your estimates in (a) and (b) in order to be 95% certain of being correct?

[26] Zvi Griliches and W. M. Mason, "Education, Income, and Ability," in Goldberger and Duncan, 1973.

4-29 Twelve plots of land are divided randomly into three groups. The first is held as a control group, while fertilizers A and B are applied to the other two groups. Yield is observed to be:

Control, C	60	64	65	55
A	75	70	66	69
B	74	78	72	68

(a) Calculate the regression of yield Y:

$$\hat{Y} = \hat{\alpha} + \hat{\beta} D_A + \hat{\gamma} D_B$$

where the dummies are defined as

$$D_A = 1 \text{ if fertilizer } A \text{ used; 0 otherwise}$$

$$D_B = 1 \text{ if fertilizer } B \text{ used; 0 otherwise}$$

(b) What is the estimated yield $\hat{Y}$
   (i) for the control C?
   (ii) for fertilizer A?
   (iii) for fertilizer B?

(c) Calculate the average yield
   (i) for the 4 C plots.
   (ii) for the 4 A plots.
   (iii) for the 4 B plots.
   How do these answers compare to (b)?

(d) What are the advantages and disadvantages of method (b) relative to (c)?

4-30 Consider the model:

$$Y = b_0 + b_1 X_1 + b_2 X_2 + \cdots + b_k X_k + bD$$

where D is 1 if the child has received flouridated water treatment, and 0 otherwise; $X_1 \cdots X_k$ are factors considered relevant, such as age, health, and socioeconomic factors; and the response Y is the annual number of cavities of each child sampled.

Choose the correct alternative.

(a) The coefficient of D (the number b) measures:

   (i) The annual number of cavities that the average child with flouridated water gets in excess of the average control child, other things being equal.

or (ii) The annual consumption of flouride by the tested group, in comparison to the control group, if other factors were held constant.

(b) b will be biased if the study omits an important regressor that is [related, unrelated] to both D and the response Y.

(c) One way to eliminate any possible bias in b is to use a randomized design that assigns the treatment and control at random (by the flip of a coin, for example). Such a randomized design makes D [correlated, uncorrelated] with all regressors, in particular the possible excluded regressors. Thus the link between D and possible excluded regressors is [broken, forged].

4-31 (a) Use multiple regression to calculate how education is related to father's income and place of residence.

(b) Graph your results.

	Years of Formal Education (E)	*Father's Income* (F)
Urban sample	15	$ 8,000
	18	11,000
	12	9,000
	16	12,000
Rural sample	13	$ 5,000
	10	3,000
	11	6,000
	14	10,000

4-32 An anthropologist sampled 4 women from a certain population, and recorded their weights and ages:

Weight W (Pounds)	*Age A (Years)*
130	30
150	50
140	60
100	20
$\bar{W} = 130$	$\bar{A} = 40$

(a) What is the equation of the line that you would use to predict W from A? Graph the line and the 4 points, to check that the line fits the data reasonably well.
(b) Predict the weight of a woman who is 40 years old. In order to give the prediction a 90% chance of being correct, by how much should the predicted value be hedged?
(c) If the regression line of W on A were computed for the whole population, in what range would you expect (with 95% confidence) to find the slope β?

4-33 (a) If a parabola were fitted to the whole population in Problem 4-32, what would you expect the sign of the coefficient of A^2 to be?
(b) Fit a parabola to the 4 data points. Does the sign of the coefficient of A^2 agree with part (a)?
(c) Do you think that the straight line or the parabola is a better model to fit the data? Why?

4-34 Answer true or false; if false, correct it.
(a) One severe limitation of multiple regression is that it cannot include factors that are categorical (nonnumerical, e.g., sex, region).
(b) Multicollinearity often is a problem in the social sciences, when the regressors have high correlation. On the other hand, in the experimental sciences, the values of the regressors often can be designed to avoid multicollinearity.

4-35 (a) Unrestrained by either food or space limitations, a bacteria colony will double within a certain period of time τ; and τ, of course, depends not on the size of the colony but on the reproductive metabolism of the individual bacteria. Write down an appropriate mathematical model to describe such growth.
(b) If the following data were observed for a particular species, fit your model by least squares, and hence estimate the doubling time τ.

Time (minutes)	0	100	200
Size of colony	2,000	6,300	18,000

APPENDIX 4-A

MLE for the Logit Model

This appendix provides the details of MLE for the simple logit model (4-50), which we briefly discussed at the end of Section 4-5.

Let us begin by looking more closely at the likelihood function. We start with a trial pair of parameters (α, β). For the first observation X_1, we can then calculate the probability of success P_1 from (4-50) [or more explicitly, from (4-51)]. Since P_1 is the probability of getting a success ($Y_1 = 1$), the probability is $1 - P_1$ of getting a failure ($Y_1 = 0$). These two cases can be combined with one formula: The probability of any value of Y_1, denoted by $p(Y_1)$, is[27]

$$p(Y_1) = P_1^{Y_1}(1 - P_1)^{1-Y_1} \tag{4-57}$$

By itself, this seems like a lot of effort just to concoct a formula; but it provides a nice stepping stone to more familiar territory.[28]

---

[27] To confirm that (4-57) works, when we substitute $Y_1 = 1$ into it, we get

$$\text{Probability of success} = P_1^1(1 - P_1)^{1-1} = P_1 \quad \checkmark$$

Similarly, when we substitute $Y_1 = 0$ into (4-57), we get

$$\text{Probability of failure} = P_1^0(1 - P_1)^{1-0} = 1 - P_1 \quad \checkmark$$

[28] To be specific, what would happen if all P_i were the same common value (π let us say)? Then (4-61) would simplify to

$$\begin{aligned} p(Y_1 \cdots Y_n) &= \prod_{i=1}^{n} \pi^{Y_i}(1 - \pi)^{1-Y_i} \\ &= \pi^{\Sigma Y_i}(1 - \pi)^{n-\Sigma Y_i} \end{aligned} \tag{4-58}$$

like (2-78)

When we regard the sample (and hence n and S) as fixed, this is called the likelihood function $L(\pi)$. And since the total number of successes $\sum Y_i$ is denoted S, we may write (4-58) as

$$L(\pi) = \pi^S(1 - \pi)^{n-S} \tag{4-59}$$

This is essentially the binomial formula and, when maximized by calculus, gives the familiar MLE:

$$\hat{\pi} = \frac{S}{n} = \text{sample proportion of successes} \tag{4-60}$$

This digression to familiar territory has given us a benchmark to judge MLE for the probit model: In (4-61) the P_i do *not* have a common value (as Figure 4-10 shows, the P_i increase with X_i), and this is what makes MLE so complicated.

Just as we calculated $p(Y_1)$, we can calculate $p(Y_2)$, ..., $p(Y_n)$; then the probability of our whole sample is obtained by multiplying together all these independent probabilities:

$$p(Y_1, Y_2, \ldots) = p(Y_1)p(Y_2)\cdots$$
$$= \prod_{i=1}^{n} P_i^{Y_i}(1 - P_i)^{1-Y_i} \tag{4-61}$$

This number, of course, depends on the trial value of (α, β) that we started with, so we call it the likelihood function $L(\alpha, \beta)$:

$$L(\alpha, \beta) = \prod_{i=1}^{n} P_i^{Y_i}(1 - P_i)^{n-Y_i} \tag{4-62}$$

We try out many pairs (α, β) on the computer, till we find the pair that maximizes $L(\alpha, \beta)$.

*APPENDIX 4-B

Intractable Nonlinear Regressions Solved by Successive Linear Approximation

To generalize (4-53), let us as usual denote the parameters to be estimated by $\beta_1 \cdots \beta_p$ (instead of α_1, α_2, i, and i_2). And let us as usual denote the observed independent variables by $X_1 \cdots X_k$ (instead of t). The number of parameters need not equal the number of independent variables ($p \neq k$). Then the general nonlinear model is

$$Y = f(X_1 \cdots X_k; \beta_1 \cdots \beta_p) + e \tag{4-63}$$

where we know the form of the equation (i.e., we know f), we have observed Y, $X_1 \ldots X_k$, and we must estimate $\beta_1 \ldots \beta_p$.

For brevity, henceforth we suppress $X_1 \cdots X_k$ in our notation, but we retain $\beta_1 \cdots \beta_p$, so that we may write (4-63) more briefly as

$$Y = f(\beta_1 \cdots \beta_k) + e \tag{4-64}$$

Now let us start with an initial guess for the parameters, $\beta_{1o} \cdots \beta_{po}$. In the neighbourhood of this guess, the following *Taylor linearization* is a reasonable approximation[29]:

$$f(\beta_1 \cdots \beta_p) = f(\beta_{1o} \cdots \beta_{po}) + \frac{\partial f}{\partial \beta_1}(\beta_1 - \beta_{1o})$$
$$+ \cdots + \frac{\partial f}{\partial \beta_p}(\beta_p - \beta_{po}) + \text{Taylor error} \tag{4-66}$$

where the partial derivatives $\partial f/\partial\beta_i$ are evaluated at $\beta_{1o}, \ldots, \beta_{po}$, just like f itself, on the right side.

Let us substitute (4-66) into (4-64) and collect the Taylor error and the stochastic error e into one term called v. Then we have

$$Y = f(\beta_{1o} \cdots \beta_{po}) + \frac{\partial f}{\partial \beta_1}(\beta_1 - \beta_{1o}) + \cdots + \frac{\partial f}{\partial \beta_p}(\beta_p - \beta_{po}) + v \quad (4\text{-}67)$$

which may be rewritten as

$$Y - f(\beta_{1o} \cdots \beta_{po}) + \frac{\partial f}{\partial \beta_1}\beta_{1o} + \cdots + \frac{\partial f}{\partial \beta_p}\beta_{po} = \beta_1 \frac{\partial f}{\partial \beta_1} + \cdots + \beta_p \frac{\partial f}{\partial \beta_p} + v \quad (4\text{-}68)$$

---

[29] The Taylor linearization for a function of one variable may be written as

$$f(\beta) = f(\beta_o) + \frac{df}{d\beta}(\beta - \beta_o) + \text{Taylor error} \quad (4\text{-}65)$$

which is illustrated in the following figure. When we extend this to a function of p variables, we obtain (4-66). For details, see for example Williamson et al., 1972.

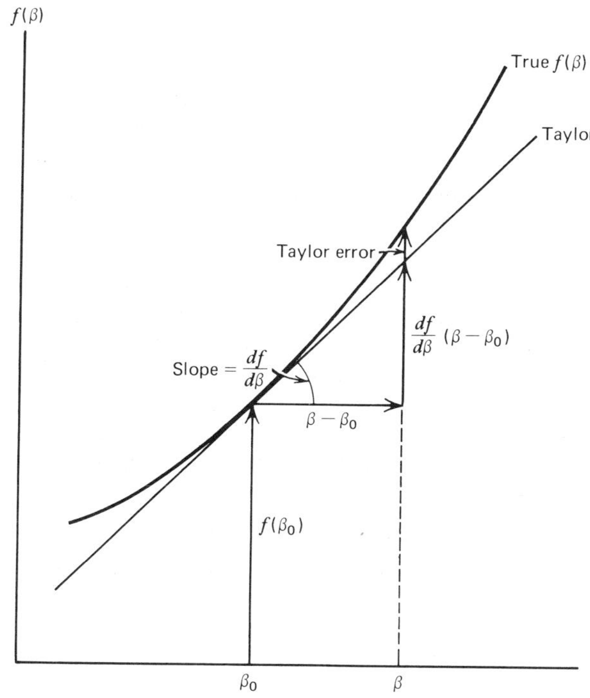

On the left, Y is observed, while all the rest can be calculated (since f and its derivatives are known, and $\beta_{1o} \cdots \beta_{po}$ are the known trial values). We may call the whole left-hand side a constructed response Y_c. Similarly, on the right, for simplicity we may denote the known partial derivatives by $Z_1 \cdots Z_p$. Then (4-68) may be briefly written as

$$Y_c = \beta_1 Z_1 + \cdots + \beta_p Z_p + v \tag{4-69}$$

In this linearized form, we can now regress Y_c on $Z_1 \cdots Z_p$, to obtain estimates of $\beta_1 \cdots \beta_p$. These new estimates are likely better than the old trial estimates, and so we can use them in place of $\beta_{1o} \cdots \beta_{po}$. Then starting at (4-66), we repeat the whole process. And we keep repeating it, every time obtaining new and better estimates, until they converge.

This iterative technique can sometimes converge to a *local* minimum for the sum of squared residuals, rather than the global minimum. Or it can even fail to converge altogether. But it usually converges fairly quickly, and from the last iteration of (4-69), the OLS regression routine will give standard errors of the estimates of $\beta_1 \ldots \beta_p$.

*PROBLEM

4-37 Consider the consumption function:

$$C = \beta_1 + \beta_2 Y^{\beta_3}$$

where C = real U.S. consumption and Y = real disposable income.

Note that this is, except for notation, the model of Problem 4-22(d) and is intractable. When it was estimated by successive linear approximations, using quarterly data from 1946 to 1973, four iterations yielded the following convergence:[30]

	β_1	β_2	β_3
Initial guess	1.0000	1.0000	1.0000
First iteration	−9.4974	1.1856	.9589
Second iteration	−10.3366	1.2400	.9539
Third iteration	−10.3517	1.2409	.9539
Fourth iteration	−10.3507	1.2409	.9539

From the last iteration, the standard errors were 4.2, .088, and .0098, respectively. Construct 95% confidence intervals for the three parameters.

[30] Quoted from Pindyck and Rubinfeld, 1976, p. 233.

APPENDIX 4-C

Another Nonlinear Example: Liquidity Preference

In Section 4-3, we gave an example (the parabolic cost function) of a model that is linear in the parameters, but nonlinear in the variables. By appropriately defining the regressors, we solved it by OLS.

Now we give a second example, which has been deferred to this appendix because it illustrates some rather subtle features. Consider the model

$$Y = \alpha + \beta\left(\frac{1}{L - L^*}\right) \tag{4-70}$$

An economic illustration of this type of relationship might be the Keynesian liquidity preference function, showing how the interest rate Y is related to the quantity of money L. Within the context of this model, L^* might be a constant independent of the interest rate, representing the transactions demand for money; $L - L^*$ represents the speculative demand for money; and α is the liquidity trap, that is, the minimum level of interest. This function is graphed in Figure 4-11; it is a rectangular hyperbola with curvature depending on β.

If L^* is known, then observations of Y and L can be used to estimate α and β. A hypothetical scatter of Y and L observations is shown in Figure 4-12*a* and in columns (1) and (2) of Table 4-5 (using a liquidity preference example, we might suppose that interest Y is measured in %, and the demand for money L is measured in units of \$50 billion). In addition, suppose we have prior information that $L^* = 2$. This scatter confirms our

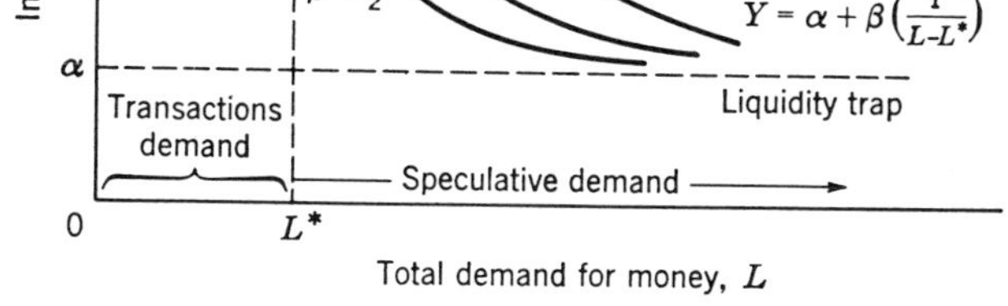

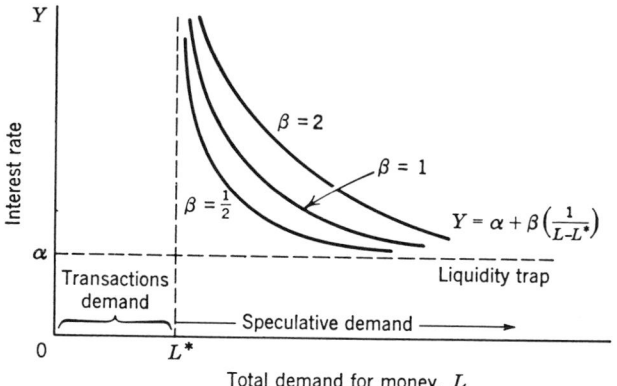

FIGURE 4-11 Possible liquidity preferences—a family of rectangular hyperbolas.

TABLE 4-5 Fitting a Rectangular Hyperbola to a Set of Observations Generated By:

$$Y_i = \alpha + \beta\left(\frac{1}{L_i - L^*}\right) + e_i$$

Step 1	Step 2
Transformation of L into X	Regression of Y on X
	Step 3 Retransformation of X back into L

(1) Y_i	(2) L_i	(3) $L_i - L^*$	(4) $X_i = \frac{1}{L_i - L^*}$	(5) $x_i = X_i - \bar{X}$	(6) $Y_i x_i$	(7) x_i^2	(8) $\hat{Y}_i = \bar{Y} + \hat{\beta}x_i = 4.07 + 1.5x_i$	(9) $\hat{e}_i = Y_i - \hat{Y}_i$	(10) $\hat{e}_i^2 = (Y_i - \hat{Y}_i)^2$
6.0	2.5	0.5	2.00	0.98	5.88	0.96	5.54	0.46	0.2116
5.5	2.4	0.4	2.50	1.48	8.14	2.19	6.29	−0.79	0.6241
5.5	2.7	0.7	1.43	0.41	2.26	0.17	4.69	0.81	0.6561
4.8	2.6	0.6	1.67	0.65	3.12	0.42	5.05	−0.25	0.0625
4.4	3.0	1.0	1.00	−0.02	−0.09	0	4.04	0.36	0.1296
3.7	3.3	1.3	0.77	−0.25	−0.93	0.06	3.69	0.01	0.0001
3.5	3.7	1.7	0.59	−0.43	−1.51	0.18	3.42	0.08	0.0064
3.2	4.4	2.4	0.42	−0.60	−1.92	0.36	3.17	0.03	0.0009
2.7	4.9	2.9	0.34	−0.68	−1.84	0.46	3.05	−0.35	0.1225
3.0	5.6	3.6	0.28	−0.74	−2.22	0.55	2.96	0.04	0.0016
2.5	6.2	4.2	0.24	−0.78	−1.95	0.61	2.90	−0.40	0.1600
$\sum Y_i = 44.8$			$\sum X_i = 11.24$	$\sum x_i = 0$	$\sum Y_i x_i = 8.94$	$\sum x_i^2 = 5.96$			$\sum (Y_i - \hat{Y}_i)^2 = 1.9745$

$$\bar{Y} = \frac{\sum Y_i}{n} = \frac{44.8}{11} = 4.07$$

$$\bar{X} = \frac{\sum X_i}{n} = 1.02$$

$$\hat{\beta} = \frac{\sum Y_i x_i}{\sum x_i^2} = \frac{8.94}{5.96} = 1.50$$

$$s^2 = \frac{\sum (Y_i - \hat{Y}_i)^2}{n-2} = 0.219$$

$$s = 0.47$$

The fitted regression is

$$\begin{aligned} Y &= \bar{Y} + \hat{\beta}x \\ &= 4.07 + 1.50x \\ &= 4.07 + 1.50(X - 1.02) \\ &= 2.54 + 1.50X \end{aligned}$$

or

$$Y = 2.54 + 1.5\left(\frac{1}{L - L^*}\right)$$

theoretical expectation that the relation between the variables is hyperbolic, rather than linear. The estimators $\hat{\alpha}$ and $\hat{\beta}$ are found in three steps.

Step 1. If, in (4-70), we let

$$X = \frac{1}{L - L^*} \tag{4-71}$$

our model becomes the simple linear regression of Y on X. It can be fitted by our standard procedure. Therefore, the first step is to transform L into X according to (4-71). This is shown in columns (3) and (4) of Table 4-5; geometrically this transformation is shown below the baseline in Figure 4-12*a*.

In Figure 4-12*b*, the new X variable is measured left to right from a zero origin, and the same observed scatter is plotted, but this time in the new (X, Y) frame of reference. As expected, this transformation of L into X has transformed our scatter into a roughly linear relation.

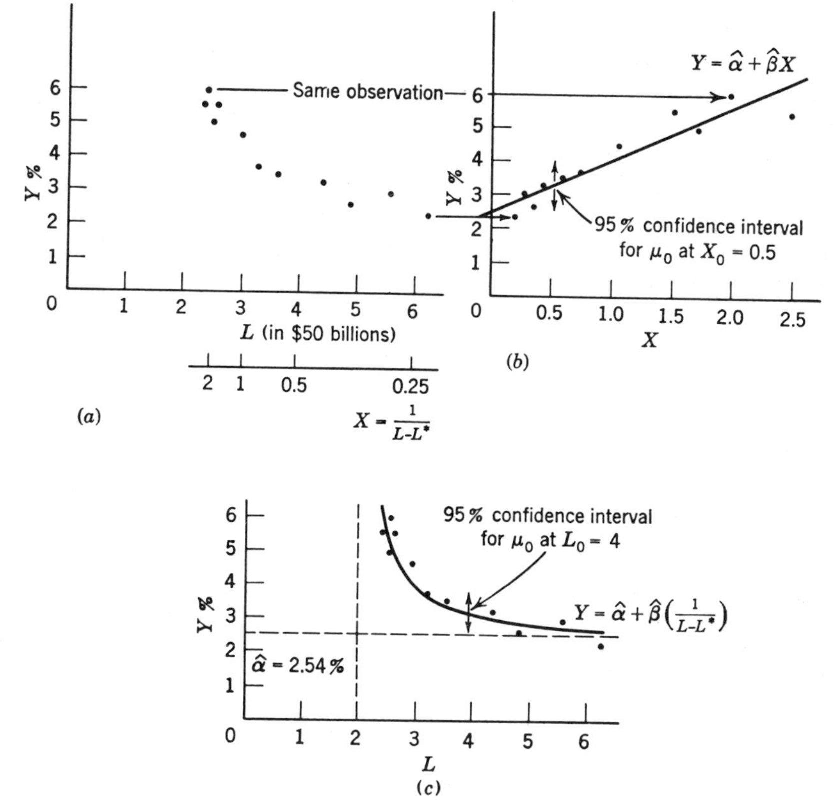

FIGURE 4-12 Fitting a rectangular hyperbola. (*a*) Step 1: transformation of L into X. (*b*) Step 2: regression of Y on X. (*c*) Step 3: retransformation of X back into L.

Step 2. Y is now regressed on X by our standard procedures, shown in columns (5) to (7) of Table 4-5. The resulting fit is

$$Y = 2.54 + 1.50X \tag{4-72}$$

shown in Figure 4-12*b*.

Step 3. We finally need to retransform X back into L. Substituting (4-71) into (4-72),

$$Y = 2.54 + 1.50\left(\frac{1}{L - L^*}\right) \tag{4-73}$$

which is the hyperbola shown in Figure 4-12*c*; thus, our least squares fit of the scatter shown in Figure 4-12*a* is complete.

In summary, it may be concluded that because the relation (4-70) is linear in the parameters α and β, standard regression procedures may be applied without complication.[31] It is only necessary before proceeding to define a new variable, and after the linear regression, to retransform. Confidence intervals, tests of hypothesis, etc., can be undertaken as outlined in Chapter 2; *it is only necessary to take great care in transforming variables.*

To illustrate: What is the 95% confidence interval for μ_0, the mean of Y when $L_0 = 4.0$? We wish to apply the standard procedure for calculating the confidence interval for a mean, set out in (2-65). But this can only be applied to the simple linear regression of Y on X given in (4-72). As a start, therefore, it is necessary to transform L_0 into X_0. From (4-71),

$$X_0 = \frac{1}{L_0 - L^*}$$

$$= \frac{1}{4.0 - 2.0} = .50$$

[31] We have considered fitting a typical rectangular hyperbola, of which Keynesian liquidity preference *might* be a special case. But any attempt in practice to estimate liquidity preference would involve further complications. For example, the transactions demand for money L^* would have to be independently estimated, and it is by no means clear, as we have assumed, that it is independent of the interest rate. Furthermore, it could not normally be assumed that the relationship is exactly a rectangular hyperbola in shape—that is, it might be necessary to start with a more general form of relation, such as

$$Y = \alpha + \beta\left(\frac{1}{L - L^*}\right)^{\gamma}$$

There are even more problems with liquidity preference, which we ignore, because our interest is in developing nonlinear econometric techniques rather than monetary theory.

But we note that (2-65) requires that X_0 be expressed as a deviation

$$\begin{aligned} x_0 &= X_0 - \bar{X} \\ &= .50 - 1.02 = -.52 \end{aligned}$$

Now we can find the point estimate for μ_0:

$$\begin{aligned} \hat{\mu}_0 &= \hat{\alpha} + \hat{\beta} x_0 \\ &= 4.07 + 1.50(-.52) = 3.29 \end{aligned} \tag{4-74}$$

And the interval estimate for μ_0 is, from (2-65),

$$\begin{aligned} \mu_0 &= \hat{\mu}_0 \pm t_{.025}\, s \sqrt{\frac{1}{n} + \frac{x_0^2}{\sum x_i^2}} \\ &= 3.29 \pm 2.26(.47)\sqrt{\frac{1}{11} + \frac{(-.52)^2}{5.96}} \\ &= 3.29 \pm .39 \end{aligned}$$

$$2.90 < \mu_0 < 3.68 \tag{4-75}$$

This 95% confidence interval is shown in Figure 4-12*c*.

5

CORRELATION

5-1 SIMPLE CORRELATION

(a) Introduction

Simple regression analysis showed us *how* variables are linearly related; correlation analysis will only show us the *degree* to which variables are linearly related. In regression analysis, a whole function is estimated (the regression equation); but correlation analysis yields only one number—an index designed to give an immediate picture of how closely two variables move together. Although correlation is a less powerful technique than regression, the two are so closely related that correlation often becomes a useful aid in interpreting regression. In fact, this is the major reason for studying it.

(b) The Sample Correlation Coefficient r

As an example, consider the marks on a verbal (Y) and mathematical (X) test scored by a sample of eight college students. Each student's performance is represented by a point in the scatter shown in Figure 5-1*a*; this information is set out in the first two columns of Table 5-1.

Since we are after a single measure of how closely these variables are related, our index should be independent of our choice of origin in Figure 5-1*a*. So we shift *both* axes in Figure 5-1*b*, just as we shifted one axis in Chapter 2. Both x and y are now defined as deviations from the mean; that is,

$$\left.\begin{aligned} x &= X - \bar{X} \\ y &= Y - \bar{Y} \end{aligned}\right\} \tag{5-1}$$

Values of the translated variables are shown in columns (3) and (4) of Table 5-1.

TABLE 5-1 Math Score (X) and Corresponding Verbal Score (Y) of a Sample of 8 Students

							Regression of Y on X			Regression of X on Y		
X	Y	$x = X - \bar{X}$	$y = Y - \bar{Y}$	xy	x^2	y^2	$\hat{Y} = \bar{Y} + \hat{\beta}x$	$Y - \hat{Y}$	$(Y - \hat{Y})^2$	$\hat{X} = \bar{X} + \hat{\beta}_* y$	$X - \hat{X}$	$(X - \hat{X})^2$
36	35	−24	−15	360	576	225	38	−3	9	48	−12	144
80	65	20	15	300	400	225	60	5	25	72	8	64
50	60	−10	10	−100	100	100	45	15	225	68	−18	324
58	39	−2	−11	22	4	121	49	−10	100	51	7	49
72	48	12	−2	−24	144	4	56	−8	64	58	14	196
60	44	0	−6	0	0	36	50	−6	36	55	5	25
56	48	−4	−2	8	16	4	48	0	0	58	−2	4
68	61	8	11	88	64	121	54	7	49	69	−1	1
$\sum X = 480$, $\bar{X} = 60$	$\sum Y = 400$, $\bar{Y} = 50$	$\sum x = 0$	$\sum y = 0$	$\sum xy = 654$	$\sum x^2 = 1304$	$\sum y^2 = 836$		$\sum (Y - \hat{Y})^2 = 508$			$\sum (X - \hat{X})^2 = 807$	

From (2-19), regression of Y on X: $\hat{\beta} = \frac{\sum xy}{\sum x^2} = .50$

Regression of X on Y: $\hat{\beta}_* = \frac{\sum xy}{\sum y^2} = .78$

$$s^2 = \frac{\sum (Y - \hat{Y})^2}{n - 2} = \frac{508}{6} = 84.7$$

$$s = 9.20$$

$$s_*^2 = \frac{\sum (X - \hat{X})^2}{n - 2} = \frac{807}{6} = 134.5$$

$$s_* = 11.60$$

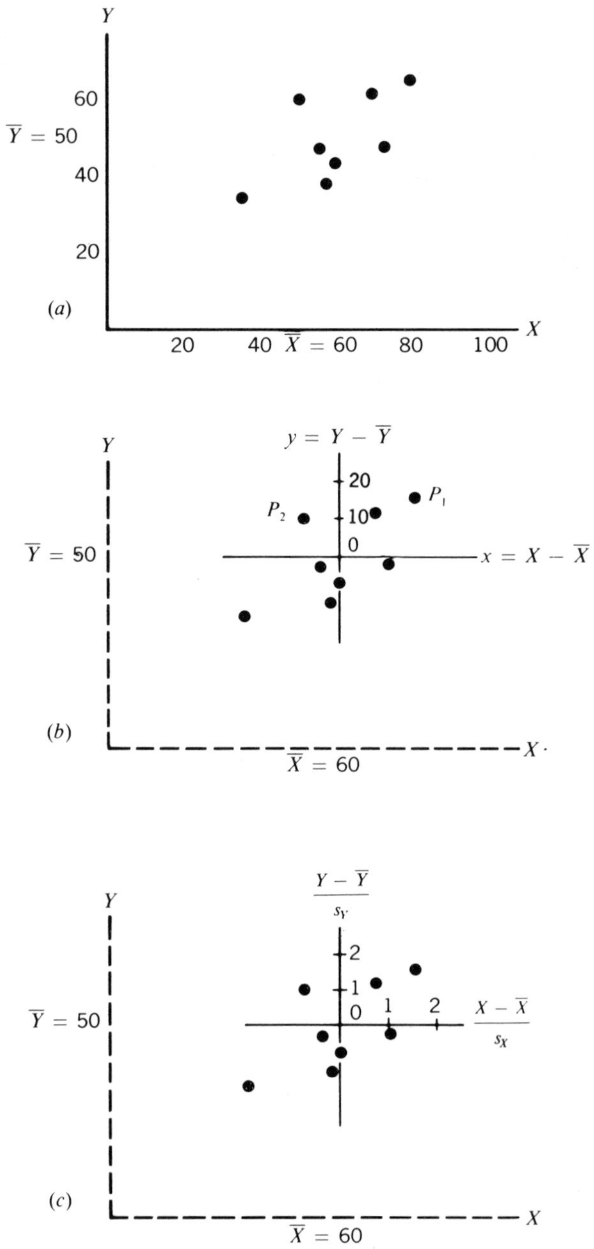

FIGURE 5-1 Scatter of math and verbal scores. (a) Original observations. (b) Axes shifted. (c) Axes rescaled to standard units.

Suppose that we multiply the x and y values for each student and sum them to get $\sum xy$. This gives us a good measure of how math and verbal results tend to move together. We can see this by referring to Figure 5-1*b*: For any observation such as P_1 in the first or third quadrant, x and y agree in sign, so their product xy is positive. Conversely, for any observation such as P_2 in the second or fourth quadrant, x and y disagree in sign, so their product xy is negative. If X and Y move together, most observations will fall in the first and third quadrants; consequently, most products xy will be positive, as will their sum—a reflection of the positive relationship between X and Y. But if X and Y are related negatively (i.e., if one rises when the other falls), most observations will fall in the second and fourth quadrants, yielding a negative value for our $\sum xy$ index. We conclude that as an index of correlation, $\sum xy$ at least carries the right sign. Moreover, when there is no relationship between X and Y, with the observations distributed evenly over the four quadrants, positive and negative terms will cancel, and $\sum xy$ will be zero.

There are just two ways that $\sum xy$ can be improved. First, it depends on sample size. (Suppose we observed exactly the same sort of scatter from a sample of double the size; then $\sum xy$ would also double, even though the picture of how these variables move together would not have changed). To avoid this problem we divide by the sample size—actually by $(n - 1)$—to yield the index:

$$\text{Sample covariance, } s_{XY} \equiv \frac{\sum xy}{n-1} \tag{5-2}$$

$$s_{XY} \equiv \frac{1}{n-1} \sum (X_i - \bar{X})(Y_i - \bar{Y}) \tag{5-3}$$

This is a highly useful concept in statistics. But it does have one remaining weakness: s_{XY} depends on the units in which x and y are measured. (Suppose the math test had been marked out of 50 instead of 100; x values and hence s_{XY} would be only half as large—even though the degree to which verbal and mathematical performance is related would not have changed.) This difficulty is avoided by measuring both variables in terms of standard units. This step is shown in Figure 5-1*c*, where both x and y are divided by their standard deviations. The resulting index is

$$\text{Sample correlation, } r \equiv \frac{1}{n-1} \sum_{i=1}^{n} \left(\frac{X_i - \bar{X}}{s_X}\right)\left(\frac{Y_i - \bar{Y}}{s_Y}\right) \tag{5-4}$$

From (5-3), we may write this more briefly as

$$\boxed{r = \frac{s_{XY}}{s_X s_Y}} \tag{5-5}$$

For computational purposes it is sometimes convenient to reexpress this as,[1]

$$r = \frac{\sum xy}{\sqrt{\sum x^2 \sum y^2}} \tag{5-6}$$

For example, to calculate the correlation coefficient between the math and verbal scores of the sample of eight students, we substitute the appropriate sums from Table 5-1 into (5-6):

$$r = \frac{654}{\sqrt{(1304)(836)}} = .63 \tag{5-7}$$

Some idea of how r behaves is given in Figure 5-2. Especially note the line in panel (*b*): When there is a perfect positive relation, the product xy is always positive. Thus $\sum xy$, and hence r, are as large as possible. A similar argument holds for the perfect negative relation shown in panel (*d*). This suggests that r has an upper limit of $+1$ and a lower limit of -1. This will be proved in Section 5-2(c) below.

Finally, consider the symmetric scatters shown in panels (*e*) and (*f*). The calculation of r in either case yields zero, because each positive product xy is offset by a corresponding negative xy in the opposite quadrant. Yet these two scatters show quite different patterns: In (*e*), there is no relation between X and Y; in (*f*), however, there is a strong relation (knowledge of X will tell us a great deal about Y).

A zero value for r therefore does not necessarily imply "no relation"; rather, it means "no *linear* relation." Thus simple correlation is a measure of linear relation only; it is of no use in describing nonlinear relations.

(c) Inference from r to ρ

In calculating r, what can we infer about the underlying population ρ? First, we must clarify our assumptions about the underlying population itself. In our example, this would be the math and verbal marks scored by *all* college

[1] To obtain (5-6), we simply substitute (5-2) into (5-5), along with the formulas for s_X and s_Y as in (2-91). Then we cancel $n - 1$. Incidentally, some authors use n instead of $n - 1$ throughout. The divisor n has the advantage of simplicity, but the disadvantage of bias in estimating corresponding population parameters.

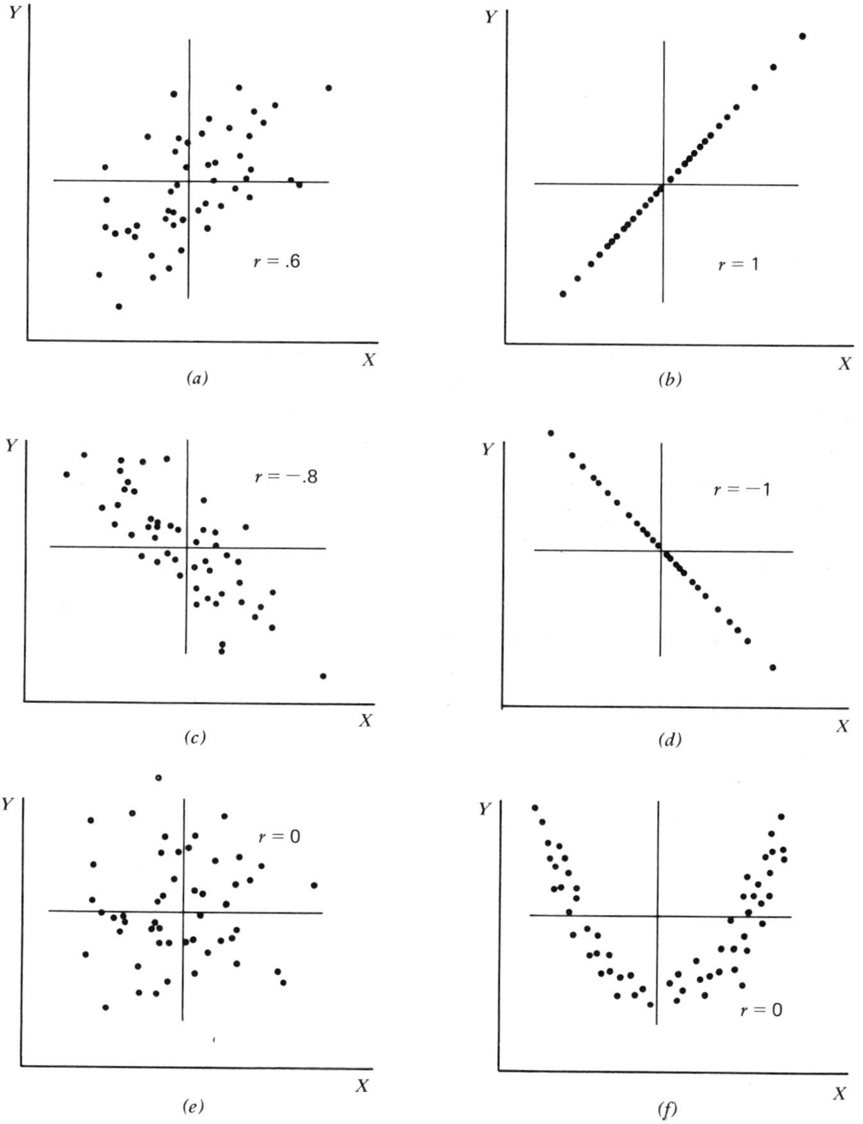

FIGURE 5-2 Some sample scatters to illustrate various values of r.

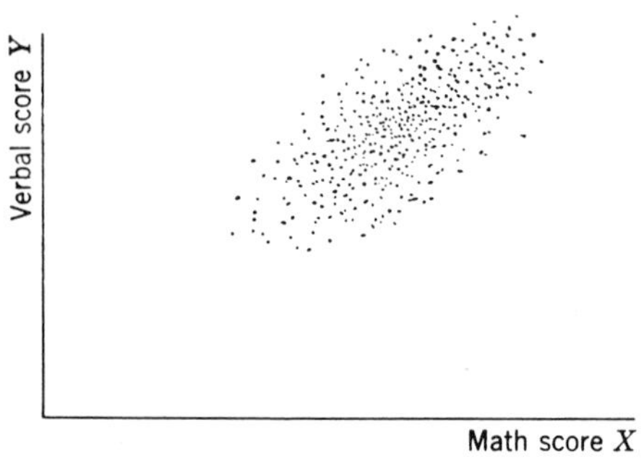

FIGURE 5-3 Bivariate population scattergram (math and verbal scores).

entrants. This population might appear as in Figure 5-3, except that there would be, of course, many more dots in this scatter, each representing another student. If we subdivide both X and Y axes into intervals, the area in our diagram will be divided up in a checkerboard pattern. From the relative frequency in each of the squares, the bar graph in Figure 5-4 is constructed. If this bar graph is approximated by a smooth surface, the result is the continuous function shown in Figure 5-5, representing the probability density of any X and Y combination.

A special kind of joint distribution of X and Y is assumed in making statistical inferences in simple correlation analysis—a bivariate normal distribution. It is called bivariate because both X and Y are random variables; one is not fixed, as fertilizer was in Chapter 2. And it is normal because the conditional distribution of X or of Y is always normal. Specifically, if we slice the surface at any value of Y (say Y_0), the shape of the resulting cross section is normal. Similarly, if we select any X value (say X_0) and slice the surface in this other direction, the resulting cross section also is normal.

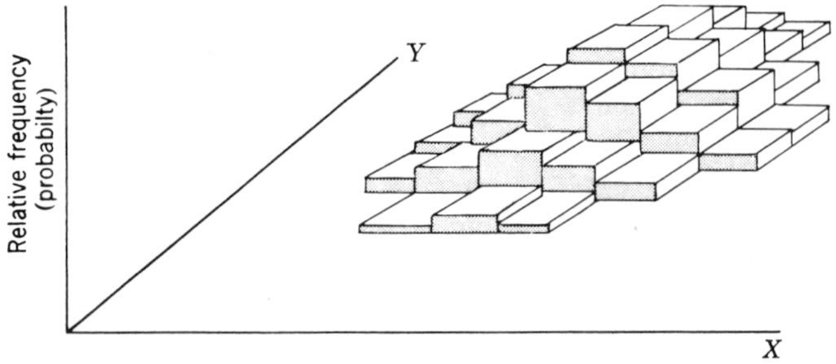

FIGURE 5-4 Bivariate population bar graph.

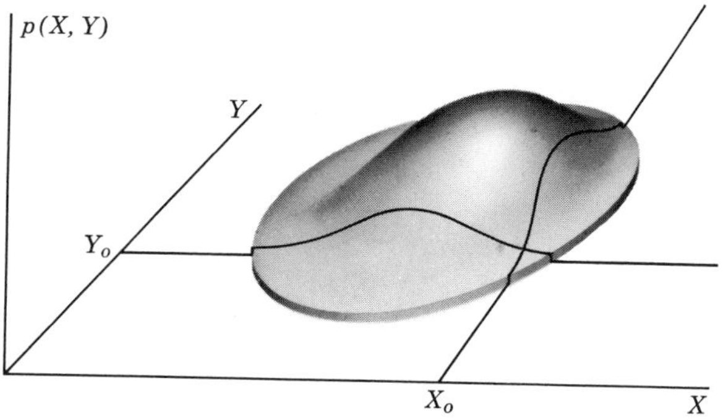

FIGURE 5-5 Bivariate normal distribution.

For the population, the correlation coefficient ρ (rho) has the same definition and interpretation as the sample correlation r. Thus, by analogy with (5-4),

$$\text{Population correlation, } \rho \equiv \frac{1}{N}\sum_{i=1}^{N}\left(\frac{X_i - \mu_X}{\sigma_X}\right)\left(\frac{Y_i - \mu_Y}{\sigma_Y}\right) \tag{5-8}$$

where N is the population size, while μ_X and σ_X are the population mean and standard deviation of X. This may be written more briefly and precisely[2] as a mathematical expectation:

$$\rho \equiv E\left(\frac{X - \mu_X}{\sigma_X}\right)\left(\frac{Y - \mu_Y}{\sigma_Y}\right) \tag{5-9}$$

It is worthwhile pausing briefly to consider the alternative way that the bivariate normal population shown in three dimensions in Figure 5-5 can be

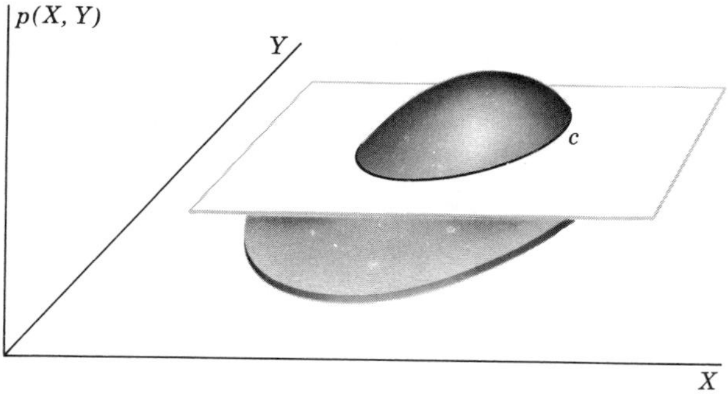

FIGURE 5-6 An isoprobability ellipse from a bivariate normal surface.

[2] The advantage of (5-8) is that it covers both the discrete case and the case where X and Y are continuous.

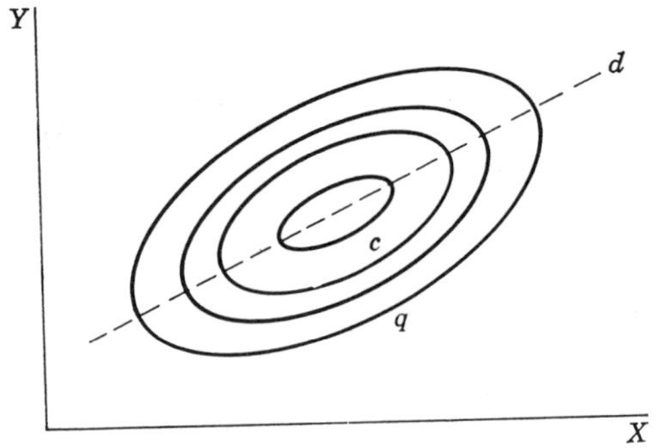

FIGURE 5-7 The bivariate normal distribution shown as a set of isoprobability or level curves.

graphed in two dimensions. Slice the surface horizontally, as in Figure 5-6 (or equivalently, you can think of flooding Figure 5-6 with water up to a certain level). The resulting cross section (or shoreline) is an ellipse, representing all (X, Y) combinations with the same probability density. It is called an *isoprobability curve* (or *level curve*). This level curve marked c is reproduced in the two-dimensional X, Y space in Figure 5-7. Level curves at higher and lower levels are also shown. (Economists will recognise this as the familiar strategy of forcing a three-dimensional function into a two-dimensional space by showing one variable as a set of isoquants.) Special attention should be directed to isoprobability ellipse q in Figure 5-7, which encloses about 85% of the distribution, and is called the ellipse of concentration.[3] Often, this single curve is used to represent an entire bivariate normal distribution.

It will also be useful in Figure 5-7 to mark the major axis (d) common to all these level curves. If the bivariate normal distribution concentrates about this major axis, ρ has a higher numerical value. Two examples of populations and their associated correlation coefficients ρ are shown in Figure 5-8.

Provided that the parent population is bivariate normal, Figure 5-9 allows us to make inferences about the population ρ from a sample correlation r. For example, if a sample of 10 students has $r = .6$, the 95% confidence interval for ρ is read vertically as

$$-.05 < \rho < .87 \tag{5-10}$$

Because of space limitations, in the balance of this chapter we will concentrate on sample correlations and ignore the corresponding popula-

[3] The ellipse of concentration is defined more precisely as that ellipse which, if filled with a probability density of constant height, would have the same means, variances, and covariance as the normal distribution that it represents.

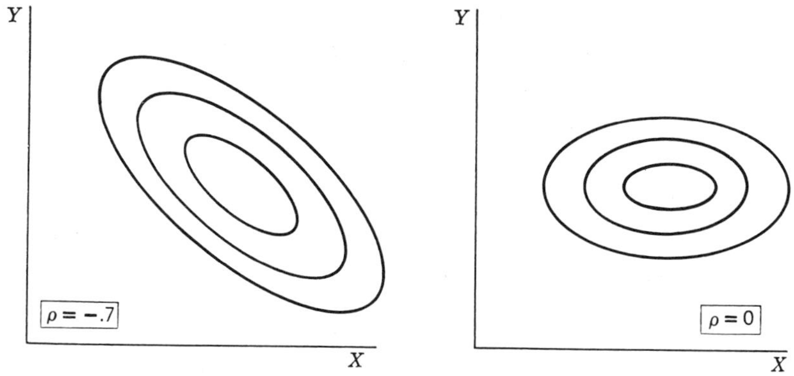

FIGURE 5-8 Examples of population correlations.

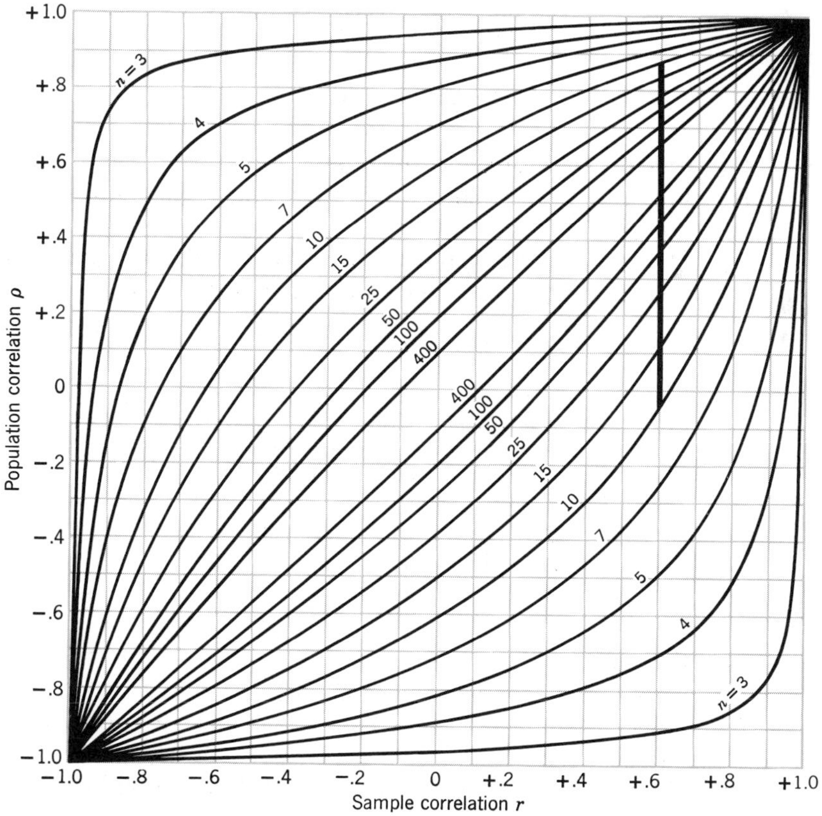

FIGURE 5-9 Ninety-five percent confidence bands for correlation ρ in a bivariate normal population, for various sample sizes n.

tion correlations. But each time a sample correlation is introduced, we should recognize that an equivalent population correlation is defined similarly, and inferences may be made about it from the sample correlation.

PROBLEMS

5-1 Over a 5-month period, a sports store sells the following quantities of tennis shorts and shirts:

	Tennis Shorts	*Shirts*
May	68	64
June	66	66
July	72	71
August	73	70
September	66	69

(a) Calculate the sample correlation r.
(b) Find the 95% confidence interval for the population correlation ρ.
(c) At the 5% level, can you reject the hypothesis that $\rho = 0$? (Test against the two-sided alternative hypothesis $\rho \neq 0$.)

⇒5-2 From a large population, 5 students' grades were sampled:

Student	*First Test X*	*Second Test Y*
A	80	90
B	60	70
C	40	40
D	30	40
E	40	60

(a) Calculate r.
(b) Find a 95% confidence interval for ρ.
(c) Calculate the regression of Y on X, and find a 95% confidence interval for β.
(d) Graph the 5 students and the estimated regression line.
(e) At the 5% level (in a two-sided test) can you reject

(i) the null hypothesis $\rho = 0$?
(ii) the null hypothesis $\beta = 0$?

5-2 CORRELATION AND REGRESSION

(a) Relation of $\hat{\beta}$ to r

If regression and correlation analysis were both applied to the same scatter of math (X) and verbal (Y) scores, how would they be related? To find out, let us recall the formulas for the regression and correlation coefficients:

$$\hat{\beta} = b = \frac{\sum xy}{\sum x^2} \qquad \text{(5-11)}$$

(2-19) repeated

$$r = \frac{\sum xy}{\sqrt{\sum x^2}\sqrt{\sum y^2}} \qquad \text{(5-12)}$$

(5-6) repeated

When (5-11) is divided by (5-12),

$$\frac{\hat{\beta}}{r} = \frac{\sqrt{\sum x^2}\sqrt{\sum y^2}}{\sum x^2} = \frac{\sqrt{\sum y^2}}{\sqrt{\sum x^2}}$$

If we divide both the numerator and denominator inside the square root sign by $(n - 1)$,

$$\frac{\hat{\beta}}{r} = \frac{\sqrt{\sum y^2/(n-1)}}{\sqrt{\sum x^2/(n-1)}} = \frac{s_Y}{s_X} \qquad \text{(5-13)}$$

or

$$\boxed{\hat{\beta} = r\frac{s_Y}{s_X}} \qquad \text{(5-14)}$$

Thus $\hat{\beta}$ and r are closely related. For example, if either is zero, the other will also be zero. Similarly, if either of the population parameters β or ρ is zero, the other will also be zero. Hence it is no surprise that in Problem 5-2, the tests for $\beta = 0$ and for $\rho = 0$ were just two equivalent ways of examining "no linear relation between X and Y."

(b) Explained and Unexplained Variation

In Figure 5-10, we reproduce the sample of math (X) and verbal (Y) scores, along with the fitted regression of Y on X, calculated in a straightforward way from the information set out in Table 5-1. Now, if we wished to predict a student's verbal score Y without knowing X, then the best prediction would be the average observed value $\bar{Y}$. At x_i, it is clear from this diagram that we would make a very large error—$(Y_i - Y)$, the deviation of Y_i from its mean. However, if X is known and the regression of Y on X has been calculated, we predict Y to be the value $\hat{Y}_i$ on the line. Note how this reduces our error,

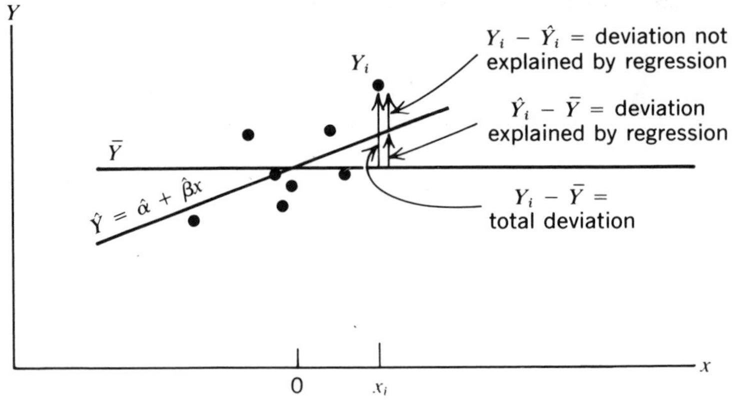

FIGURE 5-10 The value of regression in reducing variation in Y.

since $(\hat{Y}_i - \bar{Y})$—a large part of our deviation—is now "explained." This leaves only a relatively small "unexplained" deviation $(Y_i - \hat{Y}_i)$. The total deviation of Y_i is the sum:

$$\underset{\text{total deviation}}{(Y_i - \bar{Y})} = \underset{\text{explained deviation}}{(\hat{Y}_i - \bar{Y})} + \underset{\text{unexplained deviation}}{(Y_i - \hat{Y}_i)}, \quad \text{for any } i \tag{5-15}$$

It follows that:

$$\sum (Y_i - \bar{Y}) = \sum (\hat{Y}_i - \bar{Y}) + \sum (Y_i - \hat{Y}_i) \tag{5-16}$$

What is surprising is that this same equality holds true when these deviations are squared,[4] that is,

$$\underset{\text{total variation}}{\sum (Y_i - \bar{Y})^2} = \underset{\text{explained variation}}{\sum (\hat{Y}_i - \bar{Y})^2} + \underset{\text{unexplained variation}}{\sum (Y_i - \hat{Y}_i)^2} \tag{5-17}$$

where variation is defined as the sum of squared deviations.

---

[4] Square both sides of (5-15), and sum over all values of i:

$$\sum (Y_i - \bar{Y})^2 = \sum [(\hat{Y}_i - \bar{Y}) + (Y_i - \hat{Y}_i)]^2$$
$$= \sum (\hat{Y}_i - \bar{Y})^2 + \sum (Y_i - \hat{Y}_i)^2 + 2 \sum (\hat{Y}_i - \bar{Y})(Y_i - \hat{Y}_i) \tag{5-18}$$

The last term can be rewritten using (5-19):

$$2\hat{\beta} \sum x_i(Y_i - \hat{Y}_i)$$

But this sum vanishes; in fact, it was set equal to zero in equation (2-15) used to estimate the regression line. Thus, the last term in (5-18) disappears, and (5-17) is proved. This same theorem can similarly be proved in the general case of multiple regression.

A further justification of the least squares technique (not mentioned in Chapter 2) is that it results in this useful relation between explained, unexplained, and total variation.

We may rewrite (5-17) by substituting into its middle term:

$$(\hat{Y}_i - \bar{Y}) = \hat{y}_i = \hat{\beta}x_i \tag{5-19}$$

like (2-20)

We then obtain

$$\sum (Y_i - \bar{Y})^2 = \hat{\beta}^2 \sum x_i^2 + \sum (Y_i - \hat{Y}_i)^2 \tag{5-20}$$

$$\text{total variation} = \text{variation explained by } X + \text{unexplained variation}$$

This equation makes clear that explained variation is the variation accounted for by the estimated regression coefficient $\hat{\beta}$. This procedure of analyzing or decomposing total variation into its components is called *analysis of variance for regression.* The components of variance may be displayed in an ANOVA table such as Table 5-2(a). (Note that variance is variation divided by degrees of freedom.) From this, we may formulate a test of the null hypothesis $\beta = 0$. The question is whether the ratio of the explained variance to unexplained variance is sufficiently large to reject H_0.

TABLE 5-2 Analysis of Variance Table for Linear Regression

(a) General

Source of Variation	*Variation*	*d.f.*	*Variance*	*F ratio*
Explained (by regression)	$\sum (\hat{Y}_i - \bar{Y})^2$ or $\hat{\beta}^2 \sum x_i^2$	1	$\frac{\hat{\beta}^2 \sum x_i^2}{1}$	$\frac{\hat{\beta}^2 \sum x_i^2}{s^2}$
Unexplained	$\sum (Y_i - \hat{Y}_i)^2$	$n-2$	$s^2 = \frac{\sum (Y_i - \hat{Y}_i)^2}{n-2}$	
Total	$\sum (Y_i - \bar{Y})^2$	$n-1$		

(b) For the sample of math and verbal scores in Table 5-1

Source of Variation	*Variation*	*d.f.*	*Variance*	*F ratio*
Explained (by regression)	328	1	328	3.87
Unexplained (residual)	508	6	84.7	
Total	836	7		

Specifically, we form the ratio

$$F = \frac{\text{variance explained by regression}}{\text{unexplained variance}}$$

$$= \frac{\hat{\beta}^2 \sum x_i^2}{s^2} \tag{5-21}$$

This is shown as the last entry in Table 5-2(a). By referring to the critical F values in Appendix Table VI, we can calculate the prob-value for H_0, and if this is sufficiently low, reject H_0.

The F test is just an alternative way of testing the null hypothesis that $\beta = 0$. The first method—using the t ratio as in (2-46) or (2-51)—is preferable if a confidence interval also is desired. The two tests are equivalent because the t statistic is related to F (with 1 d.f. in the numerator) by

$$\boxed{t^2 = F} \tag{5-22}$$

To sum up, there are three equivalent ways of testing the null hypothesis that the regressor has no effect on Y: the F test and the t test of $\beta = 0$, and the test of $\rho = 0$ in Figure 5-9. All three will now be illustrated in an example.

Example 5-1

(a) Analyze the math and verbal scores of Table 5-1 in an ANOVA table, including the prob-value and a test of the null hypothesis $\beta = 0$ at the 5% level.

(b) Test the same null hypothesis by alternatively using the t confidence interval.

(c) Test the equivalent null hypothesis $\rho = 0$ using the confidence interval based on $r = .63$, as calculated in (5-7).

Solution

(a) The ANOVA table is set out in Table 5-2(b), yielding an F ratio of 3.87. Comparing this to the nearby critical values (in end-of-book Appendix Table VII), we find $F_{.10} = 3.59$ and $F_{.05} = 5.59$. Thus

$$.05 < \text{prob-value} < .10 \tag{5-23}$$

Since the prob-value is more than 5%, we cannot reject H_0.

(b) The appropriate estimates derived in Table 5-1 are substituted into the formula for the 95% confidence interval:

$$\beta = \hat{\beta} \pm t_{.025} \frac{s}{\sqrt{\sum x^2}} \qquad \text{(2-51) repeated}$$

Thus

$$\beta = .50 \pm 2.45\left(\frac{9.20}{\sqrt{1304}}\right)$$

$$= .50 \pm 2.45(.254) \tag{5-24}$$

$$= .50 \pm .62 \tag{5-25}$$

Since $\beta = 0$ is included in the confidence interval, we cannot reject the null hypothesis at the 5% level.

(c) In Figure 5-9, we must interpolate to find $n = 8$ and $r = .63$. This yields the approximate 95% confidence interval:

$$-.15 < \rho < +.90$$

Since $\rho = 0$ is included in the confidence interval, we cannot reject the null hypothesis at the 5% level.

(c) Coefficient of Determination, r^2

The variations in Y will now be related to r. It follows from (5-14) that

$$\hat{\beta} = r\sqrt{\frac{\sum y_i^2}{\sum x_i^2}} \tag{5-26}$$

Substituting this value for $\hat{\beta}$ in (5-20),

$$\sum (Y_i - \bar{Y})^2 = r^2 \sum y_i^2 + \sum (Y_i - \hat{Y}_i)^2 \tag{5-27}$$

Noting that $\sum y_i^2$ is by definition $\sum (Y_i - \bar{Y})^2$, the solution for r^2 is

$$\frac{\sum (Y_i - \bar{Y})^2 - \sum (Y_i - \hat{Y}_i)^2}{\sum (Y_i - \bar{Y})^2} = r^2 \tag{5-28}$$

Finally, we can reexpress the numerator by noting (5-17). Thus

$$\boxed{r^2 = \frac{\sum (\hat{Y}_i - \bar{Y})^2}{\sum (Y_i - \bar{Y})^2} = \frac{\text{explained variation of } Y}{\text{total variation of } Y}} \tag{5-29}$$

This equation provides a clear intuitive interpretation of r^2. Note that this is the *square* of the correlation coefficient r, and is often called the *coefficient of determination.*[5] *It is the proportion of the total variation in Y explained by fitting the regression.* Since the numerator cannot exceed the denominator, the maximum value of the right-hand side of (5-29) is 1; hence the limits on r are ± 1. These two limits were illustrated in Figure 5-2; in panel (b), $r = +1$ and all observations lie on a positively sloped straight line; in panel (d) $r = -1$ and all observations line on a negatively sloped straight line. In either case, a regression fit will explain 100% of the variation in Y.

At the other extreme, when $r = 0$, then the proportion of the variation of Y that is explained is $r^2 = 0$, and a regression line explains nothing. That is, when $r = 0$, then $\hat{\beta} = 0$; again note that these are just two equivalent ways of formally stating "no observed linear relation between X and Y."

(d) Regression Applied to a Bivariate Normal Population

In Figure 5-11 we show a bivariate normal distribution of math and verbal scores, represented by the ellipse of concentration that outlines most of the scatter. If we know a student's math score, say X_1, what should we predict is the verbal score Y? If we consider all possible students who scored X_1 in math, they are represented by the vertical row of dots stretching from the top edge of the ellipse to the bottom. So among these possible Y values, which is the best guess? The central one, of course, indicated by P_1.

Similarly, for any other given math score X, we could find the central Y value that is the best prediction. These best predictions, marked by the heavy dots, form a straight line,[6] called the *population regression of Y on X*:

$$Y = \alpha + \beta X \tag{5-33}$$

---

[5] From (5-29) it is easy to show that

$$1 - r^2 = \frac{\text{residual variation of } Y}{\text{total variation of } Y} \tag{5-30}$$

This is sometimes called the *coefficient of indetermination*, since it gives the proportion of the total variation of Y that remains *unexplained* by the regression. Let us divide the numerator and denominator of (5-30) by $n - 1$. In the denominator we get s_Y^2, the variance of Y; in the numerator we almost get s^2, the residual variance (the slight difference is that s^2 should have a divisor of $n - 2$). Thus

$$1 - r^2 \cong \frac{s^2}{s_Y^2} \tag{5-31}$$

or

$$s \cong \sqrt{1 - r^2}\, s_Y \tag{5-32}$$

This equation shows explicity how the residual s decreases as r increases.

[6] The line is exactly straight, as can be proved with analytical geometry.

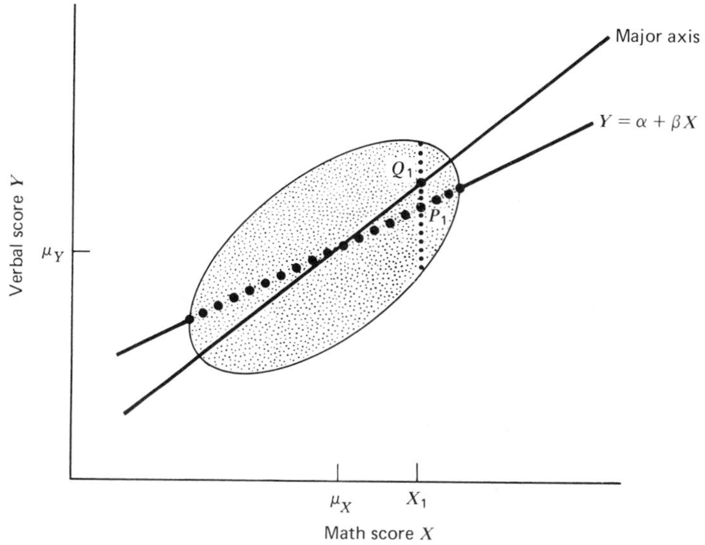

FIGURE 5-11 The regression line in a bivariate normal distribution.

This is the line that is estimated by the *sample* regression:

$$\hat{Y} = \hat{\alpha} + \hat{\beta}X \tag{5-34}$$
like (2-24)

which can then be used to predict Y [as we already did in (2-66) and (2-68)].

Referring to Figure 5-11, it is important to fully understand why we would *not* predict the point Q_1 on the major axis of the ellipse, even though Q_1 represents equivalent performance on the two tests. Since the math score X_1 is far above average, an equivalent verbal score Q_1 seems too optimistic a prediction. Recall that there is a large random element involved in performance. There are a lot of students who will do well in one exam, but not so well in the other; in other words, the correlation is less than 1 for this population. Therefore, instead of predicting at Q_1, we are more moderate and predict at P_1—a compromise between equivalent performance at Q_1 and average performance at μ_Y.

Hence we have the origin of the word regression. Whatever a student's score in math, there will be a tendency for the verbal score to regress toward the population average. It is evident from Figure 5-11 that this is equally true for a student with a very low math score; in this case, the predicted verbal score regresses upward toward the average.

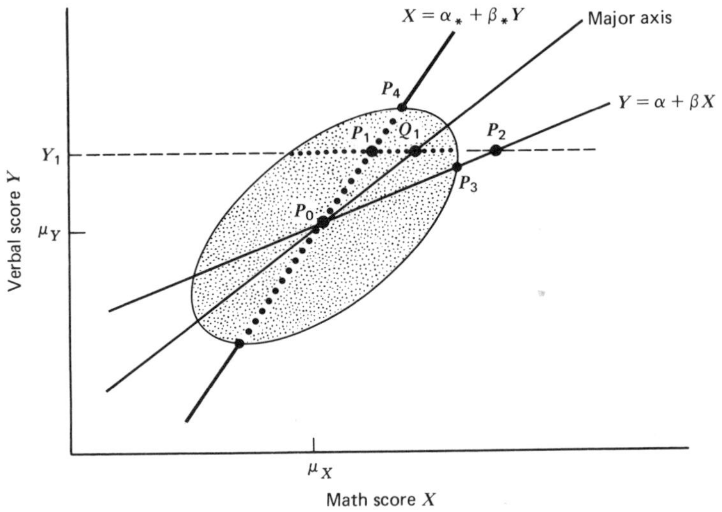

FIGURE 5-12 The two population regression lines.

(e) The Regression Line of X on Y

The bivariate distribution of Figure 5-11 is repeated in Figure 5-12. The regression line of Y on X can be obtained geometrically as the line joining the center of the ellipse P_0 to the point of vertical tangency P_3. That is, P_3 is the point on the ellipse where the tangent is completely vertical.

Now let us ask a different question: If we know a student's *verbal* score Y_1, what is the likeliest estimate of the *math* score X? Can we still use the regression line $P_0 P_3$? If we do, we obtain the estimate P_2, which is absurdly large. Instead, of course, we should use the midpoint of the possible values P_1, which also is a compromise between equivalent performance Q_1 and average performance μ_X.

Similarly, for any other given verbal score Y, we could find the central X value that is the best prediction. These best predictions, marked by heavy dots, again form a straight line, called the *regression of X on Y*. Geometrically, it is the line from the center P_0 to the point of *horizontal* tangency P_4. It may be represented algebraically by the equation

$$X = \alpha_* + \beta_* Y \tag{5-35}$$

This population line again may be estimated by the *sample* regression line:

$$\hat{X} = \hat{\alpha}_* + \hat{\beta}_* Y \tag{5-36}$$

where the estimate $\hat{\beta}_*$ is obtained from the regression formula (2-19)—interchanging X and Y, of course:

$$\hat{\beta}_* = \frac{\sum yx}{\sum y^2} \quad (5\text{-}37) \text{ like } (2\text{-}19)$$

Example 5-2

From the sample of math and verbal scores in Table 5-1,

(a) Calculate the regression of Y on X, and the regression of X on Y. Graph these two lines.

(b) For a student with a math score $X = 90$, what is the best prediction of the verbal score Y?

(c) For a student with a verbal score $Y = 10$, what is the best prediction of the math score X?

Solution:

(a) The appropriate calculations $\sum xy$, $\sum x^2$, etc., have already been carried out in Table 5-1. So we can simply substitute into the appropriate formula:

For the regression line of Y on X,

$$\hat{\beta} = \frac{\sum xy}{\sum x^2} = \frac{654}{1304} = .50 \quad (2\text{-}19) \text{ repeated}$$

$$\hat{\alpha} = \bar{Y} = 50 \quad (2\text{-}13) \text{ repeated}$$

Thus $$\hat{Y} = 50 + .50x \quad (5\text{-}38)$$

For the regression line of X on Y,

$$\hat{\beta}_* = \frac{\sum xy}{\sum y^2} = \frac{654}{836} = .78 \quad \text{like } (2\text{-}19)$$

$$\hat{\alpha}_* = \bar{X} = 60 \quad \text{like } (2\text{-}13)$$

Thus $$\hat{X} = 60 + .78y \quad (5\text{-}39)$$

These two estimated regressions are graphed in the diagram below.

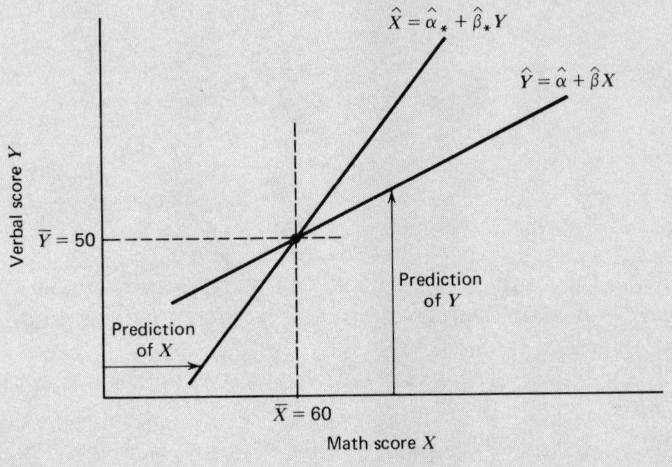

(b) We substitute $x = X - \bar{X} = 90 - 60 = 30$ into (5-38):

$$\hat{Y} = 50 + .50(30) = 65 \tag{5-40}$$

(c) We substitute $y = Y - \bar{Y} = 10 - 50 = -40$ into (5-30):

$$60 + .78(-40) = 29 \tag{5-41}$$

Remarks

Note in both (b) and (c) that the predicted grade regresses toward the average.

(f) Correlation Or Regression?

Both the standard regression and correlation models require that Y be a random variable. But the two models differ in the assumptions made about X. The regression model makes few assumptions about X, but the more restrictive correlation model of this chapter requires that X be a random variable, having with Y a bivariate normal distribution. We therefore conclude that the standard regression model has wider application. It may be used for example to describe the fertilizer-yield problem in Chapter 2 where X was fixed at prespecified levels, or the bivariate normal population of X and Y in this chapter; however, the standard correlation model describes only the latter. (It is true that r^2 can be *calculated* even when X is prespecified, as an indication of how effectively regression explains Y in (5-29); but r cannot be used for inferences about ρ in Figure 5-9.)

In addition, regression answers more interesting questions. Like correlation, it indicates if two variables move together; but it also estimates how. Moreover, the key question in correlation analysis (whether or not any relationship exists between the two variables) is answered by testing the null hypothesis $\rho = 0$; but it can alternatively be answered directly from regression analysis by testing the equivalent null hypothesis $\beta = 0$. If this is the only correlation question, then there is no need to introduce correlation analysis at all.

In conclusion, since regression answers a broader and more interesting set of questions (including some correlation questions as well), it is usually the preferred technique. Correlation is used primarily as an aid to understanding regression and as an auxiliary tool.

(g) Spurious Correlation

Even though correlation or regression may have established that two variables move together, no claim can be made that this necessarily indicates cause and effect. For example, the correlation of teachers' salaries and the consumption of liquor over a period of years turned out to be .9. This does not prove that teachers drink; nor does it prove that liquor sales increase teachers' salaries. Instead, both variables moved together, because both are influenced by a third variable—long-run growth in national income and population. If only third factors of this kind could be kept constant—or their effects fully discounted—then correlation would become more meaningful. This is the objective of multiple regression, or equivalently *partial correlation*, in the next section.

Correlations such as the above are often called spurious or nonsense correlations. It would be more accurate to say that the correlation is real enough, but any naive inference of cause and effect is nonsense. Also, as we have already suggested, the same issue occurs in regression analysis. For example, a regression applied to teachers' salaries and liquor sales would also yield a statistically significant $\hat{\beta}$ coefficient, but any inference of cause and effect from this would still be nonsense.

Although correlation and regression cannot be used as *proof* of cause and effect, these techniques are very useful in two ways. First, they can estimate a relation that theory already tells us exists (e.g., supply of wheat depends on rainfall). Second, they are often helpful in *suggesting* causal relations that were not previously suspected. For example, when cigarette smoking was found to be highly correlated with lung cancer, possible causal links between the two were investigated.

PROBLEMS

5-3 Suppose that a shoe manufacturer takes a random sample of her products in order to examine the relationship between wearing performance and cost. (Assume that the population is approximately bivariate normal.)

X = *Cost of Production*	Y = *Months of Wear*
10	8
15	10
10	6
20	12
20	9

(a) Calculate and graph the regression line of Y on X.
(b) Find the prob-value for H_0. Assume that the only difference in cost is in materials—with a very costly and durable compound being used in the more expensive shoes.
(c) Find the prob-value for H_0 under a different assumption: The more expensive shoes are made out of exactly the same materials as the cheaper shoes; the only difference is that the expensive shoes have been designed at very high cost by an internationally famous Italian designer. [Continue to use this alternative hypothesis for the remaining parts (d) to (f).]
(d) Write out the ANOVA table for the regression of Y on X. What proportion of the variation in Y is explained by this regression? What proportion is left unexplained? What is the prob-value for the null hypothesis $\beta = 0$?
(e) Calculate r. Test the null hypothesis $\rho = 0$ at the 5% level.
(f) Do you get consistent answers in (c) to (e) for the question, "Are X and Y linearly related?"
(g) What is the least squares estimate of:
  (i) Y, if $X = 12$?
  (ii) Y, if $X = 20$?
  (iii) X, if $Y = 10$?

5-4 Suppose that a bivariate normal distribution of scores is perfectly symmetric in X and Y, with $\rho = .50$ and with level curves (isoprobability ellipses) as follows:

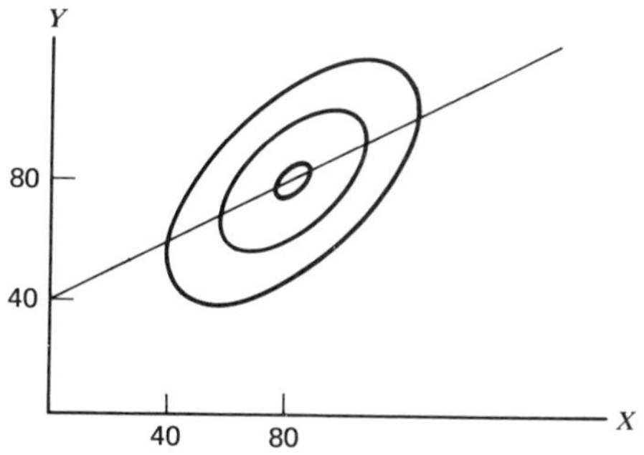

Answer true or false; if false, correct it.

(a) The regression of Y on X is

$$Y = 80 + .5(X - 80)$$

(b) The regression of Y on X is the line shown.
(c) The variance of Y is $\frac{1}{4}$ the variance of X.
(d) The proportion of the Y variation explained by X is only $\frac{1}{4}$.
(e) Thus, the residual Y values (after fitting X) would have $\frac{3}{4}$ the variation of the original Y values.
(f) For a student with a Y score of 70, the predicted X score is 60.

5-5 Let $\hat{\beta}$ and $\hat{\beta}_*$ be the sample regression slopes of Y on X, and X on Y for any given scatter of points. Answer true or false; if false, correct it.

(a) $\hat{\beta} = r\dfrac{s_Y}{s_X}$ (b) $\hat{\beta}_* = r\dfrac{s_X}{s_Y}$ (c) $\hat{\beta}\hat{\beta}_* = r^2$ (d) $\hat{\beta}_* = \dfrac{1}{\hat{\beta}}$

5-6

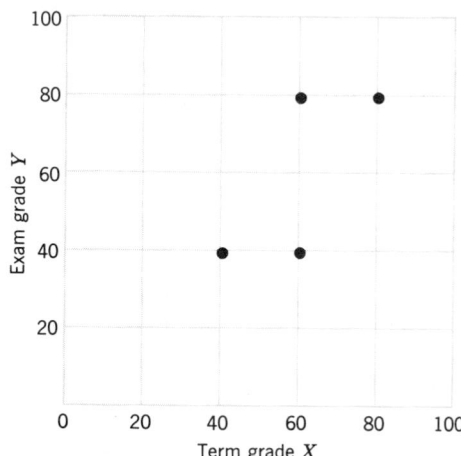

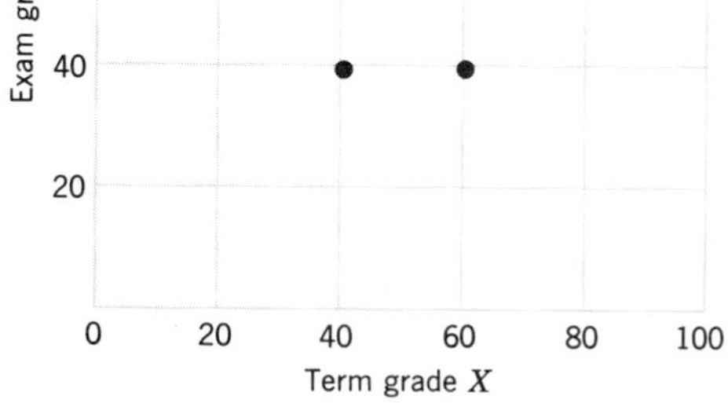

In the above graph of four students' marks, find geometrically (without doing any algebraic calculations):

(a) The regression line of Y on X.
(b) The regression line of X on Y.
(c) The correlation r [*Hint*. Problem 5-5(c)].
(d) The predicted Y for a student with $X = 70$.
(e) The predicted X for a student with $Y = 70$.

⇒ 5-7

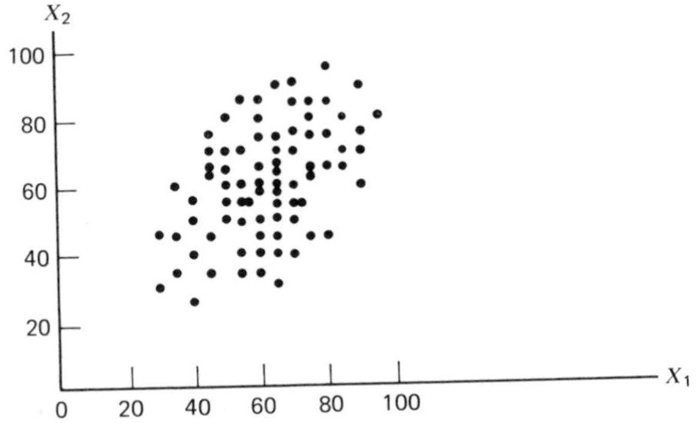

In an experimental program, 80 pilot trainees were drawn at random, and each given 2 trial landings. Their scores X_1 and X_2 were recorded in the above graph, and the following summary statistics were calculated:

$$\bar{X}_1 = 62, \qquad \bar{X}_2 = 61$$

$$\sum (X_1 - \bar{X}_1)^2 = 24{,}000, \qquad \sum (X_2 - \bar{X}_2)^2 = 26{,}000,$$

$$\sum (X_1 - \bar{X}_1)(X_2 - \bar{X}_2) = 14{,}000$$

(a) By comparison with Figure 5-2, guess the approximate correlation of X_1 and X_2. Then calculate it.
(b) Draw in the line of equivalent performance. (In this case, it is the line $X_2 = X_1$.) For comparison, calculate and then graph the regression line of X_2 on X_1.
(c) What would you predict would be a pilot's second score X_2, if his first score was $X_1 = 90$? and $X_1 = 40$?
(d) On the figure below we graph the distribution of X_1 and of X_2. The arrow indicates that the pilot who scored $X_1 = 95$ later scored $X_2 = 80$. Draw in similar arrows for all four pilots who scored $X_1 = 90$. What is the mean of their four X_2 scores? How does it compare to the answer in (c)?
(e) Repeat (d), for all the pilots who scored $X_1 = 40$.

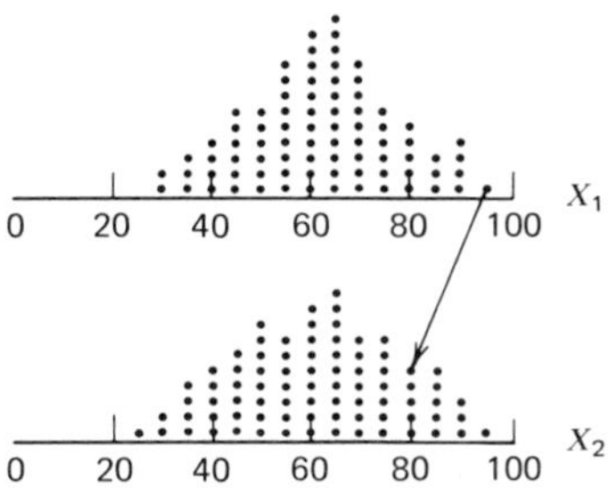

(f) Answer true or false; if false correct it:

(i) The pilots who scored very well or very badly on the first test X_1 were closer to the average on the second test X_2. Therefore, the variance of X_2 is less than the variance of X_1.

(ii) If the variances of X_1 and X_2 are approximately equal, then the regression coefficient is about equal to the correlation coefficient.

⇒5-8 Repeat Problem 5-7, parts (b) to (f), interchanging X_1 and X_2 everywhere.

⇒ 5-9 (a) When the flight instructors in Problem 5-7 graded the pilots, they praised them if they did well, or criticized them if they did poorly. They noticed that the pilots who had been praised did worse the next time, while the pilots who had been criticized did better; so they concluded that criticism works better than praise. Comment.

(b) The instructors therefore decided, for a fresh sample of 80 pilots, to criticize *every* pilot no matter how well or poorly the pilot did on the first test. They were gratified to find that this uniform criticism made the second test scores improve slightly, by 0.8 points on average. Comment.

5-10 For the data in Problem 5-7, calculate 95% confidence intervals for

(a) the correlation coefficient ρ.
(b) the regression coefficient of X_2 on $X_1(\beta)$.
(c) the regression coefficient of X_1 on $X_2(\beta_*)$.
(d) the mean of X_2, for $X_1 = 90$.
(e) an individual X_2, for $X_1 = 90$.

5-11 (a) Referring to the math and verbal scores of Table 5-1, suppose that only the students with a math score exceeding 65 were admitted to college. For this subsample of 3 students, calculate the correlation of X and Y.

(b) For the other subsample of the 5 remaining students, calculate the correlation of X and Y.

(c) Are these two correlations in the subsamples greater or less than the correlation in the whole sample? Do you think that this will be generally true?

5-12 In each part of Figure 5-2, suppose that the sample is split by the vertical line into two subsamples. Referring to Problem 5-11, but without going through the calculations again, guess how the correlations in the subsamples are related to the correlation in the whole sample.

5-13 Is the following a true summary of the preceding problem? If not, correct it:

(a) In cases (a) and (c), we find that the correlation has a smaller magnitude in each subsample than it has in the whole sample. To explain this, solve (5-31) for r^2:

$$r^2 \cong 1 - \frac{s^2}{s_Y^2}$$

where s^2 = the variance of the residuals from the fitted regression line,
and s_Y^2 = the variance of the original Y values.

For a subsample taken from one-half of the scattergram, s^2 will tend to remain the same, while s_Y^2 will tend to be much less. Thus r^2 tends to be smaller—that is, r tends to be smaller in magnitude—in the subsample.

This idea is very similar to that shown in Figure 2-12: in panel (a), where the X values are less spread out, there is less leverage to estimate the true linear relation, and hence a smaller r^2.

(b) Cases (b) and (d) in Figure 5-2 are freak cases of perfect correlation, which is maintained in the subsamples. Case (e) also is peculiar, having zero correlation in the whole sample. In each half-sample, the correlation might be slightly nonzero, due to sampling fluctuation. But this fluke will disappear in a very large sample or population.

(c) Finally, case (f) is interesting as the only case where, in splitting the data, the correlations in the two subsamples are essentially larger in magnitude than the correlation in the whole sample. This is because of the great curve (nonlinearity) in the data.

5-3 PARTIAL AND MULTIPLE CORRELATION

(a) Partial Correlation

The correlation coefficient ρ was an alternative to the regression coefficient β, for measuring the simple relation between two variables X and Y. Similarly, we now define an alternative to the multiple regression coefficient to measure the relation between X and Y *for* Z *constant*:[7] The *partial correlation coefficient* $\rho_{XY/Z}$ is defined as

$$\boxed{\rho_{XY/Z} = \text{the correlation of } X \text{ and } Y \text{, for a given (constant) } Z.} \tag{5-42}$$

In calculating the *sample* partial correlation $r_{XY/Z}$, a problem arises. Since Z is a random variable, it is usually not possible to fix a single value Z_0 and sample the corresponding conditional distribution of X and Y. Thus, unless the sample is extremely large, it is unlikely that more than a single Y, X, Z_0 combination involving Z_0 will be observed.[8] The solution is to compute $r_{YX/Z}$ as the correlation of Y and X after the influence of Z has been removed from each. By the "influence" of Z on Y, we mean the fitted regression of Y on Z:

$$\hat{Y} = \hat{\alpha} + \hat{\beta}Z \tag{5-43}$$

By "removing the influence," we mean subtracting this fitted $\hat{Y}$ from the observed Y value, obtaining the residual:

$$\hat{u} = Y - \hat{Y} = Y - (\hat{\alpha} + \hat{\beta}Z) \tag{5-44}$$

which is recognized to be that part of Y not explained by Z. Similarly we obtain $\hat{v}$, the residual deviation of X from its fitted value on Z:

$$\hat{v} = X - \hat{X} = X - (\hat{\alpha}_1 + \hat{\beta}_1 Z) \tag{5-45}$$

Then the partial correlation coefficient[9] is the simple correlation of $\hat{u}$ and $\hat{v}$:

$$\boxed{r_{XY/Z} = r_{\hat{u}\hat{v}}} \tag{5-46}$$

---

[7] In Section 5-3, for simplicity we will usually introduce only one extra regressor; but the analysis is easily generalized for the case of several extra regressors.

[8] The same problem occurred in multiple regression, as we pointed out in footnote 18 on page 95.

[9] Of course, the *population* partial correlation may also be defined like (5-46). Such a definition coincides with the original definition (5-42), if the population of all possible (X, Y, Z) values is multivariate normal.

Since it measures the same thing as multiple regression (the relation of X to Y, for Z constant), the partial correlation coefficient is related to the t ratio in multiple regression. Specifically, it can be shown that[10]:

$$r_{XY/Z} = \frac{t}{\sqrt{t^2 + (n - k - 1)}} \tag{5-47}$$

(b) Multiple Correlation, R

Whereas the partial correlations measure how Y is related to each of the regressors one by one, the multiple correlation R measures how Y is related to all the regressors at once. R is defined by first calculating the fitted values $\hat{Y}$ using all the regressors:

$$\hat{Y} = \hat{\alpha} + \hat{\beta}X + \hat{\gamma}Z$$

Then the multiple correlation R is defined as the ordinary (simple) correlation between the fitted $\hat{Y}$ and the observed Y:

$$\boxed{R \equiv r_{\hat{Y}Y}} \tag{5-50}$$

This has all the nice algebraic properties of any simple correlation. In particular, we note (5-29), which takes the form:

$$\boxed{R^2 = \frac{\sum (\hat{Y}_i - \bar{Y})^2}{\sum (Y_i - \bar{Y})^2} = \frac{\text{variation of } Y \text{ explained by all regressors}}{\text{total variation of } Y}} \tag{5-51}$$

Thus R^2 is seen to provide an overall index of how well Y can be explained by all the regressors, that is, how well a multiple regression fits the

---

[10] The partial correlation can also be calculated in terms of simple correlations:

$$r_{YX/Z} = \frac{r_{YX} - r_{YZ}r_{XZ}}{\sqrt{1 - r_{XZ}^2}\sqrt{1 - r_{YZ}^2}} \tag{5-48}$$

This formula shows explicitly that there need be no close correspondence between the partial and simple correlation coefficient; however, in the special case that both X and Y are completely uncorrelated with Z (i.e., $r_{XZ} = r_{YZ} = 0$), then (5-48) reduces to:

$$r_{YX/Z} = r_{YX} \tag{5-49}$$

that is, the partial and simple correlation coefficients are the same.

It also is instructive to note what happens at the other extreme when X becomes perfectly correlated with Z. In this case, $r_{YX/Z}$ cannot be calculated, since $r_{XZ} = 1$ and the denominator of (5-48) becomes zero as a consequence. This is recognized as the problem of perfect multicollinearity in Chapter 3, where the corresponding multiple regression estimate $\hat{\beta}$ could not be calculated.

data. Moreover, as we add additional regressors to our model, we can see how helpful they are in explaining the variation in Y, by noting how much they increase R^2.

Since the inclusion of even an irrelevant regressor will increase R^2 somewhat, it is sometimes desirable to correct for this by reducing R^2 appropriately: If there are k regressors, we define the *corrected* R^2 as[11]

$$\bar{R}^2 \equiv \left(R^2 - \frac{k}{n-1}\right)\left(\frac{n-1}{n-k-1}\right) \tag{5-52}$$

One of the many advantages of $\bar{R}^2$ is that when it is used in place of R^2, it makes (5-32) *exactly* true:

$$\boxed{s^2 = (1 - \bar{R}^2)\, s_Y^2} \tag{5-54}$$

If we add one more regressor, since s_Y^2 does not change in (5-54),

$$\boxed{s^2 \text{ decreases iff } \bar{R}^2 \text{ increases}} \tag{5-55}$$

(c) Stepwise Regression

When there are a large number of regressors, a computer is sometimes programmed to introduce them one at a time, in a so-called *stepwise regression*. The order in which the regressors are introduced may be determined in several ways, two of the commonest being:

1. The statistician may specify *a priori* the order in which he wants the regressors to be introduced. For example, if there are, among many other regressors, 3 dummy variables to take care of 4 different occupa-

---

[11] Here is the rationale for the definition (5-52): If the k regressors were entirely random (i.e., made up from random number tables), they would still produce *some* explained variation in Y—enough, in fact, to make R^2 in (5-51) on average equal to $k/(n-1)$. Our first step in correcting R^2 is therefore to subtract this "random" explanation:

$$R^2 - \frac{k}{n-1} \tag{5-53}$$

This corrected R^2 is therefore equal to zero on average, when the regressors are entirely random. But if the regressors are *not* random and actually do influence Y, then this correction overdoes it. To see why, suppose Y is *perfectly* correlated with the regressors, that is, $R^2 = 1$. Then (5-53) gives $1 - k/(n-1)$, which reduces to $(n-k-1)/(n-1)$. Instead, we would like to keep the corrected $R^2 = 1$; this requires multiplying (5-53) by the compensating factor $(n-1)/(n-k-1)$. When both these corrections are made, the result is (5-52).

tions, then it would make sense to introduce these 3 dummy variables together in succession, without interruption from other regressors.

2. If there are no prior guidelines, the statistician may want to let the data determine the order, introducing the most important regressors first. This is customarily achieved by the computer choosing the sequence that will make R^2 climb as quickly as possible.[12] Suppose, for example, that 2 regressors have already been introduced. In deciding which of the remaining regressors should be added in the next step, the computer tries each of them in turn, and selects the one that increases R^2 the most.

Whichever method is used, the computer customarily prints the regression equation after each step (after each new regressor is introduced). Then at the end, the computer prints a summary consisting of the list of regressors in the order they were introduced and the corresponding value of R^2 at each step.

Example 5-3

A recent study related lung capacity Y to several variables, including

TABLE 5-3 Summary of stepwise regression, for lung capacity Y related to 8 regressors. Based on a sample of $n = 1072$ workers.

New Regressor Introduced	*R^2 for All the Regressors Included So Far*	*ΔR^2 = Increase in R^2 Due to the New Regressor*
Physical Variables		
X_1 = age	.363	.363
X_2 = height	.467	.104
Smoking Variables		
X_3 = present smoking	.483	.016
X_4 = past smoking	.484	.001
X_5 = smoking pipes, cigars	.485	.001
Dummy Occupation Variables[a]		
X_6 = chemical work	.491	.006
X_7 = fire fighting	.496	.005
X_8 = farming	.519	.023

[a] These dummy variables compare chemical workers, fire fighters, and farmers with a reference group of physicians. For example, $X_6 = 1$ for chemical workers, 0 otherwise.

[12] A mechanical rule such as this can be a dangerous form of "data mining," especially vulnerable to misinterpretation when there are multicollinearity problems—as the discussion following Example 5-3 illustrates.

three hazardous occupations.[13] Table 5-3 was computed by stepwise regression using method 1, where the statistician specified the order *a priori*. Which steps increase R^2 the most? The least?

Solution

From the last column of Table 5-3, we see that R^2 is increased the most by the physical variables X_1 (age) and X_2 (height).[14] R^2 is increased the least by the two minor smoking variables X_4 (past smoking) and X_5 (smoking pipes, cigars). The remaining variables seem to be of moderate importance.

Although stepwise regression is a useful device to help sort out the relative importance of the regressors, there are several potential abuses to beware of:

1. Suppose a regressor is dropped simply because it increases R^2 too little (or because it is statistically insignificant in a formal test, as described below). This omission may bias the remaining regression coefficients.
2. In Table 5-3, consider the tiny increase in R^2 when X_4 (past smoking) is introduced. This does not necessarily mean that past smoking is unimportant. Instead, it might be explained by the fact that past smoking is highly correlated with X_3 (present smoking). When two regressors like this are highly correlated, the influence of one cannot clearly be sorted out from the influence of the other. Thus it is to be expected that the first one introduced (present smoking) will tend to capture the effect of both, thereby increasing R^2 on both accounts. When the second one is formally introduced (past smoking), it may have little additional effect[15] on R^2.

   On the other hand, if past smoking had been the regressor introduced first, it would have captured most of the influence of both. In this case the importance of past smoking would be overstated and the importance of present smoking understated. This illustrates an important point: The decision of which variables are most important in explaining Y may heavily depend on the order in which they are introduced.

---

[13] This is a continuation of Problem 4-8, with data based on the same sample (Lefcoe and Wonnacott, 1974).

[14] Of course it doesn't require a statistical study to establish that lung capacity depends upon age and height. These two regressors were included in the study primarily to avoid the bias that would have occurred if they had been omitted (i.e., the age and height regressors were introduced to allow for the tendency, e.g., for farmers to have a different age and height than the other occupational groups).

[15] This is a further illustration of the multicollinearity problem shown in Figure 3-3.

*(d) Simultaneous Hypothesis Tests

Consider the problem of testing the null hypothesis that a *whole set* of r regressors has no relation to the response Y (i.e., a set of r regression coefficients are all zero). Without loss of generality, we may place these r regressors last. Then we decompose the total variation into its relevant components:

$$\left.\begin{aligned}\text{Total variation} &= \text{variation explained by first regressors}\\ &\quad+\text{additional variation explained}\\ &\qquad\text{by last } r \text{ regressors}\\ &\quad+\text{unexplained variation}\end{aligned}\right\} \quad \begin{gathered}(5\text{-}56)\\ \text{like } (5\text{-}20)\end{gathered}$$

Then we form the variance ratio:

$$\boxed{F = \frac{\text{additional variance explained by last } r \text{ regressors}}{\text{unexplained variance}}} \qquad (5\text{-}57)$$

To be specific, here are the six steps involved in evaluating (5-57):

1. Calculate the increase in R^2 from adding the r regressors; call it ΔR^2.
2. Calculate the average increase in R^2 per regressor:
$$\Delta R^2/r \qquad (5\text{-}58)$$
3. Calculate the proportion of variation left unexplained after the addition of the r regressors; this is $(1 - R^2)$.
4. Divide by $n - k - 1$, the degrees of freedom in the unexplained variation; that is, calculate
$$(1 - R^2)/(n - k - 1) \qquad (5\text{-}59)$$
where $n =$ number of observations, and $k =$ total number of regressors considered (i.e., both the group of r regressors being tested and any earlier regressors already in the model.[16])
5. See how large (5-58) is relative to (5-59), by forming their ratio:
$$F = \frac{\Delta R^2/r}{(1 - R^2)/(n - k - 1)} \qquad \begin{gathered}(5\text{-}60)\\ \text{like } (5\text{-}57)\end{gathered}$$

[16] Since there is also a constant term, $k + 1$ is the number of parameters (regression coefficients) in the model; then $n - k - 1$ is the excess of observations over parameters, that is, degrees of freedom. Equation (5-59) represents, therefore, a kind of "average unexplained error per excess observation."

6. Assuming the null hyothesis is true, this F ratio can be proved to have the F distribution tabulated in end-of-book Appendix Table VII (with r degrees of freedom in the numerator, and $n-k-1$ in the denominator). Thus we can roughly calculate the prob-value in the right-hand tail, and use this for testing the null hypothesis.

For this F test to be valid, the regressors must be brought into the equation in an order specified *a priori* by the statistician. If we let the *data* select the order, then this invalidates the F test.[17]

Finally, as a special case of (5-60), we can take $r = 1$, and so test for the addition of one more regressor. The value of F obtained will be related to the t ratio $\hat{\beta}/s_{\hat{\beta}}$ by

$$\boxed{F = t^2} \tag{5-61}$$

Example 5-4

Using Table 5-3, calculate the prob-value for the null hypothesis that lung function has no relation to occupation.

Solution

For the group of the last three (occupation) regressors in Table 5-3, the above six steps yield:

1. $$\Delta R^2 = .519 - .485 = .034$$

2. $$\Delta R^2/r = .034/3 = .0113$$

3. $$1 - R^2 = 1 - .519 = .481$$

4. $$(1 - R^2)/(n-k-1) = .481/(1072 - 8 - 1)$$
$$= .481/1063 = .00045$$

5. $$F = \frac{.0113}{.00045} = 25.0$$

[17] To see why, consider for example the case of 4 regressors ($X_1 \cdots X_4$), all of which are irrelevant (i.e., all population regression coefficients are 0). What happens if the computer, at the start of its stepwise routine, searches among all 4 regressors to find the best place to begin the regression equation? If a test level of 5% is used, there is a 5% chance that X_1 will be discernible, also a 5% chance that X_2 will be discernible, and so on. The chance that at least one of the X_i will be discernible is nearly $5\% + 5\% + \cdots = 20\%$. That is, if the computer is allowed to select the juiciest regressor, there is nearly a 20% chance it will achieve statistical discernibility (significance). Thus the type I error would have nearly 20% probability, instead of the 5% claimed.

6. Now refer to Appendix Table VII, noting that the above F ratio has $r = 3$ d.f. in the numerator and $n - k - 1 = 1063$ in the denominator. We therefore consult the last line of Table VII and find $F_{.001} = 5.42$. Since the observed F of 25.0 far exceeds this,

$$\text{prob-value} \ll .001$$

and we conclude that occupation is highly discernible (statistically significant).

(e) How Many Regressors Should Be Retained?

To determine how many regressors to keep adding to our model, we might think of stopping when the regressors become statistically indiscernible (insignificant). But indiscernible at what level? This question is so difficult to answer rationally, that it is usual to fall back on the customary level of 5%. But this approach is obviously arbitrary and unsatisfactory [and even invalid, if the stepwise routine is one that lets the *data* choose the order in which the regressors are introduced—as shown in the last footnote]. We must therefore rephrase the question.

As we noted already in Section 3-6 (in particular, in footnote 9 there), it is reasonable to trade off the bias that occurs if a relevant regressor is erroneously omitted, with the extra variance that occurs if an irrelevant regressor is erroneously included. (Of course, if we *know a priori* which regressors are relevant and which are not, we should use this prior knowledge to settle the issue at once—presumably, by considering only relevant regressors in the first place. What we are concerned with here is the muddy situation that occurs all too frequently, where we are not at all sure *a priori* which regressors are really relevant, and we want the data to give us guidance.)

To keep bias and variance both low, an appropriate criterion is to minimize the MSE (mean squared error) of the response predicted by the regression equation. When this criterion is used, it can be shown that the resultant rule is approximately:

> If the *data* determines the order that the regressors are being included, add regressors until
>
> $$\frac{(1 - R^2)}{(n - k - 1)^2} \text{ is a minimum}^{18} \qquad (5\text{-}62)$$

---

[18] According to (5-30), $(1 - R^2)$ is proportional to the residual variation $\sum (Y_i - \hat{Y}_i)^2$. We may therefore rewrite (5-62) as:

(cont'd)

To explain (5-62) intuitively, when we add a regressor, we increase k, thereby decreasing the denominator. At the same time, we increase R^2, and so decrease the numerator; only if this increase in R^2 is sufficient will the ratio itself fall, and justify adding the regressor.

Example 5-5

Suppose we are using a computer program that introduces regressors in the order selected by the data, to make R^2 climb as quickly as possible. Suppose also that a sample of $n = 34$ observations yields the following stepwise regression. According to the criterion (5-62), at what point should we stop adding regressors?

k	*New Regressor Introduced*	R^2 (*explained*)	$(1 - R^2)$ (*residual*)	$(n - k - 1)$	*Criterion* $\frac{(1 - R^2)}{(n - k - 1)^2}$
1	X_1	.301	.699	32	.000642
2	X_2	.390	.610	31	.000596
3	X_3	.475	.525	30	.000546
4	X_4	.556	.444	29	.000527
5	X_5	.603	.397	28	.000472
6	X_6	.649	.351	27	.000481
7	X_7	.688	.312	26	.000461
8	X_8	.702	.298	25	.000477
9	X_9	.716	.284	24	.000493
10	X_{10}	.724	.276	23	.000522

Solution

The criterion (5-62) is calculated in the last column. It is a minimum of .000461 when $k = 7$. Thus the regression should include only 7 regressors.

$$\text{Add regressors until } \frac{\sum (Y_i - \hat{Y}_i)^2}{(n - k - 1)^2} \text{ is a minimum} \qquad (5\text{-}63)$$

It is interesting to compare (5-63) with the following more naive rule: Minimize the residual variance from the estimated regression, that is:

$$\text{Minimize } s^2 = \frac{\sum (Y_i - \hat{Y}_i)^2}{(n - k - 1)}$$

However, this criterion ignores the fact that when the *data* determines the order of including the regressors, we can go on finding discernible regressors too long. We need a criterion that stops sooner—such as (5-63), which has the *second* power of $(n - k - 1)$ appearing in the denominator.

PROBLEMS

5-14 (a) Referring to Table 5-1, using Y in column (2) and $\hat{Y}$ in column (8), calculate the multiple correlation coefficient R according to (5-50).

(b) In this example, does R agree with the simple correlation $r = .63$ [as given in (5-7)]?

*(c) Prove that R is *always* the same as r, when there is just one regressor.

Thus we may think of r as a special case of R.

5-15 For the data of Problem 3-1 relating saving S to income X and assets W, find:

(a) The multiple correlation of S on X and W.
(b) The simple correlation of S on X.
(c) What is the proportion of variation in S that is:

(i) Explained by X alone.
(ii) Explained by X and W.
(iii) Explained by the addition of W (after X).
(iv) Left unexplained (after the addition of W and X).

5-16 Use the results in Problem 5-15 to calculate the prob-value for the null hypothesis that S has no relation to W, after X has been included in the model.

5-17 Referring to Table 5-3, calculate the prob-value for the following null hypotheses about the population:[19]

(a) The smoking variables, as a group, have no relation to lung function.
(b) The 6 smoking and occupational variables as a group have no relation to lung function.
(c) Present smoking X_3 has no relation to lung function (here $r = 1$, a special but interesting case).
(d) Farming X_8 has no relation to lung function (again, $r = 1$).

5-18 In Problem 4-8, in the regression of Y (AIRCAP) on the same eight regressors as in Table 5-3, the last regressor X_8 has a coefficient of -380, with a standard error of 53.

---

[19] In each case, the model under consideration includes, as usual, just those regressors that we have listed in the table so far.

(a) Calculate the t ratio.
(b) How is this t ratio related to the F ratio in Problem 5-17 (d)?

*5-19 Fill in the blanks and the brackets with the correct choice: Suppose we recomputed Table 5-3, introducing X_3 (present smoking) last. Then:

(a) The total R^2 after all 8 regressors were included would be [the same as, different from] the value $R^2 = .519$ in Table 5-3.
(b) Because present smoking X_3 is [uncorrelated, correlated] with past smoking X_4, the increase ΔR^2 due to the inclusion of X_3 last would be [the same as, smaller, larger] than the previous value $\Delta R^2 = .016$ in Table 5-3.
(c) Suppose, continuing (b), we calculated the F ratio for the inclusion of X_3 last. It would be related to the t ratio for X_3 in Problem 4-8 ($t = -9.0/2.2 = -4.1$) by the equation

$$F = \underline{\qquad\qquad}$$

(d) Using (5-60), we could therefore work backward from F and deduce that ΔR^2 would be ________.

5-20 A 2-factor analysis of variance such as in (4-20) was carried out, to see how a response Y depended on drug type and sex. Four drugs were measured with three dummies D_A, D_B, D_C (the fourth drug being left as the reference category). The second factor (male/female) was measured with a dummy M. There were 3 patients for each combination of sex and drugs, making 24 patients in all. Stepwise regression was carried out in two different orders:

(a) Drug variables introduced first

New Regressor Introduced		*R^2 so far*
D_A	Drugs	.21
D_B		.30
D_C		.46
M	Sex	.63
MD_A	Interaction	.64
MD_B		.68
MD_C		.70

(b) Sex variable introduced first

New Regressor Introduced		*R^2 so far*
M	Sex	.17
D_A	Drugs	.38
D_B		.47
D_C		.63
MD_A	Interaction	.64
MD_B		.68
MD_C		.70

Using the stepwise routine that introduced drugs first,

(a) Calculate the prob-value for the following null hypotheses:

(i) Drugs make no difference to the average response (averaged over both sexes, in the whole population).
(ii) Sex makes no difference to the average response (averaged over all four drugs, in the whole population).
(iii) There is no interaction between the drug and sex factors, that is, drugs and sex are additive.

(b) Using the stepwise routine that introduced sex first, recalculate the prob-values in (a).

5-21 (a) In Problem 5-20, is ΔR^2 for drugs the same in both (a) and (b)? Is ΔR^2 for sex[20] the same?

(b) The test (5-60) is customarily replaced by a better test, where the average residual $(1 - R^2)/(n - k - 1)$ in the denominator is calculated for the *final residual* after *all* regressors have been added (rather than just the regressors so far). Using this improved test, recalculate Problem 5-20.

5-22 (a) In Problem 5-20 again, consider the hypothesis that sex and drugs are additive; is it acceptable at the 5% level? The 10% level? The 25% level?

(b) Assuming the hypothesis of additivity,[21] recalculate the prob-values in Problem 5-21, for the null hypotheses that drugs and sex make no difference. (*Hint*: Just erase the last 3 lines in the Table given in Problem 5-20.)

---

[20] This result is no fluke; it will be generally true in an experiment designed with the same number of observations. in each cell (in this case, 3 persons for each sex-drug combination). This is called an orthogonal design, which means a complete absence of any multicollinearity problems.

[21] This is called *pooling* the interaction with the residual, and it is often done whenever the interaction F value is satistically indiscernible at some safe level.

REVIEW PROBLEMS

5-23 Ten baseball players sampled at random had their batting averages recorded for two successive seasons, as follows:

Player	X_{77}	X_{78}
Able	300	300
Black	250	270
Costello	250	250
Donner	290	260
Efrom	260	280
Fari	270	270
Guest	230	240
Henry	280	310
Inman	260	230
Jason	310	290

(a) Graph the 10 points on the X_{77}–X_{78} plane. (Let each axis run from 200 to 320).

(b) By comparison with Figure 5-2, estimate r. Then calculate r.

(c) Calculate the regression line of Y on X. Graph it.

(d) For the 3 best players in '77, calculate their mean batting average in '77, and again in '78. Graph these 2 means as a point in the plane in (a). How far off the regression line is it?

(e) Repeat (d) for the 3 worst players in '77.

(f) Guessing from the graph in (a), about how large is the variance of X_{78} compared to X_{77}? Verify your guess by calculation.

5-24 For Problem 5-23, calculate a 95% confidence interval for ρ and for β. Do they give the same answer to the question, "Is there a statistically significant (discernible) linear relation?"

5-25 In a random sample, students' aptitude score X and achievement score Y had means $\bar{X} = 60$, $\bar{Y} = 68$, variances $s_X^2 = 100$, $s_Y^2 = 150$, and a correlation $r = .40$. Calculate each of the following, if possible; if not possible, state what further information would be necessary.

(a) The estimated slope in the regression of Y on X.

(b) The prob-value for H_0 (no linear relation between X and Y).

(c) The predicted achievement score Y of a student with an aptitude score $X = 80$.

(d) The predicted aptitude score X of a student with an achievement score $Y = 90$.

5-26 Suppose that all the firms in a certain industry recorded their profits P (after taxes) in 1975 and again in 1976, as follows:

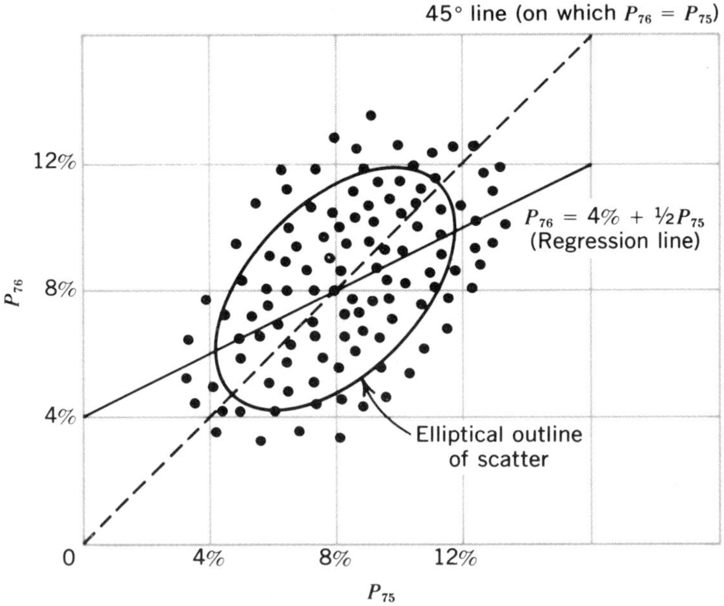

The least squares regression line also is shown in the graph. From it we would predict, for example, that a firm making a profit of 12% in 1975 would make a profit of 10% in 1976; and that a firm making a profit of 4% in 1975 would make a profit of 6% in 1976. That is, the outstandingly prosperous firms in 1975, as well as the outstandingly poor firms in 1975, tended to become less outstanding in 1976.

Select the most appropriate statement (and criticize the others).

(a) This shows that the firms tended to become more homogeneous (more stable) in their profits in 1976—fewer risks were run.

(b) This indicates, but does not prove, that some factor (perhaps a too progressive taxation policy, or a more conservative outlook by business executives, etc.) caused profits to be much less extreme in 1976 than in 1975.

(c) This shows, among other things, how difficult it is to stay near the top, from year to year (from 1975 to 1976, specifically).

(d) To predict the 1976 profit for a firm making a 1975 profit of 10%, we ought to use the 45° line and hence predict $P_{76} = P_{75} = 10\%$.

5-27 Suppose that a sociologist analyzed two demographic variables X and Y, and found the correlation r and the coefficient $\hat{\beta}$ for the regression of Y on X. A second sociologist used the same data, but with rescaled variables. Instead of using X and Y, she used:

$$X' = 1{,}000X$$

$$Y' = 100{,}000Y$$

Suppose that all her subsequent calculations also are denoted by primes (r', $\hat{\beta}'$, etc.). Are the following quantities independent of scale? (Answer yes, no, or can't say):

(a) Correlation (i.e., is $r' = r$?).
(b) Regression coefficient (i.e., is $\hat{\beta}' = \hat{\beta}$?).
(c) t ratio [i.e., is $t' = t$ in (2-60)?].
(d) Prob-value for H_0.

5-28 (a) Show that (3-11) may be rewritten as

$$s_{\hat{\beta}} = \frac{s}{\sqrt{\sum x_i^2}\sqrt{1 - r_{XZ}^2}}$$

Note that since the denominator now has the form of (5-32), it may be interpreted as the residual variation in X after the effect of Z has been removed. This is eminently reasonable, because multiple regression measures the relation of Y to X, without contamination from Z. And so this formula is comparable to (2-47).

(b) This formula is a very useful form, from which we may draw several conclusions. Answer true or false; if false, correct it:

(i) If X and Z are uncorrelated, this formula for $s_{\hat{\beta}}$ is remarkably similar to the formula (2-47) in simple regression. The only difference is that in this formula, s^2 is the residual variance left unexplained after *two* regressors have been fitted, instead of just one.
(ii) The more X and Z are positively correlated, the larger $s_{\hat{\beta}}$ will be. For example, if $r = .99$, then $s_{\hat{\beta}}$ will be about 100 times as large as if $r = 0$.
(iii) This illustrates the problem of multicollinearity: If X and Z are highly correlated, the coefficient of X will have a much larger standard error.

6

TIME SERIES

There are two major categories of statistical information: cross section and time series. To illustrate, econometricians estimating how U.S. consumer expenditure is related to national income (the consumption function) sometimes use a detailed breakdown of the consumption of individuals at various income levels at one point in time (cross section); other times they examine how total consumption is related to national income over a number of time periods (time series); and sometimes they use a combination of the two. In this chapter we will use and extend some familiar techniques (especially regression) and develop some new methods to analyze time series. Although our examples use quarterly or annual data, of course the techniques are also applicable to monthly data, weekly data, and so on.

Time series complications have provided a major challenge to statisticians. Accordingly, this will be a long chapter; but fortunately it splits conveniently into a few major parts: A Changing Variance in the Error; B Simple Time Series Decomposition and Projection; C Serially Correlated Error and Lagged Variables; and D Box Jenkins Methods.

A CHANGING VARIANCE IN THE ERROR

6-1 HETEROSCEDASTICITY

In this section, we introduce heteroscedasticity as a time series problem, since the regressor X is often related to time (or X could even be time itself). But the heteroscedasticity problem occurs in cross section studies as well.

Consider the scatter shown in Figure 6-1, where the relation between Y and X seems to be linear, but there is nevertheless a problem: The vertical spread of Y observations (i.e., the variance of the error) increases as the regressor X increases.

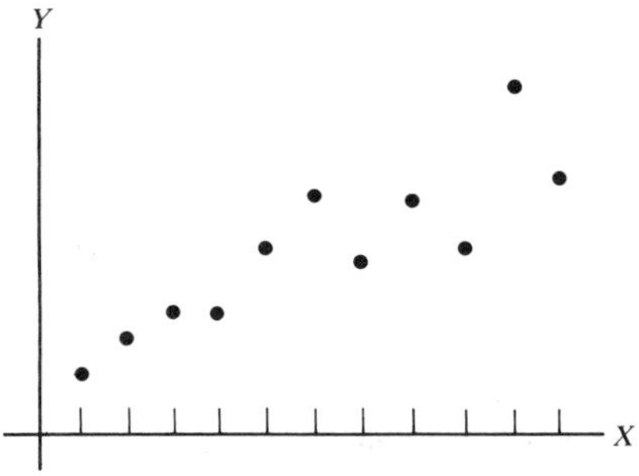

FIGURE 6-1 Linear regression scatter when σ_i is proportional to X_i

To state the problem formally, in previous chapters all disturbance terms e_i have been assumed to have the same variance; that is, we assumed

$$\text{homoscedasticity:} \quad \sigma_i^2 \text{ is constant} \tag{6-1}$$

When this assumption is unjustified, and the variance of the disturbance is not constant, we have

$$\text{heteroscedasticity:} \quad \sigma_i^2 \text{ is not constant} \tag{6-2}$$

For now, we continue to assume the errors e_i are independent (and hence uncorrelated). Furthermore, let us suppose that the Y_i have been generated by the simple linear regression model:

$$Y_i = \alpha + \beta X_i + e_i \tag{6-3}$$

We assume this satisfies all the standard assumptions cited in Chapter 2, except that the errors are heteroscedastic—in Figure 6-1, for example, σ_i^2 increases with X_i. In such circumstances, the appropriate technique is no longer the *ordinary least squares* (OLS) of Chapter 2, but instead *weighted least squares* (WLS).

(a) Weighted Least Squares (WLS)

The underlying philosophy of this technique is simple enough. A greater error occurs in the observations on the right in Figure 6-1; thus, these observations give a less precise indication of where the true regression line lies. It is therefore reasonable to pay less attention to these than to the more precise observations on the left. WLS provides a means of fitting a line by deflating the influence of the less precise observations.

Specifically, instead of minimizing the familiar

$$\sum (Y_i - \hat{\alpha} - \hat{\beta} X_i)^2 \tag{6-4}$$

we instead minimize[1]

$$\sum \frac{1}{\sigma_i^2}(Y_i - \hat{\alpha} - \hat{\beta}X_i)^2 \tag{6-5}$$

That is, each squared deviation is weighted by a factor $1/\sigma_i^2$ before summing. Thus, when the disturbance or error tends to be large (i.e., when σ_i^2 is large, as on the right-hand side of Figure 6-1), the weight $1/\sigma_i^2$ is relatively small; consequently these unreliable observations are discounted in fitting the line.

Formulas for the WLS estimators [corresponding to OLS estimators (2-13) and (2-16)] are derived by applying the calculus of minimization to (6-5). Since these formulas are awkward to develop (especially if σ_i^2 are unknown), we turn to a common special case that is easily solved.

(b) Special Case

Suppose we are estimating (6-3), and the standard deviation of the disturbance σ_i increases proportionately with X_i, that is,

$$\sigma_i = kX_i \tag{6-7}$$

or

$$\frac{\sigma_i}{X_i} = k \tag{6-8}$$

This is the kind of heteroscedasticity illustrated in Figure 6-1. Then substituting (6-7) into (6-5) leads us by WLS to minimize

$$\sum \frac{1}{k^2X_i^2}(Y_i - \hat{\alpha} - \hat{\beta}X_i)^2 \tag{6-9}$$

Rather than grinding out partial derivatives, we will develop an easier equivalent solution.

---

*[1] This criterion is justified by maximum likelihood, assuming a normal error. For any hypothetical α and β, the likelihood function for our observations $Y_1 \cdots Y_n$ is

$$L = \frac{1}{(2\pi)^{n/2}\prod^{n} \sigma_i} e^{-(1/2)\Sigma (Y_i - \alpha - \beta X_i)^2/\sigma_i^2} \tag{6-6}$$

This likelihood is maximized when the negative exponent is minimized, that is, when we select α and β to minimize

$$\sum \frac{(Y_i - \alpha - \beta X_i)^2}{\sigma_i^2}$$

Thus (6-5) yields MLE.

(c) Equivalent Solution, by Transforming the Equation

Equation (6-8) suggests that we should transform the original equation (6-3) by dividing by X_i:

$$\frac{Y_i}{X_i} = \alpha \frac{1}{X_i} + \beta + \frac{e_i}{X_i} \tag{6-10}$$

The disturbance term is now e_i/X_i, and from (6-8) its standard deviation is a constant, k; thus, it is now justified to apply OLS to this transformed equation. That is, we minimize

$$\sum \left(\frac{Y_i}{X_i} - \hat{\alpha} \frac{1}{X_i} - \hat{\beta} \right)^2 = \sum \left(\frac{Y_i - \hat{\alpha} - \hat{\beta} X_i}{X_i} \right)^2$$

$$= \sum \frac{1}{X_i^2} (Y_i - \hat{\alpha} - \hat{\beta} X_i)^2 \tag{6-11}$$

or, equivalently,[2] minimize

$$\sum \frac{1}{k^2 X_i^2} (Y_i - \hat{\alpha} - \hat{\beta} X_i)^2 \tag{6-12}$$

But this is exactly what we minimized in (6-9) in applying WLS to the original equation. Thus, in fitting (6-10) by OLS we are simply finding $\hat{\alpha}$ and $\hat{\beta}$ in a more convenient way. Specifically, we

1. Transform the data by dividing Y_i and 1 by X_i.
2. Regress Y_i/X_i on $1/X_i$ using OLS. The estimated coefficient of $1/X_i$ is $\hat{\alpha}$, and the estimated constant term is $\hat{\beta}$.

To sum up, in the population growth model in Section 4-4, we transformed the equation to make it linear; in the process we also had to transform the error term. In this example of WLS there is no problem with the linearity of the equation; we transform only to make the error term behave, so that OLS can be applied after all.

---

[2] Whatever minimizes $f(t)$ will also minimize $cf(t)$, where c is any constant.

PROBLEMS

6-1 Suppose we have the following observations of Y and X:

Y	X
4	2
7	6
4	10

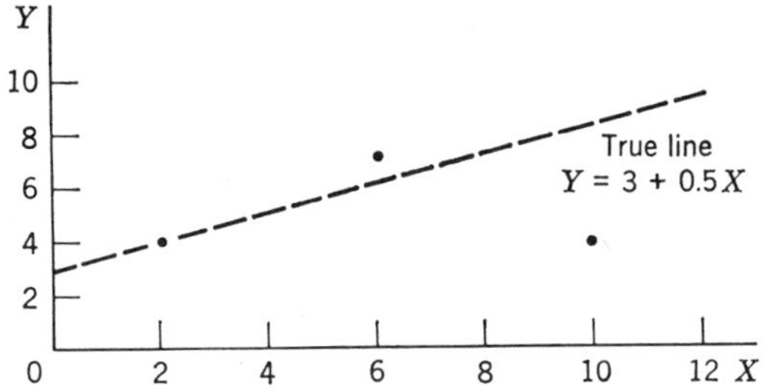

In this figure, suppose the three observations are drawn from three successive normal populations where the standard deviation increases proportionately with X.

(a) Using the transformation illustrated in the text, calculate the WLS estimate of β; then calculate the 90% confidence interval for β.

(b) Calculate the OLS estimate of β, and the subsequent 90% confidence interval.

(c) Comparing (a) and (b):

(i) Which gives an estimate $\hat{\beta}$ closer to the true β?

(ii) Which (if any) gives a valid confidence interval? That is, will 90% of such confidence intervals calculated from many different samples be true?

*6-2 (a) In Figure 4-10, is the variance of the 0–1 response Y the same at $X = 5$ and $X = 10$?

(b) When the data is partitioned so there are n observations in a cell, then the observed proportion P has a variance of $\pi(1 - \pi)/n$, where π is the true (long-run) proportion. Indicate how you might use this information to modify OLS estimation of a linear probability model, using partitioned data.[3]

[3] As we stated already, the preferred technique is MLE estimation of the logit model, without partitioning the data. However, if the range is moderate ($.2 < P < .8$), then a linear function will be a good approximation to the logit curve.

B SIMPLE TIME SERIES DECOMPOSITION AND FORECASTING

6-2 THE COMPONENTS OF A TIME SERIES

A major problem with time series is that its dependence on time may take several forms. The major ones are illustrated in Figure 6-2. Panel (*a*) shows a time series with only a trend. Panel (*b*) shows a time series with only a quarterly pattern, repeated identically every year; thus, for example, the fourth quarter of 1959 is the same as the fourth quarter of 1956 or any other year. Panel (*c*) displays a random-tracking time series of autocorrelated or serially correlated terms; that is, each value is related to the preceding

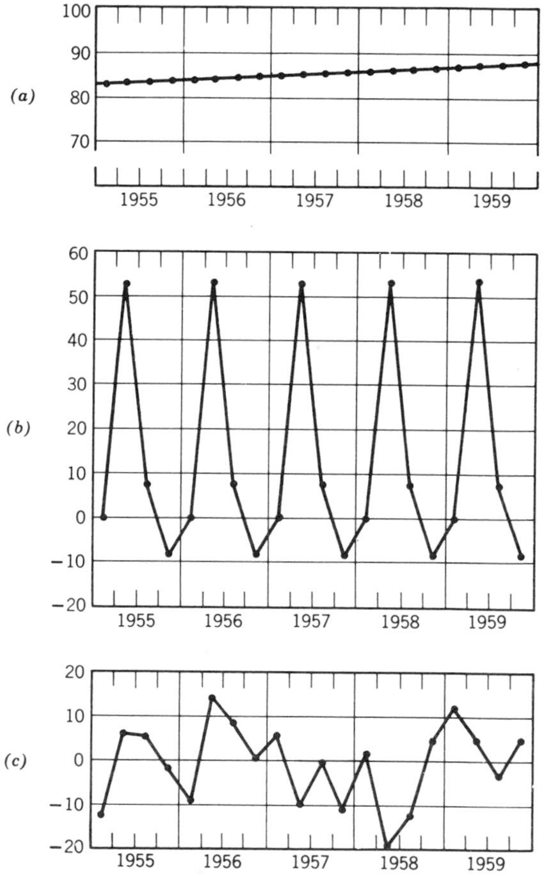

FIGURE 6-2 Three possible patterns of time dependence in a time series. (*a*) Trend. (*b*) Seasonal. (*c*) Random tracking.

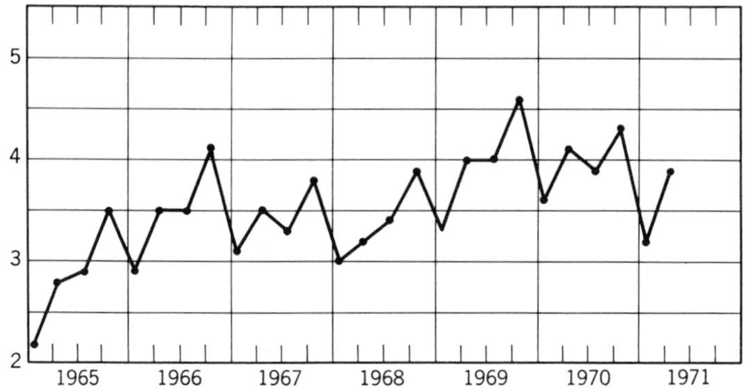

FIGURE 6-3 U.S. new plant and equipment expenditures, in durable manufacturing (in billions of dollars). *Source*. Survey of Current Business, U.S. Department of Commerce.

values, with a random disturbance added. (There are many examples of "series that follow themselves" outside of business and the social sciences; for example, a garden hose leaves a random-tracking path of water along a wall.)

If a time series followed only one of these patterns, there would be no problem. In practice, however, it is typically a mixture of all three that is very difficult to unscramble. Consider, for example, the quarterly data on plant and equipment expenditures shown in Figure 6-3. What combination of these three patterns can be perceived? There appears to be some trend, some seasonal influence, and some random element. But how much of each is a mystery.

In the rest of Part B of this chapter, we will break up a time series into these various components. We therefore consider each of the patterns in Figure 6-2 in turn.[4]

6-3 TREND

Trend is often the most important element in a time series. It may be linear, as already illustrated in Figure 6-2(a), growing at a *constant absolute amount* over time; or it may be exponential as in (4-27), growing by a *constant rate* over time. Alternatively, trend may follow a polynomial, or an even more complicated model.

[4] To complicate matters even more, there is often a fourth component in a time series: a disturbance that substantially shifts its values onto another level. For example, a war will shift bond sales, as shown in Figure 4-1. Such a displacement can often be treated with a dummy variable.

The simplest way to deal with trend is with regression, simultaneously making seasonal adjustment as discussed in the section below. We assume the trend is linear; but if it is not, it may be dealt with by using the more complicated nonlinear regression techniques set out in Chapter 4.

6-4 SEASONAL

There may be a seasonal fluctuation in time series as in Figure 6-2*b* for several reasons. A religious holiday, in particular Christmas, results in completely different economic and purchasing patterns. Or the seasons may affect economic activity; in the summer, agricultural production is high, while the sale of ski equipment is low.

(a) Extraction of Trend and Seasonal Components, Using Dummy Variables

In Figure 6-4*a* and in the first two columns of Table 6-1, we show a spectacular true life example of seasonal fluctuation—jewelry sales. We note both the possibility of a very slight upward trend and an obvious seasonal pattern marked by the sharp rise in sales every fourth quarter because of Christmas. If we made the mistake of trying to estimate only trend, say by a simple linear regression of sales S on time T as shown in Figure 6-4*b*, the result would be a substantial bias.[5] To avoid this, both trend *and* seasonal should be put into the regression model, in order to estimate their separate effects.[6]

The fourth-quarter observations may be treated in exactly the same way as the peculiar wartime observations of bond sales in Section 4-1—by the use of a dummy variable. Letting Q_4 be the fourth-quarter dummy,[7] the model becomes

$$S = \alpha + \beta_1 T + \beta_4 Q_4 + e \qquad (6\text{-}13)$$

[5] The upward bias in slope is largely caused by the fact that the last observation is a high, fourth-quarter one. (As an exercise, you can confirm that seasonal influences would exert a downward bias on slope if the first observation was for the fourth quarter of 1956 and the last was for the third quarter of 1960.)

[6] Even with this much care, least squares regression may still involve problems, because of random tracking residuals. This issue is discussed in detail in Section 6-7.

[7] There are three points in the analysis at which we might conclude that explicit account should be taken of seasonal swings. We may expect a strong seasonal influence from prior theoretical reasoning. Or, such an influence may be discovered after we plot the series. Finally, it may be discovered by examining residuals after fitting a regression; for example, after the simple regression in Figure 6-4*b* is fitted, we note that the observations indicated by arrows have consistently high residuals. To explain this, we look for something they have in common. Their common property is that they all occur in the fourth quarter. Hence the fourth quarter is introduced as a dummy regressor. This technique of "squeezing the residuals till they talk" is important in every kind of regression, not just time series; used with discretion, it indicates which further regressors may be introduced in order to reduce bias and residual variance.

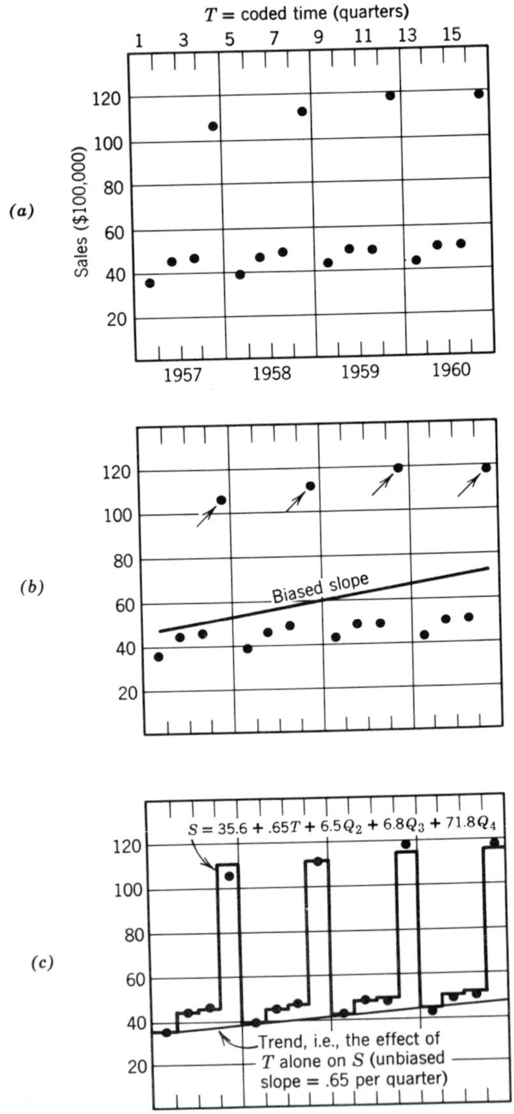

FIGURE 6-4 (*a*) Canadian jewelry sales. (*b*) Inadequate simple regression of S on T alone in which trend and seasonal influences are confounded. (*c*) Multiple regression of S on T and seasonal dummies, which explicitly distinguishes trend and seasonal effects.

TABLE 6-1 Canadian Department Store Jewelry Sales and Seasonal Dummies

Time, T (Quarter Years)		Sales, S (\$100,000's)	Q_4	Q_3	Q_2
1957	1	36	0	0	0
	2	44	0	0	1
	3	45	0	1	0
	4	106	1	0	0
1958	5	38	0	0	0
	6	46	0	0	1
	7	47	0	1	0
	8	112	1	0	0
1959	9	42	0	0	0
	10	49	0	0	1
	11	48	0	1	0
	12	118	1	0	0
1960	13	42	0	0	0
	14	50	0	0	1
	15	51	0	1	0
	16	118	1	0	0

Source. Statistics Canada, 63-002.

Even this model may not be adequate. If allowance should also be made for shifts in the other quarters, dummies Q_2 and Q_3 should be added. A dummy Q_1 is not needed for the first quarter, because Q_2, Q_3, and Q_4 measure the shift from a first-quarter base. (Whether or not to include the various regressors, Q_4, Q_3, Q_2, can be decided on statistical grounds, by testing for statistical significance. It is common to include them all in such a test, and reject or accept them as a group. But such a statistical test on data as extreme as ours would be superfluous.) Our modified model is now

$$S = \alpha + \beta_1 T + (\beta_4 Q_4 + \beta_3 Q_3 + \beta_2 Q_2) + e \tag{6-14}$$

The least squares fit is graphed in Figure 6-4*c*. Notice that our seasonal adjustment is exactly the same every year; for example, each year there is the same upward shift $\hat{\beta}_2$ in our fit between the first and second quarters. The trend is shown as the slope of the bottom line in this diagram.

This is summarized on the left-hand (unshaded) side of Figure 6-5. Panels (*a*) and (*b*) show the fitted trend and seasonal components, in sum comprising the fitted regression in panel (*d*). The difference between this and

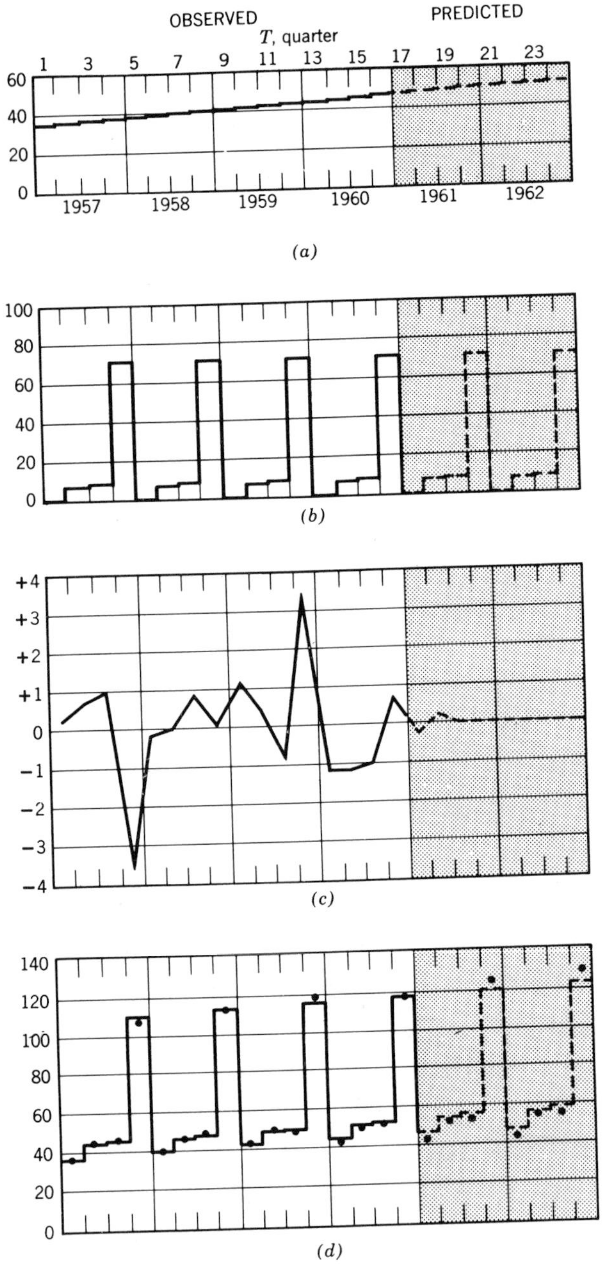

FIGURE 6-5 The three components of Canadian jewelry sales, projected with dashed lines. Compare projection of total series in (*d*) with realized sales (dots). (*a*) Trend $(35.6 + .657T)$ (*b*) Seasonal $(6.5Q_2 + 6.8Q_3 + 71.8Q_4)$. (*c*) Serially correlated residual magnified 20 times $(e_t = -.21e_{t-1})$. (*d*) Total (original) series (as in Figure 19-3*a*) projected.

the observed dots is the residual series, shown in magnified form in panel (*c*). Thus the total jewelry sales series has been broken down into its three components in panels (*a*), (*b*), and (*c*); except for the block-type artwork, this is the same sort of breakdown as shown in Figure 6-2.

(b) Seasonal Adjustment without Dummies: Moving Average

This section is a brief (and optional) digression to illustrate that dummy variables are not the only means of seasonally adjusting data. Another common method is to take a moving average (over a whole year) of the time series, as shown in Table 6-2. Notice how the wild seasonal swing is ironed out in this averaging process (because a fourth-quarter observation is included in each average value S'). The trend relation of sales to time could now be estimated by a simple regression of seasonally adjusted S' on T.

TABLE 6-2 Moving Average of Canadian Jewelry Sales

Time		*S (Unadjusted)*		*S′ (Four-Quarter Moving Average)*
	1	36		
	2	44	→ $\frac{1}{4}(36 + 44 + 45 + 106)$	$= 57.75$
1957	3	45	→ $\frac{1}{4}(44 + 45 + 106 + 38)$	$= 58.25$
	4	106	⋮	$= 58.75$
	1	38		$= 59.25$
	2	46		$= 60.75$
1958	3	47		⋮
	4	112		
	⋮	⋮		

It is interesting to compare this method with the dummy variable alternative. An apparent disadvantage is that a total of three observations are lost at the beginning and end of the time series, in order to get the moving average started and finished. However, although it is less evident, the same loss is involved in using dummy variables, since 3 d.f. are lost in estimating the shift coefficients β_2, β_3, and β_4.

An advantage of the moving average method is that it is not necessary to assume a constant seasonal shift; thus the adjustment for any quarter varies from year to year.[8] The advantage of dummy variables is that both

[8] A disadvantage of the moving average is that in smoothing out extreme observations, it may make the resulting series S' more cyclical than the original series S.

seasonal shifts *and* the trend relation of S to T are estimated simultaneously in the same regression. (A moving average adjustment is only the first stage in a two-step process; only after it is completed can trend be estimated by regressing S' on T.) Another advantage is that the dummy coefficients β_2, β_3, and β_4 give an index of the average seasonal shift, and tests of significance on them can easily be undertaken using standard procedures.

6-5 RANDOM TRACKING (AUTOCORRELATED ERROR)

We now return to Figure 6-5: With the trend and seasonal components of the time series removed by regression, this leaves the residual yet to be analyzed.

The simplest model for a random-tracking residual is to linearly relate each value e_t to its previous value e_{t-1}, with a random disturbance[9] v_t added:

$$\boxed{e_t = \rho e_{t-1} + v_t} \tag{6-15}$$

with ρ representing the strength of the tracking influence.[10]

To illustrate let us assume that $\rho = 1$, and the random disturbance v_t is standard normal; accordingly let us draw a sample of 20 independent values of v_t from Appendix Table IIb. Then, starting with an initial value of $e_0 = 5$, for example, we use (6-15) to generate $e_1, e_2, e_3 \cdots e_{20}$ as shown in Figure 6-6. The positive nature of the autocorrelation is clear; e_t tends to be high whenever the previous value e_{t-1} is high.

In practice, the parameter ρ is typically less than 1; moreover it is generally not known. However, it may be estimated by applying simple regression to (6-15). As an example, the residuals of the jewelry sales data in Figure 6-5*c* were estimated[11] to follow the autoregressive scheme:

$$\hat{e}_t = -.21\hat{e}_{t-1} \tag{6-16}$$

---

[9] In previous chapters error and disturbance may have been used synonymously; but in this chapter it is necessary to make a clear distinction between the original error e_t (which may be autocorrelated), and the further disturbance v_t (which is entirely random).

[10] It can be shown that the correlation between e_t and e_{t-1} (the so-called serial correlation) turns out to be ρ (and this is what justifies using the correlation symbol ρ).

[11] The hats in (6-16) indicate that the residuals $\hat{e}_t$ are derived from the estimated regression line. That is, $\hat{e}_t$ are the estimated residuals, whereas e_t are the unobservable true residuals.

The estimate of ρ in (6-16) was calculated to be $-.21$ as follows: $\hat{e}_t$ is given in column (1)

(cont'd)

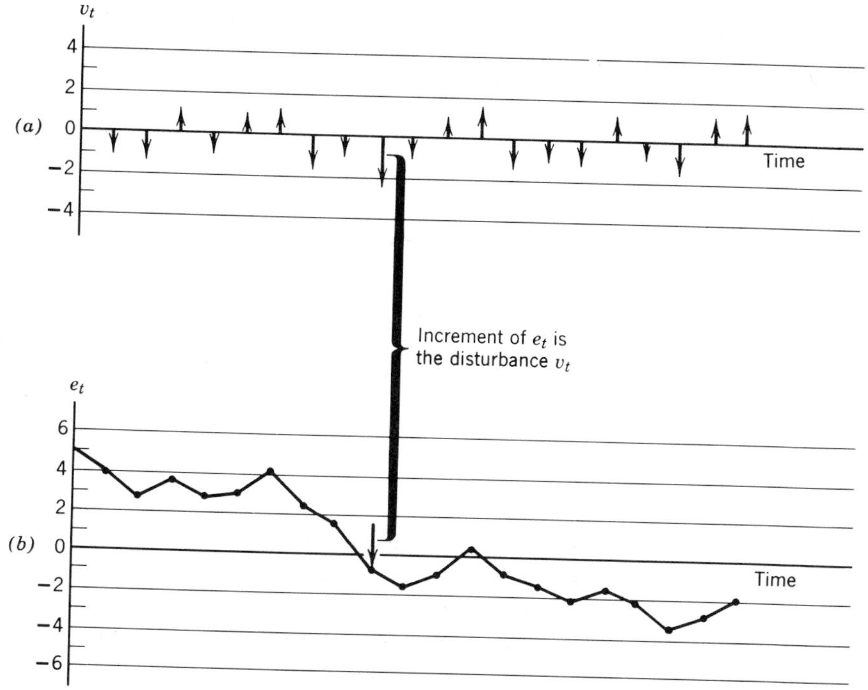

FIGURE 6-6 The construction of a serially correlated error term. (*a*) Independent disturbance v_t (*b*) Generated error: $e_t = e_{t-1} + v_t$

below; then column (2) follows directly from it; finally we regress the series in (1) on the series in (2).

	Observed		*Calculation of* $\hat{\rho}$	
Quarter *T*	(1) $\hat{e}_t$	(2) $\hat{e}_{t-1}$	(3) $\hat{e}_t \cdot \hat{e}_{t-1}$	(4) $\hat{e}^2_{t-1}$
1	+ .2			
2	+ .7	+ .2	.14	.04
3	+1.0	+ .7	.70	.49
4	−3.6	+1.0	−3.60	1.00
5	− .1	−3.6	.	.
6	.	− .1	.	.
.	.	.	.	.
.	.	.		

From (2-16)

$$\hat{\rho} = \frac{\sum \hat{e}_t \cdot \hat{e}_{t-1}}{\sum \hat{e}^2_{t-1}}$$

$$= -.21$$

This negative estimate[12] of ρ shows that autocorrelation can be negative, as well as positive. In this case, values tend to change sign (a positive value tends to be followed by a negative one), rather than track each other over time—as they did when positively correlated in Figure 6-6. (Inventory series often provide another example of negative serial correlation, if particularly large purchases for inventory result in overstocking, hence smaller purchases in the following period).

In its more general form, (6-15) becomes

$$\boxed{e_t = \rho_1 e_{t-1} + \rho_2 e_{t-2} + \cdots + \rho_k e_{t-k} + v_t} \tag{6-17}$$

which is sometimes called a kth order autoregression.

6-6 FORECASTING

One of the main reasons for decomposing a time series into its three components as in Figure 6-5 is to forecast its value into the gray future period in that diagram. A simple method suggested by that analysis is to forecast each of its components as in the extended dashed lines in panels (*a*), (*b*), and (*c*), and then sum them into the dashed line forecast[13] in panel (*d*).

Although the forecast values for the random-tracking residual in panel (*c*) are included in the forecast in panel (*d*), they quickly settle down to practically zero, since from (6-16) each is only $\frac{1}{5}$ the size of the previous one. This relatively small random tracking element in the total forecast makes good intuitive sense: In this time series it is the least predictable of the three components, and hence makes almost zero forecasted contribution beyond

---

[12] Later, in Section 6-7(e), it will be shown that (6-16) yields a biased estimate of ρ. However, this complication is initially ignored throughout the present part B in the interests of first developing a simple treatment of the various time series components.

[13] For example, using the equations of Figure 6-5, the 17th and 18th quarters are forecast to be:

Projection of	$T = 17$	$T = 18$
Trend $(35.6 + .65T)$	$35.6 + .65(17) = 46.7$	$35.6 + .65(18) = 47.3$
Seasonal $(6.5Q_2 + 6.8Q_3 + 71.8Q_4)$	Reference quarter = 0	Setting $Q_2 = 1$, $6.5(1) = 6.5$
Residual $(-.21\hat{e}_{t-1})$	$-.21(.5) = -.1$	$-.21(-.1) = .02$
Total	46.6	53.82

the first few quarters. In fact, it sometimes is reasonable enough to set this equal to zero immediately (i.e., forget about it), so that only the trend and seasonal are used. This is especially true if computational facilities are scarce, or if only long-run forecasts are desired.

To see how well the forecast worked out, we compare it in panel (*d*) with the actual values the time series took in 1961–1962, shown in dots. Although these values could not be used in the analysis (they were not yet known), they do provide a good test after the event of how well the forecast turned out. Initially the forecast is not too bad, but it tends to get worse the farther it goes into the future—one more example of the dangers of extrapolation first mentioned in Section 2-10. Thus the shorter the forecast the better; this suggests that if funds and computing facilities are available, the whole analysis should be recalculated and forecasts updated whenever new observations on the variables become available (i.e., delay your forecasts for 1962 until the 1961 figures become available; then each of the time series components in the first 3 panels of Figure 6-5 can be reestimated).

In our forecasts, we have limited ourselves to point estimates only, rather than interval estimates. The reason is not only the great complexity of a three-component time series. As well, the autocorrelation in the tracking residual invalidates prediction intervals like (2-68) that are based on the assumption of independent observations. This issue is now discussed more fully.

PROBLEMS

6-3 For the following car sales data:

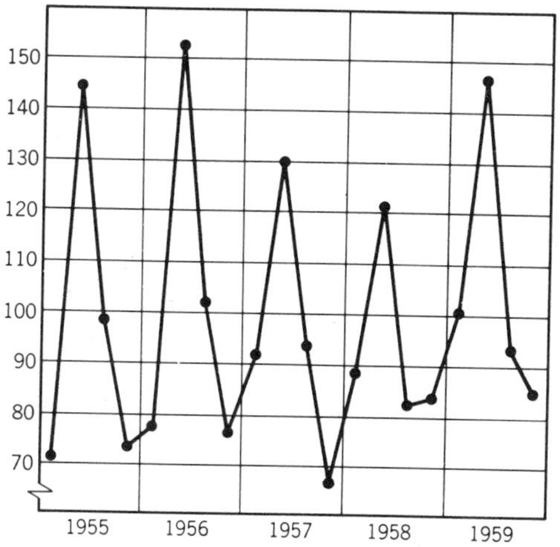

Canadian auto sales (quarterly, 1955–1959). *Source*. Statistics Canada.

(a) Fit a linear trend by eye.
(b) Shift the linear trend so that it passes as close as possible to the first quarter (reference quarter) points. Then roughly estimate how much higher the second quarters rise, on average, above this reference line. Repeat for the third and fourth quarters.
(c) For this car sales data, the standard least squares (computerized) estimates of trend and seasonal are shown in Figure 6-2*a* and *b*. Use them to judge the accuracy of your rough estimates in (*a*) and (*b*) above. (Incidentally, the residual in this series is shown in Figure 6-2*c*; in other words, Figure 6-2 is the complete decomposition of the time series above.)

6-4 (Seasonal Adjustment.)

	Auto Sales, Y (*from Problem 6-3*)	*Seasonal, S* (*from Figure 6-2b*)	(*a*) *Seasonal Deviations, s*	(*b*) *Seasonally Adjusted Auto Sales, Y − s*
1955	71	0		
	144	53		
	98	8		
	74	−9		
1956	77	0		
	153	53		
	102	8		
	76	−9		
1957	92	0		
	130	53		
	94	8		
	66	−9		
1958	89	0		
	122	53		
	82	8		
	84	−9		
1959	100	0		
	147	53		
	93	8		
	85	−9		

Auto sales *Y* and its seasonal component *S* are tabulated above. To fill in the missing columns:

(a) Calculate the mean of the seasonal series $\bar{S}$. Then calculate the seasonal series in deviation form, $s = S - \bar{S}$. This gives us a seasonal series that fluctuates up and down *around zero.*

(b) Subtract s from the original series of auto sales, Y. This new series estimates how auto sales would move if there were no seasonal component, and thus is called the *seasonally adjusted* series. In practice, the seasonal adjustment is *calculated* quite differently, but the *end result* (the seasonally adjusted series) is almost the same.

(c) Graph the seasonally adjusted series on the figure in Problem 6-3 for comparison.

(d) Comparing the second quarter of 1957 with the first quarter, what was the increase in:

  (i) Auto sales?
  (ii) Seasonally adjusted auto sales?

Which of these figures is more meaningful, in terms of indicating how well the auto industry fared in that quarter?

6-5 True or false? If false, correct it.

(a) A time series may be decomposed into three components:

  (i) Trend.
  (ii) Seasonal pattern.
  (iii) Random tracking residual.

(b) The fitting of trend and seasonal by eye, as in Problem 6-3, has the advantage of simplicity. However, if computer facilities are available, the least squares estimates have even more advantages, as follows:

  (i) They are easy to calculate, since multiple regression is a standard library program.
  (ii) They are more objective (and hence will not be biased, consciously or subconsciously, by the researcher).
  (iii) They can be used for tests and confidence intervals.

(c) The fitting of trend by multiple regression or by moving averages yields exactly the same result.

C SERIALLY CORRELATED ERROR AND LAGGED VARIABLES

6-7 SERIAL CORRELATION IN THE ERROR

(a) The Effect on Trend and Seasonal Estimates

In our initial analysis of a time series (Sections 6-3 and 6-4) we estimated the trend and seasonal components, leaving a residual series to be analyzed in Section 6-5 for autocorrelation. The problem is that the existence of a positively autocorrelated residual mixed up in the original series will reduce the reliability of our first-stage estimate of trend and seasonal (and indeed may reduce the reliability of our estimate of any other influence, for that matter). In this section we discuss this problem and suggest possible solutions. Before plunging into a lot of mathematics, it is important to understand the intuitive idea.

Autocorrelation means that the successive observations are dependent to some extent; thus, with positive autocorrelation, the second (or some later) observation tends to resemble, or repeat, the first observation, and hence gives little new information. Thus they give less information about trend (and other influences) than n independent observations would. Consequently, our estimates will be less reliable.

We turn now to the mathematical development. Our regression model is

$$Y_t = \alpha + \beta X_t + e_t \tag{6-18}$$

where X_t represents time T, or seasonal dummies, or any other time series deemed influential in determining Y_t; or for that matter, any combination of these. In addition, the error e_t is assumed to be autocorrelated. Just how e_t is related to its previous values is, of course, unknown, just as α and β are unknown. It's true that we have already estimated it in a very simple way in our example in (6-16); but now we wish to look into its theoretical properties in more detail.

(b) A Simple Explanation

Just as in Figure 6-6, we again suppose the error term e_t has the simple form of positive serial correlation given by $\rho = 1$ in (6-15); then

$$e_t = e_{t-1} + v_t \tag{6-19}$$

Now we must be even more explicit about the additional disturbance v_t, which is assumed to have the usual characteristics: zero mean, constant variance σ^2, and independence from the other disturbances v_{t-1}, v_{t-2}, etc. The initial value e_0 is also assumed to be random, with mean zero, and variance σ_0^2, say.

Suppose the true regression line (defined by α and β) is as shown in Figure 6-7*a*. Suppose further that the error terms $e_1, e_2, \ldots$ are those we generated from this same model in Figure 6-6: They are reproduced in Figure 6-7*b*. Any observed Y (e.g., Y_2) is the sum of its expected value $(\alpha + \beta X_t)$ as given by the true regression, plus the corresponding error term (e_2). Since this error e_t is positively correlated, once our observations are above this true regression, they will tend to stay above it (i.e., once e_t is positive, it will be more likely to take on a positive value in the following time period). Similarly, whenever e_t becomes negative, it tends to stay negative.

In Figure 6-7*a* we can immediately see the difficulties that this serial correlation causes, by observing how badly an ordinary regression through this scatter would estimate the true regression.[14] Specifically, in this sample, β would be underestimated and α overestimated. But in another sample we might have observed precisely the opposite pattern of errors, with e_t initially taking on negative values, followed by positive ones. In this case, we would overestimate β and underestimate α. Either of these two types of estimation error seems equally likely; and there are other possibilities as well. Intuitively, it seems that the problem is not bias, since we are as likely to get an overestimate as an underestimate. Rather, the problem is that estimates may be badly wide of the target: Although unbiased, the estimates have a large variance. Nor is this primarily the fault of the OLS regression procedure; any other estimating procedure (such as fitting by eye) would fit the "tilted" data about the same way. In fact, despite the large variance of its estimators, OLS may still be quite efficient; although there is another more sophisticated technique (generalized least squares, GLS) that is more efficient, the improvement it provides over OLS may be quite small.

We are now in a position to draw our first conclusions:

1. OLS point estimates $\hat{\alpha}$ and $\hat{\beta}$ are unbiased. (6-20)
2. OLS point estimates may be relatively efficient. (6-21)

[14] In the interests of clarity, this argument has been oversimplified, since it is assumed in Figure 6-7*a* that X_t is increasing over time regularly. Thus the argument holds best if X_t represents simply time T; but it still holds true even if X_t just tends to increase over time. On the other hand, if X_t alternates between low and high values, then our analysis would be complicated; in particular, our later conclusion about the efficiency of OLS would have to be modified.

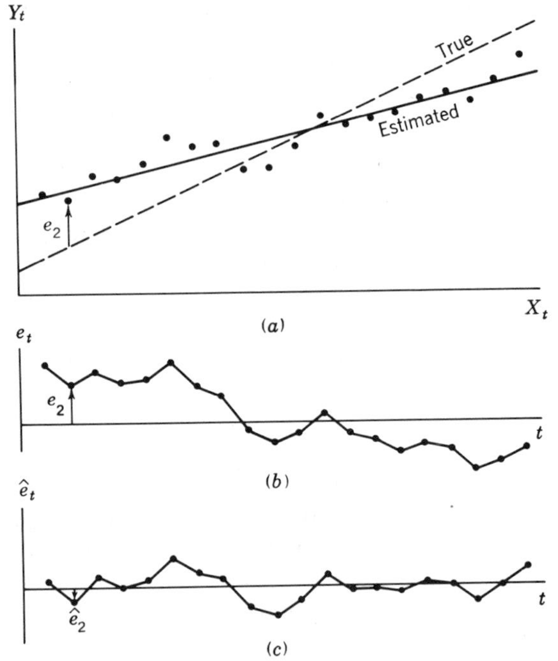

FIGURE 6-7 Regression with serially correlated error. (*a*) True and estimated regression lines. (*b*) True error terms. (*c*) Observed error terms.

However, for an *interval* estimate of β (or α), OLS would be grossly deceptive. There are two reasons for this, which will be seen in comparing the serial correlation of Figure 6-7 to the case of no serial correlation in Figure 6-8. These two figures are alike in all respects other than the serial correlation; in particular, we emphasize that they have the same variance for the error e_t.

Since Figure 6-8 satisfies the assumptions of OLS, it will provide a valid confidence interval. But this is not so for the serially correlated data of Figure 6-7; in this case the standard confidence interval

$$\beta = \hat{\beta} \pm t_{.025} \frac{s}{\sqrt{\sum x_i^2}} \tag{6-22}$$

(2-51) repeated

will err for two reasons:

1. It is likely to be centered at a more erroneous value of $\hat{\beta}$. We might hope that it would allow for this greater error by providing a wider confidence interval.

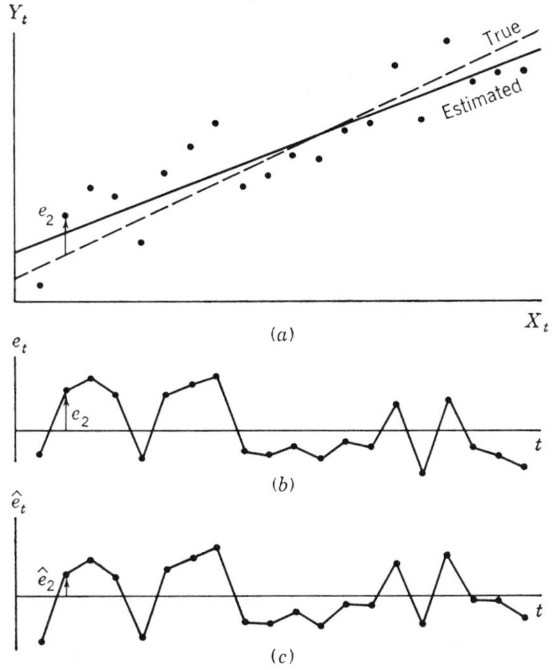

FIGURE 6-8 Regression with independent error (yet same variance as in Figure 6-7). (*a*) True and estimated regression lines. (*b*) True error terms. (*c*) Observed error terms.

2. Yet it has a *narrower* confidence interval, because it has a smaller value of s. To establish this, we recall that the variance s^2 is calculated from the observed residuals $\hat{e}_t$. In the case of serial correlation, the estimated regression line fits the tracking data rather well, leaving the small residuals $\hat{e}_t$ shown in Figure 6-7*c*.

To sum up, because the data is tracking, an OLS estimate of β is, in fact, less reliable. But it appears to the statistician to be *more* reliable because tracking data tends to yield smaller observed residuals.

(c) Regression of First Differences

To estimate β in the linear regression model (6-18), the remedy for this special case of serial correlation is to transform the data so that it does satisfy the assumptions of OLS. Since (6-18) holds true for any time t, it holds for time $t - 1$:

$$Y_{t-1} = \alpha + \beta X_{t-1} + e_{t-1} \tag{6-23}$$

We can now examine the change over time of our variables, by subtracting (6-23) from (6-18):

$$(Y_t - Y_{t-1}) = \beta(X_t - X_{t-1}) + (e_t - e_{t-1}) \tag{6-24}$$

Note from (6-19) that

$$e_t - e_{t-1} = v_t$$

and define

$$Y_t - Y_{t-1} \equiv \Delta Y_t$$

$$X_t - X_{t-1} \equiv \Delta X_t \tag{6-25}$$

which are called *first differences*. Then (6-24) can be written:

$$\boxed{\Delta Y_t = \beta\, \Delta X_t + v_t} \tag{6-26}$$

In this form, the error v_t has all the properties required by OLS. This suggests estimating β by an OLS regression of ΔY on ΔX.

(d) Generalized Differences

The model for the error term (6-19) may be made more general and realistic:

$$e_t = \rho e_{t-1} + v_t \qquad \text{(6-27)}\ \text{(6-15) repeated}$$

where[15]

$$|\rho| < 1$$

---

[15] If $\rho = 1$ as in (6-19) a major problem arises because the error becomes explosive; that is, the variance of e_t increases infinitely with time. This is proved as follows. We note that

$$\begin{aligned} e_t &= v_t + e_{t-1} \\ &= v_t + (v_{t-1} + e_{t-2}) \\ &\ \vdots \\ &= v_t + v_{t-1} + v_{t-2} + \cdots + v_1 + e_0 \end{aligned}$$

Because of independence,

$$\begin{aligned} \operatorname{var} e_t &= \sigma^2 + \sigma^2 + \cdots + \sigma^2 + \sigma_0^2 \\ &= t\sigma^2 + \sigma_0^2 \to \infty \end{aligned} \tag{6-28}$$

This means that if the relation (6-18) has been in operation over many past time periods, any Y that is now observed may be completely dominated by the explosive error e_t; thus, the relation of Y to X in (6-18) cannot be ascertained. (Of course, this problem of an exploding error becomes even worse if $|\rho| > 1$).

The specification that $|\rho| < 1$ ensures a stationary error, with finite variance independent of t, as given in (6-85).

The error e_t is again the sum of two components: its previous value *attenuated* by the factor ρ, plus the further disturbance v_t.

We continue to assume the linear regression model

$$Y_t = \alpha + \beta X_t + e_t \qquad \text{(6-29)}$$

(6-18) repeated

To estimate β, we transform the data in much the same way as before. Equation (6-29) for time $t - 1$ is multiplied by ρ:

$$\rho Y_{t-1} = \rho\alpha + \rho\beta X_{t-1} + \rho e_{t-1} \qquad \text{(6-30)}$$

Subtracting (6-30) from (6-29),

$$Y_t - \rho Y_{t-1} = \alpha(1 - \rho) + \beta(X_t - \rho X_{t-1}) + (e_t - \rho e_{t-1}) \qquad \text{(6-31)}$$

We define

$$\left.\begin{aligned} Y_t - \rho Y_{t-1} &\equiv \tau Y_t \\ X_t - \rho X_{t-1} &\equiv \tau X_t \end{aligned}\right\} \qquad \text{(6-32)}$$

These transformed values are sometimes called *generalized differences*. Then (6-31) can be written:

$$\boxed{\tau Y_t = \alpha(1 - \rho) + \beta\tau X_t + v_t} \qquad \text{(6-33)}$$

In this form the error v_t has all the properties required by OLS. Thus, with this transformation we may regress τY_t on τX_t to estimate β.

However, prior to this regression an additional adjustment must be made to the data. The *first* observed values Y_1 and X_1 cannot be transformed by (6-33), since their previous values are not available; instead the appropriate transformation is

$$\left.\begin{aligned} \sqrt{1 - \rho^2}\, Y_1 &\equiv \tau Y_1 \\ \sqrt{1 - \rho^2}\, X_1 &\equiv \tau X_1 \end{aligned}\right\} \qquad \text{(6-34)}$$

This adjustment to the data, along with a final adjustment to the regression procedure,[16] make this technique equivalent to a generally valid method called Generalized Least Squares (GLS). These final adjustments are very

---

[16] The constant regressor (whose coefficient is α) must also be transformed, just like the Y_t and X_t regressors. It becomes $(1 - \rho)$ for $t = 2, 3, \ldots, n$ in (6-33); it becomes $\sqrt{1 - \rho^2}$ for $t = 1$ by analogy with (6-34).

important; without them the regression (6-33) may be no better than OLS on (6-18), and perhaps not even as good.[17]

To sum up, if ρ is known, the data is transformed by (6-32) and (6-34), with an adjusted regression of τY_t on τX_t in (6-33) providing the estimate of β. The problem with this approach, of course, is that ρ is generally not known, and must be estimated.

(e) Statistical Estimation of ρ

To estimate ρ, equation (6-27) would be ideal if the true residuals e_t could be observed. Since they cannot, we are forced to use the fitted residuals $\hat{e}_t$ that fall out of the OLS regression of Y_t on X_t (Figure 6-7*c*). Thus ρ is estimated by applying OLS to

$$\hat{e}_t = \rho \hat{e}_{t-1} + \text{error} \qquad (6\text{-}35)$$

like (6-16)

With this regression, we obtain an estimate r for ρ which is consistent. Yet r has a bias, which can be seen from Figure 6-7*c*. The estimated residuals $\hat{e}_t$ fluctuate around zero more (and hence have a smaller serial correlation) than do the true residuals e_t. Thus r underestimates ρ on the average.

There are ways to allow for this underestimation; The most popular is *the Durbin-Watson test* for $\rho = 0$, against the alternative $\rho > 0$. Obviously H_0 should be rejected when r is high. But at what critical value? Durbin and Watson obtained an equivalent test of $\rho = 0$ by using the statistic

$$D \equiv \frac{\sum_{t=2}^{n} (\hat{e}_t - \hat{e}_{t-1})^2}{\sum_{t=1}^{n} \hat{e}_t^2} \approx 2(1 - r) \qquad (6\text{-}36)$$

What is the distribution of D? If $\rho = 0$ and there is no serial correlation, r will be close to zero and D will be close to 2. Notice also from (6-36) how r and D are inversely related; thus when there is positive serial correlation, D becomes smaller.[18] (This is easily confirmed by reexamining the ratio in the middle of (6-36); the more the serial correlation, the more the $\hat{e}$ series tends

[17] The transformation (6-34) must be used with some care. It is appropriate if and only if the process (6-27) generating the error has been going on undisturbed for a long time previous to collecting the data. In practice, however, the first observation often is taken just after a war or some other catastrophe, which seriously disturbs the error. In this case, the transformation (6-34) of the first observation should be dropped.

[18] In our jewellery sales example, D was calculated to be 2.42. Since r was calculated in (6-16) to be $-.21$, the approximate relation between D and r given by (6-36) is confirmed.

to track itself, and the smaller the numerator becomes.) There are therefore two alternative ways of establishing positive serial correlation: (1) If r is observed sufficiently above zero, or (2) if D is observed sufficiently below 2. Durbin and Watson chose the latter criterion, and tabulated the critical value of D. This is reproduced in Appendix Table VIII, which is accompanied by a graphical explanation. As well as allowing for the bias of r in estimating ρ, Durbin and Watson allowed for the dependence of r upon the configuration of X_t. Thus, there are two limiting values of D tabulated (D_L and D_U), corresponding to the two most extreme configurations of X_t; for any other configuration, the critical value of D will be somewhere between D_L and D_U.

If the existence of serial correlation has been established by the Durbin-Watson test in (6-36), there still remains the problem of estimating its value ρ. One possibility is to use the estimate that falls out of the regression (6-35); but the weakness of this estimate has already been pointed out. A number of alternatives have been suggested, none of them foolproof; one of the simplest involves rearranging (6-31) into the following regression equation:[19]

$$Y_t = \alpha(1-\rho) + \rho Y_{t-1} + \beta X_t - \beta\rho X_{t-1} + e_t - \rho e_{t-1} \qquad \text{(6-37)}$$

where $e_t - \rho e_{t-1} = v_t$ has all the attractive properties of a residual. Accordingly, run a regression of Y_t on Y_{t-1}, X_t and X_{t-1}, retaining only[20] $\hat{\rho}$, the estimated coefficient of Y_{t-1}; this provides a consistent estimate of ρ. This can then be used in equations (6-32), (6-33), and (6-34) to run a generalized difference regression—or more precisely, a GLS regression—yielding estimates of α and β.

(f) Summary of Possible Procedures

When facing time series like (6-18) with an error with an unknown amount of serial correlation, one of the many ways to proceed is:

1. Apply OLS directly to (6-18), obtaining a time series of estimated residuals $\hat{e}_t$.
2. Use this series for the Durbin-Watson test (6-36). If serial correlation in the error is not established, use the OLS estimates of α and β already derived in step 1. The task of estimation is now complete; but it is also desirable to indicate the value of D in your results.

---

[19] For an example of its performance, see the tests of alternative estimators in Griliches and Rao, 1969.

[20] We call it $\hat{\rho}$ to distinguish it from the r estimated in regression (6-35); note that the two are alternative estimators of exactly the same population parameter ρ.

On the other hand, if the Durbin-Watson test establishes serial correlation, then proceed as follows:

3. Estimate ρ by running regression (6-37) and retaining $\hat{\rho}$ (the estimated coefficient of Y_{t-1}).
4. Finally use this $\hat{\rho}$ as the missing link to calculate and regress generalized differences according to (6-32) to (6-34); or, more precisely use this $\hat{\rho}$ to apply GLS. This will provide the desired estimates of α and β. If steps 3 and 4 must be undertaken, will the result be much of an improvement over a simple and direct application of OLS to (6-18)? The answer seems to be that, while it is likely to provide an improvement, it may not be a very substantial one. Even when ρ is known, the improvement that can be achieved may be fairly modest; and when ρ is unknown, the estimation of ρ introduces a source of error that tends to erode this advantage.

Estimation is now complete. If we also wish to forecast, there are three additional steps:

5. The GLS estimates of α and β calculated in step 4 can now be used to estimate GLS residuals[22] $\hat{e}_t$, and in particular, the last residual $\hat{e}_n$.
6. The error term may now be projected. To estimate the true but unknown terms in

$$e_{n+1} = \rho e_n + v_{n+1} \qquad (6\text{-}38)$$

like (6-27)

we may use

$$\hat{e}_{n+1} = \hat{\rho}\hat{e}_n \qquad (6\text{-}39)$$

Thus the projected residual $\hat{e}_{n+1}$ is calculated using the value of $\hat{\rho}$ from step 3 and the value of $\hat{e}_n$ from step 5 (and of course ignoring the random term v_{n+1}).

7. We can now calculate $\hat{Y}_{n+1}$, the projected value of Y in the next period, as

$$\hat{Y}_{n+1} = \hat{\alpha} + \hat{\beta}X_{n+1} + \hat{e}_{n+1} \qquad (6\text{-}40)$$

where X_{n+1} is the projected value[23] of X_t, $\hat{e}_{n+1}$ has been derived in step 6, and $\hat{\alpha}$ and $\hat{\beta}$ are the GLS estimates calculated in step 4.

---

[22] In exactly the same way that we calculated OLS residuals in column (7) of Table 2-2.

[23] It is even possible that X_{n+1} may have already been observed. In many institutions like the U.S. Department of Commerce that provide business, economic, or social data to the public, there are frequent cases where some data series (say X_t) become available more quickly than others (say Y_t). Thus consider the problem a firm may face in January 1981. It may be necessary for it to use an already available X_{1980} figure in order to "predict in the past" the Y_{1980} figure that it must have but is not yet available.

Finally, note that this more complicated procedure runs parallel to our simple-minded projection in Section 6-6 above; the only differences are (1) we hope to have a better projection of the residual ($\hat{e}_{n+1}$) because we are now estimating ρ from (6-37); and (2) GLS has provided better estimates of α and β.

Again, we emphasize that this is not the only procedure available. An obvious alternative would be to estimate ρ in step 3 using the r calculated from regression (6-35), and then use this instead of $\hat{\rho}$ in steps 4 to 7. Which estimator of ρ performs better?

Both are consistent, so this provides no grounds for selection. In any case, consistency merely concerns sample sizes n that approach infinity. The important question is how these estimators behave in finite samples, which we now show with Monte Carlo methods.

(g) Monte Carlo Analysis

Throughout this book we will frequently encounter estimators that are consistent. Unfortunately, with a few exceptions it has not been possible to theoretically analyze how they behave in finite samples (as, for example, we theoretically derived the unbiasedness and variance of OLS under the conditions specified in Section 2-5). The alternative is to attack this problem with our bare hands (or, more precisely, the bare hands of a computer) using the Monte Carlo approach: We simulate a sampling experiment many times, calculating the estimator each time. This builds up the distribution of the estimator, so that we can see how close it is to its target.

Specifically, suppose we wish to compare how the consistent estimators r and $\hat{\rho}$ perform in the face of autocorrelated error. Our model is

$$Y_t = \alpha + \beta X_t + e_t \qquad \text{(6-41)}$$
(6-18) repeated

and

$$e_t = \rho e_{t-1} + v_t \qquad \text{(6-42)}$$
(6-15) repeated

where v_t are independent random variables with mean zero and variance σ^2. Monte Carlo involves the following steps:

1. Specify a value for each of the population parameters α, β, ρ, and σ^2.
2. Specify a time series of n (say $n = 20$) values for the independent variable X_t; also specify the initial error e_0.
3. "Spin the Monte Carlo wheel" by generating a random value for v_1; this (along with the specified value of e_0 and ρ) provides a value for e_1 in (6-42) and hence Y_1 in (6-41).

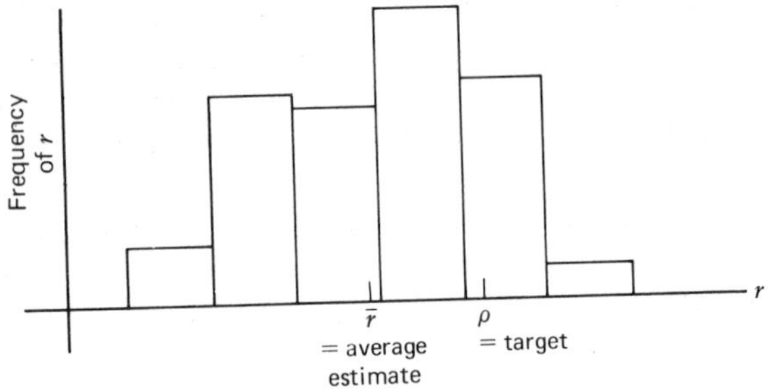

FIGURE 6-9 Monte Carlo Sampling Distribution of r.

4. Spin the Monte Carlo wheel again, generating a random value for v_2, which as before is all the additional information needed[24] to generate e_2 in (6-42) and Y_2 in (6-41). Repeat this process, generating a time series of observations $Y_1, Y_2, \ldots, Y_n$. With the data thus generated, we have finished playing the role of nature.
5. Now play the role of the statistician: Use the generated Y_t series and the specified X_t series[25] to calculate r, the estimate of ρ. [Recall that this involves an OLS fit of Y_t on X_t according to (6-41), generating a time series of estimated residuals $\hat{e}_t$; these in turn are used in an OLS regression on (6-42) to calculate r.][26]
6. Repeat steps 1 to 5, say 100 times, generating a distribution of 100 values of r (see Figure 6-9). We can thus see how close r comes to the true ρ_2 using the standard criteria for evaluating an estimator. For example, to calculate how far it is off target, on average, we use

$$\text{Observed bias} = \bar{r} - \rho \tag{6-43}$$

like (2-86)

To measure how much r fluctuates, we use

$$\text{Observed variance} = \frac{\sum_{i=1}^{100} (r_i - \bar{r})^2}{100} \tag{6-44}$$

Finally, to measure overall how far r is off its target, on average, we use

$$\text{Observed mean squared error (MSE)} = \frac{\sum_{i=1}^{100} (r_i - \rho)^2}{100} \tag{6-45}$$

like (2-104)

---

[24] Note that the required e_1 has already been generated in step 3.

[25] A preselection of X_t values is not crucial to this analysis; these could have been generated by a random process.

[26] This procedure is sometimes referred to as the two-step Cochrane-Orcutt technique.

A similar evaluation of $\hat{\rho}$ provides the remaining information necessary for comparing the two estimators—with particular importance being attached to how their MSEs compare.

$\hat{\rho}$ is tentatively recommended in the previous section because, in a Monte Carlo study involving a somewhat different model specification,[27] it outperformed r. The results from Monte Carlo studies are sometimes ambiguous,[28] and too much should not be claimed. However, to examine how the consistent estimators discussed in the balance of this book behave in small samples, Monte Carlo often provides the best available evidence.

PROBLEMS

6-6 As in Figure 6-6 and equation (6-19), construct a string of 10 serially correlated disturbances e_t. (For v_t, use the table of standard normal numbers in Appendix Table IIb. Start with $e_0 = 0$ for simplicity.) By graphing, guess whether your particular string of disturbances causes $\hat{\beta}$ to be an underestimate or overestimate of β.

*6-7 (Class exercise) Do a Monte Carlo investigation of the estimate of ρ in the model (6-41) and (6-42), as follows. Let $\alpha = 1$, $\beta = 2$, $\rho = \frac{1}{2}$, $e_0 = 2$, and $X_1 \cdots X_5 = 1, 2, \cdots 5$. Every student can start in a random place in the standard normal numbers (Appendix Table IIb) to get 5 values of v_t, thereby generating e_t and finally Y_t.

Having finished the role of nature, each student now takes on the role of statistician. First he regresses Y_t on X_t to obtain residuals $\hat{e}_t$. Then he regresses $\hat{e}_t$ on $\hat{e}_{t-1}$ to obtain r, the estimate of ρ.

Finally let the instructor collect all the estimates r, graph their frequency distribution, and calculate the observed bias (6-43) and observed MSE (6-45).

6-8 True or false? If false, correct it.
If the first observation in a residual time series is negative, then

(a) positive serial correlation means that the odds favor (i.e., probability > .50) the next observation being negative.
(b) negative serial correlation means that the odds favor the next observation being positive.
(c) no serial correlation (i.e., a purely random residual) means that the next observation is equally likely to be positive or negative.

---

[27] See Griliches and Rao, 1969.

[28] For example, the results may be sensitive to the configuration of the specified X_t series.

6-9 When $\rho = 0$, r is approximately symmetric about 0. What then is the approximate point of symmetry of D?

6-10 Suppose the serial correlation of the error is more complicated than in (6-27), with every error e_t now depending on its previous *pair* of values, that is,

$$e_t = \rho_1 e_{t-1} + \rho_2 e_{t-2} + v_t$$

where v_t has all the usual, desirable properties of a residual and ρ_1 and ρ_2 are known.

(a) How would you estimate (6-18) in this case? How is this procedure justified?
(b) Suppose ρ_1 and ρ_2 are not known. How might they be estimated?
(c) Will $\hat{e}_t$ be more or less autocorrelated than e_t?
(d) Is it true to say that the problem of a serially correlated error involves not only estimating the ρ's, but also knowing how many nonzero ρ's there are?

6-8 LAGGED X VARIABLES

Now suppose that Y_t is dependent, not only on X_t but also on previous values of X according to

$$Y_t = \beta_0 X_t + \beta_1 X_{t-1} + \beta_2 X_{t-2} + \beta_3 X_{t-3} + \cdots + e_t \tag{6-46}$$

An economic example might be dividend payments by a corporation (Y_t); these depend not only on earnings in the present period (X_t) but also on earnings in previous periods.[29]

To keep complications in dealing with this new problem of lagged variables to a minimum, we will assume in this section that the previous problem of serial correlation in the error does not exist. In other words, it is assumed that e_t has the attractive properties of a residual, being independently distributed with zero mean and constant variance σ^2. In these circumstances, the most obvious approach would be simply to apply OLS to (6-46), regressing Y_t on the most recent, presumably most important X's—say $X_t \cdots X_{t-5}$. A set of possible estimates $\hat{\beta}$ that might result is displayed, according to the lag each involves, in Figure 6-10.

The two major problems with this approach are: (1) There are many regressors that eat up a large number of degrees of freedom; and (2) these

[29] In this model we have assumed there is no intercept α. It may be confirmed that introducing such a term into (6-46) complicates the analysis slightly, but does not affect the basic argument.

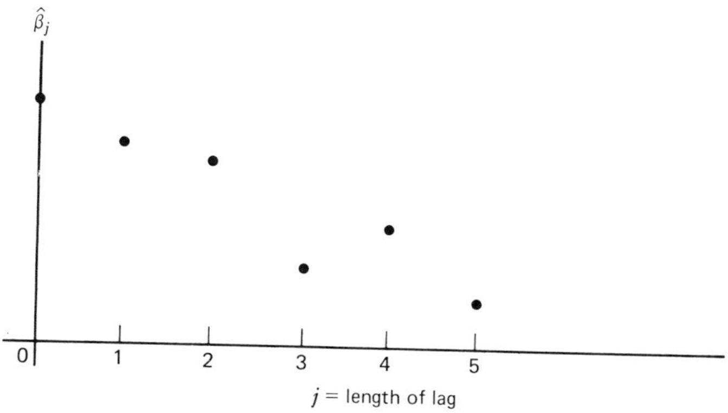

FIGURE 6-10 OLS Estimates of the Lag Model (6-46).

regressors may be closely related, making multicollinearity a serious problem. In these circumstances, it is natural to look for a simplifying assumption to make this problem more manageable.

(a) The Koyck Distributed Lag

The simplification suggested by Koyck (Koyck, 1954) was to assume the β's decrease exponentially over time:

$$\beta_j = \beta_0 \lambda^j \tag{6-47}$$

with λ being a positive fraction less than 1 (i.e., $0 < \lambda < 1$). Two examples are illustrated in Figure 6-11.

This model may provide a good representation of many economic series; to use our earlier example, it is reasonable to expect that dividends are affected more by recent earnings than earnings in the distant past. As another example, a firm is unlikely to decide on investment Y_t strictly on this year's sales level X_t, which may be temporarily out of line. Instead it is advisable to place some weight on past sales levels as well; but the further in the past, the less the weight.

While maintaining a high degree of realism, the Koyck model achieves a substantial simplification: There are only two parameters to estimate, λ and β_0, as follows:

1. Substitute (6-47) into (6-46):

$$Y_t = \beta_0 X_t + \beta_0 \lambda X_{t-1} + \beta_0 \lambda^2 X_{t-2} + \cdots + e_t \tag{6-48}$$

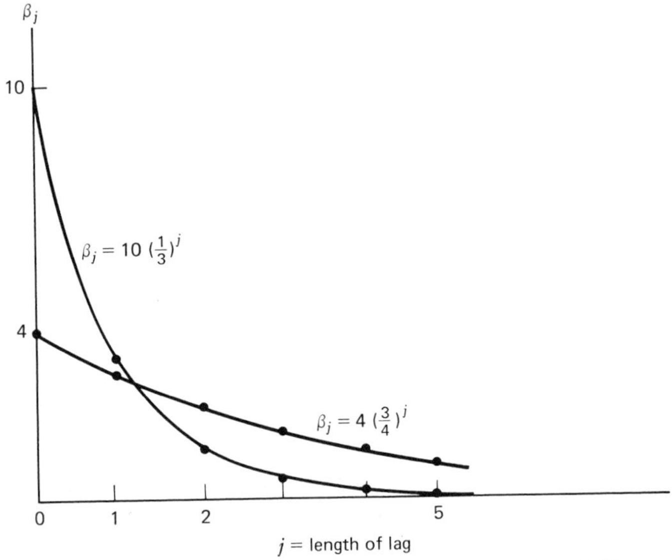

FIGURE 6-11 Two examples of Koyck lags $\beta_j = \beta_0 \lambda^j$

and for the previous t, of course,

$$Y_{t-1} = \beta_0 X_{t-1} + \beta_0 \lambda X_{t-2} + \beta_0 \lambda^2 X_{t-3} + \cdots + e_{t-1} \tag{6-49}$$

If (6-49) is multiplied by λ, and subtracted from (6-48), most of the terms drop out and we obtain

$$Y_t = \lambda Y_{t-1} + \beta_0 X_t + e_t^* \tag{6-50}$$

$$\text{where } e_t^* = e_t - \lambda e_{t-1} \tag{6-51}$$

2. Now regress Y_t on Y_{t-1} and X_t as in (6-50), to obtain the estimates of λ and β_0.
3. Finally, plug these estimates into (6-47) to generate the estimates of β_i.

Unfortunately several problems remain. The error term e_t^* in (6-51) probably is serially correlated, which makes the OLS regression in step 2 less efficient. Worse yet, the error term e_t^* is likely to be correlated with the regressor Y_{t-1} in (6-50) (since both depend on e_{t-1}^*) and this makes the OLS regression in step 2 biased (as Section 7-2 will show). While there have been a number of suggestions made for improving the estimates of β_0 and λ in step 2, they are complicated and beyond the scope of this text. Hence our discussion of the Koyck lag ends with a warning that further complications remain.

(b) Almon Distributed Lags

The Almon approach (Almon, 1965) can be viewed as falling somewhere between the two approaches already discussed: (1) a completely free OLS fit of (6-46) with no assumption imposed about the form of the lag structure, having a large number of parameters (as shown in Figure 6-10); and (2) the imposition of the Koyck assumption that the lag structure must be some exponentially decreasing function with two parameters (as shown in Figure 6-11). The intermediate Almon assumption is that the lag structure is a polynomial of some degree n, with $n + 1$ parameters. For example, the polynomial of degree 3 is

$$\beta_j = \gamma_0 + \gamma_1 j + \gamma_2 j^2 + \gamma_3 j^3 \tag{6-52}$$

with its shape depending on the four parameters $\gamma_0, \gamma_1, \gamma_2, \gamma_3$. The polynomial of degree 2 is a parabola, while the polynomial of degree 1 is a line. These polynomials provide a wide variety of shapes for the lag function β_j, as shown in Figure 6-12. To keep the model sufficiently simple, it is generally

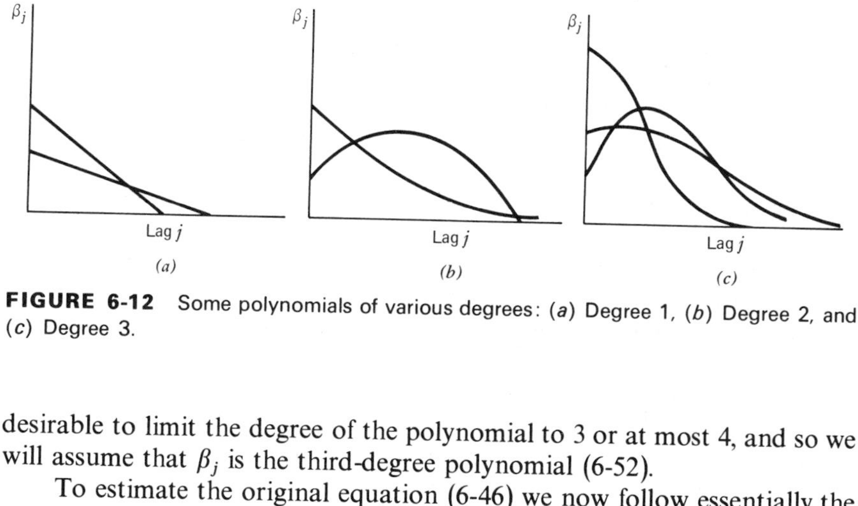

FIGURE 6-12 Some polynomials of various degrees: (*a*) Degree 1, (*b*) Degree 2, and (*c*) Degree 3.

desirable to limit the degree of the polynomial to 3 or at most 4, and so we will assume that β_j is the third-degree polynomial (6-52).

To estimate the original equation (6-46) we now follow essentially the same three steps as in the Koyck procedure:

1. Express (6-46) as a function not of the β_j, but instead of the coefficients γ_i in the lag function (6-52) [this is analogous to the Koyck case where we expressed (6-46) in terms of the coefficients β_0 and λ only]. How do we translate the β_j into the γ_i? We simply set j at each of its appropriate values in (6-52), in each case obtaining the corresponding β_j. If the

longest lag is 5, for example, so that the last coefficient is β_5, then we would have:

$$\left.\begin{aligned}
&\text{For } j=0: && \beta_0 = \gamma_0 \\
&\text{For } j=1: && \beta_1 = \gamma_0 + \gamma_1 + \gamma_2 + \gamma_3 \\
&\text{For } j=2: && \beta_2 = \gamma_0 + 2\gamma_1 + 4\gamma_2 + 8\gamma_3 \\
&\text{Similarly:}^{30} && \beta_3 = \gamma_0 + 3\gamma_1 + 9\gamma_2 + 27\gamma_3 \\
& && \beta_4 = \gamma_0 + 4\gamma_1 + 16\gamma_2 + 64\gamma_3 \\
& && \beta_5 = \gamma_0 + 5\gamma_1 + 25\gamma_2 + 125\gamma_3
\end{aligned}\right\} \tag{6-53}$$

Substitution of these β_j into (6-46) yields, after considerable rearranging,

$$\left.\begin{aligned}
Y_t = \gamma_0(X_t + X_{t-1} + X_{t-2} + X_{t-3} + X_{t-4} + X_{t-5}) \\
+ \gamma_1(X_{t-1} + 2X_{t-2} + 3X_{t-3} + 4X_{t-4} + 5X_{t-5}) \\
+ \gamma_2(X_{t-1} + 4X_{t-2} + 9X_{t-3} + 16X_{t-4} + 25X_{t-5}) \\
+ \gamma_3(X_{t-1} + 8X_{t-2} + 27X_{t-3} + 64X_{t-4} + 125X_{t-5}) + e_t
\end{aligned}\right\} \tag{6-54}$$

2. Now regress Y_t on each of the four newly constructed variables in brackets in (6-54), to estimate γ_i.
3. Finally, use (6-53) to generate the estimates of β_j. It is often helpful to graph β_j, to see whether it behaves reasonably as the lag j increases.

The two assumptions, that the length of lag in (6-46) is 5 and that the polynomial in (6-52) is of degree 3, may both be relaxed. In particular, if $\hat{\gamma}_3$ is not statistically significant in the regression (6-54), the last term in (6-52) could be dropped, leaving the lag specified as a polynomial of degree 2—after which the procedure could be rerun with appropriate modification.

Actually this is a simplified recasting of Almon's original proposal,[31] with the advantage that it is easier in most cases to understand and apply; also, like Almon's original formulation, it can be generalized to cover a great variety of special cases (two of which are included as Problems). For example, it can be used to estimate the relationship

$$Y_t = \beta_2 X_{t-2} + \beta_3 X_{t-3} + \cdots + \beta_6 X_{t-6} + e_t \tag{6-55}$$

---

[30] The first four equations in (6-53) are recognized as the appropriate set of equations to solve for $\gamma_0 \cdots \gamma_3$ (the shape of the polynomial) if $\beta_0 \cdots \beta_3$ were known.

[31] Almon used the Lagrangian interpolation form to express her polynomials, rather than the simple form (6-52).

(This might be the best model if Y_t does not depend on X_t or X_{t-1}, or if Y_t must be fitted before these values of X become available. For example, the decision to invest Y may be based on government figures X that are published only after a lag or two.) Or, a regression can be run on (6-46) using, say, X_t and X_{t-1} explicitly as regressors to estimate β_0 and β_1 if these are judged *a priori* to be the most important determinants of Y_t; simultaneously, an Almon lag can be used to approximate the remaining less important coefficients $\beta_2 \cdots \beta_5$. Alternatively, the procedure can be extended to cover several regressors, say X and Z, each being related to Y with a different length of lag j.

Finally, there is no reason for necessarily limiting this procedure to fitting a polynomial function. Equation (6-52) can be reformulated if there is prior knowledge that β is related to j in any one of many other ways. For example, it can be applied if

$$\beta_j = \psi/(j + 1) \tag{6-56}$$

with the only problem in this case being to estimate ψ. In other words, the technique as set out in steps 1, 2, and 3 above need not be restricted to polynomial estimation. Instead, it can be applied to any lag structure that is linear in the parameters to be estimated; for example, in (6-56) $\beta_j = \psi/(j + 1)$ is linear in ψ. For lag structures that are not linear, problems arise; to illustrate, any nonlinearity in the parameters $\gamma_0 \cdots \gamma_3$ introduced into (6-52) would reappear first in (6-53) and eventually in (6-54), where it would severely complicate OLS estimation of these parameters (since the parameters would appear in nonlinear form in the normal estimating equations). In some cases it may still be possible to use a transformation to break through this difficulty (as in fact we did in the Koyck case[32]); but in other cases it may not.

Of course, prior knowledge of the functional form of the lag structure is often not available; in its absence the Almon polynomial formulation (6-52) provides a very broad and flexible specification, as may be recalled from Figure 6-12.

PROBLEMS

6-11 Show how an Almon polynomial of degree 2 can be used to estimate $\beta_1, \ldots, \beta_5$ in (6-46), while simultaneously regressing Y_t on X_t directly to estimate β_0.

---

[32] Note that the Koyck lag structure (6-47) is *not* linear in the parameters to be estimated, β_0 and λ. That is why a transformation (first differencing) was necessary in the Koyck step 1 prior to the regression in step 2. But note that it was this transformation that caused the problems in the error term $(e_t - \lambda e_{t-1})$.

Graph $\hat{\beta}_0 \cdots \hat{\beta}_5$ if the Almon polynomial coefficients turned out to be $\hat{\gamma}_0 = .38$, $\hat{\gamma}_1 = -.12$, $\hat{\gamma}_2 = .01$, while the coefficient of X_t turned out to be $\hat{\beta}_0 = .45$.

6-12 Show how you would estimate $\beta_0 \cdots \beta_5$ in (6-46) if these coefficients followed the lag scheme (6-56). Graph $\hat{\beta}_0, \ldots, \hat{\beta}_5$ if $\hat{\psi}$ turned out to be 3.0.

6-9 SERIAL CORRELATION IN THE DEPENDENT VARIABLE

Consider the model[33]

$$Y_t = \alpha + \gamma Y_{t-1} + \beta X_t + e_t \tag{6-57}$$

An example might be household consumption Y_t, which might be related to other influences X_t (like income, asset holdings, etc.) and also previous consumption level Y_{t-1}—with this latter relation reflecting how past consumption habits and patterns may influence present decisions. In model (6-57) we assume that e_t is serially uncorrelated with a normal distribution:

$$e_t \sim N(0, \sigma^2) \tag{6-58}$$

These attractive properties of the error suggest that the ordinary regression model in Chapters 2 and 3 applies, and that OLS would yield unbiased consistent estimates. Unfortunately, however, this is not the case. Recall that one of the required assumptions of model (2-23) was that the variables on the left-hand side of the equation (in this case, $Y_t, Y_{t+1}, Y_{t+2}, \ldots$) should be independent. This assumption is obviously violated, since each Y depends on its previous value, according to (6-57). Therefore, it cannot automatically be concluded that OLS on (6-57) is appropriate.

But all is not lost. It is still possible to establish that applying OLS to (6-57) will be almost equivalent to MLE; hence it can be shown that, like MLE, it will be a consistent estimator. To prove this, assume that the X's are given, and the first observation Y_1 is also given.[34] Then (6-57) shows how Y_1, X_2, and e_2 determine Y_2, then Y_2, X_3, and e_3 determine Y_3, and so on.

---

[33] This model looks like the transformed Koyck model (6-50) except for one major difference: (6-57) assumes a serially uncorrelated error e_t, whereas (6-50) has a serially correlated error e_t^*—a complication that we defer to Section 6-10.

[34] This example of a peculiar first observation Y_1 is somewhat similar to the peculiar first observation referred to in footnote 17 following equation (6-34).

Thus, the complete set of observations is generated by $e_2, e_3 \cdots e_n$ (along with the given X's and the initial value of Y_1). Thus the likelihood of observing this set of sample observations is

$$p(e_2, e_3 \cdots e_n) = p(e_2)p(e_3) \cdots p(e_n)$$

From (6-58)
$$= \prod_{t=2}^{n} \left[\frac{1}{\sqrt{2\pi\sigma^2}} e^{-(1/2\sigma^2)e_t^2} \right]$$

$$= \frac{1}{(\sqrt{2\pi\sigma^2})^{n-1}} e^{-(1/2\sigma^2)\sum e_t^2}$$

From (6-57)
$$= \frac{1}{(\sqrt{2\pi\sigma^2})^{n-1}} e^{-(1/2\sigma^2)\sum (Y_t - \alpha - \gamma Y_{t-1} - \beta X_t)^2} \qquad (6\text{-}59)$$

This is maximized where the negative exponent is of smallest magnitude; that is, select α and β to

$$\text{Minimize } \sum_{t=2}^{n} (Y_t - \hat{\alpha} - \hat{\gamma} Y_{t-1} - \hat{\beta} X_t)^2 \qquad (6\text{-}60)$$

This is recognized as the least squares estimate.[35]

Thus, if Y_1 were fixed, OLS would be the MLE. The question therefore becomes, "How important is this restriction that Y_1 is fixed?" For a small sample over a short time period, this may make a difference; but this tends to disappear as sample size increases. Thus, OLS approaches MLE, and is a consistent estimator.

6-10 SERIAL CORRELATION IN BOTH THE ERROR AND THE DEPENDENT VARIABLE

The model in Section 6-7 involved serial correlation in the error only; in Section 6-9 the model involved serial correlation in the dependent variable only. In this section we consider a model in which both problems appear.

(a) The Problem and a Possible Cure

Consider our previous model with a lagged dependent variable:

$$Y_t = \alpha + \gamma Y_{t-1} + \beta X_t + e_t \qquad (6\text{-}61)$$

like (6-57)

---

[35] Note that this argument runs parallel to (2-77) to (2-80). The only difference is that here we consider the likelihood of a set of e's, whereas in (2-77) we considered the likelihood of a set of Y's. In this single equation model, these are just two alternative ways of looking at the same thing.

Suppose the error follows the simple autoregression.

$$e_t = \rho e_{t-1} + v_t \tag{6-62}$$

where v_t now has all the attractive properties of a residual (serially independent, and constant variance). Note that equation (6-50) yielded by the Koyck transformation is the same form as (6-61). Moreover, in both cases the error term is serially correlated. Of course, the Koyck transformation is not the only way we might arrive at model (6-61); alternatively, economic theory might have directly and immediately led us to specify the model in this form.

With both the error and Y following an autoregressive process, OLS on (6-61) would no longer even be consistent.[36] There are, however, several alternative ways of deriving consistent estimates: To illustrate, one is described here.

First note that (6-61) also holds at time $t - 1$, that is,

$$Y_{t-1} = \alpha + \gamma Y_{t-2} + \beta X_{t-1} + e_{t-1} \tag{6-63}$$

Multiplying this equation by ρ and subtracting the result from (6-61) yields:[37]

$$Y_t = (\gamma + \rho)Y_{t-1} + (1 - \rho)\alpha - \gamma\rho Y_{t-2} + \beta X_t - \rho\beta X_{t-1} + v_t \tag{6-64}$$

where the residual $v_t = e_t - \rho e_{t-1}$ now has the desired attractive properties. Accordingly, OLS on this equation will yield consistent estimates. Apply OLS, retaining only the last two estimated coefficients, which together provide a consistent[38] estimate of ρ. The resulting estimate $\hat{\rho}$ can now be used to apply the generalized differencing procedure[39] (6-33), which cures the condition of autocorrelated error.

---

[36] For details, see for example Goldberger, 1964 pp. 276–277.

[37] Note the similarity of this transformation to the original Koyck transformation of (6-46).

[38] The $\hat{\beta}$ coefficient estimated for X_t provides a consistent estimate of β, while the $\widehat{\rho\beta}$ coefficient estimated for X_{t-1} provides a consistent estimate of $\rho\beta$. Thus a consistent estimate of ρ is derived by taking the ratio

$$\hat{\rho} = \widehat{\rho\beta}/\hat{\beta}$$

[39] Here are the details: First use $\hat{\rho}$ to calculate the generalized differencing of (6-61):

$$(Y_t - \hat{\rho} Y_{t-1}) = \alpha(1 - \hat{\rho}) + \gamma(Y_{t-1} - \hat{\rho} Y_{t-2}) + \beta(X_t - \hat{\rho} X_{t-1}) + v_t \tag{6-65}$$

[Note also the adjustment (6-34) required for $t = 1$.] When the variables in brackets are run through an OLS regression program, consistent estimates of α, β, and γ are obtained.

(b) Serial Correlation in Its Various Forms: A Recap of Sections 6-8, 6-9, and 6-10

One view of our results is summarized in Table 6-3, where we ask: Suppose that, in ignorance, an economist applies OLS to an equation without considering the autocorrelation problems she may face; how bad will the result be?

TABLE 6-3 Some Properties of OLS in the Face of Various Kinds of Autocorrelation

If autocorrelation in:	*Then the equation to be estimated is:*	*OLS on this equation provides estimators that are:*
(i) the error only	(6-29) with error (6-27)	unbiased and consistent
(ii) the dependent variable only	(6-57) with error (6-58)	biased and consistent
(iii) both the error and dependent variable	(6-61) with error (6-62)	biased and inconsistent

Remember that if autocorrelation is limited to the error term, then OLS will provide unbiased, consistent estimators; they will however be less reliable (i.e., have greater variance) than an appropriately adjusted regression using generalized differences (GLS). If autocorrelation is limited to the dependent variable, then OLS will provide consistent estimates, but they will be biased in finite samples. If there is autocorrelation in both the error and dependent variable, then OLS loses both attractive properties: It will be neither unbiased nor consistent. To achieve consistency in this case requires a more complicated technique.

A comparison of cases (i) and (ii) in this table suggests that autocorrelation in the dependent variable may be a more critical problem than in the error term. Moreover, we emphasize that we have only scratched the surface in dealing with autocorrelation in the dependent variable; we have discussed only two methods of estimation, chosen mainly because of their relative simplicity. Many problems remain, not the least of which is that the Durbin-Watson test for whether or not the error term is autocorrelated becomes invalid in the face of autocorrelation in the dependent variable; hence it may be very difficult to establish whether or not we are dealing with case (ii) or case (iii) in Table 6-3.

*D BOX-JENKINS METHODS[40]

6-11 ARIMA MODELS

In Part B of this chapter (Sections 6-2 to 6-6), we gave one possible model of a time series—trend and seasonal components, plus a residual analyzed as a very simple autoregression. This model was useful in understanding the structure of the series, and also in forecasting it.

Now we will study an alternative model (Box-Jenkins) that is particularly useful for forecasting. To understand this model, it is first necessary to examine in detail its two components, the autoregression and the moving average.

(a) The Structure of ARMA Models

In equation (6-17) we gave the general case of random tracking, where each value depends upon several previous values. Now we study it in some detail, beginning with a change in notation. We consider any time series [perhaps a residual from a regression analysis as in (6-17), but more often the original series itself]. Denote it by y_t, and suppose it depends on p of its previous values according to a linear regression, called an autoregression (AR) of order p:

$$\text{AR}(p)\colon\ y_t = \phi_1 y_{t-1} + \phi_2 y_{t-2} + \cdots + \phi_p y_{t-p} + v_t \qquad \text{(6-66) like (6-17)}$$

where v_t are serially uncorrelated *pertubations* with an unchanging distribution over time. In particular, for all t,

$$\left.\begin{array}{l} v_t \text{ has constant mean zero} \\ v_t \text{ has constant variance } \sigma^2 \end{array}\right\} \qquad \text{(6-67)}$$

$$v_t \text{ and } v_{t+h} \text{ are uncorrelated } (h \neq 0) \qquad \text{(6-68)}$$

Another interesting way to produce a time series is with a moving average: Each time, y_t picks up one new term and drops one old term, keeping all the rest (as in the four-quarter moving average S' in Table 6-2 in

[40] The star indicates, as usual, that this is an optional section that may be skipped without losing continuity. Although it is not required for understanding the rest of the text, we nevertheless recommend reading this section because of its great practical importance. For brevity, we limit our discussion to a single time series. More detail and breadth may be found in Box and Jenkins, 1970, which includes the relation (transfer function) of one time series with another.

Section 6-4). In general, a *moving average*[41] (*MA*) *of order q* is defined as

$$\text{MA}(q)\colon\ y_t = v_t - \theta_1 v_{t-1} - \theta_2 v_{t-2} - \cdots - \theta_q v_{t-q} \qquad (6\text{-}69)$$

where v_t satisfies the same properties (6-67) and (6-68) as before.

A time series that combines the features of (6-66) and (6-69) is called a *mixture* of an autoregression and moving average:

$$\text{ARMA}(p, q)\colon\ y_t = \overbrace{\phi_1 y_{t-1} + \cdots + \phi_p y_{t-p}}^{\text{autoregression (AR)}} \\ \underbrace{+ v_t - \theta_1 v_{t-1} - \cdots - \theta_q v_{t-q}}_{\text{moving average (MA)}} \qquad (6\text{-}70)$$

(b) The Time Series Autocorrelation

The key idea in statistical inference is to look beyond the sample to the conceptual underlying population. For example, a random sample of 100 workers' wages would give a mean wage $\bar{X}$. We must recognize, however, that the sample might have turned out differently, so that $\bar{X}$ is a random variable. It merely estimates the underlying population mean μ, which is a fixed target.

Similarly, consider a time series such as the height of the water at a certain point on a dock; suppose this fluctuates in a wavy motion shown in Figure 6-13*a*. As well as the time series that was actually observed (the realized path), we must also keep in mind all the other paths that *might* have been observed if, for example, the observation point had been moved a few feet along the dock. The collection of all possible paths is what constitutes the population time series (or stochastic process). If we cut across the population of paths at some time t as shown in Figure 6-13*a*, the population of points (only 3 of which are sketched, for simplicity) has a probability distribution $p(y_t)$ with mean $E(y_t)$ and variance $\text{var}(y_t)$.

There is also a covariance of y_t and $y_{t-\ell}$, which depends of course on the lag ℓ, and is called the autocovariance γ_ℓ:

$$\gamma_\ell \equiv \text{cov}(y_t, y_{t-\ell}) \qquad (6\text{-}71)$$

When $\ell = 0$, we obtain the special case:

$$\gamma_0 = \text{cov}(y_t, y_t) = \text{var}\ y_t$$

[41] Strictly speaking, (6-69) should be called a moving *combination* of order q, because its coefficients do not sum to 1 and therefore do not form an average. However, we call it a moving average in order to conform to custom.

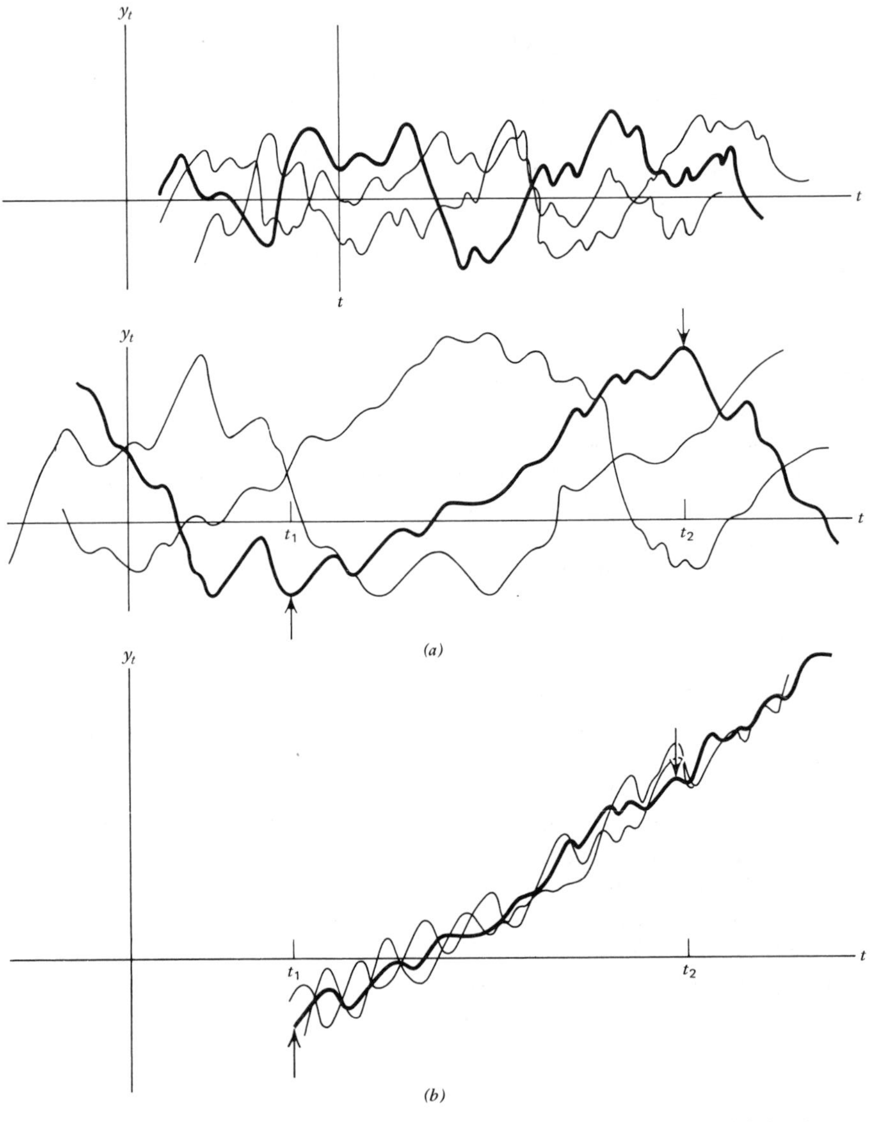

FIGURE 6-13 Time series sketched, with the realized path in heavy ink. (*a*) Stationary. (*b*) Nonstationary.

Similarly, the *autocorrelation* ρ_ℓ is defined as

$$\boxed{\rho_\ell \equiv \frac{\operatorname{cov}(y_t, y_{t-\ell})}{\sqrt{\operatorname{var} y_t \operatorname{var} y_{t-\ell}}}} \tag{6-72}$$

If the variance does not change over time, then var $y_{t-\ell} =$ var y_t and (6-72) reduces to

$$\rho_\ell = \frac{\operatorname{cov}(y_t, y_{t-\ell})}{\operatorname{var} y_t} = \frac{\gamma_\ell}{\gamma_0} \tag{6-73}$$

We now evaluate this for the moving average and the autoregression.

(c) Calculation of the Autocorrelation

(i) Moving Averages. It is easy to calculate the autocorrelation function for a moving average like (6-69). We begin by considering the simplest possible example—the first order scheme:

$$y_t = v_t - \theta v_{t-1} \tag{6-74}$$

where, for simplicity, we have let θ represent θ_1. According to (6-67) each v_t has mean zero, so that each y_t will also have mean zero. The variance is given by

$$\begin{aligned} \operatorname{var} y_t &= E(y_t^2) \\ &= E(v_t^2 + \theta^2 v_{t-1}^2 - 2\theta v_t v_{t-1}) \end{aligned}$$

According to (6-67), $E(v_t^2) = E(v_{t-1}^2) = \sigma^2$. And according to (6-68), v_t and v_{t-1} are uncorrelated, so that $E(v_t v_{t-1}) = 0$. Thus

$$\begin{aligned} \operatorname{var} y_t &= \sigma^2 + \theta^2\sigma^2 + 0 \\ &= (1 + \theta^2)\sigma^2 \end{aligned} \tag{6-75}$$

Note that this variance of y_t does not depend on time t.

For the autocovariance, at lag 1 for example, we calculate

$$\begin{aligned} E(y_t y_{t-1}) &= E(v_t - \theta v_{t-1})(v_{t-1} - \theta v_{t-2}) \\ &= E(v_t v_{t-1} - \theta v_{t-1}^2 - \theta v_t v_{t-2} + \theta^2 v_{t-1} v_{t-2}) \end{aligned} \tag{6-76}$$

Because the v_t are uncorrelated, the only term that counts is the one involving the square, v_{t-1}^2. Thus

$$E(y_t y_{t-1}) = 0 - \theta\sigma^2 + 0 + 0 = -\theta\sigma^2 \tag{6-77}$$

Substituting (6-77) and (6-75) into (6-73), we obtain the autocorrelation at lag 1:

$$\rho_1 = \frac{-\theta\sigma^2}{(1+\theta^2)\sigma^2} = \frac{-\theta}{1+\theta^2} \tag{6-78}$$

In calculating each of the other autocorrelations $\rho_2, \rho_3, \ldots$, we would find, in an equation like (6-76), that there are *no* squared terms. Thus

$$\rho_2 = \rho_3 = \cdots = 0 \tag{6-79}$$

Thus (6-78) and (6-79) define the entire autocorrelation function for the moving average (6-74). Since this autocorrelation function does not depend on time—nor as we saw earlier, does the mean or variance of y_t—the moving average is called *weakly stationary*.

For a general moving average (6-69) of order q, we could similarly show it is weakly stationary, with an autocorrelation function given by:

For MA(q),

$$\rho_\ell = \frac{-\theta_\ell + \theta_1\theta_{\ell+1} + \theta_2\theta_{\ell+2} + \cdots + \theta_{q-\ell}\theta_q}{1+\theta_1^2+\theta_2^2+\cdots+\theta_q^2}, \quad \ell = 1, 2, \ldots, q$$
$$= 0 \qquad \ell > q \tag{6-80}$$

(Of course, the autocorrelation becomes zero when the lag exceeds the order of the moving average.) Examples are shown in Figure 6-14*a*.

(ii) Autoregressions. It is a little more complicated to compute the autocorrelation function for an autoregression; for example, consider the general first-order autoregression

$$y_t = v_t + \phi y_{t-1} \tag{6-81}$$

Substituting $t-1$ for t in (6-81), we see how y_{t-1} in turn depends on its previous value y_{t-2}:

$$y_{t-1} = v_{t-1} + \phi y_{t-2} \tag{6-82}$$

Substitute (6-82) into (6-81):

$$y_t = v_t + \phi[v_{t-1} + \phi y_{t-2}]$$

Substitute for y_{t-2} in terms of *its* previous value:

$$y_t = v_t + \phi[v_{t-1} + \phi(v_{t-2} + \phi y_{t-3})]$$

Continuing to substitute, we obtain

$$y_t = v_t + \phi v_{t-1} + \phi^2 v_{t-2} + \cdots \tag{6-83}$$

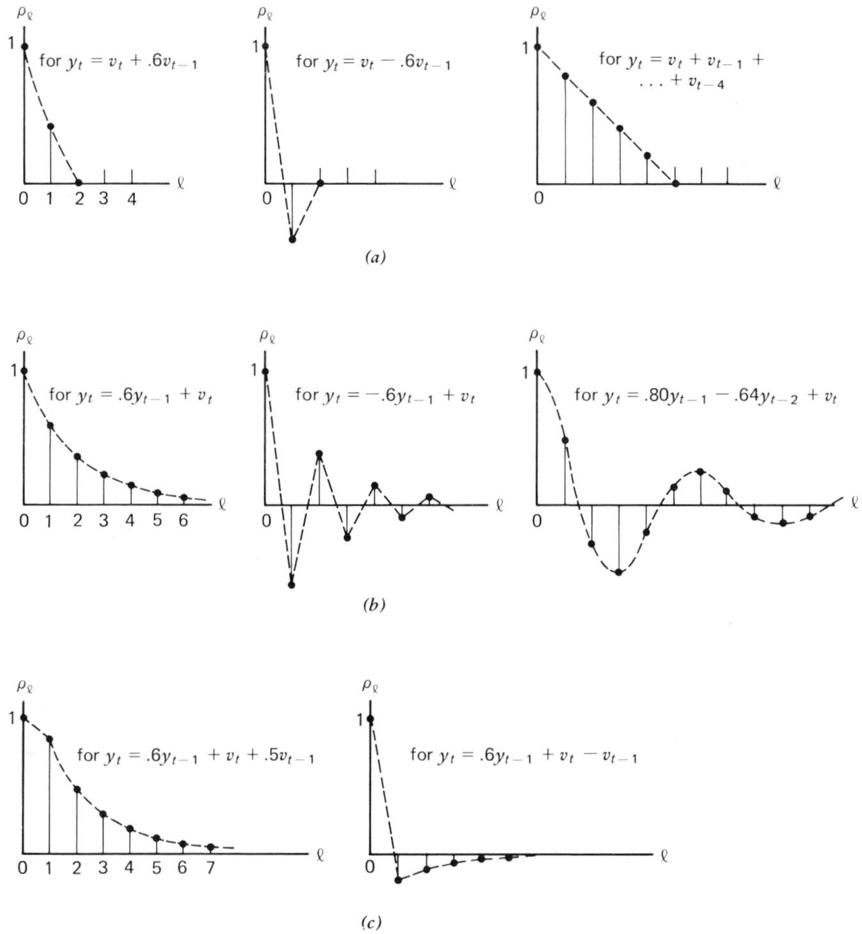

FIGURE 6-14 Some autocorrelation functions. (*a*) For moving averages. (*b*) For autoregressions. (*c*) For mixtures.

According to (6-67), each v_t has mean zero, so that each y_t will also have mean zero. Furthermore, according to (6-68), v_t are uncorrelated, and so (6-83) yields

$$\begin{aligned}\text{var}(y_t) &= \text{var } v_t + \phi^2 \text{ var } v_{t-1} + \phi^4 \text{ var } v_{t-2} + \cdots \\ &= \sigma^2 + \phi^2\sigma^2 + \phi^4\sigma^2 + \cdots \end{aligned} \tag{6-84}$$

This is an infinite geometric series, whose sum is

$$\text{var } y_t = \frac{\sigma^2}{1 - \phi^2} \tag{6-85}$$

whenever the coefficient ϕ satisfies

$$|\phi| < 1 \tag{6-86}$$

[If $|\phi| \geq 1$, then the sum (6-84) does not converge and y_t is an explosive, rather than a stationary, series. Hereafter, we assume away this possibility.]

Now consider the autocovariance: Because the mean of every y_t is zero, (6-71) may be written

$$\gamma_\ell \equiv E(y_t y_{t-\ell}) \tag{6-87}$$

$$= E(\phi y_{t-1} + v_t)(y_{t-\ell})$$

$$= \phi E(y_{t-1} y_{t-\ell}) + E(v_t y_{t-\ell}) \tag{6-88}$$

But the last term is zero because, according to (6-83), $y_{t-\ell}$ is a function of $v_{t-\ell}$, $v_{t-\ell-1}$, etc., which are earlier than v_t, and hence uncorrelated with v_t. Thus (6-88) becomes

$$\gamma_\ell = \phi E(y_{t-1} y_{t-\ell})$$

Now $y_{t-\ell}$ lags behind y_{t-1} by the amount $(t-1)-(t-\ell) = \ell - 1$. Thus, according to definition (6-87),

$$E(y_{t-1} y_{t-\ell}) = \gamma_{\ell-1}$$

Hence, it follows from the last two equations that

$$\gamma_\ell = \phi \gamma_{\ell-1} \tag{6-89}$$

With this autocovariance now in hand, how do we derive the autocorrelation? If we divide (6-89) by γ_0, according to (6-73) we obtain the autocorrelation instead of the autocovariance:

$$\rho_\ell = \phi \rho_{\ell-1} \tag{6-90}$$

Equation (6-90) says that each ρ is just a constant percentage (ϕ) of its previous value—a geometric series (decaying exponential function), whose closed formula is

$$\boxed{\rho_\ell = \phi^\ell} \tag{6-91}$$

For the general autoregression (6-66), we could similarly show the analogy to (6-90):

$$\text{For AR}(p),\ \rho_\ell = \phi_1 \rho_{\ell-1} + \phi_2 \rho_{\ell-2} + \cdots + \phi_p \rho_{\ell-p} \qquad \ell > 0 \tag{6-92}$$

This is a difference equation of order p, and its solution[43] is a sum of

[43] The conditions on the autoregression coefficients ϕ_i required for stationarity are precisely the conditions required for the solution of the difference equation (6-92) to converge (i.e., $\rho_\ell \to 0$). For the first-order autoregression (6-81), for example, the difference equation (6-90) will converge if $|\phi| < 1$ [this same condition had already been derived in (6-86)].

exponential functions and cyclical functions (sines and cosines) damped exponentially. Although the closed formula is too difficult to quote here,[44] the solution for any specific relation (involving a given set of ϕ_i) can easily be iterated[45] from the relation (6-92). Examples are shown in Figure 6-14*b*.

(iii) Mixtures. The ARMA (p, q) process (6-70) has an autocorrelation function that is complicated for the first q lags. Then, however—as we would expect—the effect of the MA(q) part is finished. Thereafter, for $\ell > q$, the autocorrelation function reflects only the AR(p) influence; thus it satisfies the difference equation[46] (6-92). Examples are shown in Figure 6-14*c*.

---

[44] See, for example, Wonnacott, 1976, Chapter 10.

[45] For example, consider the autoregression

$$y_t = .80y_{t-1} - .64y_{t-2} + v_t$$

We find from (6-92) that the autocorrelation satisfies a similar equation:

$$\rho_\ell = .80\rho_{\ell-1} - .64\rho_{\ell-2} \qquad \ell > 0$$

Thus

$$\rho_1 = .80\rho_0 - .64\rho_{-1}$$

Since $\rho_0 = 1$ and $\rho_{-1} = \rho_1$,

$$\rho_1 = .80 - .64\rho_1$$

$$\rho_1 = \frac{.80}{1.64} = .49 \qquad (6\text{-}93)$$

Next

$$\rho_2 = .80\rho_1 - .64\rho_0$$
$$= .80(.49) - .64(1) = -.25 \qquad (6\text{-}94)$$

Similarly

$$\rho_3 = .80\rho_2 - .64\rho_1$$
$$= .80(-.25) - .64(.49) = -.52 \qquad (6\text{-}95)$$

Continuing this way, we generate the last autocorrelation shown in Figure 6-14*b*—an exponentially decaying cycle.

[46] We omit the proofs, which are like the proofs of (6-80) and (6-92). For example, for the ARMA (1, 1) process, we would find

$$\rho_1 = \frac{(1 - \phi\theta)(\phi - \theta)}{1 + \theta^2 - 2\phi\theta} \qquad (6\text{-}96)$$

For lags longer than 1, the moving average effect disappears, leaving only the autoregressive influence:

$$\rho_\ell = \phi\rho_{\ell-1} \qquad \ell > 1 \qquad (6\text{-}97)$$

like (6-90)

If $\phi = .6$ and $\theta = -.5$, for example, (6-96) yields $\rho_1 = .83$; then (6-97) yields $\rho_2 = .6\rho_1 = .50$, then $\rho_3 = .6\rho_2 = .30$, etc. This is the left-hand autocorrelation shown in Figure 6-14*c*. Note how this is complicated only for the first lag, because the moving average involves only one lag. Thereafter it reflects only the autoregressive influence. (The same is true in the right-hand diagram.)

TABLE 6-4 Autocorrelations for Three Basic Box-Jenkins Models

Time Series Model, y_t	*Autocorrelation Function,* ρ_ℓ
MA(q): $y_t = v_t - \theta_1 v_{t-1} - \cdots - \theta_q v_{t-q}$ (6-69) repeated	$\rho_\ell = \dfrac{-\theta_\ell + \theta_1\theta_{\ell+1} + \theta_2\theta_{\ell+2} + \cdots + \theta_{q-\ell}\theta_q}{1 + \theta_1^2 + \theta_2^2 + \cdots + \theta_q^2}$ $\quad 1 \le \ell \le q$ $\rho_\ell = 0 \quad \ell > q$ (6-80) repeated
AR(p): $y_t = \phi_1 y_{t-1} + \phi_2 y_{t-2} + \cdots + \phi_p y_{t-p} + v_t$ (6-66) repeated	$\rho_\ell = \phi_1\rho_{\ell-1} + \phi_2\rho_{\ell-2} + \cdots + \phi_p\rho_{\ell-p}$ (6-92) repeated
ARMA(p, q): $y_t = \phi_1 y_{t-1} + \cdots + \phi_p y_{t-p} + v_t - \theta_1 v_{t-1} - \cdots - \theta_q v_{t-q}$ (6-70) repeated	$\rho_\ell =$ complicated function of θ_i and ϕ_i $\quad 1 \le \ell \le q$ $\rho_\ell = \phi_1\rho_{\ell-1} + \phi_2\rho_{\ell-2} + \cdots + \phi_p\rho_{\ell-p}$ $\quad \ell > q$ like (6-92)

In Table 6-4 we summarize the autocorrelations calculated so far, for the three models: MA(q), AR(p), and the mixed model ARMA(p, q).

(d) Differencing Nonstationary Series

Let us now consider nonstationary time series. In Figure 6-13, for example, panel (b) showed a series whose mean is increasing with time. But the problem is this: On the basis of just one realized path, observed for a finite time, it is impossible to distinguish between a stationary and nonstationary time series; for example, in Figure 6-13 the heavily outlined path in panel (b) is indistinguishable from the one in panel (a), if observed between time t_1 and t_2. So rigorously speaking, when we speak of stationarity, we must keep in mind the whole population (i.e., all the possible paths that this time series could generate).

Practically speaking, however, social scientists usually have only one realized path available.[47] And when it climbs during the whole observed time period, it is generally treated as *if*[48] it were generated by a nonstationary process. Such a nonstationary series cannot be modelled by a stationary ARMA process.

So what shall we do? If the problem is a mean that is shifting over time in a linear way[49] we can remove this from the time series by taking first differences:[50]

$$\Delta y_t = y_t - y_{t-1} \tag{6-98}$$

like (6-25)

---

[47] For example, consider the Dow-Jones average of stock prices. Does it make sense to imagine the series occurring over and over again? Historians would probably argue not—after all, historical events are unique. Thus, although historians might *conceptualize* a whole population of time series, they have to admit they will never *see* it, except for the one historical path. By contrast, physical scientists can often repeat their experiments, thereby generating as many paths as they like.

[48] Once more we see that a model is just a useful hook to hang our data on, rather than "the truth."

[49] If a time series has an exponential, rather than a linear trend, it may be appropriate to first take logs to make the trend linear, and then proceed with differencing. And other trends can sometimes be linearized with other transformations, such as the square root.

[50] In this respect, differencing is like differentiating—it reduces the degree of the polynomial. So in general, differencing an nth degree polynomial n times reduces it to degree 0, that is, a constant. Differencing one final time removes the constant.

Alternatively, the constant term (level) could be removed by subtracting the mean. However, if the level of the time series shifts to a new level, subtracting the overall mean will not work; instead, piecewise adjustment would have to be made for each new level. An easier way to remove a shifting mean is to just difference the series one last time.

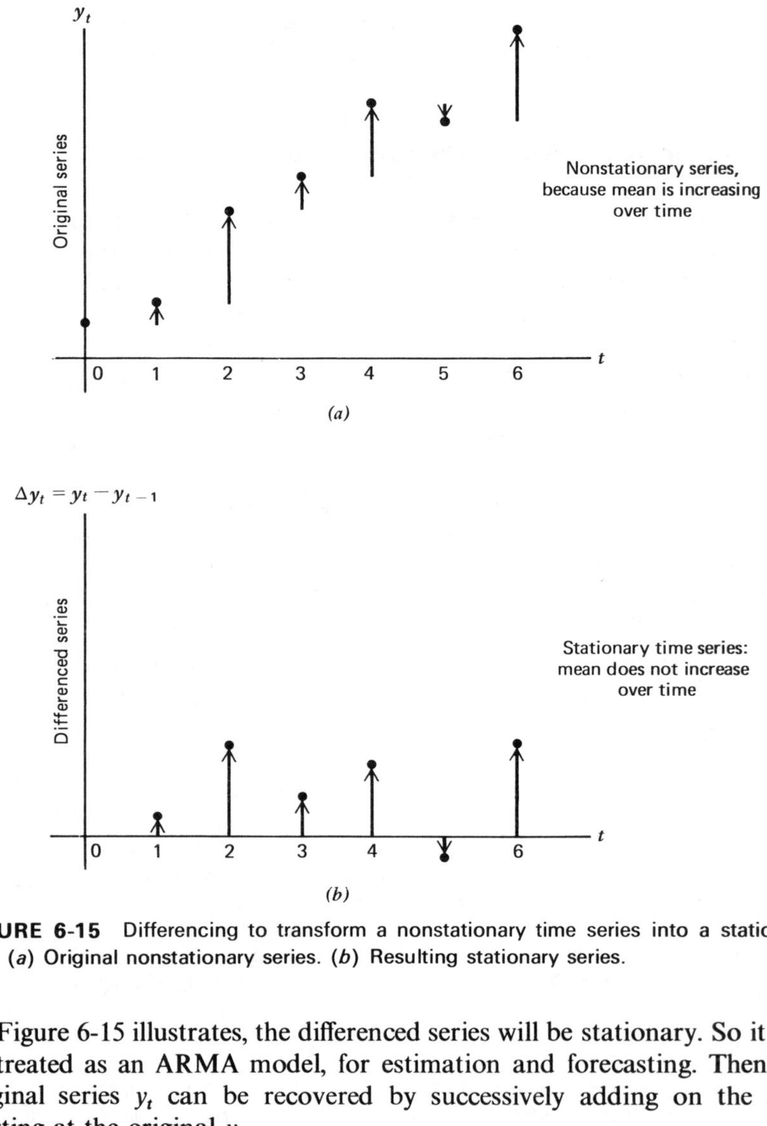

FIGURE 6-15 Differencing to transform a nonstationary time series into a stationary one. (*a*) Original nonstationary series. (*b*) Resulting stationary series.

As Figure 6-15 illustrates, the differenced series will be stationary. So it can be treated as an ARMA model, for estimation and forecasting. Then the original series y_t can be recovered by successively adding on the Δy_t, starting at the original y_0.

To generalize: Suppose a nonstationary time series can be made into a stationary ARMA (p, q) series by differencing d times. In this ARMA form it can be estimated and forecast. Then the original series can be recovered by summing d times. We shall call it an *integrated* ARMA series (since integrating is the continuous analogue of summing), and denote it by ARIMA (p, d, q).

Nonstationarity may appear in other forms as well. One of the commonest is a yearly seasonal pattern. This can be removed by taking differences with a lag of a whole year; for example, for quarterly data,[51]

$$\Delta_4 y_t = y_t - y_{t-4} \tag{6-99}$$

*PROBLEMS

6-13 (a) Prove (6-80).
(b) Graph the autocorrelation function of the MA(2) process:

$$y_t = v_t - 3v_{t-1} + 2v_{t-2}$$

6-14 (a) Prove (6-92).
(b) Graph the autocorrelation function of the AR(2) process:

$$y_t = .60y_{t-1} - .25y_{t-2} + v_t$$

[*Hint*. For ρ_1, see the derivation of (6-93).]

6-15 Using equations (6-96), graph the autocorrelation function of the ARMA (1, 1) process:

$$y_t = .5y_{t-1} + v_t - .9v_{t-1}$$

6-16 To see very simply how differencing removes trends, consider some series that are *pure* trend without a stochastic element:

(a) Suppose we have a linear trend:

$$y_t = 16, 19, 22, 25, 28, 31, 34, 37, 40, 43, 46, 49$$

Calculate Δy_t, and note that it has no trend.

(b) Suppose we have a seasonal pattern in quarterly data:

$$y_t = 2, 7, 3, 1, 2, 7, 3, 1, 2, 7, 3, 1$$

Calculate $\Delta_4 y_t$, and note that it has no trend.

(c) Suppose y_t is a sum of linear trend plus seasonal. What sort of series do you think $\Delta_4 y_t$ will reduce to? Verify your guess by adding the series in (a) to the series in (b), and then calculating $\Delta_4 y_t$.

(d) In part (a), add the calculated Δy_t successively, starting with $y_0 = 16$ (i.e., calculate the series y_0, $y_0 + \Delta y_1$, $y_0 + \Delta y_1 + \Delta y_2$, etc.). Do you recover the original series y_t?

---

[51] The differencing (6-99) will remove linear trend at the same time as it removes seasonal.

*6-12 ESTIMATION AND FORECASTING OF AN ARIMA MODEL

There are three stages in building an ARIMA model of an actual time series:

(a) *Specification* (also called identification by Box and Jenkins), which means first specifying the number of differences d to be taken in transforming the nonstationary ARIMA model into a stationary ARMA model. Then we must specify the number of lags p and q in the autoregression and moving average.
(b) *Estimation* of the parameters $\phi_1, \ldots, \phi_p$ and $\theta_1, \ldots, \theta_q$.
(c) *Diagnostic checking* to ensure that the fitted model is adequate.

Of course, if the model does not pass the diagnostic checks, then a new specification is required, and the three stages are iterated until the final model *does* pass the diagnostic checks.

(a) Specification

Do seasonal patterns, or linear trends, or even polynomial trends exist, that require differencing to remove? This issue can be often settled by prior knowledge, or by just looking at the series. If the series appears nonstationary, differences are taken until the series does appear stationary.

To then determine the lengths of the lags p and q in the autoregression and moving average, it is not sufficient just to look at the series itself; some sort of summary statistics are needed. We define the sample autocorrelation function $\hat{\rho}_\ell$ analogous to the population autocorrelation function ρ_ℓ:

$$\hat{\rho}_\ell \equiv \frac{\sum_{t=\ell+1}^{n} y_t y_{t-\ell}}{\sum_{t=1}^{n} y_t^2} \qquad \text{(6-100) like (6-72)}$$

We calculate $\hat{\rho}_\ell$ from the data[52] for lags $\ell = 1, 2, 3, \ldots$, and display the resulting function for the sample, just as we displayed various population functions in Figure 6-14. What does this graph of $\hat{\rho}_\ell$ tell us? If, for example, $\hat{\rho}_\ell$ remains near zero after one lag (like the first two panels of Figure 6-14*a*), it suggests a moving average of order 1. Or if $\hat{\rho}_\ell$ follows a damped cyclical

[52] In (6-100), we assume that y_t has zero mean, which can easily be achieved by subtracting the mean from the series.

pattern (like the last panel of Figure 6-14*b*), it suggests an autoregression of order 2. Or if $\hat{\rho}_\ell$ has a more complicated pattern (like Figure 6-14*c*) it suggests a mixed process. Because $\hat{\rho}_\ell$ is subject to sampling fluctuations, however, it is difficult to be sure, and specification remains more an art than science.[53]

In the process of specification, we must also keep in mind the general nature of models: They represent useful approximations, rather than the truth. Thus the given time series cannot be *exactly* fitted with an ARMA model. We can only hope to find a manageable model that is an adequate approximation, which forecasts reasonably well. In looking for such a model, we could get by with a pure autoregression as in Section 6-5, or alternatively a pure moving average. But we usually can do better if we allow ourselves the choice of a general mixed ARMA model (with a pure MA or pure AR as possible special cases).

(b) Estimation

There is a very naive way we could estimate the parameters of an ARMA (p, q) process: Choose the $p + q$ parameters ϕ_i and θ_i so that the autocorrelation function ρ_ℓ (given in Table 6-4) would exactly equal the calculated values of the sample autocorrelation function $\hat{\rho}_\ell$, for $\ell = 1, 2, \ldots, p + q$. This would involve $p + q$ nonlinear equations in the $p + q$ unknown parameters, which are fairly easy to solve, and would produce consistent estimators $\hat{\phi}_i$ and $\hat{\theta}_i$. In concentrating entirely on fitting the first $p + q$ lags, however, this naive approach ignores the later part of the autocorrelation function, and worse yet, pays insufficient attention to forecasting. We therefore will look at alternative methods of estimation that provide better estimates of the parameters and better forecasts.

For a pure autoregression AR(p), estimation is very easy. We simply note that in (6-83), y_t depends only on the present and *preceding* values of the disturbance, $v_t, v_{t-1}, \ldots$; thus, the even earlier y's on the right-hand side of (6-66) (i.e., $y_{t-1}, y_{t-2}, \ldots$) will be independent of v_t, and thus OLS applied to (6-66) provides consistent estimates[54] of the parameters ϕ_i.

[53] For specification, it often helps to look at other statistics as well as $\hat{\rho}_\ell$. For example, the partial autocorrelation σ_ℓ is defined as the correlation between y_t and $y_{t-\ell}$, keeping constant all the intervening values $y_{t-1}, \ldots, y_{t-\ell+1}$. Then it turns out to be a dual of the ordinary autocorrelation: σ_ℓ remains at zero after p lags for an AR(p) process [just as ρ_ℓ remains at zero after q lags for a MA(q) process]; and σ_ℓ consists of decaying exponentials and cycles for a MA(q) process [just as ρ_ℓ, for an AR(p) process]. So the sample partial autocorrelation $\hat{\sigma}_\ell$ provides information dual to $\hat{\rho}_\ell$.

[54] As we shall show in Section 7-2, OLS would be inconsistent if the error v_t were correlated with the regressors $y_{t-1}, y_{t-2}, \ldots$.

For the general ARMA (p, q) model, estimation is much more difficult. And it is customarily carried out using a canned computer program, whose details need not concern the average user. We therefore suggest that the following argument be undertaken only by the adventuresome reader; the rest can rejoin us at part (c).

If q is small (the usual case), one possible estimating technique for the ARMA model is the following special form of least squares.[55] To illustrate for $q = 2$ and $p = 3$, the ARMA model (6-70) may be written:

$$y_t - \phi_1 y_{t-1} - \phi_2 y_{t-2} - \phi_3 y_{t-3} = v_t - \theta_1 v_{t-1} - \theta_2 v_{t-2} \quad (6\text{-}101)$$

On the left side of this equation, we note that the series y_t is linearly transformed into a new series that we call Ty_t:

$$Ty_t \equiv y_t - \phi_1 y_{t-1} - \phi_2 y_{t-2} - \phi_3 y_{t-3} \quad (6\text{-}102)$$

Thus (6-101) may be written briefly as

$$Ty_t = v_t - \theta_1 v_{t-1} - \theta_2 v_{t-2} \quad (6\text{-}103)$$

or

$$y_t = T^{-1}(v_t - \theta_1 v_{t-1} - \theta_2 v_{t-2})$$

Since T is linear, its inverse T^{-1} is linear; therefore,

$$y_t = T^{-1}v_t - \theta_1 T^{-1}v_{t-1} - \theta_2 T^{-1}v_{t-2} \quad (6\text{-}104)$$

Let

$$z_t \equiv T^{-1}v_t \quad (6\text{-}105)$$

Then (6-104) simplifies to

$$y_t = z_t - \theta_1 z_{t-1} - \theta_2 z_{t-2} \quad (6\text{-}106)$$

or

$$z_t = y_t + \theta_1 z_{t-1} + \theta_2 z_{t-2} \quad (6\text{-}107)$$

The series z_t $(t = 1, 2, \ldots, n)$ can be constructed from the observed series y_t using (6-107), starting with $z_0 = z_{-1} = 0$ (the expected value 0 is the best guess when we lack any better information). Of course, we must also supply a trial pair of parameters (θ_1, θ_2).

Now rewrite (6-105) as

$$Tz_t = v_t \quad (6\text{-}108)$$

[55] Here is another possible solution: The parameters in (6-101) may be estimated by some sort of nonlinear technique such as the successive Taylor linearizations described in Appendix 4-B. (Although at first glance (6-101) may appear to be a *linear* estimation problem, we must recognize that θ_1 and θ_2 are coefficients of *unobservable* series, which complicates matters.) For details, see for example Box and Jenkins, 1970, pp. 231–233.

But T defined in (6-102) can be applied to *any* series, for example z_t. Recognizing that this is precisely what has happened on the left-hand side of (6-108), this equation becomes

$$z_t - \phi_1 z_{t-1} - \phi_2 z_{t-2} - \phi_3 z_{t-3} = v_t$$

or

$$z_t = \phi_1 z_{t-1} + \phi_2 z_{t-2} + \phi_3 z_{t-3} + v_t \tag{6-109}$$

The values of z_t constructed from (6-107) are now used in the autoregression (6-109) to estimate the parameters ϕ_i, using OLS. The estimated residuals v_t from this autoregression are squared and summed to form the criterion

$$S = \sum \hat{v}_t^2 \tag{6-110}$$

To sum up, a trial pair of parameters (θ_1, θ_2) in (6-107) has ultimately yielded an estimated set of parameters (ϕ_1, ϕ_2, ϕ_3) and a sum of squared residuals S.

We now try out a new trial pair of parameters (θ_1, θ_2) in (6-107) and repeat the whole exercise, once again obtaining an estimated set of parameters (ϕ_1, ϕ_2, ϕ_3) and a sum of squared residuals S. We continue, trying out a whole grid of possible pairs (θ_1, θ_2). We select the special pair $(\hat{\theta}_1, \hat{\theta}_2)$ that minimizes the sum of squared residuals S in (6-110). Then $(\hat{\theta}_1, \hat{\theta}_2)$, along with its estimated set of parameters $(\hat{\phi}_1, \hat{\phi}_2, \hat{\phi}_3)$, are the least squares estimates we were looking for.

(c) Diagnostic Checking

Whenever a model has been estimated, it is appropriate to check whether it is an adequate fit. A standard check that has already been suggested for multiple regression is to "overfit" the model; that is, check that a bigger model with another parameter fails to fit the data significantly better.[56]

---

[56] Another diagnostic check, particularly appropriate for ARIMA models, is to test whether the estimated residuals $\hat{v}_t$ are indeed uncorrelated. That is, test whether their autocorrelation function is zero. Box and Ljung (1978) suggest using the statistic:

$$\chi^2 = n'(n' + 2) \sum_{\ell=1}^{L} \hat{\rho}_\ell^2(\hat{v})/(n' - \ell) \tag{6-111}$$

where $n' = n - d$ = number of observations available after differencing d times,

$\hat{\rho}_\ell(\hat{v})$ = the autocorrelation function of the estimated residuals $\hat{v}_t$, for lags ℓ running from 1 up to some reasonable distance L.

If H_0 is true ($\hat{v}$ are indeed uncorrelated), then χ^2 has approximately a chi-square distribution with

$$\text{d.f.} = L - p - q \tag{6-112}$$

(d) Forecasting

Once a model has been estimated and passed through its diagnostic checks, it is ready to forecast future values of y_t—using the best available data, of course. For example, suppose data at $t = 1, 2, \ldots, n$ were used to fit the ARMA (2, 2) model

$$y_t = \phi_1 y_{t-1} + \phi_2 y_{t-2} + v_t - \theta_1 v_{t-1} - \theta_2 v_{t-2} \tag{6-113}$$

To predict the first future value y_{n+1}, we theoretically have

$$y_{n+1} = \phi_1 y_n + \phi_2 y_{n-1} + v_{n+1} - \theta_1 v_n - \theta_2 v_{n-1} \tag{6-114}$$

To use this equation, we first plug in the estimated parameters ($\hat{\phi}_1$, $\hat{\phi}_2$, $\hat{\theta}_1$, $\hat{\theta}_2$), and the estimated residuals $\hat{v}_n$ and $\hat{v}_{n-1}$ [the same residuals that appeared in (6-110)]. For the future residual v_{n+1}, the only information we have is that its expectation is zero, and so we use $v_{n+1} = 0$ as our best guess. The past values y_n and y_{n-1} are known, of course, and so the forecast of y_{n+1} in (6-114) is complete:

$$\hat{y}_{n+1} = \hat{\phi}_1 y_n + \hat{\phi}_2 y_{n-1} - \hat{\theta}_1 \hat{v}_n - \hat{\theta}_2 \hat{v}_{n-1} \tag{6-115}$$

To forecast the next future value y_{n+2}, we would theoretically have

$$y_{n+2} = \phi_1 y_{n+1} + \phi_2 y_n + v_{n+2} - \theta_1 v_{n+1} - \theta_2 v_n \tag{6-116}$$

like (6-114)

In practice, we are even more ignorant than before. The residual v_{n+2} as well as the residual v_{n+1} has to be estimated as zero. And y_{n+1} is only estimated, from (6-115). Thus the forecast is

$$\hat{y}_{n+2} = \hat{\phi}_1 \hat{y}_{n+1} + \hat{\phi}_2 y_n - \hat{\theta}_2 \hat{v}_n \tag{6-117}$$

Using a similar argument to forecast one more future value, we would use

$$\hat{y}_{n+3} = \hat{\phi}_1 \hat{y}_{n+2} + \hat{\phi}_2 \hat{y}_{n+1} \tag{6-118}$$

The pattern is now clear: Because we have predicted far enough into the future, the moving average portion (involving the future v's) has dropped out completely, and the forecast has become purely autoregressive.[57]

---

[57] If the time series had to be differenced initially (to remove a linear trend), forecasting would still be straightforward. Proceeding as above, we would obtain forecast *differences* $\hat{\Delta y}_t$ ($t = n+1, n+2, \ldots$). Then we would forecast the original series by summation as follows: Solving (6-98) for y_t,

$$y_t = y_{t-1} + \Delta y_t$$

Thus our first forecast $\hat{y}_{n+1}$ is

$$\hat{y}_{n+1} = \underset{\text{(observed)}}{y_n} + \underset{\text{(a predicted difference)}}{\hat{\Delta y}_{n+1}}$$

and in general, for $t > n + 1$,

$$\hat{y}_t = \hat{y}_{t-1} + \hat{\Delta y}_t$$

7

SIMULTANEOUS EQUATIONS, AND OTHER EXAMPLES OF CORRELATED REGRESSOR AND ERROR

In this chapter, we introduce a new method of estimation—the *covariance* or *instrumental variable* technique. Although this may seem like a digression, the reader should view it as an investment—and an important one at that, since it will provide one single means of analyzing a whole array of problems taken up in the next three chapters. Our hope is to develop one plot, rather than write a whole set of unconnected short stories.

7-1 A NEW LOOK AT OLS

(a) Covariance Operator

The covariance of X and Y as defined in Chapter 5 was a measure of how X and Y were related, similar to the correlation coefficient r:

$$\boxed{s_{XY} \equiv \frac{\sum xy}{n-1}} \qquad \text{(5-2) repeated}$$

where x and y are the deviations of X and Y about the mean.

Now, reconsider the model of Chapter 2:

$$Y = \alpha + \beta X + e \tag{7-1}$$

Taking covariances of X with each of the variables in this equation yields

$$s_{XY} = \beta s_{XX} + s_{Xe} \tag{7-2}$$

To justify this, we recall that the n sample observations of X and Y are assumed in (7-1) to be generated in the following way:

$$\left.\begin{aligned} Y_1 &= \alpha + \beta X_1 + e_1 \\ Y_2 &= \alpha + \beta X_2 + e_2 \\ &\vdots \\ Y_n &= \alpha + \beta X_n + e_n \end{aligned}\right\} \tag{7-3}$$

We can easily show[1] that with an appropriate translation of both the X- and Y-axes, the intercept term disappears and we may write

$$\left.\begin{aligned} y_1 &= \beta x_1 + e'_1 \\ y_2 &= \beta x_2 + e'_2 \\ &\vdots \\ y_n &= \beta x_n + e'_n \end{aligned}\right\} \tag{7-6}$$

where the y_i, x_i, and e'_i represent deviations from the sample mean. The first equation may be multiplied by x_1, the second by x_2, and so on:

$$\left.\begin{aligned} x_1 y_1 &= \beta x_1 x_1 + x_1 e'_1 \\ x_2 y_2 &= \beta x_2 x_2 + x_2 e'_2 \\ &\vdots \\ x_n y_n &= \beta x_n x_n + x_n e'_n \end{aligned}\right\} \tag{7-7}$$

When we sum all these equations, and divide by $n - 1$,

$$\frac{\sum xy}{n-1} = \frac{\beta \sum xx}{n-1} + \frac{\sum xe'}{n-1} \tag{7-8}$$

---

[1] Since

$$Y_i = \alpha + \beta X_i + e_i$$

taking averages,

$$\bar{Y} = \alpha + \beta \bar{X} + \bar{e}$$

Subtracting,

$$y_i = \beta x_i + e'_i \tag{7-4}$$

where

$$e'_i = e_i - \bar{e} \tag{7-5}$$

Recalling from (7-5) that e' is just e expressed as deviations from the mean, (7-8) may be written

$$s_{XY} = \beta s_{XX} + s_{Xe} \qquad \text{(7-2) proved}$$

(b) The OLS Estimate

In order to estimate β, we divide (7-2) by s_{XX} (the variance of X):

$$\frac{s_{XY}}{s_{XX}} = \beta + \frac{s_{Xe}}{s_{XX}} \tag{7-9}$$

From the observations of X and Y, s_{XY} and s_{XX} are easily calculated. But e is unobservable, so that s_{Xe} cannot be evaluated. However, if we can assume that s_{Xe} is small enough to neglect, we obtain the estimator

$$\frac{s_{XY}}{s_{XX}} = \hat{\beta} \tag{7-10}$$

We recognize this[2] as the OLS estimator (2-19).

In Chapter 2, when X was assumed fixed at various levels, the OLS estimator was justified on several grounds. Also, in Section 2-11 we concluded that even if X is random, so long as it is independent of the error e, the OLS estimator is still justified. Now we see from (7-10) that the OLS estimator is justified under conditions that are even broader; OLS is still a consistent estimator, provided

$$s_{Xe} \xrightarrow{p} 0 \tag{7-11a}$$

while

$$s_{XX} \xrightarrow{p} \text{nonzero} \tag{7-12a}$$

[2] In (2-19), the OLS estimator was given as

$$\hat{\beta} = \frac{\sum xy}{\sum x^2}$$

$$= \frac{\sum xy/(n-1)}{\sum xx/(n-1)} = \frac{s_{XY}}{s_{XX}}$$

where $\xrightarrow{p}$ means, "approaches in probability as $n \to \infty$," as defined in (2-107) and (2-108). To restate verbally,

$$\text{The sample covariance } s_{Xe} \text{ approaches zero} \tag{7-11b}$$

$$\text{while } s_{XX} \text{ approaches a nonzero limit}^3 \tag{7-12b}$$

To keep the argument simple, henceforth we will always assume that (7-12) is satisfied; this is recognized as the condition that the x's be spread out (i.e., perfect multicollinearity avoided), already discussed in Section 3-4.

Turning to condition (7-11), we note that the independence of X and e would, of course, ensure this. In fact, even the (population) uncorrelation of X and e is sufficient; hence, we abbreviate (7-11) roughly[4] by saying X and e are uncorrelated.

7-2 INCONSISTENCY OF OLS WHEN e AND X ARE CORRELATED

(a) Problem

When e is correlated with X, we see from (7-9) that the OLS estimator is no longer consistent, because s_{Xe} no longer approaches zero.

This issue is important enough to illustrate graphically. To be concrete, suppose e and X are positively correlated, as in Figure 7-1. Then positive values of e tend to be associated with positive values of the deviation x. Consequently, the OLS fit will have too large a slope. This bias in $\hat{\beta}$ will persist even with a very large sample (and, in fact, approaches σ_{Xe}/σ_{XX}).

---

[3] To be precise, we need not require s_{XX} to approach a limit; it is enough that s_{XX} be bounded away from zero (in probability), that is, there exists some fixed number $\delta > 0$ for which

$$\Pr(s_{XX} < \delta) \to 0 \tag{7-13}$$

as $n \to \infty$

* [4] The condition (7-11) includes other cases besides the case where a random sample of X and e are drawn from a population with covariance $\sigma_{Xe} = 0$. For example:

1. (7-11) will be true if X_t and e_t are stationary time series, with e_t having zero autocorrelation, and if the (population) covariance of X_t and e_t is zero for every t.
2. (7-11) will also be true even if X_t and e_t are nonstationary time series, just so long as $\sigma_e^2 \to 0$ while σ_X^2 is bounded. This can happen even while X_t and e_t maintain high correlation; according to the definition of ρ,

$$\sigma_{Xe} = \rho_{Xe}\sigma_X\sigma_e \tag{7-14}$$

so that if $\sigma_e \to 0$, it will force $\sigma_{Xe} \to 0$, even if ρ_{Xe} is as high as 1.

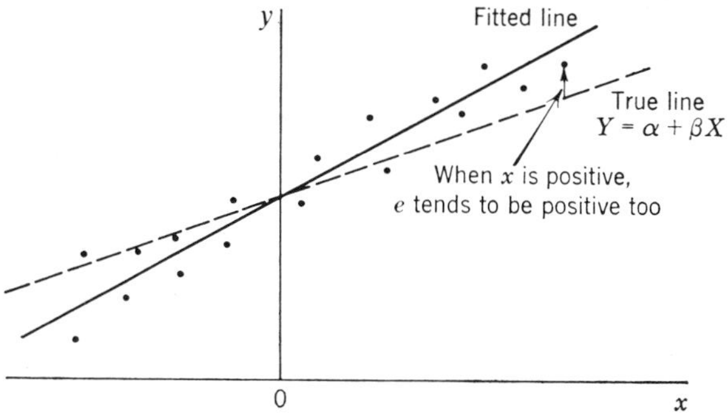

FIGURE 7-1 How correlation of e and X makes $\hat{\beta}$ biased and inconsistent.

Intuitively, the reason for this inconsistency is clear. In explaining Y, OLS gives as little credit as possible to the error, and as much credit as possible to the regressor. When the error and regressor are correlated, then some of the effect of the error is wrongly attributed to the regressor.

(b) Solution, Using Instrumental Variables (IV)

We have seen that taking covariances with X in (7-2) led us in (7-10) to the OLS estimator, which is inconsistent when X and e are correlated. If there were some random variable Z that is uncorrelated with e, then we might hope to use it instead of X to avoid the inconsistency.

To work this out in detail, we call a random variable Z an *instrumental variable* if it satisfies the following two requirements:

(1) Z and e are uncorrelated, or more precisely,

$$s_{Ze} \xrightarrow{p} 0 \qquad (7\text{-}15)$$

(2) Z and X are correlated, or more precisely,

$$s_{ZX} \xrightarrow{p} \text{nonzero} \qquad (7\text{-}16)$$

If we take covariances of Z with each of the variables in (7-1),

$$s_{ZY} = \beta s_{ZX} + s_{Ze} \qquad (7\text{-}17)$$

[This may be justified just as (7-2) was justified earlier.]

To obtain an estimate of β, divide by s_{ZX}:

$$\frac{s_{ZY}}{s_{ZX}} = \beta + \frac{s_{Ze}}{s_{ZX}}$$

By assumption, s_{Ze} approaches zero, while s_{ZX} does not, so that the last term approaches zero. Disregarding it, therefore, yields the consistent estimator

$$\boxed{\frac{s_{ZY}}{s_{ZX}} = \hat{\beta}} \tag{7-18}$$

OLS is recognized to be just the special case of instrumental variable estimation, when X itself is used as the instrumental variable.

7-3 IV EXTENDED TO MULTIPLE REGRESSION

We illustrate with two regressors, although the case of k regressors is entirely similar. The problem is to estimate the parameters of

$$Y = \beta_0 + \beta_1 X_1 + \beta_2 X_2 + e \tag{7-19}$$

In order to estimate the two unknown slope coefficients β_1 and β_2 we will need two estimating equations, which in turn requires two instrumental variables Z_1 and Z_2. Each of these two instrumental variables, of course, must satisfy the requirements of (7-15), that is, be uncorrelated with the error e, yet correlated with the regressors. In addition, the instrumental variables should avoid linear dependence among themselves, in order to avoid the problem of multicollinearity.

When we apply the first instrumental variable Z_1, that is, take covariances of Z_1 with the variables of (7-19), we obtain

$$s_{Z_1Y} = \beta_1 s_{Z_1X_1} + \beta_2 s_{Z_1X_2} + s_{Z_1e} \tag{7-20}$$

When the last term (which tends to zero) is dropped,

$$s_{Z_1Y} \stackrel{\wedge}{=} \beta_1 s_{Z_1X_1} + \beta_2 s_{Z_1X_2} \tag{7-21}$$

where $\stackrel{\wedge}{=}$ means *equals in the limit*. Similarly, by applying the second instrumental variable Z_2, we obtain

$$s_{Z_2Y} \stackrel{\wedge}{=} \beta_1 s_{Z_2X_1} + \beta_2 s_{Z_2X_2} \tag{7-22}$$

These two equations are then solved for the estimators $\hat{\beta}_1$ and $\hat{\beta}_2$.

It is interesting to note what happens if the regressors X_1 and X_2 themselves are uncorrelated with e. Then they are the best possible instrumental variables, and the estimating equations (7-21) and (7-22) become

$$s_{X_1Y} \triangleq \beta_1 s_{X_1X_1} + \beta_2 s_{X_1X_2} \tag{7-23}$$

$$s_{X_2Y} \triangleq \beta_1 s_{X_2X_1} + \beta_2 s_{X_2X_2} \tag{7-24}$$

Except for notational changes, these are the OLS estimating equations (3-6); confirming this is left as an exercise. Hence, the IV estimators coincide exactly with the OLS estimators. Thus, we confirm in multiple regression the conclusion first encountered in simple regression: when OLS is valid, it is just a special case of IV.

7-4 SIMULTANEOUS EQUATIONS—THE CONSUMPTION FUNCTION

(a) The Problem

The most common example of correlation between error and regressor occurs when the equation to be estimated is part of a whole system of simultaneous equations. We illustrate in detail with the simplest possible example: a consumption function, embedded in a very simple national income model of two equations:

$$C = \alpha + \beta Y + e \tag{7-25}$$

$$Y = C + I \tag{7-26}$$

Equation (7-25) is the standard form of the consumption function that relates consumption C to income Y. The parameters of this function that must be estimated are α (the intercept) and β (the slope, or marginal propensity to consume). The successive values of the error term e are assumed to be independent and identically distributed, with zero mean and finite variance. Equation (7-26) is an identity, which states that national income is defined as the sum of consumption and investment. Since both sides of this equation are, by definition, equal, no error term appears in this equation. Moreover, the simple equality sign can be replaced by the identity sign ($\equiv$), although in the argument that follows the more familiar equality is used.

An important distinction must be made between two kinds of variables in our system. By assumption, I is an exogenous variable. Since its value is determined *outside* the system of equations, it will often be referred to as *predetermined*; however, it should be recognized that a predetermined variable may be either fixed *or* random. The essential point is that its values are determined elsewhere, and are not influenced by C, Y, or e. In particular, we emphasize that

$$I \text{ and } e \text{ are statistically independent} \tag{7-27}$$

On the other hand, Y and C are endogenous variables; their values are determined *within* the model and thus are influenced by I and e. Since there are two equations to determine these two endogenous variables, the model is mathematically complete.[5]

Economists will immediately recognize certain oversimplifications in this model. For example, it describes a closed economy with no government sector. The assumption that I is exogenous is also an oversimplification. In fact, I is likely to depend on C or Y. You are invited to experiment in setting up a three-equation model in Y, C, and I; such a system would involve an additional endogenous variable I and an additional equation relating I to another variable that might more reasonably be regarded as exogenous (e.g., the interest rate). Economic assumptions can be made more realistic in this way by increasing the size of the model—but then its mathematical complexity also increases. Econometricians constantly must make decisions that involve this sort of trade-off between economic realism and mathematical manageability. A larger model would also be more difficult to show geometrically. Since this is our next objective, we stick to our original two-equation model.

A diagram will be useful in illustrating the statistical difficulties encountered. To highlight the problems the statistician will face, let us suppose that we have some sort of omniscient knowledge, so that we know the true consumption function $C = \alpha + \beta Y$ as shown in Figure 7-2. And let us watch what happens to the statistician—a mere mortal—who does not have this knowledge but must try to estimate this function by observing only C and Y. Specifically, let us show how badly things will turn out if he estimates α and β by fitting an OLS regression of C on Y. To find the sort of scatter of C and Y he will observe, we must remember that all observations must satisfy both equations (7-25) and (7-26).

Consider (7-25) first. Whenever e takes on a zero value, the observation of C and Y must fall somewhere along the true consumption function $C = \alpha + \beta Y$, shown in Figure 7-2. If e takes on a value greater than zero (say +\$50 billion), then consumption is greater as a consequence, and the observed C, Y combination will fall somewhere along $C = \alpha + \beta Y + 50$. Similarly, if e takes on a value of -50, he will observe a point on the line $C = \alpha + \beta Y - 50$. According to the standard assumptions, e is distributed about a zero mean. To keep the geometry simple, we further assume that e is

[5] While there must be as many linear equations as unknowns to yield a unique solution, this is not always sufficient; these equations must also be linearly independent.

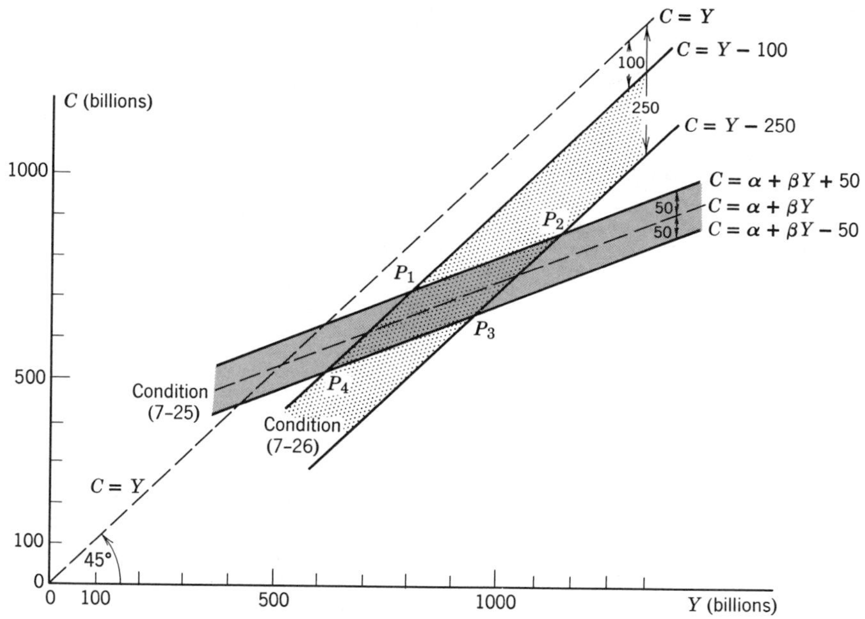

FIGURE 7-2 Problems in estimating the consumption function.

equally likely to take on any value between +50 and −50. Thus the statistician will observe C and Y falling within this band around the consumption function, shaded in Figure 7-2.

Any observed combination of C and Y must also satisfy (7-26). What does this imply? This condition can be rewritten as

$$C = Y - I$$

If I were zero, then C and Y would be equal, and any observation would fall on the familiar 45° line where $C = Y$. Let us suppose that when I is determined by outside factors it is distributed uniformly through a range of 100 to 250. If $I = 100$, then an observation of C and Y would fall along $C = Y - 100$, which is simply the line lying 100 units below the 45° line. Similarly, when $I = 250$, an observation of C and Y would fall along the line $C = Y - 250$. These two lines define the stippled band within which observations must fall to satisfy (7-26).

Since any observed combination of C and Y must satisfy *both* conditions, all observations will fall within the parallelogram $P_1 P_2 P_3 P_4$. To clarify, this parallelogram of observations is reproduced in Figure 7-3. When the statistician regresses C on Y using OLS, the result is shown as $C = \tilde{\alpha} + \tilde{\beta}Y$. When this is compared with the true consumption function

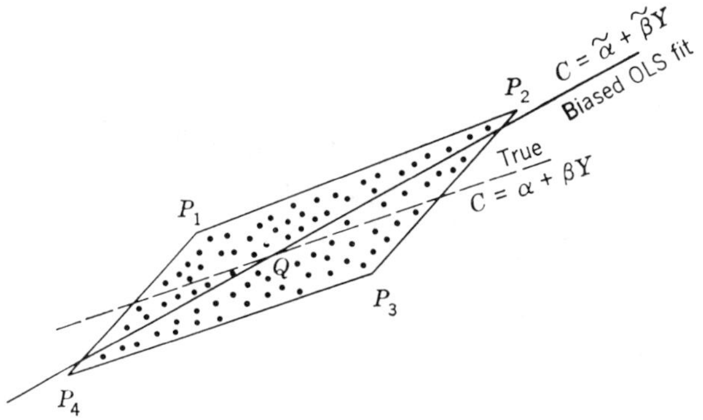

FIGURE 7-3 Biased and inconsistent OLS fit of the consumption function.

($C = \alpha + \beta Y$), it is clear that the statistician has come up with a bad fit; his estimate of the slope ($\tilde{\beta}$) has an upward bias. What has gone wrong?

The observations around P_2 have "pulled" the estimating line above the true regression; similarly, the observations around P_4 have pulled the estimating line below the true regression. It is the pull on both ends that has tilted this estimated line. Moreover, increasing sample size will not help to reduce this bias. If the number of observations in this parallelogram is doubled, this bias will remain intact.[6] Hence, OLS is inconsistent.

We notice the similarity of Figures 7-3 and 7-1. In both cases the error term is correlated with the regressor (plotted along the horizontal axis),[7] and causes the inconsistency in OLS.

[6] With an increase in sample size, the reliability of $\tilde{\beta}$ as an estimator will be increased somewhat, because its variance will decrease toward zero. But its bias will not be reduced.

It is curious that the OLS fit does not pass exactly through the tips of the parallelogram, P_2 and P_4. Although this can be verified computationally, as in Problem 7-1, we also give an intuitive reason: The OLS line provides a good fit on *all* observations. To be concrete, suppose we are fitting a line through Q, with slope to be determined. Now if P_2 were the only observation, then the line would be more tilted in order to pass right through P_2. On the other hand, if the vertical slice through P_3 were the only set of observations, then the line would be less tilted; (in fact, the line would be tilted down to the position of the true line $C = \alpha + \beta Y$). As a compromise, the OLS line fits both kinds of observations by passing somewhere between these two extremes.

[7] Although Figure 7-3 makes clear the correlation of e and the regressor Y, we shall eventually see below that this could have also been deduced from the algebra of equation (7-34): As long as $\beta < 1$, the coefficient of e is positive; hence Y and e are positively correlated.

(b) Solution by Instrumental Variable (IV)

We can obtain a consistent estimator of β if we can find an instrumental variable. The exogenous variable I is just what we need, since it satisfies the two requirements of an instrumental variable:

From (7-27), I is uncorrelated with e, and (7-15) is satisfied.

From (7-26), I affects Y; thus the two are correlated and (7-16) is satisfied.

To use I as an instrumental variable involves taking covariances in the consumption function, obtaining

$$s_{IC} = \beta s_{IY} + s_{Ie} \tag{7-28}$$

To estimate β divide by s_{IY}:

$$\frac{s_{IC}}{s_{IY}} = \beta + \frac{s_{Ie}}{s_{IY}} \tag{7-29}$$

Since the last term tends to zero, we disregard it to obtain the consistent estimator:

$$\boxed{\frac{s_{IC}}{s_{IY}} = \hat{\beta}} \tag{7-30}$$

If desired, we can derive an estimator of α, the other parameter in the consumption function. Taking expected values of all terms in the consumption function,

$$\begin{aligned} E(C) &= \alpha + \beta E(Y) + E(e) \\ &= \alpha + \beta E(Y) \end{aligned} \tag{7-31}$$

A consistent estimator $\hat{\alpha}$ is obtained by substituting consistent estimators for all other terms in (7-31):

$$\bar{C} = \hat{\alpha} + \hat{\beta}\bar{Y}$$

Solving

$$\hat{\alpha} = \bar{C} - \hat{\beta}\bar{Y} \tag{7-32}$$

(c) The Relevance of an Instrumental Variable

It is now appropriate to reconsider in detail the second requirement of the instrumental variable I—it must be correlated with the regressor Y. As is evident in (7-29), the higher the covariance s_{IY}, the smaller will be the term

s_{Ie}/s_{IY}, which is the source of estimation error; hence, the better will be the estimator.

As our instrumental variable, therefore, we should look for the most relevant variable (i.e., the instrumental variable most highly correlated with Y) to get the most statistical leverage. Thus, the exogenous variable I is a natural choice; [note in (7-26) how I directly affects Y]. Rainfall in California or even the price of haircuts in Denver might satisfy the theoretical requirements of an instrumental variable; yet either would lack statistical leverage. To state this mathematically, if California rainfall R were used as an instrumental variable, its correlation with Y would be so small that the error term s_{Re}/s_{RY} would be large. Only in extremely large samples would this ratio settle down to zero. The consistency of $\hat{\beta}$ in huge samples would be cold comfort for an economist faced with a small sample. Or, to look at it from another point of view, suppose the price of haircuts in Denver were alternatively used as an instrumental variable; since this would also involve a large estimating error, the two small-sample estimates of β might vary widely—even though in an infinitely large sample they would coincide.

In view of this relevancy requirement for an instrument, we will confine ourselves[8] to a conservative instrumental variable approach: hereafter, *we concede as instrumental only those exogenous variables that explicitly appear in our model*—that is, which appear in at least one of the equations in the system.

It is evident that neither this conservative approach, nor any other, entirely overcomes our difficulties; the decision on which variables may be used as instrumental variables is just pushed onto the econometrician who specifies the model, and in particular the exogenous variables that are included. Specification of the model remains arbitrary to a degree, and this results in some arbitrariness in statistical estimation. But this cannot be avoided. It can only be concluded that the first task of specifying the original structure of the model is a very important one, since it involves a prior judgment of which variables are "close to" C and Y, and which variables are relatively "far away."

Finally, it is important to distinguish between the term *instrument* as used by economists, and *instrumental variable* as used by statisticians. Instruments refer to variables (such as the interest rate) that are determined by policy makers with the objective of influencing *targets* (such as national income). Instrumental variable is a broader term that refers to *any* predetermined variable (including variables such as the interest rate, which are determined by the policy maker, and the weather, which is not). While only instruments can be manipulated by the policy maker, all instrumental variables can be used for estimation by the statistician.

---

[8] With the single exception of Section 7-5(c).

(d) Solution by Indirect Least Squares (ILS)

ILS is another way of deriving consistent estimates, identical to those derived by IV in this example. This alternative method is introduced because it has a very useful economic and statistical interpretation. If the problem with regressing C on Y is that Y is correlated with e, why not regress C on a variable that is not correlated with e, namely I? This is the strategy of ILS.

The first step is to take the original set of equations, called the *structural form* and transform it into its *reduced form*. This means solving the system of equations for the endogenous variables explicitly in terms of the exogenous variables and error terms.

For example, consider the original system (or structural form) (7-25) and (7-26) with structural coefficients (or parameters) α and β. When it is solved for C and Y, the result is the reduced form:

$$C = \left(\frac{\alpha}{1-\beta}\right) + \left(\frac{\beta}{1-\beta}\right)I + \left(\frac{1}{1-\beta}\right)e \tag{7-33}$$

$$Y = \left(\frac{\alpha}{1-\beta}\right) + \left(\frac{1}{1-\beta}\right)I + \left(\frac{1}{1-\beta}\right)e \tag{7-34}$$

the reduced form coefficients of course being $\alpha/(1-\beta)$, $\beta/(1-\beta)$, etc.

The reduced form equations show explicitly how exogenous investment I affects consumption C and income Y. For example, from (7-34) we see that a \$1 increase in investment causes an increase in income of $1/(1-\beta)$. This reduced form coefficient is recognized as the familiar investment multiplier, with β being the marginal propensity to consume. Similarly, the coefficient of I in (7-33) shows how consumption is affected by a \$1 increase in investment. In general, the reduced form shows the equilibrium impact of a change in any exogenous variable on each endogenous variable. Thus, both the statistician and the economist are interested in the reduced form. The statistician appreciates the advantages of transforming a system into its reduced form as a means of estimating the original structure, as we shall see directly; but even though the original structure may be estimated in some other way, the economist often finds it useful to transform it into its reduced form in order to answer policy questions.

We return to the statistical problem of estimating α and β from (7-33).[9] First, the error term, being just a constant multiple of e, is independent of I [and thus satisfies (7-27)]. Therefore, OLS on this equation yields consistent estimates. That is, an OLS fit of (7-33), namely

$$C = a + bI \tag{7-35}$$

[9] Although we choose to work with equation (7-33), it would be equally valid to work with the other reduced form equation (7-34). In fact, we would arrive at exactly the same estimators.

will yield computed coefficients a and b that are consistent estimates of the corresponding reduced form coefficients in (7-33). In other words,

$$a \triangleq \frac{\alpha}{1-\beta} \tag{7-36}$$

$$b \triangleq \frac{\beta}{1-\beta} \tag{7-37}$$

where $\triangleq$ means "is a consistent estimator of," or "equals in the limit." Our conclusion can be stated even more strongly: Since the requirements of OLS are met (in particular, e and I are independent), a and b are Gauss-Markov estimators: In the class of linear unbiased estimators, they have minimum variance.

These two equations (7-36) and (7-37) can be solved for estimates of α and β. For simplicity, we confine our attention to β, which can be consistently estimated by solving the last equation (7-37):

$$\hat{\beta} = \frac{b}{1+b} \tag{7-38}$$

This solution can be written more explicitly by noting from (7-10) that the OLS estimator b in (7-35) would be

$$b = \frac{s_{IC}}{s_{II}} \tag{7-39}$$

Substituting (7-39) into (7-38)

$$\hat{\beta} = \frac{s_{IC}/s_{II}}{1 + s_{IC}/s_{II}}$$

$$\hat{\beta} = \frac{s_{IC}}{s_{II} + s_{IC}} \tag{7-40}$$

To simplify the denominator, we return to the identity

$$Y = C + I \qquad \text{(7-26) repeated}$$

and take covariances of I with all these variables, obtaining

$$s_{IY} = s_{IC} + s_{II} \tag{7-41}$$

When this is substituted into (7-40), we obtain

$$\hat{\beta} = \frac{s_{IC}}{s_{IY}} \tag{7-42}$$

As promised, this is exactly the same as the IV estimator (7-30). This is not just a coincidence. If we had taken the trouble to estimate the other parameter α, the ILS estimator would again coincide with the IV estimator. This, in fact, is always true: Whenever ILS is feasible,[10] it will coincide with IV.

A final warning: Although b is an unbiased estimator of $\beta/(1-\beta)$ in (7-37), $b/(1+b)$ in (7-38) is a biased estimator of β, because unbiasedness is preserved only by linear transformations.[11] However, consistency is preserved, so $\hat{\beta}$ is a consistent estimator and, therefore, *asymptotically* unbiased.

To recapitulate, ILS involves transforming the original structure (7-25) and (7-26) into its reduced form (7-33) and (7-34). OLS estimation of the parameters of the reduced form [such as $\beta/(1-\beta)$] is fully justified, and provides unbiased, consistent estimates. When these are transformed back into estimates of the structural parameters (such as β), the resulting estimates are consistent, despite small-sample bias. It is not surprising that these estimates coincide with the IV estimates, since the same exogenous variable I is used as the regressor in ILS and the instrumental variable in IV.

PROBLEMS

7-1 Suppose that the true consumption function is $C = 10 + .6Y$ and the following combinations of C, Y, and I have been observed:

C	Y	I
46	60	14
31	45	14
61	75	14
58	80	22
43	65	22
73	95	22
70	100	30
55	85	30
85	115	30

[10] Cases where ILS estimation is not feasible are considered in the next chapter.

[11] To illustrate, since $6 + 2b$ is a linear transformation of b [and b is an unbiased estimator of $\beta/(1-\beta)$], it follows that $6 + 2b$ is an unbiased estimator of $6 + 2[\beta/(1-\beta)]$. On the other hand, $b/(1+b)$ is *not* a linear transformation of b; hence $b/(1+b)$ is a biased estimator of $[\beta/(1-\beta)]/\{1 + [\beta/(1-\beta)]\} = \beta$.

(a) Graph the true consumption function and the scatter of C and Y observations.

(b) Regress C on Y using OLS, and graph the estimated consumption function. Is it consistent?

(c) Estimate the consumption function:

(i) Using I as an instrumental variable (IV). Graph this estimated consumption function. Is it consistent?

(ii) Using indirect least squares (ILS).

(d) Explain why this small sample is a lucky one. What would you expect if your small sample is less lucky?

*7-2 Prove footnote 9 preceding equation (7-35).

7-3 To estimate the consumption model (7-25), suppose the covariance matrix (or table) of Y, C, I has been computed for a sample as follows:

$$\begin{bmatrix} s_{YY} & s_{CY} & s_{IY} \\ s_{YC} & s_{CC} & s_{IC} \\ s_{YI} & s_{CI} & s_{II} \end{bmatrix} = \begin{bmatrix} 130 & 100 & 30 \\ 100 & 80 & 20 \\ 30 & 20 & 10 \end{bmatrix}$$

(a) Find consistent estimates for the marginal propensity to consume, and the investment multiplier.

(b) Estimate the marginal propensity to consume by applying OLS to the consumption function directly. Is this estimate consistent? Using a diagram, explain this to a student whose statistics is limited to understanding OLS.

(c) Which of the above estimators are:

(i) Biased asymptotically?

(ii) Biased (even slightly) in small samples?

*7-5 ERRORS IN BOTH VARIABLES

While systems of simultaneous equations provide the commonest example of correlation between regressor and error, we consider another important example in this section.

(a) The Problem

Since this section has nothing to do with simultaneous equations, consider the simple single-equation model

$$Y = \alpha + \beta X + e \tag{7-43}$$

The error term e is random (stochastic), and includes measurement error as well as sampling variability. Until now it has been assumed that only the dependent variable Y has such an error term. In many applications this assumption must be questioned. When X, as well as Y, is subject to error, how does this complicate our problem of estimating the relation of Y to X? If the *exactly related* values are denoted by X_0 and Y_0, let us as usual assume a linear relation, that is,

$$Y_0 = \alpha + \beta X_0 \tag{7-44}$$

where α and β are the parameters to be estimated.[12] As before, we continue to assume that the Y_0 value is perturbed by an error e, yielding the *measured* value

$$Y = Y_0 + e \tag{7-45}$$

The new feature is that the X_0 value is also perturbed,[13] by an error v, yielding the *measured* value

$$X = X_0 + v \tag{7-46}$$

Substituting (7-45) and (7-46) into (7-44),

$$(Y - e) = \alpha + \beta(X - v)$$

$$Y = \alpha + \beta X + (e - \beta v) \tag{7-47}$$

The problem is to consistently estimate α and β, using only the measured variables X and Y.

Before developing an estimation technique when both variables are in error, consider the two limiting cases in which only one variable is subject to error.

The familiar case occurs when only Y is subject to error, and v, the error in X, is zero; then equation (7-47) reduces to the familiar model of Chapter 2:

$$Y = \alpha + \beta X + e \qquad \text{(7-48)}$$

(7-43) repeated

---

[12] It is very important to realize that this discussion is concerned with *estimation of parameters*. If we are only concerned with *prediction* (e.g., of Y from X), then there is no need to go to all this trouble. The OLS estimator of Y on X would be the optimal predictor.

[13] A classic example is Friedman's permanent income model (Friedman 1957), where permanent income is related to permanent consumption. Although he argues that this relation is precise, neither of these variables can be measured. So he measures actual income and consumption instead. And *each* includes a stochastic disturbance (which he refers to as transient income and transient consumption).

and an OLS regression of Y on X is the appropriate way of estimating α and β.

At the other extreme, suppose that only X is subject to error. Then e (the error in Y) is zero, with neither a measurement nor stochastic error in Y; then (7-47) becomes

$$Y = \alpha + \beta(X - v) \tag{7-49}$$

Or

$$X = -\frac{\alpha}{\beta} + \frac{1}{\beta} Y + v$$

which may be written

$$X = \alpha_* + \beta_* Y + v$$

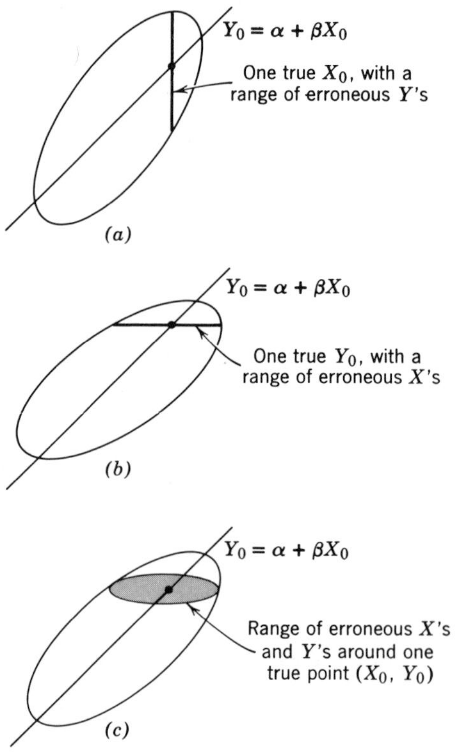

FIGURE 7-4 How a single relation of Y_0 to X_0 gives rise to different sample scatters, depending on errors in variables. (*a*) Error in Y only. (*b*) Error in X only. (*c*) Error in both variables.

In this case, an OLS regression of X on Y is the appropriate way of estimating α_* and β_*, thence estimating α and β.

These conclusions are reviewed in Figure 7-4, which shows how a single true relation of Y_0 to X_0 may generate quite different sample scatters. In Figure 7-4*a*, the error is in Y alone, and a regression of Y on X is required. On the other hand, in Figure 7-4*b*, the error is in X alone; it is easy to see that a regression of Y on X fitted to this scatter would be inappropriate, since it would underestimate[14] β. Instead, a regression of X on Y is required.

Finally, the general case in which both variables are in error is shown in Figure 7-4*c*; intuitively, it follows from panels (*a*) and (*b*) that the greater the error in Y relative to the error in X, the closer will the OLS regression of Y on X lie to the true line; and the greater the error in X relative to the error in Y, the closer will the OLS regression of X on Y lie to the true line. Clearly, if we have prior knowledge of the ratio of these errors (σ_e^2/σ_v^2, which we denote as λ), then we can use this in order to obtain the proper compromise between the two OLS regressions, as follows.

(b) Solution when the Error Ratio is Known

Suppose we know the ratio of error variances

$$\lambda = \frac{\sigma_e^2}{\sigma_v^2} \tag{7-50}$$

We emphasize, as in the footnote immediately following (7-45), that e includes both stochastic and measurement errors in Y; but v may be only measurement error in X, depending on how Y is judged to depend on X. We assume further that

$$e \text{ and } v \text{ are uncorrelated} \tag{7-51}$$

and

$$e \text{ and } v \text{ are each uncorrelated with the true values } X_0 \text{ and } Y_0 \tag{7-52}$$

It is not necessary to assume that e and v are normal.

To derive a consistent estimate of β, first take covariances of X with all variables in (7-47):

$$s_{XY} = \beta s_{XX} + s_{X(e-\beta v)} \tag{7-53}$$

[14] As an exercise, sketch in freehand a fitted regression of Y on X, observing that its slope is substantially less than the true slope β. Then in Figure 7-4*c*, sketch in the two OLS fits, noting how both are off target.

Now the sample covariance is approximately equal (in the limit, exactly equal) to the population covariance, σ; that is,

$$s_{X(e-\beta v)} \triangleq \sigma_{X(e-\beta v)} \tag{7-54}$$

From (7-46)

$$s_{X(e-\beta v)} \triangleq \sigma_{(X_0+v)(e-\beta v)}$$

From (7-51) and (7-52)

$$\triangleq \sigma_{v(-\beta v)}$$

$$\triangleq -\beta\sigma_{vv}$$

Thus

$$s_{X(e-\beta v)} \triangleq -\beta\sigma_v^2 \tag{7-55}$$

When (7-55) is substituted into (7-53),

$$s_{XY} \triangleq \beta s_{XX} - \beta\sigma_v^2 \tag{7-56}$$

Here we explicitly see how the correlation of the error with the regressor has produced the extra term $\beta\sigma_v^2$; this explicitly confirms that OLS regression of Y on X (which ignores this last term) would produce a biased estimator of β. To correctly estimate β, we need a second estimating equation because there are two unknowns, β and σ_v^2. We therefore take covariances of Y with all variables in (7-47), obtaining

$$s_{YY} \triangleq \beta s_{XY} + s_{Y(e-\beta v)} \tag{7-57}$$

Just as (7-53) was reduced to (7-56), we can now reduce (7-57) to

$$s_{YY} \triangleq \beta s_{XY} + \sigma_e^2 \tag{7-58}$$

From (7-50)

$$s_{YY} \triangleq \beta s_{XY} + \lambda\sigma_v^2 \tag{7-59}$$

Equations (7-56) and (7-59) are our two estimating equations in two unknowns β and σ_v^2. (We now see why λ must be known; if it is not, we are stuck with (7-56) and (7-58)—two equations in three unknowns, with no solution.) Before proceeding, we pause to recall the special cases diagrammed in Figure 7-4.

1. If $\sigma_v^2 = 0$ (no error in X), then $\lambda = \infty$. In this case, (7-56) can be used alone to estimate β, since the last term disappears. The solution corresponds, as expected, to the OLS regression of Y on X:

$$\hat{\beta} = \frac{s_{XY}}{s_{XX}}$$

2. If $\sigma_e^2 = 0$ (no error in Y), $\lambda = 0$ in (7-50), and (7-59) can be used alone to estimate β, since its last term disappears. As an exercise, it may be shown that the solution

$$\hat{\beta} = \frac{s_{YY}}{s_{XY}}$$

corresponds, as expected, to the OLS regression of X on Y.
3. For intermediate values of λ, it may be proved that intermediate values of $\hat{\beta}$ are obtained. Thus, an economist who doesn't know λ may at least be confident that the correct solution for β is bounded by the above two estimates. An important case occurs when the stochastic error in Y dominates the other errors in (7-50); in this case, λ becomes very large, with the appropriate estimate approaching the OLS regression of Y on X given in 1.

If λ is known, the only problem is to solve (7-56) and (7-59)—our two estimating equations in two unknowns (β and σ_v^2). Unfortunately, they are nonlinear, so their solution will be a little complicated. Let us eliminate σ_v^2 (the nuisance unknown) by first solving (7-59):

$$\sigma_v^2 \triangleq \frac{1}{\lambda}(s_{YY} - \beta s_{XY}) \tag{7-60}$$

When this is substituted into (7-56),

$$s_{XY} \triangleq \beta s_{XX} - \frac{\beta}{\lambda}(s_{YY} - \beta s_{XY}) \tag{7-61}$$

which is a quadratic equation in β. By multiplying through by λ and collecting terms, we find

$$-s_{XY}\beta^2 + (s_{YY} - \lambda s_{XX})\beta + \lambda s_{XY} \triangleq 0$$

Finally, dividing by $-s_{XY}$,

$$\beta^2 - \left(\frac{s_{YY} - \lambda s_{XX}}{s_{XY}}\right)\beta - \lambda \triangleq 0$$

or

$$\beta^2 - (2\theta)\beta - \lambda \triangleq 0 \tag{7-62}$$

where

$$\theta = \frac{s_{YY} - \lambda s_{XX}}{2s_{XY}} \tag{7-63}$$

The solution to (7-62) is given by the standard quadratic formula[15]:

$$\boxed{\hat{\beta} = \theta \pm \sqrt{\theta^2 + \lambda}} \tag{7-64}$$

Which of the two solutions is appropriate? Since λ is positive, $\sqrt{\theta^2 + \lambda}$ is greater, in absolute value, than θ. Thus, the selection of the $\pm$ sign in (7-64) determines the sign of $\hat{\beta}$. This indicates choosing the $\pm$ sign to agree with the sign of s_{XY}. For example, when s_{XY} is positive, that is, a positive relationship is observed between X and Y, then $\hat{\beta}$ is chosen to be positive too.

(c) Solution by IV

In the fortunate circumstance that an instrumental variable Z is available, we will have an alternative, simpler solution.

Specifically, we suppose that Z is uncorrelated with both errors e and v. Then it will be uncorrelated with the error term of (7-47). Assuming as required that Z is correlated with X, it then provides a consistent estimator of β; taking covariances of all terms in (7-47) with Z yields

$$\hat{\beta} = \frac{s_{ZY}}{s_{ZX}} \tag{7-65}$$

Once an adequate instrumental variable Z has been found, this is a very simple, straightforward method. The problem is finding an instrumental variable that is not only free of correlation with e and v, but also highly correlated with X. [If its correlation with X is low, then the denominator of (7-65) will be close to zero, and the resulting estimate will be unstable]. There may also, of course, be the problem of selecting between several equally good (or bad) instruments, with the resulting estimate being highly sensitive to the one arbitrarily chosen. In summary, all our earlier reservations against instrumental variables apply here. Their major justification is consistency; but this is a large sample property that may provide little comfort in small sample estimation. If only questionable instrumental variables are available (with low correlation with X), then it may be better to use the technique of subsection (b), using an arbitrary but reasonable value for λ. At least this technique guarantees an estimate bounded by the regressions of X on Y and Y on X, whereas IV does not.

[15] With the additional assumption that the errors e and v are normal, MLE yields the same solution. (For details, see Johnston, 1972.)

PROBLEMS

7-4 In Figure 7-4, it was shown how one true relation of Y to X gave rise to three different observed scatters. Draw a diagram to show how three different true relations might yield the same observed scatter. (To reemphasize, in Figure 7-4, the three lines are the same, and the scatters differ; in this problem the scatters are the same, and thus the three lines must differ.)

7-5 Assuming no error in Y, what is wrong with this analysis:

First, we may write (7-49) as

$$Y = \alpha + \beta X + (-\beta v)$$

where the error $(-\beta v)$ is just a multiple of v; hence it has zero mean, etc. We therefore take OLS regression of Y on X to estimate α and β consistently.

7-6 Suppose that from a scatter of observations,

$$s_{XY} = 60$$

$$s_{XX} = 50$$

$$s_{YY} = 100$$

In each of the following circumstances, estimate β in the model (7-47) as well as you can. Assume, from (a) to (e), that e and v are independent:

(a) $\sigma_v^2 = 0$
(b) $\sigma_e^2 = 0$
(c) $\sigma_e^2 = \sigma_v^2$
(d) $\sigma_e^2 = 2\sigma_v^2$
(e) σ_e^2 and σ_v^2 are completely unknown

Now suppose that e and v are correlated, and:

(f) $\sigma_e^2 = 2\sigma_v^2$
(g) A random variable Z is observable, which is uncorrelated with both errors e and v, yet correlated with X and Y. In fact, $s_{ZX} = 100$ and $s_{ZY} = 150$.

8

THE IDENTIFICATION PROBLEM

The previous chapter sets out the difficulties encountered by an economist fitting a consumption function to a scatter of observations of consumption and income. Even worse difficulties may be encountered if he attempts to fit a demand curve to a scatter of price and quantity observations, as we will see.

8-1 UNIDENTIFIED EQUATIONS[1]: A SUPPLY AND DEMAND EXAMPLE

In order to show how badly things may go wrong, let us again assume that we are omniscient. Thus, we can distinguish between what is really going on, and what the statistician can observe. Suppose that the price P and quantity Q demanded and supplied in a competitive market are determined by the simple model:

$$\text{Demand:} \quad Q = \alpha + \beta P + e \tag{8-1}$$

$$\text{Supply:} \quad Q = \gamma + \delta P + f \tag{8-2}$$

For simplicity, we assume that the error terms e and f have the characteristics set out in Section 2-4. Moreover, for the moment (in Section 8-1), we also assume that e and f are known to be independent, and symmetrically distributed around zero.

Before we become involved in identification problems, we must ask whether this model is mathematically complete, that is, whether there are enough equations to get a unique solution for the two endogenous variables (P, Q). To solve for these two unknowns requires two equations,[2] which we

[1] An unidentified equation is customarily called *underidentified*, as explained in Section 8-5.

[2] In general, the model will be complete if there are as many equations as unknowns. These equations, of course, must be linearly independent; in our example, β and δ must be unequal (i.e., in Figure 8-1*a* the demand and supply lines must have different slopes so that they intersect).

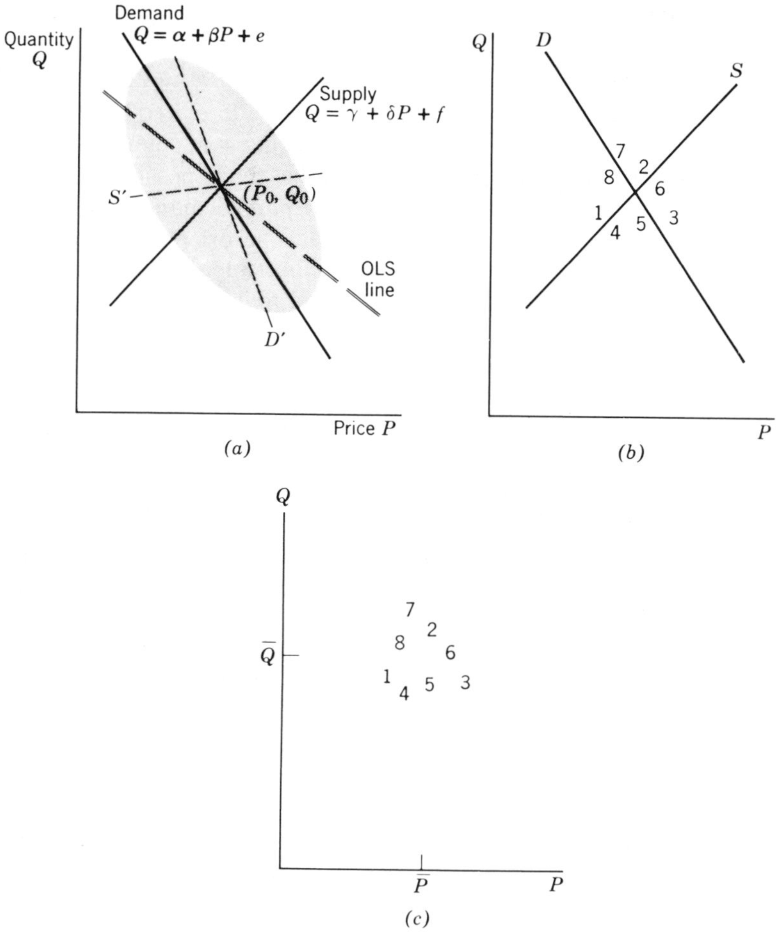

FIGURE 8-1 (*a*) Population of price and quantity determined by true D and S; or equally well by bogus D' and S'. (*b*) Sample of eight prices and quantities determined by true D and S. (*c*) The sample that the statistician observes.

have. It is important to recognize and dispose of this issue before proceeding, because the problem of identification requires a similar mathematical analysis: It, too, involves comparing equations and unknowns, although in an entirely different context. In the discussion that follows we deal only with models that are mathematically complete; that is, there are enough equations so that the endogenous variables are uniquely determined (in terms of exogenous variables and errors).

In Figure 8-1, economists are warned that their familiar Q and P axes have been switched. This is convenient so long as it is assumed (as we have for both demand and supply) that Q is a function of P. Figure 8-1*a* shows true demand D and supply S (which we assume to know through omniscience), and the ellipse of concentration for the population of generated observations. If the errors e and f are normal, then P and Q are bivariate normal[3] and the ellipse of concentration may be interpreted as a horizontal slice of the probability density function—like slice q in Figure 5-7.

The orientation of the P, Q distribution has many possibilities, depending not only on the slopes β and δ of the supply and demand curves, but also on the variances of the errors e and f. But the orientation of the P, Q distribution does have one restriction—the elliptical joint distribution must be cut into four equal quarters by the D and S lines. For if one quarter, for example the upper quarter, were more probable, then positive e and positive f would occur together more than one-quarter of the time, which violates the independence assumption.[4]

We show the whole population in Figure 8-1*a* in order to distinguish between two problems. The first we may refer to as the "statistical" problem of estimating the population from a sample. But even if this problem were solved (i.e., even if the population ellipse in Figure 8-1*a* were known), the quite different problem of *identification* would remain. For we see that a bogus demand D' and supply S' could generate exactly the same population: Note that S' and D' also cut the elliptical distribution into four equal quarters. Furthermore, there are an unlimited number of bogus demand and supply systems that we could draw in—all of which would generate this same population ellipse. And there is no way of distinguishing between bogus systems and the true one. Thus, even if the statistician knew the population, he could not reconstruct the true D and S curves, since further information is necessary.

If the statistician were to fit an OLS line in Figure 8-1*a*, he would obtain a curve that was neither D nor S, but rather a combination of the two.[5]

---

[3] To prove this, we look ahead to the reduced form equations (8-3b) and (8-4b):

$$P = P_0 + u$$

$$Q = Q_0 + v$$

where the errors u and v are linear combinations of the structural errors e and f, and hence are jointly normal with zero mean. Thus, P and Q are jointly normally distributed about the mean (P_0, Q_0).

[4] If e and f are independent, then

$$\begin{aligned}\Pr(e > 0 \text{ and } f > 0) &= \Pr(e > 0)\Pr(f > 0)\\ &= (\tfrac{1}{2})(\tfrac{1}{2})\\ &= \tfrac{1}{4}\end{aligned}$$

[5] Since the error e in demand is less than the error f in supply, the population of observations is oriented fairly close to the demand D. Since the OLS line is fairly close to the D line, the statistician might be tempted to erroneously call the OLS fit a demand curve.

In order to simplify the figures, from now on we will show only a sample of a few observations that are representative of the population. This is the kind of data that an economist observes. But remember that even if the economist were blessed with an infinite amount of data (and thus knew the population distribution of P, Q as given by the ellipse in Figure 8-1*a*), the problem of identification would remain exactly the same: There are many demand/supply systems that could generate this population, and how can the true one be discovered?

8-2 IDENTIFICATION USING PRIOR INFORMATION

A typical sample of eight observations is shown in Figure 8-1*b*. Demand and supply have generated observations in four segments, with an observation in a specific segment the result of a specific combination of signs of e and f. Thus, for example, observations 1 and 8 were the result of a negative e (dropping these observations below the demand curve) and a positive f (raising these observations above the supply curve). Similarly, observations 2 and 7 were the result of a positive e and a positive f, and so on. Note that since e and f are independent, the eight observations are distributed evenly, with two falling in each of the four segments. This is a typical pattern; although it is not guaranteed for such a small sample, it is guaranteed for the population.

The statistician will be able to estimate one or both of the D and S lines if he is lucky enough to have certain kinds of prior information. We provide three examples:

1. Suppose he has prior knowledge of the slope β of demand. In this case, he would be able to distinguish between the true demand and bogus demands. He could estimate the intercept α of demand from his scatter in Figure 8-1*c* by taking a line with slope β and raising it to just the right level so as to split the eight observed points into two equal halves with four in each. (The error e in demand was assumed to be positive and negative equally often.)

   It is very interesting that the supply line can be identified too. It would be placed so that supply, along with the known demand, would split the eight observations into four equal quarters. (This equal division follows, since e and f are assumed independent.) Although there is not a unique way to do this in a small sample, there is a unique way in the population, as can be seen in Figure 8-1*a*. Thus, we have seen how prior knowledge of β allowed us to identify demand; and the further prior knowledge that e and f are independent allowed us to identify supply also.

2. The independence of the error terms is a useful piece of prior information for identification purposes, just like knowledge of a specific parameter. However, for the balance of this discussion, we no longer assume that e and f are independent. Identification will then require some other element of prior information. Suppose that our second piece of prior information is knowledge of δ, the slope of supply; (we continue to assume prior knowledge of β). Demand can now be identified, just as before, by raising a line with slope β to split our observations into two equal halves. Moreover, supply can also now be identified in exactly the same way, by raising a line with slope δ to split our observation into halves. (Note that this does not generally divide our observations into four equal quarters; there is no necessity for doing this, since we are no longer assuming that e and f are independent.)

   This is easily verified algebraically by examining the two reduced form equations in P and Q. Substitute (8-2) into (8-1):

$$\gamma + \delta P + f = \alpha + \beta P + e$$

$$P = \frac{\gamma - \alpha}{\beta - \delta} + \frac{f - e}{\beta - \delta} \tag{8-3a}$$

or, in simpler notation,

$$P = P_0 + u \tag{8-3b}$$

Similarly

$$Q = \frac{\beta\gamma - \alpha\delta}{\beta - \delta} + \frac{\beta f - \delta e}{\beta - \delta} \tag{8-4a}$$

or

$$Q = Q_0 + v \tag{8-4b}$$

Equations (8-3a) and (8-4a) comprise the reduced form of (8-1) and (8-2). Since e and f are on average zero, u and v (being a linear combination of e and f) must also be on average zero. Thus, the average values of (8-3a) and (8-4a) provide the two estimating equations

$$\bar{P} \triangleq \frac{\gamma - \alpha}{\beta - \delta} \tag{8-5}$$

$$\bar{Q} \triangleq \frac{\beta\gamma - \alpha\delta}{\beta - \delta} \tag{8-6}$$

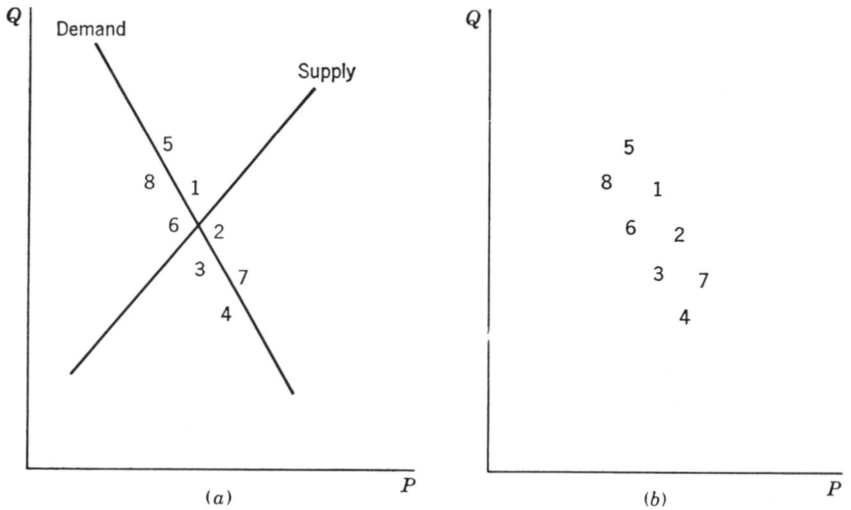

FIGURE 8-2 (*a*) How demand and supply determine a sample of eight P, Q points when supply has a much larger error variance than demand. (*b*) The sample that the statistician observes.

The statistician has no difficulty in calculating $\bar{P}$ and $\bar{Q}$ from his observations in Figure 8-1*c*; thus, he can estimate the two reduced form coefficients $[(\gamma - \alpha)/(\beta - \delta)]$ and $[(\beta\gamma - \alpha\delta)/(\beta - \delta)]$. But without further information he cannot transform these back into corresponding estimates of the four structural coefficients α, β, γ, and δ, since there is an infinite number of values for these that correspond. This is the essence of the identification problem, and it is easy to see why the problem remains even if the statistical problem of estimating the reduced form coefficients could be perfectly solved. Even if the two reduced form coefficients were known exactly, unique values for the four structural coefficients could still not be determined.

To put the problem in another way, (8-5) and (8-6) are two equations that cannot be solved for the four unknown structural coefficients. But if the statistician has prior knowledge of any two (say β and δ), he can solve for the other two (α and γ).

3. Prior information about error variance can also be used to identify. Suppose that one error is known to be zero (or, in practice, that one error is very much smaller than another). For example, suppose the statistician knows *a priori* that the error e in demand has a variance much smaller than the variance of the error u in supply. Observations typically generated by such a system are shown in Figure 8-2*a*; and the

statistician who fits a line to what he observes in Figure 8-2*b* will generally come up with a good approximation to the demand curve.[6] If there is no error in demand (σ_e^2 is known to be zero), then all observations in Figure 8-2*a* will fall exactly on the demand curve, which is, therefore, identified by the disturbances in supply. But supply remains unidentified; this would require another piece of prior information.

8-3 IDENTIFICATION USING PRIOR INFORMATION ABOUT EXOGENOUS VARIABLES

Although very useful, the kinds of prior knowledge illustrated in the previous section are seldom available to economists. We therefore turn now to a more realistic type of prior knowledge.

To begin untangling the problem of unidentification in Figure 8-1, the economist might ask about the nature of the supply error. For example, if the product is agricultural, its supply is sensitive to variations in rainfall R. Thus[7] it may be reasonable to redefine our model to explicitly include this exogenous variable:

$$\text{Demand:} \quad Q = \alpha + \beta P + e \qquad \text{(8-8)}$$
(8-1) repeated

$$\text{Supply:} \quad Q = \gamma + \delta P + \theta R + g \qquad \text{(8-9)}$$
(8-2) modified

Figure 8-3 reproduces the sample shown in Figure 8-1.

Identification is no longer hopeless, if the statistician can pin down observations 7 and 8 as occurring when rainfall was observed to be particularly heavy, and observations 3 and 5 when rainfall was light. Since the geometry is not too clear, we will see algebraically how this extended model permits identification of demand.

---

[6] Historically, research on the demand for agricultural products was undertaken before knowledge of identification difficulties. Fortunately demand for these necessities was relatively stable, while supply was subject to large shifts with weather. In such circumstances, fitted regressions turned out to be reasonably accurate approximations to demand. But had the relative shifts in the functions been reversed, these studies would have yielded estimates of supply rather than demand.

[7] Examination of residual error is a sound general technique that was recommended before—in Chapters 2 and 3. Thus, the error f of (8-2) may be thought of as

$$f = \theta R + g$$
$$= \text{part explained systematically by rainfall} + \text{residual} \qquad \text{(8-7)}$$

When (8-7) is substituted into (8-2), we obtain (8-9).

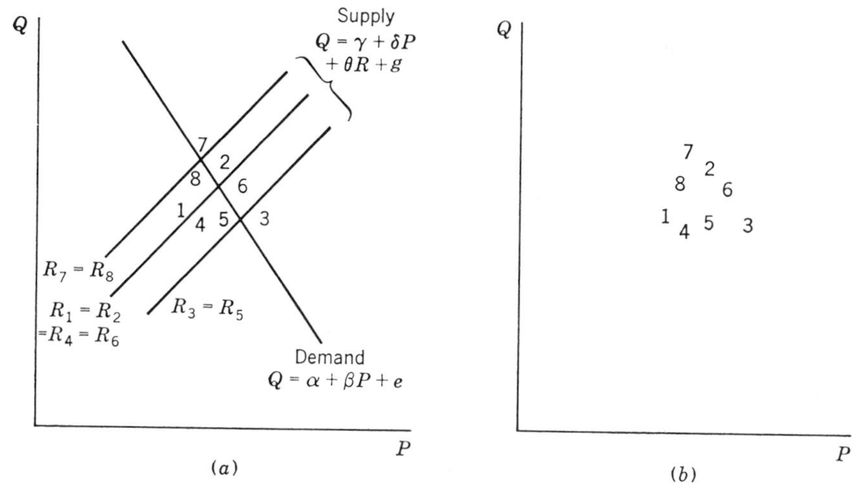

FIGURE 8-3 The same data as Figure 8-1, generated by an extended model that includes exogenous rainfall. (*a*) How demand and supply generate sample. (*b*) The sample the statistician observes.

Since R is an exogenous variable and uncorrelated with e we may use it as an instrumental variable on the demand equation (8-8), obtaining

$$s_{QR} = \hat{\beta} s_{PR} \tag{8-10}$$

Thus

$$\hat{\beta} = \frac{s_{QR}}{s_{PR}}$$

Thus, knowledge of R, as we hoped, allows us to identify and estimate demand.

When we similarly use R as an instrumental variable on the supply equation (8-9), we obtain

$$s_{QR} = \hat{\delta} s_{PR} + \hat{\theta} s_{RR} \tag{8-11}$$

Since R is the only exogenous variable available as an instrumental variable, we are confined to this single equation in the two unknowns $\hat{\delta}$ and $\hat{\theta}$, for which there is no unique solution. Thus, supply is not identified.

We can now review how the exogenous variable R helps in identification. For each of the demand and supply equations, R provided an estimating equation when used as an instrumental variable. Yet in the case of the supply equation, R appeared with an additional parameter θ that had to be estimated, in a sense canceling its benefit. Thus, R could be used to identify only demand—the equation from which it was excluded.

From another point of view, we might say that the demand equation was identified because the coefficient of R in that equation was known to be zero. Hence, we see again that it is *prior* knowledge that identifies an equation.

8-4 REQUIREMENT FOR IDENTIFICATION, IN GENERAL

We have seen how identification of an equation is made possible by an exogenous variable that is excluded from that equation. Thus, we may guess the condition required to identify an equation in general, when the only kind of prior knowledge is the exclusion of certain variables by virtue of a zero coefficient:

Order Condition Necessary to Identify an Equation

The number of *exogenous*[8] variables *excluded* from the equation must at least equal the number of *endogenous* variables *included* on the right-hand side of the equation. (8-12)

We now illustrate (8-12) with two more examples, followed by an informal proof.

Example 8-1

In Figure 8-4, supply shifts with rainfall R, and demand with national income Y. (We are careful to specify that in this model, unlike the model of the previous chapter, Y is exogenous; that is, Y affects demand for this good, but the market for this particular good does not noticeably affect Y.) Note the unpromising scatter of Q and P observations facing the statistician; it seems unlikely she can identify either demand or supply. Yet from the estimating equations shown just below the diagram, it is clear that she can generally identify *both*. For example, to identify demand, both Y and R may be used as instrumental variables. The two resulting equations are sufficient to solve for estimates of the two parameters β and η. We note that condition (8-12) is satisfied: In the demand equation, there is one excluded exogenous variable R that was instrumental in estimating the parameter of the one

[8] Strictly speaking in this chapter the term exogenous should be replaced by the broader term predetermined, which includes lagged endogenous variables as well as exogenous variables.

included endogenous variable P on the right-hand side. A similar argument shows that the supply equation can be identified.

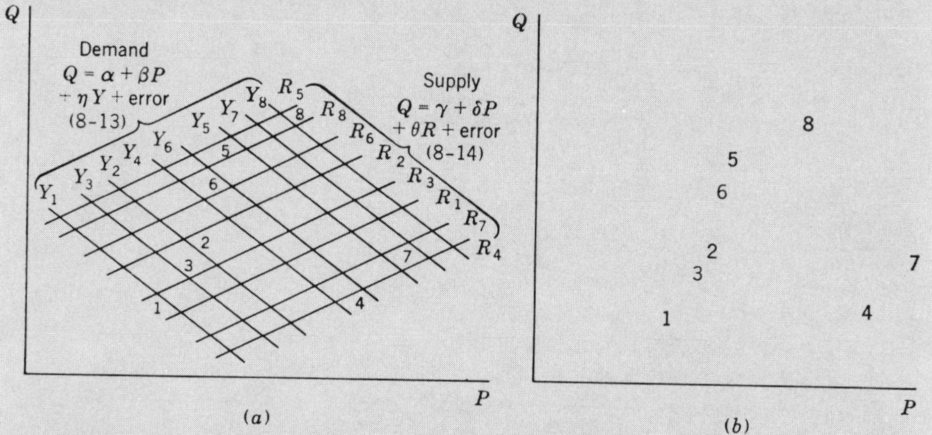

FIGURE 8-4 Supply and demand shifting with different exogenous variables. (*a*) How the sample is generated. (*b*) The sample that the statistician observes.

Estimating equations

Demand

Using Y as an instrumental variable: $s_{QY} = \hat{\beta} s_{PY} + \hat{\eta} s_{YY}$ (8-15)

Using R as an instrumental variable: $s_{QR} = \hat{\beta} s_{PR} + \hat{\eta} s_{YR}$ (8-16)

Two equations in two unknowns; solvable.

Supply

Using R as an instrumental variable: $s_{QR} = \hat{\delta} s_{PR} + \hat{\theta} s_{RR}$ (8-17)

Using Y as an instrumental variable: $s_{QY} = \hat{\delta} s_{PY} + \hat{\theta} s_{RY}$ (8-18)

Again, two equations in two unknowns; solvable.

Example 8-2

In Figure 8-5, both supply and demand shift with the same exogenous variable time (T). The scatter the statistician observes is a clearly defined one, and there seems to be some message in it. It turns out, however, that it is insufficient information; since it tells us too little about the shape of supply or demand, both remained unidentified. This is confirmed by examining the covariance equations written in directly below the diagram. Since there is now only one instrumental variable in the system (T), there is only one covariance estimating equation for demand, inadequate to determine uniquely the two unknowns, $\hat{\beta}$ and $\hat{\eta}$. The same is true for supply.

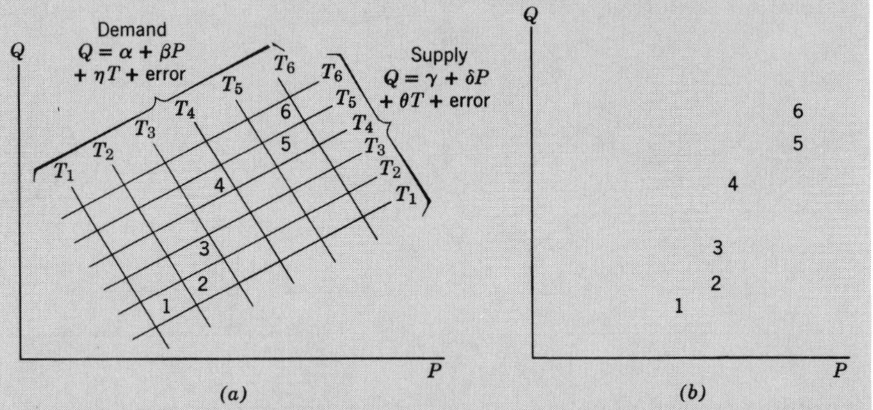

FIGURE 8-5 Supply and demand shifting with the same exogenous variable T. (*a*) How the sample is generated. (*b*) The sample that the statistician observes.

Estimating equations

Demand

Only instrumental variable available is T: $s_{QT} = \hat{\beta} s_{PT} + \hat{\eta} s_{TT}$

Only one equation in two unknowns; not uniquely solvable.

Supply

Only instrumental variable available is T: $s_{QT} = \hat{\delta} s_{PT} + \hat{\theta} s_{TT}$

Again, only one equation in two unknowns; not uniquely solvable.

To confirm statement (8-12) in general, we note that each exogenous variable included in the equation gives rise to an estimating covariance equation that will just "take care of" its parameter. But we still need an estimating equation for each parameter attached to the endogenous variables on the right-hand side of the equation. The only way to generate these estimating equations is by using *excluded* exogenous variables as instrumental variables; therefore, the number of these must at least equal the number of endogenous variables on the right-hand side.

We have now illustrated the identification problem from two points of view:

1. The reduced form was used in Section 8-2; however, this algebra would

have been far too cumbersome in the more complicated examples that followed; hence, in succeeding sections we have

2. Applied instruments.

We now pause to review the equivalence of these two approaches. It is always possible, given observations on the endogenous and exogenous variables, to estimate the coefficients of the reduced form. Unidentification means that this reduced form cannot be transformed back into a unique structure; instead there is a whole set of corresponding structures. The equivalent view of unidentification using the instrumental variable approach is that there are not enough prespecified zero coefficients in the equation being estimated; that is, there are not enough instrumental variables to estimate the nonzero coefficients.

PROBLEMS

8-1 Use the order condition (8-12) to determine which equations may be identified in this model. We denote the three exogenous variables by X_i, and the endogenous variables by Y_i:

$$Y_1 = \alpha_0 + \alpha_2 Y_2 + \alpha_3 Y_3 + \beta_1 X_1 + e_1$$

$$Y_2 = \gamma_0 + \gamma_1 Y_1 + \delta_1 X_1 + \delta_2 X_2 + \delta_3 X_3 + e_2$$

$$Y_3 = \theta_0 + \theta_1 Y_1 + \theta_2 Y_2 + \eta_1 X_1 + \eta_2 X_2 + e_3$$

8-2 Repeat Problem 8-1 using the following model:

$$Y_1 = \alpha_0 + \alpha_2 Y_2 + \beta_2 X_2 + e_1$$

$$Y_2 = \gamma_0 + \delta_1 X_1 + \delta_2 X_2 + \delta_3 X_3 + e_2$$

8-3 (a) In Problems 8-1 and 8-2, was it the long or short equations (equations with many or few terms) that were identified?

(b) True or false? If false, correct it.

(i) Prior knowledge is required to identify (pin down) the parameters of an equation. The absence of a variable from an equation may be regarded as the prior knowledge that its coefficient is zero. Thus, the short equations that have many zero coefficients are identified, while the long equations are not. To be precise, an equation may be identified if the number of terms (or number of coefficients) on the right-hand side is no more than the number of exogenous variables.

(ii) If one equation in a system can be identified, all equations can.

8-4 Referring to the model (8-8) and (8-9), suppose the following four observations have been collected:

P	Q	R
5	3	-1
4	4	1
3	3	1
4	2	-1

(a) Is demand identified?
(b) Calculate the deviations $p_i = P_i - \bar{P}$ and $q_i = Q_i - \bar{Q}$.
(c) Estimate β with the instrument R.
(d) Estimate β with OLS.
(e) Graph the four sample values of P, Q and show the two slopes calculated in (c) and (d). Which slope is appropriate?
(f) What is the sample correlation between R and the fitted residuals $\hat{e}$ when we use:

(i) The instrumental variable R.
(ii) OLS.

(g) What is the population correlation between R and e assumed to be? Which answer to part (f) does this match?

8-5 Suppose true D and S are given by:

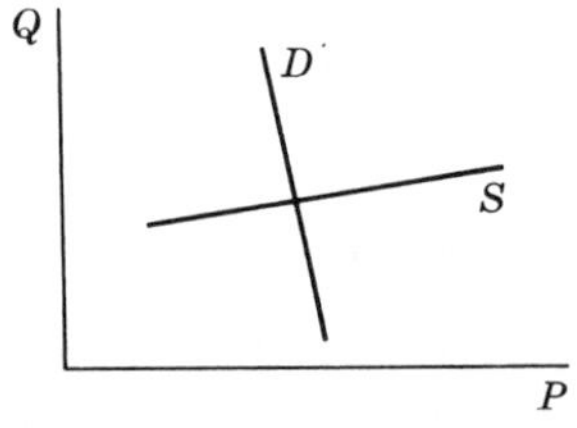

(a) Further suppose that the errors e and f are independent, with rectangular distributions with equal variance. As in the consumption function example in the previous chapter, draw in the parallelogram within which the population observations must fall. Note how this parallelogram is oriented along the demand line—even though error variances are equal. Why?
*(b) If e and f were normal with equal variance, sketch in the ellipse of concentration of P and Q.

8-5 OVERIDENTIFICATION

So far we have investigated primarily the algebraic problem of how many prior restrictions are necessary to identify the parameters of an equation. Suppose that we have established that a given equation is identified.[9] Thus, we know that its statistical estimation is possible. How should we proceed?

We first review some of our previous work with some additional geometry.

(a) An Unidentified Equation Reconsidered

In Section 8-3, we saw that supply was not identified, because there was only one estimating equation (8-11) for the two unknowns $\hat{\delta}$ and $\hat{\theta}$. This is illustrated in Figure 8-6*a*.

(b) Identified Equation

(i) Exactly Identified Equation. In Figure 8-4, supply was identified because there were two estimating equations (8-17) and (8-18) for the two unknowns $\hat{\delta}$ and $\hat{\theta}$ (see Figure 8-6*b*).

(ii) Overidentified Equation. Now consider a model where there is one more exogenous variable than we need to identify supply:

$$\text{Demand:} \quad Q = \alpha + \beta P + \eta T + \xi Y + e \tag{8-19}$$

$$\text{Supply:} \quad Q = \gamma + \delta P + \theta R + f \tag{8-20}$$

When we use the three exogenous variables T, Y, and R as instrumental variables on the supply equation (8-20), we obtain

$$s_{QT} = \hat{\delta} s_{PT} + \hat{\theta} s_{RT} \tag{8-21}$$

$$s_{QY} = \hat{\delta} s_{PY} + \hat{\theta} s_{RY} \tag{8-22}$$

$$s_{QR} = \hat{\delta} s_{PR} + \hat{\theta} s_{RR} \tag{8-23}$$

---

[9] Here we must be very careful. Equation (8-12) is only a necessary condition and, therefore, does not guarantee identification. The sufficient condition must also be fulfilled; but this is so complicated that it is deferred to Chapter 18.

For illustration, however, we can show how an equation may remain unidentified, even though the necessary condition (8-12) is just barely satisfied (so that there are exactly as many excluded exogenous variables as there are coefficients of endogenous variables to be estimated). Suppose two of the excluded exogenous variables are linearly related (e.g., one is a variable measured in feet, the other is the same variable measured in inches, as in Chapter 3). In this case, we get information essentially from only one of these instrumental variables, not both, and as a consequence we don't have enough information to identify.

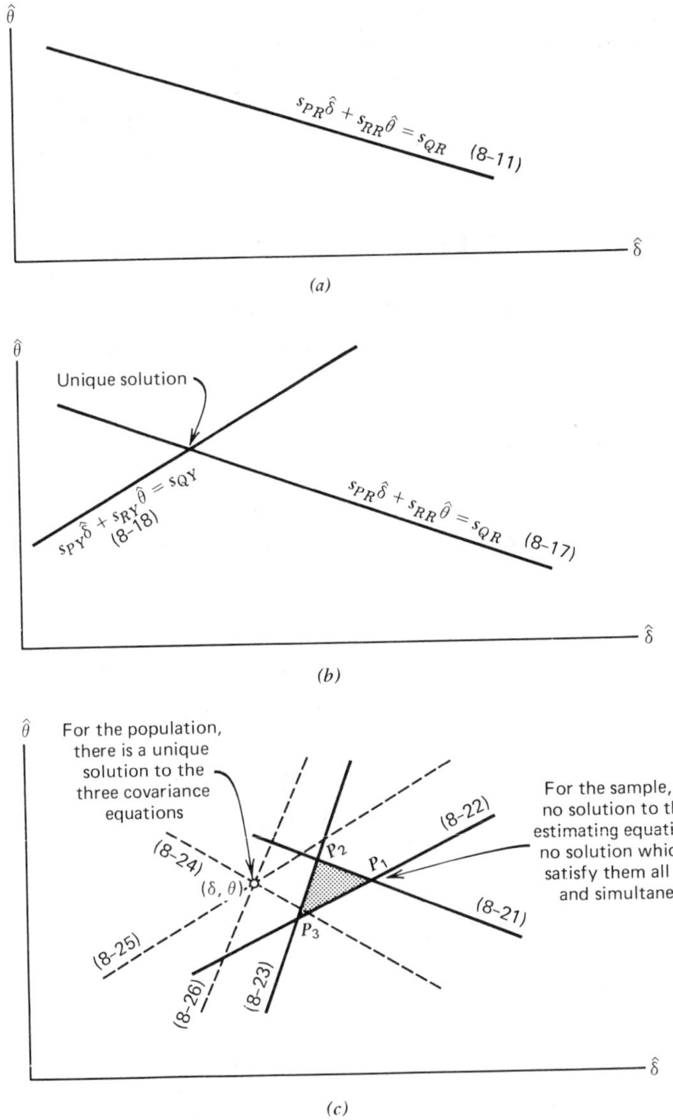

FIGURE 8-6 Graphs of estimating equations for the two unknown parameters in the supply equation. (*a*) Unidentified case, equation (8-11). (*b*) Exactly identified case, equations (8-17) and (8-18). (*c*) Overidentified case, equations (8-21) to (8-23).

We must remember that identification is not primarily a statistical issue. If an equation is unidentified, even an infinite sample won't help; on the other hand, if an equation is identified, δ and θ can be estimated—approximately if the sample is small, or exactly if it is infinite. Consider this latter case where the population (i.e., the set of σ's) is known. The three equations to estimate δ and θ become

$$\sigma_{QT} = \delta\sigma_{PT} + \theta\sigma_{RT} \quad (8\text{-}24)$$

$$\sigma_{QY} = \delta\sigma_{PY} + \theta\sigma_{RY} \quad (8\text{-}25)$$

$$\sigma_{QR} = \delta\sigma_{PR} + \theta\sigma_{RR} \quad (8\text{-}26)$$

[Note how these three population equations correspond to the sample equations (8-21) to (8-23).] These three equations (8-24) to (8-26) will have a unique solution[10]—the true parameters (δ, θ)—designated by the empty dot in Figure 8-6*c*.

So far, cases (i) and (ii) seem similar—they both are identified equations. But when we ask about *statistical* estimation, we see a difference. In case (ii) there are three statistical estimating equations (8-21) to (8-23) for only two unknowns; generally they will not have a unique solution because of statistical fluctuation; that is, the three lines in Figure 8-6*c* will not have a common intersection point.

What should the statistician do with these three equations (remember that he is not omniscient; he does not know σ_{QT}, but only the sample s_{QT}, etc.)? A naive answer is to use the first two equations (8-21) and (8-22), ignoring the information given by the third instrumental variable R. This means using solution P_1. It is the simplest answer to the "embarrassment of riches—more than enough instrumental variables." Yet another statistician might choose to use two different equations—(8-21) and (8-23)—thereby obtaining the estimate P_2. A third statistician might argue for point P_3.

Which of these three points is the best estimate? Or is there yet another point in or near the triangle $P_1 P_2 P_3$ that is even better? This is a tough problem to answer; it takes up most of Chapter 9, and has been the area of a vast amount of econometric research.

---

[10] *Proof.* Applying the *population* covariance operator for the instrumental variable T, to (8-20),

$$\sigma_{QT} = \delta\sigma_{PT} + \theta\sigma_{RT} + \sigma_{fT}$$

But the instrumental variable T and error f, by definition, have $\sigma_{fT} = 0$, so it must be true that

$$\sigma_{QT} = \delta\sigma_{PT} + \theta\sigma_{RT}$$

This equation states that (δ, θ) must satisfy (8-24). Similarly, (δ, θ) must satisfy (8-25) and (8-26), and so is a solution to the system.

We finally must explain the terms *exactly* identified and *over* identified. In Figure 8-6*c* we have just shown that two instrumental variables would have been enough to get some kind of estimate of the two parameters. In a naive sense, the third instrumental variable might be called "more than enough" or "too much."[11] For this reason, this case is called the overidentified case. By contrast, the case in Figure 8-6*b* is called the exactly identified case. Finally, the case in Figure 8-6*a* is sometimes called underidentified as well as unidentified.

PROBLEMS

8-6 Of the equations in Problem 8-2, which are exactly identified, and which are overidentified?

8-6 SUMMARY: IDENTIFICATION IN CONTEXT

There are three distinct issues in model-building:

1. Mathematical completeness of the model.
2. Identification of the parameters of an equation in the model.
3. Statistical estimation of the parameters of the equation.

Each issue must be settled satisfactorily before going on to the next. Whereas the first issue of completeness is pretty trivial, the second issue of identification takes up most of this chapter, while the third issue of statistical estimation is just introduced in this chapter and is developed in detail in Chapter 9.

We illustrate these issues by referring again to the supply-demand model of Section 8-5:

$$\text{Demand:} \quad Q = \alpha + \beta P + \eta T + \xi Y + e \qquad \text{(8-19) repeated}$$

$$\text{Supply:} \quad Q = \gamma + \delta P + \theta R + f \qquad \text{(8-20) repeated}$$

It is useful to describe this system with the flow diagram shown in Figure 8-7. Values of the exogenous variables and disturbances are fed into the structural system, and yield values for the endogenous variables. To further amplify these three issues:

[11] Yet, in a truer sense, all sample information is helpful in estimation, so that the third instrument is not too much. It is only too much for someone who is unprepared to use it wisely.

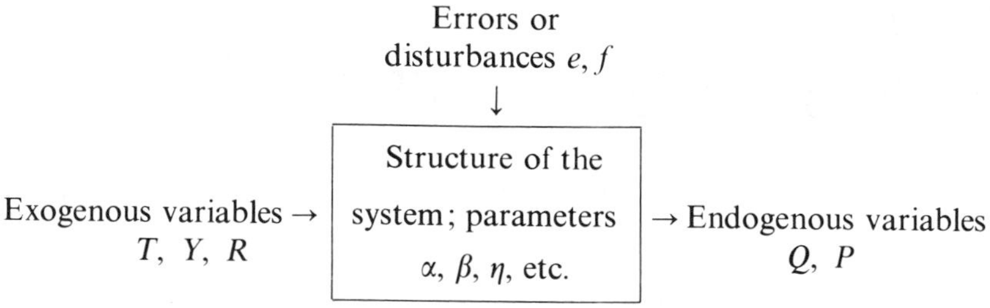

FIGURE 8-7 A schematic view of an econometric system.

1. *Mathematical completeness* means that if the errors, exogenous variables, and structural parameters are known, the endogenous variables are uniquely determined. It requires that the model have as many independent equations as endogenous variables.
2. *Identification* means that if the errors, exogenous variables, and endogenous variables are known, the structural parameters are uniquely determined. Unidentification occurs when a given set of disturbances and exogenous variables may be "passed through" several different structures, each yielding the same values for the endogenous variables. In this case, the true structure cannot be identified from a whole set of bogus structures.

   Identification of a single structural equation requires that there be enough prior information that some parameters are zero[12] to pin down the other parameters of the equation uniquely. Specifically, the order condition (8-12) for identification is that there must be at least as many omitted exogenous variables as there are endogenous variables included on the right-hand side.
3. Finally, suppose realistically that only a *sample* of the values of the exogenous and endogenous variables is known. *Statistical estimation* is the problem of estimating the structural parameters in such a way as to minimize the (estimated) errors in some sense; (compare to the estimation of parameters in Chapter 2—the objective is the same in either case).

   Statistical estimation is simple if there are exactly as many estimating covariance equations as unknown parameters (the exactly identified case). However, when we have more estimating covariance equations (the overidentified case), there remains a major problem of how to use all this information effectively.

---

[12] Or, alternatively, prior information about the error terms.

9

SELECTED ESTIMATING TECHNIQUES

9-1 TWO-STAGE LEAST SQUARES (2SLS)

Two-stage least squares, developed independently by Bassman (1957) and Thiel (1957), is one of the simplest solutions to the problem of overidentification. It provides estimators in the situation described in Figure 8-6*c*, where use of all available instrumental variables results in a set of estimating equations with no unique solution.

To show how 2SLS works, consider again the demand-supply model of Section 8-5:

$$\text{Demand:}\quad Q = \alpha + \beta P + \eta T + \xi Y + e \qquad (9\text{-}1)$$
(8-19) repeated

$$\text{Supply:}\quad Q = \gamma + \delta P + \theta R + f \qquad (9\text{-}2)$$
(8-20) repeated

where P, Q are endogenous, and T, Y, R are exogenous and independent of the errors e, f. Suppose we wish to estimate the second equation, which has the overidentified parameters. But suppose we had missed the whole point that supply is one equation in a simultaneous system, and had applied OLS to (9-2). What would happen? As shown in Chapter 7, we would get inconsistent estimates of γ, δ, and θ because one of our regressors (P) is an endogenous variable, hence is dependent on f. However, we can eliminate this problem if we can purge P of its dependence on f. This is the first stage, and it allows us then, in the second stage, to apply OLS.

First stage

Find a modified regressor $\hat{P}$ that resembles P, yet is independent of f. To find $\hat{P}$, regress P on all the exogenous variables (T, Y, R), obtaining the fitted variable

$$\hat{P} = b_0 + b_1 T + b_2 Y + b_3 R \qquad (9\text{-}3)$$

Since T, Y, and R are exogenous, each is independent of the error f; hence any function of them (in particular, the linear combination $\hat{P}$) will also be independent[1] of f.

Second stage

Substituting $\hat{P}$ for P in equation (9-2), *estimate the parameters* (γ, δ, θ) *by applying OLS to this equation*, which has become

$$Q = \gamma + \delta\hat{P} + \theta R + f^* \tag{9-4}$$

This procedure is now legitimate, since $\hat{P}$ is uncorrelated with the adjusted error term f^*.

Figure 8-6*c* provides an intuitive view of what 2SLS involves. Recall that this diagram showed how the use of instrumental variables Y, T, and R would result in three estimating equations for the two parameters δ and θ. There was no unique solution for this overdetermined system, because there were no guidelines for discarding one of these equations, or for attaching relative weights to them. But suppose one of our instrumental variables (T) cannot properly be regarded as an exogenous variable affecting this system, that is, suppose it does not enter the demand equation and, hence, has no effect on either P or Q. Therefore, its covariance with either P or Q is zero,[2] and it makes no sense to estimate (8-21) in Figure 8-6*c*. With this equation eliminated, a unique estimate for δ and θ exists at P_3. This instrumental variable technique now does yield a unique solution, with T disappearing entirely from the calculations.

Under these circumstances, P_3 can also be shown to be the 2SLS solution: Since T has no effect on P (nor on Q), T should not be included in the first stage (9-3), nor does T appear in the second stage (9-4); thus T disappears from 2SLS calculations also.

This limiting case is not of great interest in itself because with T disqualified as an instrumental variable, supply becomes exactly identified. But it does illustrate what occurs in the less extreme case in which T has some effect on the system, but much less than Y or R. Supply is again

[1] Not quite independent. Since the coefficients b_i in (9-3) are not absolute constants, but are estimates depending on f, $\hat{P}$ depends slightly on f. This reservation holds true in small sample estimation. But with an infinite sample, any dependence of the b_i on the error terms disappears, making 2SLS a consistent estimator.

[2] Strictly speaking, it is only the population covariances σ_{QT} and σ_{PT} that are zero. There is no reason to expect that their sample estimators s_{QT} and s_{PT} will be precisely zero, especially if the sample is very small. But if they are not zero, this is a reflection only of sampling error, and our conclusion that it makes no sense to evaluate equation (8-21) still holds.

overidentified. In these circumstances the 2SLS solution will not be P_3, but some point close to it. Thus 2SLS may be regarded as a method of selecting a unique solution point in Figure 8-6*c*, with the exact position of this point depending on the relative effect of the instrumental variables T, Y, and R on the endogenous variables.

2SLS is, in fact, instrumental variable estimation, with $\hat{P}$ being used as an instrumental variable along with R. These are the two instrumental variables required to estimate (9-2), and the problem of oversupply of instrumental variables is solved. In the general case where the equation to be estimated includes several endogenous variables (on the right-hand side), the instrumental variables used are the fitted values of each of these endogenous variables (along with the exogenous variables in the equation, of course). It is evident that this always provides just the right number of instrumental variables for estimation purposes.

To sum up, overidentification means an oversupply of instrumental variables. 2SLS reduces this to just the right number, by taking linear combinations of the original instrumental variables in the first stage.

9-2 OTHER PROCEDURES

(a) Equation Versus System Estimation

There are many other procedures available for estimating an equation in a simultaneous system, such as Limited Information/Maximum Likelihood and Least Generalized Variance. Like 2SLS, they are called limited information techniques since they involve estimating only one equation; hence, they do not require observing all variables in all equations in the system.

It is true, of course, that these techniques can be used to estimate a whole system, one equation at a time. But if the whole system is to be estimated, there are other—even more complicated—procedures available for *simultaneously* estimating all equations. These are called *full information* methods, since they require observations on all variables in the system. They include methods such as Three-Stage Least Squares (3SLS) and Full Information/Maximum Likelihood.

(b) The Degrees of Freedom Problem

With the advent of computers, policymakers have increasingly turned to very large models to describe the economy. Such a model may involve fifty, one hundred, or even more equations, with a correspondingly large number of variables and parameters to be estimated. But data in economics is limited. If the number of sample observations on each variable in the system is less than the number of unknown parameters (as is frequently the case) the simultaneous estimation of all these parameters (using, say, 3SLS) is impossible. When there are too many parameters for the limited amount of data, it is sometimes called the *problem of too few degrees of freedom*, or more simply, the *d.f. problem*.

One obvious way of reducing this problem would be to estimate one equation at a time, using a single-equation technique such as 2SLS. But this may not help enough. Recall that in the first stage of estimating (9-1) with 2SLS, the endogenous variable P was regressed on all the exogenous variables that appear *anywhere in the system*. While in that simple model there were only three such exogenous variables (T, Y, and R), in large systems of equations there may literally be hundreds. Thus it may be impossible to accomplish even the first stage of 2SLS unless the number of instrumental variables can somehow be reduced.

One suggestion for reducing this number is philosophically clear and simple enough to introduce next, as an illustration of the imaginative but very simple approach econometricians often bring to very difficult problems.

(c) Structurally Ordered Instrumental Variables (SOIV)

To illustrate the basic idea, first developed by F.M. Fisher (1965c), consider a simple example. Suppose we wish to estimate the first equation in the following system:

$$\left.\begin{aligned} Y_1 &= \gamma_{12} Y_2 + \beta_{11} X_1 + \beta_{12} X_2 + e_1 && \text{(a)} \\ Y_2 &= \gamma_{23} Y_3 + \beta_{23} X_3 + e_2 && \text{(b)} \\ Y_3 &= \gamma_{31} Y_1 + \gamma_{32} Y_2 + \beta_{34} X_4 + e_3 && \text{(c)} \end{aligned}\right\} \quad \text{(9-5)}$$

where γ_{ij} (or β_{ij}) is the coefficient attached to endogenous (or exogenous) variable j in equation i. The first stage of 2SLS would involve regressing Y_2 on X_1, X_2, X_3, and X_4; but suppose, for degrees of freedom reasons, this number of regressors must somehow be reduced. Instead of doing this in a completely arbitrary fashion, why not ask: In our specified structure (9-5), which X is most influenced in explaining Y_2? The answer is X_3, since it is the only X that directly affects Y_2 by appearing in equation (b). Accordingly, X_3 is one of the regressors we will retain. Pursuing this approach one step further, we see that X_4 is the next closest influence: It is only one stage removed in influencing Y_2, since it influences Y_3 [in equation (c)], and this in turn influences Y_2 [in equation (b)]. Finally, the influence of X_1 and X_2 is even less direct; you can confirm that we would have to sort our way through all three equations in the system before being able to establish their influence.

We can schematically summarize how each X affects Y_2 in the following three statements [where, for example, the first is read as "X_3 affects Y_2 as shown in equation (b)."]

$$\left.\begin{array}{l} X_3 \xrightarrow[\text{(b)}]{} Y_2 \\ X_4 \xrightarrow[\text{(c)}]{} Y_3 \xrightarrow[\text{(b)}]{} Y_2 \\ X_1 \text{ and } X_2 \xrightarrow[\text{(a)}]{} Y_1 \xrightarrow[\text{(c)}]{} Y_3 \xrightarrow[\text{(b)}]{} Y_2 \end{array}\right\} \qquad (9\text{-}6)$$

The basic philosophy of *Structurally Ordered Instrumental Variables* (SOIV) may be summed up as follows: Since Y_2 cannot be regressed on all the X's, a smaller number of X's can be selected by examining which ones are structurally closest to Y_2. Thus, from (9-6), X_3 and perhaps X_4 would be selected. Again, this illustrates the importance of model specification. Just as the original specification of any model determines the instrumental variables that will be available (i.e., all the X's in all the equations), SOIV is a way of letting the specification of the model determine which instrumental variables should be used, when all cannot be.[3]

9-3 RECURSIVE SYSTEMS

As a final topic, consider the much easier problem when the equations in a system are not simultaneous, but recursive.

(a) The Simple Recursive System

In such a system, the endogenous variables are determined one at a time, in sequence. Thus, the first endogenous variable is determined from the first equation, independent of the other endogenous variables; its solution then appears in the second equation to determine the value of the second endogenous variable, and so on.

The successive or sequential nature of this solution is illustrated in the following recursive system:

[3] Further problems remain with this approach; for example, even though according to (9-6), X_4 has a more *direct* influence on Y_2, it is still possible that X_1 may have a *greater* influence.

$$\left.\begin{aligned}
&Y_1 &&= \beta_{11}X_1 + \beta_{12}X_2 + \cdots + \beta_{1M}X_M + e_1\\
&\gamma_{21}Y_1 + Y_2 &&= \beta_{21}X_1 + \cdots \qquad\qquad + \beta_{2M}X_M + e_2\\
&\gamma_{31}Y_1 + \gamma_{32}Y_2 + Y_3 &&= \beta_{31}X_1 + \cdots \qquad\qquad + \beta_{3M}X_M + e_3\\
&\vdots\\
&\gamma_{Q1}Y_1 + \cdots \qquad + Y_Q &&= \beta_{Q1}X_1 + \cdots \qquad\qquad + \beta_{QM}X_M + e_Q
\end{aligned}\right\} \qquad (9\text{-}7)$$

where X_i = exogenous variables

Y_i = endogenous variables

and, most important,

e_i = *independent* error terms[4]

Given the structural coefficients in the system (all the γ's and β's), how would each of the Y's be determined? From the exogenous variables (X_i), and a randomly determined value for e_1, the first equation yields a solution for Y_1; note that this value of Y_1 is logically independent of all the other Y_i values in the system. With the value of Y_1 thus determined, the second equation yields a solution for Y_2.[5] And as we move through successive steps, each equation yields one more Y in terms of the previously determined Y's and the exogenous variables.

A recursive system is easier to deal with than a simultaneous system: in particular, OLS can be used to estimate its parameters. To justify its application, recall that OLS is appropriate if the error term in the equation is independent of the regressors. Clearly, it can be applied to the first equation, since the only regressors are exogenous variables, which are—by assumption—independent of e_1. Moreover, OLS can be applied to the second equation, where Y_2 is regressed on Y_1, and the exogenous X's; all these regressors are independent of e_2. Specifically, the X's are independent of e_2 because they are exogenous. Y_1 is also independent of e_2 since, from the first equation, the only error term affecting Y_1 is e_1. Because e_1 and e_2 are assumed independent, it follows that Y_1 and e_2 are independent.[6] The

[4] This is the crucial assumption that defines a recursive system. *Any* system can have its left side put into triangular form (9-7) by simple manipulations of linear algebra. But these same manipulations usually will so entangle the errors on the right side that the errors will no longer be independent. When this happens, we will call the system nonrecursive, because the recursive OLS solution to be discussed is no longer valid.

[5] That is, $Y_2 = -\gamma_{21}Y_1 + \beta_{21}X_1 + \cdots + \beta_{2M}X_M + e_2$

[6] Contrast this with a simultaneous system in which both Y_1 and Y_2 appear in the first equation, as well as the second. Thus, Y_1 and Y_2 depend on both e_1 and e_2. In particular, the dependence of the regressor Y_1 on e_2 would mean that OLS applied to the second equation would result in biased and inconsistent estimates.

justification of OLS on each succeeding equation follows a similar argument.

(b) Bloc Recursive Systems

A system of equations becomes bloc recursive if any of the individual endogenous variables in (9-7) is replaced with a whole bloc of simultaneously determined endogenous variables. The simple example in Figure 9-1 will illustrate. The first bloc is made up of Y_1 and Y_2; these are simultaneously determined by the first two equations. These solved values are then conceptually plugged into the last three equations to determine the solution for Y_3, Y_4, and Y_5—the second bloc of endogenous variables. Errors e_1 and e_2 associated with the first bloc are assumed independent of errors e_3, e_4, and e_5 associated with the second bloc; (however, the errors within a bloc

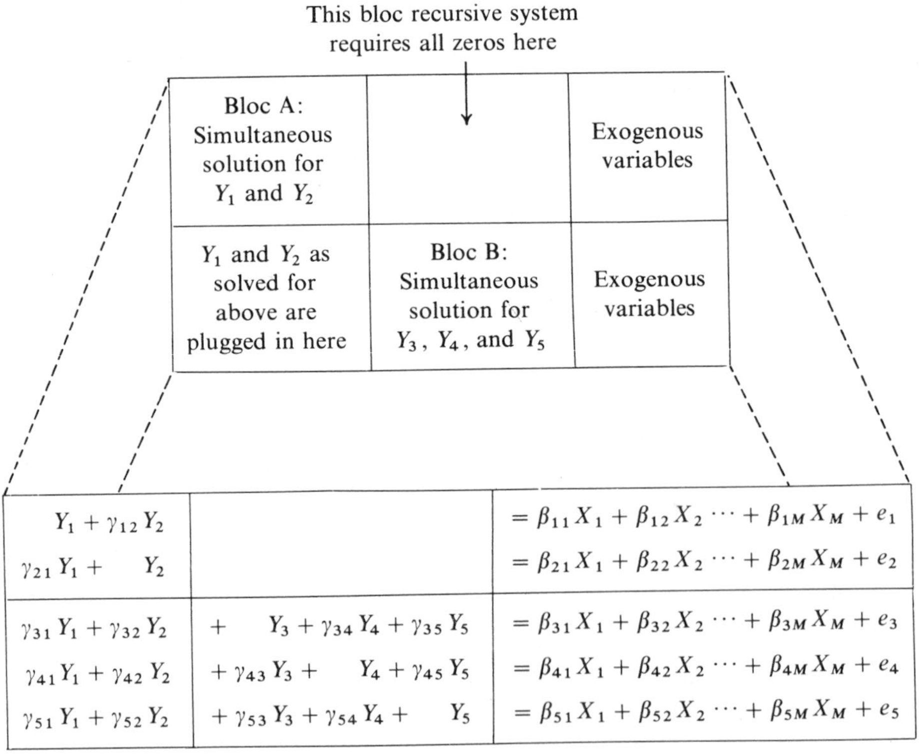

FIGURE 9-1 A bloc recursive system.

may be dependent—i.e., e_1 and e_2 may be dependent). OLS is no longer valid, because the system now involves elements of simultaneity.[7] Hence, a more sophisticated, bloc-by-bloc approach is required: In each bloc, the Y variables from the previous blocs are treated as exogenous (predetermined), and the bloc coefficients are estimated by 2SLS (described in Section 9-1), equation by equation, or by some similar method.

In summary, a bloc recursive system is one that has a very special combination of zero coefficients attached to the endogenous variables, and the assumption that every error term is independent of errors in another bloc.

[7] Specifically, OLS cannot be used on the first equation to (consistently) regress Y_1 on Y_2, $X_1, \ldots, X_M$, because the regressor Y_2 is not independent of e_1.

10

BAYESIAN INFERENCE

In the first nine chapters, we have discussed how to make estimates based on data alone. Bayesian statistics shows how estimates should be modified in the light of knowledge that may be available prior to the gathering of data.

10-1 POSTERIOR PROBABILITIES IN GENERAL

(a) Introduction

Since Bayesian statistics are not regularly covered in a first course in statistics, we develop them from first principles. We begin with an elementary example.

Example 10-1

In a certain country, suppose that it rains 40% of the days and shines 60% of the days. A barometer manufacturer, in testing her instrument, has found that although it is fairly reliable, it sometimes errs: On rainy days it erroneously predicts "shine" 10% of the time, and on shiny days it erroneously predicts "rain" 30% of the time.

TABLE 10-1 Prior Probabilities, $p(\theta)$

State θ	$p(\theta)$
θ_1 (Rain)	.40
θ_2 (Shine)	.60

The best prediction of tomorrow's weather *before* looking at the barometer would be the *prior distribution* in Table 10-1. But *after* looking at the barometer and seeing it predict "rain," what is the *posterior distribution*? That is, with this new information in hand, can't we quote better odds on rain than Table 10-1? Intuitively, the answer should be yes; let's prove it.

Solution

We first set out the reliability of the barometer in Table 10-2.

TABLE 10-2 Conditional Probabilities, $p(X/\theta)$

Prediction X / *State θ*	X_1 (*Rain*)	X_2 (*Shine*)	Σ
θ_1 (Rain)	.90	.10	1.00
θ_2 (Shine)	.30	.70	1.00

This information is combined with the prior probabilities in Table 10-1 to define the sample space that is shown as the entire rectangle in Figure 10-1. If you like, you can think of this as an abstract representation of the millions of days that could occur. Now consider the proportion of those days in which the state of nature (θ) is rain and also in which the prediction X is "rain." 40% of the time, the state of nature is rain (Table 10-1), and when this occurs there is a 90% probability that the prediction will be "rain" (Table 10-2); accordingly, this combination occurs 90% of 40% = 36% of the time. This probability is shown in the upper-left corner of Figure 10-1. It may be written more formally[1]:

$$p(\theta_1, X_1) = p(\theta_1)p(X_1/\theta_1) \tag{10-3}$$

$$= (.4)(.9) = .36 \tag{10-4}$$

[1] Equation (10-3) uses the standard probability formula:

$$p(x, y) = p(x)p(y/x) \tag{10-1}$$

which comes from the definition of conditional probability:

$$p(y/x) \equiv \frac{p(x, y)}{p(x)} \tag{10-2}$$

For details, see a standard introductory text such as Wonnacott and Wonnacott, 1977.

Similarly, the probability of the state shine and the prediction "rain" is

$$p(\theta_2, X_1) = p(\theta_2)p(X_1/\theta_2) \tag{10-5}$$

$$= (.6)(.3) = .18 \tag{10-6}$$

Of course, after "rain" has been predicted, the whole sample space in Figure 10-1 is no longer relevant; instead, only that shaded part covering the days in which there is a "rain" prediction is relevant. In that smaller sample space, we see that rain is twice as probable as shine (.36 versus .18). This produces the posterior distribution in Table 10-3.

TABLE 10-3 Posterior Probabilities, $p(\theta/X_1)$

State θ	$p(\theta/X_1)$
θ_1 (Rain)	.67
θ_2 (Shine)	.33

Table 10-3 may be deduced more formally, as follows. From (10-4) and (10-6):

$$p(\text{prediction "rain"}) = p(X_1) = .36 + .18 = .54 \tag{10-7}$$

According to (10-2),

$$p(\theta_1/X_1) = \frac{p(\theta_1, X_1)}{p(X_1)} = \frac{.36}{.54} = .67$$

Similarly, (10-8)

$$p(\theta_2/X_1) = \frac{p(\theta_2, X_1)}{p(X_1)} = \frac{.18}{.54} = .33$$

To keep the mathematical manipulations in perspective, we repeat the physical interpretation for emphasis. Before the evidence (barometer) is seen, the prior probabilities $p(\theta)$ give the proper betting odds on the weather. But after the evidence X_1 is available, we can do better; the posterior probabilities $p(\theta/X_1)$ now give the proper betting odds.

To generalize this example, we may write (10-8) in one equation, as follows:

$$p(\theta/X_1) = \frac{p(\theta, X_1)}{p(X_1)}$$

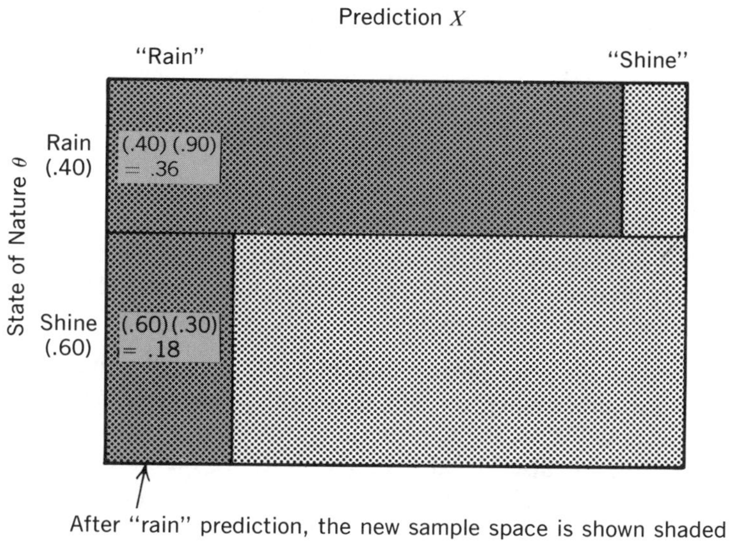

FIGURE 10-1 How posterior probabilities are determined.

By (10-3) or (10-5),

$$p(\theta/X_1) = \frac{p(\theta)p(X_1/\theta)}{p(X_1)} \tag{10-9}$$

Now in this formula, as in Table 10-3, θ varies over all possible states, whereas X_1 is the fixed observation. Since X_1 is a constant, $p(X_1)$ also is a constant, and so we may write (10-9) as

$$p(\theta/X_1) = cp(\theta)p(X_1/\theta) \tag{10-10}$$

where

$$c = \frac{1}{p(X_1)}$$

is a constant (that will make the total probability sum to 1 over all θ).

There is another interesting consequence of θ varying while the observation X_1 is fixed. As we mentioned in Section 2-12, $p(X_1/\theta)$ is then called the *likelihood* function. Thus we may summarize (10-10) verbally, as follows:

$$\text{(Posterior distribution)} \propto \text{(prior distribution) (likelihood function)} \tag{10-11}$$

where $\propto$ means *equals, except for a constant*, or *is proportional to*. In conclusion, (10-11) states precisely how the final (posterior) distribution is calculated by combining the prior distribution with the observed sample information.

PROBLEMS

10-1 Suppose that another barometer is used: On shiny days it erroneously predicts "rain" 35% of the time, but on rainy days it always predicts "rain" correctly.

(a) With the prior probabilities in Table 10-1, calculate the posterior probability of rain, once this barometer has predicted "rain." What is the posterior probability of shine?

(b) True or false? If false, correct it. Since the barometer always predicts "rain" when it does rain, a "rain" prediction means that it is dead certain that it will rain.

(c) Explain why the posterior probability of rain is now *less* than in Table 10-3, even though this new barometer is a better predictor when it rains.

10-2 Suppose that you are in charge of the nationwide leasing of a specific car model. Your service agent in a certain city has not been perfectly reliable: He has shortcut his servicing in the past about $\frac{1}{10}$ of the time. Whenever such shortcutting occurs, the probability that an individual will cancel his lease increases from .2 to .5.

(a) If an individual has canceled his lease, what is the probability that he received shortcut servicing?

(b) Suppose that the service agent is even more unreliable, shortcutting half the time. What is your answer to (a) in this case?

10-3 A factory has three machines (θ_1, θ_2, and θ_3) making bolts. The newer the machine, the larger and more accurate it is, according to the following table:

Machine	*Proportion of Total Output Produced by this Machine*	*Rate of Defective Bolts*
θ_1 (Oldest)	10%	5%
θ_2	40%	2%
θ_3 (Newest)	50%	1%
	100%✓	

Thus, for example, θ_3 produces half of the factory's output, and of all the bolts it produces, 1% are defective.

(a) Suppose that a bolt is selected at random; *before* it is examined, what is the chance that it was produced by machine θ_1? by θ_2? by θ_3?

(b) Suppose that the bolt is examined and found to be defective; *after* this examination, what is the chance that it was produced by machine θ_1? by θ_2? by θ_3?

*10-4 (a) Suppose that, in an earlier quality control study, 100 steel bars had been selected at random from a firm's output, with each subjected to strain until it broke:

Breaking strength, θ	200	210	220	230	240	250
Relative frequency	.10	.30	.20	.20	.10	.10

Suppose that this is the only available prior distribution of θ. Graph it.

(b) Now suppose that a strain gauge becomes available that gives a crude measurement X of any bar's breaking strength θ (without breaking it). By "crude," we mean that the measurement error ranges from -20 to $+20$, so that X has the following distribution:

X	$\theta - 20$	$\theta - 10$	θ	$\theta + 10$	$\theta + 20$
$p(X/\theta)$	.2	.2	.3	.2	.1

Suppose that the measurement X of a bar purchased at random turns out to be $X_1 = 240$. What is the (posterior) distribution of θ, now that this estimate is available? Graph the likelihood, and posterior distributions. Where does the posterior distribution lie relative to the prior distribution and the likelihood?

*10-2[2] POPULATION PROPORTION

Now we apply the general principle (10-11) to an example in which there are many, many "states of nature," rather than just two. And each state of nature (formerly called θ) is now a population proportion π.

[2] This section requires familiarity with the binomial distribution. For example, see Wonnacott and Wonnacott, 1977, Section 4-3.

Example 10-2

Over the past year, the Radex Corporation has achieved a notorious reputation for bad quality control, having produced shipments of radios of widely varying quality. To be specific, let π represent the proportion of defective raj in a shipment. Then the past record of π for all shipments from Radex (i.e., the prior distribution of π) is given in Table 10-4(a).

TABLE 10-4 Calculating the Posterior Distribution of a Population Proportion π

(a) Given Prior Distribution of π			*(b) Calculations to Obtain Posterior Distribution*		
(1) *Proportion of Defectives* π	(2) *Number of Shipments*	(3) *Relative Number of Shipments*	(4) *Likelihood of π [from Table III(b) given sample $n = 5$, $S = 3$]*	(5) *Prior times Likelihood* (3) × (4)	(6) *Divide by .160, yields Posterior*
0%	2	.01	0*	0	0
10%	30	.15	.01	.002	.01
20%	40	.20	.05	.010	.06
30%	42	.21	.13	.027	.17
40%	34	.17	.23	.039	.24
50%	26	.13	.31	.040	.25
60%	16	.08	.35	.028	.18
70%	8	.04	.31	.012	.08
80%	2	.01	.20	.002	.01
90%		0	.07	0	0
100%		0	0*	0	0
	200	1.00✓		.160	1.00✓

* If the shipment proportion of defective radios were $\pi = 0\%$ (or $\pi = 100\%$), then the likelihood of the sample having $S = 3$ defective radios (and $n - S = 2$ good radios) would be zero — — such a sample just could not occur.

Now suppose that you have just been appointed purchaser for a large department store. Your first job is to make a decision on whether to return a shipment of radios from Radex that has been lying in your warehouse for 2 weeks. Your decision, of course, will depend upon what you guess is the proportion of defectives π.

(a) Graph the prior distribution of π.

(b) Now suppose that you examine 5 radios at random to get sample evidence on π, and that 3 of the 5 turn out to be defective. Now what is the (posterior) distribution of π? Calculate it and graph it.

(c) Suppose that your department store will regard the shipment as satisfactory only if π is less than 25%. What would you say is the probability of this:

(i) Before the sample?
(ii) After the sample?

Solution

(a) The distribution of π prior to the sample is taken from Table 10-4(a) and graphed in Figure 10-2.

(b) To calculate the posterior distribution in Table 10-4(b), we use (10-11). We first need the likelihood function, that is, the likelihood of getting the 3 defectives that we observed in our sample of 5. This, of course, is given by the binomial formula, for a fixed $S = 3$, and various values of π. That is, we read[3] Appendix Table III(b) horizontally along the row where $n = 5$ and $S = 3$, and record it in column (4) of Table 10-4(b).

Now, following (10-11), we multiply this likelihood function by the prior distribution. Finally, to "norm" the probabilities so they sum to 1.00, we must divide through by the constant[4] .160. This gives us the posterior distribution in the last column of Table 10-4(b) which, along with the likelihood function, is also graphed in Figure 10-2.

(c) (i) From Table 10-4(a), the prior probability of less than 25% defectives is

$$\Pr(\pi < 25\%) = .01 + .15 + .20 = .36$$

---

[3] Alternatively, we could calculate the likelihood the hard way from the binomial formula:

$$p(S/\pi) = \binom{n}{S}\pi^S(1-\pi)^{n-S}$$

where $S = 3$, $n = 5$, and π varies. We rename it $L(\pi)$ for simplicity:

$$L(\pi) = \binom{5}{3}\pi^3(1-\pi)^2$$

[4] Just as we divided both probabilities in (10-8) by .54.

(ii) From the last column of Table 19-4(b), the posterior probability is

$$\Pr(\pi < 25\%/S = 3) = 0 + .01 + .06 = .07$$

Thus the sample, with its large proportion of defectives, has lowered the probability of a satisfactory lot from .36 to .07.

This example displays several features that generally will be found to be true:

1. The posterior distribution is a compromise, peaking between the prior distribution and the likelihood function.
2. If we had multiplied either the prior or the likelihood by some convenient constant, it merely would have changed the second-last column of Table 10-4 by the same constant. But the adjusted or normed values in the last column[5] would be exactly as before. Accordingly:

Multiplying the prior or likelihood function by a convenient constant does not affect the posterior	(10-12)

3. The problem as stated had discrete values for π (that is, $\pi = 0, .1, .2, \ldots$). However, this was just a convenient way of tabulating a variable π that really is continuous. So we have sketched all the graphs as continuous.[6]

To generalize Example 10-2, let us consider first the possible prior distributions for π. There is a whole family of distributions, called the β distributions, that serve as a convenient approximation for almost any prior that we might encounter in practice; and the formula for the β-family is simple:[7]

$$\boxed{\beta \text{ distribution for the prior, } p(\pi) = \pi^a(1 - \pi)^b} \qquad (10\text{-}13)$$

[5] Even if we do not norm the posterior distribution, we would get a graph that still is the right shape (it merely would be the wrong height). Therefore, we may omit the norming in our graphs. [However, we must remember to do the norming if probabilities are to be calculated as in part (c) of Example 10-2.]

[6] Is it really legitimate to shift the argument back and forth between discrete and continuous models? For our purposes, yes. The essential difference between a discrete probability function and the analogous continuous probability density is simply a constant multiplier, the constant being the cell width. And constant multipliers do not really matter, as stated in (10-12) above.

[7] In view of our remark (10-12) above, we have omitted in (10-13) the awkward multiplier $(a + b + 1)!/a!b!$, which would make the total integral (probability) 1.

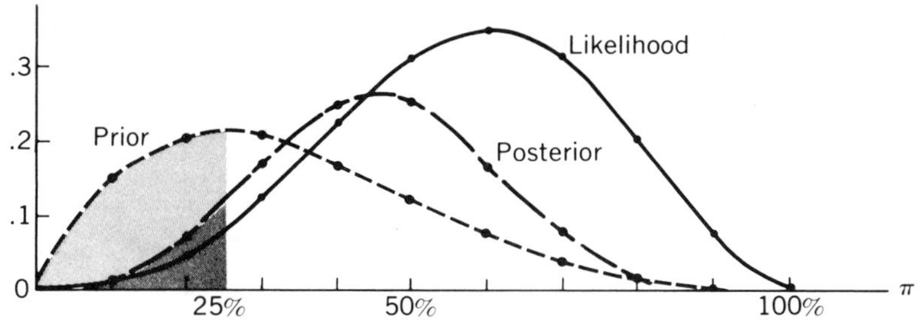

FIGURE 10-2 The prior distribution and likelihood function (based on sample information) are multiplied together to give the compromise posterior distribution of π.

[Note that this formula is remarkably similar to the likelihood function (10-15) below. In fact, this similarity will prove very convenient in the subsequent calculation of the posterior distribution.] In (10-13), the parameters (constants) a and b may be any numbers, although positive small integers are most common. For example, you may verify that the prior in column (3) of Table 10-4 is approximately[7] the β distribution with $a = 1$ and $b = 3$:

$$p(\pi) \simeq \pi(1 - \pi)^3 \tag{10-14}$$

Next, to generalize the likelihood function, consider a sample of n observations that results in S "successes" and F "failures" (where $F = n - S$, of course). The likelihood function then is given by the general binomial formula:

$$p(S/\pi) = \binom{n}{S}\pi^S(1 - \pi)^F \tag{10-15}$$

Since only π is varying, we may write this as

$$\boxed{\text{Likelihood, } L(\pi) \propto \pi^S(1 - \pi)^F}$$

(10-16) like (4-72)

When the prior (10-13) is multiplied by the likelihood (10-16), we obtain the posterior:

$$p(\pi/S) \propto \pi^a(1 - \pi)^b \pi^S(1 - \pi)^F$$

$$\boxed{\text{Posterior, } p(\pi/S) \propto \pi^{a+S}(1 - \pi)^{b+F}} \tag{10-17}$$

Thus we see the real advantage of using a prior model of the β-function form: It has made the computation of the posterior distribution very simple.[8] In fact, all three distributions—prior, likelihood, and posterior—now have the same β-function form: $\pi^i(1-\pi)^j$ for some i and j. Furthermore, many such β functions are already tabulated, by reading across Appendix Table III(b) (ignoring the constant binomial coefficient, which does not really matter). This greatly simplifies computation, as the next example illustrates.

Example 10-3

Referring back to Example 10-2, suppose that your engineering expert tells you that Radex is now using a better technique; in fact, the prior distribution has so improved that it now may be approximated with a β function with $a = 0$, and $b = 4$:

$$p(\pi) \propto \pi^0(1-\pi)^4$$
$$\propto (1-\pi)^4$$

But suppose that the sample turns out the same way (3 defectives out of 5). Without worrying about constant multipliers, graph the prior, the likelihood, and the posterior.

Solution

As already remarked, we may overlook constants such as binomial coefficients, which do not depend on π.

First we extract each distribution from the appropriate row of Appendix Table III(b). For example, the likelihood function is $L(\pi) \propto \pi^3(1-\pi)^2$, which we find in Table III(b)—under $n = 5$ and $S = 3$. The prior distribution is $p(\pi) \propto \pi^0(1-\pi)^4$, which we can also find in Table III(b)—under $n = 4$ and $S = 0$. Finally, the posterior distribution is $p(\pi/S) \propto \pi^3(1-\pi)^6$, which we can again find in Table III(b)—under $n = 9$ and $S = 3$. Thus:

π	0	.1	.2	.3	.4	.5	.6	.7	.8	.9	1.0
$L(\pi)$	0	.01	.05	.13	.23	.31	.35	.31	.20	.07	0
$p(\pi)$	1.00	.66	.41	.24	.13	.06	.03	.01	.00	.00	0
$p(\pi/S)$	0	.04	.18	.27	.25	.16	.07	.02	.00	.00	0

---

[8] Because the β prior distribution conveniently makes the posterior distribution turn out to be of the same β form, it is known technically as a *conjugate* prior.

The graphs of all three distributions are given in Figure 10-3. Note again that the posterior is a compromise, peaking between the prior and the likelihood.

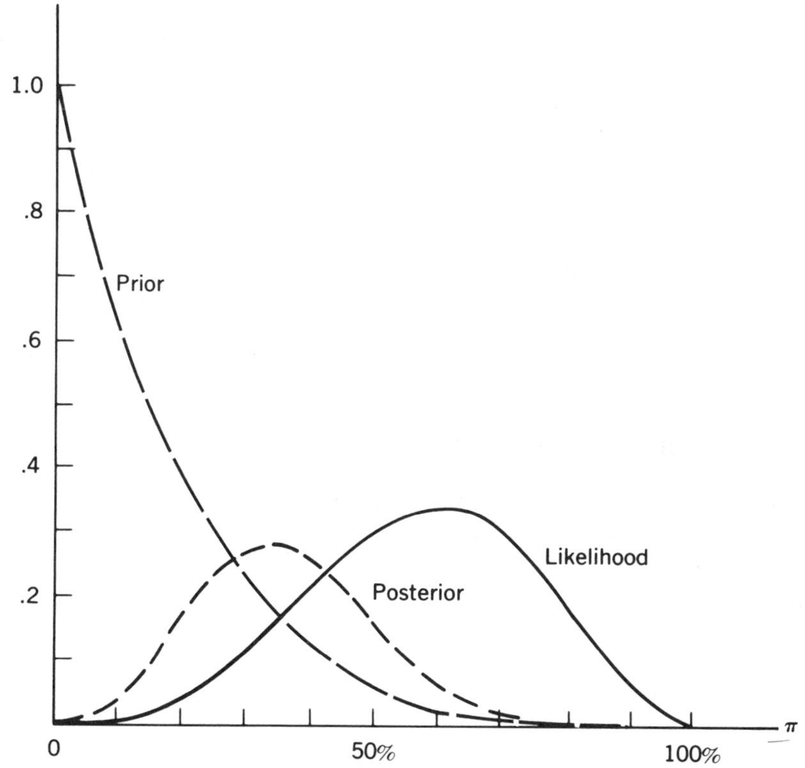

FIGURE 10-3 Different prior, hence different posterior, than in Figure 10-2.

PROBLEMS

⇒ 10-5 (Continuation of Example 10-3.) In each of the following cases, graph the prior, likelihood, and posterior.

	Prior	*Sample*
(a)	$\pi^0(1-\pi)^0$	3 defective, 6 good
(b)	$\pi^1(1-\pi)^3$	2 defective, 3 good

⇒ 10-6 True or false? If false, correct it.

(a) In Problem 10-5(a), we started with an informationless prior[9] in the sense that no values of π were more probable than others; and we combined it with a relatively large sample of 9 observations. In Problem 10-5(b), on the other hand, we started with information in the prior, and a sample of 4 fewer observations. Yet we got the same posterior distribution, that is, the same conclusion about the shipment in the warehouse. So this prior may be thought of as providing the same information as an extra 4 observations—1 defective and 3 good.

(b) We therefore may think of a prior distribution as a *quasi-sample* of extra observations. In general, the prior distribution of (10-13) may be considered a quasi-sample of a defective radios and b good radios.

(c) A person who insists on using only the sample, and ignores the prior, may be viewed just like a person who throws away part of a sample (insofar as statistical inference is concerned).

10-3 MEAN μ OF A NORMAL POPULATION

Once more, we apply the general principle (10-11), this time to an example where each state of nature is a mean μ of a normal population.

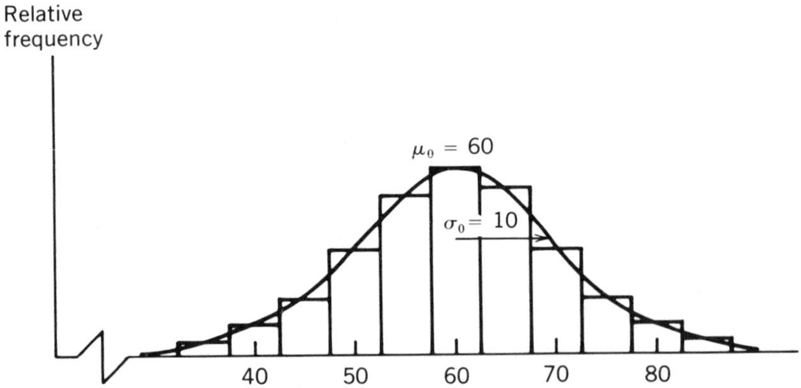

FIGURE 10-4 The distribution of shipment means is approximately normal.

[9] There is some room for argument about what constitutes an informationless prior. Some authors (Box and Tiao, 1973) give good reasons (too subtle for this text) for defining the informationless prior as

$$p(\pi) = \pi^{-.5}(1 - \pi)^{-.5}$$

Example 10-4

Suppose that Steelcorp sells steel beams; within each shipment, the breaking strengths of the beams are distributed normally around a mean μ, with variance $\sigma^2 = 300$. But μ changes from shipment to shipment because of poor quality control. In fact, suppose that when all shipment means μ are recorded in a bar graph, they turn out to be like Figure 10-4. That is, the distribution of μ is approximately normal, with mean $\mu_0 = 60$ and standard deviation[10] $\sigma_0 = 10$.

Now suppose that you have to make a decision on whether to return a specific shipment of beams that you bought from Steelcorp. Your decision, of course, will depend on what you guess is the mean strength μ. To guide you, you have the information contained in Figure 10-4 about what μ might be. Suppose that you also have available a sample of 12 beams from this particular shipment, and $\bar{X}$ turns out to be 70.

(a) Sketch the likelihood function.

(b) Sketch the posterior distribution obtained by multiplying the prior distribution of Figure 10-4 by the likelihood function.

(c) Suppose that the shipment must be regarded as unsatisfactory if μ is less than 62.5. What would you say is the probability of this, as estimated from the sketched distributions:

(i) Before the sample was taken?

(ii) After the sample?

Solution

We will use the previous footnote to sketch normal curves on the basis of their moments. And for simplicity, we will ignore the constant multiplier in the normal distribution $(1/\sqrt{2\pi}\,\sigma)$; this will make each curve have a maximum value of 1.

(a) What is the likelihood of getting $\bar{X} = 70$? The distribution of $\bar{X}$ is normal, with a variance of $\sigma^2/n = 300/12 = 25$. Thus its equation is, from (10-18),

$$p(\bar{X}/\mu) \propto e^{-(1/2)(\bar{X}-\mu)^2/25}$$

---

[10] The moments of a normal distribution may be roughly obtained from the graph as follows: A normal curve peaks at its mean, of course. At a distance of 1σ from its mean, the curve falls to 60% of its peak value (and at a distance of 2σ from its mean, the curve falls to 14% of its peak value). These facts may be algebraically verified from the formula for a normal curve with mean μ and standard deviation σ:

$$p(x) = \frac{1}{\sqrt{2\pi}\,\sigma}\, e^{(-1/2\sigma^2)(x-\mu)^2} \qquad (10\text{-}18)$$

where $\bar{X} = 70$ and μ varies. We rename it $L(\mu)$ for simplicity:

$$L(\mu) \propto e^{-(1/2)(\mu-70)^2/25} \tag{10-19}$$

We recognize this likelihood as a normal curve, centered at 70 with a standard deviation $\sqrt{25} = 5$. Its graph is sketched in Figure 10-5.

(b) For the posterior distribution, we must multiply the prior times the likelihood. We do this for several values[11] of μ, to obtain several points on the posterior distribution. From them, we sketch the graph of the posterior distribution shown in Figure 10-5.

(c) The probability that μ is below 62.5 can be estimated as the relative area under the distribution, shown shaded in Figure 10-5. This appears to be:

(i) For the prior, approximately .60.
(ii) For the posterior, approximately .10.

In this example, the posterior seems to be distributed normally. This is no surprise, since it comes from a normal prior and normal likelihood. (This is just like our previous example: The posterior distribution for π was a β function, just like the prior and likelihood.) Again, we note that the posterior peaks between the prior and the likelihood, and that it is closer to the curve with the least variance. That is, the more concentrated curve that accordingly provides the more precise and reliable information (in this case, the likelihood) has the greater influence in determining the posterior. These features generally are true, and may be stated more precisely, as follows.

We calculate the posterior distribution from two pieces of information:

1. The *actual* sample centered at $\bar{X}$, which is the basis of the likelihood function.
2. The prior distribution, which is equivalent to the information in *another* sample (often called a *hypothetical* or *quasi*-sample).[12]

This quasi-sample is, of course, centered on the prior mean μ_0, and is made up of n_0 hypothetical observations. The question is: How large is n_0? To answer this, note that the smaller the variance σ_0^2 of the prior distribution (relative to σ^2, the variance of an observation), the more influential the

[11] For example, consider $\mu = 65$ as shown in Figure 10-5. We read off the prior probability (.9) and likelihood (.6) of $\mu = 65$ from the two appropriate graphs. Their product, $.9 \times .6 = .54$, is the desired point on the posterior distribution.

[12] Recall that this concept already has been encountered in Problem 10-6. Of course, the prior distribution is not *really* a sample. But its effect on the posterior distribution is exactly equivalent to the effect of a sample with n_0 observations; and such a quasi-sample provides a nice intuitive way to understand and remember the posterior formula (10-27).

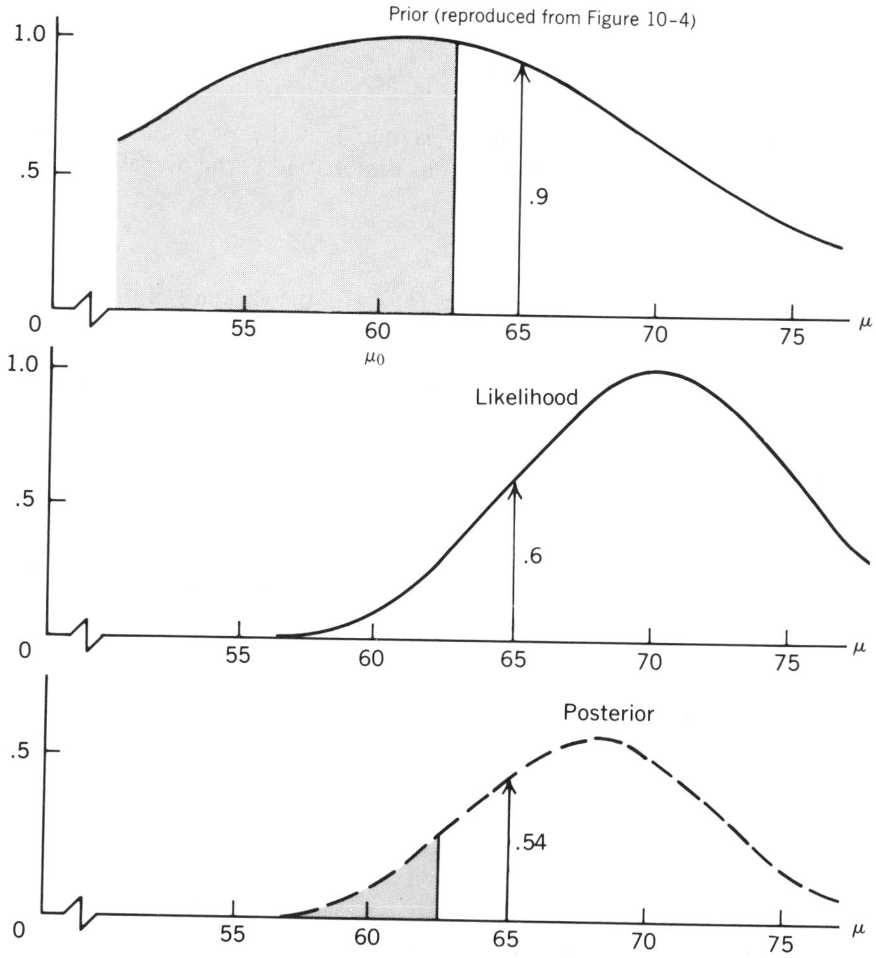

FIGURE 10-5 The prior distribution and likelihood function are multiplied to give the compromise posterior distribution of μ.

prior will be, and the larger n_0 consequently will be. So it is no surprise that the quasi-sample size n_0 is given by the formula:[13]

$$n_0 = \frac{\sigma^2}{\sigma_0^2} \tag{10-20}$$

[13] Here is the *rigorous* proof that definition (10-20) leads to the posterior distribution (10-27): We are given the prior distribution and likelihood function:

$$p(\mu) = K_1 e^{-(1/2\sigma_0{}^2)(\mu-\mu_0)^2} \qquad \text{(10-22) like (10-18)}$$

(*cont'd*)

That is:

$$\sigma_0^2 = \frac{\sigma^2}{n_0} \tag{10-21}$$

When the n_0 quasi-observations centered at the prior mean μ_0 are combined with the n actual observations centered at $\bar{X}$, the overall mean is

$$\text{Posterior mean} = \frac{n_0\mu_0 + n\bar{X}}{n_0 + n} \tag{10-25}$$

Since the total number of observations is $n_0 + n$, the variance of the posterior distribution is

$$\text{Posterior variance} = \frac{\sigma^2}{n_0 + n} \tag{10-26}$$

In conclusion, therefore,

$$\boxed{\text{Posterior distribution, } \mu \sim N\left(\frac{n_0\mu_0 + n\bar{X}}{n_0 + n}, \frac{\sigma^2}{n_0 + n}\right)} \tag{10-27}$$

---

[13] *(continued)*

$$p(\bar{X}/\mu) = K_2\, e^{-(n/2\sigma^2)(\bar{X}-\mu)^2} \tag{10-23}$$

$$\text{posterior} = (\text{prior})(\text{likelihood}) = K_1 K_2\, e^{-(1/2\sigma_0{}^2)(\mu-\mu_0)^2 - (n/2\sigma^2)(\bar{X}-\mu)^2}$$

(10-11) repeated

Let us consider in detail the exponent, which may be rearranged as a quadratic function of μ:

$$\text{exponent} = -\frac{1}{2}\left[\mu^2\left(\frac{1}{\sigma_0^2} + \frac{n}{\sigma^2}\right) - 2\mu\left(\frac{\mu_0}{\sigma_0^2} + \frac{n\bar{X}}{\sigma^2}\right) + K_3\right] \tag{10-24}$$

Now we exploit the definition of n_0; we substitute (10-21) into (10-24):

$$\text{exponent} = -\frac{1}{2}\left[\mu^2\left(\frac{n_0 + n}{\sigma^2}\right) - 2\mu\left(\frac{n_0\mu_0 + n\bar{X}}{\sigma^2}\right) + K_3\right]$$

$$= -\frac{1}{2}\left(\frac{n_0 + n}{\sigma^2}\right)\left[\mu^2 - 2\mu\left(\frac{n_0\mu_0 + n\bar{X}}{n_0 + n}\right) + K_4\right]$$

$$= -\frac{1}{2}\left(\frac{1}{\sigma^2/(n_0 + n)}\right)\left[\mu - \left(\frac{n_0\mu_0 + n\bar{X}}{n_0 + n}\right)\right]^2 + K_5$$

This exponent is recognized as that of a normal distribution, with:

$$\text{variance} = \sigma^2/(n_0 + n)$$

(10-26) proved

and

$$\text{mean} = \left(\frac{n_0\mu_0 + n\bar{X}}{n_0 + n}\right)$$

(10-25) proved

where

$$n_0 = \frac{\sigma^2}{\sigma_0^2} \qquad \text{(10-20) repeated}$$

and equation (10-27) is read: μ has a normal distribution with mean $(n_0\mu_0 + n\bar{X})/(n_0 + n)$ and variance $\sigma^2/(n_0 + n)$.

Example 10-5

Let us rework Example 10-4 with formulas instead of graphs:

(a) Express the value of the prior distribution in terms of quasi-observations.

(b) Calculate the posterior distribution.

(c) Calculate exactly the probability that μ is below 62.5,

(i) before the sample is taken.

(ii) after the sample has been taken.

Solution

(a) From (10-20):

$$n_0 = \frac{\sigma^2}{\sigma_0^2} = \frac{300}{100} = 3$$

That is, the prior distribution is equivalent to a quasi-sample of 3 observations.

(b) From (10-27), the posterior distribution is normal, with:

$$\text{Posterior mean} = \frac{n_0\mu_0 + n\bar{X}}{n_0 + n}$$

$$= \frac{3(60) + 12(70)}{3 + 12} = 68 \qquad \text{(10-28)}$$

$$\text{Posterior variance} = \frac{\sigma^2}{n_0 + n} = \frac{300}{3 + 12} = 20 \qquad \text{(10-29)}$$

(c)

(i) Before the sample, we use the prior distribution:

$$\Pr(\mu < 62.5) = \Pr\left(\frac{\mu - \mu_0}{\sigma_0} < \frac{62.5 - 60}{10}\right)$$

$$= \Pr(Z < .25) = 1 - .40 = .60$$

(ii) After the sample, we use the posterior distribution calculated in (b):

$$\Pr(\mu < 62.5) = \Pr\left(\frac{\mu - 68}{\sqrt{20}} < \frac{62.5 - 68}{\sqrt{20}}\right)$$

$$= \Pr(Z < -1.23) = .11$$

Remarks

Note that the precise answers calculated from formulas in (b) and (c) correspond very nicely to the shaded graphical approximations that we found before in Example 10-4. Since the formula answers are easier and more accurate, from now on we will use formulas instead of sketching.

From the posterior distribution, we can calculate an interval that has a 95% chance of containing μ:

$$\mu = \text{posterior mean} \pm 1.96 \text{ posterior standard deviations} \tag{10-30}$$

Noting (10-25) and (10-26), we finally obtain:

95% Bayesian confidence interval:[14]

$$\mu = \left(\frac{n_0 \mu_0 + n\bar{X}}{n_0 + n}\right) \pm 1.96\sqrt{\frac{\sigma^2}{n_0 + n}} \tag{10-31}$$

where $n_0 = \sigma^2/\sigma_0^2$.

It is interesting to compare this with the classical confidence interval, based on $\bar{X}$ alone:

95% classical confidence interval:

$$\mu = \bar{X} \pm 1.96\frac{\sigma}{\sqrt{n}} \tag{10-32}$$

Compared with the classical confidence interval, the Bayesian confidence interval is centered at a compromise between μ_0 and $\bar{X}$, and is shorter because of the extra n_0 quasi-observations provided by prior information.

[14] The words credibility interval sometimes also are used, because it may be argued that it is an interval that can really be believed. By contrast, the 95% confidence interval is based only on the sample, and is not so credible if it conflicts with prior information.

Example 10-6

For Example 10-5, calculate:
(a) The 95% Bayesian confidence interval.
(b) The 95% classical confidence interval.

Solution

(a) Substitute (10-28) and (10-29) into (10-30):

$$\mu = 68 \pm 1.96\sqrt{20} = 68 \pm 8.8$$

(b)
$$\mu = \bar{X} \pm 1.96\sqrt{\frac{\sigma^2}{n}} \qquad \text{(10-32) repeated}$$

$$= 70 \pm 1.96\sqrt{\frac{300}{12}} = 70 \pm 9.8$$

Note that this classical confidence interval is wider, since it takes no account of the information in the prior.

PROBLEMS

10-7 (Continuation of Example 10-4.) Suppose that the sample size is $n = 48$ instead of $n = 12$, but everything else is the same, namely: $\mu_0 = 60$, $\sigma_0^2 = 100$, $\sigma^2 = 300$, and the sample mean $\bar{X} = 70$.

(a) Calculate the posterior distribution, and graph it.
(b) Graph the prior and likelihood also. Does the posterior lie between them? Which is the posterior closer to? How much closer?
(c) On the basis of all the available evidence, find the probability that the shipment mean μ is below 62.5.
(d) Calculate the 95% Bayesian confidence interval for μ, and contrast it to the 95% classical confidence interval.

10-8 Repeat Problem 10-7, if the sample size is $n = 2$.

⇒ 10-9 Suppose that it is essential to estimate the length θ of a beetle that accidentally gets caught in a delicate piece of machinery. A measurement X is possible, using a crude device that is subject to considerable error: X is distributed normally about the true value θ, with a standard deviation $\sigma = 5$ mm. Suppose that a sample of 6 such observations yields an average $\bar{X} = 20$ mm.

Some information also is available from the local agricultural station. They tell us that this species of beetle has length that is distributed normally about a mean of 25 mm with a standard deviation of 2.5 mm.

(a) Find a 95% Bayesian confidence interval for the beetle's length θ.

(b) What is the probability that θ is at least 26 mm.?

10-10 The value of wheat falls with its moisture content, measured by the electrical conductivity of the wheat. Suppose that the measured moisture value is distributed normally about the true value, with an error that has a standard deviation of only one-fifth of a percentage point.

Suppose that the loads of wheat that are brought to a grain elevator during a certain week have moisture contents m varying from 14% to 16%, roughly; specifically, the values of m are distributed normally about a mean of 15%, with a standard deviation of .5%.

If a load has a measured value of 13.8%, what is the chance that its true value of m is less than 14%?

10-4 BAYESIAN REGRESSION

In the simple regression model, suppose that the slope β has a prior distribution[15]:

$$\text{Prior distribution, } \beta \sim N(\beta_0, \sigma_0^2) \tag{10-33}$$

The sample provides an estimator $\hat{\beta}$ that also is normal,[16] with mean β and variance $\sigma^2/\sum x^2$, as given in (2-27) and (2-28). If, as in Problem 2-17, we denote

$$\sigma_X^2 = \frac{1}{n} \sum x^2$$

then the variance of $\hat{\beta}$ can be written as

$$\frac{\sigma^2/\sigma_X^2}{n}$$

[15] For simplicity, we assume that any prior information about α is independent of β, and so can be ignored in constructing inferences about β.

[16] For $\hat{\beta}$ to be normal, we must make the same assumptions as in Section 2-7: The Y observations are distributed normally, or the sample size n is large enough.

and so

$$\hat{\beta} \sim N\left(\beta, \frac{\sigma^2/\sigma_X^2}{n}\right) \tag{10-34}$$

When the prior information is combined with the sample information, we obtain a result[17] that is remarkably like the formula for μ:

$$\boxed{\text{Posterior distribution, } \beta \sim N\left(\frac{n_0\beta_0 + n\hat{\beta}}{n_0 + n}, \frac{\sigma^2/\sigma_X^2}{n_0 + n}\right)} \tag{10-35}$$

like (10-27)

where

$$n_0 = \frac{\sigma^2/\sigma_X^2}{\sigma_0^2}$$

From this, we can construct a confidence interval:

95% Bayesian confidence interval:

$$\beta = \left(\frac{n_0\beta_0 + n\hat{\beta}}{n_0 + n}\right) \pm 1.96\sqrt{\frac{\sigma^2/\sigma_X^2}{n_0 + n}} \tag{10-36}$$

like (10-31)

Example 10-7

Suppose that the prior distribution for β is distributed normally about a central value of 5 with a variance of .25. A sample of 8 points provides the following statistics for estimating the slope β:

$$\sum xy = 2400, \qquad \sum x^2 = 400, \qquad \text{residual } s^2 = 25.$$

Using s^2 to approximate σ^2, find:

(a) The quasi-sample size n_0 that is equivalent to the prior.

(b) The 95% Bayesian confidence interval (10-36).

(c) The 95% Bayesian confidence interval, correcting (10-36) by replacing 1.96 with $t_{.025}$ with d.f. $= n_0 + n - 2$.

(d) The 95% classical confidence interval, for comparison.

[17] To derive (10-35), we can appeal to the general normal case (10-27), with the following substitutions:

β for μ

$\hat{\beta}$ for $\bar{X}$

σ^2/σ_X^2 for σ^2

Solution

In standard notation, the prior information is

$$\beta_0 = 5, \sigma_0^2 = .25 \tag{10-37}$$

And from the sample we can calculate:

$$\hat{\beta} = \frac{\sum xy}{\sum x^2} = \frac{2400}{400} = 6.0 \tag{10-38}$$

$$\sigma_X^2 = \frac{1}{n}\sum x^2 = \frac{400}{8} = 50$$

(a)
$$n_0 = \frac{\sigma^2/\sigma_X^2}{\sigma_0^2} \simeq \frac{25/50}{.25} = 2$$

(b)
$$\beta = \left(\frac{n_0\beta_0 + n\hat{\beta}}{n_0 + n}\right) \pm 1.96\sqrt{\frac{\sigma^2/\sigma_X^2}{n_0 + n}} \qquad \text{(10-36) repeated}$$

$$= \frac{2(5) + 8(6)}{2 + 8} \pm 1.96\sqrt{\frac{25/50}{2 + 8}}$$

$$= 5.80 \pm 1.96(.224)$$

$$= 5.80 \pm .44$$

(c) From Appendix Table V, with d.f. $= n_0 + n - 2 = 8$, we find $t_{.025} = 2.306$, and hence

$$\beta = 5.80 \pm 2.306(.224)$$

$$= 5.80 \pm .52$$

(d) Now we use d.f. $= n - 2 = 6$, and find $t_{.025} = 2.447$. Thus

$$\beta = \hat{\beta} \pm t_{.025}\sqrt{\frac{s^2}{\sum x^2}} \qquad \text{(2-51) repeated}$$

$$= 6.00 \pm 2.447\sqrt{\frac{25}{400}}$$

$$= 6.00 \pm .61$$

Remarks

The Bayesian confidence interval in (c) is shorter than the classical confidence interval in (d), reflecting the value of the prior information. The Bayesian confidence interval also is centered at a compromise between $\hat{\beta}$ and

β_0—but 4 times closer to $\hat{\beta}$ because the sample has 4 times as much information ($n = 8$ while $n_0 = 2$).

Incidentally, replacing $z_{.025}$ with $t_{.025}$ [as we did in the Bayesian confidence interval in part (c)] is an approximation that is also useful in applying (10-31) when s^2 has to be used as an estimator for σ^2.

Finally, Bayesian techniques can easily be applied to multiple regression, too. Since the calculations customarily are carried out by computer, however, we will not attempt to do an example by hand.

PROBLEMS

10-11 A consulting economist was given a prior distribution for a regression slope β that was distributed normally about a mean of 2.0 with a standard deviation of .80. Calculate the Bayesian 95% confidence intervals for β as she successively gathers more data:

(*a*) $n = 5, \sum xy = 50, \sum x^2 = 25, s^2 = 12.8.$

(*b*) $n = 10, \sum xy = 80, \sum x^2 = 50, s^2 = 8.0.$

(*c*) $n = 20, \sum xy = 150, \sum x^2 = 100, s^2 = 9.6.$

REVIEW PROBLEMS

10-12 Suppose that your firm has just purchased a major piece of machinery, and that your engineers have judged it to be substandard. You know that the firm that produced it substitutes inferior domestic components for the standard imported components $\frac{1}{4}$ of the time. You further know that such substitution of domestic components increases the probability that the machine will be substandard from .2 to .3. What is the probability that your machine has imported components?

10-13 A shipment of natural sponges is to be sampled to determine three characteristics:

(1) The proportion of defectives π.
(2) The mean weight μ.
(3) The slope β of the graph of absorbency Y as a linear function of weight X.

Suppose, on the basis of past shipments, that the following priors are deemed appropriate:

(1) $p(\pi) = \pi^3(1 - \pi)^{12}$.
(2) $\mu \sim N(150, 400)$.
(3) $\beta \sim N(4.0, .25)$.

A sample of $n = 20$ sponges yielded the following statistics:

(1) Sample proportion of defectives $P = 10\%$.
(2) For weight, $\bar{X} = 140$, $\sum (X_i - \bar{X})^2 = 22{,}800$.
(3) For regression, $\sum (X_i - \bar{X})^2 = 22{,}800$, $\sum (X_i - \bar{X})(Y_i - \bar{Y}) = 114{,}000$, and residual $s^2 = 2{,}850$.

On the basis of the prior and the data, find:

(a) The posterior distribution for π.
(b) The posterior distribution for μ, and its 95% Bayesian confidence interval.
(c) The posterior distribution for β, and its 95% Bayesian confidence interval.

PART 2

MORE ADVANCED ECONOMETRICS

11

INTRODUCTION: SOME BACKGROUND MATHEMATICS

In Part 2 we now change gears: The rest of this book is a much more mathematical treatment of the material in earlier chapters. It is assumed before proceeding that readers will have had a college course in calculus, and another in matrix algebra. We make no attempt to teach these; it is our view that this background should not be rushed, and can be learned most effectively in courses given by math departments from good existing texts.

However, from time to time we will build on these prerequisites. For example, we develop vector differentiation in this chapter, and vector geometry in Chapter 14.

Although Part 2 generalizes the material in earlier chapters, and hence provides a reasonably self-contained introduction to more advanced econometrics, it is by no means a comprehensive survey of this very broad area. Students specializing in this field will also wish to consult textbooks like Malinvaud 1970, or Theil 1971, as well as many other references provided at the back of this book. Although a course in mathematical statistics is not a prerequisite, it may be valuable to have at hand a text such as Lindgren 1968, or Hoel 1971. A review of statistical distributions is given in Chapter 13.

A prerequisite for OLS estimation in the next chapter is partial differentiation of linear and quadratic forms. So differentiation will be the main topic of this brief introductory chapter.

11-1 NOTATION

In matrix algebra, a boldface capital letter such as **A** or **X** represents a matrix; a boldface small letter such as **a** or **x** represents a vector; to avoid too many transpose signs, a vector may be either row *or* column, depending on the context in which it is introduced. Thus, several observations on one variable are introduced as a column, for example,

$$\mathbf{y} = \begin{bmatrix} y_1 \\ y_2 \\ \cdot \\ \cdot \\ \cdot \\ y_n \end{bmatrix}$$

while one observation on several variables is introduced as a row, for example,

$$\mathbf{x} = \begin{bmatrix} x_1, x_2, \ldots, x_k \end{bmatrix}$$

Note that a single entry in a matrix or vector is designated by an ordinary small letter such as y_1 or x_k. The reader is warned that from now on, the variables x and y may refer to *either* their actual observed values or deviations from their mean. Following Chapters 2 and 3, it is recommended that the reader regard the y's as actual observed values, and all the x's as deviations from the mean. But this is not absolutely necessary. Both sets of variables could be treated as original observed variables or, for that matter, both could be treated as deviations from their means—provided that the different definition of the intercept constant is kept in mind (as in Figure 2-7), and other minor adjustments are made.

11-2 PARTIAL DERIVATIVES OF LINEAR AND QUADRATIC FORMS

(a) Linear Form

Consider the linear form in the variables β_i (where a_i are constants):

$$L = a_1\beta_1 + a_2\beta_2 + \cdots + a_k\beta_k \tag{11-1}$$

This may be written as

$$L = \mathbf{a}\,\boldsymbol{\beta} \tag{11-2}$$

i.e.

$$\boxed{L} = \boxed{\quad \mathbf{a} \quad}\ \begin{bmatrix} \\ \boldsymbol{\beta} \\ \\ \end{bmatrix}$$

The partial derivatives of (11-1) with respect to each variable are

$$\begin{aligned}
\frac{\partial L}{\partial \beta_1} &= a_1 \\
\frac{\partial L}{\partial \beta_2} &= a_2 \\
&\vdots \\
\frac{\partial L}{\partial \beta_k} &= a_k
\end{aligned} \tag{11-3}$$

Let us stack these partial derivatives in a column vector denoted by $\partial L/\partial \boldsymbol{\beta}$ or $(\partial/\partial\boldsymbol{\beta})(\mathbf{a}\ \boldsymbol{\beta})$. Then (11-3) may be written more concisely as

$$\boxed{\frac{\partial}{\partial \boldsymbol{\beta}}(\mathbf{a}\ \boldsymbol{\beta}) = \mathbf{a}'} \tag{11-4}$$

Note the similarity to the formula in ordinary calculus:

$$\frac{d}{dx}(ax) = a \tag{11-5}$$

(b) Quadratic Form

Consider next the quadratic form in the same variables β_i (where a_{ij} are constants):

$$Q = a_{11}\beta_1^2 + a_{12}\beta_1\beta_2 + \cdots + a_{21}\beta_2\beta_1 + a_{22}\beta_2^2 + \cdots + a_{ij}\beta_i\beta_j + \cdots + a_{k1}\beta_k\beta_1 + \cdots + a_{kk}\beta_k^2 \tag{11-6}$$

where $a_{ij} = a_{ji}$ without loss of generality. In matrix notation, this may be rewritten as

$$Q = \boldsymbol{\beta}'\mathbf{A}\boldsymbol{\beta} \tag{11-7}$$

i.e.

$$\boxed{Q} = \boxed{\beta_1 \ \cdots \ \beta_k} \ \boxed{\begin{matrix} a_{11} & \cdots & a_{1k} \\ \vdots & & \\ a_{k1} & \cdots & a_{kk} \end{matrix}} \ \boxed{\begin{matrix} \beta_1 \\ \vdots \\ \beta_k \end{matrix}}$$

where $\mathbf{A} = \mathbf{A}'$ without loss of generality.

If we take the partial derivatives of (11-6) with respect to each variable, and remember $a_{21} = a_{12}$ etc., then

$$\frac{\partial Q}{\partial \beta_1} = 2a_{11}\beta_1 + a_{12}\beta_2 + \cdots + a_{1k}\beta_k + a_{21}\beta_2 + \cdots + a_{k1}\beta_k$$

Similarly

$$\left.\begin{aligned} \frac{\partial Q}{\partial \beta_1} &= 2(a_{11}\beta_1 + a_{12}\beta_2 + \cdots + a_{1k}\beta_k) \\ \frac{\partial Q}{\partial \beta_2} &= 2(a_{21}\beta_1 + a_{22}\beta_2 + \cdots + a_{2k}\beta_k) \\ &\;\;\vdots \\ \frac{\partial Q}{\partial \beta_k} &= 2(a_{k1}\beta_1 + \qquad \cdots + a_{kk}\beta_k) \end{aligned}\right\} \tag{11-8}$$

As before, these partial derivatives stacked in a column are denoted by $\partial Q/\partial \boldsymbol{\beta}$ or $(\partial/\partial \boldsymbol{\beta})(\boldsymbol{\beta}'\mathbf{A}\boldsymbol{\beta})$. Since the right side of (11-8) is the matrix product $2\mathbf{A}\boldsymbol{\beta}$, (11-8) may be written concisely as

$$\boxed{\frac{\partial}{\partial \boldsymbol{\beta}}(\boldsymbol{\beta}'\mathbf{A}\boldsymbol{\beta}) = 2\mathbf{A}\boldsymbol{\beta}} \tag{11-9}$$

Note again the similarity to the formula in ordinary calculus:

$$\frac{d}{dx}(ax^2) = 2ax \tag{11-10}$$

With this mathematics in hand, we can now turn to the full matrix development of the regression model.

12

MULTIPLE REGRESSION USING MATRICES (A Generalization of Chapters 1, 2, and 3)

During the course of this chapter, it is advisable to consult Table 12-1 frequently, since it summarizes results for the simple and multivariate cases, side by side, for easy comparison.

12-1 INTRODUCTION TO THE GENERAL LINEAR MODEL

If y is a linear function of the independent variables $x_2, x_3, \ldots, x_k$, plus error, then the ith observation y_i can be written as

$$y_i = \beta_1 + \beta_2 x_{i2} + \cdots + \beta_k x_{ik} + e_i \qquad (12\text{-}1)$$

where the subscript i refers to the ith observation. Notice that β_1 is not a slope, but is, in fact, the constant term in the equation—that is, what we have called α in earlier chapters. One of the great virtues of matrices is that this constant term will no longer require special treatment. In vector notation, (12-1) is

$$\boxed{y_i} = \boxed{1 \quad x_{i2} \quad \cdots \quad x_{ik}} \begin{bmatrix} \beta_1 \\ \beta_2 \\ \cdot \\ \cdot \\ \cdot \\ \beta_k \end{bmatrix} + \boxed{e_i} \qquad (12\text{-}2)$$

TABLE 12-1 Comparison of Simple and Multiple Regression

Simple	*Multiple*
1. *Model*	
$Y = \alpha + x\beta + e$ (2-23)	$\mathbf{y} = \mathbf{X}\boldsymbol{\beta} + \mathbf{e}$ (12-3)
2. *Least squares maximum likelihood estimates*	
$\hat{\beta} = (\sum x^2)^{-1}(\sum xy)$ (2-19)	$\hat{\boldsymbol{\beta}} = (\mathbf{X}'\mathbf{X})^{-1}\mathbf{X}'\mathbf{y}$ (12-4)
3. *Distribution of* $\hat{\beta}$	
$\hat{\beta}$ is normal with $E(\hat{\beta}) = \beta$ (2-27) and var $(\hat{\beta}) = \sigma^2(\sum x^2)^{-1}$ (2-28) $= \sigma^2 v$	$\hat{\boldsymbol{\beta}}$ is multivariate normal with $E(\hat{\boldsymbol{\beta}}) = \boldsymbol{\beta}$ (12-5) and cov $(\hat{\boldsymbol{\beta}}) = \sigma^2(\mathbf{X}'\mathbf{X})^{-1}$ (12-6) $= \sigma^2\mathbf{V}$
4. *Standardized distribution*	
$z = \dfrac{\hat{\beta} - \beta}{\sqrt{\sigma^2 v}}$ (2-43) or $z^2 = (\hat{\beta} - \beta)(\sigma^2 v)^{-1}(\hat{\beta} - \beta)$ has χ^2 distribution with 1 d.f.	$\chi^2 = (\mathbf{C}\hat{\boldsymbol{\beta}} - \mathbf{C}\boldsymbol{\beta})'(\sigma^2\mathbf{CVC}')^{-1}(\mathbf{C}\hat{\boldsymbol{\beta}} - \mathbf{C}\boldsymbol{\beta})$ has χ^2 distribution with r d.f. (12-7)
5. *Quasi-standardized distribution (using* s^2 *for* σ^2*)*	
$t = \dfrac{(\hat{\beta} - \beta)}{\sqrt{s^2 v}}$ (2-46) has t distribution on $(n - 2)$ d.f. or $t^2 = (\hat{\beta} - \beta)(s^2 v)^{-1}(\hat{\beta} - \beta)$ has F distribution on $(1, n - 2)$ d.f.	$F = \dfrac{1}{r}(\mathbf{C}\hat{\boldsymbol{\beta}} - \mathbf{C}\boldsymbol{\beta})'(s^2\mathbf{CVC}')^{-1}(\mathbf{C}\hat{\boldsymbol{\beta}} - \mathbf{C}\boldsymbol{\beta})$ (12-8) has F distribution on $(r, n - k)$ d.f. where k is the number of regressors, and r the number of simultaneous tests on the regressors.

If we stack all y observations into a column vector, we have

$$\mathbf{y} = \mathbf{X}\boldsymbol{\beta} + \mathbf{e} \qquad (12\text{-}9)$$

like (12-3)

$$\begin{bmatrix} y_1 \\ y_2 \\ \cdot \\ \cdot \\ \cdot \\ y_i \\ \cdot \\ \cdot \\ \cdot \\ y_n \end{bmatrix} = \begin{bmatrix} 1 & x_{12} & \cdots & x_{1k} \\ 1 & x_{22} & \cdots & x_{2k} \\ & \cdot & & \cdot \\ & \cdot & & \cdot \\ & \cdot & & \cdot \\ 1 & x_{i2} & & x_{ik} \\ & \cdot & & \cdot \\ & \cdot & & \cdot \\ & \cdot & & \cdot \\ 1 & x_{n2} & \cdots & x_{nk} \end{bmatrix} \begin{bmatrix} \beta_1 \\ \beta_2 \\ \cdot \\ \cdot \\ \cdot \\ \beta_k \end{bmatrix} + \begin{bmatrix} e_1 \\ e_2 \\ \cdot \\ \cdot \\ \cdot \\ e_i \\ \cdot \\ \cdot \\ \cdot \\ e_n \end{bmatrix}$$

We assume the e_i are independent errors, with mean zero and variance σ^2, so that

$$E(\mathbf{e}) = \mathbf{0} \qquad (12\text{-}10)$$

and the covariance matrix of $\mathbf{e}$ is

$$\mathrm{cov}(\mathbf{e}) \equiv E(\mathbf{e}\mathbf{e}') = \sigma^2\mathbf{I} \qquad (12\text{-}11)$$

$$\begin{bmatrix} E(e_1 e_1) & E(e_1 e_2) & \cdots & E(e_1 e_n) \\ E(e_2 e_1) & E(e_2 e_2) & \cdots & \cdot \\ \cdot & & & \cdot \\ \cdot & & & \cdot \\ \cdot & & & \\ E(e_n e_1) & E(e_n e_2) & \cdots & E(e_n e_n) \end{bmatrix} = \begin{bmatrix} \sigma^2 & & & & 0 \\ & \sigma^2 & & & \\ & & \cdot & & \\ & & & \cdot & \\ & & & & \cdot \\ 0 & & & & \sigma^2 \end{bmatrix} \qquad (12\text{-}12)$$

Since the e distribution is, in fact, the y distribution translated onto a zero mean, the only difference in these two sets of variables is their mean value. Thus:

$$E(\mathbf{y}) = \mathbf{X}\boldsymbol{\beta} \qquad (12\text{-}13)$$

$$\text{and } \mathrm{cov}(\mathbf{y}) = \sigma^2\mathbf{I} \qquad (12\text{-}14)$$

Note that the covariance matrix of $\mathbf{e}$ in (12-11) and of $\mathbf{y}$ in (12-14) are identical.

Example 12-1

In the wheat yield model in Table 3-1, we assume that our seven observations of y were generated as follows:

$$\begin{bmatrix} y_1 \\ y_2 \\ y_3 \\ y_4 \\ y_5 \\ y_6 \\ y_7 \end{bmatrix} = \begin{bmatrix} 1 & -300 & -10 \\ 1 & -200 & 0 \\ 1 & -100 & -10 \\ 1 & 0 & 10 \\ 1 & 100 & 0 \\ 1 & 200 & 0 \\ 1 & 300 & 10 \end{bmatrix} \begin{bmatrix} \beta_1 \\ \beta_2 \\ \beta_3 \end{bmatrix} + \begin{bmatrix} e_1 \\ e_2 \\ e_3 \\ e_4 \\ e_5 \\ e_6 \\ e_7 \end{bmatrix} \tag{12-15}$$

in which the β's are unknowns to be estimated, and the error terms are drawn from the normal distribution described in (12-10) and (12-11).

12-2 LEAST SQUARES ESTIMATION (OLS)

OLS involves minimizing the sum of squared deviations, expressed in matrix form; that is, minimize

$$(\mathbf{y} - \mathbf{X\beta})'(\mathbf{y} - \mathbf{X\beta}) \tag{12-16}$$

This may be written[1]:

$$\mathbf{y}'\mathbf{y} - 2\mathbf{y}'\mathbf{X\beta} + \mathbf{\beta}'\mathbf{X}'\mathbf{X\beta} \tag{12-17}$$

The minimum occurs where the partial derivatives with respect to $\mathbf{\beta}$ are zero. The vector of partial derivatives may be obtained by applying the results of Section 11-2 to equation (12-17), since its three terms in $\mathbf{\beta}$ are constant, linear, and quadratic. Thus, the vector of partial derivatives is

$$\mathbf{0} - 2\mathbf{X}'\mathbf{y} + 2\mathbf{X}'\mathbf{X\beta}$$

Setting this equal to zero yields[2] the least squares estimate:

$$\boxed{\hat{\mathbf{\beta}} = (\mathbf{X}'\mathbf{X})^{-1}\mathbf{X}'\mathbf{y}} \tag{12-19}$$

like (12-4)

[1] The expansion of (12-16) into (12-17) is analogous to the expansion of the scalar quantity $(y - xb)^2$ into $y^2 - 2y(xb) + (xb)^2$. The details are as follows:

Equation (12-16) may be written

$$\{\mathbf{y}' - (\mathbf{X\beta})'\}\{\mathbf{y} - \mathbf{X\beta}\} = \mathbf{y}'\mathbf{y} - \mathbf{y}'\mathbf{X\beta} - (\mathbf{X\beta})'\mathbf{y} + (\mathbf{X\beta})'\mathbf{X\beta} \tag{12-18}$$

But since $\mathbf{y}'\mathbf{X\beta}$ is a 1×1 matrix, it is identical to its transpose $(\mathbf{X\beta})'\mathbf{y}$. Thus, the two middle terms may be collected together and (12-17) follows.

By a generalization of the Gauss-Markov theorem, $\hat{\boldsymbol{\beta}}$ can be proved to be the Best Linear Unbiased Estimator (BLUE); moreover this requires no assumption about the distribution of **e** (normal, or otherwise).

12-3 MAXIMUM LIKELIHOOD ESTIMATION (MLE)

Here it is explicitly assumed that

$$\mathbf{e} \text{ is normally distributed} \tag{12-21}$$

MLE estimates are derived by trying out all possible values for $\boldsymbol{\beta}$ and σ and selecting the set that maximizes the likelihood of our observed sample. For any $\boldsymbol{\beta}$ and σ we consider, the likelihood of our observed sample $\mathbf{y}$ is

$$L(\boldsymbol{\beta}, \sigma^2) = \frac{1}{(2\pi\sigma^2)^{n/2}} e^{-(1/2\sigma^2)(\mathbf{y}-\mathbf{X}\boldsymbol{\beta})'(\mathbf{y}-\mathbf{X}\boldsymbol{\beta})} \tag{12-22}$$

This is simply a generalization of (2-79), with the mean $\alpha + \beta x_i$ being replaced by the mean $\beta_1 + \beta_2 x_{i2} + \cdots + \beta_k x_{ik}$ of (12-1), and dressed up in matrix notation.

As remarked after equation (2-79), whatever the value of σ we try, we can maximize (12-22) with respect to $\boldsymbol{\beta}$ by minimizing the magnitude of the exponent; that is, minimize

$$(\mathbf{y} - \mathbf{X}\boldsymbol{\beta})'(\mathbf{y} - \mathbf{X}\boldsymbol{\beta}) \tag{12-23}$$

Since this is precisely the same criterion (12-16) used in deriving OLS estimates, MLE and OLS are identical.

As in Appendix 2-D it can be shown that the MLE of σ^2 (the variance of e) is a biased estimator. It is the result of simply averaging the squared residuals between the observed and fitted values of y:

$$\hat{\sigma}^2 = \frac{1}{n}(\mathbf{y} - \hat{\mathbf{y}})'(\mathbf{y} - \hat{\mathbf{y}}) \tag{12-24}$$

---

[2] We assume that $\mathbf{X}$ is of full rank (complete multicollinearity is avoided) so that $\mathbf{X}'\mathbf{X}$ is invertible. We might be tempted to rewrite (12-19) as

$$\hat{\boldsymbol{\beta}} = (\mathbf{X}^{-1}\mathbf{X}'^{-1})\mathbf{X}'\mathbf{y} = \mathbf{X}^{-1}\mathbf{y} \tag{12-20}$$

This is *only* justified, however, when $\mathbf{X}$ is *square* so that $\mathbf{X}^{-1}$ exists. In this case, where $k = n$, there are as many parameters as observations, and the problem is no longer a statistical problem of best fit, but rather a mathematical problem of the *only* fit.

where $\hat{\mathbf{y}} = \mathbf{X}\hat{\boldsymbol{\beta}}$. Because $\hat{\sigma}^2$ is biased, in the development below we prefer to use the unbiased estimator:

$$\boxed{s^2 = \frac{1}{n-k}(\mathbf{y} - \hat{\mathbf{y}})'(\mathbf{y} - \hat{\mathbf{y}})} \tag{12-25}$$

The ratio s^2/σ^2 has a C^2 (modified chi-squared) distribution with only $(n-k)$ d.f., since k d.f. out of the total n have been used in deriving the k estimators $\hat{\boldsymbol{\beta}}$. The details of this, and other distributions, will be given in Chapter 13.

Example 12-2

In the wheat yield example in Table 3-2, $\hat{\boldsymbol{\beta}}$ is estimated from (12-19) by

$$\begin{bmatrix} \hat{\beta}_1 \\ \hat{\beta}_2 \\ \hat{\beta}_3 \end{bmatrix} = (\mathbf{X}'\mathbf{X})^{-1}\mathbf{X}'\mathbf{y}$$

$$= \left(\begin{bmatrix} 1 & 1 & \cdots & 1 \\ -300 & -200 & \cdots & 300 \\ -10 & 0 & \cdots & 10 \end{bmatrix} \begin{bmatrix} 1 & -300 & -10 \\ 1 & -200 & 0 \\ & \cdot & \\ & \cdot & \\ & \cdot & \\ 1 & 300 & 10 \end{bmatrix} \right)^{-1} \begin{bmatrix} 1 & 1 & \cdots & 1 \\ -300 & -200 & \cdots & 300 \\ -10 & 0 & \cdots & 10 \end{bmatrix} \begin{bmatrix} 40 \\ 50 \\ \cdot \\ \cdot \\ \cdot \\ 80 \end{bmatrix}$$

$$= \begin{bmatrix} 7 & 0 & 0 \\ 0 & 28_4 & 7_3 \\ 0 & 7_3 & 4_2 \end{bmatrix}^{-1} \begin{bmatrix} 420 \\ 165_2 \\ 600 \end{bmatrix} = \begin{bmatrix} \frac{1}{7} & 0 & 0 \\ 0 & {}_5635 & -{}_3111 \\ 0 & -{}_3111 & {}_2444 \end{bmatrix} \begin{bmatrix} 420 \\ 165_2 \\ 600 \end{bmatrix} = \begin{bmatrix} 60.0 \\ .038 \\ .833 \end{bmatrix} \tag{12-26}$$

where the subscript represents the number of omitted zeros; for example, 28_4 means 280,000, while $.{}_5635$ means .00000635. Note how the measurement of

x values as deviations has resulted in zeros in all but one of the elements of the first row and column of $\mathbf{X'X}$. This greatly simplifies its inversion. $\hat{\boldsymbol{\beta}}$ now defines our estimated regression plane, from which fitted y values can be calculated:

$$\hat{\mathbf{y}} = \mathbf{X}\hat{\boldsymbol{\beta}} \qquad (12\text{-}27)$$

In our example:

$$\begin{bmatrix} \hat{y}_1 \\ \hat{y}_2 \\ \cdot \\ \cdot \\ \cdot \\ \\ \hat{y}_7 \end{bmatrix} = \begin{bmatrix} 1 & -300 & -10 \\ 1 & -200 & 0 \\ 1 & -100 & -10 \\ 1 & 0 & 10 \\ 1 & 100 & 0 \\ 1 & 200 & 0 \\ 1 & 300 & 10 \end{bmatrix} \begin{bmatrix} 60.0 \\ .038 \\ .833 \end{bmatrix} = \begin{bmatrix} 40.2 \\ 52.4 \\ 47.9 \\ 68.3 \\ 63.8 \\ 67.6 \\ 79.8 \end{bmatrix}$$

These estimated values $\hat{y}$, along with the observed values y, allow us to estimate the variance of our error from (12-25):

$$s^2 = \frac{1}{(7-3)} \begin{bmatrix} -.2 & -2.4 & 2.1 & 1.7 & 1.2 & -2.6 & .2 \end{bmatrix} \begin{bmatrix} -.2 \\ -2.4 \\ 2.1 \\ 1.7 \\ 1.2 \\ -2.6 \\ .2 \end{bmatrix}$$

$$= 21.34/4 = 5.35 \qquad (12\text{-}28)$$

which agrees with the computer output in Table 3-3, incidentally.

PROBLEMS

12-1 Show that (2-13) and (2-16) represent the special case of (12-19) for simple regression.

12-4 DISTRIBUTION OF $\hat{\boldsymbol{\beta}}$

Because $\mathbf{X}$ is fixed, $\hat{\boldsymbol{\beta}}$ estimated in (12-19) is just a linear transformation of normal, independent variables $\mathbf{y}$. To emphasize this, we rewrite (12-19) as

$$\hat{\boldsymbol{\beta}} = \mathbf{My} \tag{12-29}$$

where

$$\mathbf{M} = (\mathbf{X'X})^{-1}\mathbf{X'} \tag{12-30}$$

As stated in Table 12-2, such a linear transformation keeps $\hat{\boldsymbol{\beta}}$ normal, with mean

$$E(\hat{\boldsymbol{\beta}}) = E(\mathbf{My}) = \mathbf{M}E(\mathbf{y})$$

Noting (12-30) and (12-13)

$$E(\hat{\boldsymbol{\beta}}) = \{(\mathbf{X'X})^{-1}\mathbf{X'}\}\mathbf{X}\boldsymbol{\beta}$$

$$\boxed{E(\hat{\boldsymbol{\beta}}) = \boldsymbol{\beta}} \tag{12-31}$$

like (12-5)

Thus, $\hat{\boldsymbol{\beta}}$ is a normal, unbiased estimator of $\boldsymbol{\beta}$. The covariance matrix of $\hat{\boldsymbol{\beta}}$ is also found from Table 12-2, and is

$$\operatorname{cov}(\hat{\boldsymbol{\beta}}) = \mathbf{M}(\operatorname{cov}\,\mathbf{y})\mathbf{M'}$$

Noting[3] (12-30) and (12-14),

$$\operatorname{cov}(\hat{\boldsymbol{\beta}}) = \{(\mathbf{X'X})^{-1}\mathbf{X'}\}\sigma^2\mathbf{I}\{(\mathbf{X'X})^{-1}\mathbf{X'}\}'$$

$$\boxed{\operatorname{cov}(\hat{\boldsymbol{\beta}}) = \sigma^2(\mathbf{X'X})^{-1}} \tag{12-32}$$

like (12-6)

Note how the inverse $(\mathbf{X'X})^{-1}$ keeps reappearing. Since it will continue to be of fundamental importance in our estimating procedures, we introduce the abbreviation

$$\mathbf{V} \equiv (\mathbf{X'X})^{-1} \tag{12-33}$$

Thus

$$\operatorname{cov}\,\hat{\boldsymbol{\beta}} = \sigma^2\mathbf{V} \tag{12-34}$$

[3] Also noting that the transpose of an inverse equals the inverse of the transpose, and that $(\mathbf{X'X})' = \mathbf{X'X}$, that is, $\mathbf{X'X}$ is symmetric.

TABLE 12-2 Linear Transformations and Their Distributions (Extension of Appendix 2-A)

	Variable	*Mean*	*Variance*	*Distribution*
(a) *Univariate case*				
Original variable	y	μ	σ^2	normal
				↓
Its transformation	$z = my$	$m\mu$	$m^2\sigma^2$	normal
(b) *Bivariate case*				
Original variables	y_1	μ_1	σ_1^2	normal
	y_2	μ_2	σ_2^2	normal
			and covariance σ_{12}	↓
Transformation	$z = m_1 y_1 + m_2 y_2$	$m_1\mu_1 + m_2\mu_2$	$m_1^2\sigma_1^2 + m_2^2\sigma_2^2 + 2m_1 m_2 \sigma_{12}$	normal
(In matrix notation)	$\begin{bmatrix} z \end{bmatrix} = \begin{bmatrix} m_1 & m_2 \end{bmatrix} \begin{bmatrix} y_1 \\ y_2 \end{bmatrix}$	$\begin{bmatrix} m_1 & m_2 \end{bmatrix} \begin{bmatrix} \mu_1 \\ \mu_2 \end{bmatrix}$	$\begin{bmatrix} m_1 & m_2 \end{bmatrix} \begin{bmatrix} \sigma_1^2 & \sigma_{12} \\ \sigma_{12} & \sigma_2^2 \end{bmatrix} \begin{bmatrix} m_1 \\ m_2 \end{bmatrix}$	
(c) *Multivariate case*			covariance matrix	
Original variables	$\mathbf{y}$	$\boldsymbol{\mu}$	$\boldsymbol{\Sigma}$	normal
				↓
Transformation	$\mathbf{z} = \mathbf{M}\mathbf{y}$	$\mathbf{M}\boldsymbol{\mu}$	$\mathbf{M}\boldsymbol{\Sigma}\mathbf{M}'$	normal
(In matrix notation)	$\begin{bmatrix} \mathbf{z} \end{bmatrix} = \begin{bmatrix} \mathbf{M} \end{bmatrix} \begin{bmatrix} \mathbf{y} \end{bmatrix}$	$\begin{bmatrix} \mathbf{M} \end{bmatrix} \begin{bmatrix} \boldsymbol{\mu} \end{bmatrix}$	$\begin{bmatrix} \mathbf{M} \end{bmatrix} \begin{bmatrix} \boldsymbol{\Sigma} \end{bmatrix} \begin{bmatrix} \mathbf{M}' \end{bmatrix}$	

Example 12-3

For the wheat yield example, $\text{cov}(\hat{\boldsymbol{\beta}})$ can be obtained easily from (12-32), noting that $(\mathbf{X}'\mathbf{X})^{-1}$ has already been calculated in (12-26):

$$\text{cov}\,\hat{\boldsymbol{\beta}} = \sigma^2 \begin{bmatrix} \frac{1}{7} & 0 & 0 \\ 0 & ._{5}635 & -._{3}111 \\ 0 & -._{3}111 & ._{2}444 \end{bmatrix} \tag{12-35}$$

and σ^2 can be estimated by $s^2 = 5.35$ in (12-28).

PROBLEMS

12-2 Consider a simple regression based on only three observations. Suppose $\sigma^2 = 10$, and the single regressor is to be set at three values—4, 6, 8.

(a) Expressing the regressor in deviation form, calculate $\text{cov}(\hat{\boldsymbol{\beta}})$ using (12-32). Does this illustrate the principle that the estimators of the slope and intercept are uncorrelated?

(b) This time do not define the regressor as deviations from the mean. Set up (12-32) again in this case, and calculate the covariance between the estimators of the slope and intercept.

12-3 Prove (3-11), using the theory of this chapter.

12-5 CONFIDENCE REGIONS AND HYPOTHESIS TESTING

With the distribution of the estimator $\hat{\boldsymbol{\beta}}$ in hand, we are now in a position to develop confidence intervals and hypothesis tests for $\boldsymbol{\beta}$. But we choose instead to slow down, and generalize our argument. In the following section, we consider a general linear transformation of $\hat{\boldsymbol{\beta}}$, which will be useful in constructing a whole array of confidence intervals about some or all of the β's. The student who finds this concept a bit difficult is advised that this is a high-return investment. From this general procedure, many specific confidence intervals and tests will be easily derived.

Let us consider the distribution of $\hat{\boldsymbol{\gamma}}$, a general linear transformation of $\hat{\boldsymbol{\beta}}$:

$$\hat{\boldsymbol{\gamma}} = \mathbf{C}\hat{\boldsymbol{\beta}} \tag{12-36}$$

$$\begin{bmatrix} \hat{\gamma}_1 \\ \vdots \\ \hat{\gamma}_r \end{bmatrix} = \begin{bmatrix} c_{11} & \cdots & c_{1k} \\ \vdots & & \\ c_{r1} & & c_{rk} \end{bmatrix} \begin{bmatrix} \hat{\beta}_1 \\ \vdots \\ \hat{\beta}_k \end{bmatrix}$$

where **C** is any arbitrary matrix of constants, subject only to the restriction that it be of rank r. This means that the rows must be linearly independent, and in particular, that $r \leq k$. Looking ahead, we see that if we let **C** be the identity, for example, (12-36) will enable us to find the distribution of $\hat{\boldsymbol{\beta}}$ itself; or if we let $\mathbf{C} = (1\ 0\ 0 \cdots 0)$, the result is the distribution of a single variable $\hat{\beta}_1$. While k is the total number of regressors in the model, r is the number we will be testing.

To find the distribution of $\mathbf{C}\hat{\boldsymbol{\beta}}$, we appeal once more to the theory of linear transformations described in Table 12-2. Also noting (12-31), it follows that

$$E(\mathbf{C}\hat{\boldsymbol{\beta}}) = \mathbf{C}E(\hat{\boldsymbol{\beta}}) = \mathbf{C}\boldsymbol{\beta}$$

and from (12-34)

$$\operatorname{cov}(\mathbf{C}\hat{\boldsymbol{\beta}}) = \mathbf{C}(\operatorname{cov} \hat{\boldsymbol{\beta}})\mathbf{C}' = \sigma^2\mathbf{CVC}' \tag{12-37}$$

Just as we found a standardized normal variable (z) in the univariate case, so we now standardize in this multivariate case. It may be shown that

$$\chi^2 = (\mathbf{C}\hat{\boldsymbol{\beta}} - \mathbf{C}\boldsymbol{\beta})'(\sigma^2\mathbf{CVC}')^{-1}(\mathbf{C}\hat{\boldsymbol{\beta}} - \mathbf{C}\boldsymbol{\beta}) \tag{12-38}$$

like (12-7)

has a χ_r^2 distribution (chi-square with r d.f.).

We remind the reader again that the distributions in this chapter are discussed more systematically in Chapter 13, and the interpretation of χ^2 in (12-38) as a generalization of the familiar standard normal z is summarized in row 4 of Table 12-1. (A student without a background in statistical theory should consult this table and read Chapter 13 concurrently.)

Notice that our standardization procedure in (12-38)—just as in the simpler case of z—involves measuring the variables as deviations from their means $(\mathbf{C}\hat{\boldsymbol{\beta}} - \mathbf{C}\boldsymbol{\beta})$, and expressing them in terms of standard units by dividing by their variance[4] [or more specifically their covariance matrix $\sigma^2\mathbf{CVC}'$].

---

[4] We divide by the variance rather than the standard deviation because we have squared all our r normal variables $(\mathbf{C}\hat{\boldsymbol{\beta}} - \mathbf{C}\boldsymbol{\beta})$ in (12-38). This complicated quadratic function involves r normal variables—but they are correlated because each $\hat{\gamma}_i$ is a linear function of $\hat{\boldsymbol{\beta}}$. Nevertheless, the distribution of (12-38) is equivalent to a simple sum of r squared uncorrelated normal variates, whose sum by definition is a χ^2 variate with r d.f. The reason for this equivalence is that the correlation of $\hat{\gamma}_1, \ldots, \hat{\gamma}_r$ is compensated for, or "undone," by the complexity of the matrix $(\sigma^2\mathbf{CVC}')^{-1}$. In other words, the covariance matrix describes how the variables $\hat{\gamma}_1, \ldots, \hat{\gamma}_r$ are related; hence multiplying by its inverse "unrelates" them.

If we divide (12-38) by r (degrees of freedom), the χ^2 variable becomes a C^2 variable (d.f. $= r$). Since σ^2 is unknown, its unbiased estimator s^2 (d.f. $= n - k$) is substituted; in the process (12-38) becomes a ratio of two independent C^2 variables, that is, an F variable. Note again in Table 12-1 (row 5) the similarity of this to the univariate case where replacement of σ^2 by s^2 changed a normal variable to a t variable. Thus

$$F = \frac{1}{r}(\mathbf{C}\hat{\boldsymbol{\beta}} - \mathbf{C}\boldsymbol{\beta})'(\mathbf{CVC}')^{-1}(\mathbf{C}\hat{\boldsymbol{\beta}} - \mathbf{C}\boldsymbol{\beta})/s^2 \tag{12-39}$$

like (12-8)

has an F distribution, with r and $(n - k)$ degrees of freedom. F is the basic statistic we will be using for constructing confidence intervals or for testing hypotheses about $\boldsymbol{\beta}$. Furthermore, we can construct any number of diverse tests from this fundamental result—simply by using an appropriately specified $\mathbf{C}$ matrix.

The F statistic has a well-tabulated distribution, whose critical 5% point is denoted by $F_{.05}$ (Appendix Table VII). Thus, from (12-39), the following probability statement can be made:

$$\Pr\left[\frac{1}{r}(\mathbf{C}\hat{\boldsymbol{\beta}} - \mathbf{C}\boldsymbol{\beta})'(\mathbf{CVC}')^{-1}(\mathbf{C}\hat{\boldsymbol{\beta}} - \mathbf{C}\boldsymbol{\beta})/s^2 \leq F_{.05}\right] = 95\% \tag{12-40}$$

From the inequality within the brackets, we obtain a 95% confidence region for $\mathbf{C}\boldsymbol{\beta}$:

$$\boxed{(\mathbf{C}\boldsymbol{\beta} - \mathbf{C}\hat{\boldsymbol{\beta}})'(\mathbf{CVC}')^{-1}(\mathbf{C}\boldsymbol{\beta} - \mathbf{C}\hat{\boldsymbol{\beta}}) \leq s^2 r F_{.05}} \tag{12-41}$$

As well as this general confidence region, we now find it useful to develop several special cases.

(a) Confidence Region for all β_i

To obtain a simultaneous (joint) confidence region for all the β_i, set $\mathbf{C} = \mathbf{I}$. In this special case, $(\mathbf{CVC}')^{-1} = \mathbf{V}^{-1} = \mathbf{X}'\mathbf{X}$, and thus the 95% confidence region (12-41) reduces to:

$$\boxed{(\boldsymbol{\beta} - \hat{\boldsymbol{\beta}})'\mathbf{X}'\mathbf{X}(\boldsymbol{\beta} - \hat{\boldsymbol{\beta}}) \leq s^2 k F_{.05}} \tag{12-42}$$

In (12-42) everything is known except $\boldsymbol{\beta}$. The values of $\boldsymbol{\beta}$ that satisfy this inequality form a k-dimensional ellipsoid.

Example 12-4

For the wheat yield in Example 12-2, the right side of (12-42) is (5.35)(3)(6.59) = 105.8. Thus (12-42) altogether is:

$$\begin{bmatrix} \beta_1 - 60.0 & \beta_2 - .038 & \beta_3 - .833 \end{bmatrix} \begin{bmatrix} 7 & 0 & 0 \\ 0 & 280{,}000 & 7{,}000 \\ 0 & 7{,}000 & 400 \end{bmatrix} \begin{bmatrix} \beta_1 - 60.0 \\ \beta_2 - .038 \\ \beta_3 - .833 \end{bmatrix} \leq 105.8 \qquad (12\text{-}43)$$

which is an ellipsoid in three-dimensional space, with center (60.0, .038, .833).

Since we haven't estimated a joint confidence region before, it may be a bit difficult for you to get an intuitive grasp of what is going on; so let's consider the simpler example of Chapter 2 in which yield is related to fertilizer only. In this case there are only two parameters to simultaneously estimate—β_1 (which we denoted in Chapter 2 as α) and β_2 (which we denoted in Chapter 2 simply as β). The 95% confidence region equivalent to (12-43) in this case would be a two-dimensional ellipse, something like the ellipse[5] in Figure 12-1*a*. This ellipse could have fallen in any one—or any combination—of the four quadrants in the β_1, β_2 space.

In Figure 12-1*b*, this 95% confidence region is translated into our original *Y*, *x* space. Since β_1 represents the *Y* intercept, the limiting restrictions on its values are easily translated, using dotted horizontal lines. Since β_2 is a slope parameter, the restrictions on its possible values cannot be so easily translated. However, note from the left-hand diagram that β_2 is limited to positive values—and you can confirm that the only regressions that can be fitted into the confidence band in the right-hand diagram are those with a positive slope. This suggests the appropriate way of thinking about the joint confidence band in Figure 12-1*b*; at a 95% level of confidence it can be stated that this band will cover the true regression line *throughout its entire length.*[6]

---

[5] The advantage of measuring *x* as deviations from the mean is that this ensures that the axes of the ellipse in Figure 12-1*a* will be parallel to the β_1 and β_2 axes (i.e., $\hat{\beta}_1$ and $\hat{\beta}_2$ will be uncorrelated).

[6] The equation of this band is given by (2-72).

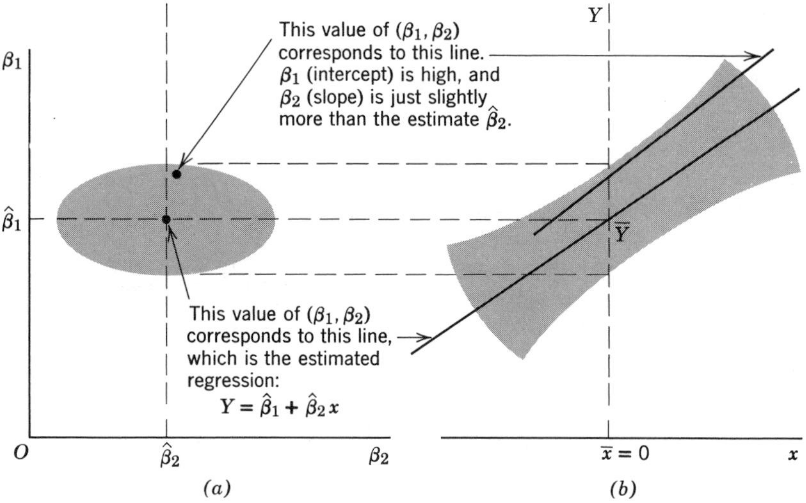

FIGURE 12-1 Interpretation of joint confidence region in simple regression. (*a*) β_1, β_2 space. (*b*) x, Y space.

(b) Confidence Region for Several β_i

Without loss of generality, we can rearrange our x variables so that the ones of interest are put last; let us suppose there are r of these, and we wish to obtain a simultaneous confidence region for them: Let $\boldsymbol{\beta}_r$ be the column vector of the last r β's and

$$\mathbf{C} = \left[\begin{array}{c|cccc} & 1 & & & \\ & & 1 & & 0 \\ 0 & & & \ddots & \\ & & 0 & & \ddots \\ & & & & 1 \end{array}\right] \tag{12-44}$$

so that

$$\mathbf{C}\boldsymbol{\beta} = \boldsymbol{\beta}_r \tag{12-45}$$

The estimator for these r β's, of course, is

$$\mathbf{C}\hat{\boldsymbol{\beta}} = \hat{\boldsymbol{\beta}}_r \tag{12-46}$$

The final step necessary before we can apply (12-41) is to compute the covariance matrix $\mathbf{CVC}'$, which is designated $\mathbf{V}_r$:

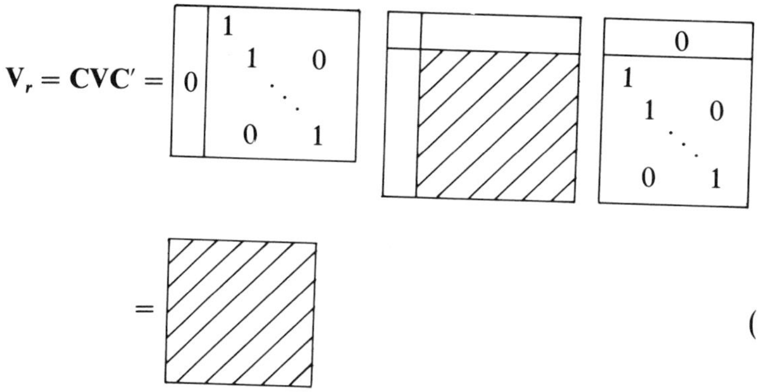

$$\mathbf{V}_r = \mathbf{C}\mathbf{V}\mathbf{C}' = \begin{bmatrix} 1 & & & \\ & 1 & & 0 \\ 0 & & \ddots & \\ & 0 & & 1 \end{bmatrix} \boxed{/\!/\!/\!/} \begin{bmatrix} & 0 & & \\ 1 & & & \\ & 1 & & 0 \\ & & \ddots & \\ & 0 & & 1 \end{bmatrix}$$

$$= \boxed{/\!/\!/\!/} \tag{12-47}$$

Thus $\mathbf{V}_r$ is the lower right-hand $r \times r$ block of $\mathbf{V}$. This is just what we feel intuitively: Only the covariances of the last r $\hat{\beta}$'s are relevant. Substituting into (12-41), we derive the 95% joint confidence region for the last r β's:

$$\boxed{(\boldsymbol{\beta}_r - \hat{\boldsymbol{\beta}}_r)'\mathbf{V}_r^{-1}(\boldsymbol{\beta}_r - \hat{\boldsymbol{\beta}}_r) \le s^2 r F_{.05}} \tag{12-48}$$

Example 12-5

Suppose in the wheat yield problem we are interested in a joint confidence region for only the two slope parameters β_2 and β_3 (i.e., we are interested only in the marginal effects of fertilizer and rainfall on yield). Then the two-dimensional 95% confidence ellipse is obtained from (12-48) and, noting that $\mathbf{V}$ is given in (12-35),

$$\begin{bmatrix} \beta_2 - .038 & \beta_3 - .833 \end{bmatrix} \begin{bmatrix} .5635 & -.3111 \\ -.3111 & .2444 \end{bmatrix}^{-1} \begin{bmatrix} \beta_2 - .038 \\ \beta_3 - .833 \end{bmatrix} \le (5.35)(2)(6.94)$$
$$= 74.3 \tag{12-49}$$

In passing, we note that the development of the previous section (a) and the next section (c) are, in fact, just two interesting special cases of this analysis. Thus, if we set $r = k$ in (12-48), we obtain equation (12-42) of section (a). This special case was treated separately not only because it is the limiting case in which all β_i are simultaneously estimated, but also because the central matrix $\mathbf{V}^{-1}$ was so easy to deal with. [Since it is the inverse of $(\mathbf{X}'\mathbf{X})^{-1}$, it is simply $\mathbf{X}'\mathbf{X}$ itself, that is, no inversion or reinversion is necessary. The same is not true for $\mathbf{V}_r^{-1}$ in this section, unfortunately.]

(c) Confidence Interval for One β_i

The second special case to which we now turn is obtained by setting $r = 1$ in (12-48). The resulting confidence ellipsoid is one dimensional; it reduces to the following confidence interval for a single β (which without loss of generality we take as β_k):

$$(\beta_k - \hat{\beta}_k)^2 \frac{1}{v_k} \leq s^2 F_{.05} \tag{12-50}$$

where $v_k =$ the lower right element of $\mathbf{V}$. This confidence interval may be reexpressed to bring it into more familiar form:

$$(\beta_k - \hat{\beta}_k)^2 \leq v_k s^2 F_{.05} \tag{12-51}$$

$$|\beta_k - \hat{\beta}_k| \leq \sqrt{v_k s^2 F_{.05}} \tag{12-52}$$

We may further reexpress this in terms of the t-distribution, if we like, by noting that $F_{.05}$ with 1 and $(n - k)$ d.f. is just the square of the $t_{.025}$ value on $(n - k)$ d.f.:

$$F_{.05} = t_{.025}^2 \tag{12-53}$$

Thus, (12-52) becomes

$$|\beta_k - \hat{\beta}_k| \leq \sqrt{v_k}\, s\, t_{.025} \tag{12-54}$$

or the confidence interval

$$\beta_k = \hat{\beta}_k \pm \sqrt{v_k}\, s\, t_{.025} \tag{12-55}$$

The way in which it appears in this equation suggests that $\sqrt{v_k}\, s$ must be s_k, the standard error of $\hat{\beta}_k$; in other words, (12-55) may be rewritten in the familiar form:

$$\beta_k = \hat{\beta}_k \pm t_{.025}\, s_k \tag{12-56}$$

like (2-51)

$$\text{where } s_k = \sqrt{v_k}\, s \tag{12-57}$$

Example 12-6

Suppose we are interested in the marginal effect of rainfall in the wheat-yield example—that is, a 95% confidence interval for β_3. From (12-57),

$$s_3 = \sqrt{v_3}\, s$$

Noting that **V** is given in (12-35), and s right after,

$$s_3 = \sqrt{.00444}\,\sqrt{5.35} = .154 \tag{12-58}$$

which agrees with Table 3-3, incidentally. Thus, noting the $\hat{\beta}_3$ value estimated in Example 12-2, (12-56) becomes

$$\beta_3 = .833 \pm 2.776(.154) \tag{12-59}$$

$$= .833 \pm .428 \tag{12-60}$$

A similar set of calculations for the other coefficient β_2 would yield an equation customarily set out as follows:

	YIELD = 60.0 + .0381 FERT + .833 RAIN		
standard error	.0058	.154	(12-61)
95% confidence interval	±.0161	±.428	

(d) Hypothesis Testing

To test an hypothesis, we merely note whether the hypothesis lies within the confidence interval—as we noted already in (2-59). We illustrate with some examples.

Example 12-7

In (12-61), suppose we wish to test the null hypothesis that rainfall has no effect on yield, that is,

$$H_0\colon \beta_3 = 0$$

$$\text{vs } H_1\colon \beta_3 \neq 0$$

We note that $\beta_3 = 0$ is not included in the confidence interval ($\beta_3 = .833 \pm .428$), so we can reject the null hypothesis at the 5% level.

Next, suppose we wish to test the null hypothesis that the marginal effect of fertilizer is .050. That is,

$$H_0: \beta_2 = .050$$

$$\text{vs } H_1: \beta_2 \neq .050$$

We note that $\beta_2 = .050$ is included in the confidence interval ($\beta_2 = .0381 \pm .0161$), so we cannot reject the null hypothesis at the 5% level. Of course, it would be rash indeed to accept H_0. Instead, we ought to conclude, "case not proven."

Example 12-8

In the wheat yield example, suppose we wish to test (at a 5% level) the null hypothesis that the average yield is 65 and is unaffected by fertilizer and rainfall. That is,

$$H_0: \boldsymbol{\beta} = \begin{bmatrix} 65 \\ 0 \\ 0 \end{bmatrix} = \boldsymbol{\beta}_0 \text{ say}$$

$$\text{vs } H_1: \boldsymbol{\beta} \neq \begin{bmatrix} 65 \\ 0 \\ 0 \end{bmatrix}$$

Solution

We see whether $\boldsymbol{\beta}_0$ satisfies the 95% confidence region (12-43). Accordingly, we calculate the left side (L.S.) of (12-43):

$$\text{L.S.} = \begin{bmatrix} 65-60 & 0-.038 & 0-.833 \end{bmatrix} \begin{bmatrix} 7 & 0 & 0 \\ 0 & 280{,}000 & 7{,}000 \\ 0 & 7{,}000 & 400 \end{bmatrix} \begin{bmatrix} 65-60 \\ 0-.038 \\ 0-.833 \end{bmatrix}$$

$$= 1303.2 \tag{12-62}$$

Since this vastly exceeds the R.S. = 105.8, $\boldsymbol{\beta}_0$ does not lie within the confidence region (12-43), and thus we reject it at the 5% level.

Example 12-9

Continuing the previous example, suppose we wish to test (at a 5% level) the null hypothesis that the marginal effect of a pound of fertilizer is one-tenth the marginal effect of an inch of rain. That is,

$$H_0\colon \beta_2 = .10\beta_3$$
$$\text{vs } H_1\colon \beta_2 \neq .10\beta_3$$

Solution

We just reexpress H_0 in the usual form:

$$\beta_2 - .10\beta_3 = 0 \tag{12-63}$$

which is a linear transformation of $\boldsymbol{\beta}$, with $\mathbf{C}$ in (12-36) defined as

$$\mathbf{C} = \begin{bmatrix} 0 & 1 & -.10 \end{bmatrix}$$

The 95% confidence region for $\mathbf{C}\boldsymbol{\beta}$ is given by (12-41), and we check whether the null hypothesis is contained within it. That is, we see whether (12-41) is satisfied by substituting into it

$$\mathbf{C}\boldsymbol{\beta} = 0$$

and

$$\mathbf{C}\hat{\boldsymbol{\beta}} = \begin{bmatrix} 0 & 1 & -.10 \end{bmatrix} \begin{bmatrix} 60.0 \\ .038 \\ .833 \end{bmatrix} = -.0452$$

and, using $\mathbf{V} = (\mathbf{X}'\mathbf{X})^{-1}$ calculated in (12-35)

$$\mathbf{CVC}' = \begin{bmatrix} 0 & 1 & -.10 \end{bmatrix} \begin{bmatrix} \frac{1}{7} & 0 & 0 \\ 0 & ._{5}635 & -._{3}111 \\ 0 & -._{3}111 & ._{2}444 \end{bmatrix} \begin{bmatrix} 0 \\ 1 \\ -.10 \end{bmatrix}$$

$$= .000073$$

After all these substitutions are made, the L.S. of (12-41) becomes:

$$(\mathbf{C\beta} - \mathbf{C\hat{\beta}})'(\mathbf{CVC}')^{-1}(\mathbf{C\beta} - \mathbf{C\hat{\beta}})$$
$$= (0 + .0452)(.000073)^{-1}(0 + .0452) = 28.0 \tag{12-64}$$

And the R.S. of (12-41) is

$$s^2 r F_{.05} = 5.35(1)7.71 = 41.2 \tag{12-65}$$

Thus the null hypothesis does lie within the confidence interval (12-41), and so H_0 cannot be rejected at the 5% level.

PROBLEMS

12-4 Referring to Problem 3-1, we are now in a position to find confidence intervals for the model

$$S = \beta_1 + \beta_2 x + \beta_3 w + e$$

where x and w are income and wealth, measured as deviations from the mean. Then you may verify

$$\mathbf{X'X} = \begin{bmatrix} 5 & 0 & 0 \\ 0 & 18 & -18 \\ 0 & -18 & 144 \end{bmatrix}$$

and

$$\mathbf{X'y} = \begin{bmatrix} 3.8 \\ 2.6 \\ -6.3 \end{bmatrix}$$

where $\mathbf{y}$ of course is the vector of the dependent variable (saving). Then

$$\mathbf{V} = (\mathbf{X'X})^{-1} = \begin{bmatrix} 1/5 & 0 & 0 \\ 0 & 8/126 & 1/126 \\ 0 & 1/126 & 1/126 \end{bmatrix}$$
$$= \begin{bmatrix} .2 & 0 & 0 \\ 0 & .0635 & .00794 \\ 0 & .00794 & .00794 \end{bmatrix}$$

and finally

$$s^2 = \frac{1}{n-k}(\mathbf{y} - \hat{\mathbf{y}})'(\mathbf{y} - \hat{\mathbf{y}}) = .0039$$

(a) Construct a 95% confidence region for:

(i) β_1
(ii) β_2
(iii) β_3
(iv) β_2 and β_3 simultaneously
(v) β_1 and β_2 simultaneously

(b) Write out the estimated regression in the standard form (12-61).

12-5 Continuing Problem 12-4, test the following hypotheses at the 5% level (2-sided):

(i) $\beta_2 = 0$ (i.e., income does not affect saving).
(ii) $\beta_3 = 0$ (i.e., wealth does not affect saving).
(iii) $\beta_2 = 0$ and $\beta_3 = 0$ simultaneously.
(iv) $\beta_2 = .10$ (This may be a colleague's claim, for example).
(v) $\beta_2 = -5\beta_3$ (i.e., the income effect is opposite to the wealth effect, and 5 times as strong).

12-6 Consider a Cobb-Douglas production function relating quantity produced Q to labor L and capital K:

$$Q = AL^{\beta}K^{\gamma}$$

Taking logs, this becomes

$$y = \alpha + \beta x + \gamma z$$

where $y = \log Q$, $\alpha = \log A$, $x = \log L$, and $z = \log K$ (and let x and z be measured as deviations from the mean). Suppose the estimated coefficients and their covariance matrix, based on a sample of 25 observations, are:

$$\hat{\boldsymbol{\beta}} = \begin{bmatrix} -1.26 \\ .61 \\ .46 \end{bmatrix}$$

$$\text{cov}\,\hat{\boldsymbol{\beta}} = s^2(\mathbf{X}'\mathbf{X})^{-1} = .015 \begin{bmatrix} 25 & 0 & 0 \\ 0 & 9.3 & 5.4 \\ 0 & 5.4 & 12.7 \end{bmatrix}^{-1}$$

$$= .015 \begin{bmatrix} .040 & 0 & 0 \\ 0 & .1428 & -.0607 \\ 0 & -.0607 & .1046 \end{bmatrix}$$

(a) Constant returns to scale may be stated as

$$H_0: \beta + \gamma = 1$$

Test this hypothesis at a 5% test level. What is the prob-value for H_0?

(b) Equal marginal productivity of capital and labor may be stated as:

$$H_0: \beta = \gamma$$

Test this hypothesis at a 5% test level. What is the prob-value for H_0?

12-7 Suppose a regression includes a constant term plus 3 independent variables (x_1, x_2, and x_3), all measured as deviations from the mean, and:

$$(\mathbf{X'X}) = \begin{bmatrix} 37 & ? & ? & ? \\ ? & 8.813 & 0 & .048 \\ ? & ? & .214 & -.076 \\ ? & ? & ? & .028 \end{bmatrix}$$

(a) Fill in the missing elements.
(b) Of the three independent variables, which two are uncorrelated? Which two are nearly collinear?
(c) What was the sample size n?

12-6 MULTICOLLINEARITY

Multicollinearity occurs, for example, if the variables x_2 and x_3 measure nearly the same thing; in terms of the matrix

$$\mathbf{X} = \begin{bmatrix} 1 & x_{12} & x_{13} & \cdots & x_{1k} \\ 1 & x_{22} & x_{23} & \cdots & x_{2k} \\ \cdot & & & & \cdot \\ \cdot & & & & \cdot \\ \cdot & & & & \cdot \\ 1 & x_{n2} & x_{n3} & \cdots & x_{nk} \end{bmatrix} \tag{12-66}$$

this means that the second and third columns are almost linearly dependent. If, as another example, the variable x_4 is almost the sum of x_2 and x_3, then

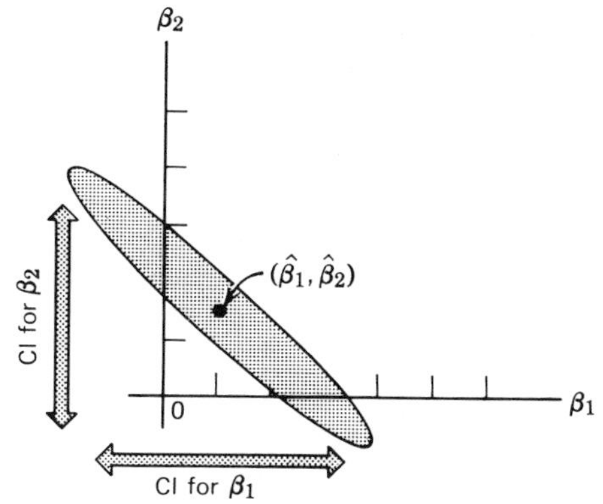

FIGURE 12-2 Joint confidence ellipse and individual confidence intervals in the case of two multicollinear regressors.

the second, third, and fourth columns of **X** will be almost linearly dependent. Such multicollinearity results in the inverse matrix $(\mathbf{X}'\mathbf{X})^{-1}$ having some extremely large entries. (In the limiting case of perfect collinearity, the determinant of **X′X** is zero, and its inverse does not exist.) Since $\sigma^2(\mathbf{X}'\mathbf{X})^{-1}$ is the covariance matrix of $\hat{\boldsymbol{\beta}}$, we therefore obtain some very large variances and covariances, and hence broad confidence intervals. In such circumstances, it becomes very difficult to establish that an individual regressor influences y. Intuitively, when two regressors are nearly the same, the influence on y of one of them may be erroneously attributed to the other.

This can be shown more rigorously by examining in detail the joint confidence region for when there are just two parameters, β_1 and β_2. If the two regressors are almost linearly dependent, then β_1 and β_2 have very large variances and covariance. Geometrically, this means that the elliptical confidence region given by (12-48) is very tilted, as in Figure 12-2. This is a striking contrast to the level confidence region of Figure 12-1*a*.

Now consider the individual confidence intervals for each of the parameters if they are tested one at a time. These are shown as the arrows in Figure 12-2; (it can be proved that the interval for any parameter, say β_k, is slightly narrower than the projection of the joint confidence ellipse onto the β_k axis.[7]) Since each of these confidence intervals includes zero, it is not possible to reject the null hypothesis for either regressor. In this case, then, no relationship can be statistically established between y and the regressors if individual tests are run.

---

[7] Intuitively this is no surprise. The joint confidence ellipse uses the sample to make a statement about both regressors; the individual confidence interval uses the same sample to make a statement about only one regressor—hence it can be more precise.

But if a joint test is run, then a relationship can be established. Specifically, the null hypothesis that *both* coefficients are zero can be rejected, since the origin falls in the rejection area outside the joint confidence ellipse. Thus we conclude that y is related to these regressors in some way—although because of multicollinearity it is very difficult to sort out whether it is one, or the other, or both. This illustrates the conclusion that, in the face of multicollinearity, tests on individual regressors may be very weak; in many cases the only way of statistically confirming causal relationships may be with a joint test.

Multicollinearity is avoided if the regressors differ as much as possible. In Figure 3-3, this meant that the points in the x-z plane are not clustered near line L. Algebraically, it means that the columns of $\mathbf{X}$ are orthogonal;[8] that is, the product $\mathbf{X'X}$ is diagonal. Or, to put the same point the other way around: multicollinearity *does* occur when $\mathbf{X'X}$ has large off-diagonal elements, and relatively small diagonal elements. In this case, a technique called *ridge regression* is often used. (It is so-named, because in the case of multicollinearity, the bivariate distribution of two regression coefficients is the sort of narrow ridge shown in Figure 12-2.) Roughly speaking, ridge regression augments the main diagonal of $\mathbf{X'X}$ by adding a matrix $\mathbf{D}$ consisting of positive diagonal elements (and zeros elsewhere). Then the ridge regression estimate of $\boldsymbol{\beta}$ is

$$\hat{\boldsymbol{\beta}} = (\mathbf{X'X} + \mathbf{D})^{-1}\mathbf{X'y}$$

In the face of multicollinearity, this estimator is much more stable (i.e., has much smaller variance) than the OLS estimator (12-19). But the cost of this procedure is that it introduces bias; so the elements of $\mathbf{D}$ are chosen to keep this bias small enough so that the overall mean squared error (2-105) is still reduced.

Economists and other social scientists often have to take the data as it comes—and it often contains a substantial degree of multicollinearity. But when they can design their experiments they should make their regressors orthogonal, in order to exploit the following advantages:

1. In avoiding multicollinearity, they get more precise confidence intervals and more certainty about which regressors are relevant.
2. If a smaller model with only j regressors (rather than the original k) is appropriate, then the coefficients $\hat{\beta}_1 \cdots \hat{\beta}_j$ of this new model will be exactly the same as the coefficients in the old extended model. In other words, coefficients do not change as some variables are dropped from the model. This is more satisfactory, philosophically as well as computationally.

[8] For an extended discussion of orthogonality, see Chapter 14.

PROBLEMS

12-8 Redo Problem 12-2(a), if the three values of the regressor are 3.9, 4.0, and 4.1. Now how much greater is the standard error of the coefficient of the regressor?

12-9 ("Dummy Variable Trap").

To give a concrete example of where *perfect* multicollinearity can inadvertently occur, consider the data in Problem 4-31, for example. Suppose we regressed education E on F, U, and R, where

$$F = X_2 = \text{father's income}$$
$$U = X_3 = 1 \text{ if urban; } 0 \text{ otherwise}$$
$$R = X_4 = 1 \text{ if rural; } 0 \text{ otherwise.}$$

(a) Write out the matrix of regressors, including the constant regressor $X_1 = 1$.
(b) Can X_1 be written as a linear combination of X_3 and X_4? That is, does perfect multicollinearity exist?
(c) Calculate $\mathbf{X'X}$. Can it be inverted (to calculate $\hat{\boldsymbol{\beta}} = (\mathbf{X'X})^{-1}\mathbf{X'y}$)?
(d) Suggest several ways to break this perfect multicollinearity.

12-10 In Figure 12-2, let us see why the individual confidence intervals are as long as they are. If we drew in the confidence regions for various confidence levels, Figure 12-2 would look like this:

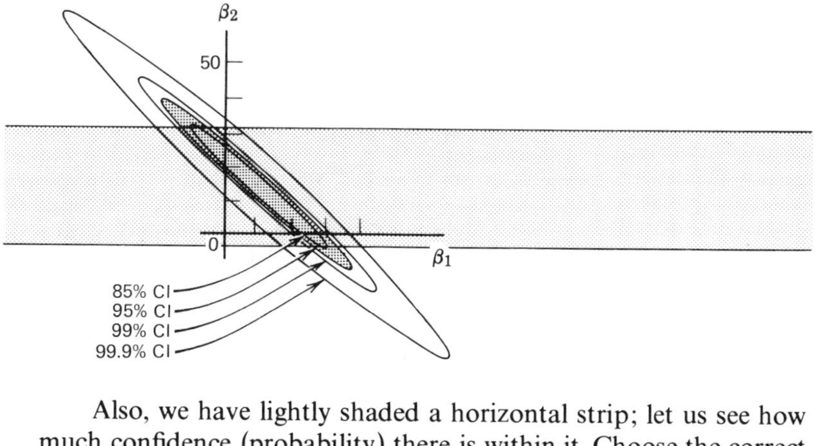

Also, we have lightly shaded a horizontal strip; let us see how much confidence (probability) there is within it. Choose the correct alternative in square brackets:

(a) Since the strip includes the 85% confidence ellipse, plus some more, its confidence is [more, less] than 85%.

(b) On the other hand, the strip omits a substantial chunk of probability in the tips of the 95% confidence ellipse. So its confidence [can, cannot] be as high as 100%.

(c) We have shown so far that the strip has confidence somewhere between 85% and 100%. It seems reasonable to guess its confidence level is about [95%, 99.9%].

(d) To express the strip algebraically, its equation is

$$[-5 < \beta_1 < 33, \quad -5 < \beta_2 < 33, \quad \beta_1^2 + \beta_2^2 \le 1]$$

(e) Thus the strip represents a confidence interval for $[\beta_1, \beta_2]$, and so may be represented more briefly in Figure 12-2 as the [horizontal, vertical] arrow.

12-7 INTERPOLATION AND PREDICTION

Consider a new set of values for the independent variables $\mathbf{x}_0 = (1, x_{02}, x_{03}, \ldots, x_{0k})$. What will be (a) the confidence interval for the *mean* value of the corresponding y_0? (b) The prediction interval for a *single* corresponding y_0?

(a) Confidence Interval for the Mean of y_0

We use

$$\hat{\mu}_0 \equiv \mathbf{x}_0 \hat{\boldsymbol{\beta}} \tag{12-67}$$

to estimate the mean of y_0 given by

$$\mu_0 \equiv \mathbf{x}_0 \boldsymbol{\beta} \tag{12-68}$$

To find its confidence interval, we simply set

$$\mathbf{C} = \mathbf{x}_0$$

so that (12-36) reduces to (12-67). Continuing with this substitution, we obtain from (12-41) a 95% confidence interval for $\mathbf{x}_0\boldsymbol{\beta}$:

$$(\mathbf{x}_0 \boldsymbol{\beta} - \mathbf{x}_0 \hat{\boldsymbol{\beta}})'(\mathbf{x}_0 \mathbf{V} \mathbf{x}_0')^{-1}(\mathbf{x}_0 \boldsymbol{\beta} - \mathbf{x}_0 \hat{\boldsymbol{\beta}}) \le s^2 F_{.05}$$

Noting (12-67) and (12-68), and that $(\mathbf{x}_0 \mathbf{V} \mathbf{x}_0')$ is a scalar, this 95% confidence interval reduces to

$$(\mu_0 - \hat{\mu}_0)^2 \le s^2 F_{.05}(\mathbf{x}_0 \mathbf{V} \mathbf{x}_0')$$

If we substitute $t_{.025}^2$ for $F_{.05}$, and take the square root,

$$|\mu_0 - \hat{\mu}_0| \le t_{.025} s \sqrt{\mathbf{x}_0 \mathbf{V} \mathbf{x}_0'}$$

In other words:

The 95% confidence interval for the mean of y_0 is

$$\mu_0 = \hat{\mu}_0 \pm t_{.025}\, s\sqrt{\mathbf{x}_0 \mathbf{V} \mathbf{x}_0'} \qquad (12\text{-}69)$$

where $\hat{\mu}_0 = \hat{\beta}_1 + \hat{\beta}_2 x_{02} + \cdots + \hat{\beta}_k x_{0k}$ and $t_{.025}$ is the critical t value with $(n-k)$ d.f.

(b) Prediction Interval for an Individual Observation y_0

This is the same as the confidence interval for the mean of y_0, except that the variance term must be augmented because of the estimated dispersion (s^2) of an individual y value about its mean. Thus, we obtain:

95% prediction interval for an individual y_0

$$y_0 = \hat{\mu}_0 \pm t_{.025}\, s\sqrt{\mathbf{x}_0 \mathbf{V} \mathbf{x}_0' + 1} \qquad (12\text{-}70)$$

where $\hat{\mu}_0$, s, and t are the same as in (12-69).

Example 12-10

In the wheat yield example, if 550 pounds of fertilizer are applied and rainfall is 25 inches, what is:

(a) The 95% confidence interval for the mean yield?

(b) The 95% prediction interval for the yield on one plot?

Solution

(a) We must express fertilizer as a deviation from its mean of 400, and rainfall as a deviation from its mean of 20. Thus

$$\mathbf{x}_0 = \begin{bmatrix} 1 & 550-400 & 25-20 \end{bmatrix} = \begin{bmatrix} 1 & 150 & 5 \end{bmatrix}$$

and

$$\hat{\boldsymbol{\beta}} = \begin{bmatrix} 60 \\ .038 \\ .833 \end{bmatrix}$$

Thus, from (12-67),

$$\hat{\mu}_0 = \mathbf{x}_0 \hat{\boldsymbol{\beta}} = 69.88$$

Using **V** from (12-35), we also calculate

$$\mathbf{x}_0 \mathbf{V} \mathbf{x}_0' = \begin{bmatrix} 1 & 150 & 5 \end{bmatrix} \begin{bmatrix} 1/7 & 0 & 0 \\ 0 & ._5635 & -._3111 \\ 0 & -._3111 & ._2444 \end{bmatrix} \begin{bmatrix} 1 \\ 150 \\ 5 \end{bmatrix} = .229$$

We substitute these [as well as $s^2 = 5.35$ from (12-28)] into (12-69):

$$\begin{aligned} \mu_0 &= \hat{\mu}_0 \pm t_{.025}\, s\sqrt{\mathbf{x}_0 \mathbf{V} \mathbf{x}_0'} \\ &= 69.88 \pm 2.776\sqrt{5.35}\,\sqrt{.229} \\ &= 69.88 \pm 3.07 \end{aligned} \qquad (12\text{-}71)$$

(b) To predict a single plot, we use the same calculation except for adding 1 under the square root, which yields

$$\begin{aligned} y_0 &= 69.88 \pm 2.776\sqrt{5.35}\sqrt{.229 + 1} \\ &= 69.88 \pm 7.12 \end{aligned} \qquad (12\text{-}72)$$

Remarks

Note that (12-71) and (12-72) are more precise (involve smaller sampling allowances) than the estimates that ignored rainfall [specifically (2-71) and the equation below it]. Thus, the additional information on rainfall has improved the estimates.

PROBLEMS

12-11 In Problem 12-4, for a family earning $x = 2$ thousand above average, and having assets $w = 6$ thousand above average.

(i) What would you predict saving to be?

(ii) Construct an interval that is 95% sure of correctly predicting this family's saving.

REVIEW PROBLEMS

12-12 Referring to Problem 4-31, we are now in a position to find confidence intervals for the model

$$E = \beta_1 + \beta_2 f + \beta_3 d$$

where E is child's education (in years), f is father's annual income (in thousands, above average), and d is a dummy, also in deviation form ($d = -\frac{1}{2}$ for urban, $d = \frac{1}{2}$ for rural). Then you may verify that

$$(\mathbf{X}'\mathbf{X}) = \begin{bmatrix} 8 & 0 & 0 \\ 0 & 68 & -8 \\ 0 & -8 & 2 \end{bmatrix}$$

and

$$\mathbf{X}'\mathbf{y} = \begin{bmatrix} 109 \\ 47 \\ -6.5 \end{bmatrix}$$

hence

$$\mathbf{V} = (\mathbf{X}'\mathbf{X})^{-1} = \begin{bmatrix} 1/8 & 0 & 0 \\ 0 & 1/36 & 4/36 \\ 0 & 4/36 & 34/36 \end{bmatrix} = \begin{bmatrix} .125 & 0 & 0 \\ 0 & .0278 & .111 \\ 0 & .111 & .944 \end{bmatrix}$$

Finally

$$s^2 = \frac{1}{n-k}(\mathbf{y} - \hat{\mathbf{y}})'(\mathbf{y} - \hat{\mathbf{y}}) = 3.30$$

(a) Construct a 90% [*not* 95%] confidence interval for:

(i) β_2
(ii) β_3
(iii) β_2 and β_3 simultaneously.

(b) Write out the estimated regression equation in standard form (12-61).

(c) Test the following hypotheses at the 10% level (2-sided):

(i) $\beta_2 = 0$ (i.e., father's income is irrelevant).
(ii) $\beta_3 = 0$ (i.e., urban-rural factor is irrelevant).
(iii) $\beta_2 = 0$ and $\beta_3 = 0$ simultaneously.

(d) In part (c), how can you reconcile the answers to parts (i) and (ii) with the answer to part (iii)?

(e) For a rural child whose father's annual income is 1.5 thousand below average, find a 90% prediction interval for her education E.

(f) For all rural residents whose father's annual income is 1.5 thousand below average, find a 90% confidence interval for their mean education.

*(g) For a child picked at random, on whom no information is available, construct a 90% prediction interval for her education E. (Assume that the data of Problem 4-31 is a random sample from the same population from which the child is picked). Compare to part (e).

12-13 True or false? If false, correct it:

(a) Multicollinearity between X_2 and X_3 may mean that we cannot reject $\beta_2 = 0$; nor can we reject $\beta_3 = 0$. Nonetheless we may be able to reject the hypothesis that *both* are zero.

(b) If and only if the stochastic term e is normal, the likelihood function is:

$$L(\boldsymbol{\beta}, \sigma^2) = \frac{1}{(2\pi\sigma^2)^{n/2}} e^{-(1/2\sigma^2)(\mathbf{y}-\mathbf{X}\boldsymbol{\beta})'(\mathbf{y}-\mathbf{X}\boldsymbol{\beta})}$$

(c) If and only if e is normal, the OLS estimator of β is

$$\hat{\boldsymbol{\beta}} = (\mathbf{X}'\mathbf{X})'\mathbf{X}^{-1}\mathbf{y}$$

12-14 Suppose there are exactly as many observations as unknown parameters ($n = k$), so that the matrix $\mathbf{X}$ is square and invertible.

(a) Prove that the OLS solution (12-19) reduces to

$$\hat{\boldsymbol{\beta}} = \mathbf{X}^{-1}\mathbf{y}$$

(b) Another way to derive the solution is as follows: With as many parameters as observations, we should be able to fit the model perfectly, with zero residuals. That is, the fitted values $\hat{\mathbf{y}} = \mathbf{X}\hat{\boldsymbol{\beta}}$ should be exactly equal to $\mathbf{y}$ itself:

$$\mathbf{X}\hat{\boldsymbol{\beta}} = \mathbf{y}$$

Solve this equation for $\hat{\boldsymbol{\beta}}$. Do you get the same answer as in (a)?

13

DISTRIBUTION THEORY: HOW THE NORMAL, t, χ^2, AND F DISTRIBUTIONS ARE RELATED

13-1 INTRODUCTION

In this chapter we shall show the close relationship between the important distributions that are used in statistical tests. As you read, it is advisable to frequently consult Tables 13-1 and 13-2 at the end of the chapter, since they provide a guide to the relations among the variables.

The distribution of the standard normal variable z is assumed to be well known. (It is discussed in every elementary statistics text; for example, Wonnacott and Wonnacott, 1977, Chapter 4.) Normal variables are the building blocks of the other variables in this chapter. The first of these is the χ^2, to which we now turn.

13-2 χ^2, THE CHI-SQUARE DISTRIBUTION

(a) Definition

If n independent standard normal variables are squared and added, we obtain a random variable that appears in many applications (though in slightly disguised form). It is denoted χ_n^2, and is called a chi-square variable with n d.f. Thus

$$\chi_n^2 \equiv z_1^2 + z_2^2 + \cdots + z_n^2 \tag{13-1}$$

$$= \sum_{i=1}^{n} z_i^2$$

where the z_i are independent variables, with distributions that are standard normal and therefore identical.

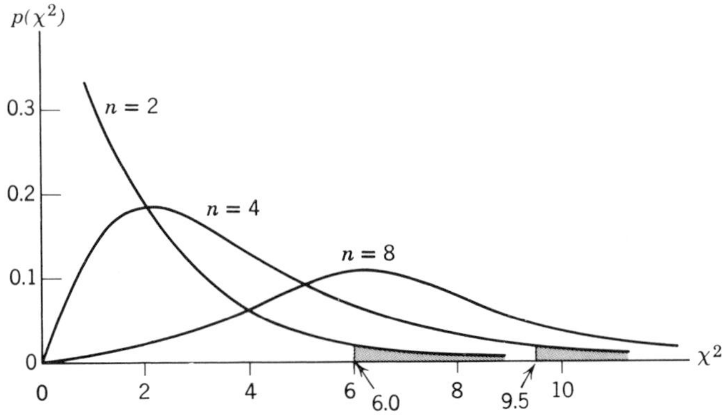

FIGURE 13-1 Probability distribution of χ_n^2.

The probability distribution of χ_n^2 is shown in Figure 13-1. Of course, for each different n, we get a different probability distribution; the larger the n, the larger will this χ^2 sum of n terms tend to be. Although the χ^2 distribution requires sophisticated mathematics to derive in detail, its most important general features are easily deduced. Since χ^2 is a sum of squares, it must be positive. Moreover, we note from (13-1) that it is a sum of independent and identically distributed variables (the sum of what may be regarded as a sample from the z^2 population). Thus, the formulas for sample sums can be applied [alternatively Table 12-2(b) can be extended]:

$$E(\chi_n^2) = nE(z^2)$$

Since z is standard, its variance is one. That is,

$$E(z^2) = 1 \tag{13-2}$$

Thus

$$E(\chi_n^2) = n \tag{13-3}$$

Similarly

$$\text{var } \chi_n^2 = n \text{ var } (z^2) \tag{13-4}$$

It may be proved with advanced calculus that

$$\text{var}(z^2) = 2 \tag{13-5}$$

Thus

$$\text{var } \chi_n^2 = 2n \tag{13-6}$$

Finally, the central limit theorem assures us that as n grows large, the distribution of χ_n^2 approaches the normal. This can be seen in Figure 13-1.

(b) Other Views and Uses of χ^2

(i) If we take a sample from a normal distribution, $y_1, y_2, \ldots, y_n$, and standardize,

$$z_i = \frac{y_i - \mu}{\sigma}$$

then from (13-1)

$$\sum_{i=1}^{n} \left(\frac{y_i - \mu}{\sigma}\right)^2 \sim \chi_n^2 \tag{13-7}$$

$$\frac{\sum_{i=1}^{n} (y_i - \mu)^2}{\sigma^2} \sim \chi_n^2 \tag{13-8}$$

where the symbol $\sim$ means *is distributed as*. Thus $\sim \chi_n^2$ is read "is distributed as chi-square with n d.f."

(ii) We may generalize (13-8). First, we reexpress it in vector notation:

$$\frac{1}{\sigma^2}(\mathbf{y} - \boldsymbol{\mu})'(\mathbf{y} - \boldsymbol{\mu}) \sim \chi_n^2$$

$$(\mathbf{y} - \boldsymbol{\mu})'(\sigma^2\mathbf{I})^{-1}(\mathbf{y} - \boldsymbol{\mu}) \sim \chi_n^2 \tag{13-9}$$

The middle factor $\sigma^2\mathbf{I}$ represents the covariance matrix of the y_i, which were assumed to be independent and identically distributed with variance σ^2 (as, for example, in a sample). We now wonder what can be done if we relax this assumption about the y_i. Suppose, in fact, that there are r normal variates in the vector $\mathbf{y}$, having a mean vector $\boldsymbol{\mu}$ with perhaps different components, and a covariance matrix, no longer based on the identity, but now the more general $\sigma^2\mathbf{W}$. We will prove that:

$$\boxed{(\mathbf{y} - \boldsymbol{\mu})'(\sigma^2\mathbf{W})^{-1}(\mathbf{y} - \boldsymbol{\mu}) \sim \chi_r^2} \tag{13-10}$$

where the r variates[1] $\mathbf{y} \sim N(\boldsymbol{\mu}, \sigma^2\mathbf{W})$.

Proof of (13-10). Without loss of generality, assume $\boldsymbol{\mu} = \mathbf{0}$. In linear algebra, it may be proved that since $\sigma^2\mathbf{W}$ is a covariance matrix, and hence $\mathbf{W}$ is positive definite, there exists a "square root" matrix $\mathbf{R}$ that satisfies

$$\mathbf{R}\mathbf{R}' = \mathbf{W} \tag{13-11}$$

Now let

$$\mathbf{q} = \mathbf{R}^{-1}\mathbf{y} \tag{13-12}$$

[1] Since we no longer interpret the y_i as a sample, we use r instead of n for the number of y_i.

The covariance matrix of $\mathbf{q}$ is obtained by the theory of linear transformations of Table 12-2, and is

$$\begin{aligned}\operatorname{cov}(\mathbf{q}) &= \mathbf{R}^{-1}(\operatorname{cov}\,\mathbf{y})\mathbf{R}^{-1'} \\ &= \mathbf{R}^{-1}(\sigma^2\mathbf{W})\mathbf{R}^{-1'}\end{aligned}$$

Substituting[2] for $\mathbf{W}$ as given by (13-11),

$$= \sigma^2\mathbf{I} \tag{13-13}$$

This proves $\mathbf{q}$ is an independent set of variables, with variance σ^2. Moreover, since $\mathbf{q}$ is the linear transformation (13-12) of the normal $\mathbf{y}$, it has the same $\mathbf{0}$ mean (recall that we assumed $\boldsymbol{\mu} = \mathbf{0}$), and it is normal. Hence $(1/\sigma)\mathbf{q}$ is a set of fully standardized normal variates, and

$$\frac{1}{\sigma^2}\mathbf{q}'\mathbf{q} \sim \chi_r^2 \tag{13-14}$$

Substituting (13-12) into (13-14),

$$\frac{1}{\sigma^2}(\mathbf{y}'\mathbf{R}^{-1'})(\mathbf{R}^{-1}\mathbf{y}) \sim \chi_r^2$$

$$\frac{1}{\sigma^2}\mathbf{y}'(\mathbf{R}^{-1'}\mathbf{R}^{-1})\mathbf{y} \sim \chi_r^2$$

$$\frac{1}{\sigma^2}\mathbf{y}'(\mathbf{R}\mathbf{R}')^{-1}\mathbf{y} \sim \chi_r^2$$

By (13-11),

$$\mathbf{y}'(\sigma^2\mathbf{W})^{-1}\mathbf{y} \sim \chi_r^2$$

This establishes (13-10) for $\boldsymbol{\mu} = \mathbf{0}$, and there are no problems involved in translating this into the general case where $\boldsymbol{\mu}$ is nonzero.

The primary example of (13-10) is the vector of k regression estimators $\hat{\boldsymbol{\beta}}$ that occurs in (12-42); from (13-10) and (12-34) it follows that

$$(\hat{\boldsymbol{\beta}} - \boldsymbol{\beta})'(\sigma^2\mathbf{V})^{-1}(\hat{\boldsymbol{\beta}} - \boldsymbol{\beta}) \sim \chi_k^2 \tag{13-15}$$

and, more generally, following (12-37),

$$(\mathbf{C}\hat{\boldsymbol{\beta}} - \mathbf{C}\boldsymbol{\beta})'(\sigma^2\mathbf{C}\mathbf{V}\mathbf{C}')^{-1}(\mathbf{C}\hat{\boldsymbol{\beta}} - \mathbf{C}\boldsymbol{\beta}) \sim \chi_r^2 \tag{13-16}$$

(12-38) proved

(iii) Going back to the idea of the sample of y_i that occur in (13-8), we may ask what happens when we substitute $\bar{y}$ for the unknown μ. It was

[2] Noting also that $\mathbf{R}^{-1'} = \mathbf{R}'^{-1}$.

remarked in Section 2-6 that $\bar{y}$ is the best fit to the sample, in the least squares sense. Thus, the squared deviations measured from $\bar{y}$ are less than from any other value, even slightly less than from μ; that is, $\sum_{i=1}^{n} (y_i - \bar{y})^2$ is slightly less than $\sum_{i=1}^{n} (y_i - \mu)^2$. Thus, the distribution of $\sum (y_i - \bar{y})^2/\sigma^2$ is a little below the χ_n^2 distribution of $\sum (y_i - \mu)^2/\sigma^2$. In fact, it turns out[3] to be the distribution of χ_{n-1}^2; that is,

$$\frac{\sum_{i=1}^{n} (y_i - \bar{y})^2}{\sigma^2} \sim \chi_{n-1}^2 \tag{13-17}$$

[3] Equation (13-17) and its generalization (13-23) are proved in advanced texts in mathematical statistics, such as Cramer 1946, or Kendall and Stuart 1963. Since the proof is simple and instructive in the special case when $n = 2$, we give it here:

In the left side of (13-17),

$$\begin{aligned}\sum_{i=1}^{2} (y_i - \bar{y})^2 &= (y_1 - \bar{y})^2 + (y_2 - \bar{y})^2 \\ &= \left(y_1 - \frac{y_1 + y_2}{2}\right)^2 + \left(y_2 - \frac{y_1 + y_2}{2}\right)^2 \\ &= \left(\frac{y_1 - y_2}{2}\right)^2 + \left(\frac{y_2 - y_1}{2}\right)^2 \\ &= \frac{(y_1 - y_2)^2}{2}\end{aligned} \tag{13-18}$$

Dividing by σ^2

$$\frac{\sum_{i=1}^{2} (y_i - \bar{y})^2}{\sigma^2} = \frac{(y_1 - y_2)^2}{2\sigma^2} \tag{13-19}$$

Since $y_i \sim N(\mu, \sigma^2)$ and are independent, then the variable $(y_1 - y_2)$ is normal,

with mean $\mu - \mu = 0$

and variance $\sigma^2 + \sigma^2 = 2\sigma^2$

so that its standardized value is

$$z = \frac{(y_1 - y_2) - 0}{\sqrt{2\sigma^2}}$$

that is,

$$z^2 = \frac{(y_1 - y_2)^2}{2\sigma^2} \tag{13-20}$$

Substituting (13-20) into (13-19),

$$\begin{aligned}\frac{\sum_{i=1}^{2} (y_i - \bar{y})^2}{\sigma^2} &= z^2 \\ &= \chi_1^2 = \chi_{n-1}^2\end{aligned} \tag{13-21}$$

This completes our proof of (13-17) for $n = 2$.

(iv) In the previous section, we used $\bar{y}$ as the best fit to a simple sample. Regression theory extended this same concept of best fit to the case in which there are k explanatory variables, or regressors. [We include the dummy regressor (1, 1, 1, 1, ..., 1), so that there are altogether k parameters to be estimated in the linear regression.] In equation (12-25) the residual sum of squares was given as

$$(\mathbf{y} - \hat{\mathbf{y}})'(\mathbf{y} - \hat{\mathbf{y}}) = \sum_{i=1}^{n} (y_i - \hat{y}_i)^2 \tag{13-22}$$

By definition, the least squares estimators made the sum of squared deviations from $\hat{y}_i$ less than from any other value, even less than from μ_i. Thus the distribution of $\sum (y_i - \hat{y}_i)^2/\sigma^2$ is below the χ_n^2 distribution of $\sum (y_i - \mu_i)^2/\sigma^2$. In fact, there was so much freedom of choice in selecting all k estimates, that $\sum_{i=1}^{n} (y_i - \hat{y}_i)^2/\sigma^2$ has the distribution of χ_{n-k}^2, that is,

$$\frac{\sum (y_i - \hat{y}_i)^2}{\sigma^2} \sim \chi_{n-k}^2 \tag{13-23}$$

(c) C^2, the Modified χ^2

Let χ_r^2 be a chi-square variable with r d.f. The "modified χ_r^2" is defined by dividing by the degrees of freedom:

$$\boxed{C_r^2 \equiv \frac{\chi_r^2}{r}} \tag{13-24}$$

Just as χ_r^2 may be regarded as a sample sum, so C_r^2 may be regarded as a sample mean from the z^2 population. Thus, its expectation is the population mean $E(z^2)$ given by (13-2) as 1. Thus

$$E(C_r^2) = 1 \tag{13-25a}$$

Similarly, from (13-5),

$$\text{var } C_r^2 = \frac{2}{r} \tag{13-25b}$$

These two equations establish that C_r^2 has zero bias and a variance that approaches zero; by (2-109), therefore, its probability limit is the population mean

$$C_r^2 \xrightarrow{p} 1 \tag{13-25c}$$

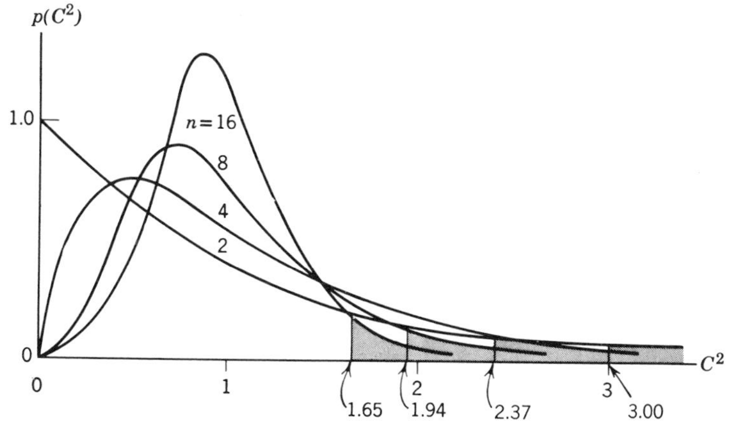

FIGURE 13-2 Probability distribution of C_n^2 (modified χ_n^2).

Equation (13-25c) may alternatively be derived by noting that the sample mean is a consistent estimator of the population mean. This is shown in Figure 13-2.

The value of modifying χ_r^2 to C_r^2 is to simplify formulas (13-17) and (13-23). If we divide (13-17) by $n - 1$ on both sides, we obtain

$$\boxed{\frac{s^2}{\sigma^2} \sim C_{n-1}^2} \tag{13-26}$$

where s^2 is the residual variance after fitting the sample mean.

Similarly, if we divide (13-23) by $n - k$ on both sides, we obtain

$$\boxed{\frac{s^2}{\sigma^2} \sim C_{n-k}^2} \tag{13-27}$$

where s^2 is the residual variance after fitting k parameters in the regression analysis. This is a generalization of (13-26).

(d) χ^2-Estimators

We now show that s^2 is a consistent and unbiased estimator of σ^2. In view of its distribution, it is appropriate to call it a χ^2-estimator of σ^2.

To establish its consistency, we consider a fixed number of regressors (k), and let $n \to \infty$; hence, $(n - k) \to \infty$. Then from (13-25c)

$$C_{n-k}^2 \xrightarrow{p} 1$$

and from (13-27), therefore,

$$\frac{s^2}{\sigma^2} \xrightarrow{p} 1$$

that is,

$$\boxed{s^2 \xrightarrow{p} \sigma^2} \tag{13-28}$$

Next, to establish its unbiasedness, we begin with the fact that C^2 is scaled to have a mean of 1; from (13-25a)

$$E(C_{n-k}^2) = 1$$

From (13-27)

$$E\left(\frac{s^2}{\sigma^2}\right) = 1$$

Since σ^2, the population variance, is constant,

$$\frac{1}{\sigma^2} E(s^2) = 1$$

$$\boxed{E(s^2) = \sigma^2} \tag{13-29}$$

This unbiasedness, of course, is the reason for using $n - k$ instead of n as the divisor for s^2.

13-3 *t* DISTRIBUTION

(a) Definition

The mathematical definition of "student's" t with r d.f. is

$$\boxed{t_r \equiv \frac{z}{C_r}} \tag{13-30}$$

where z is a standard normal variable, and

$$C_r = \sqrt{C_r^2} \tag{13-31}$$

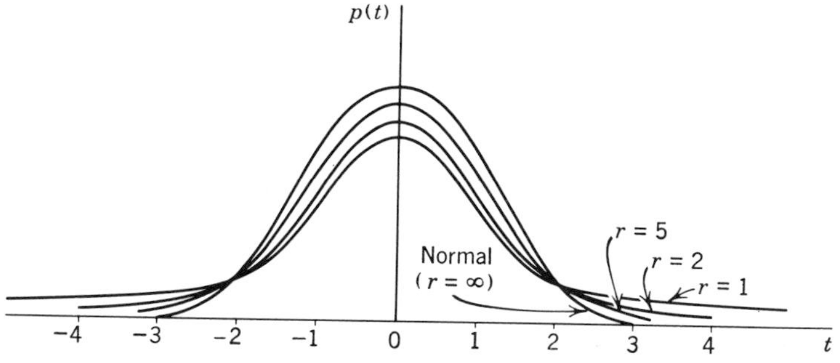

FIGURE 13-3 Probability distribution of t_r.

It is also assumed that the modified chi-square variable C_r^2 is *statistically independent of z*. C_r is called a modified chi variable.

The probability distribution of t_r is shown in Figure 13-3. Of course, for each different r there is a different C_r^2, and hence a different t_r. The critical values of the *t*-distribution for each *r* are given in Table V in the end-of-book Appendix. Although the *t*-distribution requires sophisticated mathematics to derive in detail, we can easily deduce its most important features. From (13-25c) as $r \to \infty$,

$$C_r \xrightarrow{p} 1$$

hence, from (13-30),

$$t_r \xrightarrow{p} z \tag{13-32}$$

This is seen in Figure 13-3; the *t*-distribution gradually approaches the normal as *r* increases. This is also verified in end-of-book Appendix Table V; as *r* gets very large, the *t* percentiles get very close to the *z* percentiles (given in the last row, for reference). In fact, if $r > 30$, there is very little error in approximating *t* with *z*.

On the other hand, as long as *r* is finite, C_r is not precisely 1; instead, it is distributed around 1. It is this variability of C_r in the denominator of (13-30) that spreads the *t*-distribution out more than the normal. In Figure 13-2, the student will note that the smaller is *r*, the greater is the variability of C_r^2 (hence C_r); this causes greater variability in the corresponding *t* distribution in Figure 13-3.

(b) Uses of *t*

(i) Sample Mean. In practice, the *t* distribution occurs in quasistandardizing a normal variate. As the commonest example, we consider a sample mean $\bar{y}$.

If $y \sim N(\mu, \sigma^2)$, then the sample mean $\bar{y} \sim N(\mu, \sigma^2/n)$ and in its standardized form is

$$z = \frac{\bar{y} - \mu}{\sigma/\sqrt{n}} \tag{13-33}$$

Moreover, when s was substituted for σ, we called it the *quasi*-standardized

$$z^* = \frac{\bar{y} - \mu}{s/\sqrt{n}} \tag{13-34}$$

To prove this has a t distribution, we introduce two canceling occurrences of σ into (13-34):

$$z^* = \frac{\bar{y} - \mu}{(s/\sigma)(\sigma/\sqrt{n})}$$

$$= \frac{(\bar{y} - \mu)/(\sigma/\sqrt{n})}{(s/\sigma)}$$

by (13-33) and (13-26)

$$z^* = \frac{z}{C_{n-1}} \tag{13-35}$$

By (13-30) this has the t distribution, provided that the numerator and denominator are independent, that is, that $\bar{y}$ and s are independent. At first glance there seems to be doubt about this independence, because s and $\bar{y}$ are calculated from the same sample; indeed, $\bar{y}$ occurs explicitly in the formula $s^2 = \sum (y_i - \bar{y})^2/(n - 1)$. Yet there is a surprising theorem that proves that s and $\bar{y}$ in fact are independent,[4] and this completes our argument.

---

[4] This is proved in advanced texts such as Cramer 1946, or Kendall and Stuart 1963. The proof is simple and instructive enough in the special case when $n = 2$, that we give it here:

From (13-18) it follows that

$$s^2 = \frac{(y_1 - y_2)^2}{2}$$

while, by definition,

$$\bar{y} = \frac{y_1 + y_2}{2}$$

Since constants can be ignored without loss of generality, it is enough to prove that $(y_1 - y_2)$ is independent of $(y_1 + y_2)$.

We therefore consider the covariance of these variables, obtaining

$$\begin{aligned} E(y_1 - y_2)(y_1 + y_2) &= E(y_1^2 - y_2^2) \\ &= E(y_1^2) - E(y_2^2) \\ &= 0 \end{aligned} \tag{13-36}$$

since (by assumption) y_1 and y_2 have identical distributions. Also, since both y_1 and y_2 are normal, $(y_1 - y_2)$ and $(y_1 + y_2)$ are also normal. Hence, their zero covariance in (13-36) establishes their independence.

(ii) General Case. It is not only the sample mean that can be quasi-standardized to produce a t statistic. It may be similarly proved that whenever any normal variate is quasi-standardized, it becomes a t variable rather than a z variable. The estimated regression coefficients $\hat{\beta}_i$ are prime examples. The substituted s, being a random variable, makes the t distribution a little more widespread than the z distribution. This causes confidence intervals to be a little wider (vaguer)—the price paid for not knowing σ exactly.

13-4 THE F DISTRIBUTION

(a) Definition

The mathematical definition of an F variable with m and n d.f. is rather like the definition of t:

$$\boxed{F_{m,n} \equiv \frac{C_m^2}{C_n^2}} \tag{13-37}$$

where C_m^2, C_n^2 are *independent* modified Chi-square variables. This is the same sort of independence of numerator and denominator specified in the definition of t. As an extreme example of what could conceivably happen were this independence not assured, suppose $m = n$, and C_m^2 and C_n^2 are perfectly dependent by being identical; then their ratio must be 1 exactly, which is not a very interesting random variable.

Some of the limiting properties of the F distribution are obvious from the limiting properties of C^2. From (13-25), as $n \to \infty$,

$$C_n^2 \xrightarrow{p} 1$$

Thus, from (13-37), as $n \to \infty$

$$\boxed{F_{m,n} \xrightarrow{p} C_m^2} \tag{13-38}$$

Figure 13-4 shows how the F distribution approaches the corresponding C_m^2 distribution as n increases. This is also borne out in end-of-book Appendix Table VII; as n gets large, the percentiles of $F_{m,n}$ get close to the percentiles of C_m^2 (given in the last row, for reference).

Finally, as $m \to \infty$ as well as $n \to \infty$,

$$F_{m,n} \xrightarrow{p} 1 \tag{13-39}$$

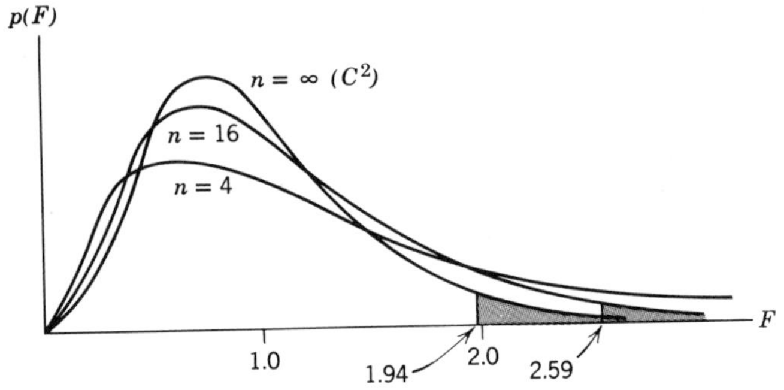

FIGURE 13-4 Probability distribution of $F_{m,n}$ for $m = 8$, and various n.

In other words, the critical values of F approach 1 as both m and n become very large, that is, as we move towards the lower right-hand corner of end-of-book Appendix Table VII.

(b) Use of F in Regression

When σ^2 is known, regression tests may be made using the modified chi-square statistic:

$$C_r^2 = \frac{1}{r}(\mathbf{C}\hat{\boldsymbol{\beta}} - \mathbf{C}\boldsymbol{\beta})'(\mathbf{CVC}')^{-1}(\mathbf{C}\hat{\boldsymbol{\beta}} - \mathbf{C}\boldsymbol{\beta})/\sigma^2 \tag{13-40}$$
(13-16) modified

But in the usual case, s^2 must be substituted for the unknown σ^2. We will establish that the resulting

$$F = \frac{1}{r}(\mathbf{C}\hat{\boldsymbol{\beta}} - \mathbf{C}\boldsymbol{\beta})'(\mathbf{CVC}')^{-1}(\mathbf{C}\hat{\boldsymbol{\beta}} - \mathbf{C}\boldsymbol{\beta})/s^2 \tag{13-41}$$
(12-39) repeated

does have an F distribution according to the definition (13-37). We merely introduce canceling occurrences of σ^2 into (13-41):

$$F = \frac{(\mathbf{C}\hat{\boldsymbol{\beta}} - \mathbf{C}\boldsymbol{\beta})'(\sigma^2\mathbf{CVC}')^{-1}(\mathbf{C}\hat{\boldsymbol{\beta}} - \mathbf{C}\boldsymbol{\beta})/r}{s^2/\sigma^2} \tag{13-42}$$

The numerator and denominator have already [in (13-16) and (13-27) respectively] been shown to be C^2 variates. Their independence can be proved in advanced texts such as Cramer 1946, so that (13-41) indeed does follow the F distribution, with r and $(n - k)$ d.f.

In conclusion, the substitution of s for σ changed a C^2 variable in (13-40) into an F variable (13-41), just as it changed a z into a t in Section 13-3.

13-5 COMPARISON AND REVIEW

A summary is presented in Table 13-1.

A briefer summary is given in Table 13-2, where we note that each variable in column (1) is just a special case ($r = 1$) of the corresponding variable in column (2). Thus

$$z^2 = C_1^2 \tag{13-43}$$

and

$$t_{n-k}^2 = F_{1,\,n-k} \tag{13-44}$$

It is also interesting to note that in a sense each variable in row (1) is a special case ($n = \infty$) of the corresponding variable in row (2). Thus

$$z = t_\infty \tag{13-45}$$

and

$$C_r^2 = F_{r,\,\infty} \tag{13-46}$$

This information is summarized in Figure 13-5, which shows how the F table includes these other distributions as well.

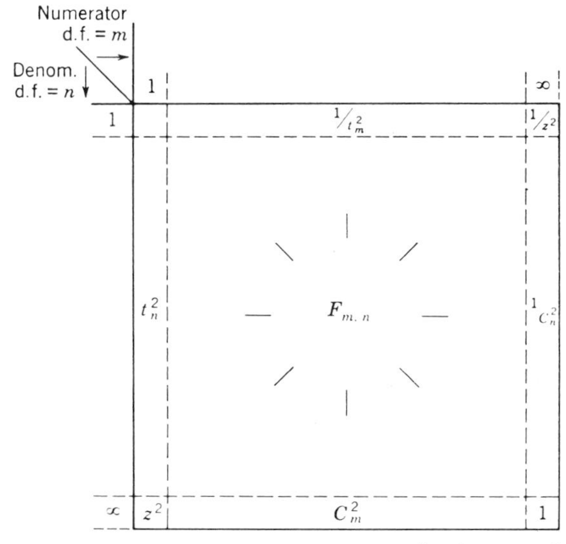

FIGURE 13-5 Relation of the F distribution to C^2, t^2, and z^2 (as found in Appendix Table VII).

TABLE 13-1 Summary of How Variables in this Chapter are Distributed

(a) *Chi-Square* (χ_r^2)

Definition:

$$\sum_{i=1}^{n} z_i^2 = \frac{\sum (y_i - \mu)^2}{\sigma^2} \sim \chi_n^2 \qquad (13\text{-}1)$$

or, in matrix terms,

$$(\mathbf{y} - \boldsymbol{\mu})'(\sigma^2\mathbf{I})^{-1}(\mathbf{y} - \boldsymbol{\mu}) \sim \chi_n^2 \qquad (13\text{-}9)$$

This remains true even if we consider an entirely different set of variables that are not independent, with cov $\mathbf{y} = \sigma^2\mathbf{W}$. Then

$$(\mathbf{y} - \boldsymbol{\mu})'(\sigma^2\mathbf{W})^{-1}(\mathbf{y} - \boldsymbol{\mu}) \sim \chi_n^2 \qquad (13\text{-}10)$$

Now suppose that in (13-1) μ is unknown and is replaced with $\bar{y}$:

$$\sum_{i=1}^{n} \frac{(y_i - \bar{y})^2}{\sigma^2} \sim \chi_{n-1}^2 \qquad (13\text{-}17)$$

and in the general case with k regressors,

$$\sum_{i=1}^{n} \frac{(y_i - \hat{y}_i)^2}{\sigma^2} \sim \chi_{n-k}^2 \qquad (13\text{-}23)$$

(b) *Modified Chi-Square* (C_r^2)

Definition:

$$\frac{\chi_r^2}{r} \sim C_r^2 \qquad (13\text{-}24)$$

In the single (constant) regressor case, when μ is estimated by $\bar{y}$,

$$\frac{s^2}{\sigma^2} \sim C_{n-1}^2 \qquad (13\text{-}26)$$

In the general case, with k regressors

$$\frac{s^2}{\sigma^2} \sim C_{n-k}^2 \qquad (13\text{-}27)$$

s^2 is used to estimate σ^2, below.

(c) *Student's t*

Definition:

$$\frac{z}{C_r} \sim t_r \qquad (13\text{-}30)$$

Used in quasi-standardizing:

$$\frac{\bar{y} - \mu}{s/\sqrt{n}} \sim t_{n-1} \qquad (13\text{-}34)$$

(d) *F*

Definition:

$$\frac{C_m^2}{C_n^2} \sim F_{m,n} \qquad (13\text{-}37)$$

Also used for quasi-standardizing, in regression:

$$\frac{(\mathbf{C}\hat{\boldsymbol{\beta}} - \mathbf{C}\boldsymbol{\beta})'(\mathbf{CVC}')^{-1}(\mathbf{C}\hat{\boldsymbol{\beta}} - \mathbf{C}\boldsymbol{\beta})/r}{s^2} \sim F_{r,n-k} \qquad (13\text{-}41)$$

TABLE 13-2 Relation of Various Distributions for Practical Work[a]

↓ *Available knowledge* / *Purpose* →	(1) *Confidence Interval or Test for* One *Parameter*	(2) *Confidence Interval or Test for* Several (r) *Parameters*
(1) σ^2 known	Use z (or z^2)	C_r^2
(2) σ^2 unknown, s^2 used instead	t_{n-k} (or t_{n-k}^2)	$F_{r,n-k}$

[a] n = sample size, k = number of regressors, and r = number of simultaneous tests on the parameters.

PROBLEMS

13-1 It is possible to find the critical points of C_1^2 using only the z table (Table IV). In this way, find the critical point of C_1^2 that

(a) marks off 5% in the upper tail
(b) marks off 1% in the upper tail.

13-2 Using only the F table (Table VII) find the critical point of C_r^2 that

(a) when $r = 5$, marks off 5% in the upper tail
(b) when $r = 15$, marks off 5% in the upper tail.

13-3 Construct a 90% confidence interval for σ^2 from this sample of n observations from $N(\mu, \sigma^2)$: 28, 31, 21, 28, 22

(a) Assume μ is known to be 25. [*Hint*. (13-8)]
(b) Assume, more realistically, that μ is unknown. [*Hint*. (13-26)]

14

*VECTOR GEOMETRY

The star means that strictly speaking, instructors may skip this chapter and later starred sections that are also geometrically oriented. However, many students find a picture worth a thousand words. So those who find that geometry makes a difficult subject easier to follow, are encouraged to study this starred material.

14-1 THE GEOMETRIC INTERPRETATION OF VECTORS

(a) Introduction

Assuming the reader is familiar with vector algebra, we develop its corresponding geometric interpretation in this chapter; this is then used to reinterpret regression and correlation theory. Readers with matrix algebra will have simultaneously taken varying amounts of geometry; hence, some may be able to pick up this argument at a midway point. But for the sake of those who have very little background, this geometry is developed from first principles. For simplicity, we begin by showing vectors in only two or three dimensions. However, interpretations in any number of dimensions are equally valid; thus, we can drop explicit reference to the dimension of the space later on.

Consider the vector

$$\mathbf{x} = (x_1, x_2, \ldots, x_n) \tag{14-1}$$

For example,

$$\mathbf{x} = (2, 4, 3) \tag{14-2}$$

which may be plotted as a point in three dimensions (Figure 14-1). Sometimes it is more convenient to represent it as an arrow from the origin to the point. If a vector is designated as an arrow, it may be shifted, provided its length and direction are maintained—that is, it may be shifted in a

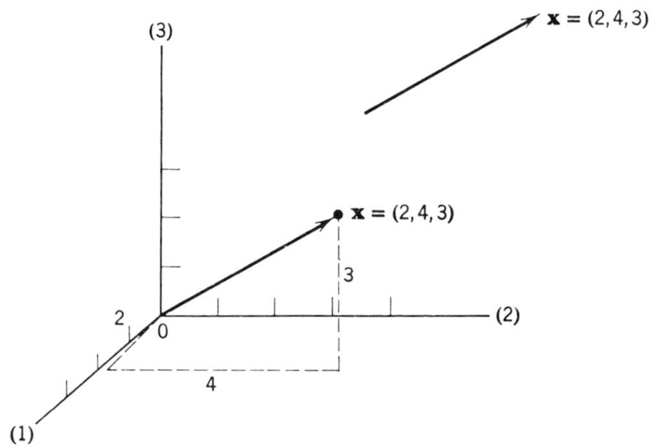

FIGURE 14-1 A three-dimensional vector. This vector is the direction and distance defined by moving two units in the first direction, four units in the second direction, and three units in the third direction.

parallel way. But if a vector is designated as a point only, then of course this point may *not* be shifted.

The simple algebraic manipulations of vectors are set out in Table 14-1, along with the corresponding geometric interpretation. In addition, each geometric operation is detailed in Figures 14-2 to 14-4.

In review, in Figure 14-5 we see that the sum $(\mathbf{x} + \mathbf{y})$ is one diagonal of the parallelogram formed from $\mathbf{x}$ and $\mathbf{y}$, while the difference $(\mathbf{x} - \mathbf{y})$ is the other diagonal.

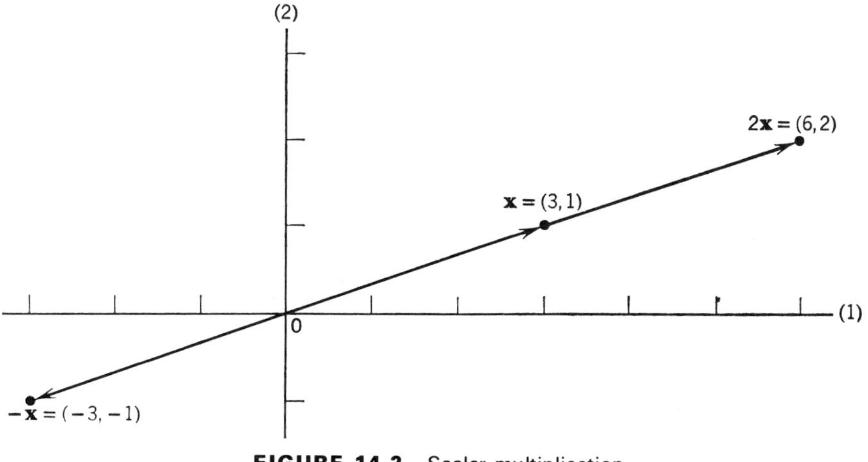

FIGURE 14-2 Scalar multiplication

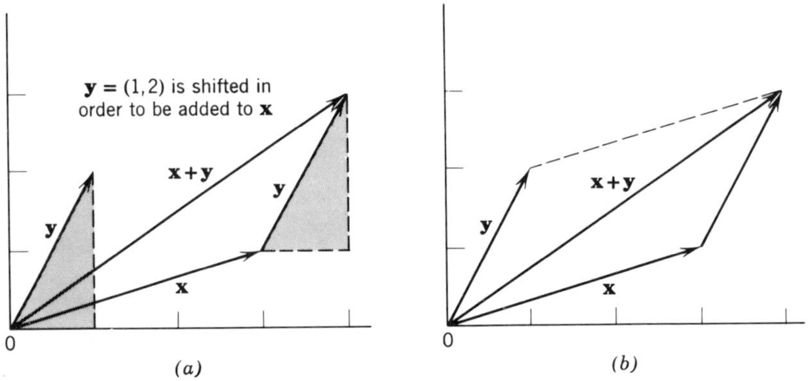

FIGURE 14-3 Vector addition, which in (*b*) is seen to be equivalent to constructing a diagonal of the parallelogram defined by **x** and **y**.

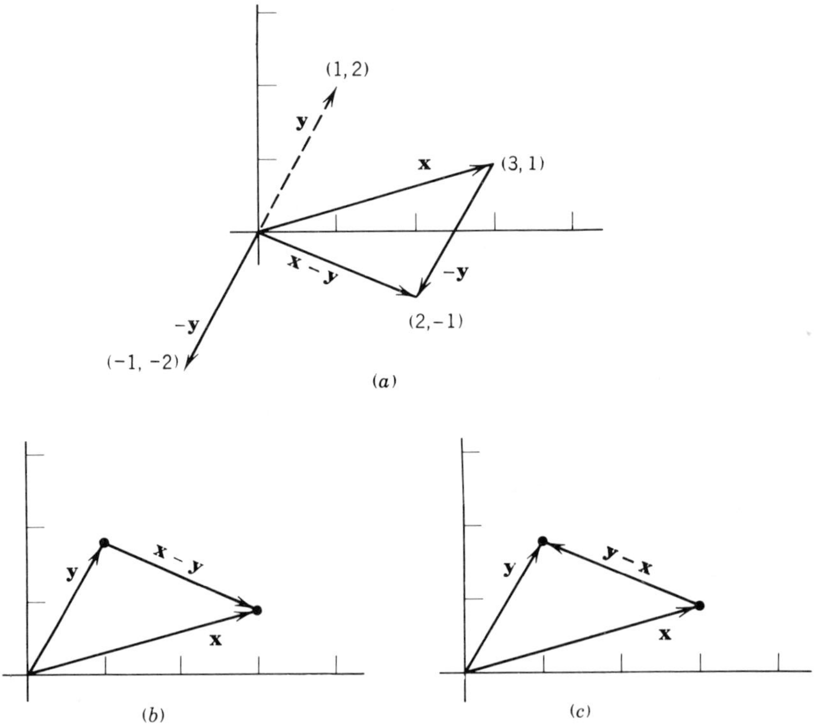

FIGURE 14-4 Vector subtraction ($\mathbf{x} - \mathbf{y}$), which in (*b*) is seen to be equivalent to moving from point **y** to point **x**. (*c*) The reader can confirm that ($\mathbf{y} - \mathbf{x}$) is similarly obtained by moving from point **x** to point **y**.

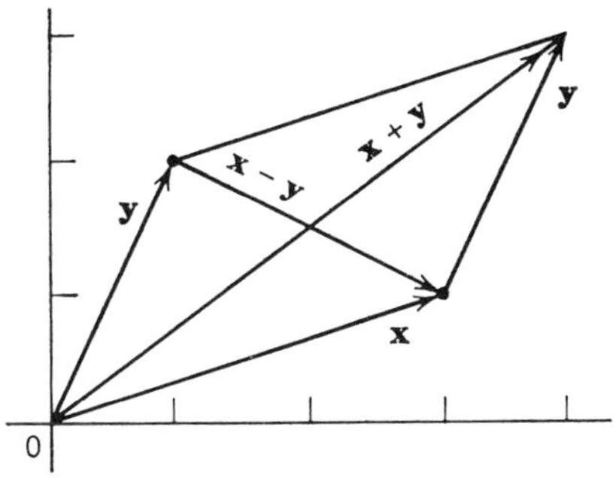

FIGURE 14-5 Vector addition and subtraction compared. Addition is the diagonal obtained by shifting the arrow **y** to follow the arrow **x**; subtraction is the diagonal obtained by moving from the point **y** to the point **x**.

TABLE 14-1 Comparison of the Algebra and Geometry of Vectors

	Since each manipulation is defined algebraically in this way:	*It follows that it has this geometric interpretation:*
Scalar multiplication by a positive constant	2(3, 1) = (6, 2)	Changes length (Figure 14-2)
Scalar multiplication by −1	−1(3, 1) = (−3, −1)	Changes direction (Figure 14-2)
Addition	(3, 1) + (1, 2) = (4, 3)	Shifts the arrow **y** to follow the arrow **x** (Figure 14-3); this is seen to yield the diagonal of the parallelogram constructed from **x** and **y**
Subtraction	(3, 1) − (1, 2) = (2, −1)	Is equivalent to summing **x** + (−**y**), that is, shifting the arrow (−**y**) to follow the arrow **x** in Figure 14-4*a*. This is also seen to be the arrow obtained in Figure 14-4*b* by moving from the *point* **y** to the *point* **x**

(b) Dot Product

(i) Definition and Properties. The dot product (also called inner product or scalar product) of two vectors is defined as a simple kind of matrix multiplication:

$$\mathbf{x} \cdot \mathbf{y} = \begin{bmatrix} x_1 & x_2 & \cdots & x_n \end{bmatrix} \begin{bmatrix} y_1 \\ y_2 \\ \cdot \\ \cdot \\ \cdot \\ y_n \end{bmatrix} = x_1 y_1 + x_2 y_2 + \cdots + x_n y_n \qquad (14\text{-}3)$$

For example,

$$(3, 1, -1) \cdot (2, -3, 0) = 3$$

The dot product, of course, obeys all the rules of matrix multiplication; for example,

$$\mathbf{x} \cdot (\mathbf{y} + \mathbf{z}) = \mathbf{x} \cdot \mathbf{y} + \mathbf{x} \cdot \mathbf{z} \quad \text{(distributive law)} \qquad (14\text{-}4)$$

$$\mathbf{x} \cdot (c\mathbf{y}) = (c\mathbf{x}) \cdot \mathbf{y} = c(\mathbf{x} \cdot \mathbf{y}) \qquad (14\text{-}5)$$

But, it also satisfies in addition:

$$\mathbf{x} \cdot \mathbf{y} = \mathbf{y} \cdot \mathbf{x} \quad \text{(commutative law)} \qquad (14\text{-}6)$$

(ii) Length. A special case is the dot product of a vector with itself:

$$\mathbf{x} \cdot \mathbf{x} = x_1^2 + x_2^2 + \cdots + x_n^2 \qquad (14\text{-}7)$$

This is called $\|\mathbf{x}\|^2$. In two dimensions we recognize it as the squared length of the vector, according to the theorem of Pythagoras in Figure 14-6*a*. For example, the vector $\mathbf{x} = (3, 1)$ has squared length

$$\mathbf{x} \cdot \mathbf{x} = 3^2 + 1^2 = 10$$

Thus, its length is $\sqrt{10} = 3.16$.

It is easy to also confirm in three dimensions that $\|\mathbf{x}\|^2$ is the squared length of the vector. For example, in Figure 14-6*b*, first apply the Pythagorean theorem to the horizontal ΔABC, obtaining $x_1^2 + x_2^2$ as the squared length of AC. Then apply the Pythagorean theorem again to the vertical ΔACD, confirming that the squared length of the vector AD is

$$(x_1^2 + x_2^2) + x_3^2 = \|\mathbf{x}\|^2 \qquad (14\text{-}8)$$

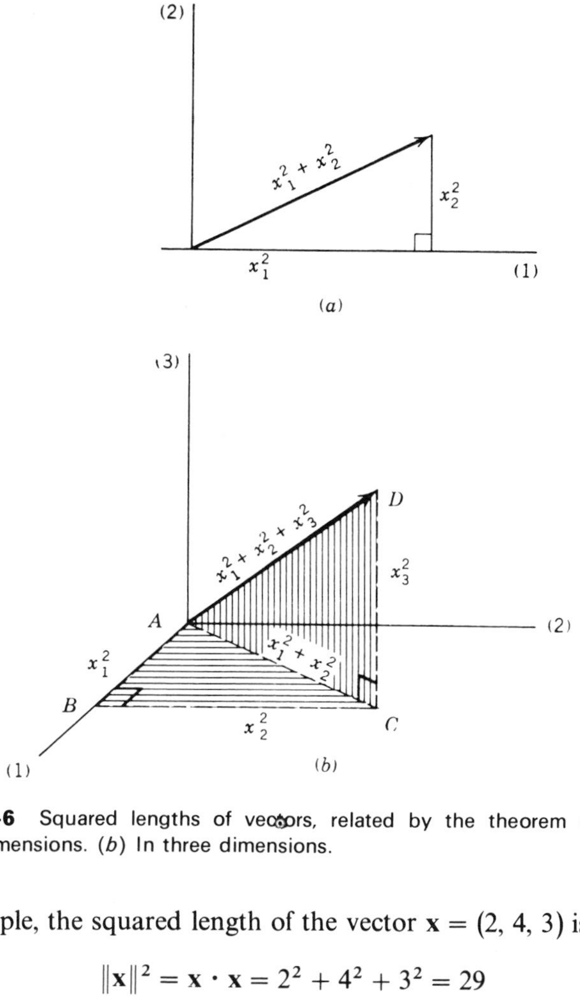

FIGURE 14-6 Squared lengths of vectors, related by the theorem of Pythagoras. (*a*) In two dimensions. (*b*) In three dimensions.

As an example, the squared length of the vector $\mathbf{x} = (2, 4, 3)$ is

$$\|\mathbf{x}\|^2 = \mathbf{x} \cdot \mathbf{x} = 2^2 + 4^2 + 3^2 = 29 \tag{14-9}$$

Thus, its length is $\sqrt{29} = 5.39$.

$\|\mathbf{x}\|$ has turned out to be length wherever it is physically meaningful (in 1, 2, or 3 dimensions). We will use a little mathematical imagination and call $\|\mathbf{x}\|$ the *length* (or *norm*) in any number of dimensions.

To review:

$$\|\mathbf{x}\|^2 = \mathbf{x} \cdot \mathbf{x} \tag{14-10}$$

$$= x_1^2 + x_2^2 \cdots + x_n^2 = \text{squared length} \tag{14-11}$$

while

$$\|\mathbf{x}\| = \text{length}$$

One of the most frequently used facts about length is that, if c is positive,

$$\|c\mathbf{x}\| = c\|\mathbf{x}\| \tag{14-12a}$$

This is obvious from Figure 14-2, and may be proved more rigorously in n dimensions.[1] When c is negative, equation (14-12a) cannot be correct because the right side is negative while the left side is positive. By taking the absolute value (magnitude) of c, we may write a generally correct form of (14-12a):

$$\|c\mathbf{x}\| = |c|\;\|\mathbf{x}\| \tag{14-12b}$$

(iii) Perpendicularity. Also called *orthogonality*, and symbolized by $\perp$, this is easily expressed in terms of vector length. From Figure 14-7, it is evident that $\mathbf{x} \perp \mathbf{y}$ iff the length of $(\mathbf{x}+\mathbf{y})$ equals the length of $(\mathbf{x}-\mathbf{y})$, that is, iff

$$\|\mathbf{x}+\mathbf{y}\|^2 = \|\mathbf{x}-\mathbf{y}\|^2$$

$$(\mathbf{x}+\mathbf{y})\cdot(\mathbf{x}+\mathbf{y}) = (\mathbf{x}-\mathbf{y})\cdot(\mathbf{x}-\mathbf{y})$$

$$\mathbf{x}\cdot\mathbf{x} + 2\mathbf{x}\cdot\mathbf{y} + \mathbf{y}\cdot\mathbf{y} = \mathbf{x}\cdot\mathbf{x} - 2\mathbf{x}\cdot\mathbf{y} + \mathbf{y}\cdot\mathbf{y}$$

$$4\mathbf{x}\cdot\mathbf{y} = 0$$

$$\mathbf{x}\cdot\mathbf{y} = 0$$

$$\boxed{\mathbf{x} \perp \mathbf{y} \text{ iff } \mathbf{x}\cdot\mathbf{y} = 0} \tag{14-13}$$

That is, two vectors are perpendicular if and only if their dot product is zero.

(c) Subspaces

(i) Generation of Subspaces. In Figure 14-8, we show that when a fixed vector $\mathbf{x}_1$ is multiplied by every possible scalar c_1, a straight line is generated running through $\mathbf{x}_1$ and the origin. Each vector $c_1\mathbf{x}_1$ may be

---

[1] ***Proof of* (14-12a).** Since $c\mathbf{x} = (cx_1, cx_2, \ldots)$, from definition (14-11),

$$\|c\mathbf{x}\|^2 = (cx_1)^2 + (cx_2)^2 + \cdots$$
$$= c^2(x_1^2 + x_2^2 + \cdots) = c^2\|\mathbf{x}\|^2$$

Thus

$$\|c\mathbf{x}\| = c\|\mathbf{x}\|$$

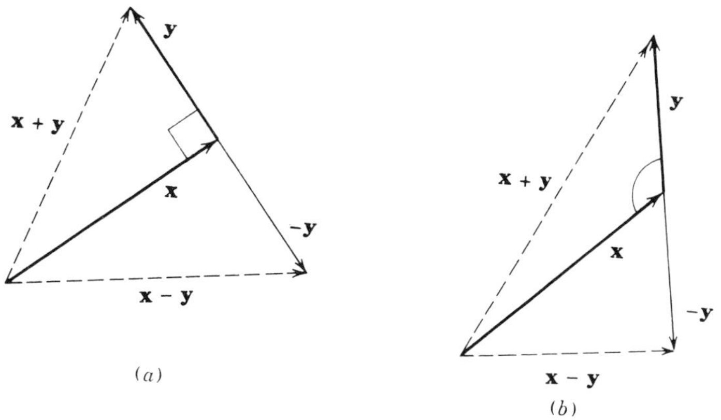

FIGURE 14-7 $\mathbf{x} \perp \mathbf{y}$ iff $\|\mathbf{x}+\mathbf{y}\| = \|\mathbf{x}-\mathbf{y}\|$. (Note that the diagrams are valid in any number of dimensions.) (*a*) $\mathbf{x} \perp \mathbf{y}$. (*b*) $\mathbf{x}$ not $\perp$ $\mathbf{y}$.

represented as an arrow or a point, but the picture is less cluttered if we simply use a point. In summary we write

$$L: \qquad c_1\mathbf{x}_1 \qquad -\infty < c_1 < \infty \tag{14-14}$$

In Figure 14-9, we increase dimension by one. In this figure, we use for the first time two conventions about arrowheads. First, arrows within the plane have a light arrowhead, and arrows outside the plane have a dark arrowhead. Second, arrowheads are shown as cones so that when the arrow is pointing away from the reader, the circular base of the cone can be seen. Finally, we represent the plane as a slab, although mathematically speaking,

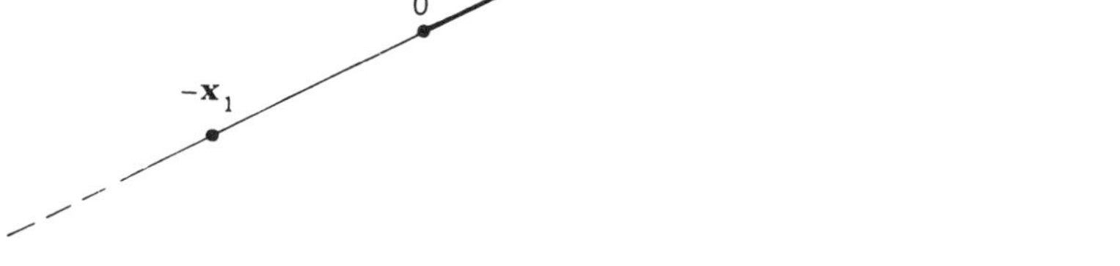

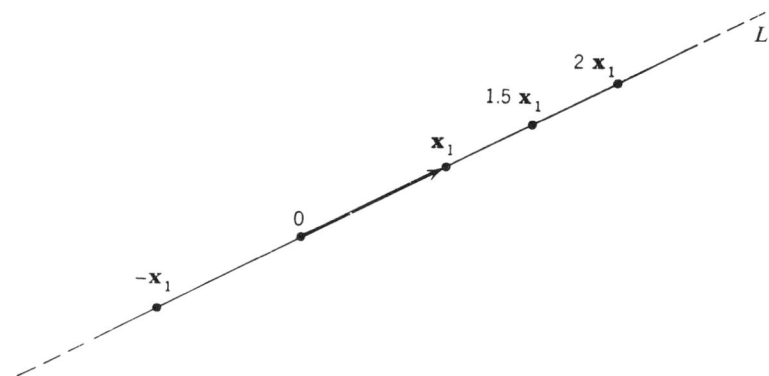

FIGURE 14-8 The line L generated by $\mathbf{x}_1$. (The diagram may be pictured in either two or three dimensions.) L is $c_1\mathbf{x}_1$, where c_1 takes on all values, so that the line extends to infinity.

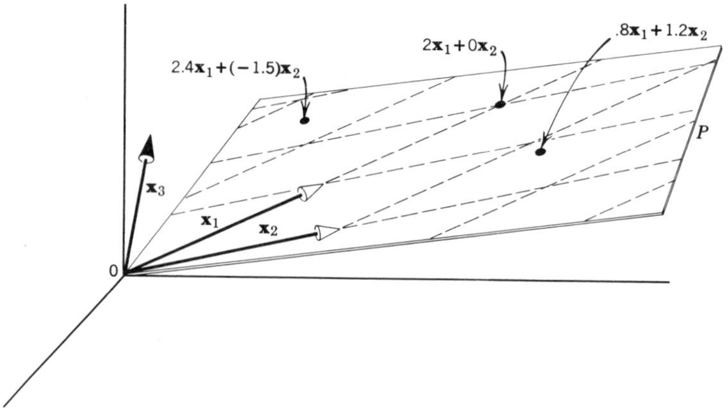

FIGURE 14-9 The plane P generated by $\mathbf{x}_1$ and $\mathbf{x}_2$. P is $c_1\mathbf{x}_1 + c_2\mathbf{x}_2$, where c_1, c_2 take on all values, so that the plane extends to infinity.

it has no thickness. These conventions make it much easier to visualize geometry in n-dimensional space (n-space).

In Figure 14-9, we show the set of points generated by two fixed vectors in 3-space,

$$P: \qquad c_1\mathbf{x}_1 + c_2\mathbf{x}_2 \qquad -\infty < c_1, c_2 < \infty \tag{14-15}$$

This is called the *set of all possible linear combinations of* $\mathbf{x}_1$ *and* $\mathbf{x}_2$, and is the plane running through $\mathbf{x}_1$, $\mathbf{x}_2$, and the origin.[2] Geometrically, we see that we can generate (i.e., get to) any point on this plane P by taking the appropriate linear combination of $\mathbf{x}_1$ and $\mathbf{x}_2$, that is, by appropriately selecting c_1 and c_2 in (14-15); but we cannot generate any point above or below this plane.

To generate the whole 3-space requires a third independent vector, such as $\mathbf{x}_3$, to take us off the plane P. Thus, the whole set of points in this 3-space could be generated by

$$c_1\mathbf{x}_1 + c_2\mathbf{x}_2 + c_3\mathbf{x}_3 \qquad -\infty < c_i < \infty \tag{14-16}$$

This is often stated as: $\mathbf{x}_1$, $\mathbf{x}_2$, and $\mathbf{x}_3$ generate (or span) this 3-space. Or: $\mathbf{x}_1$, $\mathbf{x}_2$, and $\mathbf{x}_3$ are a *basis* of this 3-space.

This generalizes into n-space; consider the set of points

$$c_1\mathbf{x}_1 + c_2\mathbf{x}_2 + \cdots + c_m\mathbf{x}_m \qquad -\infty < c_i < \infty \tag{14-17}$$

[2] Unless $\mathbf{x}_1$, $\mathbf{x}_2$, and the origin all lie on a straight line, in which case we can generate only this line. Or worse yet, if $\mathbf{x}_1$, $\mathbf{x}_2$, and the origin all coincide (i.e., $\mathbf{x}_1 = \mathbf{x}_2 = \mathbf{0}$) then we can generate only one point—the origin. These degenerate cases are called "linear dependence of $\mathbf{x}_1$ and $\mathbf{x}_2$." For simplicity, we will assume throughout this chapter that linear dependence does not occur.

This set of all possible linear combinations of these m fixed vectors is called an m-dimension *subspace*. If $m = 1$, then the subspace is a straight line. If $m = 2$, then the subspace is a plane. If $m > 2$, the subspace is called a hyperplane. Only if $m = n$, and we thus have n linearly independent vectors ($\mathbf{x}_1$, $\mathbf{x}_2 \cdots \mathbf{x}_n$) will we generate all of our n-space. For any vector or point $\mathbf{y}$ in this n-space, a unique set of coefficients $c_1, c_2 \cdots c_n$ can be found such that

$$\mathbf{y} = c_1\mathbf{x}_1 + c_2\mathbf{x}_2 + \cdots + c_n\mathbf{x}_n \tag{14-18}$$

These values $\langle c_1, c_2, \ldots, c_n \rangle$ are called *the coordinates of* $\mathbf{y}$ *with respect to the basis* $(\mathbf{x}_1, \mathbf{x}_2, \ldots, \mathbf{x}_n)$.

For example, in two-space, the vectors $\mathbf{x}_1 = (1, -1)$ and $\mathbf{x}_2 = (2, 1)$ will generate the whole space. We now use (14-18) to find the coordinates (with respect to this basis $\mathbf{x}_1$, $\mathbf{x}_2$) of a given vector, say $\mathbf{y} = (4, -1)$; this involves selecting c_1 and c_2 so that

$$c_1\mathbf{x}_1 + c_2\mathbf{x}_2 = \mathbf{y} \tag{14-19}$$

that is[3]

$$c_1 \begin{bmatrix} 1 \\ -1 \end{bmatrix} + c_2 \begin{bmatrix} 2 \\ 1 \end{bmatrix} = \begin{bmatrix} 4 \\ -1 \end{bmatrix} \tag{14-20}$$

that is,

$$c_1 + 2c_2 = 4$$

$$-c_1 + c_2 = -1$$

The algebraic solution to this set of equations is $c_1 = 2$, $c_2 = 1$. We have expressed $\mathbf{y}$ as a linear combination of $\mathbf{x}_1$ and $\mathbf{x}_2$, with the coefficients $\langle 2, 1 \rangle$ being the coordinates of $\mathbf{y}$ with respect to $\mathbf{x}_1$ and $\mathbf{x}_2$.

This is seen geometrically in Figure 14-10: The line (subspace) L_1 generated by $\mathbf{x}_1$ is shown, along with the subspace L_2 generated by $\mathbf{x}_2$. Then we complete the parallelogram, confirming that c_1 must be 2, and c_2 must be 1.

In other words, to find the coordinates of $\mathbf{y}$, we project; to find c_1, we project $\mathbf{y}$ onto L_1 in the direction parallel to L_2; or, stated briefly, we project $\mathbf{y}$ *onto* $\mathbf{x}_1$ *along* (parallel to) $\mathbf{x}_2$. Similarly, to find c_2 we project $\mathbf{y}$ onto $\mathbf{x}_2$ along $\mathbf{x}_1$.

The simplest kind of projection occurs when $\mathbf{x}_1 \perp \mathbf{x}_2$; this is called an *orthogonal* projection, as in Figure 14-11.

[3] For convenience, we sometimes write our vectors as columns instead of rows. More formally, we can easily justify (14-20) by transposing (14-19).

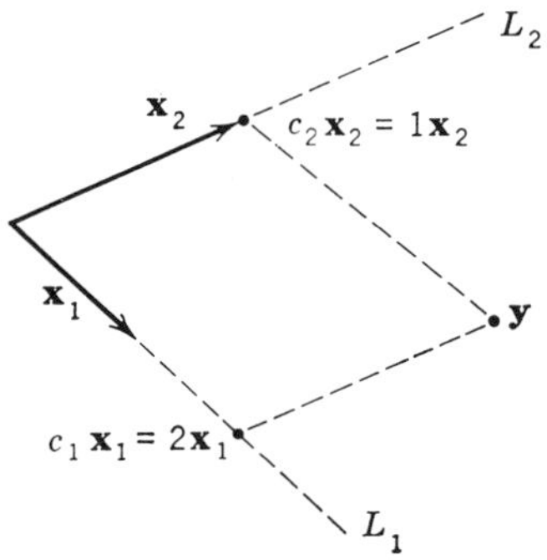

FIGURE 14-10 Finding the coordinates of $\mathbf{y}$ (with respect to $\mathbf{x}_1, \mathbf{x}_2$) geometrically by projection.

(d) Perpendicular Projections and Least Distance

Perpendicular projections are particularly easy to calculate, because the condition for perpendicularity (14-13) is so simple. To work out $\mathbf{y}_1$, the ⊥ projection of $\mathbf{y}$ onto $\mathbf{x}_1$, consider Figure 14-12, which is valid in any dimension. Of course, since the projection vector $\mathbf{y}_1$ lies on L_1, it is just a (scalar) multiple of $\mathbf{x}_1$; that is,

$$\mathbf{y}_1 = c\mathbf{x}_1 \tag{14-21}$$

with the problem being to determine c. Moreover, we note (Figure 14-5) that $\mathbf{y} - \mathbf{y}_1$ is the vector defined by moving from $\mathbf{y}_1$ to $\mathbf{y}$. But we must keep this perpendicular to $\mathbf{x}_1$, that is, we must find c, so that

$$(\mathbf{y} - \mathbf{y}_1) \perp \mathbf{x}_1 \tag{14-22}$$

Substitute (14-21) into (14-22) and use (14-13):

$$(\mathbf{y} - c\mathbf{x}_1) \cdot \mathbf{x}_1 = 0$$

$$(\mathbf{y} \cdot \mathbf{x}_1) - c(\mathbf{x}_1 \cdot \mathbf{x}_1) = 0$$

$$\boxed{c = \frac{\mathbf{y} \cdot \mathbf{x}_1}{\mathbf{x}_1 \cdot \mathbf{x}_1}} \tag{14-23}$$

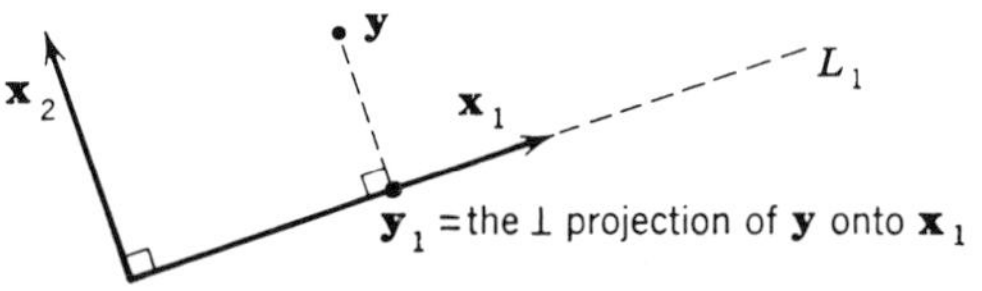

FIGURE 14-11 The orthogonal projection of $\mathbf{y}$ onto $\mathbf{x}_1$.

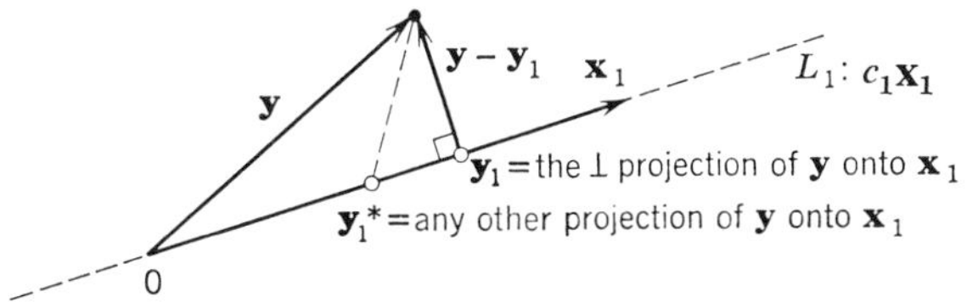

FIGURE 14-12 Orthogonal projection in two dimensions: $\mathbf{y}$ projected onto $\mathbf{x}_1$.

Substituting (14-23) into (14-21) establishes that

$$\boxed{\mathbf{y}_1 = \left(\frac{\mathbf{y} \cdot \mathbf{x}_1}{\mathbf{x}_1 \cdot \mathbf{x}_1}\right)\mathbf{x}_1} \tag{14-24}$$

where $\mathbf{y}_1$ is the $\perp$ projection of $\mathbf{y}$ onto $\mathbf{x}_1$.

The length of this projected vector has a simple formula too:

$$\begin{aligned} \|\mathbf{y}_1\|^2 &= \mathbf{y}_1 \cdot \mathbf{y}_1 \\ &= c^2\mathbf{x}_1 \cdot \mathbf{x}_1 \\ &= \left[\frac{\mathbf{y} \cdot \mathbf{x}_1}{\mathbf{x}_1 \cdot \mathbf{x}_1}\right]^2 \mathbf{x}_1 \cdot \mathbf{x}_1 \end{aligned}$$

$$\boxed{\|\mathbf{y}_1\|^2 = \frac{(\mathbf{y} \cdot \mathbf{x}_1)^2}{\mathbf{x}_1 \cdot \mathbf{x}_1}} \tag{14-25}$$

Hence, the norm or length of $\mathbf{y}_1$ is

$$\|\mathbf{y}_1\| = \frac{|\mathbf{y} \cdot \mathbf{x}_1|}{\|\mathbf{x}_1\|} \tag{14-26}$$

Referring again to Figure 14-12, we see that the *perpendicular* projection $\mathbf{y}_1$ is the point on L_1 closest to $\mathbf{y}$; any nonperpendicular projection, say $\mathbf{y}_1^*$, is farther from $\mathbf{y}$. The proof is simple: The distance $\|\mathbf{y} - \mathbf{y}_1^*\|$ must be greater than the distance $\|\mathbf{y} - \mathbf{y}_1\|$, because the hypotenuse of a right-angled triangle is greater than either side.

This theorem is important enough for regression and correlation theory that it is shown in the three-dimensional case in Figure 14-13.

> The perpendicular projection of $\mathbf{y}$ onto the subspace
>
> $$c_1\mathbf{x}_1 + c_2\mathbf{x}_2 + \cdots + c_m\mathbf{x}_m \tag{14-27}$$
>
> is the one point on this subspace closest to $\mathbf{y}$.

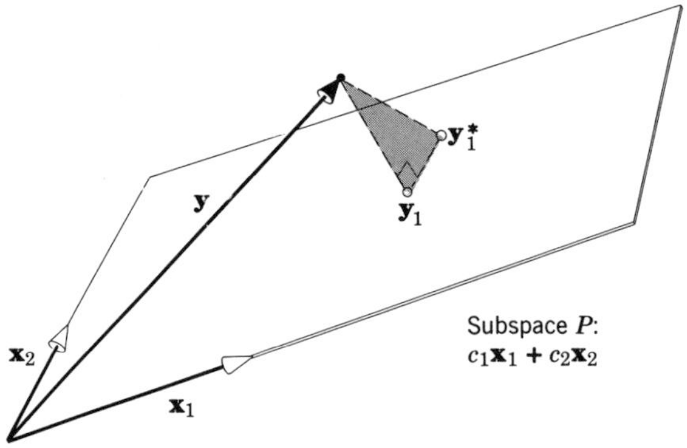

FIGURE 14-13 Orthogonal projection in three dimensions: $\mathbf{y}$ projected onto $(\mathbf{x}_1, \mathbf{x}_2)$ subspace.

(e) Cos θ

We can now obtain a simple formula for the cosine of the angle between any two vectors $\mathbf{x}_1$ and $\mathbf{y}$. Referring to Figure 14-14, we first $\perp$ project $\mathbf{y}$ onto $\mathbf{x}_1$; then, by definition from trigonometry,

$$\cos\theta = \pm\frac{\|\mathbf{y}_1\|}{\|\mathbf{y}\|} \tag{14-28}$$

Moreover, from Figure 14-14, it is clear that the sign of cos θ agrees with the sign of the coefficient c in (14-21). Using this equation, we may rewrite (14-28) as

$$\cos\theta = \frac{c\|\mathbf{x}_1\|}{\|\mathbf{y}\|} \tag{14-29}$$

Substituting (14-23)

$$\cos\theta = \frac{\mathbf{y}\cdot\mathbf{x}_1}{\|\mathbf{x}_1\|^2}\frac{\|\mathbf{x}_1\|}{\|\mathbf{y}\|} \tag{14-30}$$

$$\cos\theta = \frac{\mathbf{y}\cdot\mathbf{x}_1}{\|\mathbf{x}_1\|\,\|\mathbf{y}\|} \tag{14-31}$$

To free our notation somewhat, we rename $\mathbf{x}_1$ by $\mathbf{x}$:

$$\boxed{\cos\theta = \frac{\mathbf{x}\cdot\mathbf{y}}{\|\mathbf{x}\|\,\|\mathbf{y}\|}} \tag{14-32}$$

where θ is the angle between $\mathbf{x}$ and $\mathbf{y}$.

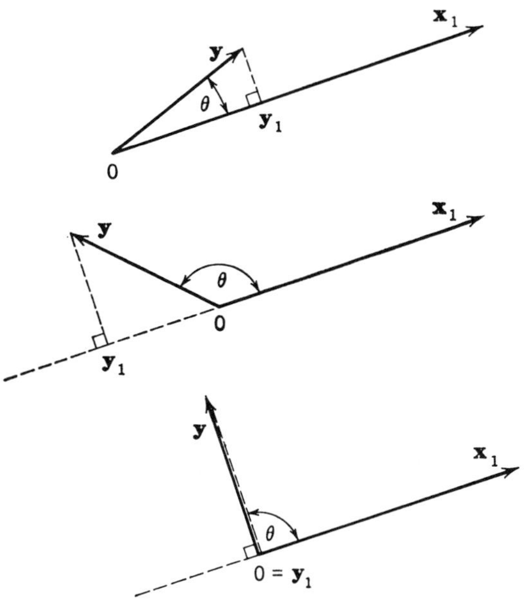

FIGURE 14-14 Cos θ. (*a*) θ acute, cos $\theta > 0$, $\mathbf{y}_1 = c\mathbf{x}_1$, where $c > 0$. (*b*) θ obtuse, cos $\theta < 0$; $\mathbf{y}_1 = c\mathbf{x}_1$, where $c < 0$. (*c*) θ is $90°$ ($\mathbf{y} \perp \mathbf{x}_1$), cos $\theta = 0$; $\mathbf{y}_1 = c\mathbf{x}_1$, where $c = 0$.

PROBLEMS

14-1 Let $\mathbf{x} = (1, -2)$ and $\mathbf{y} = (3, 1)$. Graph as arrows $\mathbf{x}$ and $\mathbf{y}$ and the following:

(a) $2\mathbf{x}$.
(b) $\mathbf{x} + \mathbf{y}$.
(c) $\mathbf{x} - \mathbf{y}$.
(d) $(\mathbf{x} + \mathbf{y}) + (\mathbf{x} - \mathbf{y})$. Check that this equals $2\mathbf{x}$.
(e) $(\mathbf{x} + \mathbf{y}) - (\mathbf{x} - \mathbf{y})$. Check that this equals $2\mathbf{y}$.
(f) $-3\mathbf{x} + 2\mathbf{y}$.

14-2 Which of the following pairs are orthogonal?

(a) $(1, 3)$ and $(-6, 2)$.
(b) $(1, -2)$ and $(1, 2)$.
(c) $(1, 2, -2)$ and $(2, 3, 2)$.
(d) $(1, -2, 1, 0, 1)$ and $(2, 0, 1, -1, -1)$; call these $\mathbf{x}_1$ and $\mathbf{x}_2$.

14-3 Find c so that $(\mathbf{x}_2 - c\mathbf{x}_1)$ will be perpendicular to $\mathbf{x}_1$ in Problem 14-2(d) above.

14-4 Using the basis $\mathbf{x}_1 = (1, -1)$, $\mathbf{x}_2 = (2, 1)$, find algebraically the coordinates of each of the following points. Then verify your result geometrically (work approximately).

(a) $(-1, -2)$.
(b) $(0, 3)$.
(c) $(-1, 1)$.
(d) $(3, -1)$.

14-5 Find the coordinates of the point $(1.2, .3)$ with respect to

(a) the basis $\mathbf{x}_1 = (.5, .1)$, $\mathbf{x}_2 = (.1, .2)$
(b) the orthogonal basis $\mathbf{x}_1 = (-.4, .2)$, $\mathbf{x}_2 = (.1, .2)$
(c) the orthonormal basis $\mathbf{x}_1 = (-.6, -.8)$, $\mathbf{x}_2 = (-.8, .6)$, where each vector is normalized, that is, of length 1. Which basis is easiest?

14-6 Consider the basis $\mathbf{x}_1 = (1, 0, 2)$ and $\mathbf{x}_2 = (2, -1, 1)$, which generates a plane P in three-space. For each point below, find whether it lies on the plane; if it does, then find its coordinates with respect to $(\mathbf{x}_1, \mathbf{x}_2)$:

(a) $(5, -1, 7)$.
(b) $(4, 0, 1)$.
(c) $(3, -2, 0)$.

14-7 Consider vectors $\mathbf{x}_1, \mathbf{x}_2$ in the two-space: $c_1\mathbf{x}_1 + c_2\mathbf{x}_2$:

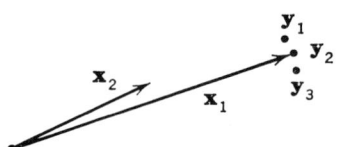

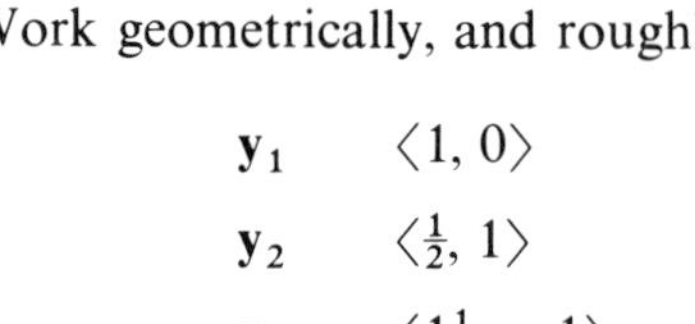

(a) Match the point with the correct pair of coordinates with respect to $(\mathbf{x}_1, \mathbf{x}_2)$. Work geometrically, and roughly.

$\mathbf{y}_1$	$\langle 1, 0 \rangle$
$\mathbf{y}_2$	$\langle \frac{1}{2}, 1 \rangle$
$\mathbf{y}_3$	$\langle 1\frac{1}{2}, -1 \rangle$

(b) The three points are close together. Are their coordinates close? Give an intuitive reason why.

14-8

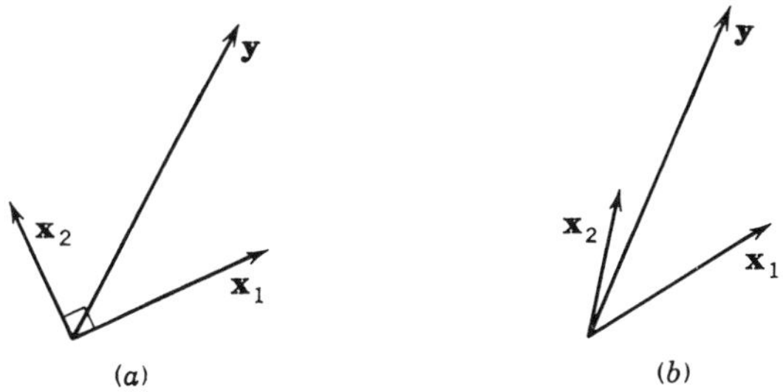

Work geometrically in two-space. In each case, find the ⊥ projection of $\mathbf{y}$ onto $\mathbf{x}_1$, and $\mathbf{y}$ onto $\mathbf{x}_2$. Call them $\mathbf{y}_1$ and $\mathbf{y}_2$. Under what circumstances does $\mathbf{y} = \mathbf{y}_1 + \mathbf{y}_2$?

14-2 LEAST SQUARES FIT

With this geometry in hand, we now turn to its application to regression. First, consider the problem of fitting a line, as in Chapter 2. To keep the geometry simple, our example in Figure 14-15 consists of only three observed points. The values of x are centered at 0; this can always be achieved by using deviations from the mean (y may or may not be also translated to a zero mean). The mathematical model may be written as

$$\mathbf{y} = \mathbf{X}\boldsymbol{\beta} + \mathbf{e} \tag{14-33}$$

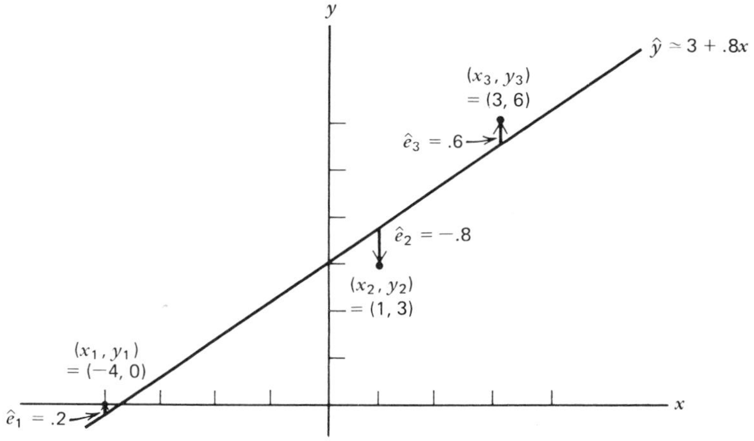

FIGURE 14-15 Regression scatter: points are observations; axes are variables.

The sample values used for estimating $\boldsymbol{\beta}$ are displayed in the form:

$$\mathbf{y} = \mathbf{X}\hat{\boldsymbol{\beta}} + \hat{\mathbf{e}} \tag{14-34}$$

$$\begin{bmatrix} 0 \\ 3 \\ 6 \end{bmatrix} = \begin{bmatrix} 1 & -4 \\ 1 & 1 \\ 1 & 3 \end{bmatrix} \begin{bmatrix} \hat{\beta}_1 \\ \hat{\beta}_2 \end{bmatrix} + \begin{bmatrix} \hat{e}_1 \\ \hat{e}_2 \\ \hat{e}_3 \end{bmatrix}$$

or

$$\mathbf{y} = \hat{\mathbf{y}} + \hat{\mathbf{e}} \tag{14-35}$$

$$\text{observed } y = \text{fitted } y + \text{residual}$$

where the fitted vector is

$$\hat{\mathbf{y}} = \hat{\beta}_1 \; \mathbf{x}_1 + \hat{\beta}_2 \; \mathbf{x}_2$$

$$\hat{\mathbf{y}} = \hat{\beta}_1 \begin{bmatrix} 1 \\ 1 \\ 1 \end{bmatrix} + \hat{\beta}_2 \begin{bmatrix} -4 \\ 1 \\ 3 \end{bmatrix} \tag{14-36}$$

Figure 14-16 displays exactly this same information in alternative vector geometry. Whereas in Figure 14-15 each *observation* was plotted as a point in "variable" space (i.e., the space defined by variables on the axes), in Figure 14-16 each *variable* is now plotted as a point or arrow in an "observation" space. Whereas each point in Figure 14-15 was drawn from a *row* of (14-34) [e.g., the first point (−4, 0) was drawn from the first row], each point or vector in Figure 14-16 is a *column* of (14-34).

In our example we also note that $\mathbf{x}_1$ and $\mathbf{x}_2$ are perpendicular. This follows because

$$\mathbf{x}_1 \cdot \mathbf{x}_2 = (1, 1, 1) \cdot (x_1, x_2, x_3) \tag{14-37}$$

$$= x_1 + x_2 + x_3 \tag{14-38}$$

$$= n\bar{x} \tag{14-39}$$

Recall that x was translated so that $\bar{x} = 0$; therefore

$$\mathbf{x}_1 \cdot \mathbf{x}_2 = 0 \tag{14-40}$$

This establishes that $\mathbf{x}_1 \perp \mathbf{x}_2$. This was the motive for translating x onto a zero mean.

Algebraically in (14-36) our problem is to find a fitted value of $\mathbf{y}$ that is a linear combination of $\mathbf{x}_1$ and $\mathbf{x}_2$. Geometrically, in Figure 14-16, this means that we must select a fit somewhere on the plane P generated by $\mathbf{x}_1$ and $\mathbf{x}_2$. If we wish to determine the point or vector on this plane P that best fits, or is closest to the observed $\mathbf{y}$, we should drop a perpendicular from $\mathbf{y}$ onto P. Is

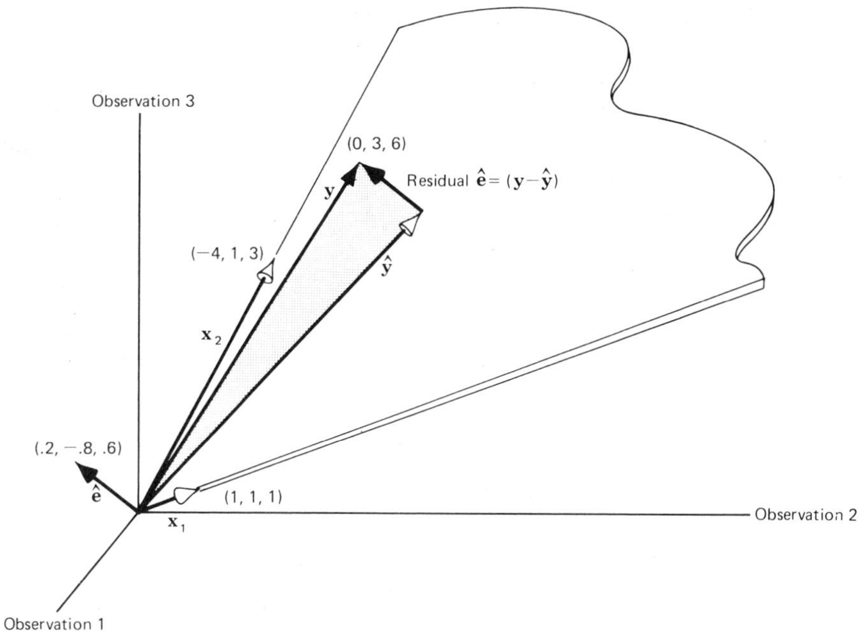

FIGURE 14-16 Same information as in Figure 14-15; but here points (vectors) are variables, axes are observations.

this the least squares solution? The answer is: yes. Recall that least squares involves selecting $\hat{y}_i$ to minimize

$$\sum (y_i - \hat{y}_i)^2 \tag{14-41}$$

In vector notation, according to (14-11), this is:

$$\|\mathbf{y} - \hat{\mathbf{y}}\|^2 \tag{14-42}$$

That is, least squares involves minimizing the squared distance (i.e., minimizing the distance) between $\mathbf{y}$ and $\hat{\mathbf{y}}$, which is accomplished by perpendicular projection according to (14-27).

It is also important to note that the vector of estimated residuals

$$\hat{\mathbf{e}} = (\mathbf{y} - \hat{\mathbf{y}})$$

is perpendicular (orthogonal) to the $(\mathbf{x}_1, \mathbf{x}_2)$ plane; hence $\hat{\mathbf{e}}$ is orthogonal to each of the regressors $\mathbf{x}_1$ and $\mathbf{x}_2$ in the plane. This means

$$\mathbf{x}_1 \cdot \hat{\mathbf{e}} = 0 \qquad \text{and} \qquad \mathbf{x}_2 \cdot \hat{\mathbf{e}} = 0$$

Finally the equivalence of Figures 14-15 and 14-16 may be confirmed by noting how the estimated residuals $(\hat{e}_1, \hat{e}_2, \hat{e}_3) \simeq (.2, -.8, .6)$ appear in each.

14-3 ORTHOGONAL REGRESSORS

If the regressors are orthogonal, as in Figure 14-16, we can then find simple formulas for $\hat{\beta}_1$ and $\hat{\beta}_2$. Referring to Figure 14-17, for notation, we find that $\hat{\mathbf{y}}$ is just the sum of $\hat{\mathbf{y}}_1$ and $\hat{\mathbf{y}}_2$, the individual $\perp$ projections of $\mathbf{y}$ onto $\mathbf{x}_1$ and $\mathbf{x}_2$, respectively. That is,

$$\hat{\mathbf{y}} = \hat{\mathbf{y}}_1 + \hat{\mathbf{y}}_2 \tag{14-43}$$

From (14-24)

$$\hat{\mathbf{y}} = \left(\frac{\mathbf{y} \cdot \mathbf{x}_1}{\|\mathbf{x}_1\|^2}\right)\mathbf{x}_1 + \left(\frac{\mathbf{y} \cdot \mathbf{x}_2}{\|\mathbf{x}_2\|^2}\right)\mathbf{x}_2 \tag{14-44}$$

Comparing (14-44) with (14-36), we conclude that the coefficient

$$\hat{\beta}_1 = \frac{\mathbf{y} \cdot \mathbf{x}_1}{\|\mathbf{x}_1\|^2} \tag{14-45}$$

Now recall from (14-37) that $\mathbf{x}_1$ is just the unit vector. Thus

$$\mathbf{y} \cdot \mathbf{x}_1 = y_1 + y_2 + y_3, \qquad \text{and in general} = \sum_{i=1}^{n} y_i$$

$$\|\mathbf{x}_1\|^2 = 1 + 1 + 1, \qquad \text{and in general} = n$$

Thus (14-45) reduces to

$$\hat{\beta}_1 = \bar{y} \tag{14-46}$$

(2-13) confirmed

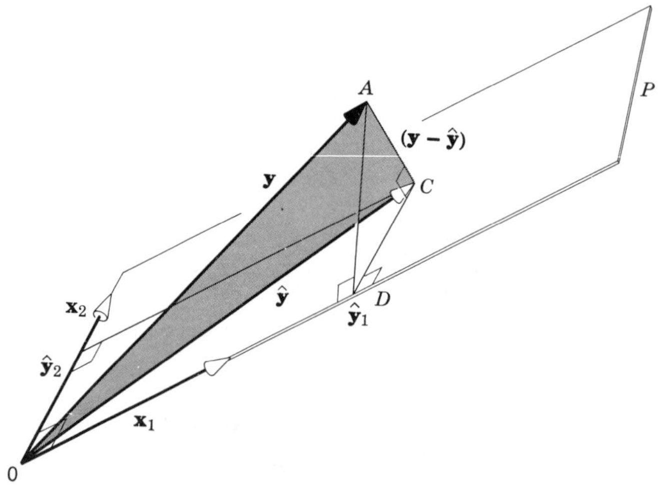

FIGURE 14-17 The projected $\hat{\mathbf{y}}$ is the sum of the individual projections $\hat{\mathbf{y}}_1$ and $\hat{\mathbf{y}}_2$, because $\mathbf{x}_1 \perp \mathbf{x}_2$. Note that $\hat{\mathbf{y}}_1$ (or $\hat{\mathbf{y}}_2$) is that part of $\mathbf{y}$ explained by $\mathbf{x}_1$ (or $\mathbf{x}_2$).

Similarly, we conclude that

$$\hat{\beta}_2 = \frac{\mathbf{x}_2 \cdot \mathbf{y}}{\|\mathbf{x}_2\|^2} \tag{14-47}$$

and noting that $\mathbf{x}_2$ is, in fact, the variable $\mathbf{x}$ appearing in Chapter 2

$$\hat{\beta}_2 = \frac{\sum x_i y_i}{\sum x_i^2} \tag{14-48}$$

(2-16) confirmed

14-4 ANOVA FOR SIMPLE REGRESSION

If we apply the Pythagorean theorem to Figure 14-17, it turns out to be the ANOVA table in disguise. Specifically, consider ΔADC, reproduced again in Figure 14-18 (noting that the vector $DC = \hat{\mathbf{y}}_2 = \hat{\beta}_2 \mathbf{x}_2$). From the theorem of Pythagoras,

$$\|\mathbf{y} - \hat{\mathbf{y}}_1\|^2 = \|\hat{\beta}_2 \mathbf{x}_2\|^2 + \|\mathbf{y} - \hat{\mathbf{y}}\|^2 \tag{14-49}$$

When we recognize that $\mathbf{x}_2$ here is just the x in Chapter 5, this equation begins to look suspiciously like equation (5-20) expressed in vector notation. This can easily be verified; since

$$\hat{\mathbf{y}}_1 = \hat{\beta}_1 \mathbf{x}_1 \tag{14-50}$$

by (14-46)

$$= \bar{y} \begin{bmatrix} 1 \\ 1 \\ 1 \end{bmatrix}$$

$$= \begin{bmatrix} \bar{y} \\ \bar{y} \\ \bar{y} \end{bmatrix}$$

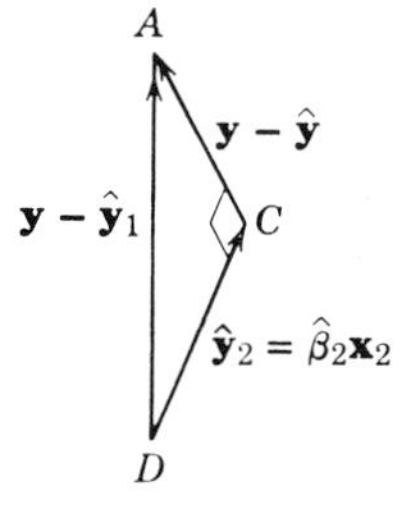

FIGURE 14-18 Pythagorean theorem and ANOVA, for the little triangle of Figure 14-17.

Thus

$$(\mathbf{y} - \hat{\mathbf{y}}_1) = \boxed{\begin{matrix} y_1 - \bar{y} \\ y_2 - \bar{y} \\ y_3 - \bar{y} \end{matrix}} \tag{14-51}$$

Thus fitting $\mathbf{y}$ on the dummy regressor $\mathbf{x}_1$ is just expressing $\mathbf{y}$ in terms of deviations from its mean. The various components of (5-20) are therefore as follows: From (14-51),

$$\|\mathbf{y} - \hat{\mathbf{y}}_1\|^2 = \text{total variation} \tag{14-52}$$

Similarly we can express the right side of (14-49):

$$\begin{aligned} \|\hat{\beta}_2 \mathbf{x}_2\|^2 &= \hat{\beta}_2^2 \|\mathbf{x}_2\|^2 \\ &= \text{explained variation,} \end{aligned} \tag{14-53}$$

and

$$\|\mathbf{y} - \hat{\mathbf{y}}\|^2 = \text{unexplained (residual) variation}$$

Thus, (14-49) becomes

$$\text{Total variation} = \text{explained variation} + \text{unexplained variation} \tag{14-54}$$

(5-20) proved again

More formally, this can be written:

$$\begin{aligned} &\text{total variation after } \mathbf{y} \text{ regressed on } \mathbf{x}_1 \\ &\quad = \text{variation explained by adding regressor } \mathbf{x}_2 \\ &\qquad + \text{variation still left unexplained} \end{aligned} \tag{14-55}$$

14-5 THE STATISTICAL MODEL

In applying statistical tests, we use a mathematical model, that is, a set of assumptions about the parent population of *all* possible outcomes, not just the one outcome we happened to observe. Referring to (14-33), we note that the population consists of all possible observed $\mathbf{y}$ vectors, generated by all possible errors. This is shown schematically in Figure 14-19. If errors are assumed normal, the possible $\mathbf{y}$'s we might observe would be spread out in a boundless cloud, thick around $E(\mathbf{y})$, but thinning out in the distance. But to make the geometry manageable, it is necessary to draw an ellipsoid that delimits most of the observed $\mathbf{y}$'s, the so-called ellipsoid of concentration. For the independent errors specified in (12-14), the ellipsoid is simply a

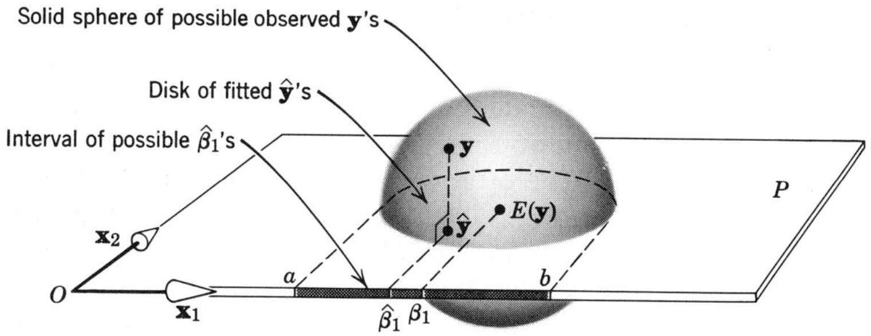

FIGURE 14-19 The distributions of $\mathbf{y}$, $\hat{\mathbf{y}}$ and $\hat{\beta}_1$ (assuming $\mathbf{x}_1 \perp \mathbf{x}_2$).

sphere. This sphere of **y** observations (vectors, points) is centered at the mean $E(\mathbf{y})$, which according to (12-13) or (14-33) lies in the plane P generated by $\mathbf{x}_1$ and $\mathbf{x}_2$. Of course, the statistician doesn't know where in this plane $E(\mathbf{y})$ lies; he can only estimate it by observing a sample vector such as the **y** vector shown. Note that this observation involves substantial error; that is, **y** is quite distant from $E(\mathbf{y})$.

Least squares estimation consists of orthogonally projecting this observed vector **y** onto the plane P, the resulting $\hat{\mathbf{y}}$ becoming the estimate of $E(\mathbf{y})$. To derive $\hat{\beta}_1$, the estimate of the true population coefficient β_1, we project $\hat{\mathbf{y}}$ along $\mathbf{x}_2$ onto[4] $\mathbf{x}_1$; similarly, $\hat{\beta}_2$ is derived by projecting $\hat{\mathbf{y}}$ along $\mathbf{x}_1$ onto $\mathbf{x}_2$. We note in this example, that $\hat{\beta}_1$ happened to underestimate β_1, because of the particular error in the observed vector **y**.

Our more general observations on Figure 14-19 are: $E(\mathbf{y})$ is fixed, while the disk around it, lying in P, represents possible fitted values of $\hat{\mathbf{y}}$, corresponding to the possible observed **y**'s falling in the sphere. *ab* is the projection of this whole disk along $\mathbf{x}_2$ onto $\mathbf{x}_1$. This is the interval of $\hat{\beta}_1$'s around the fixed true β_1. This sampling distribution of $\hat{\beta}_1$ intuitively seems to be unbiased and normal, since the possible observed **y**'s are normally distributed in the sphere centered on $E(\mathbf{y})$; these properties in fact have already been rigorously established in Section 12-4.

---

[4] To be precise, such a projection gives us, for example, $\hat{\beta}_1\mathbf{x}_1$, rather than the $\hat{\beta}_1$ shown in Figure 14-19. But to keep things simple, we have cheated a little and assumed $\mathbf{x}_1$ is of *unit* length, so that $\hat{\beta}_1\mathbf{x}_1$ is a vector of length $\hat{\beta}_1$. Thus $\hat{\beta}_1$ may be easily interpreted as the distance along $\mathbf{x}_1$. The target β_1 is similarly interpreted.

But suppose $\mathbf{x}_1$ is not of unit length. (Usually it will not be; indeed in our example, $\mathbf{x}_1$ is the dummy regressor of 1's, so that its length is $\sqrt{n}$.) Then to be precise we must interpret β_1 and β_2 as the coordinates of $E(\mathbf{y})$ on the plane P [i.e., the solution to $E(\mathbf{y}) = \beta_1\mathbf{x}_1 + \beta_2\mathbf{x}_2$]. Thus β_1 is found by projecting $E(\mathbf{y})$ along $\mathbf{x}_2$ onto $\mathbf{x}_1$, and seeing how many times longer than $\mathbf{x}_1$ this is.

14-6 MULTICOLLINEARITY

Thus far we have only considered two regressors, $\mathbf{x}_1$ and $\mathbf{x}_2$, with $\mathbf{x}_1$ being the unit variable used to estimate the regression intercept $\hat{\beta}_1$, and $\mathbf{x}_2$ being the only bona fide regressor. So long as $\mathbf{x}_2$ is measured as deviations from the mean, $\mathbf{x}_1$ and $\mathbf{x}_2$ must be orthogonal, and Figure 14-19 applies: The projection of $\hat{\mathbf{y}}$ along $\mathbf{x}_2$ onto $\mathbf{x}_1$ is just the $\perp$ projection. Now suppose both $\mathbf{x}_1$ and $\mathbf{x}_2$ are bona fide regressors, in which case they need not be orthogonal. Figure 14-20*a* shows what happens when they are not; the skewed projection of the disk of possible $\hat{\mathbf{y}}$'s along $\mathbf{x}_2$ onto $\mathbf{x}_1$ spreads out the interval of $\hat{\beta}_1$'s.

As the vectors $\mathbf{x}_1$ and $\mathbf{x}_2$ become more nearly collinear, the problem gets worse, as in Figure 14-20*b*; here the interval of $\hat{\beta}_1$'s is dispersed on both sides of the origin. The point estimate $\hat{\beta}_1$ may be positive—but there is now a good chance it may be negative. Moreover, although we see from Figure 14-20*b* that the true β_1 is *not* zero, this is very difficult to establish statistically; usually $H_0(\beta_1 = 0)$ will not be rejected because of the huge standard deviation of $\hat{\beta}_1$.

Although multicollinearity causes a huge spread in $\hat{\beta}_1$, the other attractive properties of $\hat{\beta}_1$ (normality, unbiasedness) are not affected.

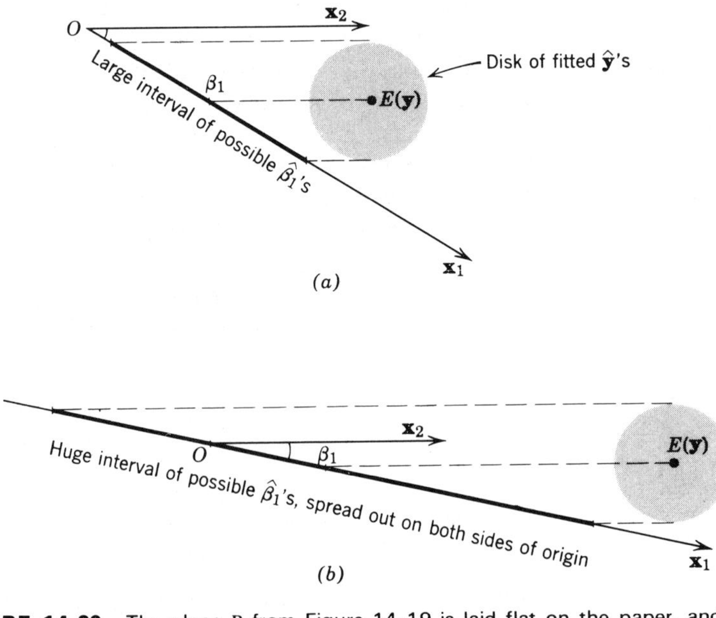

FIGURE 14-20 The plane P from Figure 14-19 is laid flat on the paper, and viewed from above. (*a*) The distributions of $\hat{\mathbf{y}}$ and $\hat{\beta}_1$ when $\mathbf{x}_1$ and $\mathbf{x}_2$ are not $\perp$. (*b*) When $\mathbf{x}_1$ and $\mathbf{x}_2$ are nearly collinear.

14-7 CORRELATION AND COS θ

In (14-51) it was established that

$$(\mathbf{y} - \hat{\mathbf{y}}_1) = \boxed{\begin{matrix} y_1 - \bar{y} \\ y_2 - \bar{y} \\ y_3 - \bar{y} \end{matrix}} \tag{14-56}$$

$$= \text{deviations of } \mathbf{y} \tag{14-57}$$

Throughout the rest of the chapter, we will be interested only in this deviation form for every vector. Also note that since **y** as well as **x** is expressed in deviation form, according to (2-20) the intercept now disappears, along with the unit regressor used to estimate it. In other words, all **x**'s now become bona fide regressors.

If we consider two such deviation vectors, **x** and **y**, it would be interesting to measure how closely they correspond. The standard geometric measure of the closeness of the direction of two vectors is

$$\cos\theta = \frac{\mathbf{x} \cdot \mathbf{y}}{\|\mathbf{x}\| \, \|\mathbf{y}\|} \tag{14-58}$$

(14-32) repeated

Writing the dot product explicitly in terms of components,

$$\cos\theta = \frac{\sum x_i y_i}{\sqrt{\sum x_i^2}\sqrt{\sum y_i^2}} \tag{14-59}$$

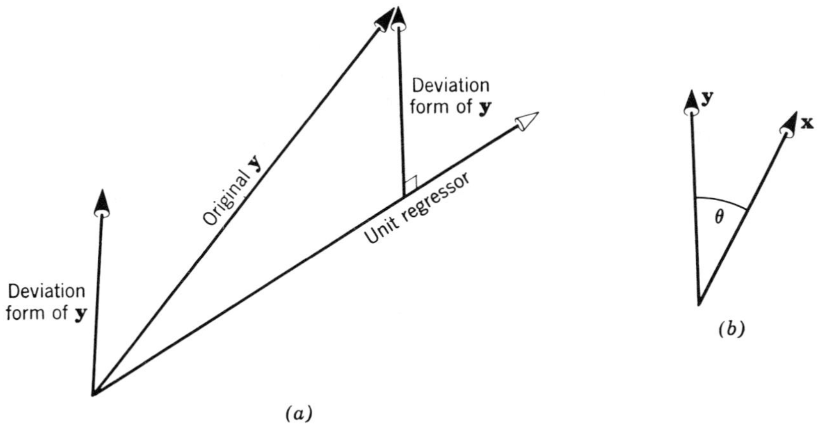

FIGURE 14-21 (*a*) Relation of a vector **y** to its derivation form. (*b*) Correlation = cos θ, where **x** and **y** are in deviation form.

Since the x_i and y_i values are deviations, we recognize this as the correlation coefficient of (5-6). Thus,

$$\boxed{r = \cos\theta} \tag{14-60}$$

where θ is the angle between the deviation vectors **x** and **y**. In other words, the geometric interpretation of correlation is the closeness of the angle θ. This is shown in Figure 14-21.

Thus, for every geometrical statement about $\cos\theta$, there is an equivalent statistical statement about r. A few such examples are given in Table 14-2. Similarly, the equivalence of the geometry and statistics of regression is given in Table 14-3.

14-8 CORRELATIONS—SIMPLE, MULTIPLE, AND PARTIAL

With all vectors hereafter expressed in deviation form, we see in Figure 14-22 that the correlation r_{YX_2} is just $\cos\theta_2$. To distinguish it from the multiple and partial correlations, r_{YX_2} is sometimes called the simple correlation.

The multiple correlation coefficient R is defined as the simple correlation between **y** and $\hat{\mathbf{y}}$—that is, $\cos\lambda$ in Figure 14-22. This provides an index of how well **y** can be explained by both regressors[5] $\mathbf{x}_1$ and $\mathbf{x}_2$.

The partial correlation of **y** and $\mathbf{x}_2$, designated $r_{YX_2|X_1}$, is the simple correlation of **y** and $\mathbf{x}_2$ after the influence of $\mathbf{x}_1$ has been removed from each. The influence of $\mathbf{x}_1$ on **y** is the fitted value $(\hat{\mathbf{y}}_1)$ when **y** is regressed on $\mathbf{x}_1$. When this influence is removed, or subtracted from **y**, the result is the residual vector $(\mathbf{y} - \hat{\mathbf{y}}_1)$. Similarly, $\mathbf{x}_2$ is regressed on $\mathbf{x}_1$ (at A), and when this influence is removed from $\mathbf{x}_2$, the result is the vector AB; this is shifted to CD, forming the angle ϕ_2. Then $\cos\phi_2$ is the partial correlation $r_{YX_2|X_1}$. Similarly, we could show that $\cos\phi_1$ is $r_{YX_1|X_2}$.

In Table 14-4, we extend Table 14-2 to a comparison of the geometry and statistics of multiple and partial correlation.

---

[5] Specifically,

$$R \equiv r_{\mathbf{y}\hat{\mathbf{y}}} = \cos\lambda = \frac{\|\hat{\mathbf{y}}\|}{\|\mathbf{y}\|}$$

Bearing in mind that **y**, like all other variables, is defined as deviations from the mean, $\|\mathbf{y}\|^2$ is its total variation, and we may write

$$R^2 = \frac{\|\hat{\mathbf{y}}\|^2}{\|\mathbf{y}\|^2} = \frac{\text{variation explained by all regressors}}{\text{total variation}} \qquad \text{like (5-51)}$$

TABLE 14-2 Comparison of the Geometrical Interpretation of Cos θ and the Statistical Interpretation of Correlation r (All variables are in deviation form)

Geometry	*Statistics*
$\cos\theta$	r
$-1 \le \cos\theta \le 1$	$-1 \le r \le 1$
$\cos\theta = +1$ iff $\mathbf{x}$ and $\mathbf{y}$ agree perfectly in direction.	$r = +1$ iff x and y move together perfectly
$\cos\theta = -1$ iff $\mathbf{x}$ and $\mathbf{y}$ are in perfectly opposite directions	$r = -1$ iff x and y move together perfectly, but in opposite directions.
$\cos\theta = 0$ iff $\mathbf{x}$ and $\mathbf{y}$ are $\perp$	$r = 0$ iff x and y have no linear relation; iff x and y are uncorrelated

TABLE 14-3 Comparison of the Geometry and Statistics of Regression and ANOVA (All variables are in deviation form).

Geometry	*Statistics*
Squared length of $\mathbf{y}$ Length of $\mathbf{y}$	Variation of y Standard deviation of y (except for the divisor $\sqrt{n-1}$)
$\perp$ projection, yielding $\mathbf{y} - \hat{\mathbf{y}}$ of minimum length	Statistical least squares fit, yielding minimum sum of squared deviations.
Pythagorean theorem: $\|\mathbf{y} - \hat{\mathbf{y}}_1\|^2 = \|\hat{\beta}_2 \mathbf{x}_2\|^2 + \|\mathbf{y} - \hat{\mathbf{y}}\|^2$	ANOVA: Total variation = explained variation + unexplained variation

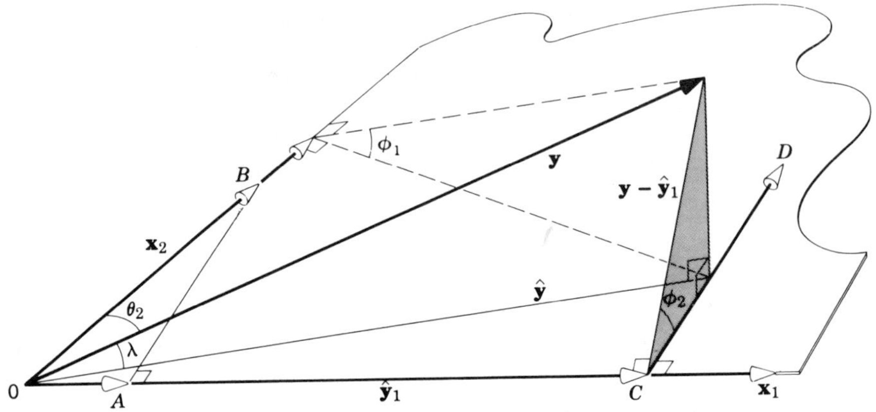

FIGURE 14-22 Multiple correlation coefficient ($R = \cos\lambda$) compared with simple correlation coefficient ($r_{YX_2} = \cos\theta_2$) and partial correlation coefficient ($r_{YX_2|X_1} = \cos\phi_2$).

TABLE 14-4 Comparison of the Geometry and Statistics of Correlations—Simple, Partial, and Multiple (An Extension of Table 14-2. Also refer to Figure 14-22.)

Geometry	*Statistics*
$\cos\theta_2$	Simple correlation r_{YX_2}
$\cos\phi_2$	Partial correlation $r_{YX_2\mid X_1}$
$\cos\lambda$	Multiple correlation R
$\cos\lambda = 1$ iff **y** and $\hat{\mathbf{y}}$ coincide; iff **y** lies in the $(\mathbf{x}_1, \mathbf{x}_2)$ subspace.	$R = 1$ iff x_1 and x_2 explain y exactly, leaving no residual.
$\cos\lambda = 0$ iff **y** orthogonal to the $(\mathbf{x}_1, \mathbf{x}_2)$ subspace.	$R = 0$ iff $\hat{y} = 0x_1 + 0x_2 = 0$ i.e., x_1 and x_2 do not explain y at all.
$\lvert\cos\theta_2\rvert \le \lvert\cos\lambda\rvert$	$r_{YX_2} \le R$
$\lvert\cos\phi_2\rvert \le \lvert\cos\lambda\rvert$	$r_{YX_2\mid X_1} \le R$

14-9 TESTS WHEN THERE ARE k REGRESSORS

(a) ANOVA for Last g Regressors

With a little imagination, in Figure 14-22 we can think of replacing $\mathbf{x}_1$ with a set of regressors $\mathbf{x}_1, \mathbf{x}_2 \cdots \mathbf{x}_{k-g}$, and $\mathbf{x}_2$ with the remaining set of g regressors $\mathbf{x}_{k-g+1} \cdots \mathbf{x}_k$. We now wish to simultaneously test this latter set of g regressors. The only change this causes in the theory of the previous section is that the lines generated by $\mathbf{x}_1$ and $\mathbf{x}_2$ are replaced by subspaces. These subspaces are impossible to draw, so they are still represented in Figure 14-23 by lines. How can we test the null hypothesis that the last g

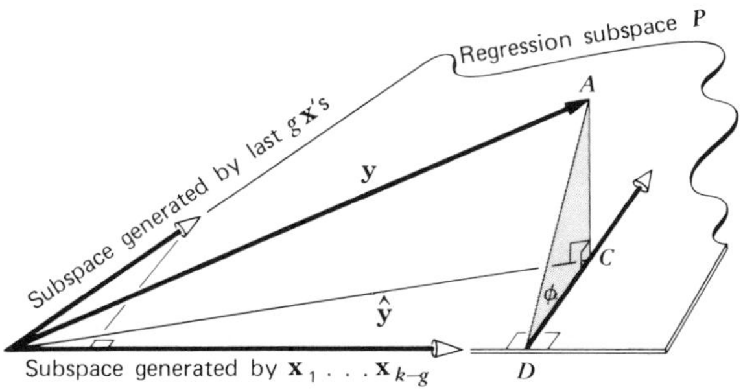

FIGURE 14-23 Multiple regression with k regressors, with the last g being tested.

regressors are all irrelevant, that is, the last g regression coefficients are zero? One method is to apply the Pythagorean theorem to the triangle ADC to obtain the ANOVA identity

$$\|AD\|^2 = \|CD\|^2 + \|AC\|^2$$

unexplained variation after y is regressed on $x_1 \ldots x_{k-g}$
= variation explained by introducing g more regressors
+ unexplained variation that still remains (14-61)

The two variations on the right side of (14-61) are statistically independent χ^2 variables, with g and $(n-1-k)$ d.f. respectively.[6] When we divide by

[6] For proof, see for example, H. Scheffé, 1959. Of course, we are assuming that the true coefficients of the last g regressors are all zero, since this is the null hypothesis being tested.

Our convention in this chapter is to let k represent the number of regressors *excluding* the constant regressor of 1's. This disagrees with Chapter 12 (where k *included* the constant regressor).

these d.f., the variations become variances, and their ratio is

$$F = \frac{\text{additional variance explained by introducing the } g \text{ regressors}}{\text{residual variance}} \tag{14-62}$$

which follows the F distribution and can be used to test the statistical significance of the last g regressors [(14-62) confirms (5-57) noting, that in that earlier chapter, the number of regressors being tested was called r, rather than g.]

When there is just one regressor to be tested, we set $g = 1$ in (14-62), and so obtain:

$$F = \frac{\text{additional variance explained by the last regressor } \mathbf{x}_k}{\text{unexplained variance}} \tag{14-63}$$

(b) Partial Correlation

Alternatively we could test the last regressor by examining the partial correlation $r_{YX_k|X_1X_2,\ldots,X_{k-1}}$, which we shall abbreviate to r in this discussion. In Figure 14-24, when $g = 1$, the partial correlation r is cos ϕ (just as in Figure 14-22). Instead of asking [as in (14-63)] whether the squared length of CD in Figure 14-24 is large enough (relative to AC) to reject H_0, why not ask the equivalent question: Is angle ϕ close enough, that is, is r large enough? To

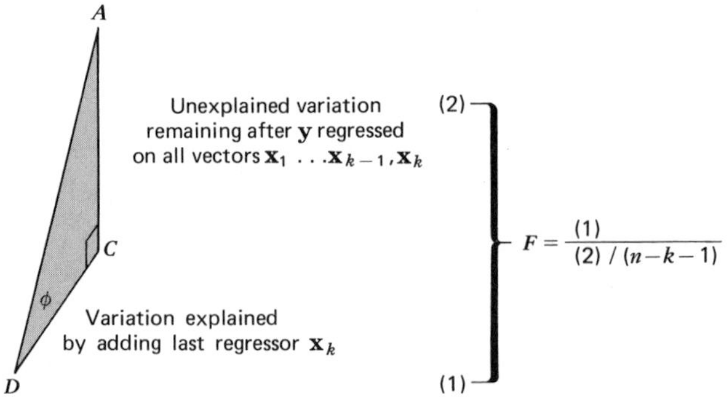

FIGURE 14-24 ANOVA. showing the vectors in triangle ADC in Figure 14-23 when $g = 1$.

do this we simply express F in (14-63) in terms of r, rather than squared lengths, as follows. From (14-63), or Figure 14-24, we may write

$$F = \frac{\|CD\|^2}{\|AC\|^2/(n-k-1)} \tag{14-64}$$

Thus
$$\frac{F}{n-k-1} = \frac{\|CD\|^2}{\|AC\|^2}$$

Dividing the numerator and denominator on the RHS by $\|AD\|^2$ and noting that $r^2 = (\cos\phi)^2 = \|CD\|^2/\|AD\|^2$,

$$\frac{F}{n-k-1} = \frac{\|CD\|^2/\|AD\|^2}{\|AC\|^2/\|AD\|^2} = \frac{r^2}{\dfrac{\|AD\|^2 - \|CD\|^2}{\|AD\|^2}} = \frac{r^2}{1-r^2} \tag{14-65}$$

Therefore,

$$F = \frac{r^2(n-k-1)}{1-r^2} \tag{14-66}$$

As expected, the closer is ϕ, the greater is r, and the greater is F. Thus (14-66) and (14-63) are seen to be alternative ways of testing the null hypothesis that $\mathbf{y}$ is not related to the last regressor $\mathbf{x}_k$.

Finally, if we take the square root of (14-66), according to (13-44) we then have

$$t = \sqrt{F} = \frac{r\sqrt{n-k-1}}{\sqrt{1-r^2}} \tag{14-67}$$

This is the same t that appeared in our tests in Chapters 2 and 3. Note that (14-67) nicely shows the relation of t, F, and the partial correlation r.

PROBLEMS

14-9 True or false? If false, correct it:

(a) In studying the relation of three variables, if $\mathbf{x}$ and $\mathbf{y}$ are each uncorrelated with $\mathbf{z}$, then $r_{XY|Z} = r_{XY}$, that is, the partial and simple correlations coincide.

(b) If the multiple correlation of $\mathbf{y}$ with $\mathbf{x}_1 \cdots \mathbf{x}_k$ is zero, then the partial correlation of $\mathbf{y}$ with $\mathbf{x}_k$ is also zero, as is the simple correlation of $\mathbf{y}$ with $\mathbf{x}_k$.

(c) The partial correlation of $\mathbf{y}$ and $\mathbf{x}_k$ is the simple correlation of $\mathbf{y}$ and $\hat{\mathbf{y}}$ after the influence of $\mathbf{x}_k$ has been removed from each.

14-10 Suppose 50 observations were used to regress $\mathbf{y}$ on 3 regressors $\mathbf{x}_1$, $\mathbf{x}_2$, and $\mathbf{x}_3$. If the partial correlation of $\mathbf{y}$ and $\mathbf{x}_3$ was .28, is this statistically significant (discernible) at the 5% level (2-sided)?

14-11 Refer to Figure 14-23, with $g = 1$. Suppose that instead of observing $\mathbf{x}_k$, an economist observed a variable $\mathbf{z}_k$ that was more closely correlated to the previous variables $\mathbf{x}_1 \cdots \mathbf{x}_{k-1}$, yet still generated the same regression subspace P. Suppose further that there is no doubt that the previous variables $\mathbf{x}_1 \cdots \mathbf{x}_{k-1}$ belong in the model. The only question is whether the last variable ($\mathbf{x}_k$ or $\mathbf{z}_k$) belongs. True or false? If false, correct it, giving a brief reason.

(a) The multiple correlation of $\mathbf{y}$ with $\mathbf{x}_1 \cdots \mathbf{x}_{k-1}, \mathbf{z}_k$ would equal the multiple correlation of $\mathbf{y}$ with $\mathbf{x}_1 \cdots \mathbf{x}_{k-1}, \mathbf{x}_k$.

(b) The partial correlation of $\mathbf{y}$ with $\mathbf{z}_k$ would equal the partial correlation of $\mathbf{y}$ with $\mathbf{x}_k$.

14-12 Referring to Figure 14-22, suppose the regressors $\mathbf{x}_1$ and $\mathbf{x}_2$ were more correlated, so that the picture was like this:

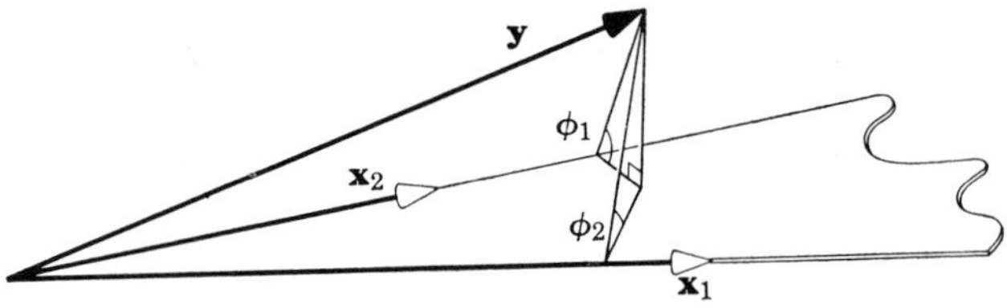

Suppose two economists, using the same sample of 24 observations, made the following two different analyses of the model:

$$\mathbf{y} = \beta_0 + \beta_1 \mathbf{x}_1 + \beta_2 \mathbf{x}_2 + \text{error} \tag{14-68}$$

1. The first economist makes a test of the null hypothesis $\beta_2 = 0$. She calculates the t value, which turns out to be only 1.1 (reflecting a small partial correlation, i.e., a wide angle ϕ_2). At the 5% level, the null hypothesis is not rejected, and so she recommends using the model

$$\mathbf{y} = \beta_0 + \beta_1 \mathbf{x}_1 + \text{error} \tag{14-69}$$

The estimated coefficients turn out to be

$$\mathbf{y} = 1.70 + 1.3\mathbf{x}_1 + \text{residual} \tag{14-70}$$

with the coefficient 1.3 being statistically significant (discernible).

2. In the model (14-68) the second economist makes a test of the null hypothesis $\beta_1 = 0$. In this case, the t value turns out to be only 1.4 (reflecting a small partial correlation, i.e., a wide angle ϕ_1). At the 5% level, the null hypothesis is not rejected, and so he recommends the model

$$\mathbf{y} = \beta_0 + \beta_2 \mathbf{x}_2 + \text{error} \tag{14-71}$$

The estimated coefficients turn out to be

$$\mathbf{y} = 1.70 + 4.7\mathbf{x}_2 + \text{error} \tag{14-72}$$

with the coefficient 4.7 being statistically significant.

(a) Is it possible that the two economists could validly arrive at such different conclusions as (14-70) and (14-72), or can the discrepancy be explained away as a computational error?
(b) Which economist has the better model? Or is there an even better model than these two? If you cannot answer this categorically, list the possible criteria for choosing between models.

*14-10 FORWARD STEPWISE REGRESSION[7]

In this section we will discuss in more detail the stepwise procedure introduced in Section 5-3. Consider a forward stepwise regression[8] of $\mathbf{y}$ on $\mathbf{x}_1$ and $\mathbf{x}_2$, where we start from scratch, adding one regressor at a time; initially suppose that we have specified *a priori* that $\mathbf{x}_1$ will be tested first, and $\mathbf{x}_2$ second.

Before examining this procedure, in Figure 14-25 we show the result of applying the standard multiple regression of $\mathbf{y}$ on $\mathbf{x}_1$ and $\mathbf{x}_2$. (Although our remarks are illustrated for two regressors, they are easily generalized to k regressors.) Although the true coefficients β_1 and β_2 are not shown, they must be kept in mind as the targets; we suppose that β_1 and β_2 are both nonzero, so that $\mathbf{y}$ depends on both $\mathbf{x}_1$ and $\mathbf{x}_2$. The near collinearity between $\mathbf{x}_1$ and $\mathbf{x}_2$ results in large standard errors for the estimators $\hat{\beta}_1$ and $\hat{\beta}_2$; but at least $\hat{\beta}_1$ and $\hat{\beta}_2$ are unbiased, and the residual $\mathbf{y} - \hat{\mathbf{y}}$ is minimized.

---

[7] This section is starred because of its difficulty. Also, it includes a fallacy that fortunately appears in the literature less often today than in the past.

[8] In practice, the forward procedure is typically used by computer programs in the interest of cost, since alternative stepwise procedures involve fitting regressions of larger dimension. For more detail on alternatives, see Draper and Smith, 1966.

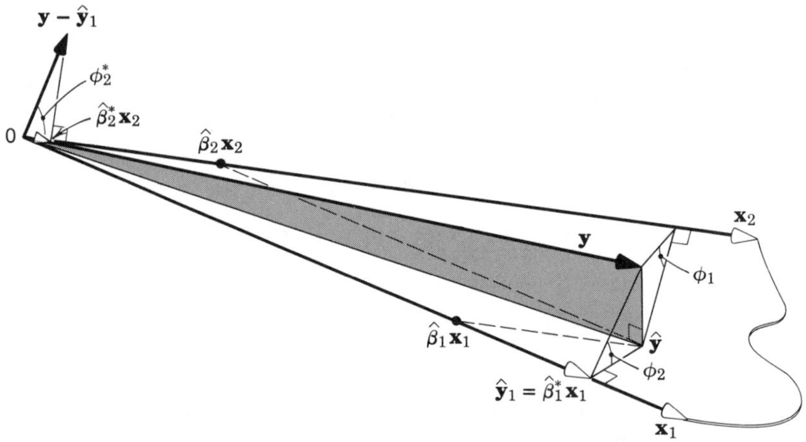

FIGURE 14-25 Problems in stepwise regression.

In stepwise regression, the first step is to regress $\mathbf{y}$ on $\mathbf{x}_1$ alone, yielding the fit $\hat{\mathbf{y}}_1 = \hat{\beta}_1^* \mathbf{x}_1$. Clearly, so long as the regressors $\mathbf{x}_1$ and $\mathbf{x}_2$ are not orthogonal, $\hat{\beta}_1^*$ will be a biased estimate of β_1. (In the case shown in Figure 14-25 it is larger than the unbiased $\hat{\beta}_1$.)

The second step is to consider the second regressor $\mathbf{x}_2$. If we are not careful we may follow the natural temptation, now that $\mathbf{x}_1$ has been "netted out," to regress the rest of $\mathbf{y}$ still left unexplained, that is, the residual $\mathbf{y} - \hat{\mathbf{y}}_1$, on $\mathbf{x}_2$. In Figure 14-25 we shift this residual vector to the origin, and show the resulting estimate $\hat{\beta}_2^*$. Again, as long as $\mathbf{x}_1$ and $\mathbf{x}_2$ are not orthogonal, $\hat{\beta}_2^*$ will be a biased estimator of β_2 (in the case shown it is smaller than the unbiased $\hat{\beta}_2$). Furthermore, a test of significance on $\hat{\beta}_2^*$ would be very weak, being based on cos ϕ_2^*, which is nearly zero.[9]

(And there is even more damage: The final residual $\mathbf{y} - \hat{\beta}_1^* \mathbf{x}_1 - \hat{\beta}_2^* \mathbf{x}_2$ will not be as small as in the standard multiple regression.)[10]

We have earlier concluded that with multicollinear regressors, it is difficult in any case to establish statistical significance; here we are using a biased method that makes it even more difficult to establish the significance of regressors that are tested last.

The correct unbiased test of the relationship between $\mathbf{y}$ and $\mathbf{x}_2$ involves a test of $r_{YX_2|X_1}$, or cos ϕ_2. But this is the angle between the residual $\mathbf{y} - \hat{\mathbf{y}}_1$

---

[9] *Reason.* Since the residual $\mathbf{y} - \hat{\mathbf{y}}_1$ is perpendicular to $\mathbf{x}_1$, and since $\mathbf{x}_1$ and $\mathbf{x}_2$ are nearly parallel, $\mathbf{y} - \hat{\mathbf{y}}_1$ will be nearly perpendicular to $\mathbf{x}_2$, that is, ϕ_2^* will be nearly 90°.

[10] The standard least squares regression coefficients $\hat{\beta}_1$ and $\hat{\beta}_2$ were chosen, by definition, to make $\mathbf{y} - \hat{\beta}_1 \mathbf{x}_1 - \hat{\beta}_2 \mathbf{x}_2$ a minimum, and thus smaller than $\mathbf{y} - \hat{\beta}_1^* \mathbf{x}_1 - \hat{\beta}_2^* \mathbf{x}_2$. (Unless, of course, $\mathbf{x}_1$ and $\mathbf{x}_2$ are orthogonal, in which case the two residuals coincide.)

and the vector $\hat{\mathbf{y}} - \hat{\mathbf{y}}_1$, not $\mathbf{x}_2$. If this test leads to the decision to include $\mathbf{x}_2$, then we obtain the correct $\hat{\beta}$ coefficients by a full multiple regression of $\mathbf{y}$ on $\mathbf{x}_1$ and $\mathbf{x}_2$. (In larger models, after each such test, a multiple regression is run on all the x's that have so far been included.)

In summary, we consider several major problems involved in stepwise regression when regressors are not orthogonal. *Even if the correct procedure is used* (i.e., even if the relationship between $\mathbf{y}$ and $\mathbf{x}_2$ is tested by examining $\cos \phi_2$, not $\cos \phi_2^*$) there are two problems:

1. In the initial step of testing whether $\mathbf{x}_1$ should be included, $\hat{\beta}_1^*$ is a biased estimate.
2. Suppose in the initial step we have tested $\mathbf{x}_1$ and decided to include it;[11] then we test the significance of $\mathbf{x}_2$ by examining $\cos \phi_2$ in Figure 14-25. Although the multiple correlation of $\mathbf{y}$ on $\mathbf{x}_1$ and $\mathbf{x}_2$ is high, the partial correlation ($\cos \phi_2$) may be statistically insignificant because of multicollinearity. Then the final regression fit would include only $\mathbf{x}_1$. On the other hand, consider what would happen if we took up the regressors in the other order. In the first step we would include[12] $\mathbf{x}_2$; then, in testing the significance of $\mathbf{x}_1$, we might find the partial correlation ($\cos \phi_1$) statistically insignificant. In this case, the final regression equation would include only $\mathbf{x}_2$. Thus, the variables appearing in our final model may depend on the order in which they are brought into consideration. For this reason, in the absence of prior grounds to justify a prescribed ordering of the variables, a computer program should be selected that will automatically pick up first the regressor that is most highly correlated with $\mathbf{y}$.

Now suppose an incorrect procedure is used (i.e., suppose we have already decided to include $\mathbf{x}_1$, and in then testing $\mathbf{x}_2$ we erroneously examine $\cos \phi_2^*$, rather than $\cos \phi_2$; or equivalently, suppose we erroneously regress $\mathbf{y} - \hat{\mathbf{y}}_1$ on $\mathbf{x}_2$). Then there are two additional problems:

1. $\hat{\beta}_2^*$ will be a severely biased estimate of the effect of the second regressor $\mathbf{x}_2$, and any test based on it will find it very difficult to establish its statistical significance.
2. The test will also be weak because of the excessively large residual.

---

[11] In the first step of regressing $\mathbf{y}$ on $\mathbf{x}_1$ only, the test of $\mathbf{x}_1$ could be viewed either as examining the biased $\hat{\beta}_1^*$, or alternatively examining $\cos \theta_1$, where θ_1 is the angle between $\mathbf{y}$ and $\mathbf{x}_1$ in Figure 14-25. This close angle leads us to conclude that $\mathbf{x}_1$ is a statistically significant regressor.

[12] Note that this test of $\mathbf{x}_2$ would be statistically significant for the same reason as our initial test of $\mathbf{x}_1$ in footnote 11 above.

In conclusion, if there are clear prior guidelines indicating that a few specific regressors are appropriate, then they should all be used right away in a full multiple regression, rather than tested one at a time with any sort of stepwise approach. If there are no such prior guidelines, but the number of regressors must be kept small to provide a more manageable model, then a stepwise technique may be reasonable. But it must be recognized that this procedure tends to discriminate against regressors tested last, even if correctly applied; and if incorrectly applied, it discriminates even more.

*PROBLEMS

14-13 As in Figure 14-25 suppose $\mathbf{x}_1$ and $\mathbf{x}_2$ are highly collinear. In addition, suppose that the true (as opposed to observed) $\mathbf{y}$ has a perfect positive correlation with $\mathbf{x}_2$, that is, the true model is: $\mathbf{y} = 0\mathbf{x}_1 + \beta_2 \mathbf{x}_2$. Also, suppose that we are lucky enough in our sample to observe $\mathbf{y}$ being perfectly correlated with $\mathbf{x}_2$, that is, $\mathbf{y}$ is perfectly explained by this single regressor. Hence, the fitted standard multiple regression of $\mathbf{y}$ on $\mathbf{x}_1$ and $\mathbf{x}_2$ is

$$\mathbf{y} = 0\mathbf{x}_1 + \hat{\beta}_2 \mathbf{x}_2 \tag{14-77}$$

(a) Show this geometrically.
(b) Is $\hat{\beta}_2$ unbiased?
(c) What is the vector of residuals?
Now, to show how badly a stepwise analysis can go wrong if applied carelessly, suppose an erroneous stepwise procedure is undertaken and in the first step $\mathbf{y}$ is regressed on $\mathbf{x}_1$ as follows:

$$\mathbf{y}_1 = \hat{\beta}_1^* \mathbf{x}_1$$

(d) Is $\hat{\beta}_1^*$ biased? Is it possible for us to conclude that $\hat{\beta}_1^*$ is significantly different from zero?
(e) Suppose after erroneously including $\mathbf{x}_1$ as a regressor, we further err by regressing the residual vector $(\mathbf{y} - \hat{\mathbf{y}}_1)$ on $\mathbf{x}_2$. Is the resulting estimate of β_2 biased? Is it possible that we will therefore, reject $\mathbf{x}_2$ as a regressor (even though $\mathbf{x}_2$ in fact perfectly explains $\mathbf{y}$)?
(f) How does the resulting fitted equation compare with (14-77)?
(g) How does the final residual vector resulting from this stepwise procedure compare with the residual vector in (c)?
(h) Could this disastrous result have occurred if, in the first step, we had used a computer routine that introduced the regressor most highly correlated with $\mathbf{y}$ first?

14-14 Suppose an economist is examining the effect of socioeconomic background (x_1) and education (x_2) on income (Y). After explaining Y by regressing it on x_1 only, he states that no further significant explanation of Y can be established using x_2. He concludes that income is related to socioeconomic background, but not education. You are to discuss his paper. What has gone wrong? Illustrate using vector geometry; also point out under what special circumstances this sort of two-step approach could be justified. Are these circumstances present in this case?

REVIEW PROBLEMS

14-15

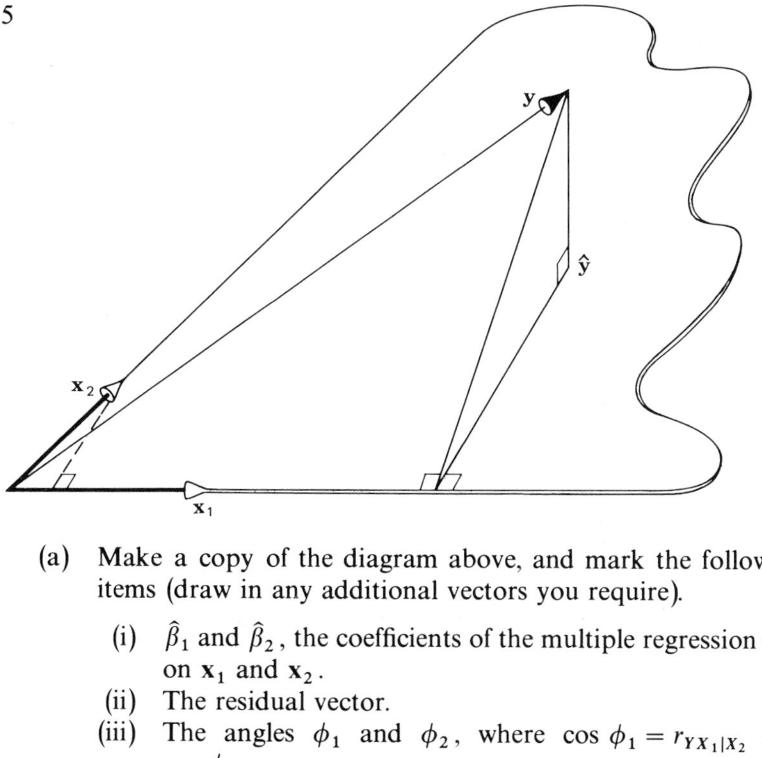

(a) Make a copy of the diagram above, and mark the following items (draw in any additional vectors you require).

(i) $\hat{\beta}_1$ and $\hat{\beta}_2$, the coefficients of the multiple regression of **y** on $\mathbf{x}_1$ and $\mathbf{x}_2$.

(ii) The residual vector.

(iii) The angles ϕ_1 and ϕ_2, where $\cos \phi_1 = r_{YX_1|X_2}$ and $\cos \phi_2 = r_{YX_2|X_1}$.

(iv) The angle λ, where $\cos \lambda = R$.

(v) $\hat{\beta}$, the coefficient of simple regression of **y** on $\mathbf{x}_1$. Is $\hat{\beta}$ the same as the multiple regression coefficient $\hat{\beta}_1$? Under what conditions would $\hat{\beta} = \hat{\beta}_1$?

(vi) θ_1, where $\cos \theta_1 = r_{YX_1}$.

(b) Using this diagram, what is the F test for $\beta_2 = 0$? What is the F test for $\beta_1 = 0$?

14-16 An economist fitted the simple regression

$$\mathbf{y} = a + b\mathbf{x} + \hat{\mathbf{e}} \text{ (residual)}$$

The next day she decided that she should include another explanatory variable $\mathbf{z}$, for the same data; she therefore fitted the multiple regression

$$\mathbf{y} = a' + b'\mathbf{x} + c'\mathbf{z} + \hat{\mathbf{e}}'$$

The letters a, b, a', etc., refer to the fitted (OLS) values, not the true (population) values. Under what circumstances will the following be true? (Answer very carefully; for example: never, or always, or usually, except when . . . , or rarely; only when . . .). In each case, explain why.

(a) $b' = b$

(b) $\sum_{i=1}^{n} (\hat{e}_i')^2 \leq \sum_{i=1}^{n} (\hat{e}_i)^2$

(c) b' is statistically significant (discernible) at the 5% level, yet b is not.

(d) b is statistically significant at the 5% level, yet b' is not.

14-17 (a) In a sample of 30 observations, suppose the multiple correlation of $\mathbf{y}$ with 5 variables is .72. Including a sixth variable x_6 increases the multiple correlation to .75.
Test the hypothesis $\beta_6 = 0$ ($\mathbf{x}_6$ is irrelevant) at the 5% level (2-sided).

(b) If $R = .75$ does not achieve statistical significance (discernability), what value of R would?

(c) What is the partial correlation of $\mathbf{y}$ with $\mathbf{x}_6$?

15

OTHER REGRESSION TOPICS

15-1 SPECIFICATION ERROR

How much do estimates err when the model is misspecified? For example, a relationship that is actually nonlinear may be specified to be linear; the problem this raises has already been briefly discussed in Section 2-10. The present section is devoted to another kind of misspecification, the kind that occurs if too many or too few regressors are included in the model (a model is "too long" or "too short").

(a) Too Many Regressors: A Model that is Too Long

The problem of too many regressors may be formulated as follows: Suppose some regressors really don't belong in the model (12-9), that is, their coefficients should have been set equal to zero, *a priori*. If we inadvertently keep these extraneous regressors in the model, that is, estimate their coefficients, will this raise any problems?

In terms of bias, the answer is: no problems. According to (12-31), regression coefficients are unbiased. So the extraneous regressors will have coefficients whose expectation is zero, while the relevant regressors will have coefficients whose expectation is also correct. Thus, no bias is introduced by too many regressors.

However, making the model too long does increase the variance of the estimators. Obviously this is true for the extraneous regressors: Because these β_i are zero, it would be better to specify them as zero exactly, rather than use estimates $\hat{\beta}_i$ that fluctuate around zero. Moreover, the inclusion of irrelevant regressors will also increase the variance for the *relevant* regressors—to the degree that the extraneous regressors produced multicollinearity problems [although we do not prove this, we illustrate it geometrically in part (c)].

(b) Too Few Regressors: A Model that is Too Short

The problem of too few regressors is in many ways the dual of too many regressors: In the model (12-9), suppose some coefficients are wrongly forced to be zero *a priori*. Then of course they are biased. And the remaining coefficients will be biased too, as they are forced to carry the effect of the omitted regressors. As compensation, however, the *variance* of all the coefficients will be reduced, to the extent that the omission of regressors cuts back on multicollinearity problems [although we do not prove this, we illustrate it geometrically in part (d)].

Let us work out an algebraic expression for the bias. Without loss of generality, we may suppose it is the last regressors that are inadvertently omitted. Thus in the correct model (12-9), let $\mathbf{X} = [\mathbf{X}_1, \mathbf{X}_2]$, where $\mathbf{X}_2$ are the erroneously omitted regressors, and $\mathbf{X}_1$ are the correctly included regressors. If we correspondingly partition $\boldsymbol{\beta}$, then (12-9) may be written as

$$E(\mathbf{y}) = \mathbf{X}\boldsymbol{\beta} = [\mathbf{X}_1, \mathbf{X}_2]\begin{bmatrix}\boldsymbol{\beta}_1 \\ \boldsymbol{\beta}_2\end{bmatrix} = \mathbf{X}_1\boldsymbol{\beta}_1 + \mathbf{X}_2\boldsymbol{\beta}_2 \tag{15-1}$$

When we inadvertently regress $\mathbf{y}$ on $\mathbf{X}_1$ alone, the regression coefficients ($\hat{\boldsymbol{\beta}}_1^*$ say) are given by (12-19):

$$\hat{\boldsymbol{\beta}}_1^* = (\mathbf{X}_1'\mathbf{X}_1)^{-1}\mathbf{X}_1'\mathbf{y} \tag{15-2}$$

To see whether $\hat{\boldsymbol{\beta}}_1^*$ is unbiased, we calculate its expectation:

$$E(\hat{\boldsymbol{\beta}}_1^*) = (\mathbf{X}_1'\mathbf{X}_1)^{-1}\mathbf{X}_1' E(\mathbf{y}) \tag{15-3}$$

by (15-1),

$$= (\mathbf{X}_1'\mathbf{X}_1)^{-1}\mathbf{X}_1'(\mathbf{X}_1\boldsymbol{\beta}_1 + \mathbf{X}_2\boldsymbol{\beta}_2)$$

$$E(\hat{\boldsymbol{\beta}}_1^*) = \boldsymbol{\beta}_1 + (\mathbf{X}_1'\mathbf{X}_1)^{-1}\mathbf{X}_1'\mathbf{X}_2\boldsymbol{\beta}_2 \tag{15-4}$$

The bias is $(\mathbf{X}_1'\mathbf{X}_1)^{-1}\mathbf{X}_1'\mathbf{X}_2\boldsymbol{\beta}_2$ (the extent to which $E(\hat{\boldsymbol{\beta}}_1^*)$ misses its target $\boldsymbol{\beta}_1$ in the equation above). How can we interpret this bias?

First of all, let $\mathbf{x}_i$ denote a typical omitted regressor in $\mathbf{X}_2$. If we regress $\mathbf{x}_i$ on $\mathbf{X}_1$, let us denote the column of coefficients by $\hat{\boldsymbol{\beta}}_i$. Then, from (12-19), $\hat{\boldsymbol{\beta}}_i$ is given by

$$\hat{\boldsymbol{\beta}}_i = (\mathbf{X}_1'\mathbf{X}_1)^{-1}\mathbf{X}_1'\mathbf{x}_i \tag{15-5}$$

Now let us do this for each of the omitted regressors $\mathbf{x}_i$; and when we are finished, stack all these results side by side. All the stacked regressors $\mathbf{x}_i$ of course form $\mathbf{X}_2$, and all the stacked coefficients $\hat{\boldsymbol{\beta}}_i$ we shall denote $\mathbf{B}_{21}$. Thus (15-5) produces

$$\mathbf{B}_{21} = (\mathbf{X}_1'\mathbf{X}_1)^{-1}\mathbf{X}_1'\mathbf{X}_2 \tag{15-6}$$

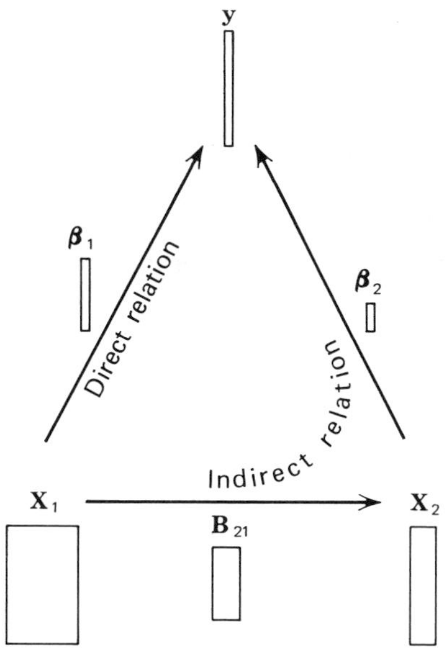

FIGURE 15-1 Coefficients of X_1 are biased when X_2 is erroneously omitted (compare to Figure 3-5).

We may call $\mathbf{B}_{21}$ the regression of $\mathbf{X}_2$ on $\mathbf{X}_1$. Note that it occurs in (15-4), which may therefore be written simply as

$$\boxed{E(\hat{\boldsymbol{\beta}}_1^*) = \boldsymbol{\beta}_1 + \mathbf{B}_{21}\boldsymbol{\beta}_2} \tag{15-7}$$

like (3-23)

This is illustrated in Figure 15-1, which is analogous to Figure 3-5. The bias $\mathbf{B}_{21}\boldsymbol{\beta}_2$ may also be called the indirect relation, because it is a chain that consists of two links. This chain of bias will be zero if either link is zero, that is, if $\mathbf{B}_{21} = 0$ (that is, if $\mathbf{X}_1$ and $\mathbf{X}_2$ are unrelated, i.e., orthogonal) or if $\boldsymbol{\beta}_2 = 0$ (that is, if the model is correctly specified, and is not too short after all).

*(c) Vector Geometry of too Many Regressors

We now return to the case in part (a) above where the model is *too long*, that is, there are *too many* regressors included. In Figure 15-2, for example, an extraneous regressor $\mathbf{x}_2$ has been included, as well as the relevant regressor $\mathbf{x}_1$. (We refer to $\mathbf{x}_1$ and $\mathbf{x}_2$ as single vectors, but you can think of each as being a whole set of vectors.) The page represents the $(\mathbf{x}_1, \mathbf{x}_2)$ plane. The sphere of possible $\mathbf{y}$'s has been projected onto it, forming the given disk of

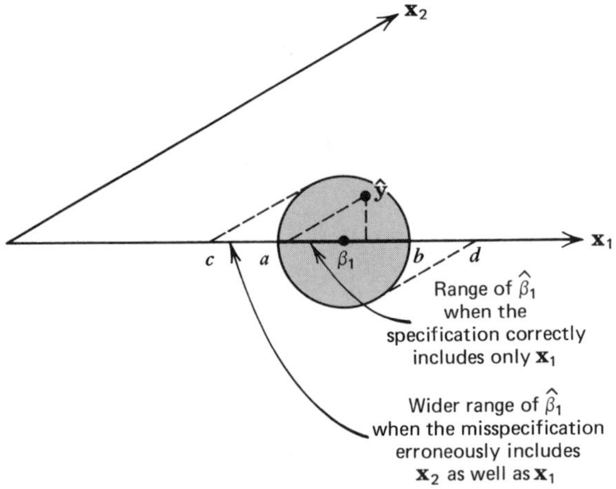

FIGURE 15-2 Including an extraneous regressor $\mathbf{x}_2$ produces a more variable, but still unbiased, estimator of β_1.

possible fitted $\hat{\mathbf{y}}$'s. The correct specification projects $\hat{\mathbf{y}}$ orthogonally[1] onto $\mathbf{x}_1$, producing an estimator in the range *ab*.

The incorrect specification, however, projects $\hat{\mathbf{y}}$ in the direction of $\mathbf{x}_2$ onto $\mathbf{x}_1$ (compare to Figure 14-20). This skewed projection produces an estimator $\hat{\beta}_1$ in the range *cd*; although this range is unbiased, it has wider variance.

In addition, of course, the incorrect specification produces an estimator $\hat{\beta}_2$, obtained by projecting $\hat{\mathbf{y}}$ in the direction of $\mathbf{x}_1$ onto $\mathbf{x}_2$. This estimator is also unbiased (centered at 0), and of wider variance than necessary. (If it were correctly specified to be zero, it would have no variance at all). Finally, although it has no simple geometric interpretation, including too many regressors cuts back on the degrees of freedom in the residuals to estimate σ^2.

We have assumed so far that the misspecified model is the one that is actually retained by the statistician. But suppose it is put forth tentatively, and β_2 is tested at the 5% level. This means there is only a 5% chance of $\hat{\beta}_2$ achieving significance (discernibility) and hence being retained. In other words, there is a 95% chance that the erroneous regressor β_2 will be

---

[1] The correct specification is simply a one-shot ⊥ projection of $\mathbf{y}$ onto $\mathbf{x}_1$. But this is equivalent to the two-stage ⊥ projection, first of $\mathbf{y}$ onto the $(\mathbf{x}_1, \mathbf{x}_2)$ plane (producing $\hat{\mathbf{y}}$), followed by a further ⊥ projection onto $\mathbf{x}_1$.

Incidentally, in Figures 15-2 and 15-3 we assume as usual that $\mathbf{x}_1$ and $\mathbf{x}_2$ are of unit length, to achieve the same simplification as described in footnote 4 in chapter 14.

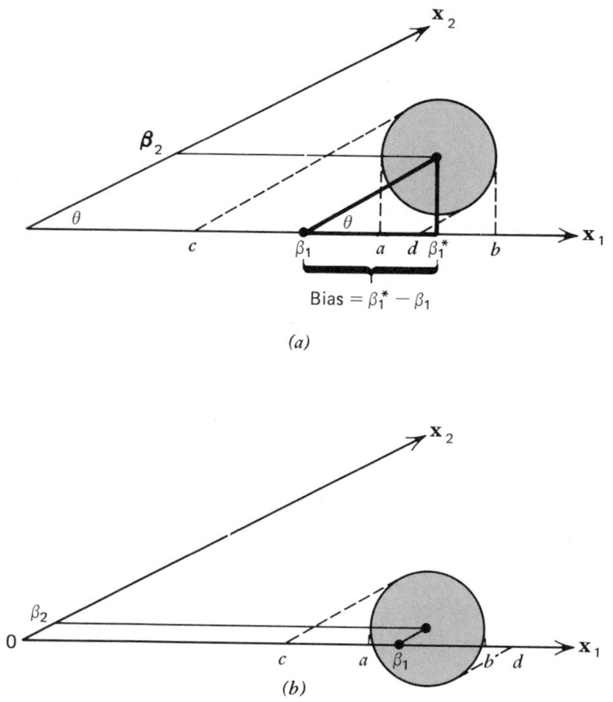

FIGURE 15-3 Excluding a relevant regressor $\mathbf{x}_2$ produces a less variable but biased estimator of β_1. (*a*) Where bias is large. (*b*) Where bias is small enough to make total error (MSE) smaller.

dropped from the model—in which case the correct specification would be achieved after all. Thus the data would correct an error of prior misspecification.[2]

*(d) Vector Geometry of too Few Regressors

In Figure 15-3*a* we see what happens when a relevant regressor $\mathbf{x}_2$ is excluded. Although this is similar to Figure 15-2 in many ways, the differences must be kept clear: In Figure 15-3*a*, $\mathbf{x}_2$ is really *relevant* (i.e., $\beta_2 \neq 0$), so that the disk of $\hat{\mathbf{y}}$ is no longer centered on the $\mathbf{x}_1$ axis. And the skewed projection of $\hat{\mathbf{y}}$ in the direction of $\mathbf{x}_2$ onto $\mathbf{x}_1$ now produces the *correct* estimator $\hat{\beta}_1$ in the range *cd*, centered on the true β_1. On the other hand, when

[2] If we were trying on *several* extraneous regressors at the 5% level, then the chance of erroneously retaining one or more would rise.

we erroneously exclude $\mathbf{x}_2$, our resulting orthogonal projection of $\hat{\mathbf{y}}$ onto $\mathbf{x}_1$ produces the biased estimator in the range *ab*, centered on β_1^*, say. The difference $\beta_1^* - \beta_1$ is the bias. It is easy to find geometrically an expression for this bias:

Consider the heavily outlined triangle whose base is the bias. Its hypotenuse is of length β_2, and its angle is θ (we can see all this by shifting our attention left to the $\mathbf{x}_2$ axis). Thus

$$\text{Bias} = \beta_2 \cos\theta \tag{15-8}$$

Now what is the regression coefficient of $\mathbf{x}_2$ on $\mathbf{x}_1$? As in Figure 3-5, we denote it by β_{21}. We can express it as

$$\beta_{21} = r\frac{s_{x2}}{s_{x1}} \tag{15-9}$$

like (5-14)

But $\mathbf{x}_1$ and $\mathbf{x}_2$ were normalized to unit length, so that $s_{x_1}/s_{x_2} = 1$. Furthermore, according to (14-60), the correlation r is just $\cos\theta$. Thus

$$\beta_{21} = \cos\theta \tag{15-10}$$

Substituting (15-10) into (15-8),

$$\boxed{\text{Bias} = \beta_2\beta_{21}} \tag{15-11}$$

which agrees nicely with (3-23) or (15-7).

Although excluding a relevant regressor introduces bias, it reduces variance. In other words, in Figure 15-3*a*, the admittedly biased interval *ab* is narrower than the unbiased interval *cd*. Yet on the whole, the biased interval *ab* is farther from the target β_1 than is the unbiased interval *cd* (when judged in terms of mean squared error (MSE) in (2-104)).

In Figure 15-3*b*, however, we see a case where the bias is so small that the interval *ab* is a better estimator than *cd*. That is, when β_2 is *nearly* zero,[3] we can get a better estimator of β_1 by assuming that β_2 actually *is* zero. (And we get a better estimator of β_2 as well: zero is better than a projection of the disk of $\hat{\mathbf{y}}$ along $\mathbf{x}_1$ onto $\mathbf{x}_2$). Thus we conclude: When β_2 is *nearly* zero, a strong case can be made for assuming it *is* zero, thus shortening the model.

[3] Of course, the problem is that, in our prior specification, we usually have to *guess* how small β_2 really is. If our guess can be summarized by a prior distribution for β_2, then this can be combined with the empirical estimate $\hat{\beta}_2$ to produce a Bayesian compromise. As noted in Chapter 10, this is better than relying on the prior guess alone, or on the data alone.

(e) Conclusions

Briefly speaking, in this section we have shown:

> It never helps to have a model that is too long.[4] But it *may* help to have a model too short (whenever the reduction in variance more than compensates for the introduction of bias).

(15-12)

In other words, it helps to make a model too short if there are multicollinearity problems (high variance) and the omitted coefficient is nearly zero (so that assuming it is exactly zero does not produce a large bias). These are the same issues discussed in footnote 9 in Chapter 3.

In conclusion, it cannot be emphasized too strongly that sound prior specification of the model is very important—in many ways at least as important as the details of the statistical techniques to which this book is devoted.

*15-2 PRINCIPAL COMPONENTS

(a) Definition and Derivation

This technique is often used when there are too many regressors relative to too little data (sometimes called the problem of *too few degrees of freedom*, or simply the *d.f. problem*), and when there is multicollinearity between the regressors. Suppose the problem is to regress

$$\mathbf{y} = \mathbf{X}\boldsymbol{\beta} + \mathbf{e}$$

and we have the following data matrix:

$$\mathbf{X} = \begin{bmatrix} x_{11} & \cdots & x_{k1} \\ \cdot & & \\ \cdot & & \\ \cdot & & \\ x_{1n} & & x_{kn} \end{bmatrix} = \begin{bmatrix} \mathbf{x}_1 & \cdots & \mathbf{x}_k \\ & & \\ & & \\ & & \end{bmatrix} \tag{15-13}$$

Briefly stated, principal components is a technique for reexpressing the **x**'s with a smaller number of new **z** variables that are linear combinations of

[4] Of course, by "too long" we mean that the model includes regressors whose true coefficients are zero. By "too short" we mean that the model excludes regressors whose true coefficients are nonzero.

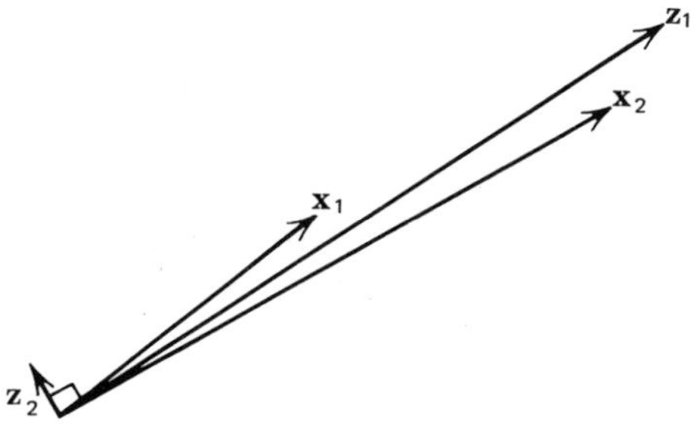

FIGURE 15-4 Principal component $\mathbf{z}_1$, for the original regressors $\mathbf{x}_1, \mathbf{x}_2$.

the **x**'s. These **z**'s will be orthogonal (and so have no multicollinearity problem) and will capture as much as possible of the variation in the **x**'s, with the first **z** capturing the maximum amount, the second **z** the maximum remaining, and so on.

As an example, consider the simple case where there are two regressors, $\mathbf{x}_1$ and $\mathbf{x}_2$; these are reexpressed with the components $\mathbf{z}_1$ and $\mathbf{z}_2$ (Figure 15-4). The larger one, which captures most of the variation, is called the *principal component.*

The requirement that $\mathbf{z}_1$ be a linear function of $\mathbf{x}_1$ and $\mathbf{x}_2$ means that

$$\boxed{\mathbf{z}_1} = a_{11}\boxed{\mathbf{x}_1} + a_{21}\boxed{\mathbf{x}_2} \tag{15-14}$$

that is

$$\mathbf{z}_1 = \mathbf{X}\mathbf{a}_1 \tag{15-15}$$

where $$\mathbf{a}_1 = \begin{bmatrix} a_{11} \\ a_{21} \end{bmatrix}$$

Similarly $$\mathbf{z}_2 = \mathbf{X}\mathbf{a}_2 \tag{15-16}$$

By stacking the **z** columns into a matrix **Z**, and the **a** columns into a matrix **A**, (15-15) and (15-16) may be written more briefly as

$$\mathbf{Z} = \mathbf{X}\mathbf{A} \tag{15-17}$$

with the problem being to appropriately select the matrix **A**.

Although we will continue thinking geometrically in terms of just two regressors (as in Figure 15-4) our argument from now on will be valid for any number of regressors.

What are the restraints on selecting the vector $\mathbf{a}_1$? First we maximize the variation (or squared length) of $\mathbf{z}_1$. From (15-15) we see that this implies:

$$\text{Maximize } \mathbf{z}_1'\mathbf{z}_1 = \mathbf{a}_1'\mathbf{X}'\mathbf{X}\mathbf{a}_1 \tag{15-18}$$

But this variation can obviously be made arbitrarily large by selecting a huge $\mathbf{a}_1$. So we restrict $\mathbf{a}_1$ to be of length 1, that is,

$$\mathbf{a}_1'\mathbf{a}_1 = 1 \tag{15-19}$$

The reason for this particular restriction is not yet obvious; but later we will show that this restriction—along with similar restrictions on the other **a**'s—is necessary to satisfy our second constraint that the total variation in all the **z**'s be equal to the total variation in all the **x**'s.

Maximization of (15-18) subject to (15-19) involves setting up the Lagrangian:

$$\phi = \mathbf{a}_1'\mathbf{X}'\mathbf{X}\mathbf{a}_1 - \lambda_1(\mathbf{a}_1'\mathbf{a}_1 - 1) \tag{15-20}$$

We set the partial derivatives with respect to $\mathbf{a}_1$ equal to $\mathbf{0}$; from (11-9),

$$\frac{\partial\phi}{\partial\mathbf{a}_1} = 2\mathbf{X}'\mathbf{X}\mathbf{a}_1 - 2\lambda_1\mathbf{a}_1 = \mathbf{0} \tag{15-21}$$

Thus

$$(\mathbf{X}'\mathbf{X})\mathbf{a}_1 = \lambda_1\mathbf{a}_1 \tag{15-22}$$

With the equation in this form, the solution is seen to involve finding a latent root λ_1 and corresponding latent vector[5] $\mathbf{a}_1$ of $\mathbf{X}'\mathbf{X}$.

But there are many latent roots. The question is: which one? Substituting (15-22) into (15-18) yields:

$$\text{Maximize } \mathbf{z}_1'\mathbf{z}_1 = \mathbf{a}_1'\lambda_1\mathbf{a}_1 = \lambda_1\mathbf{a}_1'\mathbf{a}_1 = \lambda_1 \tag{15-23}$$

by virtue[6] of (15-19). Thus maximizing $\mathbf{z}_1'\mathbf{z}_1$ implies maximizing λ_1. Therefore, we select the largest latent root and associated latent vector. This latent vector $\mathbf{a}_1$ then provides the precise specification for the first component $\mathbf{z}_1$ in (15-15).

---

[5] Latent vectors (also called eigenvectors) are discussed in standard linear algebra texts. For our purposes, we need the following theorems:

I. If a matrix (such as $\mathbf{X}'\mathbf{X}$) is positive semidefinite, its latent roots will be positive or 0.
II. If a matrix (such as $\mathbf{X}'\mathbf{X}$) is real and symmetric, latent vectors corresponding to distinct latent roots will be orthogonal.

[6] Note another advantage of imposing restriction (15-19): It simplifies our interpretation of λ_1, making it equal to the squared length (or variation) of $\mathbf{z}_1$.

We now turn to the second component $\mathbf{z}_2$, which involves specifying $\mathbf{a}_2$. First we ask: What are the restrictions in selecting $\mathbf{a}_2$? As before, we wish to

$$\text{Maximize } \mathbf{z}_2'\mathbf{z}_2 = \mathbf{a}_2'\mathbf{X}'\mathbf{X}\mathbf{a}_2 \tag{15-24}$$

subject to the restriction that

$$\mathbf{a}_2'\mathbf{a}_2 = 1 \tag{15-25}$$

But now it is also required that $\mathbf{z}_2$ be orthogonal to $\mathbf{z}_1$:

$$\mathbf{z}_2'\mathbf{z}_1 = 0 \tag{15-26}$$

which implies[7]:

$$\mathbf{a}_2'\mathbf{a}_1 = 0 \tag{15-29}$$

Accordingly, to determine $\mathbf{a}_2$ we form the Lagrangian:

$$\phi = \mathbf{a}_2'\mathbf{X}'\mathbf{X}\mathbf{a}_2 - \lambda_2(\mathbf{a}_2'\mathbf{a}_2 - 1) - \mu(\mathbf{a}_2'\mathbf{a}_1) \tag{15-30}$$

We set the partial derivative equal to zero:

$$\frac{\partial \phi}{\partial \mathbf{a}_2} = 2\mathbf{X}'\mathbf{X}\mathbf{a}_2 - 2\lambda_2\mathbf{a}_2 - \mu\mathbf{a}_1 = 0 \tag{15-31}$$

Since μ can be shown to be zero,[8] (15-31) reduces to

$$(\mathbf{X}'\mathbf{X})\mathbf{a}_2 = \lambda_2\mathbf{a}_2 \tag{15-32}$$

which like (15-22) involves a latent root λ_2 and corresponding latent vector $\mathbf{a}_2$. Moreover, just as λ_1 was selected as the largest latent root, so λ_2 is chosen as the next largest latent root. Its associated latent vector $\mathbf{a}_2$ then determines the second component $\mathbf{z}_2$, according to (15-16).

---

[7] From (15-16) and (15-15) it follows that (15-26) can be written

$$\mathbf{a}_2'\mathbf{X}'\mathbf{X}\mathbf{a}_1 = 0 \tag{15-27}$$

or, noting (15-22),

$$\mathbf{a}_2'\lambda_1\mathbf{a}_1 = 0 \tag{15-28}$$

Since $\lambda_1 \neq 0$, (15-29) follows.

[8] Premultiplying (15-31) by $\mathbf{a}_1'$ yields

$$2\mathbf{a}_1'\mathbf{X}'\mathbf{X}\mathbf{a}_2 - 2\lambda_2\mathbf{a}_1'\mathbf{a}_2 - \mu\mathbf{a}_1'\mathbf{a}_1 = 0 \tag{15-33}$$

But the second term disappears because of (15-29), while the first term also disappears because this scalar can be transposed, and hence—using (15-22) and (15-29)—reduced to

$$2\mathbf{a}_2'\mathbf{X}'\mathbf{X}\mathbf{a}_1 = 2\mathbf{a}_2'\lambda_1\mathbf{a}_1 = 0 \tag{15-34}$$

Thus the last term in (15-33) must also disappear; finally, since $\mathbf{a}_1'\mathbf{a}_1 \neq 0$, $\mu = 0$.

This process continues until all k latent roots and vectors are determined, in appropriate order. These orthogonal[9] vectors are then assembled in the matrix:

$$\mathbf{A} = \begin{bmatrix} \mathbf{a}_1 & \cdots & \mathbf{a}_k \\ & & \\ & & \end{bmatrix} \tag{15-35}$$

At the same time, noting conditions (15-23) and (15-26) (and all other similar conditions), and also noting (15-17), we may write

$$\mathbf{Z'Z} = \begin{bmatrix} \lambda_1 & & & 0 \\ & \lambda_2 & & \\ & & \ddots & \\ 0 & & & \lambda_k \end{bmatrix} = \mathbf{A'X'XA} \tag{15-36}$$

Note in this equation how the matrix $\mathbf{X'X}$ has been diagonalized by an appropriate premultiplication and postmultiplication by its latent vectors in $\mathbf{A}$; also note that in the resulting diagonalized matrix the latent roots of $\mathbf{X'X}$ appear along the diagonal.

Since one of the problems we were trying to solve was multicollinearity, let us see what would happen if there were perfect multicollinearity in $\mathbf{X}$, resulting in $\mathbf{X'X}$ being less than full rank. To illustrate simply, consider our original example in which $\mathbf{X}$ has only two vectors, $\mathbf{x}_1$ and $\mathbf{x}_2$, and suppose they are collinear. In this case λ_2, the squared length of $\mathbf{z}_2$, will be equal to zero. This is easily confirmed by referring back to Figure 15-4. If perfect collinearity exists, $\mathbf{x}_1$ and $\mathbf{x}_2$ coincide; since $\mathbf{z}_1$ is a linear function of $\mathbf{x}_1$ and $\mathbf{x}_2$, it must also coincide. Accordingly $\mathbf{z}_1$ can capture all the variation in $\mathbf{x}_1$ and $\mathbf{x}_2$, and there will be no variation in the $\mathbf{z}_2$ direction (i.e., λ_2, the squared length of $\mathbf{z}_2$, will be zero). In general, perfect multicollinearity in the $\mathbf{X}$ matrix will be reflected in one or more zero latent roots in the southeast corner of (15-36); and a high degree of multicollinearity in the $\mathbf{X}$ matrix will be reflected in one or more very small latent roots.

It is also important to review how the $\mathbf{z}$'s have exactly captured the variation in the original $\mathbf{x}$'s. Since the variation of $\mathbf{x}_1$ is $\mathbf{x}_1'\mathbf{x}_1$, (and so on) the total variation of all the $\mathbf{x}$'s may be written

$$\mathbf{x}_1'\mathbf{x}_1 + \mathbf{x}_2'\mathbf{x}_2, \ldots, \mathbf{x}_k'\mathbf{x}_k = \mathrm{tr}(\mathbf{X'X}) \tag{15-37}$$

---

[9] These vectors were constrained to be orthogonal by (15-29), etc. In any case, from linear algebra we know that latent vectors corresponding to distinct latent roots must be orthogonal—since $\mathbf{X'X}$ is real and symmetric.

where tr means *trace* (the sum of the diagonal elements). Because of (15-17) and the fact that $\mathbf{A}'\mathbf{A}$ is an identity matrix,[10]

$$\operatorname{tr}(\mathbf{X}'\mathbf{X}) = \operatorname{tr}(\mathbf{Z}'\mathbf{Z}) \tag{15-40}$$

$$= \mathbf{z}_1'\mathbf{z}_1 + \mathbf{z}_2'\mathbf{z}_2 + \cdots + \mathbf{z}_k'\mathbf{z}_k \tag{15-41}$$

It follows from (15-37) and (15-41) that the total variation (sum of the squared lengths) of all the components $\mathbf{z}$ is equal to the total variation (sum of the squared lengths) of all the original $\mathbf{x}$'s. [Now we can see the other important reason for imposing the restriction (15-19) in maximizing $\mathbf{z}_1'\mathbf{z}_1$. This condition guaranteed equality in the total variation of the two sets of variables.]

Finally, recalling the set of conditions represented by (15-23), etc., the total variation in all the $\mathbf{z}$'s (or $\mathbf{x}$'s) may be expressed as

$$\text{Total variation in all } \mathbf{z}\text{'s (or } \mathbf{x}\text{'s)} = \lambda_1 + \lambda_2 + \cdots + \lambda_k \tag{15-42}$$

Thus the proportion of the variation in all the $\mathbf{x}$'s that we have been able to capture in the first few components, $\mathbf{z}_1, \mathbf{z}_2 \cdots \mathbf{z}_f$, say, is $(\lambda_1 + \lambda_2 + \cdots + \lambda_f)/(\lambda_1 + \lambda_2 + \cdots + \lambda_k)$. Since λ_1 is largest, λ_2 next largest, etc., we see that $\mathbf{z}_1 \cdots \mathbf{z}_f$ capture a disproportionately large share of the total variation. Consequently, they are called the *principal components*.

(b) Use in Regression

Let $\mathbf{Z}^*$ denote the first f principal components of $\mathbf{Z}$—obtained by keeping only the first f columns of $\mathbf{A}$, the matrix $\mathbf{A}^*$, say. That is,

$$\mathbf{Z}^* = \mathbf{X}\mathbf{A}^* \tag{15-43}$$

like (15-17)

When $\mathbf{y}$ is regressed on $\mathbf{Z}^*$, let us denote the regression coefficients by $\hat{\boldsymbol{\beta}}^*$, so that

$$\hat{\mathbf{y}} = \mathbf{Z}^*\hat{\boldsymbol{\beta}}^* \tag{15-44}$$

---

[10] Specifically, (15-40) can be shown by noting that

$$\operatorname{tr}(\mathbf{Z}'\mathbf{Z}) = \operatorname{tr}(\mathbf{A}'\mathbf{X}'\mathbf{X}\mathbf{A}) = \operatorname{tr}(\mathbf{X}'\mathbf{X}\mathbf{A}\mathbf{A}') \tag{15-38}$$

[This follows because $\operatorname{tr}(\mathbf{BC}) = \operatorname{tr}(\mathbf{CB})$.] But from the set of conditions represented by (15-19) and (15-29),

$$\mathbf{A}\mathbf{A}' = \mathbf{I} \tag{15-39}$$

Accordingly, (15-38) reduces to

$$\operatorname{tr}(\mathbf{Z}'\mathbf{Z}) = \operatorname{tr}(\mathbf{X}'\mathbf{X}) \qquad \text{(15-40) proved}$$

How can we translate this regression result from **z**'s back into **x**'s? Substitute (15-43) into (15-44):

$$\hat{\mathbf{y}} = \mathbf{X}\mathbf{A}^*\hat{\boldsymbol{\beta}}^* \tag{15-45}$$

Thus $\mathbf{A}^*\hat{\boldsymbol{\beta}}^*$ are the desired regression coefficients of **X**.

Note how this procedure has alleviated our original problem of too many regressors by reducing the number of regressors[11] from k to f. It also appears that any multicollinearity problem that may have originally existed will also be solved, since the **z**'s are an orthogonal set of regressors. But this raises a puzzle: If perfect multicollinearity existed in the **x**'s it is not possible to run a straightforward regression of **y** on **X**, since a solution for $\hat{\boldsymbol{\beta}}$ simply does not exist. Yet the use of the principal components will allow us always to get a solution in (15-45)—even in this case. The mystery is solved by referring again to Figure 15-4. In the limiting case of perfect multicollinearity, $\mathbf{x}_1$ and $\mathbf{x}_2$ would coincide; in addition, $\mathbf{z}_1$ would also coincide. Then $\mathbf{z}_1$ would be the (only) principal component, and a regression of **y** on $\mathbf{z}_1$ will clearly yield a solution. This procedure is seen to be equivalent to regressing **y** on $\mathbf{x}_1$ while discarding $\mathbf{x}_2$—that is, setting $\beta_2 = 0$. Because this prior restriction allows us to pin down β_2, we can estimate β_1. This suggests that principal components is equivalent to multiple regression subject to restraints. In this case of perfect multicollinearity there is no advantage of the principal component method over arbitrarily discarding $\mathbf{x}_2$ (or, for that matter, $\mathbf{x}_1$). But in the case of partial multicollinearity the advantage of the principal component method is easily seen, referring again to Figure 15-4. Rather than using $\mathbf{x}_1$ or $\mathbf{x}_2$ while totally discarding the other, using the principal component $\mathbf{z}_1$ is seen to be a means of capturing the essence of *both* $\mathbf{x}_1$ and $\mathbf{x}_2$, without totally discarding either.

(c) Reservations

There are several reservations about using principal components in regression. First, principal components do not enjoy the important property of being invariant to scale. That is, if $\mathbf{x}_1$ were to be scaled in inches rather than feet, the length of $\mathbf{x}_1$ in Figure 15-4 would increase 12 times, the direction of $\mathbf{z}_1$ would consequently shift toward $\mathbf{x}_1$, and $\mathbf{z}_1$ would no longer be the same regressor. Since the result depends on the arbitrary scale in which each of the $\mathbf{x}_i$ is measured, it is common to reduce this arbitrariness by rescaling each $\mathbf{x}_i$ into standardized form (i.e., with mean 0 and standard deviation 1).

---

[11] Of course, omitting regressors introduces bias, as indicated in Section 15-1. However, at the same time variance may be reduced enough so that overall, MSE is reduced.

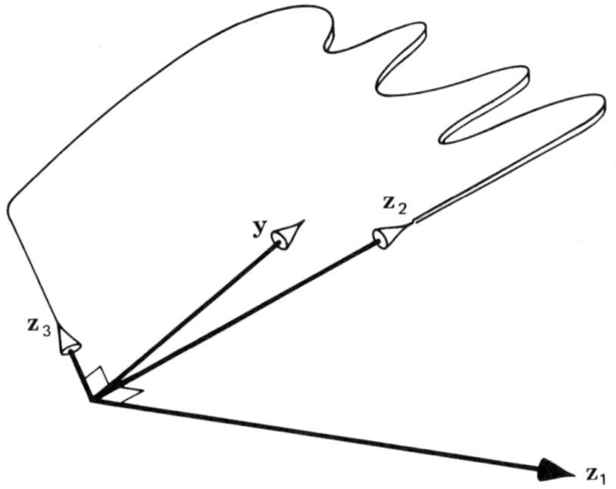

FIGURE 15-5 A limitation of the principal component technique.

Second, principal components is a two-step procedure, and it is possible that the **z**'s discarded in the first step (because they are relatively unimportant in capturing the variation in the **x**'s) could nonetheless have been important in explaining **y** in the second step. In Figure 15-5 this difficulty is illustrated in its most extreme form, by considering the case in which **y** lies in the ($\mathbf{z}_2$, $\mathbf{z}_3$) plane. In this case, we would obviously hope to discard $\mathbf{z}_1$ and choose $\mathbf{z}_2$ and $\mathbf{z}_3$ as our principal components, since they perfectly explain **y** ($\mathbf{z}_1$ is completely irrelevant). The problem is that there is simply no guarantee of this: If, for example, the **x**'s are concentrated in (or near) the ($\mathbf{z}_1$, $\mathbf{z}_2$) plane, then $\mathbf{z}_1$ and $\mathbf{z}_2$ will unfortunately be selected as our two principal components. To summarize the difficulty: in the first step, the **z**'s are selected as principal components because of their ability to explain the **x**'s; but they may or may not be the best set for the eventual objective of explaining **y**.

This suggests another strategy for applying principal components. The **x** variables that are judged relatively important in explaining **y** can be used as they stand. The remaining less important variables can be reduced to a few principal components. Finally, **y** is explained by regressing it on these principal components, along with the origional important variables.

PROBLEMS

15-1 Use a diagram such as Figure 15-3(a) to illustrate how the rainfall coefficient in (3-22) is so severely biased when the temperature regressor is omitted, that this coefficient actually changes sign in (3-21). (Hint: Are $\mathbf{x}_1$ and $\mathbf{x}_2$ negatively correlated? How is this represented geometrically?)

16

TIME SERIES PROBLEMS AND GENERALIZED LEAST SQUARES (GLS)

In this chapter we develop GLS to generalize our discussion of heteroscedasticity and serially correlated error in Chapter 6. We later discuss in detail another time series problem, involving seasonal adjustment.

16-1 GLS IS MLE

We begin by generalizing the linear model in Chapter 12. Suppose

$$\mathbf{y} = \mathbf{X}\boldsymbol{\beta} + \mathbf{e} \tag{16-1}$$

where

$$\mathbf{e} \text{ has mean zero} \tag{16-2}$$

and

$$\text{known covariance matrix } \mathbf{U} \tag{16-3}$$

$\mathbf{U}$ may be *any* covariance matrix, rather than the special covariance matrix $\sigma^2\mathbf{I}$ previously assumed in (12-14). If we assume that $\mathbf{e}$ has a multivariate normal distribution, the likelihood of the sample is the multivariate normal probability function

$$L(\boldsymbol{\beta}) = \frac{1}{(2\pi)^{n/2}\,|\mathbf{U}|^{1/2}}\, e^{-(1/2)(\mathbf{y}-\mathbf{X}\boldsymbol{\beta})'\mathbf{U}^{-1}(\mathbf{y}-\mathbf{X}\boldsymbol{\beta})} \tag{16-4}$$

This is a maximum when the magnitude of the negative exponent is a minimum, that is, when the generalized sum of squares (quadratic form)

$$(\mathbf{y} - \mathbf{X}\boldsymbol{\beta})'\mathbf{U}^{-1}(\mathbf{y} - \mathbf{X}\boldsymbol{\beta}) \tag{16-5}$$

is a minimum. Thus, we see that "generalized least squares" provides maximum likelihood estimates. Using an argument similar to that used in Chapter 12, we set the partial derivatives (with respect to $\boldsymbol{\beta}$) equal to zero to obtain the GLS/MLE estimate:

$$\boxed{\hat{\boldsymbol{\beta}} = (\mathbf{X}'\mathbf{U}^{-1}\mathbf{X})^{-1}\mathbf{X}'\mathbf{U}^{-1}\mathbf{y}} \tag{16-6}$$

We can further verify that $\hat{\boldsymbol{\beta}}$ is normally distributed with:

$$E(\hat{\boldsymbol{\beta}}) = \boldsymbol{\beta} \tag{16-7}$$

$$\text{cov}(\hat{\boldsymbol{\beta}}) = (\mathbf{X}'\mathbf{U}^{-1}\mathbf{X})^{-1} \tag{16-8}$$

Equation (16-7) states that $\hat{\boldsymbol{\beta}}$ is unbiased. In the next section we will see that its variance in (16-8) is optimal too, in a certain sense.

PROBLEMS

16-1 The model for OLS assumes that e_i are uncorrelated and of constant variance, that is,

$$\mathbf{U} = \sigma^2\mathbf{I}$$

(a) Show that the likelihood function (16-4) reduces to the likelihood function for OLS in (12-22).

(b) Show that the GLS estimators (16-6) reduce to the OLS estimators (12-19).

16-2 Prove (16-6) to (16-8), using methods analogous to Chapter 12.

16-2 GAUSS-MARKOV THEOREM

Now we generalize the theory of Section 2-6, establishing that even without the normality assumption, the estimators (16-6) are justified by:

The Gauss-Markov Theorem:

Within the class of linear unbiased estimators of the parameters, it is the GLS estimators (16-6) that minimize the variance of each[1] estimator.	(16-9)

[1] That is, GLS minimizes each of the diagonal elements in the covariance matrix of $\hat{\boldsymbol{\beta}}$. But because of the multivariate nature of $\hat{\boldsymbol{\beta}}$, we perhaps should be concerned with minimizing the *generalized variance*—defined as the determinant $|\text{cov}\ \hat{\boldsymbol{\beta}}|$. From (16-18) it follows that GLS also minimizes this generalized variance. For proof, see Goldberger, 1964, Chapters 2 and 4.

In fact, an even stronger conclusion is possible. If we consider any linear transformation of $\boldsymbol{\beta}$, say $\mathbf{L}\boldsymbol{\beta}$ [as in equation (12-36)], we would naturally be interested in the unbiased linear estimator of $\mathbf{L}\boldsymbol{\beta}$ that has minimum generalized variance. The answer is $\mathbf{L}\hat{\boldsymbol{\beta}}$, where $\hat{\boldsymbol{\beta}}$ is the GLS estimator in (16-6).

Proof. Denote the estimators (16-6) by

$$\hat{\boldsymbol{\beta}} = \mathbf{A}\mathbf{y} \tag{16-10}$$

where

$$\mathbf{A} = (\mathbf{X}'\mathbf{U}^{-1}\mathbf{X})^{-1}\mathbf{X}'\mathbf{U}^{-1} \tag{16-11}$$

To prove that the vector **Ay** is indeed the minimum variance estimator, we consider whether it could possibly be improved. That is, we try to find a better linear estimator

$$(\mathbf{A} + \mathbf{C})\mathbf{y} \tag{16-12}$$

with **C** the "improvement" to be determined.

Our objective is to choose **C** to minimize variance; but our choice is restricted. Specifically, the condition of unbiasedness puts some limitation on **C**; the addition of **Cy** (to hopefully reduce variance) must not change the expected value of our unbiased[2] estimator **Ay**, that is,

$$E(\mathbf{C}\mathbf{y}) = \mathbf{0} \tag{16-13}$$

But

$$E(\mathbf{C}\mathbf{y}) = \mathbf{C}E(\mathbf{y})$$

by (16-2)

$$= \mathbf{C}\mathbf{X}\boldsymbol{\beta}$$

Thus, we must have

$$\mathbf{C}\mathbf{X}\boldsymbol{\beta} = \mathbf{0} \text{ for all possible vectors } \boldsymbol{\beta} \tag{16-14}$$

Hence, we must set

$$\mathbf{C}\mathbf{X} = \mathbf{0} \tag{16-15}$$

This is the restriction on **C** that keeps (16-12) unbiased.

Now we turn to the crucial calculation of the variance of the new estimator. From Table 12-2

$$\begin{aligned} \operatorname{cov}(\mathbf{A} + \mathbf{C})\mathbf{y} &= (\mathbf{A} + \mathbf{C})(\operatorname{cov}\ \mathbf{y})(\mathbf{A} + \mathbf{C})' \\ &= (\mathbf{A} + \mathbf{C})\mathbf{U}(\mathbf{A} + \mathbf{C})' \\ &= \mathbf{AUA}' + \mathbf{CUA}' + \mathbf{AUC}' + \mathbf{CUC}' \end{aligned} \tag{16-16}$$

Now consider just the second term; substituting (16-11)

$$\begin{aligned} \mathbf{CUA}' &= \mathbf{CU}\{(\mathbf{X}'\mathbf{U}^{-1}\mathbf{X})^{-1}\mathbf{X}'\mathbf{U}^{-1}\}' \\ &= \mathbf{CU}\{\mathbf{U}^{-1\prime}\mathbf{X}(\mathbf{X}'\mathbf{U}^{-1}\mathbf{X})^{-1\prime}\} \end{aligned} \tag{16-17}$$

[2] **Ay** is unbiased by (16-7).

Because it is a covariance matrix, $\mathbf{U}' = \mathbf{U}$. It follows from this[3] that $\mathbf{U}^{-1\prime} = \mathbf{U}^{-1}$ and $(\mathbf{X}'\mathbf{U}^{-1}\mathbf{X})^{-1\prime} = (\mathbf{X}'\mathbf{U}^{-1}\mathbf{X})^{-1}$. Equation (16-17) can, therefore, be rewritten:

$$\mathbf{CUA}' = \mathbf{CX}(\mathbf{X}'\mathbf{U}^{-1}\mathbf{X})^{-1}$$

Noting (16-15)

$$= \mathbf{0}$$

Of course, the third term of (16-16), being the transpose of the second term, is also zero, so that (16-16) becomes

$$\operatorname{cov}(\mathbf{A} + \mathbf{C})\mathbf{y} = \mathbf{AUA}' + \mathbf{CUC}' \tag{16-18}$$

To see if $\mathbf{C}$ may reduce the variance of a single (say the ith) estimator, we look at the ith diagonal term in the covariance matrix. It will be the sum of the diagonal term from $\mathbf{AUA}'$ (the old variance[4] for $\hat{\beta}_i$) and the diagonal term from $\mathbf{CUC}'$. Since $\mathbf{CUC}'$ is positive semidefinite,[5] however, its diagonal term will be positive or zero, and hence will *increase* (or leave unchanged) the variance.

Since we wish to keep the variance to a minimum, we set $\mathbf{CUC}'$ equal to zero. This can be accomplished by setting

$$\mathbf{C} = \mathbf{0} \tag{16-19}$$

that is, the "improvement" $\mathbf{C}$ is zero. Thus, there is no improvement possible in the GLS estimator, and the Gauss-Markov theorem is established: GLS is the best linear unbiased estimator (BLUE).

Let us review the GLS estimator (16-6). By definition, it is the estimator that minimized the generalized sum of squares (16-5). It turns out to be MLE, if the errors $\mathbf{e}$ have a multivariate normal distribution. Even without the normality assumption, however, GLS is the estimator with the smallest variance, in the class of linear unbiased estimators (Gauss-Markov theorem).

As a special case, we may set $\mathbf{U} = \sigma^2\mathbf{I}$ to obtain the classical OLS estimator, thus proving its attractive properties (BLUE, MLE).

In the next two sections, we will develop two other special cases—heteroscedasticity and serial correlation.

---

[3] We also use the matrix theorem that the transpose of an inverse equals the inverse of the transpose.

[4] When the original (unaugmented) $\mathbf{Ay}$ was used to estimate $\boldsymbol{\beta}$.

[5] $\mathbf{CUC}'$ is positive semidefinite because $\mathbf{U}$ itself is positive definite, being a covariance matrix. For details, see Goldberger, 1964, Chapter 2.

PROBLEMS

16-3 Prove the Gauss-Markov theorem for the special case of OLS. Compared to the proof in Appendix 2-C, is this proof easier? More or less rigorous?

16-3 HETEROSCEDASTICITY

(a) WLS Solution

This section is a generalization of Section 6-1. We assume as usual that each observation is generated by the model:

$$y_i = \mathbf{x}_i\boldsymbol{\beta} + e_i \qquad i = 1, 2, \ldots, n \tag{16-20a}$$

that is,

$$\mathbf{y} = \mathbf{X}\boldsymbol{\beta} + \mathbf{e} \tag{16-20b}$$

But the components e_i of $\mathbf{e}$ have

$$\text{Unequal variances } \sigma_i^2 \tag{16-21}$$

We still assume, however, that the e_i are uncorrelated with each other and with the x_i. Thus $\mathbf{e}$ has a diagonal covariance matrix

$$\mathbf{U} = \begin{bmatrix} \sigma_1^2 & & & & 0 \\ & \sigma_2^2 & & & \\ & & \cdot & & \\ & & & \cdot & \\ & & & & \cdot \\ 0 & & & & \sigma_n^2 \end{bmatrix} \tag{16-22}$$

The GLS estimator by definition minimizes

$$(\mathbf{y} - \mathbf{X}\boldsymbol{\beta})'\mathbf{U}^{-1}(\mathbf{y} - \mathbf{X}\boldsymbol{\beta}) \tag{16-23}$$

(16-5) repeated

Because $\mathbf{U}$ is diagonal, so is $\mathbf{U}^{-1}$:

$$\mathbf{U}^{-1} = \begin{bmatrix} 1/\sigma_1^2 & & & & 0 \\ & 1/\sigma_2^2 & & & \\ & & \cdot & & \\ & & & \cdot & \\ & & & & \cdot \\ 0 & & & & 1/\sigma_n^2 \end{bmatrix} \tag{16-24}$$

Thus (16-23) reduces to minimizing

$$\sum_{i=1}^{n} \frac{(y_i - \mathbf{x}_i\boldsymbol{\beta})^2}{\sigma_i^2} \tag{16-25}$$

(6-5) generalized

This is just the generalization of the weighted least squares (WLS) criterion (6-5) to the case of multiple regression.

The explicit WLS solution is given by (16-6):

$$\hat{\boldsymbol{\beta}} = (\mathbf{X}'\mathbf{U}^{-1}\mathbf{X})^{-1}\mathbf{X}'\mathbf{U}^{-1}\mathbf{y} \tag{16-26}$$

(16-6) repeated

where $\mathbf{U}^{-1}$ is given by (16-24) above. Since these WLS estimators are a special case of GLS, they are Gauss-Markov estimators, as well as MLE when normality is assumed.

(b) Equivalent Solution by Transformation

Alternatively, we may transform the system of equations (16-20) so that the errors have constant variance, and hence satisfy the OLS model. This may be achieved by dividing the ith equation by σ_i, that is, multiplying the system (16-20) by the *dividing matrix*:

$$\mathbf{D} = \begin{bmatrix} 1/\sigma_1 & & & & 0 \\ & 1/\sigma_2 & & & \\ & & \cdot & & \\ & & & \cdot & \\ & & & & \cdot \\ 0 & & & & 1/\sigma_n \end{bmatrix} \tag{16-27}$$

Then we have

$$(\mathbf{Dy}) = (\mathbf{DX})\boldsymbol{\beta} + (\mathbf{De}) \tag{16-28}$$

where

$$\mathbf{De} = \begin{bmatrix} e_1/\sigma_1 \\ e_2/\sigma_2 \\ \cdot \\ \cdot \\ \cdot \\ e_n/\sigma_n \end{bmatrix} \text{ has covariance matrix } \mathbf{I} \tag{16-29}$$

$$\mathbf{Dy} = \begin{bmatrix} y_1/\sigma_1 \\ y_2/\sigma_2 \\ \cdot \\ \cdot \\ \cdot \\ y_n/\sigma_n \end{bmatrix} \tag{16-30}$$

and

$$\mathbf{DX} = \begin{bmatrix} x_{11}/\sigma_1 & x_{12}/\sigma_1 & \cdots \\ x_{21}/\sigma_2 & x_{22}/\sigma_2 & \\ \cdot & & \\ \cdot & & \\ \cdot & & \\ x_{n1}/\sigma_n & \cdots & x_{nk}/\sigma_n \end{bmatrix} \tag{16-31}$$

Now because of (16-29), OLS may be applied to (16-28); this solution is given by substituting **Dy** and **DX** for **y** and **X** in (12-19):

$$\begin{aligned}\hat{\boldsymbol{\beta}} &= \{(\mathbf{DX})'\mathbf{DX}\}^{-1}(\mathbf{DX})'(\mathbf{Dy}) \\ &= \{\mathbf{X}'(\mathbf{D}'\mathbf{D})\mathbf{X}\}^{-1}\mathbf{X}'(\mathbf{D}'\mathbf{D})\mathbf{y}\end{aligned} \tag{16-32}$$

Now

$$\mathbf{D}'\mathbf{D} = \begin{bmatrix} 1/\sigma_1^2 & & & & 0 \\ & 1/\sigma_2^2 & & & \\ & & \cdot & & \\ & & & \cdot & \\ & & & & \cdot \\ 0 & & & & 1/\sigma_n^2 \end{bmatrix}$$

which is the same as $\mathbf{U}^{-1}$ in (16-24). Thus this procedure of first transforming as in (16-28) so that the error behaves, then applying OLS as in (16-32), is seen to be exactly equivalent to the GLS/WLS solution (16-26). And this procedure provides advantages. We can use the concepts (such as vector geometry) or the computer routines (such as stepwise regression) available for OLS.

PROBLEMS

16-4

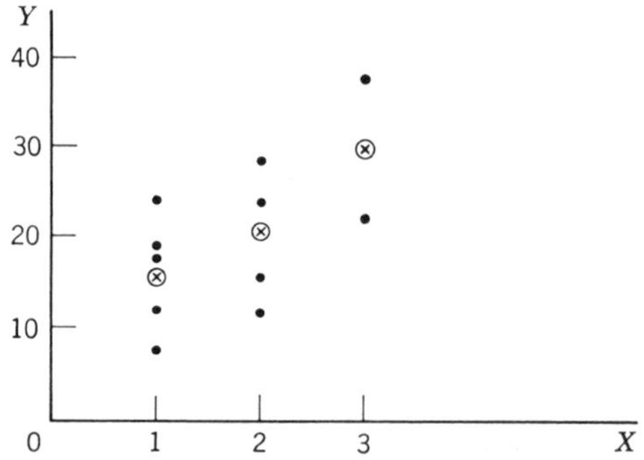

Suppose we have collected data as in the graph above. For each X, there are several sample values of Y, and their mean $\bar{Y}$ is graphed. Suppose that each conditional distribution of Y has the same variance σ^2, as in the model (2-22). We give a summary of this data in table form:

X_i	n_i	$\bar{Y}_i$
1	5	15
2	4	20
3	2	30

Suppose the individual observations Y_i have been lost, and only the $\bar{Y}_i$ retained.

(a) What is the variance of each of the $\bar{Y}_i$?
(b) Find the GLS estimate of the slope β.
(c) Estimate β by applying OLS to the values of $\bar{Y}_i$.
(d) Which estimator is better, (b) or (c)?
(e) Can you describe briefly why the OLS estimate is slightly higher than the GLS estimate?

16-4 SERIALLY CORRELATED ERROR

(a) GLS Solution

In the linear regression model,

$$y_t = \mathbf{x}_t \boldsymbol{\beta} + e_t \qquad t = 1, 2, \ldots, n \tag{16-33}$$

that is,

$$\mathbf{y} = \mathbf{X}\boldsymbol{\beta} + \mathbf{e} \tag{16-34}$$

let us assume that the errors e_t are no longer uncorrelated. In fact, we assume that e_t are serially correlated in the simplest type of autoregressive scheme (or so-called Markov chain):

$$e_t = \rho e_{t-1} + v_t \qquad (t = \cdots -2, -1, 0, 1, 2, \ldots) \tag{16-35}$$

where $|\rho| < 1$, and the process has been going on for a long time.[6] (16-36)

Also, the disturbance v_t is assumed to have the usual characteristics

$$E(\mathbf{v}) = \mathbf{0} \tag{16-37}$$

and

$$\operatorname{cov}(\mathbf{v}) = \sigma^2 \mathbf{I} \tag{16-38}$$

These assumptions about $\mathbf{v}$ ensure that $\mathbf{e}$ has a zero expected value:

$$E(\mathbf{e}) = \mathbf{0} \tag{16-39}$$

[6] If the data starts after a catastrophe, this assumption is not true of course, and our subsequent analysis is invalid. For the same issue from a slightly different viewpoint, see also the footnote to (16-72) and footnote 17 in Chapter 6.

but its covariance matrix is[8]

$$\mathbf{U} = \sigma_e^2 \begin{bmatrix} 1 & \rho & \rho^2 & \cdot & \cdot & \cdot \\ \rho & 1 & \rho & & & \\ \rho^2 & \rho & 1 & & & \\ \cdot & & & \cdot & & \\ \cdot & & & & \cdot & \\ \cdot & & & & & \cdot \\ \cdot & & & & & 1 \end{bmatrix} \tag{16-40}$$

where

$$\sigma_e^2 = \frac{\sigma^2}{1-\rho^2} \tag{16-41}$$

σ^2 being the variance of the disturbance v_t. It may be easily verified, by multiplying $\mathbf{U}^{-1}\mathbf{U} = \mathbf{I}$, that

$$\mathbf{U}^{-1} = \frac{1}{\sigma_e^2}\left(\frac{1}{1-\rho^2}\right) \begin{bmatrix} 1 & -\rho & & & & 0 \\ -\rho & 1+\rho^2 & -\rho & & & \\ & -\rho & 1+\rho^2 & -\rho & & \\ & & \cdot & \cdot & \cdot & \\ & & & \cdot & \cdot & \cdot \\ & & & \cdot & \cdot & \cdot \\ & & & -\rho & 1+\rho^2 & -\rho \\ 0 & & & & -\rho & 1 \end{bmatrix} \tag{16-42}$$

Thus, the GLS solution is obtained by substituting this value of $\mathbf{U}^{-1}$ into (16-6):

$$\hat{\boldsymbol{\beta}} = (\mathbf{X}'\mathbf{U}^{-1}\mathbf{X})^{-1}\mathbf{X}'\mathbf{U}^{-1}\mathbf{y} \tag{16-43}$$

(16-6) repeated

(b) Equivalent Solution by Transformation

Alternatively, we would like to transform the system of equations (16-34) so that the errors become uncorrelated, and hence satisfy the OLS model. In view of (16-35), which may be reexpressed as

$$-\rho e_{t-1} + e_t = v_t \tag{16-44}$$

[8] Note that model (16-35) can be obtained from (6-81); we merely set $y_t = e_t$, $v_t = v_t$, and $\phi = \rho$ in (6-81). Making these same substitutions, the variance σ_e^2 in (16-41) is found from (6-85), and the autocorrelations in (16-40) are found from (6-91).

we are motivated to multiply the system (16-34) by the differencing matrix:

$$\mathbf{D} = \begin{bmatrix} \sqrt{1-\rho^2} & & & & 0 \\ -\rho & 1 & & & \\ & \cdot & \cdot & & \\ & & \cdot & \cdot & \\ & & & \cdot & \cdot \\ 0 & & & -\rho & 1 \end{bmatrix} \tag{16-45}$$

(The first row is exceptional, and will be explained later. For the moment, let us just accept the fact that some such first row is necessary to keep the matrix square, $n \times n$.)

Then we have (16-34) transformed to

$$(\mathbf{Dy}) = (\mathbf{DX})\,\boldsymbol{\beta} + (\mathbf{De}) \tag{16-46}$$

where

$$\mathbf{De} = \begin{bmatrix} \sqrt{1-\rho^2}\, e_1 \\ -\rho e_1 + e_2 \\ -\rho e_2 + e_3 \\ \cdot \\ \cdot \\ \cdot \\ -\rho e_{n-1} + e_n \end{bmatrix} \tag{16-47}$$

According to (16-44)

$$\mathbf{De} = \begin{bmatrix} \sqrt{1-\rho^2}\, e_1 \\ v_2 \\ v_3 \\ \cdot \\ \cdot \\ \cdot \\ v_n \end{bmatrix} \tag{16-48}$$

which is an uncorrelated set of errors, as we intended. **Dy** and **DX** are defined like (16-47); for example:

$$\mathbf{Dy} = \begin{bmatrix} \sqrt{1-\rho^2}\, y_1 \\ -\rho y_1 + y_2 \\ \cdot \\ \cdot \\ \cdot \\ -\rho y_{n-1} + y_n \end{bmatrix} \tag{16-49}$$

The OLS solution of (16-46) is given by substituting **Dy** and **DX** for **y** and **X** in (12-19):

$$\begin{aligned} \hat{\boldsymbol{\beta}} &= \{(\mathbf{DX})'\mathbf{DX}\}^{-1}(\mathbf{DX})'\mathbf{Dy} \\ &= \{\mathbf{X}'(\mathbf{D}'\mathbf{D})\mathbf{X}\}^{-1}\mathbf{X}'(\mathbf{D}'\mathbf{D})\mathbf{y} \end{aligned} \tag{16-50}$$

Now from (16-45),

$$\mathbf{D}'\mathbf{D} = \begin{bmatrix} 1 & -\rho & & & & & 0 \\ -\rho & 1+\rho^2 & -\rho & & & & \\ & -\rho & 1+\rho^2 & -\rho & & & \\ & & \cdot & \cdot & \cdot & & \\ & & & \cdot & \cdot & \cdot & \\ & & & & \cdot & \cdot & \cdot \\ & & & & -\rho & 1+\rho^2 & -\rho \\ 0 & & & & & -\rho & 1 \end{bmatrix} \tag{16-51}$$

which is the same as[9] $\mathbf{U}^{-1}$ in (16-42). Thus (16-50) is exactly the same as the GLS solution (16-43). In fact, it was precisely for this reason that the first row of **D** was defined as it was; it made $\mathbf{D}'\mathbf{D} = \mathbf{U}^{-1}$ essentially.

(c) Generalized Differencing

Our solution (16-50) using the **D** transformation is recognized to be the method of generalized differencing introduced in Chapter 6-7*d*. It involves the following steps.

---

[9] Except for a scalar that cancels out in the reciprocal appearances of $\mathbf{U}^{-1}$ in (16-43).

1. Use (16-49) to calculate the generalized differences

$$\left.\begin{aligned} \tau y_t &= y_t - \rho y_{t-1} \\ \text{and} \qquad & \qquad\qquad t = 2, 3, 4, \ldots, n \\ \tau \mathbf{x}_t &= \mathbf{x}_t - \rho \mathbf{x}_{t-1} \end{aligned}\right\} \tag{16-52}$$

(6-32) generalized

2. Adjust the first observed $\mathbf{x}$ and y values

$$\left.\begin{aligned} \tau y_1 &= \sqrt{1-\rho^2}\, y_1 \\ \text{and} \qquad & \\ \tau \mathbf{x}_1 &= \sqrt{1-\rho^2}\, \mathbf{x}_1 \end{aligned}\right\} \tag{16-53}$$

(6-34) generalized

   This adjustment—which may have been a bit of a mystery when introduced in (6-34)—must be made in order to keep this procedure equivalent to GLS, with all its attractive properties. [Note from (16-46) that $\mathbf{DX}$ involves using $\mathbf{D}$ to transform the *entire* $\mathbf{X}$ matrix, including the constant regressor of 1's.]
3. Apply OLS to the set of all n generalized differences, regressing $\tau\mathbf{y}$ on $\tau\mathbf{X}$.

16-5 GENERALIZATION: GLS ALWAYS EQUIVALENT TO A TRANSFORMATION AND OLS

In the last two sections we have seen two examples of how GLS estimates could be obtained by first transforming in order to make the error satisfy the standard assumptions of Chapter 12, and then applying OLS. This approach will be generalized in this section.

Recall that the GLS model is

$$\mathbf{y} = \mathbf{X}\boldsymbol{\beta} + \mathbf{e} \tag{16-1 repeated}$$

where

$$\text{cov}\ \mathbf{e} = \mathbf{U} \tag{16-3 repeated}$$

Whatever the covariance matrix $\mathbf{U}$ may be, it is possible to linearly transform the errors $\mathbf{e}$ by a matrix $\mathbf{M}$ so that

$$\text{cov}(\mathbf{Me}) = \mathbf{I} \tag{16-54}$$

Proof. Since $\mathbf{U}$ is a covariance matrix, it is positive definite and symmetric;[10] therefore there exists an invertible matrix $\mathbf{M}$ such that

$$\mathbf{MUM}' = \mathbf{I} \tag{16-55}$$

---

[10] For details on the properties of a covariance matrix, see Goldberger, 1964, p. 87.

(The proof is given in standard linear algebra texts. The matrix **M** is not unique, but this does not cause any difficulty.) It is easily verified that[11]

$$\mathbf{M}'\mathbf{M} = \mathbf{U}^{-1} \tag{16-56}$$

Thus **M** is sometimes denoted by $\mathbf{U}^{-1/2}$.

From Table 12-2,

$$\text{cov}(\mathbf{Me}) = \mathbf{M}(\text{cov } \mathbf{e})\mathbf{M}' \tag{16-57}$$

$$= \mathbf{MUM}'$$

$$= \mathbf{I} \tag{16-58}$$

and (16-54) is proved.

We therefore transform (16-1) by premultiplying by **M**:

$$(\mathbf{My}) = (\mathbf{MX})\boldsymbol{\beta} + (\mathbf{Me})$$

that is,

$$\mathbf{y}^* = \mathbf{X}^*\boldsymbol{\beta} + \mathbf{e}^* \tag{16-59}$$

obtaining a model where the error $\mathbf{e}^*$ satisfies the assumptions of OLS.

The OLS estimates are given by (12-19) as

$$\hat{\boldsymbol{\beta}} = (\mathbf{X}^{*\prime}\mathbf{X}^*)^{-1}\mathbf{X}^{*\prime}\mathbf{y}^* \tag{16-60}$$

$$= \{(\mathbf{MX})'\mathbf{MX}\}^{-1}(\mathbf{MX})'(\mathbf{My})$$

$$= \{\mathbf{X}'(\mathbf{M}'\mathbf{M})\mathbf{X}\}^{-1}\mathbf{X}'(\mathbf{M}'\mathbf{M})\mathbf{y}$$

by (16-56)

$$= (\mathbf{X}'\mathbf{U}^{-1}\mathbf{X})^{-1}\mathbf{X}'\mathbf{U}^{-1}\mathbf{y} \tag{16-61}$$

which are just the GLS estimates in (16-6).

In conclusion, an **M** must always exist, such that this transformation followed by OLS will yield the GLS result; in fact, GLS is sometimes referred to as the Aitken transformation. Thus GLS may be viewed as simply an extension of OLS.

PROBLEMS

*16-5 Suppose the following four points were observed in a time series, whose errors e_t form a simple autocorrelated process with $\rho = -.9$. Suppose also that $e_t \sim N(0, .5^2)$.

---

[11] From (16-55), $\mathbf{U} = \mathbf{M}^{-1}\mathbf{I}\mathbf{M}'^{-1} = \mathbf{M}^{-1}\mathbf{M}'^{-1}$. Therefore,

$$\mathbf{U}^{-1} = \mathbf{M}'\mathbf{M}$$

t	x_t	y_t	e_t
1	0	0	
2	0	−1	
3	0	0	
4	1	0	

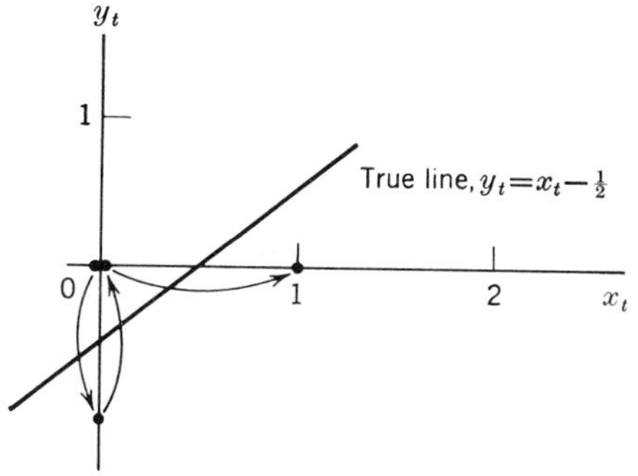

(a) Fill out the table of e_t. Are these errors very negatively correlated?

(b) Calculate the slope estimate using:

(i) OLS
(ii) GLS
(iii) Which is nearer the correct value $\beta = 1$?

16-6 Consider the model

$$\mathbf{y} = \mathbf{X}\boldsymbol{\beta} + \mathbf{e} \tag{1}$$

(16-1) repeated

where $\mathbf{e}$ has covariance matrix $\mathbf{A}$, which can be written as $\mathbf{A} = \mathbf{B}\mathbf{B}'$ where $\mathbf{B}$ is invertible, and we denote $\mathbf{B}^{-1} = \mathbf{C}$. Without any real loss of generality, suppose all variables are measured as deviations from the mean. Finally, suppose there are n observations and k regressors, so that $\mathbf{X}$ is of dimension $n \times k$.

True or false? If false, correct it:

(a) One way to find the BLUE estimate of $\boldsymbol{\beta}$ is to:

(i) Transform equation (1) into a simple model having uncorrelated error, by multiplying (transforming) by the Aitken matrix $\mathbf{C}$, obtaining

$$(\mathbf{C}\mathbf{y}) = (\mathbf{C}\mathbf{X})\boldsymbol{\beta} + (\mathbf{C}\mathbf{e}) \tag{2}$$

(ii) Then apply OLS to the transformed variables, that is, regress $(\mathbf{C}\mathbf{y})$ on the regressors $(\mathbf{C}\mathbf{X})$. The resulting regression coefficients constitute the BLUE estimate $\hat{\boldsymbol{\beta}}$.

(b) Alternatively, we can calculate the BLUE estimate of $\boldsymbol{\beta}$ in one step by the GLS formula:

$$\hat{\boldsymbol{\beta}} = (\mathbf{X}'\mathbf{A}^{-1}\mathbf{X})^{-1}\mathbf{X}'\mathbf{A}^{-1}\mathbf{y}$$

(c) The estimator in (a) has a slightly larger variance than the estimator in (b). However, the estimator in (a) has a much smaller bias.

(d) One advantage of method (a) is this: After transforming, all the properties of OLS can be exploited. This is both a theoretical and practical benefit: the well-known theory of OLS, including the geometry such as Figure 14-19, can be used; the practical aspects of OLS, such as computer programs for OLS regression, can also be used.

For part (e), fill in the blanks:

(e) One aspect of the GLS model (16-1) that causes considerable practical difficulty is that the covariance matrix $\mathbf{A}$ is usually not known. $\mathbf{A}$ has n^2 elements, some of which are necessarily equal because of symmetry. Yet there remain __________ distinct elements, which are far too many parameters to sensibly try to estimate without some simplifying assumptions. (Besides, the elements of $\mathbf{A}$ are not really of primary interest, since it is $\boldsymbol{\beta}$ that we wanted to estimate in the first place.) It is therefore customary to make some simplifying assumptions about $\mathbf{A}$, such as:

   (i) $\mathbf{A}$ is zero everywhere except on the diagonal, that is, the errors $\mathbf{e}_i$ are __________. Furthermore, in simple regression (with only one regressor), it is often assumed that σ_i is proportional to X_i, that is, $\sigma_i = kX_i$, which is called a __________ model. Then $\mathbf{A}$ has only one unknown parameter, k. And k does not even have to be estimated, since its two occurrences in (16-6) cancel.

   (ii) The errors are serially correlated, according to the simple first-order autoregression (16-35). Then according to (16-42), there are only two unknown parameters, ρ and σ_e^2. And σ_e^2 does not have to be estimated, since its two occurrences in (16-6) cancel. This leaves only the serial correlation ρ to be estimated.

   An estimate $\hat{\rho}$ may be obtained by regressing $\hat{e}_t$ on __________, where $\hat{e}_t$ is the series of estimated residuals after OLS estimation on (16-1). Allowance should be made for the bias in $\hat{\rho}$, as is made in the __________ test for $\rho = 0$.

16-6 FORECASTING, IF SERIALLY CORRELATED ERROR

Recall the simplest case of serial correlation (6-15). If ρ were known, the forecast in the first future period $n + 1$ would be given by (6-39) and (6-40) as:

$$\hat{Y}_{n+1} = \hat{\alpha} + \hat{\beta}X_{n+1} + \rho\hat{e}_n \tag{16-62}$$

This may be generalized to

$$\hat{Y}_{n+1} = \mathbf{x}_{n+1}\hat{\boldsymbol{\beta}} + \mathbf{w}'\mathbf{U}^{-1}\hat{\mathbf{e}} \tag{16-63}$$

which has been shown (Goldberger, 1964) to be the best linear unbiased forecast (BLUE) in *any* GLS application (serial correlation, heteroscedasticity, etc.). As before, $\mathbf{x}_{n+1}$ is the row of regressor values for which we wish to predict Y; $\hat{\boldsymbol{\beta}}$ and $\hat{\mathbf{e}}$ are the estimates that fall out of the GLS regression, and $\mathbf{U}$ is the covariance matrix of the error $\mathbf{e}$, assumed known *a priori*. One additional new piece of prior information is required:

$$\mathbf{w} \equiv \begin{bmatrix} \text{cov}(e_{n+1}, e_1) \\ \text{cov}(e_{n+1}, e_2) \\ \cdot \\ \cdot \\ \cdot \\ \text{cov}(e_{n+1}, e_n) \end{bmatrix} \tag{16-64}$$

that is, the covariance vector showing how the error in the projection period e_{n+1} is related to the errors over the sample period, $\mathbf{e} = (e_1, e_2 \cdots e_n)$.

When we examine it in detail, (16-63) is just exactly what we would expect. To the forecasted trend $\mathbf{x}_{n+1}\hat{\boldsymbol{\beta}}$ we are again adding some sort of forecasted error. Exactly what should this forecasted error be? The most obvious suggestion is to use $\mathbf{w}'\hat{\mathbf{e}}$; in other words, take $\hat{\mathbf{e}}$, our best estimate of the error terms over the sample, and apply our prior knowledge $\mathbf{w}'$ of how the error in the projection period is related to them. But the estimated errors $\hat{\mathbf{e}}$ should first be weighted according to their reliability, as given by the inverse covariance matrix $\mathbf{U}^{-1}$. (A similar situation occurred in the case of heteroscedasticity: in (16-25) we saw that it was appropriate to pay more attention to some observations than others.)

To sum up. Once again, in a more complicated context, we are pursuing a very simple principle: If the disturbance can be forecast, then forecast it. This means that the burden of prior knowledge is increased; our prior knowledge of $\mathbf{U}$ must now be augmented by prior knowledge of $\mathbf{w}$.

PROBLEMS

16-7 (a) Show that in the case of simple regression and simple serial correlation (6-15), the general forecast (16-63) reduces to (16-62). (*Hint*. $\mathbf{w}'$ will just be the last row of $\mathbf{U}$, multiplied by ρ.)

(b) What would (16-63) reduce to, in the case of multiple regression and simple serial correlation?

16-7 HOW MUCH IS GLS WORTH?

(a) In General

Whenever our data follows the model (16-1) to (16-3), we have shown that GLS estimates have certain desirable properties. They are:

1. Unbiased.
2. MLE, if normality assumed.
3. BLUE even if normality is not assumed; that is, within the class of linear unbiased estimators, they have the smallest variance (Gauss-Markov theorem).

We now ask how much damage would be done if OLS were applied directly to the data,[12] even though it may not be theoretically justified.

First of all, we are pleasantly surprised to find that OLS estimators would be unbiased. To prove this, we merely repeat the argument that established (12-31). This argument is still valid because the covariance matrix $\mathbf{U}$ does not appear anywhere in this computation of expected values; the crucial issue is that $\mathbf{E(e)} = 0$, and this is still true in our model, by (16-2).

However (by Gauss-Markov), GLS estimators have smaller variance than other linear unbiased estimators, including OLS. How much variance would OLS have?

To derive the actual formula for the variance of the OLS estimators, we recall that the OLS estimator is

$$\hat{\boldsymbol{\beta}}_0 = (\mathbf{X}'\mathbf{X})^{-1}\mathbf{X}'\mathbf{y} \tag{16-65}$$

(12-19) repeated

From Table 12-2,

$$\text{cov}(\hat{\boldsymbol{\beta}}_0) = (\mathbf{X}'\mathbf{X})^{-1}\mathbf{X}'(\text{cov } \mathbf{y})\{(\mathbf{X}'\mathbf{X})^{-1}\mathbf{X}'\}'$$

---

[12] In other words, suppose we apply OLS directly to (16-1), rather than *after* the GLS transformation $\mathbf{M}$.

From (16-3), and noting that $\mathbf{X'X}$ is symmetric,

$$\operatorname{cov}(\hat{\boldsymbol{\beta}}_0) = (\mathbf{X'X})^{-1}\mathbf{X'UX}(\mathbf{X'X})^{-1} \tag{16-66}$$

We will show in some special cases how much this exceeds the optimal variance of the GLS estimator

$$\operatorname{cov}(\hat{\boldsymbol{\beta}}) = (\mathbf{X'U}^{-1}\mathbf{X})^{-1} \tag{16-67}$$

(16-8) repeated

To be simple and concrete, we will consider the case of simple regression (2-21) where the independent variable x takes on five successive values.

(b) Heteroscedasticity

Suppose the values of x_i are 1, 2, 3, 4, 5, and that the standard deviation[13] of y_i is proportional to x_i. The optimal GLS estimators have covariance computed in (16-67):

$$\operatorname{cov}\hat{\boldsymbol{\beta}} = \begin{bmatrix} 2.4 & -1.1 \\ -1.1 & 0.7 \end{bmatrix} \tag{16-68}$$

whereas from (16-66), the OLS estimators have

$$\operatorname{cov}\hat{\boldsymbol{\beta}}_0 = \begin{bmatrix} 6.2 & -2.5 \\ -2.5 & 1.2 \end{bmatrix} \tag{16-69}$$

which is far worse. In this case, GLS is worth a great deal.

(c) Serial Correlation

Suppose the values of x_i are $-2, -1, 0, 1, 2$, and that the errors in y follow a simple autocorrelated process (16-35) with[14] $\rho = \frac{1}{2}$. Then for GLS

$$\operatorname{cov}\hat{\boldsymbol{\beta}} = \begin{bmatrix} .57 & 0 \\ 0 & .154 \end{bmatrix} \tag{16-70}$$

---

[13] It is also assumed that the standard deviation of y_1 is 1, for simplicity. Furthermore, the x_i are not shifted to a zero mean, that is, x_i are not in deviation form.

[14] And $\operatorname{var}(v_t) = 1$, for simplicity.

whereas for OLS,

$$\text{cov}\ \hat{\boldsymbol{\beta}}_0 = \boxed{\begin{matrix} .59 & 0 \\ 0 & .160 \end{matrix}} \qquad (16\text{-}71)$$

which is only slightly worse. Thus, in this example with x increasing regularly and ρ positive, OLS is quite efficient. [Note that this provides support for our statement (6-21).]

Finally, suppose we calculated GLS by transformation; but after calculating all generalized differences (16-52), we forgot to adjust the first observations as in (16-53). The result is

$$\text{cov}\ \hat{\boldsymbol{\beta}}_* = \boxed{\begin{matrix} 2.80 & -1.20 \\ -1.20 & .80 \end{matrix}} \qquad (16\text{-}72)$$

which is worse than OLS.[15] This confirms our earlier statement [following (6-34)] that this adjustment in the first observation may be crucial; without it, the result may be worse than OLS.

This discussion of serial correlation must be kept in perspective with the following three observations.

1. In concluding that OLS is often a reasonably good estimation procedure for serial correlation, we emphasize that we have only considered its efficiency in *point* estimation. OLS *interval* estimates may be highly misleading (see the discussion of Figures 6-7 and 6-8).
2. Chapter 16 has been devoted exclusively to the case where ρ is known. But it almost always must be estimated. In such circumstances, the case for using OLS is strengthened, not because it becomes a better estimating technique, but rather because the application of alternative more complicated techniques becomes less justified.
3. Finally, recall that there may be other time series problems such as lagged variables (discussed in Chapter 6); if so, they must, if possible, be dealt with at the same time.

[15] This spectacular result is, of course, in part due to the small sample. With a larger sample, the effect of an adjustment in the first observation tends to fade out. We should also keep in mind the possibility that the first observation may occur after a discontinuity in the process generating the error, as described in footnote 17 in chapter 6. Then the GLS transformation (16-53) is not valid.

PROBLEMS

16-8 Comparing (16-68) and (16-69), what is the efficiency of OLS relative to GLS for the slope estimate?

16-9 Calculate the covariance matrices as in (16-68) and (16-69), assuming just three x values (1, 2, 3).

16-10 Calculate the covariance matrices as in (16-70) and (16-71), assuming just three x values $(-1, 0, 1)$.

16-8 SEASONAL ADJUSTMENT PROBLEMS

(a) Regressions With and Without Seasonally Adjusted Data

If a variable **y** is subject to quarterly seasonal influence, then the argument of Section 6-4 can be generalized in the following way:

$$\mathbf{y} = \mathbf{X}\boldsymbol{\beta} + \mathbf{D}\boldsymbol{\gamma} + \mathbf{e} \qquad \text{(16-73) like (6-14)}$$

where **X** includes all the other regressors (including the unit vector to pick up the intercept estimate), and **D** includes the three required seasonal dummies, that is,

$$\mathbf{D} = \begin{bmatrix} 0 & 0 & 0 \\ 1 & 0 & 0 \\ 0 & 1 & 0 \\ 0 & 0 & 1 \\ 0 & 0 & 0 \\ 1 & 0 & 0 \\ 0 & 1 & 0 \\ 0 & 0 & 1 \\ 0 & 0 & 0 \\ 1 & 0 & 0 \\ \vdots & & \end{bmatrix}$$

Suppose the data for **X** and **y** is available only in deseasonalized form, however. Then it would be appropriate for deseasonalized **y** to be regressed on deseasonalized **X**, without the seasonal dummies. How would the regression coefficient $\hat{\boldsymbol{\beta}}$ compare to $\hat{\boldsymbol{\beta}}$ in (16-73)? The very same, as the following theorem states[16]:

[16] This result is certainly reasonable in view of what was said at the beginning of Section 5-3: Like the partial correlation, the multiple regression coefficient measures the relation of the regressor **X** to the response, *with the effect of the other regressors netted out.*

Theorem

(16-73) will yield the same estimate of $\boldsymbol{\beta}$ as the following three-step procedure:

1. Deseasonalize $\mathbf{y}$ into $\mathbf{y}^a$. (16-74)
2. Deseasonalize $\mathbf{X}$ into $\mathbf{X}^a$.
3. Proceed with a standard regression using only seasonally adjusted data; in other words regress $\mathbf{y}^a$ on $\mathbf{X}^a$.

We have stated our theorem in terms of seasonal adjustment, because this is the commonest type of adjustment. But our proof (and hence the theorem) will be perfectly valid for any kind of adjustment, involving *any* kind of dummy variables *or* ordinary variables—for example, age adjustment.

To illustrate how geometry can sometimes simplify proofs, in part (b) we will contrast a geometric proof with a much more complicated algebraic proof.[17] We could also prove three more similar theorems: Compared to the full regression (16-73),

(1) if we regress $\mathbf{y}^a$ on $\mathbf{X}^a$, we get the same residual $\mathbf{s}^2$ as well as the same $\hat{\boldsymbol{\beta}}$.
(2) if we regress $\mathbf{y}$ on $\mathbf{X}^a$, we get a larger residual, but the same $\hat{\boldsymbol{\beta}}$.
(3) if we regress $\mathbf{y}^a$ on $\mathbf{X}$, we get a larger residual, and a different $\hat{\boldsymbol{\beta}}$.

Of course, if the available data consists of the unadjusted variables $\mathbf{X}$ and $\mathbf{y}$, it is easiest and most appropriate to analyze them as they stand using (16-73). We give the other methods merely to show what happens if it is *adjusted* variables that are available. Note particularly that combination (3) (regressing $\mathbf{y}^a$ on $\mathbf{X}$) is unfortunate: It gives the wrong $\hat{\boldsymbol{\beta}}$ (and incidentally the wrong s^2 too).

*(b) Proof of (16-74)[18]

To prove the theorem, we will first estimate $\boldsymbol{\beta}$ by the three steps given in (16-74). Then we will show that this estimate is identical to the estimate of $\boldsymbol{\beta}$ in (16-73).

1. Seasonally adjust $\mathbf{y}$ by regressing it on $\mathbf{D}$. This will yield

$$\mathbf{y} = \mathbf{D}\hat{\boldsymbol{\phi}} + \mathbf{y}^a \tag{16-75}$$

[17] Our algebraic proof follows that of Lovell 1963, who first proved this theorem.

[18] Part (b) is starred because the algebra is a bit difficult, while the simpler vector geometry is optional.

where the residual $\mathbf{y}^a$ represents the deseasonalized $\mathbf{y}$ series, and

$$\hat{\boldsymbol{\phi}} = (\mathbf{D}'\mathbf{D})^{-1}\mathbf{D}'\mathbf{y} \tag{16-76}$$

Thus, using (16-75), we may express the deseasonalized $\mathbf{y}$ as

$$\mathbf{y}^a = \mathbf{y} - \mathbf{D}\hat{\boldsymbol{\phi}} \tag{16-77}$$

and noting (16-76),

$$= \mathbf{y} - \mathbf{D}(\mathbf{D}'\mathbf{D})^{-1}\mathbf{D}'\mathbf{y} \tag{16-78}$$

$$= \mathbf{A}\mathbf{y} \tag{16-79}$$

where

$$\mathbf{A} = [\mathbf{I} - \mathbf{D}(\mathbf{D}'\mathbf{D})^{-1}\mathbf{D}'] \tag{16-80}$$

2. Deseasonalize $\mathbf{X}$ by regressing it also on $\mathbf{D}$. It may be easily confirmed, using exactly the same sort of argument as in step 1, that

$$\mathbf{X}^a = \mathbf{A}\mathbf{X} \tag{16-81}$$

These first two steps can be shown geometrically. In Figure 16-1, $\mathbf{D}$ represents the subspace generated by the dummy vectors, while $\mathbf{X}$ represents the subspace generated by the other regressors. Step 1 involves the perpendicular projection of $\mathbf{y}$ onto $\mathbf{D}$ at M, with the difference between this and $\mathbf{y}$ being $\mathbf{y}^a$. Similarly in Step 2, $\mathbf{X}^a$ represents the difference between $\mathbf{X}$ and its fitted value on $\mathbf{D}$.

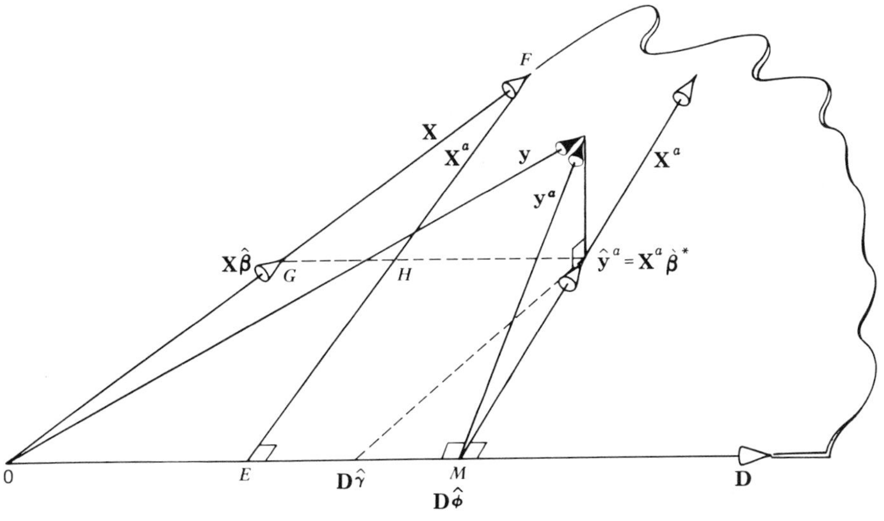

FIGURE 16-1 Why **X** and **y** need not initially be deseasonalized.

3. Now regress $\mathbf{y}^a$ on $\mathbf{X}^a$, which yields

$$\hat{\mathbf{y}}^a = \mathbf{X}^a\hat{\boldsymbol{\beta}}^* \tag{16-82}$$

This is seen to involve shifting $\mathbf{X}^a$ from its origin at E to a new origin at M, followed by a perpendicular projection of $\mathbf{y}^a$ onto $\mathbf{X}^a$ at $\hat{\mathbf{y}}^a$. $\hat{\boldsymbol{\beta}}^*$ is the relative length of $\hat{\mathbf{y}}^a$ along $\mathbf{X}^a$.

Now turn to the much simpler alternative method of estimating $\boldsymbol{\beta}$. Simply regress $\mathbf{y}$ on both $\mathbf{X}$ and $\mathbf{D}$ as in (16-73), which yields

$$\hat{\mathbf{y}} = \mathbf{X}\hat{\boldsymbol{\beta}} + \mathbf{D}\hat{\boldsymbol{\gamma}} \tag{16-83}$$

Geometrically this involves a perpendicular projection of $\mathbf{y}$ onto the subspace spanned by $\mathbf{X}$ and $\mathbf{D}$, yielding $\hat{\mathbf{y}}$—which coincides with $\hat{\mathbf{y}}^a$ derived in the previous alternative. Then this $\hat{\mathbf{y}}$ is projected in a parallel fashion onto $\mathbf{X}$ and $\mathbf{D}$ yielding the estimated coefficients in (16-83). In particular we note that $\hat{\boldsymbol{\beta}}$ is the relative length of this projection along $\mathbf{X}$.

The final step is to prove that $\hat{\boldsymbol{\beta}}^*$ in (16-82) is exactly the same as $\hat{\boldsymbol{\beta}}$ in (16-83). Although there may have been no great advantage in the geometric method so far, in this last step it will be far simpler than the algebraic alternative.

The geometric proof is simple: $\hat{\boldsymbol{\beta}}^*$ is the relative length of $\hat{\mathbf{y}}^a$ along $\mathbf{X}^a$, which is easily confirmed to be EH/EF; at the same time we have already concluded that $\hat{\boldsymbol{\beta}}$ is OG/OF. Are these two ratios equal? The answer is yes, because GH is parallel to OE in the triangle OEF.

Now consider the algebraic proof. First note that the residual from regression (16-83) is

$$\mathbf{y} - \mathbf{X}\hat{\boldsymbol{\beta}} - \mathbf{D}\hat{\boldsymbol{\gamma}} \tag{16-84}$$

But a residual is always orthogonal to all its regressors—in particular, (16-84) must be orthogonal to the regressor subspace $\mathbf{X}$, and also to the subspace $\mathbf{D}$; that is,

$$\mathbf{X}'(\mathbf{y} - \mathbf{X}\hat{\boldsymbol{\beta}} - \mathbf{D}\hat{\boldsymbol{\gamma}}) = 0 \tag{16-85}$$

$$\mathbf{D}'(\mathbf{y} - \mathbf{X}\hat{\boldsymbol{\beta}} - \mathbf{D}\hat{\boldsymbol{\gamma}}) = 0 \tag{16-86}$$

Similarly, from regression (16-82), and the orthogonality of its residual to the regressor $\mathbf{X}^a$, it follows that

$$\mathbf{X}^{a'}(\mathbf{y}^a - \mathbf{X}^a\hat{\boldsymbol{\beta}}^*) = \mathbf{0} \tag{16-87}$$

This may be rewritten using (16-81) and (16-79) as

$$(\mathbf{X}'\mathbf{A}')(\mathbf{A}\mathbf{y} - \mathbf{A}\mathbf{X}\hat{\boldsymbol{\beta}}^*) = \mathbf{0} \tag{16-88}$$

To prove that $\hat{\boldsymbol\beta}^* = \hat{\boldsymbol\beta}$, we must show that $\hat{\boldsymbol\beta}$ will also satisfy equation (16-88)[20]; in other words our problem is to prove

$$(\mathbf{X}'\mathbf{A}')(\mathbf{A}\mathbf{y} - \mathbf{A}\mathbf{X}\hat{\boldsymbol\beta}) \overset{?}{=} \mathbf{0} \tag{16-89}$$

Since[21] $\mathbf{AD} = \mathbf{0}$, the left side of (16-89) may be written

$$\text{L.S.} = \mathbf{X}'\mathbf{A}'(\mathbf{A}\mathbf{y} - \mathbf{A}\mathbf{X}\hat{\boldsymbol\beta} - \mathbf{A}\mathbf{D}\hat{\boldsymbol\gamma}) \tag{16-90}$$

Now it can be verified that $\mathbf{A}$ is symmetric[22] and idempotent.[23] Using these properties, (16-90) can be rewritten

$$\text{L.S.} = \mathbf{X}'\mathbf{A}'(\mathbf{y} - \mathbf{X}\hat{\boldsymbol\beta} - \mathbf{D}\hat{\boldsymbol\gamma}) \tag{16-91}$$

Substituting for $\mathbf{A}' = \mathbf{A}$ from (16-80):

$$\text{L.S.} = \underbrace{\mathbf{X}'\mathbf{I}(\mathbf{y} - \mathbf{X}\hat{\boldsymbol\beta} - \mathbf{D}\hat{\boldsymbol\gamma})}_{=\,\mathbf{0},\ \text{from (16-85)}} - \mathbf{X}'\mathbf{D}(\mathbf{D}'\mathbf{D})^{-1}\underbrace{\mathbf{D}'(\mathbf{y} - \mathbf{X}\hat{\boldsymbol\beta} - \mathbf{D}\hat{\boldsymbol\gamma})}_{=\,\mathbf{0},\ \text{from (16-86)}} \tag{16-92}$$

$$= \mathbf{0} = \text{R.S. of (16-89)}$$

Thus $\hat{\boldsymbol\beta}$ does after all satisfy (16-89) and, comparing this with (16-88), establishes that

$$\hat{\boldsymbol\beta} = \hat{\boldsymbol\beta}^* \tag{16-93}$$

Just as this establishes (16-74) we can also prove (in problem 16-12) the other three theorems (1)-(3) on p. 448 In each case, the geometric proof follows from Fig. 16-1, and is considerably easier than the corresponding algebraic proof.

PROBLEMS

16-11 Suppose $\mathbf{X}$ is completely explained by $\mathbf{D}$.

- (a) What is this situation called?
- (b) Is it possible to estimate $\boldsymbol\beta$ in (16-73) using either of the alternative methods in Section 16-8? Explain.

16-12 Prove the three theorems on page 448 geometrically, using Figure 16-1.

---

[20] Equation (16-88) has a *unique* solution for $\hat{\boldsymbol\beta}^*$, because its coefficient matrix $\mathbf{X}'\mathbf{A}'\mathbf{A}\mathbf{X}$ is of full rank (since $\mathbf{X}$ is assumed to be of full rank).

[21] From (16-80): $\mathbf{AD} = [\mathbf{I} - \mathbf{D}(\mathbf{D}'\mathbf{D})^{-1}\mathbf{D}']\mathbf{D} = \mathbf{D} - \mathbf{D} = \mathbf{0}$.

[22] This follows because both $\mathbf{I}$ and $\mathbf{D}(\mathbf{D}'\mathbf{D})^{-1}\mathbf{D}'$ are symmetric.

[23] Idempotent means that $\mathbf{AA} = \mathbf{A}$. This is easy to verify from the definition (16-80). In view of the symmetry of $\mathbf{A}$, it then follows that $\mathbf{A}'\mathbf{A} = \mathbf{A}'$, from which (16-91) follows.

17

INSTRUMENTAL VARIABLES (IV) (A Generalization of Chapter 7)

*17-1 REVIEW OF OLS GEOMETRY

In Figure 14-19 we showed how a least squares fit corresponded geometrically to a perpendicular projection. In order to simplify this review, we now consider the regression of $\mathbf{y}$ on just one regressor $\mathbf{x}$, according to the model

$$y_t = \beta x_t + e_t, \qquad (t = 1, 2, \ldots, n) \tag{17-1}$$

that is,

$$\mathbf{y} = \beta\mathbf{x} + \mathbf{e} \tag{17-2}$$

where the e_t are independent and identically distributed with zero mean and variance σ^2. We regard $\mathbf{x}$ as fixed, or else independent of $\mathbf{e}$, so that when we look at the conditional distribution of $\mathbf{e}$, for a given $\mathbf{x}$,

$$E(\mathbf{x} \cdot \mathbf{e}) = 0 \tag{17-3}$$

The expected value of $\mathbf{y}$ is $\beta\mathbf{x}$, shown in Figure 17-1 as a multiple of the vector $\mathbf{x}$ ($\beta = \frac{2}{3}$). The possible errors $\mathbf{e}$ are delimited by the sphere of concentration, centered at the origin [since $E(\mathbf{e}) = \mathbf{0}$]. A typical error vector $\mathbf{e}$ is shown. Its correlation with $\mathbf{x}$, which is $\cos\theta$, happens to be positive. But other errors such as $\mathbf{e}^*$ would have a negative correlation with $\mathbf{x}$, so that if we averaged over all possible errors, the correlation of $\mathbf{x}$ and $\mathbf{e}$ would be zero, as stated in (17-3).

The typical observed $\mathbf{y}$ is given algebraically by (17-2); geometrically, we add $\mathbf{e}$ to $\beta\mathbf{x}$ to obtain $\mathbf{y}$ in Figure 17-1. Now OLS is the technique that $\perp$ projects $\mathbf{y}$ onto $\mathbf{x}$ at $\hat{\beta}\mathbf{x}$. Although this happens to slightly overestimate the target $\beta\mathbf{x}$, this procedure is just as likely to underestimate; on the average, $\hat{\beta}\mathbf{x}$ exactly equals $\beta\mathbf{x}$, that is, $\hat{\beta}$ is an unbiased estimator of β.

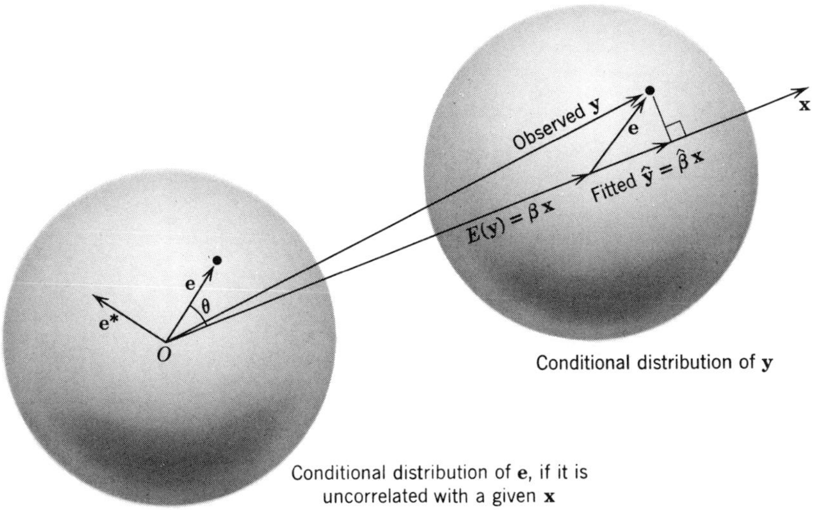

FIGURE 17-1 OLS gives an unbiased, consistent estimator when **x** and **e** are uncorrelated.

*17-2 GEOMETRY OF INSTRUMENTAL VARIABLES (IV)

We next consider the model

$$\mathbf{y} = \beta \mathbf{x} + \mathbf{e} \tag{17-4}$$

where the error vector is different; now **e** is correlated with **x**. As shown in Figure 17-2, for a given **x** the distribution of **e** will tend to be in the same direction as **x**. The conditional $E(\mathbf{e})$, at the center of the sphere of concentration of **e**, will be no longer **0**.

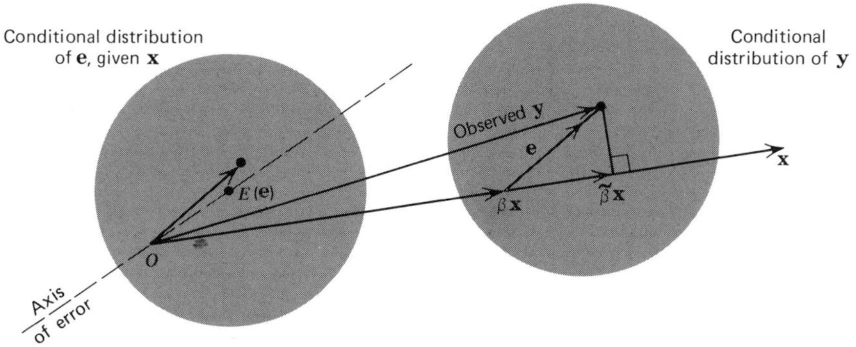

FIGURE 17-2 OLS gives a biased and inconsistent estimator when **x** and **e** are correlated.

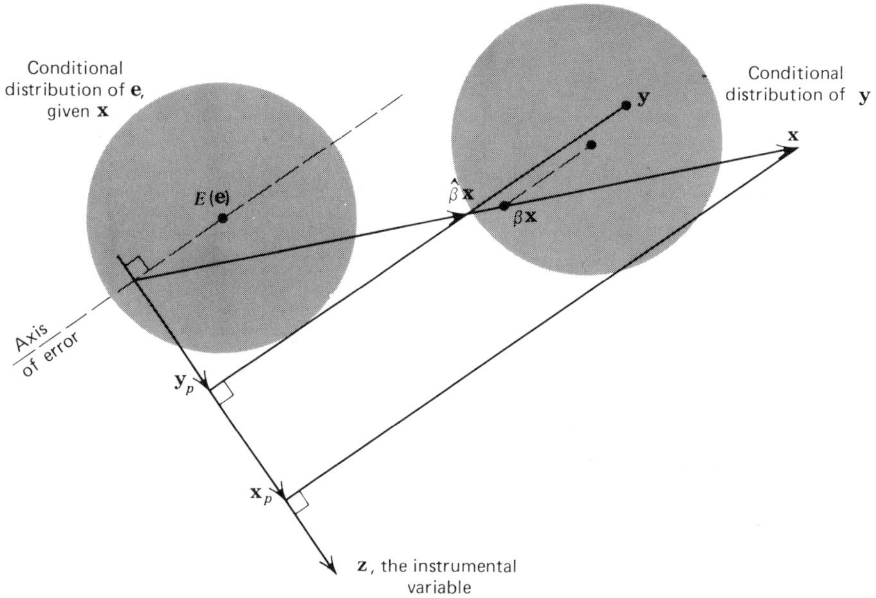

FIGURE 17-3 Instrumental variable gives a consistent estimator when **e** and **x** are correlated.

The OLS or ⊥ projection of **y** onto **x** yields an estimate $\tilde{\beta}$**x**, which happens to be too large. Furthermore, most of these estimates will be too large, because of the eccentric disposition of the errors (which is due, in turn, to the correlation of **e** with **x**). Thus $\tilde{\beta}$ is a biased, inconsistent estimator.

A consistent estimator $\hat{\beta}$ could be obtained if we projected **y** onto **x**, not in a ⊥ direction, but instead *in the direction of the broken line joining O and* $E(\mathbf{e})$, which we shall refer to as the direction of the error or the *axis of the error*. Then our estimates would be distributed evenly above and below the target, making the estimator consistent. In Figure 17-3 we will see that application of an instrument gives us just exactly this skewed projection.

But first we review the algebraic conditions of an instrumental variable **z** as given in equations (7-15) and (7-16). Their geometric equivalents as shown in Figure 17-3, are roughly:

1. **z** and **e** are perpendicular, in an infinite sample, and on average.[1]
2. **z** and **x** are not perpendicular, in an infinite sample, and on average.

[1] To illustrate the geometry easily, we have imposed this stronger condition; requiring **z** and **e** to be perpendicular *on average* is slightly stronger than the condition of (7-15). It means that, over all the possible samples shown as the ellipse of concentation in Figure 17-3, **z** and **e** are perpendicular on average. Thus, an individual error **e** may not be ⊥ to **z**, that is, the enclosed angle does not have $\cos\theta = 0$; however, the distribution of **e** on both sides of its axis makes $\cos\theta$ sometimes positive, and sometimes negative, so that on average $\cos\theta = 0$.

We now examine the estimate that results when $\mathbf{y}$ is $\perp$ projected onto such an instrument, that is, when $\mathbf{y}$ is correctly projected in the direction of the error, to the point $\hat{\beta}\mathbf{x}$ on $\mathbf{x}$, and to the point $\mathbf{y}_p$ on $\mathbf{z}$ itself. (Also, $\mathbf{x}$ is projected to $\mathbf{x}_p$ on $\mathbf{z}$.)

The consistent estimate $\hat{\beta}$ is given, according to (14-12b), by

$$|\hat{\beta}| = \frac{\|\hat{\beta}\mathbf{x}\|}{\|\mathbf{x}\|} \tag{17-5}$$

Because of similarity of triangles, it is equally well given by

$$|\hat{\beta}| = \frac{\|\mathbf{y}_p\|}{\|\mathbf{x}_p\|} \tag{17-6}$$

from (14-26)

$$= \frac{|\mathbf{z} \cdot \mathbf{y}|/\|\mathbf{z}\|}{|\mathbf{z} \cdot \mathbf{x}|/\|\mathbf{z}\|}$$

$$= \frac{|\mathbf{z} \cdot \mathbf{y}|}{|\mathbf{z} \cdot \mathbf{x}|} \tag{17-7}$$

It is easily confirmed that $\hat{\beta}$ will be given correctly, in sign as well as magnitude, by

$$\boxed{\hat{\beta} = \frac{\mathbf{z} \cdot \mathbf{y}}{\mathbf{z} \cdot \mathbf{x}}} \tag{17-8}$$

But this is just the instrumental variable estimate in (7-18). Thus, the instrumental variable technique is seen to be a projection of $\mathbf{y}$ onto $\mathbf{x}$ in the direction of the error.

17-3 ALGEBRAIC GENERALIZATION

Now consider extending the use of instruments to the general case of k regressors

$$\mathbf{y} = \mathbf{X}\boldsymbol{\beta} + \mathbf{e} \tag{17-9}$$

(12-9) repeated

where $\mathbf{X}$ is the full matrix of n observations, $\mathbf{X} = [\mathbf{x}_1, \mathbf{x}_2, \ldots, \mathbf{x}_k]$. Now estimation of the k parameters[2] in $\boldsymbol{\beta}$ requires k instruments, say $\mathbf{z}_1, \mathbf{z}_2, \ldots, \mathbf{z}_k$. Let the n observations on these instruments be marshalled

[2] Hereafter, whenever instruments are used, we will express all variables in deviation form. Thus, there is no intercept term, and all k regressors are variables. In any case, there is no problem in estimating the intercept at the end.

into the matrix **Z**, which we note has the same dimension as **X**. We now show that, to provide consistent estimates of $\boldsymbol{\beta}$, it is sufficient that the set of instrumental variables **Z** satisfy the following two conditions, which generalize (7-15) and (7-16):

1. z_i and e are uncorrelated, or more precisely, $s_{z_i e} \xrightarrow{p} 0$ (17-10)

   that is,

$$\frac{1}{n}\mathbf{z}_i'\mathbf{e} \xrightarrow{p} 0 \qquad \text{for} \qquad i = 1, 2, \ldots, k$$

   that is,

$$\boxed{\frac{1}{n}\mathbf{Z}'\mathbf{e} \xrightarrow{p} \mathbf{0}} \tag{17-11}$$

2. z_i and the x's are correlated, or more precisely

$$\boxed{\frac{1}{n}\mathbf{Z}'\mathbf{X} \xrightarrow{p} \text{a nonsingular limit } \Sigma} \tag{17-12}$$

   This condition implies that the **x** variables must be linearly independent, and the **z** variables also.

To obtain consistent estimators of $\boldsymbol{\beta}$ we apply all k instruments to (17-9), obtaining

$$\frac{1}{n}\mathbf{Z}'\mathbf{y} = \frac{1}{n}\mathbf{Z}'\mathbf{X}\boldsymbol{\beta} + \frac{1}{n}\mathbf{Z}'\mathbf{e} \tag{17-13}$$

Because of (17-11), as n increases

$$\frac{1}{n}\mathbf{Z}'\mathbf{y} \xrightarrow{p} \left(\frac{1}{n}\mathbf{Z}'\mathbf{X}\right)\boldsymbol{\beta} \tag{17-14}$$

Because of the invertibility specified in (17-12), we may solve (17-14):

$$\left(\frac{1}{n}\mathbf{Z}'\mathbf{X}\right)^{-1}\left(\frac{1}{n}\mathbf{Z}'\mathbf{y}\right) \xrightarrow{p} \boldsymbol{\beta} \tag{17-15}$$

Noting that the two occurrences of n cancel, the estimator is

$$\hat{\boldsymbol{\beta}} = (\mathbf{Z}'\mathbf{X})^{-1}(\mathbf{Z}'\mathbf{y}) \xrightarrow{p} \boldsymbol{\beta} \tag{17-16}$$

that is, $\hat{\boldsymbol{\beta}}$ is consistent.

If **X** is asymptotically uncorrelated with **e** (condition 1) and not multicollinear (condition 2), **X** qualifies as the instrument set **Z**. Substituting into (17-16) yields the consistent estimator

$$\hat{\boldsymbol{\beta}} = (\mathbf{X}'\mathbf{X})^{-1}(\mathbf{X}'\mathbf{y}) \tag{17-17}$$

which is, of course, the OLS estimator in (12-19).

Finally, now that this procedure is justified, we notice that by multiplying by n, our original covariance estimating equations (17-13) can be written in the simpler form

$$\mathbf{Z}'\mathbf{y} = \mathbf{Z}'\mathbf{X}\boldsymbol{\beta} + \mathbf{Z}'\mathbf{e} \tag{17-18}$$

17-4 NOTATION

In Table 17-1, we review the different notations for instrumental variables used in Chapters 7 and 17. One central idea stands out. Whether we call it "taking covariances," "taking dot product," etc., we are doing the same calculation and obtaining exactly the same estimator in each case.

TABLE 17-1 A Summary of Instrumental Variable Estimation

Section	*"Application" of the Instrument to the Model Equation (7-1) or Its Generalization Means:*	*Which in turn Yields the Estimator:*
Chapter 7 (simple algebra)	Taking covariances with Z, $s_{ZY} = \beta s_{ZX} + s_{Ze}$ (7-17)	$\hat{\beta} = \dfrac{s_{ZY}}{s_{ZX}}$ (7-18)
Chapter 17-2	Taking dot product with $\mathbf{z}$, $\mathbf{z} \cdot \mathbf{y} = \beta \mathbf{z} \cdot \mathbf{x} + \mathbf{z} \cdot \mathbf{e}$	$\hat{\beta} = \dfrac{\mathbf{z} \cdot \mathbf{y}}{\mathbf{z} \cdot \mathbf{x}}$ (17-8)
Chapter 17-3	Premultiplying by $\mathbf{z}'$, to estimate one parameter β $\mathbf{z}'\mathbf{y} = \beta \mathbf{z}'\mathbf{x} + \mathbf{z}'\mathbf{e}$	$\hat{\beta} = \dfrac{\mathbf{z}'\mathbf{y}}{\mathbf{z}'\mathbf{x}}$
	Premultiplying by $\mathbf{Z}'$, to estimate k parameters $\boldsymbol{\beta}$ $\mathbf{Z}'\mathbf{y} = \mathbf{Z}'\mathbf{X}\boldsymbol{\beta} + \mathbf{Z}'\mathbf{e}$ (17-18)	$\hat{\boldsymbol{\beta}} = (\mathbf{Z}'\mathbf{X})^{-1}(\mathbf{Z}'\mathbf{y})$ (17-16)

PROBLEMS

17-1 (a) What does the geometry of Figure 17-1 look like when the e_t are serially correlated, although e_t and x_t are still uncorrelated?

(b) Is the OLS estimate still unbiased?

*(c) What is wrong with the OLS confidence interval?

18

IDENTIFICATION (A Generalization of Chapter 8)

This chapter will consider what form the mathematical model (i.e., the system of equations) must take in order to identify the parameters of an equation. Before beginning it must be recognized, as in Section 8-2, that prior knowledge of the relative variance of the error terms—or more generally, prior knowledge of the covariance matrix of the error terms—can help identify an equation. While readers are referred to extensive analysis of this elsewhere,[1] it is not analyzed here. Instead, we limit ourselves to a discussion of the conditions for identification in the absence of prior information on covariance structure, where the only prior knowledge is that certain parameters are zero (i.e., certain terms in the equation are missing).

We begin by comparing the structural and reduced forms of the model.

18-1 STRUCTURAL AND REDUCED FORMS

(a) The Structural Form

This is diagrammed in Figure 18-1; it consists of a system of linear equations relating Q current endogenous variables $\mathbf{y}$ to the errors $\mathbf{e}$ and M predetermined variables[2] $\mathbf{x}$. These latter must be defined broadly to include both exogenous variables with values determined outside the system, *and* lagged endogenous variables, whose values are, of course, also predetermined. (In the rest of this book, we will often loosely use the term

[1] See, for example, Fisher 1966(a).

[2] The constant term is accounted for by a dummy exogenous variable that always takes on the value 1, or else the constant term may be ignored. Either convention is satisfactory for this chapter, if followed consistently. That is, if the constant term is kept in, then there will also be associated with it the dummy exogenous variable, as the instrument to "just take care of" estimating the constant term.

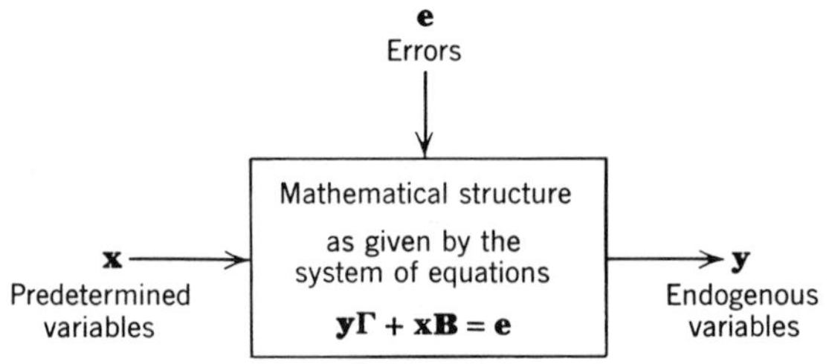

FIGURE 18-1 A schematic view of an econometric model

exogenous variables when we mean more accurately predetermined variables.) Thus, our model is

$$\boxed{\mathbf{y}\boldsymbol{\Gamma} + \mathbf{x}\mathbf{B} = \mathbf{e} \qquad \text{Structural form}} \tag{18-1}$$

$$\underbrace{\boxed{\mathbf{y}}}_{Q}\ \boxed{\boldsymbol{\Gamma}} + \underbrace{\boxed{\mathbf{x}}}_{M}\ \boxed{\mathbf{B}} = \boxed{\mathbf{e}}$$

Mathematical completeness requires that there be as many linearly independent equations as endogenous variables; hence the matrix $\boldsymbol{\Gamma}$ must be square and invertible.

An example will illustrate. In Chapter 8, we considered the following demand and supply equations:

$$\begin{aligned} &\text{Demand} \quad \nu Q = \alpha + \beta P + \eta T + \xi Y + e_1 \\ &\text{Supply} \quad \lambda Q = \gamma + \delta P + \theta R + e_2 \end{aligned} \tag{18-2a}$$

where the exogenous variables T, Y, and R determine the endogenous variables P and Q. The notation of (18-2a) is a little different from that used in (8-19) and (8-20). The errors are denoted e_1 and e_2. The coefficients ν and λ have been introduced to emphasize that an equation can be identified only up to a factor of proportionality; that is, we can only hope to identify the *ratios* α/ν, β/ν, etc. This idea of uniqueness up to a factor of proportionality will persist as far as equation (18-11). Equation (18-2a) in matrix form is

$$\begin{bmatrix} P & Q \end{bmatrix} \begin{bmatrix} -\beta & -\delta \\ \nu & \lambda \end{bmatrix} + \begin{bmatrix} 1 & T & Y & R \end{bmatrix} \begin{bmatrix} -\alpha & -\gamma \\ -\eta & 0 \\ -\xi & 0 \\ 0 & -\theta \end{bmatrix} = \begin{bmatrix} e_1 & e_2 \end{bmatrix} \tag{18-2b}$$

The specification of this model involves setting three elements in **B** equal to zero *a priori.*

(b) The Reduced Form

This is the explicit solution of the structural form (18-1) for **y**. Since $\mathbf{\Gamma}$ is invertible, this solution is obtained by postmultiplying (18-1) by $\mathbf{\Gamma}^{-1}$:

$$\mathbf{y} = -\mathbf{x}\mathbf{B}\mathbf{\Gamma}^{-1} + \mathbf{e}\mathbf{\Gamma}^{-1}$$

This is written simply as:

$$\boxed{\mathbf{y} = \mathbf{x}\mathbf{\Pi} + \mathbf{v} \qquad \text{Reduced form}} \tag{18-3}$$

in which

$$\mathbf{v} = \mathbf{e}\mathbf{\Gamma}^{-1}$$

and

$$\mathbf{\Pi} = -\mathbf{B}\mathbf{\Gamma}^{-1} \tag{18-4a}$$

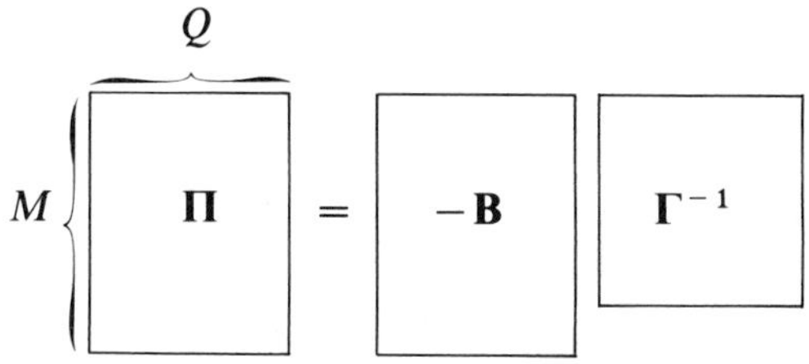

Postmultiplying (18-4a) by $-\mathbf{\Gamma}$, the relation may be written

$$-\mathbf{\Pi}\mathbf{\Gamma} = \mathbf{B} \tag{18-4b}$$

18-2 IDENTIFICATION—NECESSARY AND SUFFICIENT CONDITIONS

(a) Introduction

Consider the identification problem as stated in Section 8-6. We supposed that we know how the endogenous variables are related to the predetermined variables, that is, the reduced form (18-3). (In assuming the true reduced form is known, we emphasize that identification precedes statistical problems.) Without prior restrictions, that is, without adequate specification, there would be many possible corresponding structures (18-1); accordingly, (18-1) is said to be unidentified.

To illustrate, we ask: Can we translate the known reduced form coefficients back into a unique set of structural coefficients? In other words, can we plug the $\mathbf{\Pi}$ matrix of coefficients into the left-hand side of (18-4a) and then solve for the coefficients in **B** and $\mathbf{\Gamma}$? The mechanics of answering this are obviously somewhat complicated, but intuitively it may be immediately seen that if none of the elements of **B** and **Γ** have *a priori* been restricted to zero, the information in **Π** (i.e., MQ coefficients) will not be sufficient to allow us to solve for all the coefficients in **B** and **Γ** (note that MQ coefficients would have to be solved for in **B** alone). Thus **B** and **Γ** are unidentified.[3] But as we prespecify more and more of the coefficients in **B** and **Γ**, we have fewer and fewer to solve for. Thus eventually the information in **Π** will become sufficient to determine this shrinking numbers of unknowns; at this point **B** and **Γ** become exactly identified.[4] Finally, if even more coefficients in **B** and **Γ** are prespecified (as, for example, our prior theory and knowledge of these economic relations might dictate), then the estimate $\hat{\mathbf{\Pi}}$ would provide more than enough information. Some elements of $\hat{\mathbf{\Pi}}$ could be discarded, and still yield an estimate of **B** and **Γ**; or, different elements of $\hat{\mathbf{\Pi}}$ could be discarded,

---

[3] Here is another view: If **B** and **Γ** are not restricted, then both the true structure *and* various bogus structures will correspond to the true reduced form. To prove this, suppose the true structure is

$$\mathbf{y\Gamma}_0 + \mathbf{xB}_0 = \mathbf{e} \qquad (18\text{-}5a)$$

According to (18-4a), its reduced form is

$$\mathbf{\Pi}_0 = -\mathbf{B}_0\mathbf{\Gamma}_0^{-1} \qquad (18\text{-}5b)$$

Now a bogus system of structural equations can easily be constructed by postmultiplying the true structure (18-5*a*) by any invertible matrix **M**, as follows:

$$\mathbf{y}(\mathbf{\Gamma}_0\mathbf{M}) + \mathbf{x}(\mathbf{B}_0\mathbf{M}) = \mathbf{eM} \qquad (18\text{-}5c)$$

Even though this structure is a bogus one, we can show that it will still have the same reduced form (18-5*b*): Again noting (18-4a), its reduced form will be:

$$\begin{aligned}&(-\mathbf{B}_0\mathbf{M})(\mathbf{\Gamma}_0\mathbf{M})^{-1}\\ &= -\mathbf{B}_0\mathbf{M}\mathbf{M}^{-1}\mathbf{\Gamma}_0^{-1}\\ &= -\mathbf{B}_0\mathbf{\Gamma}_0^{-1} = \mathbf{\Pi}_0\end{aligned}$$

Thus $\mathbf{\Pi}_0$ is the reduced form for both the true *and* bogus structures.

There are many bogus structures of the form (18-5*c*), since **M** can be any invertible matrix. We therefore conclude that $\mathbf{\Pi}_0$ corresponds to the true structure (18-5*a*) *and* to a whole set of bogus structures (18-5*c*). Even if we know the true $\mathbf{\Pi}_0$, there are many structures that correspond; and there is no way of sorting out the true one from the bogus ones.

Another way of stating this problem is that the true and bogus structures are observationally equivalent in the sense that they will give rise to the same pattern of *y*'s (as earlier illustrated in Figure 8-1*a* where the true and bogus supply/demand systems generated the same population ellipse of *y*'s); or more precisely, they will yield an identical likelihood function for the *y*'s.

[4] Following the argument of the previous footnote, we note that the process of specifying zeros in the structure involves declaring inadmissible some of the bogus structures encountered in the previous case—namely those bogus structures with non-zero elements where we now specify zeros. Exact identification means that this process of restricting the admissible structures (by imposing zeros) has continued to the point there is now only one remaining structure that corresponds to the reduced form, and that must be the true structure.

yielding a different estimate of $\mathbf{B}$ and $\boldsymbol{\Gamma}$. In the face of this excess of information, $\mathbf{B}$ and $\boldsymbol{\Gamma}$ are said to be overidentified.

Clearly, the issue is far more complicated than this brief overview suggests[5]; for example, certain structural equations (i.e., columns of $\mathbf{B}$ and $\boldsymbol{\Gamma}$) may be identified, while others may not. Thus it is necessary to answer the identification problem one equation at a time. In conclusion, then,

Definition

An equation of the structure (18-1) is identified if there are unique (up to a factor of proportionality) values of its parameters corresponding to a given reduced form (and satisfying the prior restrictions, of course).	(18-6)

The discussion so far has been intuitive, to provide a feel for the identification problem: Can we translate knowledge of $\boldsymbol{\Pi}$ back into knowledge of $\mathbf{B}$ and $\boldsymbol{\Gamma}$? It is now time for a more precise, and hence more complicated, treatment of the problem.

(b) Condition on the Reduced Form

Without loss of generality, we can suppose that it is the first equation we wish to identify. We thus concentrate on the first column of $\boldsymbol{\Gamma}$ and $\mathbf{B}$ in (18-1). Furthermore, we order the variables so that the zero coefficients in the first column of $\boldsymbol{\Gamma}$ and $\mathbf{B}$ appear first; thus the structure is

$$\mathbf{y}\boldsymbol{\Gamma} + \mathbf{x}\mathbf{B} = \mathbf{e} \tag{18-7}$$

$$\overbrace{[\quad \mathbf{y} \quad]}^{Q}\ \begin{matrix} q_0 \\ q \end{matrix}\Bigg\{\overbrace{\begin{bmatrix} \mathbf{0} & \boldsymbol{\Gamma}_0 \\ \boldsymbol{\gamma} & \end{bmatrix}}^{Q}\Bigg\} Q + \overbrace{[\quad \mathbf{x} \quad]}^{M}\ \begin{matrix} m_0 \\ m \end{matrix}\Bigg\{\overbrace{\begin{bmatrix} \mathbf{0} & \mathbf{B}_0 \\ \boldsymbol{\beta} & \end{bmatrix}}^{Q}\Bigg\} M = \overbrace{[\quad \mathbf{e} \quad]}^{Q}$$

m_0 is the number of predetermined variables excluded from the first equation, while q is the number of endogenous variables included.[6] We will soon see the important way in which they are related.

---

[5] We emphasize that this is purely an intuitive view of identification, and is not meant to imply that an econometrician should prespecify coefficients in her model with the sole objective of identifying her equations. Instead she must formulate her model on the grounds of good economic theory, and this formulation will give her a certain number of zeros. She then has to ask, "Will this given pattern of zeros allow me to identify the equations?"

In practice, in large economic models many exogenous variables appear in some equations but not in others; since this in turn implies a large number of prespecified zeros, overidentification is what frequently occurs.

[6] Other terms in (18-7) are defined in a straightforward way. Thus, $\mathbf{0}$ is an appropriately dimensioned zero vector, $\boldsymbol{\gamma}$ is the set of q nonzero coefficients in the first column of $\boldsymbol{\Gamma}$, etc.

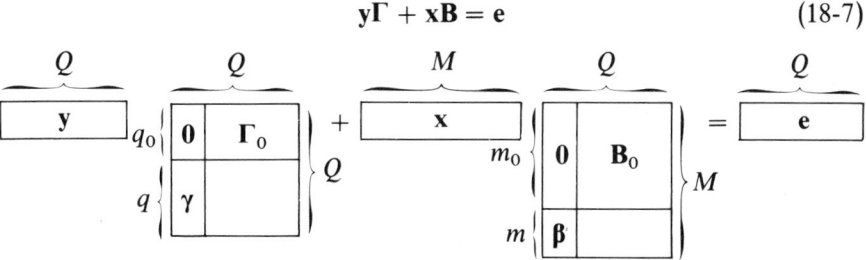

The form of $\boldsymbol{\Gamma}$ and $\mathbf{B}$ as given in (18-7) is now substituted into (18-4b):

$$-\boldsymbol{\Pi}\boldsymbol{\Gamma} = \mathbf{B} \tag{18-8}$$

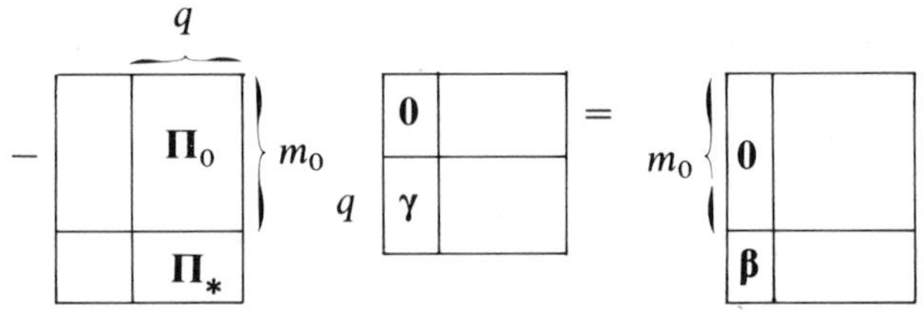

When the first column on the left side is equated to the first column on the right side, we obtain[7] the two matrix equations:

$$-\boldsymbol{\Pi}_0 \boldsymbol{\gamma} = \mathbf{0} \tag{18-9}$$

$$-\boldsymbol{\Pi}_* \boldsymbol{\gamma} = \boldsymbol{\beta} \tag{18-10}$$

For a given reduced form $\boldsymbol{\Pi}$, under what conditions will these equations yield a unique (up to a factor of proportionality) solution for $\boldsymbol{\gamma}$ and $\boldsymbol{\beta}$? Answering first the question for $\boldsymbol{\gamma}$, we note that (18-9) is a homogeneous system of equations in q unknowns. The theory of linear equations tells[8] us that the necessary and sufficient condition for a unique solution is:

$$\text{Rank } \boldsymbol{\Pi}_0 = q - 1 \tag{18-11}$$

(necessary and sufficient condition for identifying the first equation)

Of course, once $\boldsymbol{\gamma}$ is uniquely determined, then $\boldsymbol{\beta}$ is uniquely determined according to (18-10), and the first equation is identified.

(c) Condition on the Structural Form

It is more useful to reexpress condition (18-11) in terms of the structural form. Looking back to (18-7) we see that $\boldsymbol{\Gamma}_0$ and $\mathbf{B}_0$ are the coefficient matrices for the variables omitted from the first equation, and for all equations except the first.

We will show that when these two matrices are combined, a necessary and sufficient condition for the identification of the first equation is

---

[7] Because of the zeros in the first column of $\boldsymbol{\Gamma}$, only the last q elements ($\boldsymbol{\gamma}$) come into play.

[8] Outline of the argument:

If $\boldsymbol{\Pi}_0$ were of full rank q, then an invertible $q \times q$ submatrix $\boldsymbol{\Pi}_s$ could be found that would give the absolutely unique solution $\boldsymbol{\gamma} = -\boldsymbol{\Pi}_s^{-1}\mathbf{0} = \mathbf{0}$ for (18-9). But this is no use. Instead, we want to be able to specify one γ (usually $\gamma_1 = 1$ is the specification) and then solve uniquely for the other γ's in terms of it (uniqueness up to a factor of proportionality). This means the rank of $\boldsymbol{\Pi}_0$ must be $q - 1$.

$$\text{Rank}\begin{bmatrix}\boldsymbol{\Gamma}_0\\ \mathbf{B}_0\end{bmatrix} = Q - 1 \tag{18-12}$$

(necessary and sufficient condition for identifying the first equation)

that is, $\begin{bmatrix}\boldsymbol{\Gamma}_0\\ \mathbf{B}_0\end{bmatrix}$ is of full rank.[9]

To prove this, we note that rank will be unchanged if we augment this combined matrix with the corresponding zero coefficients in the first equation. Moreover, rank remains unchanged if the result is postmultiplied by the invertible matrix $\boldsymbol{\Gamma}^{-1}$. Thus, we obtain

$$\begin{matrix} q_0\{ \\ m_0\{ \end{matrix}\left[\begin{array}{c|c} \mathbf{0} & \boldsymbol{\Gamma}_0 \\ \hline \mathbf{0} & \mathbf{B}_0 \end{array}\right]\left[\;\boldsymbol{\Gamma}^{-1}\;\right] \quad \text{which reduces}^{10} \text{ to} \quad \begin{matrix} q_0\{ \\ m_0\{ \end{matrix}\overset{\quad q_0 \qquad q}{\left[\begin{array}{c|c} \mathbf{I} & \mathbf{O} \\ \hline * & -\boldsymbol{\Pi}_0 \end{array}\right]} \tag{18-13}$$

---

[9] It is impossible that rank $\begin{bmatrix}\boldsymbol{\Gamma}_0\\ \mathbf{B}_0\end{bmatrix} > Q - 1$, because this matrix has only $Q - 1$ columns.

[10] The star indicates a submatrix whose form is unimportant in the subsequent argument.

We establish (18-13) in two parts—top and bottom. To prove the top part, express $\boldsymbol{\Gamma}$ as in (18-7), and write

$$\boldsymbol{\Gamma}\boldsymbol{\Gamma}^{-1} = \mathbf{I}$$

$$q_0\{\left[\begin{array}{c|c} \mathbf{0} & \boldsymbol{\Gamma}_0 \\ \hline & \end{array}\right]\left[\;\boldsymbol{\Gamma}^{-1}\;\right] = q_0\{\overset{\quad q_0 \qquad q}{\left[\begin{array}{c|c} \mathbf{I} & \mathbf{O} \\ \hline & \end{array}\right]} \tag{18-14}$$

The shaded top part of (18-14) is exactly the top part of (18-13).

To prove the bottom part of (18-13), express $\mathbf{B}$ as in (18-7) and $\boldsymbol{\Pi}$ as in (18-8), and write (18-4*a*):

$$\mathbf{B}\boldsymbol{\Gamma}^{-1} = -\boldsymbol{\Pi}$$

$$m_0\{\left[\begin{array}{c|c} \mathbf{0} & \mathbf{B}_0 \\ \hline & \end{array}\right]\left[\;\boldsymbol{\Gamma}^{-1}\;\right] = -\left[\begin{array}{c|c} * & \boldsymbol{\Pi}_0 \\ \hline & \end{array}\right] \tag{18-15}$$

The shaded top part of (18-15) is exactly the bottom part of (18-13), and the proof is complete.

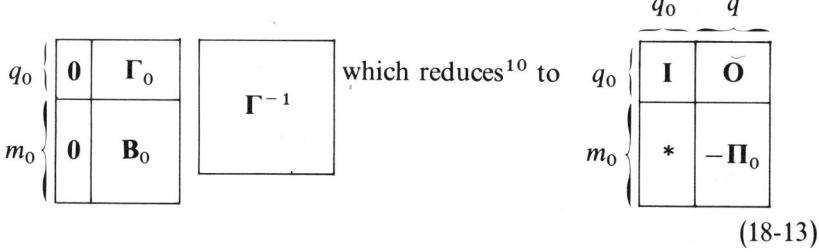

Because the rank of $\mathbf{I}$ is obviously q_0, the rank of the right-hand matrix in (18-13) is $q_0 + \text{rank}\ \mathbf{\Pi}_0$. Therefore,

$$\text{Rank} \begin{bmatrix} \mathbf{\Gamma}_0 \\ \mathbf{B}_0 \end{bmatrix} = q_0 + \text{rank}\ \mathbf{\Pi}_0 \tag{18-16}$$

We finally substitute the condition (18-11) for identifiability:

$$\text{Rank} \begin{bmatrix} \mathbf{\Gamma}_0 \\ \mathbf{B}_0 \end{bmatrix} = q_0 + (q - 1)$$

$$= Q - 1 \tag{18-17}$$

and (18-12) is proved.

We next prove the order condition required for identification, first given in Section 8-4:

$$m_0 \geq q - 1$$

(the order condition necessary for identifying the first equation)

(18-18)
(8-12) repeated

To prove this, we go back to (18-11) to see that identification requires

$$\text{Rank}\ \mathbf{\Pi}_0 = q - 1 \tag{18-19}$$

(18-11) repeated

But the rank of a matrix cannot exceed the number of its rows; thus,

$$\text{Rank}\ \mathbf{\Pi}_0 \leq m_0 \tag{18-20}$$

Combining these last two equations, we see that identification requires

$$q - 1 \leq m_0 \qquad \text{(18-18) proved}$$

(d) Interpretation

We can use the rank condition (18-12) to investigate when the first equation is not identified. This occurs if

$$\text{Rank} \begin{bmatrix} \mathbf{\Gamma}_0 \\ \mathbf{B}_0 \end{bmatrix} < Q - 1 \tag{18-21}$$

In practice, there are several ways this can occur:

1. When $\begin{bmatrix} \mathbf{\Gamma}_0 \\ \mathbf{B}_0 \end{bmatrix}$ has too few rows; that is,

$$m_0 + q_0 < Q - 1$$

that is,

$$m_0 < (Q - q_0) - 1$$

that is,

$$m_0 < q - 1$$

This is merely stating that the order condition (18-18) has been violated—there are too few excluded exogenous variables (instrumental variables) to identify the first equation.

In the other cases to which we now turn, the necessary order condition (18-18) is satisfied, but the sufficient rank condition (18-12) is not.

2. When some specific column of $\begin{bmatrix} \mathbf{\Gamma}_0 \\ \mathbf{B}_0 \end{bmatrix}$ is identically zero.

This means that this specific equation of the system can confuse the first equation; referring to (18-7) for example, if this specific equation is added to the first, a bogus first equation is created that destroys the identity of the first equation.

For example, for our structural model we might take the following extension of the demand-supply system (18-2b); (we indicate nonzero parameters with an * to avoid proliferation of letters):

$$\begin{bmatrix} P & Q & S \end{bmatrix} \begin{bmatrix} * & * & * \\ * & * & 0 \\ 0 & 0 & * \end{bmatrix} + \begin{bmatrix} 1 & T & Y & R & Z \end{bmatrix} \begin{bmatrix} * & * & * \\ * & 0 & 0 \\ * & 0 & * \\ 0 & 0 & * \\ * & 0 & * \end{bmatrix} = \begin{bmatrix} e_1 & e_2 & e_3 \end{bmatrix} \tag{18-22}$$

To investigate the identification of the first equation, we have indicated by dotted lines the matrix

$$\begin{bmatrix} \mathbf{\Gamma}_0 \\ \mathbf{B}_0 \end{bmatrix} = \begin{bmatrix} 0 & * \\ 0 & * \end{bmatrix} \tag{18-23}$$

This matrix has property (2)—a zero column—and hence the first equation is not identified. We see how reasonable this is; if the second equation were added to the first, a bogus first equation would be created. In terms of which variables are specified to be zero, this bogus equation would look like the first equation; only S and R are excluded. If the first equation were to be estimated, there would be no way of knowing whether the resulting fit was an estimate of the first equation, or a bogus combination of the first two equations.

3. When the columns of $\begin{bmatrix} \mathbf{\Gamma}_0 \\ \mathbf{B}_0 \end{bmatrix}$ are linearly dependent in some more subtle way, making the rank $< Q - 1$. We illustrate with an example:

$$\begin{bmatrix} y_1 & y_2 & y_3 & y_4 \end{bmatrix} \begin{bmatrix} * & * & 0 & 0 \\ * & * & 0 & * \\ * & 0 & * & * \\ 0 & 0 & * & 0 \end{bmatrix} + \begin{bmatrix} x_1 & x_2 & x_3 \end{bmatrix} \begin{bmatrix} 0 & * & 0 & * \\ 0 & 0 & * & 0 \\ * & * & * & * \end{bmatrix} = \begin{bmatrix} e_1 & e_2 & e_3 & e_4 \end{bmatrix} \tag{18-24}$$

To investigate the identifiability of the first equation, we have indicated by dotted lines the matrix

$$\begin{bmatrix} \mathbf{\Gamma}_0 \\ \mathbf{B}_0 \end{bmatrix} = \begin{bmatrix} 0 & * & 0 \\ * & 0 & * \\ 0 & * & 0 \end{bmatrix} \tag{18-25}$$

which has linearly dependent columns,[11] so that

$$\text{Rank} \begin{bmatrix} \mathbf{\Gamma}_0 \\ \mathbf{B}_0 \end{bmatrix} < 3$$
$$< Q - 1$$

which violates (18-12).

This result is also reasonable. When the three columns (c_1, c_2, c_3) of (18-25) are linearly dependent, this means that some linear combination of the columns,

$$k_1 c_1 + k_2 c_2 + k_3 c_3 = 0$$
$$\text{for some } k_i \neq 0$$

Then if the same linear combination of the last three equations is added to the first equation, a bogus first equation would result, just as before.

---

[11] *Proof.* If we denote the columns by c_1, c_2, and c_3, we see that

$$c_1 = kc_3$$
$$\text{i.e.,} \quad c_1 + 0c_2 - kc_3 = 0$$

(e) A Final Subtlety

The rank requirement (18-12) depends on the matrix $\begin{bmatrix}\mathbf{\Gamma}_0\\ \mathbf{B}_0\end{bmatrix}$, some of whose elements (parameters) are known to be zero. The remaining elements are not known (in fact, their estimation is precisely the task of the econometrician). For example, we may have, in estimating the third equation of (18-24),

$$\begin{bmatrix}\mathbf{\Gamma}_0\\ \mathbf{B}_0\end{bmatrix} = \begin{array}{|ccc|}\hline \gamma_{11} & \gamma_{12} & 0\\ \gamma_{21} & \gamma_{22} & \gamma_{24}\\ 0 & \beta_{12} & \beta_{14}\\ \hline\end{array} \tag{18-26}$$

Although prespecified zeros no longer ensure it, it is still logically possible that the parameters are so related[12] as to make the matrix less than full rank, that is, rank $< Q - 1$. However, we consistently suppose throughout this chapter that no such relation between the parameters is known to exist *a priori*. And for such a relation to hold by coincidence would be practically impossible; it happens "almost nowhere," in mathematical language. The reader can appreciate this by giving the parameters of (18-26) values at random (taking the values out to two or three decimal places), and noting that condition (18-27) fails, that is, the matrix is indeed of full rank.

In conclusion, the cases where rank could "collapse by coincidence" are so rare, that they are ignored in practice.

PROBLEMS

18-1 Find which equations are identified. Of those equations that are identified, classify them as exactly identified or overidentified.

$$\boxed{\quad \mathbf{y} \quad} \begin{array}{|ccc|}\hline 0 & * & *\\ * & * & *\\ * & * & *\\ \hline\end{array} + \boxed{\quad \mathbf{x} \quad} \begin{array}{|ccc|}\hline * & * & *\\ * & 0 & 0\\ * & 0 & 0\\ 0 & * & 0\\ * & * & *\\ * & * & 0\\ \hline\end{array} = \boxed{\quad \mathbf{e} \quad}$$

[12] To be specific, the relation

$$\gamma_{11}\gamma_{22}\beta_{14} - \gamma_{21}\gamma_{12}\beta_{14} - \gamma_{11}\beta_{12}\gamma_{24} = 0 \tag{18-27}$$

makes the determinant zero, hence the rank <3.

18-2 Repeat for

$$
\boxed{\quad \mathbf{y} \quad}
\begin{bmatrix} * & * & * & 0 \\ * & * & 0 & * \\ * & * & * & * \\ * & * & * & * \end{bmatrix}
+
\boxed{\quad \mathbf{x} \quad}
\begin{bmatrix} * & 0 & * & * \\ 0 & 0 & * & 0 \\ 0 & * & 0 & * \\ 0 & 0 & * & 0 \\ * & * & * & 0 \\ * & * & * & * \end{bmatrix}
=
\boxed{\quad \mathbf{e} \quad}
$$

18-3 ESTIMATION REQUIREMENTS: INDEPENDENCE OF VARIABLES

The conditions for identification are strictly algebraic, and apply to the *parameters* in the system. These conditions must be satisfied prior to looking at any statistical information. Statistical estimation of the parameters then requires overcoming another hurdle: In the case of exact identification the *variables* must be linearly independent. To illustrate, consider the following system:

$$
\begin{bmatrix} y_1 & y_2 & y_3 \end{bmatrix}
\begin{bmatrix} 1 & 0 & \gamma_{13} \\ \gamma_{21} & 1 & \gamma_{23} \\ 0 & \gamma_{32} & 1 \end{bmatrix}
+
\begin{bmatrix} x_1 & x_2 \end{bmatrix}
\begin{bmatrix} 0 & \beta_{12} & \beta_{13} \\ \beta_{21} & 0 & \beta_{23} \end{bmatrix}
=
\begin{bmatrix} e_1 & e_2 & e_3 \end{bmatrix}
\tag{18-28}
$$

We have set one coefficient in each equation equal to one, so that we can discuss simple uniqueness, rather than uniqueness up to a factor of proportionality. The first equation is exactly identified; therefore, we may use our instrumental variables x_1 and x_2 on the first equation to obtain estimating equations:

$$
\begin{bmatrix} s_{X_1Y_2} & s_{X_1X_2} \\ s_{X_2Y_2} & s_{X_2X_2} \end{bmatrix}
\begin{bmatrix} \hat{\gamma}_{21} \\ \hat{\beta}_{21} \end{bmatrix}
= -
\begin{bmatrix} s_{X_1Y_1} \\ s_{X_2Y_1} \end{bmatrix}
\tag{18-29}
$$

There will be a unique solution iff the left-hand matrix **S** of covariances is of full rank, 2. This requires:

1. No linear dependence among the rows of **S**, caused by the exogenous variables[13] (x_1, x_2) being linearly dependent.
2. No linear dependence among the columns in **S**, caused by the included variables[14] (y_2, x_2) being linearly dependent.

Thus, once again we encounter the familiar problem of multicollinearity first discussed in Chapter 3. The condition that **S** be of full rank, is simply the condition that collinearity does not exist. However, in estimating systems of equations it may appear in either of the two above forms. It is interesting to note that these two conditions reduce to a single condition in multiple regression in the single equation model. In this special case, the requirement (see Chapter 3) that there be no collinearity between exogenous variables automatically satisfies conditions (1) and (2) above. Condition (1) is clearly met since the only exogenous variables in a single equation model are those that appear in that equation; and (2) is satisfied since the only included variables on the right-hand side of a single equation model are all the exogenous variables. Hence, the two collinearity conditions in multiple equation estimation reduce to a single collinearity condition in a single equation model.

18-4 SUMMARY: COMPLETENESS, IDENTIFICATION, AND ESTIMATION PROBLEMS

Formulating and estimating an econometric model requires that three successive conditions be met; each involves examining the rank of a different matrix. The three requirements are set out in Table 18-1.

---

[13] Both included in *and* excluded from the first equation. If, for example

$$x_1 = kx_2$$

then, in (18-29),

$$s_{X_1Y_2} = ks_{X_2Y_2}$$

$$s_{X_1X_2} = ks_{X_2X_2}$$

and the rows of **S** are linearly dependent.

[14] Both endogenous and exogenous. Here we define included variables as all those variables appearing in the equation *except* the variable determined by this equation—that is, in this case, y_1. This definition is equivalent to the definition used in Chapter 8 of "included variables on the right-hand side."

TABLE 18-1 Conditions for Completeness, Identification, and Estimation

	Mathematical Completeness	*Identification*	*Estimation*
Question	Does the system of equations provide a unique solution for the endogenous variables?	Do the prior restrictions on parameters of the model allow us to identify the first equation?	Assuming exact identification, are problems of multicollinearity avoided?
I System of equations	*Necessary and sufficient condition* $\mathbf{\Gamma}$ is of full rank, that is, Rank $\mathbf{\Gamma} = Q$	(In the absence of prior restrictions on the covariance of the error terms, or on the nonzero coefficients), the *necessary condition* is: Enough zero coefficients in the first equation; that is, $m_0 \geq q - 1$ The *necessary and sufficient* condition is: Rank $\begin{bmatrix} \mathbf{\Gamma}_0 \\ \mathbf{B}_0 \end{bmatrix} = Q - 1$ that is, this matrix is of full rank.	*Necessary and sufficient condition* Estimating covariance matrix [$\mathbf{S}$ in (18-29)] must be of full rank, that is, Rank $\mathbf{S} = m + q - 1$ This implies (1) no linear dependence between exogenous variables, included *and* excluded from first equation.[a] (2) no linear dependence between endogenous and exogenous variables included in the first equation.[b]
II Single equation model	Completeness and identification problems do not exist, provided of course that the equation is correctly specified as one endogenous variable as a function of several exogenous variables.		(1) and (2) above reduce to the single condition that there be no linear dependence among the exogenous variables in the equation.

[a] If the equation is overidentified, some linear dependence between the exogenous variables (instruments) is allowed, since there is a surplus of instrumental variables.

[b] Except the endogenous variable determined by this equation, on the left-hand side.

1. First, the model must be mathematically complete. If this requirement is not met, then the model provides no solution for the endogenous variables, that is, the model cannot tell us how changes in exogenous variables influence endogenous variables; hence it is not an interesting economic model. Therefore, throughout this chapter we have tacitly assumed that this completeness condition was met.
2. The second requirement is identification; this also is an algebraic condition that should be established prior to any examination of statistical evidence. If this condition is not met, then there is no hope of estimating a specific equation, since there will be no way of knowing whether we are estimating this equation or some bogus combination of equations in the model. The condition

$$\text{Rank} \begin{bmatrix} \mathbf{\Gamma}_0 \\ \mathbf{B}_0 \end{bmatrix} = Q - 1 \qquad \text{(18-12) repeated}$$

is the necessary and sufficient condition for identification, when the only prior knowledge is that certain variables have a zero coefficient.
3. Finally, in the exactly identified case, estimation of the parameters of a given equation requires that there be no statistical problem of multicollinearity among the relevant observed variables.

For emphasis we reiterate that the problems of mathematical completeness and identification relate only to the parameters to be estimated, and are problems that must be disposed of prior to any estimation. On the other hand, the problem of multicollinearity involves the observed variables (rather than the parameters) and, therefore, does not arise until the actual estimation is undertaken.

To summarize the identification issue as simply as possible, let us momentarily overlook sufficiency [i.e., the more demanding condition (18-12)] and return to the simple order condition (18-18) relating the number of excluded exogenous variables (m_0) to the number of included endogenous variables (q). We distinguish several cases:

1. If $m_0 < q - 1$, the equation is unidentified (also called underidentified).
2. If the equation is identified, we distinguish two subcases:
   (a) If $m_0 = q - 1$, the equation is called *exactly identified.*
   (b) If $m_0 > q - 1$, the equation is called *overidentified*, because there are more instrumental variables available than is absolutely necessary. Thus, a statistical problem occurs as to how to use them all effectively. Some solutions are given in Chapter 19.

PROBLEMS

18-3 Recall in Section 8-3 how we argued that identification may be achieved by adding exogenous variables. Explain this using (18-4a) and the argument we developed in Section 18-2a. (*Hint*. Note that this case involves changing matrix dimensions, as well as introducing zero restrictions.)

18-4 To emphasize that the identification problem is algebraic, rather than statistical, suppose each of the following relationships hold without error:

$$\text{Demand:} \quad Q = \alpha + \beta P + \mu Y$$

$$\text{Supply:} \quad Q = \gamma + \delta P + \theta Y$$

where Y is exogenous.

(a) With a three-dimensional diagram, show the graph of each equation; the line of intersection would contain the scatter of observed (Q, P, Y) values. (Note certain similarities to Figure 3-3 illustrating multicollinearity.)

(b) Use this diagram to answer: Is demand identified? Is supply? Check your answers with the algebraic criteria (18-18) or (18-12) of this chapter.

19

SINGLE EQUATION ESTIMATION (An Extension of Chapter 9)

19-1 INTRODUCTION

Certain sections of this chapter are starred, as optional. However, students who like geometry will find in these starred sections the motivation for the austere algebraic arguments in the other sections.

This chapter describes methods to estimate the parameters of a single overidentified equation within a simultaneous system. (Recall that if an equation is unidentified, it cannot be estimated. If it is exactly identified, it can be estimated without difficulty using the exogenous variables as instrumental variables, or equivalently using ILS.) Without loss of generality, we place the single equation of interest first. The other equations now matter only insofar as they specify the other exogenous variables.

Consider, for example, the estimation of the first equation in the following simple system:

$$y_1 = \gamma_1 y_2 + e_1 \tag{19-1}$$

$$y_2 = \gamma_2 y_1 + \beta_1 x_1 + \beta_2 x_2 + e_2 \tag{19-2}$$

where

y_i = endogenous variables

x_i = exogenous variables

e_i = errors

To emphasize that the importance of the second equation is the exogenous variables that it specifies, we could write the system as

$$y_1 = \gamma_1 y_2 + e_1 \tag{19-3}$$

x_1, x_2 are the exogenous variables in the system (19-4)

We note that the subscripts on γ and e could be omitted in (19-3), since this is the only equation that will be considered henceforth. We further realize that for each variable, for example either of the y's, there is a column of observed values $\mathbf{y} = (y_1, y_2, \ldots, y_t, \ldots, y_n)'$, often a time series. Thus, we finally write the system as

$$\mathbf{y}_1 = \gamma \mathbf{y}_2 + \mathbf{e} \tag{19-5}$$

$$\mathbf{x}_1 \text{ and } \mathbf{x}_2 \text{ are the exogenous variables in the system} \tag{19-6}$$

We assume as usual that every exogenous variable x is uncorrelated with e, so that the conditions in Chapter 17 for using x as an instrumental variable are satisfied. This means the *population* correlation of x and e is zero. The sample correlation, of course, will likely be slightly different from zero, because of sampling fluctuation; yet the sample correlation will be zero on the average, and in an infinite sample.

In fact, for our instrumental variables we can use *any* variables that are uncorrelated with e, including sometimes the lagged endogenous variables as well as the exogenous variables; these variables altogether constitute the predetermined variables.

19-2 TWO-STAGE LEAST SQUARES (2SLS)

*(a) Geometry

We now show geometrically, in the simple system (19-5) and (19-6), that the two stages of 2SLS are:

1. Selection of the best instrumental variable.
2. The application of this IV.

1. Equation (19-5) is overidentified, since there are two extra exogenous variables to use as instrumental variables, but only one is needed to estimate γ. It may be estimated by selecting either $\mathbf{x}_1$ or $\mathbf{x}_2$ as an instrumental variable and disregarding the other. This alternative is shown in Figure 19-1. On the one hand, the use of $\mathbf{x}_1$ as an instrumental variable (shown by shading) involves the projection[1] of the observed vectors $\mathbf{y}_1$ and $\mathbf{y}_2$ onto $\mathbf{x}_1$—at A and B. As in Chapter 17, the estimator is just the ratio of distances along this instrumental variable, that is,

$$\hat{\gamma} = \frac{0A}{0B} \tag{19-7}$$

[1] From now on, to simplify, *projection* is used to designate $\perp$ *projection*, unless stated otherwise.

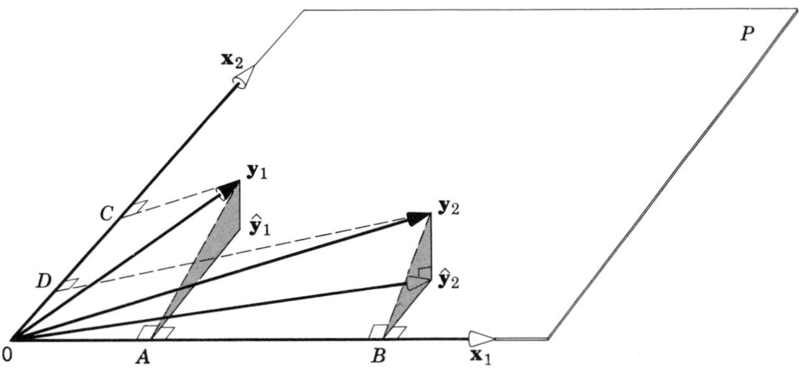

FIGURE 19-1 How alternative instrumental variables can be used to estimate γ in (19-5).

On the other hand, use of $\mathbf{x}_2$ as an instrumental variable involves the projection of $\mathbf{y}_1$ and $\mathbf{y}_2$ onto $\mathbf{x}_2$; this yields a different estimator:

$$\hat{\gamma} = \frac{0C}{0D} \tag{19-8}$$

Since we assumed the error term $\mathbf{e}$ is perpendicular (on the average) to both $\mathbf{x}_1$ and $\mathbf{x}_2$, either of the above estimates is consistent. There is one other important observation: $\mathbf{x}_1$ and $\mathbf{x}_2$ generate a whole plane P of vectors perpendicular to $\mathbf{e}$. Hence, we could have used *any vector in P* as an instrumental variable.

If we had to choose between the two estimates (19-7) and (19-8), it would be reasonable to select the former (using $\mathbf{x}_1$ as the instrumental variable), since $\mathbf{y}_2$ is more correlated to $\mathbf{x}_1$ than to $\mathbf{x}_2$. (The desirability of a high correlation between $\mathbf{y}_2$ and the instrumental variable has already been established in Chapter 7.) Now it is immediately evident that we can find an even better instrumental variable than $\mathbf{x}_1$—namely the vector in P closest to $\mathbf{y}_2$. This is, of course $\hat{\mathbf{y}}_2$, the projection (i.e., least squares fit) of $\mathbf{y}_2$ onto P. This regression of $\mathbf{y}_2$ on the exogenous variables $\mathbf{x}_1$ and $\mathbf{x}_2$ is the first step in the two-stage procedure; it involves selecting as the new instrumental variable that linear combination of the original instrumental variables that best fits $\mathbf{y}_2$. In selecting a better instrumental variable, we also eliminate our oversupply of instrumental variables.

2. The second stage, shown in Figure 19-2, is to apply this instrument $\hat{\mathbf{y}}_2$ to the equation (19-5) to be estimated. Thus, we obtain $\hat{\gamma}$ as the ratio of distances along the instrumental variable when $\mathbf{y}_1$ and $\mathbf{y}_2$ are projected onto $\hat{\mathbf{y}}_2$.

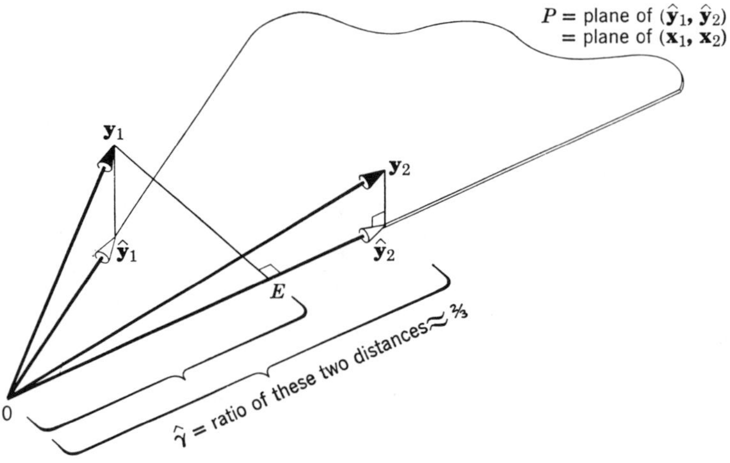

FIGURE 19-2 2SLS estimate of γ in equation (19-5).

We now prove that the IV approach given above coincides with the 2SLS of Section 9-1 [$\hat{\mathbf{y}}_2$ substituted into (19-5), followed by OLS]. We first write out the IV solution $\hat{\gamma}$ explicitly: In the notation of (17-8), when we use $\hat{\mathbf{y}}_2$ as an instrumental variable on (19-5):

$$\hat{\mathbf{y}}_2 \cdot \mathbf{y}_1 = \gamma \hat{\mathbf{y}}_2 \cdot \mathbf{y}_2 + \hat{\mathbf{y}}_2 \cdot \mathbf{e} \tag{19-9}$$

which yields the estimator

$$\hat{\gamma} = \frac{\hat{\mathbf{y}}_2 \cdot \mathbf{y}_1}{\hat{\mathbf{y}}_2 \cdot \mathbf{y}_2} \tag{19-10}$$

But it may be seen geometrically[2] that

$$\hat{\mathbf{y}}_2 \cdot \mathbf{y}_2 = \hat{\mathbf{y}}_2 \cdot \hat{\mathbf{y}}_2 \tag{19-11}$$

2

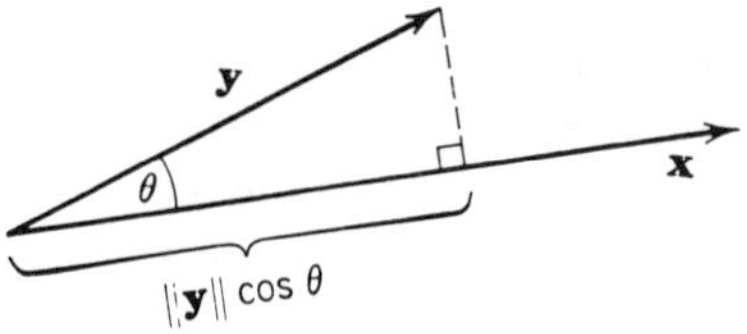

From (14-32), for any two vectors $\mathbf{x}$ and $\mathbf{y}$,

$$\mathbf{x} \cdot \mathbf{y} = \|\mathbf{x}\|(\|\mathbf{y}\| \cos \theta)$$
$$= (\text{length of } \mathbf{x})\ (\text{length of projection of } \mathbf{y} \text{ on } \mathbf{x}).$$

(Cont'd)

When this is substituted into the denominator of (19-10)

$$\hat{\gamma} = \frac{\hat{\mathbf{y}}_2 \cdot \mathbf{y}_1}{\hat{\mathbf{y}}_2 \cdot \hat{\mathbf{y}}_2} \tag{19-12}$$

which is the OLS coefficient of regression of $\mathbf{y}_1$ on $\hat{\mathbf{y}}_2$. $\hat{\gamma}$ is, therefore, the 2SLS estimate of Section 9-1.

As a second example, we change (19-5) slightly by introducing a third exogenous variable $\mathbf{x}_3$ into the first equation, obtaining

$$\mathbf{y}_1 = \gamma \mathbf{y}_2 + \beta_3 \mathbf{x}_3 + \mathbf{e} \tag{19-13}$$

$\mathbf{x}_1$, $\mathbf{x}_2$, and $\mathbf{x}_3$ are the exogenous variables in the system.

Except for notation, this is exactly the supply-demand system of (9-2) and (9-1) of Chapter 9.

In the first stage, we fit $\mathbf{y}_2$ to the $(\mathbf{x}_1, \mathbf{x}_2, \mathbf{x}_3)$ subspace generated by all the exogenous variables in the system regardless of whether or not they appear in the equation to be estimated,[3] obtaining the instrumental variable $\hat{\mathbf{y}}_2$. In the second stage, $\hat{\mathbf{y}}_2$, along with $\mathbf{x}_3$, are used as instrumental variables on (19-13), to obtain estimates of γ and β_3.

In part (b) we will prove in general that this IV approach coincides with the 2SLS described in Section 9-1.

This is a very useful interpretation of the dot product. If we put $\mathbf{y}_2$ in the role of $\mathbf{y}$, and $\hat{\mathbf{y}}_2$ in the role of $\mathbf{x}$, we obtain

$$\begin{aligned} \hat{\mathbf{y}}_2 \cdot \mathbf{y}_2 &= (\text{length of } \hat{\mathbf{y}}_2)\,(\text{length of projection of } \mathbf{y}_2 \text{ on } \hat{\mathbf{y}}_2) \\ &= (\text{length of } \hat{\mathbf{y}}_2)\,(\text{length of } \hat{\mathbf{y}}_2) \\ &= \|\hat{\mathbf{y}}_2\|^2 \\ &= \hat{\mathbf{y}}_2 \cdot \hat{\mathbf{y}}_2 \end{aligned} \qquad \text{(19-11) proved}$$

[3] The student may wonder why $\mathbf{x}_3$ is used in the first stage, since it also appears later in the second stage. A simple answer is: because it is required in order to fit an adequate proxy for $\mathbf{y}_2$. Elaborating on this idea, we realize that in the reduced form, $\mathbf{y}_2$ will be a linear combination of *all* the x's, plus an error term. The first stage of 2SLS yields a consistent estimate of this linear combination.

Another viewpoint may be useful: If, in the first stage, we regress all the variables on the right side of the equation (both $\mathbf{y}_2$ and $\mathbf{x}_3$) on all the exogenous variables, then we obtain all the instrumental variables we need for the second stage: $\hat{\mathbf{y}}_2$, and $\hat{\mathbf{x}}_3 = \mathbf{x}_3$ itself.

(b) Algebraic Generalization

To generalize (19-13), we first make some notational changes. Remembering that there is a vector of n observations for each variable, we let:

$\mathbf{y}$ = the endogenous variable on the left-hand side (which is determined by the first equation, and was formerly denoted in (19-13) by $\mathbf{y}_1$).

$\mathbf{Y}_1$ = the other endogenous variables in the first equation, on the right-hand side (formerly a single variable denoted by $\mathbf{y}_2$).

$\mathbf{X}_1$ = the exogenous variables included in the first equation (formerly a single variable denoted by $\mathbf{x}_3$). (19-14)

$\mathbf{X}_1^*$ = the exogenous variables in the system that are excluded from the first equation (formerly $[\mathbf{x}_1, \mathbf{x}_2]$). Thus $\mathbf{X} \equiv [\mathbf{X}_1, \mathbf{X}_1^*]$ = all the exogenous variables in the whole system of equations.

Then the generalization of (19-13) may be written:

$$\mathbf{y} = \mathbf{Y}_1\boldsymbol{\gamma}_1 + \mathbf{X}_1\boldsymbol{\beta}_1 + \mathbf{e} \tag{19-15}$$

which may alternatively be written in partitioned matrix notation as

$$\mathbf{y} = [\mathbf{Y}_1, \mathbf{X}_1]\begin{bmatrix}\boldsymbol{\gamma}_1 \\ \boldsymbol{\beta}_1\end{bmatrix} + \mathbf{e} \tag{19-16}$$

The stages of 2SLS, as described in Chapter 9-1, are:

1. Regress each variable in $\mathbf{Y}_1$ on $\mathbf{X}$ (all the exogenous variables in the system). We let the theoretical relation be denoted

$$\mathbf{Y}_1 = \mathbf{X}\boldsymbol{\Pi}_1 + \mathbf{V}_1 \qquad \text{(19-17) like (18-3)}$$

Note that since we are fitting a *set* of variables $\mathbf{Y}_1$, we have a *matrix* of coefficients $\boldsymbol{\Pi}_1$. Then the OLS estimator is

$$\hat{\mathbf{Y}}_1 = \mathbf{X}\hat{\boldsymbol{\Pi}}_1 \qquad \text{(19-18}a\text{)}$$

where

$$\hat{\boldsymbol{\Pi}}_1 = (\mathbf{X}'\mathbf{X})^{-1}\mathbf{X}'\mathbf{Y}_1 \qquad \text{(19-18}b\text{)}$$

2. Substituting this $\hat{\mathbf{Y}}_1$ for $\mathbf{Y}_1$ in (19-16), we have

$$\mathbf{y} = [\hat{\mathbf{Y}}_1, \mathbf{X}_1]\begin{bmatrix}\boldsymbol{\gamma}_1 \\ \boldsymbol{\beta}_1\end{bmatrix} + \mathbf{e}^* \tag{19-19}$$

We now apply OLS to this equation,[4] obtaining

2SLS solution:

$$\begin{bmatrix} \hat{\gamma}_1 \\ \hat{\boldsymbol{\beta}}_1 \end{bmatrix} = ([\hat{\mathbf{Y}}_1, \mathbf{X}_1]'[\hat{\mathbf{Y}}_1, \mathbf{X}_1])^{-1}[\hat{\mathbf{Y}}_1, \mathbf{X}_1]'\mathbf{y} \tag{19-20}$$

which is a generalization of (19-12).

We now prove its consistency by showing that it is equivalent to using the instruments $[\hat{\mathbf{Y}}_1, \mathbf{X}_1]$ on (19-16), which would yield

$$[\hat{\mathbf{Y}}_1, \mathbf{X}_1]'\mathbf{y} = [\hat{\mathbf{Y}}_1, \mathbf{X}_1]'[\mathbf{Y}_1, \mathbf{X}_1]\begin{bmatrix} \hat{\gamma}_1 \\ \hat{\boldsymbol{\beta}}_1 \end{bmatrix} \tag{19-21}$$

which is a generalization of (19-9). When solved by matrix inversion, it yields

IV solution, using $\hat{\mathbf{Y}}_1$ and $\mathbf{X}_1$ as instrumental variables:

$$\begin{bmatrix} \hat{\gamma}_1 \\ \hat{\boldsymbol{\beta}}_1 \end{bmatrix} = ([\hat{\mathbf{Y}}_1, \mathbf{X}_1]'[\mathbf{Y}_1, \mathbf{X}_1])^{-1}[\hat{\mathbf{Y}}_1, \mathbf{X}_1]'\mathbf{y} \tag{19-22}$$

which is a generalization of (19-10). We note that (19-22) corresponds exactly to (19-20), except for a single appearance of $\mathbf{Y}_1$ in place of $\hat{\mathbf{Y}}_1$. Equivalence of these two procedures thus hinges on showing that

$$[\hat{\mathbf{Y}}_1, \mathbf{X}_1]'[\hat{\mathbf{Y}}_1, \mathbf{X}_1] = [\hat{\mathbf{Y}}_1, \mathbf{X}_1]'[\mathbf{Y}_1, \mathbf{X}_1] \tag{19-23}$$

that is, that

$$\hat{\mathbf{Y}}_1'\hat{\mathbf{Y}}_1 = \hat{\mathbf{Y}}_1'\mathbf{Y}_1 \tag{19-24}$$

which is a generalization of (19-11), and also showing that

$$\mathbf{X}_1'\hat{\mathbf{Y}}_1 = \mathbf{X}_1'\mathbf{Y}_1 \tag{19-25}$$

To establish these, we return to our first-stage solution for $\hat{\mathbf{Y}}_1$; from (19-18*a*) and (19-18*b*)

$$\hat{\mathbf{Y}}_1 = \mathbf{X}(\mathbf{X}'\mathbf{X})^{-1}\mathbf{X}'\mathbf{Y}_1 \tag{19-26}$$

Thus the left side of (19-24) can be written

$$\hat{\mathbf{Y}}_1'\hat{\mathbf{Y}}_1 = \{\mathbf{Y}_1'\mathbf{X}(\mathbf{X}'\mathbf{X})^{-1}\mathbf{X}'\}\{\mathbf{X}(\mathbf{X}'\mathbf{X})^{-1}\mathbf{X}'\mathbf{Y}_1\} \tag{19-27}$$

$$= \mathbf{Y}_1'\mathbf{X}(\mathbf{X}'\mathbf{X})^{-1}\mathbf{X}'\mathbf{Y}_1 \tag{19-28}$$

[4] Noting, of course, that the $[\hat{\mathbf{Y}}_1, \mathbf{X}_1]$ and $\begin{bmatrix} \gamma_1 \\ \boldsymbol{\beta}_1 \end{bmatrix}$ in (19-19) correspond to the $\mathbf{X}$ and $\boldsymbol{\beta}$ in (12-19). We also note in (19-19) that $\mathbf{e}^*$ is the error term $\mathbf{e}$ adjusted for the substitution of $\hat{\mathbf{Y}}_1$ for $\mathbf{Y}_1$.

Again noting (19-26):

$$= \hat{\mathbf{Y}}_1'\mathbf{Y}_1 \qquad \text{(19-24) proved}$$

To establish (19-25), we note from (19-26) that

$$\mathbf{X}'\hat{\mathbf{Y}}_1 = \mathbf{X}'\{\mathbf{X}(\mathbf{X}'\mathbf{X})^{-1}\mathbf{X}'\mathbf{Y}_1\} \tag{19-29}$$

$$= \mathbf{X}'\mathbf{Y}_1 \tag{19-30}$$

From (19-14) we substitute for $\mathbf{X}$:

$$[\mathbf{X}_1, \mathbf{X}_1^*]'\hat{\mathbf{Y}}_1 = [\mathbf{X}_1, \mathbf{X}_1^*]'\mathbf{Y}_1 \tag{19-31}$$

whose first component is

$$\mathbf{X}_1'\hat{\mathbf{Y}}_1 = \mathbf{X}_1'\mathbf{Y}_1 \qquad \text{(19-25) proved}$$

Thus, the 2SLS solution in (19-20) is proven equivalent to the IV solution in (19-22). The final question is: Are $[\hat{\mathbf{Y}}_1, \mathbf{X}_1]$ bona fide instrumental variables to use on (19-16), that is, do they satisfy the conditions of relevancy, and uncorrelation with the error?

Since the instrumental variables are the fitted values of the right-hand variables in (19-16), the condition of relevancy (17-12) is satisfied. The other condition (17-11) is that the instrumental variables be uncorrelated[5] with the error. Since, by assumption, $\mathbf{X}_1$ satisfies this requirement, we need only ensure that $\hat{\mathbf{Y}}_1$ also qualifies, that is, we must prove

$$\frac{1}{n}\hat{\mathbf{Y}}_1'\mathbf{e} \xrightarrow{p} \mathbf{0} \tag{19-32}$$

To prove this, we first substitute for $\hat{\mathbf{Y}}_1'$ as given by (19-18*a*):

$$\frac{1}{n}\hat{\mathbf{Y}}_1'\mathbf{e} = \frac{1}{n}(\mathbf{X}\hat{\mathbf{\Pi}}_1)'\mathbf{e}$$

$$= \hat{\mathbf{\Pi}}_1'\left(\frac{1}{n}\mathbf{X}'\mathbf{e}\right) \tag{19-33}$$

Since the exogenous variables are uncorrelated with the error,

$$\frac{1}{n}\mathbf{X}'\mathbf{e} \xrightarrow{p} \mathbf{0} \tag{19-34}$$

Also the OLS estimate (19-18*b*) from the first stage is consistent, that is,

$$\hat{\mathbf{\Pi}}_1 \xrightarrow{p} \mathbf{\Pi}_1 \tag{19-35}$$

[5] We remind the reader that *asymptotic* uncorrelation is understood throughout this chapter, even when the word asymptotic is omitted.

Substituting (19-35) and (19-34) into (19-33)

$$\frac{1}{n}\hat{\mathbf{Y}}_1\mathbf{e} \xrightarrow{p} \mathbf{\Pi}_1'\mathbf{0} = \mathbf{0} \qquad (19\text{-}36)$$

(19-32) proved

Thus $[\hat{\mathbf{Y}}_1, \mathbf{X}_1]$ is established as a bona fide set of instrumental variables, and it follows that 2SLS can be regarded as a special application of IV.

*19-3 THE GEOMETRY OF LEAST WEIGHTED VARIANCE (LWV)

(a) Introduction

To illustrate the basic ideas as easily as possible, we return to the simple model of the introduction

$$\mathbf{y}_1 = \gamma\mathbf{y}_2 + \mathbf{e} \qquad (19\text{-}37)$$

(19-5) repeated

$\mathbf{x}_1$ and $\mathbf{x}_2$ are the exogenous variables in the system (19-38)

(19-6) repeated

The 2SLS solution in Figure 19-2 is reproduced in Figure 19-3. Note how the projection of $\mathbf{y}_1$ onto $\hat{\mathbf{y}}_2$ (at E) is equivalent to:

1. Regressing $\mathbf{y}_1$ onto P, obtaining $\hat{\mathbf{y}}_1$; then
2. Regressing $\hat{\mathbf{y}}_1$ onto $\hat{\mathbf{y}}_2$. (19-39)

We now ask: Suppose we had expressed the first equation differently, with $\mathbf{y}_2$ rather than $\mathbf{y}_1$ on the left-hand side? Then

$$\mathbf{y}_2 = \left(\frac{1}{\gamma}\right)\mathbf{y}_1 + \left(\frac{-1}{\gamma}\right)\mathbf{e}$$

that is,

$$\mathbf{y}_2 = \left(\frac{1}{\gamma}\right)\mathbf{y}_1 + \mathbf{u} \qquad (19\text{-}40)$$

Although $(1/\gamma)$ is the reciprocal of γ, the estimator $\widehat{(1/\gamma)}$ need not be the reciprocal of $\hat{\gamma}$. This is shown in Figure 19-3. Whereas γ in (19-37) is estimated by 2SLS by projecting $\mathbf{y}_1$ onto $\hat{\mathbf{y}}_2$, $(1/\gamma)$ in (19-40) is estimated by projecting $\mathbf{y}_2$ onto $\hat{\mathbf{y}}_1$. In the special case shown in the diagram, the resulting $\hat{\gamma}$ is about 2/3; but $\widehat{(1/\gamma)}$ is about 5/4, implying an estimate of γ of 4/5. Which estimate is preferable? Or would some other estimate somewhere between (e.g., 3/4) be better?

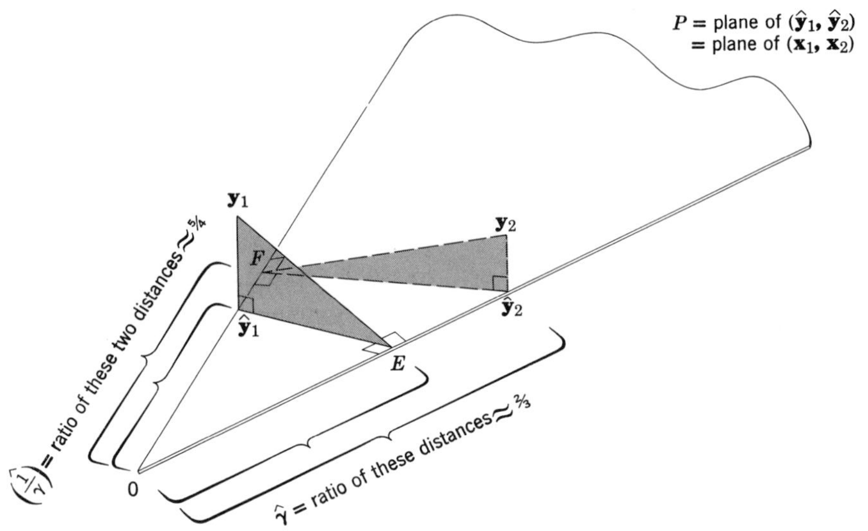

FIGURE 19-3 Alternative 2SLS solutions.

We recognize this to be similar to the problem of errors in variables, first discussed in Section 7-5; those conclusions may now be translated into this more complicated case. Thus, if $\mathbf{y}_1$ is subject to error, but $\mathbf{y}_2$ is not, then the equation should be written in the form (19-37) and we should regress $\mathbf{y}_1$ on $\hat{\mathbf{y}}_2$. On the other hand, if only $\mathbf{y}_2$ is subject to error, then (19-40) is the appropriate form, and we should regress $\mathbf{y}_2$ on $\hat{\mathbf{y}}_1$. But if both $\mathbf{y}_1$ and $\mathbf{y}_2$ are subject to error, we should seek an estimate somewhere between.

(b) Minimizing the Variances of Several Estimated Errors

To resolve this dilemma, we cast the system (19-37) and (19-38) into reduced form

$$\mathbf{y}_1 = \pi_{11}\mathbf{x}_1 + \pi_{12}\mathbf{x}_2 + \mathbf{v}_1 \tag{19-41}$$

$$\mathbf{y}_2 = \pi_{21}\mathbf{x}_1 + \pi_{22}\mathbf{x}_2 + \mathbf{v}_2 \tag{19-42}$$

where the π coefficients give the true relation of each $\mathbf{y}_i$ to $\mathbf{x}_1$ and $\mathbf{x}_2$, while $\mathbf{v}_i$ is the error in $\mathbf{y}_i$. If we have no prior knowledge of the relative size of these error terms, it might seem reasonable to select estimates of the π coefficients so as to minimize

$$\|\hat{\mathbf{v}}_1\|^2 + \|\hat{\mathbf{v}}_2\|^2 \tag{19-43}$$

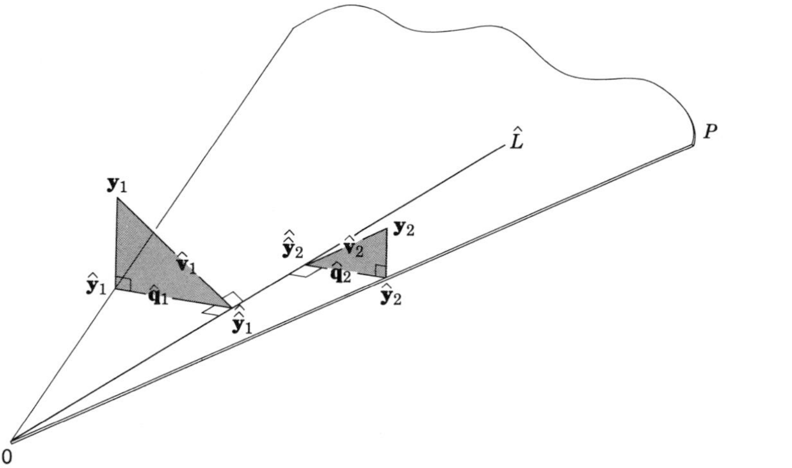

FIGURE 19-4 Minimizing the estimated errors in the reduced form, subject to the constraint of the structural form.

(This must, of course, involve *estimated* error terms $\hat{\mathbf{v}}_i$ rather than the unknown true error terms $\mathbf{v}_i$.) Minimizing this sum of two squared vector lengths is similar to the familiar least squares criterion, extended to include two sets of error terms. The only new feature is that the π coefficients are not freely chosen; they are constrained to make the fitted $\hat{\hat{\mathbf{y}}}_i$ conform to the structural relation (19-37)

$$\hat{\hat{\mathbf{y}}}_1 = \hat{\gamma}\hat{\hat{\mathbf{y}}}_2 \tag{19-44}$$

That is, $\hat{\hat{\mathbf{y}}}_1$ is a multiple of $\hat{\hat{\mathbf{y}}}_2$; in other words, $\hat{\hat{\mathbf{y}}}_1$ and $\hat{\hat{\mathbf{y}}}_2$ lie on a common line $\hat{L}$.

The geometric interpretation of such a fit is shown in Figure 19-4. We consider all possible lines $\hat{L}$ in the plane P generated by $\mathbf{x}_1$ and $\mathbf{x}_2$ (or equally well by $\hat{\mathbf{y}}_1$ and $\hat{\mathbf{y}}_2$).

The projection of the observed $\mathbf{y}_i$ onto $\hat{L}$ provides the estimate[6] $\hat{\hat{\mathbf{y}}}_i$. The estimated error $\hat{\mathbf{v}}_i$ is the difference between these observed and estimated vectors, $i = 1, 2$. We select the $\hat{L}$ that minimizes the sum of these squared lengths, as specified in (19-43). The estimate $\hat{\gamma}$ is, of course, the ratio of lengths along $\hat{L}$—specifically, the ratio of the lengths of $\hat{\hat{\mathbf{y}}}_1$ and $\hat{\hat{\mathbf{y}}}_2$. As we had hoped, this does yield $\hat{\gamma}$ between the pair of 2SLS estimates (i.e., between 2/3 and 4/5).

Because of the form of the equation (19-37), we had to restrict the estimate $\hat{\hat{\mathbf{y}}}_1$ to be a multiple of $\hat{\hat{\mathbf{y}}}_2$; thus both estimates fall on $\hat{L}$, simplifying

[6] The vector $\hat{\hat{\mathbf{y}}}_1$ is denoted with two hats to indicate that it has two constraints: (1) it must be a linear combination of the $\mathbf{x}_j$, and (2) it must be a linear combination (multiple) of $\hat{\hat{\mathbf{y}}}_2$. Geometrically, in Figure 19-4 this means that $\hat{\hat{\mathbf{y}}}_1$ must not only lie in P, but on $\hat{L}$ as well.

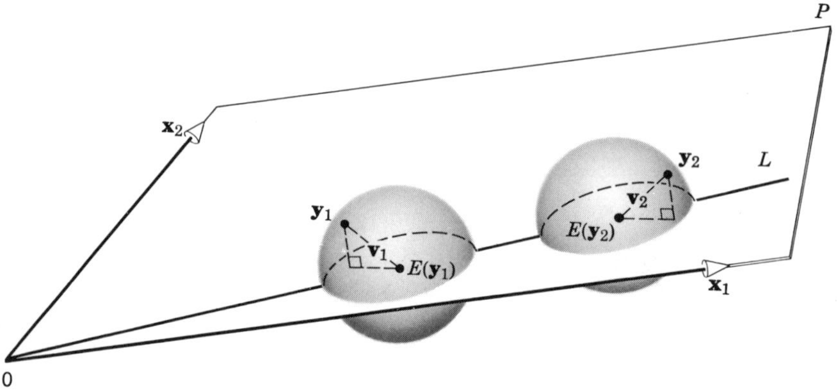

FIGURE 19-5 Assumptions underlying Figure 19-4.

the analysis. But if (19-37) included another exogenous variable $\mathbf{x}_3$, then $\hat{\hat{\mathbf{y}}}_1$ and $\hat{\hat{\mathbf{y}}}_2$ would have to be selected in a more complicated way. But the principle of minimizing (19-43) would remain the same.[7]

Finally, before leaving Figure 19-4, we emphasize that $\hat{\hat{\mathbf{y}}}_1$ and $\hat{\hat{\mathbf{y}}}_2$ represent the restricted fit of $\mathbf{y}_1$ and $\mathbf{y}_2$ onto the $(\mathbf{x}_1, \mathbf{x}_2)$ subspace, that is, the least squares fit of the reduced form (19-41) and (19-42) *restricted* to satisfy the structural relation (19-44). On the other hand, $\hat{\mathbf{y}}_1$ and $\hat{\mathbf{y}}_2$ represent the least squares fit of the reduced form that is free and *unrestricted*.

We now pause to consider the underlying assumptions of this model. In Figure 19-5 we show the parent populations from which the observed $\mathbf{y}_1$ and $\mathbf{y}_2$ are assumed to be drawn. $\mathbf{x}_1$ and $\mathbf{x}_2$ and the reduced form parameters π_{ij} are fixed. $\mathbf{v}_1$ is a linear combination of the **e**'s in the structural equations, so that $E(\mathbf{v}_1) = \mathbf{0}$. When we take expected values of (19-41), we therefore obtain

$$E(\mathbf{y}_1) = \pi_{11}\mathbf{x}_1 + \pi_{12}\mathbf{x}_2 \tag{19-47}$$

Similarly, from (19-42)

$$E(\mathbf{y}_2) = \pi_{21}\mathbf{x}_1 + \pi_{22}\mathbf{x}_2 \tag{19-48}$$

---

[7] Note that minimizing (19-43) is equivalent to minimizing

$$\|\hat{\mathbf{q}}_1\|^2 + \|\hat{\mathbf{q}}_2\|^2 \tag{19-45}$$

where $\hat{\mathbf{q}}_i$ in Figure 19-4 is the projection of $\mathbf{v}_i$ onto P.

Proof. Because the critical two triangles in Figure 19-4 have right angles, minimizing (19-43) is equivalent to minimizing

$$\|\hat{\mathbf{q}}_1\|^2 + \|\mathbf{y}_1 - \hat{\mathbf{y}}_1\|^2 + \|\hat{\mathbf{q}}_2\|^2 + \|\mathbf{y}_2 - \hat{\mathbf{y}}_2\|^2 \tag{19-46}$$

But the second and fourth terms in this equation remain constant for all possible $\hat{L}$. Therefore, minimizing (19-46) is equivalent to minimizing (19-45).

That is, $E(\mathbf{y}_1)$ and $E(\mathbf{y}_2)$ lie in the instrumental variable plane as shown in Figure 19-5. Moreover, taking expected values of the structural equation (19-37),

$$E(\mathbf{y}_1) = \gamma E(\mathbf{y}_2) \tag{19-49}$$

That is, $E(\mathbf{y}_1)$ and $E(\mathbf{y}_2)$ lie on the same line through the origin, designated L.

In Figure 19-5, individual observed $\mathbf{y}_1$ and $\mathbf{y}_2$ are also shown, differing from their expected values because of the errors $\mathbf{v}_1$ and $\mathbf{v}_2$. The distributions of $\mathbf{y}_1$ and $\mathbf{y}_2$ are shown schematically as the two spheres of concentration with equal size if we assume that the error terms ($\mathbf{v}_1$ and $\mathbf{v}_2$) have equal variance.

The statistician, of course, only knows the location of $\mathbf{y}_1$, $\mathbf{y}_2$, and the instrumental variable plane. He estimates L in Figure 19-5 with $\hat{L}$ in Figure 19-4. In the process, he estimates $\mathbf{v}_1$, $\mathbf{v}_2$, $E(\mathbf{y}_1)$, and $E(\mathbf{y}_2)$ with $\hat{\mathbf{v}}_1$, $\hat{\mathbf{v}}_2$, $\hat{\hat{\mathbf{y}}}_1$, and $\hat{\hat{\mathbf{y}}}_2$, respectively.[8]

To sum up, if we assume the variances of $\mathbf{v}_1$ and $\mathbf{v}_2$ are equal, the parent population is shown in Figure 19-5, with estimation shown in Figure 19-4. But if we assume $\mathbf{v}_2$ is nearly zero, then the true line L is near $\mathbf{y}_2$, and the 2SLS estimation, shown at E in Figure 19-3, would be more appropriate. Or if we assume instead that $\mathbf{v}_1$ is nearly zero, then the true line L is near $\mathbf{y}_1$, and the 2SLS estimation shown at F in Figure 19-3 would be more appropriate. It would seem desirable to avoid any arbitrary prior assumption about the relative size of $\mathbf{v}_1$ and $\mathbf{v}_2$. Instead, we *estimate* the relative size by observing how far $\mathbf{y}_1$ and $\mathbf{y}_2$ lie off the plane P, shown in Figure 19-6 as $\|\mathbf{w}_1\|$ and $\|\mathbf{w}_2\|$, respectively.

We thus arrive at the following criterion that generalizes (19-43). We choose the line $\hat{\hat{L}}$ (and with it $\hat{\hat{\mathbf{y}}}_1$, $\hat{\hat{\mathbf{y}}}_2$, and their ratio $\hat{\gamma}$) so as to minimize

$$\frac{\|\hat{\mathbf{v}}_1\|^2}{\|\mathbf{w}_1\|^2} + \frac{\|\hat{\mathbf{v}}_2\|^2}{\|\mathbf{w}_2\|^2} \tag{19-50}$$

We call this the criterion of *least weighted variance* (LWV). We must examine how it solves the problems that motivated it. We note that when $\|\mathbf{w}_1\| = \|\mathbf{w}_2\|$, that is, when $\|\mathbf{v}_1\|$ seems about equal to $\|\mathbf{v}_2\|$, criterion (19-50) reduces to (19-43), as it should. When $\|\mathbf{w}_2\|$ is nearly zero, the second term of (19-50) becomes dominant. Then $\|\hat{\mathbf{v}}_2\|$ is minimized with little regard for $\|\hat{\mathbf{v}}_1\|$, so that the line $\hat{\hat{L}}$ is chosen below $\mathbf{y}_2$. Thus, the 2SLS solution is generated, as desired.

---

[8] We observe in passing that the assumption that $\mathbf{v}_1$ and $\mathbf{v}_2$ have the same variance does *not* generally lead to estimates $\hat{\mathbf{v}}_1$ and $\hat{\mathbf{v}}_2$ that are equal. In fact minimizing (19-43) leads, in our example, to $\|\hat{\mathbf{v}}_1\| > \|\hat{\mathbf{v}}_2\|$. (This is similar to the result of Chapter 2, that the assumed constant variance of the error in simple regression does not generally lead to *estimated* errors that are equal.)

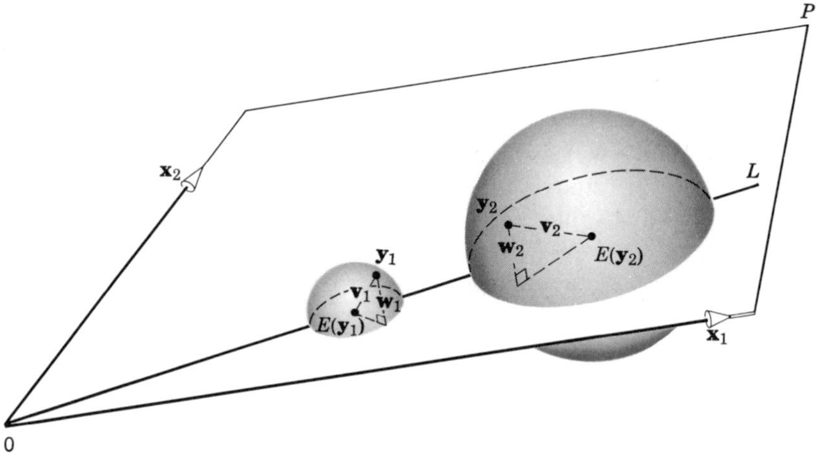

FIGURE 19-6 Assumptions of least weighted variance (LWV) allowing errors of any relative size.

We note that LWV of (19-50) is very similar to the least weighted sum of squares of equation (6-5), which also arose out of heteroscedasticity assumptions. In both cases, our estimate is drawn toward the more reliable observation having less variance.

As shown in equation (19-45) of a previous footnote, minimizing (19-50) is equivalent to minimizing

$$\frac{\|\hat{\mathbf{q}}_1\|^2}{\|\mathbf{w}_1\|^2} + \frac{\|\hat{\mathbf{q}}_2\|^2}{\|\mathbf{w}_2\|^2} \tag{19-51}$$

The geometry is shown in Figure 19-7. The weights $\|\mathbf{w}_1\|$ and $\|\mathbf{w}_2\|$ are the observed distances of $\mathbf{y}_1$ and $\mathbf{y}_2$ from the instrumental variable plane, which provide the best indication of the relative size of the unknown $\|\mathbf{v}_1\|$ and $\|\mathbf{v}_2\|$. Once these fixed weights are found, $\hat{\hat{L}}$ is determined within the instrumental variable plane P, by selecting those vectors $\hat{\mathbf{q}}_1$ and $\hat{\mathbf{q}}_2$ that minimize (19-51).

Moreover, since $\hat{\hat{L}}$ is a vector in the instrumental variable plane, it is a bona fide instrumental variable. Thus, we obtain a consistent estimator $\hat{\gamma}$, calculated as before from relative lengths measured along the instrumental variable $\hat{\hat{L}}$. Whereas $\hat{\mathbf{y}}_2$ was used in 2SLS because it was the instrumental variable closest to $\mathbf{y}_2$, we may regard $\hat{\hat{L}}$ in LWV as the instrumental variable closest, in some sense, to both $\mathbf{y}_1$ *and* $\mathbf{y}_2$. Otherwise our strategy remains the same: (1) find the appropriate instrumental variable; (2) use it. The next

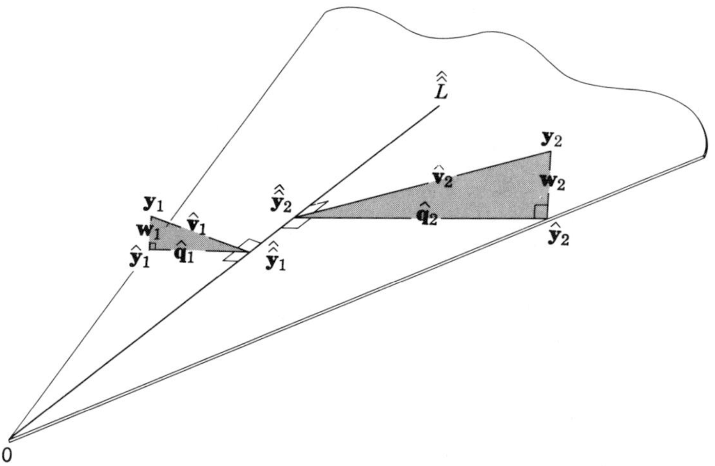

FIGURE 19-7 Estimation, using least weighted variance (LWV).

method we will consider in Section 19-4 follows this same pattern, with L again being estimated closest to both $\mathbf{y}_1$ and $\mathbf{y}_2$, but in a somewhat different sense. But first, our progress so far should be summarized.

(c) The Various Methods Compared

In Figure 19-8 we show how each method involves the selection of a different instrumental variable. (Since the specific solutions cannot be shown without hopelessly cluttering the diagram, we limit ourselves to the instrumental variable plane.)[9]

First, our single equation can be estimated using either $\mathbf{x}_1$ or $\mathbf{x}_2$ as an instrumental variable. By reviewing Figure 19-1, we can see the difficulties that arise. Using $\mathbf{x}_1$ as an instrumental variable yields the estimate

$$\hat{\gamma} = \frac{0A}{0B} \approx \frac{2}{5}$$

[9] Of course this instrumental variable plane is a fixed plane only while $\mathbf{x}_1$ and $\mathbf{x}_2$ are fixed. But since our instrumental variables are typically random variables, the instrumental variable plane takes on various random positions in space. Yet the geometry remains valid; whatever the position of the instrumental variable plane, the *conditional* distribution of $\mathbf{y}_1$ and $\mathbf{y}_2$ around it is validly shown in Figure 19-6. (This is similar to the argument of Section 2-11.)

Difficulties do arise, however, if there are errors in measuring the instrumental variables $\mathbf{x}_1$ and $\mathbf{x}_2$. Then the geometry no longer remains valid, and a whole new set of econometric problems is introduced. Throughout this book (except for Section 7-5), it is assumed that all instrumental variables are measured without error.

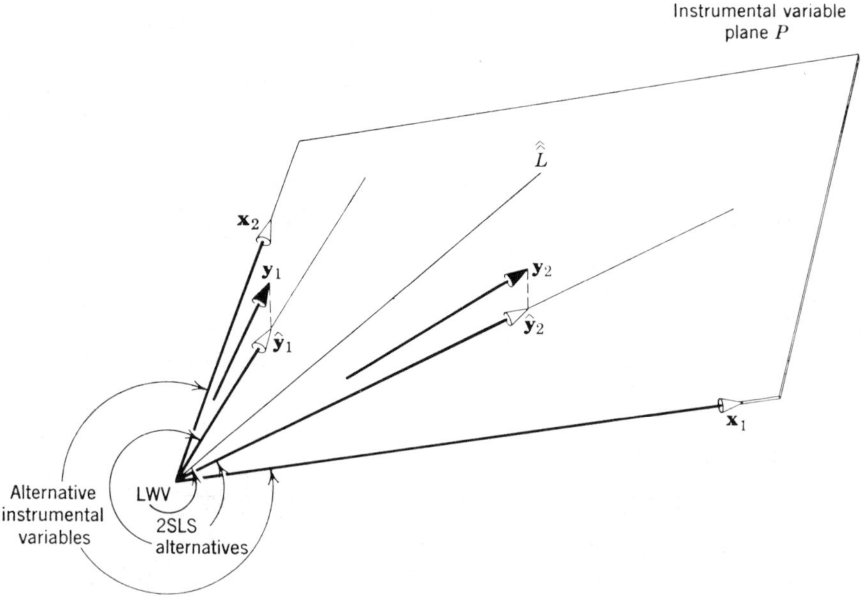

FIGURE 19-8 Review of single equation solutions, defined on the instrumental variable subspace.

while $\mathbf{x}_2$ as an instrumental variable yields the quite different estimate

$$\frac{0C}{0D} \approx 2$$

Naive IV thus appears to be a very unstable estimating procedure, with the result very sensitive to the instrumental variable chosen. It is true that either estimator is consistent; in an infinite sample, $\hat{\mathbf{y}}_1$ and $\hat{\mathbf{y}}_2$ would both lie on the true line (L in Figure 19-5), and either instrumental variable would yield the same estimate. But in the small sample estimation in Figure 19-1, this is little comfort. Sample fluctuation has resulted in $\hat{\mathbf{y}}_1$ and $\hat{\mathbf{y}}_2$ lying off the true line. This, plus the fact that each instrumental variable is so far away from L, results in two widely differing estimates.

It also follows that although all the techniques we have discussed are consistent—they perform equally well in infinite samples—in small samples they do not. Therefore, rather than use either $\mathbf{x}_1$ or $\mathbf{x}_2$ alone, we prefer to combine them into a new instrumental variable. Specifically, either $\hat{\mathbf{y}}_1$ or $\hat{\mathbf{y}}_2$ are better (i.e., closer); in Figure 19-3, we show the pair of 2SLS estimators they generate.

Finally, LWV involves the selection of the unique instrument $\hat{\hat{L}}$ lying somewhere between.

19-4 LIMITED INFORMATION/LEAST GENERALIZED VARIANCE (LI/LGV); LIMITED INFORMATION/MAXIMUM LIKELIHOOD (LI/ML); LIMITED INFORMATION/LEAST VARIANCE RATIO (LI/LVR)

(a) Introduction

These three approaches all lead to exactly the same estimator (as proved in advanced texts). They share a common feature with LWV: We do not require a prior specification of whether $\mathbf{y}_1$ should be viewed as a function of $\mathbf{y}_2$, or $\mathbf{y}_2$ as a function of $\mathbf{y}_1$.

*(b) The Geometry of LI/LGV

We illustrate the first approach, LI/LGV, by considering the covariance matrix[10] of the estimated errors $\hat{\mathbf{v}}_1$ and $\hat{\mathbf{v}}_2$:

$$\hat{\boldsymbol{\Omega}} = \begin{bmatrix} \hat{\mathbf{v}}_1 \cdot \hat{\mathbf{v}}_1 & \hat{\mathbf{v}}_1 \cdot \hat{\mathbf{v}}_2 \\ \hat{\mathbf{v}}_2 \cdot \hat{\mathbf{v}}_1 & \hat{\mathbf{v}}_2 \cdot \hat{\mathbf{v}}_2 \end{bmatrix} \tag{19-52}$$

In LWV we minimized (19-43), which is recognized as the trace[11] of $\hat{\boldsymbol{\Omega}}$. On the other hand, LI/LGV, which we now consider, involves minimizing the *determinant* of $\hat{\boldsymbol{\Omega}}$, that is, minimizing

$$|\hat{\boldsymbol{\Omega}}| = \begin{vmatrix} \hat{\mathbf{v}}_1 \cdot \hat{\mathbf{v}}_1 & \hat{\mathbf{v}}_1 \cdot \hat{\mathbf{v}}_2 \\ \hat{\mathbf{v}}_2 \cdot \hat{\mathbf{v}}_1 & \hat{\mathbf{v}}_2 \cdot \hat{\mathbf{v}}_2 \end{vmatrix} = \tag{19-53}$$

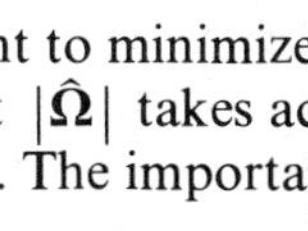

We might ask why anyone would want to minimize the determinant of $\hat{\boldsymbol{\Omega}}$ rather than its trace. The answer is that $|\hat{\boldsymbol{\Omega}}|$ takes account of the covariance as well as the variances of $\hat{v}_1$ and $\hat{v}_2$. The importance of this is shown

---

[10] Except for the scalar divisor n. This constant can be ignored in the minimization procedures that will be discussed.

[11] This follows, since the trace is defined as the sum of the main diagonal elements, $\hat{\mathbf{v}}_1 \cdot \hat{\mathbf{v}}_1 + \hat{\mathbf{v}}_2 \cdot \hat{\mathbf{v}}_2 = \|\hat{\mathbf{v}}_1\|^2 + \|\hat{\mathbf{v}}_2\|^2$.

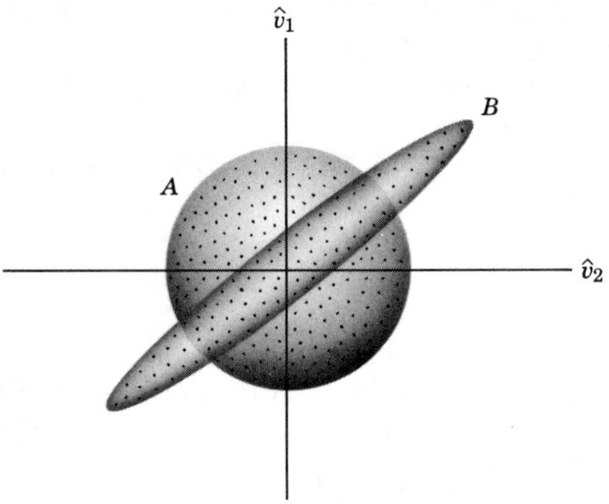

FIGURE 19-9 Scatter diagram of alternative selections of $\hat{v}_1$ and $\hat{v}_2$. This is a scatter diagram in the variable space, rather than the observation space.

in Figure 19-9, where we revert to a scatter diagram in which the axes refer to $\hat{v}_1$ and $\hat{v}_2$, rather than the n observations. We ask, "Would we prefer a fitting procedure that results in error pattern A, or error pattern B?" Our intuition tells us that pattern B might be preferred because it involves error spread over a smaller area.

Before proceeding, we note that the variances of the two *individual* errors are larger for B, since this scatter extends slightly farther in both the horizontal ($\hat{v}_2$) and vertical ($\hat{v}_1$) direction. Moreover, the covariance of $\hat{v}_1$ and $\hat{v}_2$ is also larger for B (in A the errors are uncorrelated, while in B they are highly correlated). In fact, it is the high covariance that tilts the ellipse and gives it smaller area.

Which estimation method would tell us to select B rather than A? If, as in LWV, we only minimize the variances of $\hat{v}_1$ and $\hat{v}_2$, we would select A with its smaller variances. But if, as in LI/LGV, we minimize the determinant of $\hat{\boldsymbol{\Omega}}$, we will select B. For in B it is true that the variances in the diagonal d in (19-53) are greater; but this is more than offset by the relatively large covariance terms in e that are subtracted. Thus, LI/LGV is a selection procedure that allows variances (of estimated error) to increase, provided this is more than offset by increased covariance. In conclusion, the idea is to select the error scatter in Figure 19-9 with the smallest area; and algebraically this is accomplished by minimizing $|\hat{\boldsymbol{\Omega}}|$.

This determinant is called the generalized variance; hence the name least generalized variance. A possible solution that this criterion might yield is illustrated in Figure 19-10. The instrumental variable $\hat{\hat{L}}$ is selected by choosing $\hat{\mathbf{v}}_1$ and $\hat{\mathbf{v}}_2$ to minimize $|\hat{\boldsymbol{\Omega}}|$; then, as before, we estimate $\hat{\gamma}$ from relative lengths along this instrumental variable; (in this example, $\hat{\gamma}$ is a little

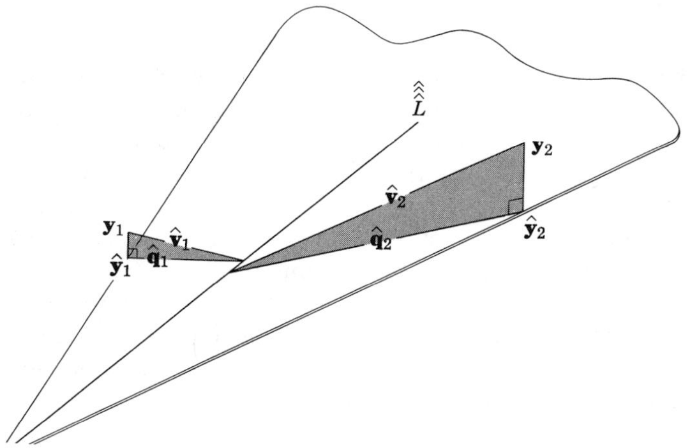

FIGURE 19-10 Limited information/least generalized variance (LI/LGV). (We return to plotting vectors in the observation space.)

more than 1). Since we no longer minimize $\|\mathbf{v}_1\|^2$ and $\|\mathbf{v}_2\|^2$, these vectors are no longer selected perpendicular to $\hat{\hat{\hat{L}}}$.

Like LWV, LI/LGV may be regarded as a compromise between the two different 2SLS estimates; it is also similar in the sense that we fit $\mathbf{y}_1$ and $\mathbf{y}_2$ to the reduced form equations (19-41) and (19-42), while keeping in mind the restrictions imposed by the structural equation (19-37). LI/LGV differs from LWV only in using as its criterion of good fit the determinant rather than the weighted trace of $\hat{\boldsymbol{\Omega}}$. An advantage of LI/LGV is that it takes into account covariance[12] as well as variance terms; moreover, it provides a less restricted fit, since it does not require that $\hat{\mathbf{q}}_1$ be parallel to $\hat{\mathbf{q}}_2$. But we wonder whether this might prove a disadvantage. Once the vectors $\hat{\mathbf{v}}_1$ and $\hat{\mathbf{v}}_2$ are allowed to swing freely, may they not in special cases end up in odd directions? We notice in our example how this could result in a very strange estimate of γ, since this is defined by relative lengths along $\hat{\hat{\hat{L}}}$. Later on we will see that this problem is not nearly as serious as this geometry suggests[13]; nevertheless, the occasional occurrence of estimates far off target remains a major weakness of LI/LGV, especially in small samples.

An algebraic development of LI/LGV is deferred to the Appendix of Chapter 20.

---

[12] While LWV does not take account of the covariance of the errors $\mathbf{v}_1$ and $\mathbf{v}_2$ in the reduced form, it does reflect to some degree the covariance of the errors $\mathbf{e}_1$ and $\mathbf{e}_2$ in the original structure; this follows since each $\mathbf{v}_i$ depends on both $\mathbf{e}_1$ and $\mathbf{e}_2$.

[13] In some other contexts as well, the three-dimensional geometry of LI/LGV may be misleading.

(c) LI/ML

We recall that in an exactly identified system, we could estimate the reduced form, and then infer the structural form (indirect least squares). If we attempt this procedure in the overidentified case, we would find that after estimating the reduced form, there would be no corresponding structural form that satisfies the constraints (zero coefficients in specified places). A natural solution is to estimate the reduced form, subject to constraints specified by the structural equations. Geometrically, we have shown that this is precisely what LI/LGV involves. If we assume that the errors are multivariate normal, then the criterion of maximum likelihood (LI/ML) would give exactly the same estimates as LI/LGV. The proof would be similar to that of Section 2-12, although much more complex.

(d) Algebraic Generalization, LI/LVR

We turn finally to a third criterion for generating the same estimate of a single equation. It permits the easiest algebraic treatment, which we develop now in full generality.

The structural equation to be estimated was first given in (19-15); now we change notation slightly. As in the identification chapter, we will collect all the endogenous variables together on the left side, so that the structural equation to be estimated is

$$\mathbf{Y}\boldsymbol{\gamma} = \mathbf{X}_1\boldsymbol{\beta}_1 + \mathbf{X}_1^*\mathbf{0} + \mathbf{e} \tag{19-54}$$

where $\mathbf{Y}$ includes all endogenous variables in the first equation ($\mathbf{Y} = [\mathbf{y}, -\mathbf{Y}_1]$ in our previous notation). By writing a zero coefficient, we emphasize that certain exogenous variables $\mathbf{X}_1^*$ are specifically excluded.

Let us consider some estimator $\hat{\boldsymbol{\gamma}}$, and the corresponding linear combination

$$\tilde{\mathbf{y}} = \mathbf{Y}\hat{\boldsymbol{\gamma}} \tag{19-55}$$

This we call the composite endogenous variable, which will be our estimate of $\mathbf{Y}\boldsymbol{\gamma}$ in (19-54). Referring to that equation, we hope to choose $\hat{\boldsymbol{\gamma}}$ so that $\tilde{\mathbf{y}}$ depends on $\mathbf{X}_1$ alone, not on all of $\mathbf{X} = [\mathbf{X}_1, \mathbf{X}_1^*]$. In terms of regression analysis, $\tilde{\mathbf{y}}$ should be explained by $\mathbf{X}_1$ just about as well as by $\mathbf{X}$. (Not *quite* as well, because the addition of more regressors $\mathbf{X}_1^*$ will improve the explanation *slightly* even when $\mathbf{X}_1^*$ is irrelevant.) Putting this algebraically, we would expect the ratio

$$\frac{\text{the residual variation, using } \mathbf{X}_1 \text{ only}}{\text{the residual variation, using all } \mathbf{X}} \tag{19-56}$$

to be only slightly greater than unity. Thus we have motivated a precise definition of the least-variance ratio (LI/LVR) estimator:

$$\boxed{\hat{\gamma} \text{ is chosen to make the variance ratio (19-56) a minimum}} \tag{19-57}$$

In order to develop the formula for $\hat{\gamma}$, we first express the ratio (19-56) algebraically. Using (19-61) in the footnote below,[14] the denominator becomes

$$\text{Residual variation (using } \mathbf{X}) = \tilde{\mathbf{y}}'\{\mathbf{I} - \mathbf{X}(\mathbf{X}'\mathbf{X})^{-1}\mathbf{X}'\}\tilde{\mathbf{y}} \tag{19-62}$$

Substituting (19-55)

$$= \hat{\gamma}'\mathbf{Y}'\{\mathbf{I} - \mathbf{X}(\mathbf{X}'\mathbf{X})^{-1}\mathbf{X}'\}\mathbf{Y}\hat{\gamma}$$

$$= \hat{\gamma}'\mathbf{R}\hat{\gamma} \tag{19-63}$$

where

$$\mathbf{R} = \mathbf{Y}'\{\mathbf{I} - \mathbf{X}(\mathbf{X}'\mathbf{X})^{-1}\mathbf{X}'\}\mathbf{Y} \tag{19-64}$$

Similarly, the numerator is

$$\text{Residual variation (using } \mathbf{X}_1 \text{ only}) = \hat{\gamma}'\mathbf{R}_1\hat{\gamma} \tag{19-65}$$

where

$$\mathbf{R}_1 = \mathbf{Y}'\{\mathbf{I} - \mathbf{X}_1(\mathbf{X}_1'\mathbf{X}_1)^{-1}\mathbf{X}_1'\}\mathbf{Y} \tag{19-66}$$

Thus (19-56), the variance ratio to be minimized, may be written

$$\text{Residual variance ratio} = \frac{\hat{\gamma}'\mathbf{R}_1\hat{\gamma}}{\hat{\gamma}'\mathbf{R}\hat{\gamma}} \tag{19-67}$$

---

[14] Applying the Pythagorean theorem to ΔDAC in Figure 14-18,

$$\|\mathbf{y} - \hat{\mathbf{y}}\|^2 = \|\mathbf{y} - \hat{\mathbf{y}}_1\|^2 - \|\hat{\beta}_2\mathbf{x}_2\|^2 \qquad \text{(14-49) repeated}$$

This also holds true in higher dimensions, regardless of how many regressors are used. When deviations from the mean are denoted by $\mathbf{y}$ (rather than $\mathbf{y}$-$\hat{\mathbf{y}}_1$), then

$$\text{Residual variation} = \text{total variation in } \mathbf{y} - \text{variation explained by all regressors} \tag{19-59}$$

$$= \mathbf{y}'\mathbf{y} - (\mathbf{X}\hat{\boldsymbol{\beta}})'(\mathbf{X}\hat{\boldsymbol{\beta}}) \tag{19-60}$$

Substituting (12-19) for $\hat{\boldsymbol{\beta}}$, and noting the canceling occurrences of $(\mathbf{X}'\mathbf{X})$,

$$= \mathbf{y}'\mathbf{y} - \mathbf{y}'\mathbf{X}(\mathbf{X}'\mathbf{X})^{-1}\mathbf{X}'\mathbf{y}$$

that is,

$$\text{Residual variation} = \mathbf{y}'\{\mathbf{I} - \mathbf{X}(\mathbf{X}'\mathbf{X})^{-1}\mathbf{X}'\}\mathbf{y} \tag{19-61}$$

We now show that the minimization of any such ratio of two quadratic forms requires only that we solve

$$\mathbf{R}_1\hat{\gamma} = \lambda\mathbf{R}\hat{\gamma} \tag{19-68}$$

that is,

$$\boxed{(\mathbf{R}_1 - \lambda\mathbf{R})\hat{\gamma} = \mathbf{0}} \tag{19-69}$$

for the smallest eigenvalue[15] λ, and corresponding eigenvector $\hat{\gamma}$.

Proof. To minimize (19-67) we could just as well minimize

$$\hat{\gamma}'\mathbf{R}_1\hat{\gamma} \tag{19-71}$$

subject to the constraint

$$\hat{\gamma}'\mathbf{R}\hat{\gamma} = c \tag{19-72}$$

where c is any constant. Solving by Lagrange multiplier, we form

$$g(\hat{\gamma}) = \hat{\gamma}\mathbf{R}_1\hat{\gamma} - \lambda(\hat{\gamma}'\mathbf{R}\hat{\gamma} - c) \tag{19-73}$$

$$= \hat{\gamma}'(\mathbf{R}_1 - \lambda\mathbf{R})\hat{\gamma} + \lambda c \tag{19-74}$$

and partially differentiate with respect to each component of $\hat{\gamma}$. According to (11-9), we find the vector of partial derivatives

$$\frac{\partial g}{\partial \hat{\gamma}} = 2(\mathbf{R}_1 - \lambda\mathbf{R})\hat{\gamma} = \mathbf{0} \qquad \text{(19-69) almost proved}$$

We need now only show why the *smallest* value of λ is chosen. Substitute (19-68) into (19-67):

$$\text{Residual variance ratio} = \frac{\hat{\gamma}'(\lambda\mathbf{R}\hat{\gamma})}{\hat{\gamma}'\mathbf{R}\hat{\gamma}} = \lambda \tag{19-75}$$

Clearly, to minimize this ratio, the *smallest* value of λ should be selected, and our proof is complete.

As we argued in (19-56), this variance ratio λ will generally exceed 1 and cannot in any case fall below it. Thus, minimization of λ involves selecting the λ closest to 1. We have designated this variance ratio as λ, since it appears

---

[15] One way to solve is to set the determinant of the coefficient matrix of (19-69) equal to zero (a necessary and sufficient condition for nontrivial solutions for $\hat{\gamma}$); that is, set

$$|\mathbf{R}_1 - \lambda\mathbf{R}| = 0 \tag{19-70}$$

The solution of this polynomial yields various values of λ, with the smallest being selected. This is substituted into (19-69), which is then solved for $\hat{\gamma}$, noting, of course, that $\hat{\gamma}$ can be solved only up to a scale factor (i.e., fix one $\hat{\gamma}_i$, and solve for the rest).

as both a Lagrange multiplier and a latent root (eigenvalue). However, in the econometrics literature it is frequently referred to as $\hat{l}$.

In conclusion, to find the LI/LVR estimator:

1. Calculate the *residual matrices* $\mathbf{R}_1$ and $\mathbf{R}$, given by (19-66) and (19-64). (Recall that $\mathbf{R}_1$ uses only those **x**'s appearing in the structural equation to be estimated, whereas $\mathbf{R}$ uses *all* the **x**'s.)
2. Solve the characteristic equation (19-69), thereby obtaining $\hat{\boldsymbol{\gamma}}$. But $\hat{\boldsymbol{\gamma}}$ can be determined only up to a scale factor; hence it must be normalized by setting some appropriate component (usually the first) equal to 1. Thus, we determine our composite endogenous variable to be

$$\tilde{\mathbf{y}} = \mathbf{y}_1 + \hat{\gamma}_2 \mathbf{y}_2 + \hat{\gamma}_3 \mathbf{y}_3 + \cdots \tag{19-76}$$

3. Using (19-76), calculate the vector of values of the *composite* endogenous variable $\tilde{\mathbf{y}}$, substitute this for $\mathbf{Y}\boldsymbol{\gamma}$ in (19-54), and use OLS on this equation to regress $\tilde{\mathbf{y}}$ on $\mathbf{X}_1$. Since the regressors $\mathbf{X}_1$ and error **e** satisfy all the OLS requirements, this will yield a consistent estimator $\hat{\boldsymbol{\beta}}_1$. This, along with the previously calculated $\hat{\boldsymbol{\gamma}}$, completes the estimation of the equation.

We will hereafter designate any of the equivalent LI/LVR, LI/ML, LI/LGV as simply LI, although strictly speaking, *all* the methods developed in this chapter are *limited information*, in the sense that they estimate one equation at a time.

19-5 *k*-CLASS ESTIMATORS

This is simply a new view of the estimators considered so far, again using the instrumental variable technique. In estimating the single equation

$$\mathbf{y} = \mathbf{Y}_1\boldsymbol{\gamma}_1 + \mathbf{X}_1\boldsymbol{\beta}_1 + \mathbf{e} \tag{19-77}$$

(19-15) repeated[16]

we recall that

1. OLS used the illegitimate instrumental variables $[\mathbf{Y}_1, \mathbf{X}_1]$
2. 2SLS used the instrumental variables $[\hat{\mathbf{Y}}_1, \mathbf{X}_1]$ where $\hat{\mathbf{Y}}_1$ was the unrestricted reduced-form fit. Since $\mathbf{X}_1$ is common to both methods, the difference lies in the illegitimate use of $\mathbf{Y}_1$ in OLS versus the legitimate use of $\hat{\mathbf{Y}}_1$ in 2SLS.

---

[16] Note that we return to the definition of **y** and $\mathbf{Y}_1$ in (19-15).

We now generalize this, and take a weighted average of these two methods (with weights $1 - k$ and k); this yields the instrumental variables

$$(1 - k)\mathbf{Y}_1 + k\hat{\mathbf{Y}}_1 = \mathbf{Y}_1 + k(\hat{\mathbf{Y}}_1 - \mathbf{Y}_1) \tag{19-78}$$

Of course, we retain $\mathbf{X}_1$ as our second set of instruments.[17] We see that by definition,

1. When $k = 0$, we get OLS.
2. When $k = 1$, we get 2SLS.

The surprising thing is that[18]

3. When $k = \lambda$ of equation (19-75), we get LI.

Note how frequently this term ($k = \lambda = \hat{l}$) keeps reappearing. We now show another useful interpretation. Recall how λ (hereafter referred to as $\hat{l}$) appeared as the variance ratio in (19-75). Its closeness to 1 is interpreted as how well $\tilde{\mathbf{y}}$ is explained by $\mathbf{X}_1$, compared to how well $\tilde{\mathbf{y}}$ is explained by all the regressors $\mathbf{X}$. To restate: If we have correctly specified the model, in the sense of including all the relevant regressors in $\mathbf{X}_1$, then $\hat{l}$ will be very close to 1,

---

[17] For a more explicit description of k-class estimators, apply the k-class instruments $[\mathbf{Y}_1 + k(\hat{\mathbf{Y}}_1 - \mathbf{Y}_1), \mathbf{X}_1]$ on equation (19-77). Dropping the error term, and exchanging the two sides of the equation, we obtain

$$\begin{bmatrix} \mathbf{Y}_1' + k(\hat{\mathbf{Y}}_1 - \mathbf{Y}_1)' \\ \mathbf{X}_1' \end{bmatrix} (\mathbf{Y}_1\hat{\boldsymbol{\gamma}}_1 + \mathbf{X}_1\hat{\boldsymbol{\beta}}_1) = \begin{bmatrix} \mathbf{Y}_1' + k(\hat{\mathbf{Y}}_1 - \mathbf{Y}_1)' \\ \mathbf{X}_1' \end{bmatrix} \mathbf{y} \tag{19-79}$$

On the left side, we may reexpress

$$(\mathbf{Y}_1\hat{\boldsymbol{\gamma}}_1 + \mathbf{X}_1\hat{\boldsymbol{\beta}}_1) = [\mathbf{Y}_1, \mathbf{X}_1] \begin{bmatrix} \hat{\boldsymbol{\gamma}}_1 \\ \hat{\boldsymbol{\beta}}_1 \end{bmatrix} \tag{19-80}$$

Substitution of (19-80) into (19-79) and appropriate matrix multiplication yields the following "k-class normal equations":

$$\left[\begin{array}{c|c} \mathbf{Y}_1'\mathbf{Y}_1 + k(\hat{\mathbf{Y}}_1 - \mathbf{Y}_1)'\mathbf{Y}_1 & \mathbf{Y}_1'\mathbf{X}_1 + k(\hat{\mathbf{Y}}_1 - \mathbf{Y}_1)'\mathbf{X}_1 \\ \hline \mathbf{X}_1'\mathbf{Y}_1 & \mathbf{X}_1'\mathbf{X}_1 \end{array}\right] \begin{bmatrix} \hat{\boldsymbol{\gamma}}_1 \\ \hat{\boldsymbol{\beta}}_1 \end{bmatrix} = \begin{bmatrix} \mathbf{Y}_1'\mathbf{y} + k(\hat{\mathbf{Y}}_1 - \mathbf{Y}_1)'\mathbf{y} \\ \mathbf{X}_1'\mathbf{y} \end{bmatrix} \tag{19-81}$$

which may be solved for $\begin{bmatrix} \hat{\boldsymbol{\gamma}}_1 \\ \hat{\boldsymbol{\beta}}_1 \end{bmatrix}$ by matrix inversion.

[18] For proofs in this section, see Goldberger 1964, pp. 341–344.

exceeding it only because of random fluctuation. On the other hand, if we have misspecified the model, then $\hat{l}$ will exceed 1 both because of random fluctuation and because of misspecification.

This suggests a statistical test for correct specification. Letting l represent the true parameter[19] estimated by $\hat{l}$, and noting that $l = 1$ if the equation is correctly specified, we test

$$H_0: l = 1 \tag{19-82}$$

versus the alternative (i.e., the misspecification)

$$H_1: l > 1 \tag{19-83}$$

If H_0 is true, the estimator $\hat{l}$ follows an adjusted[20] chi-square distribution. Thus, a sufficiently large observed $\hat{l}$ would lead us to reject H_0 and search for a better specification.

An interesting and related question is, "How does the *k*-class estimate behave as we change the value of *k*?" Recent studies indicate that the estimator varies little as long as *k* does not greatly exceed 1. But if it does, then the estimator may assume quite unreasonable values. This means that if we are using LI, and $\hat{l}$ greatly exceeds 1 (because of, say, misspecification), then LI may yield a quite unreasonable estimate. Some insurance against this, of course, is to avoid LI estimation when we fear misspecification or $\hat{l}$ turns out to be quite large; thus, the desirability of the test given in (19-82) is confirmed.

As already pointed out, LI and 2SLS are both *k*-class estimators. There is another interesting way in which they are related. Recall the discussion leading up to the definition of LI/LVR in (19-56); in asking that the residual variation (using $\mathbf{X}_1$ only) be just about as small as the residual variation (using all $\mathbf{X}$), we minimized the ratio of these two variances. Alternatively, why not minimize their *difference*? It can be shown that this difference criterion yields the 2SLS estimator.

A review of single equation estimation is given in Table 19-1. LWV is not shown in this table since it has not yet been used in practical estimation; it was introduced into this discussion as a pedagogical device, useful in bridging the gap between 2SLS and LI.

---

[19] More precisely, let l be the ratio of population (as opposed to sample) variances.

[20] Not to be confused with modified chi-square. For the adjustment required, see Goldberger 1964.

TABLE 19-1 How Single Equation Methods Are Related

Estimate of γ in our example was, let us say,	.60	.67	.75	.80	.85
Estimator used:	OLS	2SLS	LI	2SLS	OLS
		on (19-37)		on (19-40)	
Corresponding k values:	0	1 →	$\hat{l}$	← 1	0

PROBLEMS

19-1 Can OLS be used to estimate (19-15)? Why, or why not?

*19-2 Show the equivalence of 2SLS and IV as techniques for estimating the exactly identified consumption function (7-25). What is the direction of bias if OLS is used? Answer two ways: (a) algebraically (b) using vector geometry.

*19-3 In estimating the exactly identified demand equation below, use vector geometry to guess the answer to the following questions:

$$Q = \alpha + \beta P + \eta Y + \text{error} \qquad \text{(demand)} \qquad \text{(8-13) repeated}$$

$$Q = \gamma + \delta P + \theta R + \text{error} \qquad \text{(supply)} \qquad \text{(8-14) repeated}$$

Y and R are the exogenous variables in the system.

(a) Do 2SLS and IV involve projecting P and Q onto the same instrumental variable subspace?
(b) Are $\hat{Q}$ and the residual vector the same in both techniques?
(c) Is $\hat{Q}$ the same in the supply equation (8-14) as it is in the demand equation (8-13)?

*19-4 (a) Consider the equation

$$\mathbf{y}_1 = \gamma \mathbf{y}_2 + \beta_1 \mathbf{x}_1 + \beta_2 \mathbf{x}_2 + \mathbf{e} \qquad (19\text{-}84)$$

where there are *no* other exogenous variables in the system; hence this equation is not identified.

Show with vector geometry why 2SLS will not yield unique estimates of γ, β_1, and β_2. Would it be true to say, "The problem is that in the second stage one is trying to project $\mathbf{y}_1$ onto a 2-space, and then express it in terms of 3 vectors (one too many vectors)?

(b) Suppose $\mathbf{x}_2$ appears in another equation in the system, but not in (19-84). Hence this equation is exactly identified. With the same diagram show that unique estimates of γ and β_1 can now be obtained, precisely because $\mathbf{x}_2$ is not used in the second stage.

(c) Using this same vector geometry, illustrate the statement: Even if we knew the *true* reduced form, this would still not allow us to uniquely determine the structural equation in part (a). Hence identification is a problem that exists even if statistical estimation is no problem.

*19-5 Suppose you wish to estimate the overidentified equation (19-5), and you know none of the techniques explained in this chapter. So you experiment, estimating the reduced form equations:

$$\hat{\mathbf{y}}_1 = \hat{\pi}_{11}\mathbf{x}_1 + \hat{\pi}_{12}\mathbf{x}_2$$

$$\hat{\mathbf{y}}_2 = \hat{\pi}_{21}\mathbf{x}_1 + \hat{\pi}_{22}\mathbf{x}_2$$

which is of course exactly how you would start if you were applying ILS to an exactly identified equation. Then you ask, "Suppose I replace $\mathbf{y}_1$ and $\mathbf{y}_2$ in (19-5) with their fitted values above, and then apply OLS?" Would you, in fact, be applying one of the techniques explained in this chapter? Why?

20

SYSTEMS ESTIMATION

Whereas in the previous chapter we estimated one or a few equations in a simultaneous system, we now consider the problem of estimating *all* the equations.

20-1 2SLS APPLIED TO EACH EQUATION

As pointed out in Section 9-2, the simplest and most obvious suggestion is to estimate the system one equation at a time using 2SLS (or another limited information method). Although this may not be the best approach in theory, it sometimes is in practice. Accordingly, it is worth briefly reviewing what a 2SLS estimation of each equation would involve. We illustrate with the three-equation model from Chapter 9, with each variable now representing a vector of n observations:

$$\left.\begin{aligned} \mathbf{y}_1 &= \gamma_{12}\mathbf{y}_2 + \beta_{11}\mathbf{x}_1 + \beta_{12}\mathbf{x}_2 + \mathbf{e}_1 && \text{(a)} \\ \mathbf{y}_2 &= \gamma_{23}\mathbf{y}_3 + \beta_{23}\mathbf{x}_3 + \mathbf{e}_2 && \text{(b)} \\ \mathbf{y}_3 &= \gamma_{31}\mathbf{y}_1 + \gamma_{32}\mathbf{y}_2 + \beta_{34}\mathbf{x}_4 + \mathbf{e}_3 && \text{(c)} \end{aligned}\right\} \quad \begin{array}{r}(20\text{-}1) \\ (9\text{-}5)\text{ repeated}\end{array}$$

The first stage is accomplished for all equations at once by freely fitting the *entire* reduced form[1]:

$$\hat{\mathbf{Y}} = \mathbf{X}\hat{\mathbf{\Pi}} \tag{20-2}$$

that is

$$\left.\begin{aligned} \hat{\mathbf{y}}_1 &= \hat{\pi}_{11}\mathbf{x}_1 + \hat{\pi}_{12}\mathbf{x}_2 + \hat{\pi}_{13}\mathbf{x}_3 + \hat{\pi}_{14}\mathbf{x}_4 \\ \hat{\mathbf{y}}_2 &= \hat{\pi}_{21}\mathbf{x}_1 + \hat{\pi}_{22}\mathbf{x}_2 + \hat{\pi}_{23}\mathbf{x}_3 + \hat{\pi}_{24}\mathbf{x}_4 \\ \hat{\mathbf{y}}_3 &= \hat{\pi}_{31}\mathbf{x}_1 + \hat{\pi}_{32}\mathbf{x}_2 + \hat{\pi}_{33}\mathbf{x}_3 + \hat{\pi}_{34}\mathbf{x}_4 \end{aligned}\right\} \tag{20-3}$$

[1] Rather than just part of it, as in, for example, (19-18a).

This single fitting procedure provides all the fitted $\hat{\mathbf{y}}$'s to be plugged into all the equations in (20-1); then the second-stage estimates of all these equations can proceed. This will in turn provide a set of estimated residuals $\hat{\mathbf{e}}_1$, $\hat{\mathbf{e}}_2$, $\hat{\mathbf{e}}_3$.

There are two theoretical reasons why we might be able to improve upon this one-equation-at-a-time procedure in estimating the system.

Estimation of the first equation in (20-1) does not exploit our prior information about other equations in the system—in particular, the zero restrictions we have imposed in other equations.[2] (20-4)

Our estimate of the first equation might be improved further if we could allow for possible correlation between the errors in each structural equation (i.e., between $\mathbf{e}_1$, $\mathbf{e}_2$, and $\mathbf{e}_3$); the possibility of such correlation may have become evident from a cursory examination of the fitted $\hat{\mathbf{e}}_1$, $\hat{\mathbf{e}}_2$, and $\hat{\mathbf{e}}_3$. (20-5)

20-2 THREE STAGE LEAST SQUARES (3SLS)

(a) Introduction

Three stage least squares (3SLS) is a systems method developed by Zellner and Theil 1962, which adds a third stage to take both (20-4) and (20-5) into account. It is called a *full information* method, since it exploits all available information as it simultaneously estimates all equations in the system. By contrast, a single equation method like 2SLS is referred to as a *limited information* method.

The first two stages of 3SLS have already been described: the 2SLS estimation of each equation in the system—one at a time, as in (20-2) and (20-1). This generates a set of observed errors $\hat{\mathbf{e}}_1$, $\hat{\mathbf{e}}_2$, $\hat{\mathbf{e}}_3$, which is used to estimate the covariance matrix of the errors in the system (in fact, when this has been calculated, the entire battery of 2SLS estimates has no further use and may be discarded).

The third stage is, of course, the problem. What should it achieve? First, if it is to be a solution using full information it must be a single, once-and-for-all simultaneous solution of the whole system (20-1)—*not* one equation at a time. Second, if it is to exploit the covariance matrix of the errors that we have just estimated, it should use the technique we have already developed to handle this—GLS. And this is the best way to briefly describe the third

---

[2] For example, $\beta_{21} = 0$ [i.e., $\mathbf{x}_1$ does not appear in (20-1b)].

stage: a large GLS solution of the entire system simultaneously. Before developing this third stage in detail, however, we need to take another look at GLS and 2SLS.

(b)   2SLS Reconsidered

We will show that 2SLS can be interpreted as a transformation using all the exogenous variables **X**, followed by GLS. To establish this, let us begin with the equation to be estimated, the first let us say:

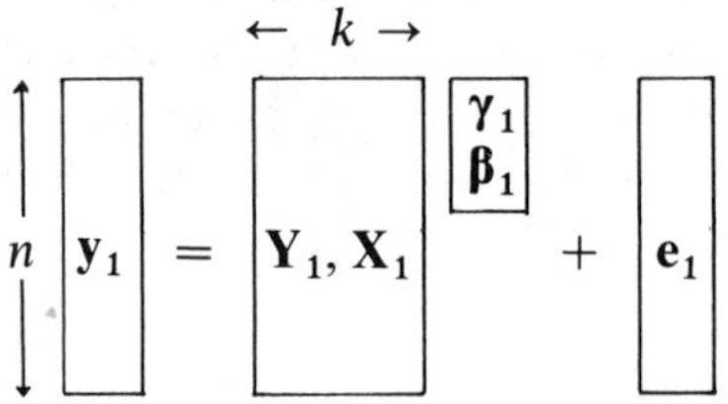

$$n \; \mathbf{y}_1 = \overset{\leftarrow \; k \; \rightarrow}{\mathbf{Y}_1, \mathbf{X}_1} \begin{bmatrix} \gamma_1 \\ \beta_1 \end{bmatrix} + \mathbf{e}_1$$

$$\text{(20-6)} \\ \text{like (19-16)}$$

To reduce terminology, we write this more briefly as:

$$\mathbf{y}_1 = \mathbf{S}_1 \boldsymbol{\alpha}_1 + \mathbf{e}_1 \tag{20-7}$$

with the subscript emphasizing that all terms belong to the first equation; thus $\mathbf{S}_1$ is made up of all the variables on the right side of this equation, and $\boldsymbol{\alpha}_1$ is the vector of all the coefficients. Now let us transform (20-7) with $\mathbf{X}'$ (all M exogenous variables in all the equations):

$$\mathbf{X}'\mathbf{y}_1 = \mathbf{X}'\mathbf{S}_1\boldsymbol{\alpha}_1 + \mathbf{X}'\mathbf{e}_1 \tag{20-8}$$

$$M \; \overset{\leftarrow \; n \; \rightarrow}{\mathbf{X}'} \; \mathbf{y}_1 = \mathbf{X}' \; \mathbf{S}_1 \begin{bmatrix} \boldsymbol{\alpha}_1 \end{bmatrix} + \mathbf{X}' \; \mathbf{e}_1$$

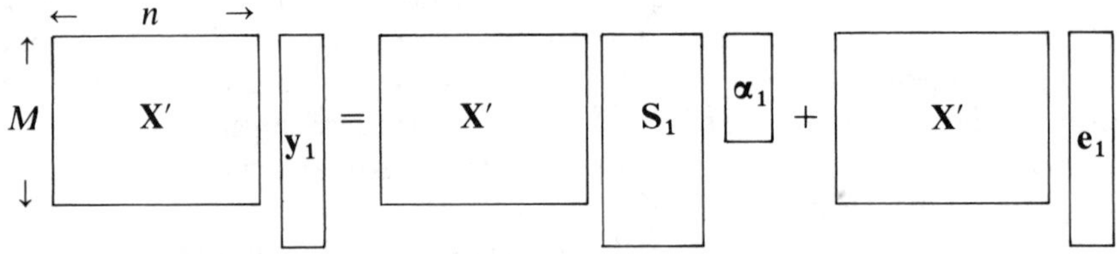

When $\mathbf{X}'\mathbf{y}_1$ is multiplied out, we obtain a vector of M transformed observations, which we will denote by $\underline{\mathbf{y}}_1$; that is

$$\text{let} \quad \underline{\mathbf{y}}_1 = \mathbf{X}'\mathbf{y}_1 \tag{20-9}$$

$$\text{Similarly let} \quad \underline{\mathbf{S}}_1 = \mathbf{X}'\mathbf{S}_1 \tag{20-10}$$

$$\text{and} \quad \underline{\mathbf{e}}_1 = \mathbf{X}'\mathbf{e}_1 \tag{20-11}$$

Then (20-8) may be written briefly as

$$M\left\{\ \underline{\mathbf{y}}_1 = \underline{\mathbf{S}}_1 \boldsymbol{\alpha}_1 + \underline{\mathbf{e}}_1 \right. \tag{20-12}$$

Next, to apply GLS to (20-12), we need the covariance matrix of the error $\underline{\mathbf{e}}_1$. If we make the standard assumption that

$$\text{cov}(\mathbf{e}_1) = \sigma_{11}\mathbf{I} \tag{20-13}$$

then, from Table 12-2,

$$\begin{aligned}\text{cov}(\underline{\mathbf{e}}_1) &= \text{cov}(\mathbf{X}'\mathbf{e}_1) = \mathbf{X}'(\text{cov } \mathbf{e}_1)\mathbf{X} \\ &= \sigma_{11}\mathbf{X}'\mathbf{X}\end{aligned} \tag{20-14}$$

Then the GLS estimate is given by applying (16-6) to (20-12); noting how reciprocal occurrences of σ_{11} cancel, we obtain

$$\hat{\alpha}_1 = \{\underline{\mathbf{S}}_1'(\mathbf{X}'\mathbf{X})^{-1}\underline{\mathbf{S}}_1\}^{-1}\underline{\mathbf{S}}_1'(\mathbf{X}'\mathbf{X})^{-1}\underline{\mathbf{y}}_1 \tag{20-15}$$

which can be proved to be just the 2SLS solution.[3] We have established, then, that 2SLS can be interpreted as a transformation using all exogenous variables in the system, followed by the application of GLS.

---

[3] ***Proof.*** First, substitute (20-9) and (20-10) into (20-15), obtaining:

$$\hat{\boldsymbol{\alpha}}_1 = \{(\mathbf{X}'\mathbf{S}_1)'(\mathbf{X}'\mathbf{X})^{-1}(\mathbf{X}'\mathbf{S}_1)\}^{-1}\{(\mathbf{X}'\mathbf{S}_1)'(\mathbf{X}'\mathbf{X})^{-1}(\mathbf{X}'\mathbf{y}_1)\} \tag{20-16}$$

By bringing half the right side of (20-16) over to the left, and by expanding transposed products, we obtain

$$\mathbf{S}_1'\mathbf{X}(\mathbf{X}'\mathbf{X})^{-1}\mathbf{X}'\mathbf{S}_1\hat{\boldsymbol{\alpha}}_1 = \mathbf{S}_1'\mathbf{X}(\mathbf{X}'\mathbf{X})^{-1}\mathbf{X}'\mathbf{y}_1 \tag{20-17}$$

Recalling how $\mathbf{S}_1$ and $\boldsymbol{\alpha}_1$ were defined in (20-7), we may rewrite this as

$$\begin{bmatrix}\mathbf{Y}_1' \\ \mathbf{X}_1'\end{bmatrix}\mathbf{X}(\mathbf{X}'\mathbf{X})^{-1}\mathbf{X}'\mathbf{S}_1\begin{bmatrix}\hat{\boldsymbol{\gamma}}_1 \\ \hat{\boldsymbol{\beta}}_1\end{bmatrix} = \begin{bmatrix}\mathbf{Y}_1' \\ \mathbf{X}_1'\end{bmatrix}\mathbf{X}(\mathbf{X}'\mathbf{X})^{-1}\mathbf{X}'\mathbf{y}_1$$

which partitions into

$$\mathbf{Y}_1'\mathbf{X}(\mathbf{X}'\mathbf{X})^{-1}\mathbf{X}'\mathbf{S}_1\begin{bmatrix}\hat{\boldsymbol{\gamma}}_1 \\ \hat{\boldsymbol{\beta}}_1\end{bmatrix} = \mathbf{Y}_1'\mathbf{X}(\mathbf{X}'\mathbf{X})^{-1}\mathbf{X}'\mathbf{y}_1 \tag{20-18}$$

and

$$\mathbf{X}_1'\mathbf{X}(\mathbf{X}'\mathbf{X})^{-1}\mathbf{X}'\mathbf{S}_1\begin{bmatrix}\hat{\boldsymbol{\gamma}}_1 \\ \hat{\boldsymbol{\beta}}_1\end{bmatrix} = \mathbf{X}_1'\mathbf{X}(\mathbf{X}'\mathbf{X})^{-1}\mathbf{X}'\mathbf{y}_1 \tag{20-19}$$

Similarly, the 2SLS solution in (19-20) may be written

$$\begin{bmatrix}\hat{\mathbf{Y}}_1' \\ \mathbf{X}_1'\end{bmatrix}[\hat{\mathbf{Y}}_1, \mathbf{X}_1]\begin{bmatrix}\hat{\boldsymbol{\gamma}}_1 \\ \hat{\boldsymbol{\beta}}_1\end{bmatrix} = \begin{bmatrix}\hat{\mathbf{Y}}_1' \\ \mathbf{X}_1'\end{bmatrix}\mathbf{y}_1 \tag{20-20}$$

(continued)

The final important conclusion is that some sort of instrumental variable treatment (such as transformation by $\mathbf{X}'$) is an essential prerequisite for applying GLS in a system of simultaneous equations. If we had tried to apply GLS to (20-7) without the transformation by $\mathbf{X}'$ in (20-8), then GLS (just like OLS) would be an inconsistent procedure[4] because of the correlation between $\mathbf{e}_1$ and $\mathbf{S}_1$.

---

which partitions into

$$\hat{\mathbf{Y}}_1'[\hat{\mathbf{Y}}_1, \mathbf{X}_1]\begin{bmatrix}\hat{\boldsymbol{\gamma}}_1\\ \hat{\boldsymbol{\beta}}_1\end{bmatrix} = \hat{\mathbf{Y}}_1'\mathbf{y}_1 \tag{20-21}$$

and

$$\mathbf{X}_1'[\hat{\mathbf{Y}}_1, \mathbf{X}_1]\begin{bmatrix}\hat{\boldsymbol{\gamma}}_1\\ \hat{\boldsymbol{\beta}}_1\end{bmatrix} = \mathbf{X}_1'\mathbf{y}_1 \tag{20-22}$$

We now show the equivalence of (20-17) and 2SLS in (20-20) by establishing that (20-18) is equivalent to (20-21) and (20-19) to (20-22). To establish the first, we note that in the regression of Y_1 on X in (19-18a), we obtain the fitted values

$$\hat{\mathbf{Y}}_1 = \mathbf{X}(\mathbf{X}'\mathbf{X})^{-1}\mathbf{X}'\mathbf{Y}_1 \tag{20-23}$$

Transposing this, and noting that $\mathbf{X}'\mathbf{X}$ is symmetric, (20-18) can be written

$$\hat{\mathbf{Y}}_1'\mathbf{S}_1\begin{bmatrix}\hat{\boldsymbol{\gamma}}_1\\ \hat{\boldsymbol{\beta}}_1\end{bmatrix} = \hat{\mathbf{Y}}_1'\mathbf{y}_1 \tag{20-24}$$

Finally, noting that $\mathbf{S}_1 = [\mathbf{Y}_1, \mathbf{X}_1]$, and using (19-24) this is seen to be equivalent to (20-21).

To show the equivalence of (20-19) to (20-22) we let

$$\mathbf{X}(\mathbf{X}'\mathbf{X})^{-1}\mathbf{X}' = \mathbf{P} \tag{20-25}$$

and noting that $\mathbf{X}'\mathbf{P} = \mathbf{X}'$, we conclude that $\mathbf{P}$ acts like the identity matrix when postmultiplying $\mathbf{X}'$. ($\mathbf{P}$ is a projection operator onto the subspace generated by the columns of $\mathbf{X}$). Furthermore, if we partition $\mathbf{X}$ into its parts that are included and excluded from the first equation, we obtain

$$\begin{bmatrix}\mathbf{X}_1'\\ \mathbf{X}_1^{*\prime}\end{bmatrix}\mathbf{X}(\mathbf{X}'\mathbf{X})^{-1}\mathbf{X}' = \begin{bmatrix}\mathbf{X}_1'\\ \mathbf{X}_1^{*\prime}\end{bmatrix} \tag{20-26}$$

Noting only the first part,

$$\mathbf{X}_1'\mathbf{X}(\mathbf{X}'\mathbf{X})^{-1}\mathbf{X}' = \mathbf{X}_1'$$

This allows us to simplify (20-19) to

$$\mathbf{X}_1'[\mathbf{Y}_1, \mathbf{X}_1]\begin{bmatrix}\hat{\boldsymbol{\gamma}}_1\\ \hat{\boldsymbol{\beta}}_1\end{bmatrix} = \mathbf{X}_1'\mathbf{y}_1$$

which, using (19-25), reduces to (20-22).

[4] It is the application of $\mathbf{X}'$ that gives the zero (asymptotic) covariance between the error ($\mathbf{X}'e_1$) and the other variables on the right-hand side ($\mathbf{X}'\mathbf{S}_1$) that GLS requires.

The problem may be reviewed in its simplest possible context by recalling that OLS (or GLS) could not be consistently applied to (7-25) because of the correlation between $\mathbf{e}$ and $\mathbf{Y}$. Instead, a transformation using $\mathbf{I}$ as an instrumental variable was required, as given in (7-28).

(c) The Third Stage of 3SLS

In this development, we will assume that there are no identities in the system, and all equations are identified.[5] If these assumptions do not hold, then a more advanced treatment is required.

Now suppose that we have completed the first two stages of 3SLS. That is, we have derived the 2SLS estimate of each equation in the system, and from it calculated the residual (estimated error) vector $\hat{\mathbf{e}}_i$. We may now discard the 2SLS estimates of each equation, but we keep the error vectors $\hat{\mathbf{e}}_i$ to use in the third stage.

The third stage involves the same procedure that we described in part (b): We transform *all* the equations by $\mathbf{X}'$, and then use GLS. In using GLS, of course, we must use the error vectors $\hat{\mathbf{e}}_i$ from the second stage. Furthermore, we must apply GLS *simultaneously* to all equations in the system.

Here then are the details: Just as in (20-8) we transformed the first equation, we now apply the instrumental variable $\mathbf{X}$ to transform the whole system:

$$\mathbf{X}'\mathbf{y}_1 = \mathbf{X}'\mathbf{S}_1\boldsymbol{\alpha}_1 + \mathbf{X}'\mathbf{e}_1$$

$$\mathbf{X}'\mathbf{y}_2 = \mathbf{X}'\mathbf{S}_2\boldsymbol{\alpha}_2 + \mathbf{X}'\mathbf{e}_2$$

$$\vdots \qquad\qquad \vdots \qquad\qquad \vdots$$

$$\mathbf{X}'\mathbf{y}_Q = \mathbf{X}'\mathbf{S}_Q\boldsymbol{\alpha}_Q + \mathbf{X}'\mathbf{e}_Q \tag{20-27}$$

---

[5] In fact, it is assumed that at least one equation is overidentified. Since equations are usually overidentified, however, this presents no problem in practice. For more details, see for example, Zellner and Theil 1962.

We write this as a huge simultaneous system:

$$\begin{bmatrix} \mathbf{X}'\mathbf{y}_1 \\ \mathbf{X}'\mathbf{y}_2 \\ \cdot \\ \cdot \\ \cdot \\ \mathbf{X}'\mathbf{y}_Q \end{bmatrix} = \begin{bmatrix} \mathbf{X}'\mathbf{S}_1 & & & 0 \\ & \mathbf{X}'\mathbf{S}_2 & & \\ & & \ddots & \\ 0 & & & \mathbf{X}'\mathbf{S}_Q \end{bmatrix} \begin{bmatrix} \boldsymbol{\alpha}_1 \\ \boldsymbol{\alpha}_2 \\ \cdot \\ \cdot \\ \cdot \\ \boldsymbol{\alpha}_Q \end{bmatrix} + \begin{bmatrix} \mathbf{X}'\mathbf{e}_1 \\ \mathbf{X}'\mathbf{e}_2 \\ \cdot \\ \cdot \\ \cdot \\ \mathbf{X}'\mathbf{e}_Q \end{bmatrix} \tag{20-28}$$

or, even more simply, as

$$\underline{\mathbf{y}} = \underline{\mathbf{S}}\boldsymbol{\alpha} + \underline{\mathbf{e}} \tag{20-29}$$

We now apply GLS to this system, which requires an estimate of the covariance of the error $\underline{\mathbf{e}}$. This, in turn, requires knowledge of the covariance of the original unknown errors $\mathbf{e}_i$. Suppose the n observations occur over n time periods, and that contemporaneous errors (i.e., occurring at the same time) are correlated. In fact, let the covariance between contemporaneous errors in the ith and jth equation be denoted σ_{ij}. And we will assume that noncontemporaneous errors are uncorrelated. Then in matrix terms this means that the set of all nQ errors $\mathbf{e}$ defined as

$$\mathbf{e} \equiv \begin{bmatrix} \mathbf{e}_1 \\ \mathbf{e}_2 \\ \cdot \\ \cdot \\ \cdot \\ \mathbf{e}_Q \end{bmatrix} \tag{20-30}$$

has a covariance matrix

$$\text{cov } \mathbf{e} = \sum = \begin{bmatrix} \sigma_{11}\mathbf{I} & \sigma_{12}\mathbf{I} & \cdots \\ \sigma_{21}\mathbf{I} & & \\ \vdots & \ddots & \\ & & \sigma_{QQ}\mathbf{I} \end{bmatrix} \tag{20-31}$$

We showed in (20-14) that, if σ_{11} is the variance of the error in the first equation,

$$\text{cov}(\mathbf{X}'\mathbf{e}_1) = \sigma_{11}\mathbf{X}'\mathbf{X} \tag{20-32}$$

We can now similarly show[6] that

$$\text{cov}\,\underline{\mathbf{e}} = \mathbf{U} = \text{cov}\begin{bmatrix} \mathbf{X}'\mathbf{e}_1 \\ \mathbf{X}'\mathbf{e}_2 \\ \cdot \\ \cdot \\ \cdot \\ \mathbf{X}'\mathbf{e}_Q \end{bmatrix} = \begin{bmatrix} \sigma_{11}\mathbf{X}'\mathbf{X} & \sigma_{12}\mathbf{X}'\mathbf{X} & \cdots & \\ \sigma_{21}\mathbf{X}'\mathbf{X} & & & \\ \cdot & \cdot & & \\ \cdot & & \cdot & \\ \cdot & & & \cdot \\ & & & \sigma_{QQ}\mathbf{X}'\mathbf{X} \end{bmatrix} \tag{20-36}$$

---

[6] ***Proof.*** Comparing (20-28) and (20-29) we note that $\underline{\mathbf{e}}$ can be expressed with the following block multiplication:

$$\underline{\mathbf{e}} = \begin{bmatrix} \mathbf{X}' & & & & 0 \\ & \mathbf{X}' & & & \\ & & \cdot & & \\ & & & \cdot & \\ & & & & \cdot \\ 0 & & & & \mathbf{X}' \end{bmatrix} \begin{bmatrix} \mathbf{e}_1 \\ \mathbf{e}_2 \\ \cdot \\ \cdot \\ \cdot \\ \mathbf{e}_Q \end{bmatrix} \tag{20-33}$$

From Table 12-2,

$$\text{cov}\,\underline{\mathbf{e}} = \mathbf{U} = \begin{bmatrix} \mathbf{X}' & & & & 0 \\ & \mathbf{X}' & & & \\ & & \cdot & & \\ & & & \cdot & \\ & & & & \cdot \\ 0 & & & & \mathbf{X}' \end{bmatrix} (\text{cov}\,\mathbf{e}) \begin{bmatrix} \mathbf{X} & & & & 0 \\ & \mathbf{X} & & & \\ & & \cdot & & \\ & & & \cdot & \\ & & & & \cdot \\ 0 & & & & \mathbf{X} \end{bmatrix} \tag{20-34}$$

$$= \begin{bmatrix} \mathbf{X}' & & & & 0 \\ & \mathbf{X}' & & & \\ & & \cdot & & \\ & & & \cdot & \\ & & & & \cdot \\ 0 & & & & \mathbf{X}' \end{bmatrix} \begin{bmatrix} \sigma_{11}\mathbf{I} & \sigma_{12}\mathbf{I} & \cdots & \\ \sigma_{21}\mathbf{I} & & & \\ \cdot & \cdot & & \\ \cdot & & \cdot & \\ \cdot & & & \cdot \\ & & & \sigma_{QQ}\mathbf{I} \end{bmatrix} \begin{bmatrix} \mathbf{X} & & & & 0 \\ & \mathbf{X} & & & \\ & & \cdot & & \\ & & & \cdot & \\ & & & & \cdot \\ 0 & & & & \mathbf{X} \end{bmatrix} \tag{20-35}$$

When multiplied out, this becomes

$$\mathbf{U} = \begin{bmatrix} \mathbf{X}'\sigma_{11}\mathbf{X} & \cdots & \\ \mathbf{X}'\sigma_{21}\mathbf{X} & & \\ \cdot & \cdot & \\ \cdot & & \cdot \\ \cdot & & & \cdot \\ & & \mathbf{X}'\sigma_{QQ}\mathbf{X} \end{bmatrix} = \begin{bmatrix} \sigma_{11}\mathbf{X}'\mathbf{X} & \cdots & \\ \sigma_{21}\mathbf{X}'\mathbf{X} & & \\ \cdot & \cdot & \\ \cdot & & \cdot \\ \cdot & & & \cdot \\ & & \sigma_{QQ}\mathbf{X}'\mathbf{X} \end{bmatrix} \quad \text{(20-36) proved}$$

where σ_{ij} is the covariance between the errors of the ith and jth equation. It is consistently estimated by using those residuals $\hat{\mathbf{e}}_i$ kept from the second stage:

$$\hat{\sigma}_{ij} = \frac{1}{n}\hat{\mathbf{e}}_i'\hat{\mathbf{e}}_j \tag{20-37}$$

When the estimates in (20-37) are plugged into (20-36), the resulting $\hat{\mathbf{U}}$ provides the missing link in applying GLS to (20-29); hence we now can calculate:

The 3SLS solution:

$$\hat{\boldsymbol{\alpha}} = (\underline{\mathbf{S}}'\hat{\mathbf{U}}^{-1}\underline{\mathbf{S}})^{-1}\underline{\mathbf{S}}'\hat{\mathbf{U}}^{-1}\underline{\mathbf{y}} \tag{20-38}$$

where $\underline{\mathbf{S}}$ and $\underline{\mathbf{y}}$ are defined in (20-29).

We have completed the chain of logic underlying 3SLS. To summarize, the actual calculations typically proceed in the following sequence: 3SLS follows 2SLS through the first two stages, and the third stage is GLS estimation of the transformed system (20-29). These three stages, in detail, are:

1. Estimate the whole reduced form, to get fitted values corresponding to all the observed $\mathbf{Y}$. By obtaining all the $\hat{\mathbf{Y}}$ instrumental variables, we have completed the first stage of 2SLS—for *all* equations in the system.
2. Using the relevant instruments we proceed with the second stage of the 2SLS fit, again for each equation. So far, we have accomplished no more or no less than estimating the system by 2SLS, one equation at a time. These estimated equations then yield estimated errors $\hat{\mathbf{e}}_1, \hat{\mathbf{e}}_2, \ldots, \hat{\mathbf{e}}_Q$, used to calculate $\hat{\mathbf{U}}$.
3. Use $\hat{\mathbf{U}}$ to apply GLS to the transformed system (20-29), obtaining (20-38).

PROBLEM

20-1 True or false; if false, correct it:

OLS, 2SLS, and 3SLS can all be interpreted as the application of instrumental variables, followed by GLS.

20-3 3SLS OR 2SLS? FULL INFORMATION VERSUS LIMITED INFORMATION ESTIMATION ON A SYSTEM OF EQUATIONS

If an entire system of equations is to be estimated, is it better in practice to use 2SLS one equation at a time, or use 3SLS? Since 3SLS follows 2SLS through both its first two stages, this question can be rephrased: Is the third stage of 3SLS worth it? And if so, is it feasible?

In Section 20-1 several theoretical reasons for preferring a systems method to a single-equation method were cited. In comparing 3SLS to 2SLS, (20-5) seems particularly important. If there is no correlation in residuals between equations, then 3SLS and 2SLS asymptotically coincide; thus the major gain provided by 3SLS occurs only if there is correlation between the residuals that can be exploited.

In certain circumstances this may provide a strong incentive for using 3SLS. However, there are two important reasons why 2SLS may still be preferred. Recall that 3SLS involved using the prior specification (and observed information) in *all* equations—a point that was cited earlier as an advantage. But if there is misspecification in the model (and there is a constant risk that this will occur in at least some equations in a system) then this may turn to a disadvantage. 2SLS estimation tends[7] to limit the damage done by misspecification to the equation in which misspecification occurs, whereas 3SLS "spreads around" this misspecification in estimating all equations in the system.

The second possible reason for preferring 2SLS has already been alluded to in Section 9-2: a shortage of degrees of freedom. If 3SLS is applied to a large system, there will be a large number of parameters to estimate; the number of observations may fall short of this (making estimation impossible) or just barely exceed it (making estimation unreliable). In that case, 2SLS one equation at a time becomes the more attractive option.

20-4 MODIFIED 2SLS

(a) The Problem

In an economy-wide model with a very large number of equations, even 2SLS one equation at a time may not overcome the degrees of freedom problem. The reason is that such a large number of equations will contain a

[7] Although 2SLS reduces the damage of misspecification elsewhere in the system, it does not guarantee against it. For example, if the misspecification involves overlooking an exogenous variable that should appear in some of the other equations, then this may involve a cost in estimating (and perhaps even identifying) the first equation.

very large number of exogenous variables. If this number exceeds the number of observations, then it is not even possible to get the first-stage, 2SLS fit on the reduced form such as (20-3). The number of regressors must somehow be reduced; the question is: How?

One suggestion is SOIV (structurally ordered instrumental variables) already discussed in Chapter 9. For each equation, this procedure selects the **x**'s in the system that are in some sense closest to the **y** being explained. A second suggestion, instead of discarding some of the **x**'s, is to select a smaller number that best captures the information provided by *all* of them,[8] using principal components.

(b) 2SLS Using Principal Components

This approach involves replacing the **x**'s in the first stage of 2SLS with their principal components (PC). As we saw in Section 15-2, PC is a useful way of curing the degrees of freedom (d.f.) problem. The number of principal components, although somewhat arbitrary, must nevertheless satisfy two guidelines: (1) Obviously the number must be small enough to solve the d.f. problem; and (2) the number must be large enough to guarantee identification [recall that identification requires a sufficient number of exogenous variables, according to (8-12)].

PC can be used in several alternative ways for the first stage of 2SLS. In (20-3), suppose we are estimating the first reduced form equation for $\hat{\mathbf{y}}_1$. Instead of replacing all the **x**'s with PC,[9] we can retain the **x**'s included in the first structural equation[10] [i.e., $\mathbf{x}_1$ and $\mathbf{x}_2$, or $\mathbf{X}_1$ using the notation of (19-14)] and supplement these with the PC of $\mathbf{X}_1^*$—the exogenous variables excluded.[11] But this will introduce multicollinearity if some of the PC are closely related to $\mathbf{X}_1$. Accordingly, selection of PC should compromise between maximizing the variation of $\mathbf{X}_1$ explained (the standard guideline for selecting PC in any case), and minimizing the correlation of the PC with the variables in $\mathbf{X}_1$.

---

[8] This approach is sometimes referred to as *data reduction*, to distinguish it from *truncation*, which refers to the discard of some of the **x**'s. Thus SOIV and similar methods are sometimes referred to as *truncated 2SLS*.

[9] Examples of this approach include Klein 1969 and Mitchell and Fisher 1970.

[10] Note how this is similar to the SOIV approach.

[11] Alternatively, $\mathbf{X}_1$ could be supplemented with the PC's of *all* the exogenous variables **X**.

20-5 LIMITED INFORMATION INSTRUMENTAL VARIABLES (LIVE)

The above modifications of 2SLS are designed to overcome the d.f. problem that would otherwise make traditional 2SLS out of the question—and would even more certainly preclude a systems method like 3SLS. Now consider a single-equation method aimed at solving this d.f. problem that also captures one of the advantages of a systems method: In the estimation of any individual equation, it exploits prior information (i.e., zero restrictions) on *all* the equations in the system.

This approach, referred to as LIVE,[12] was simultaneously developed by Brundy and Jorgenson 1971, and Dhrymes 1971(b); it can be clarified by considering two alternative ways of estimating the reduced form $\mathbf{\Pi}$. The first is an unrestricted fit $\hat{\mathbf{\Pi}}$ in (20-2), which is now not feasible because of a shortage of d.f. The second is to note that for any system of equations, the reduced form (18-3) is related to the structural form (18-1) according to (18-4a). Thus if we could somehow get estimates $\hat{\mathbf{B}}$ and $\hat{\mathbf{\Gamma}}$ (complete with their prespecified zero components) we could estimate

$$\hat{\mathbf{\Pi}}_R = -\hat{\mathbf{B}}\hat{\mathbf{\Gamma}}^{-1} \tag{20-39}$$

where the subscript R is used to emphasize that $\hat{\mathbf{\Pi}}_R$ is a restricted estimate of the reduced form, since it must incorporate the prior restrictions[13] imposed on $\mathbf{B}$ and $\mathbf{\Gamma}$. (Accordingly, this approach is sometimes referred to as *restricted reduced form* estimation.)

How do we get the initial required estimates $\hat{\mathbf{B}}$ and $\hat{\mathbf{\Gamma}}$? Since this is just an initial step, almost any way will do (provided, of course, that it overcomes the d.f. problem). Thus LIVE involves the following iterative procedure:

Step 1. Estimate $\hat{\mathbf{B}}$ and $\hat{\mathbf{\Gamma}}$ for the entire system using any consistent method that conserves d.f. While an obvious suggestion might be 2SLS using PC, or SOIV (i.e., select the subset of instrumental variables nearest to the equation being estimated), an even simpler, computationally less costly approach is recommended: Use *any* sufficiently small subset of instrumental variables in the system.

Step 2. Plug the estimates of $\hat{\mathbf{B}}$ and $\hat{\mathbf{\Gamma}}$ from step 1 into (20-39), thereby estimating the restricted reduced form $\hat{\mathbf{\Pi}}_R$.

---

[12] Brundy and Jorgenson call it LIVE (Limited Information Instrumental Variables Efficient) while Dhrymes refers to it as LIIV (Limited Information Instrumental Variables).

[13] As stated earlier, these restrictions need not be zero restrictions; but for simplicity the point is illustrated this way.

Step 3. Use this to calculate the whole battery of fitted **y** values for the entire system according to

$$\hat{\mathbf{Y}}^* = \mathbf{X}\hat{\mathbf{\Pi}}_R \tag{20-40}$$

like (20-2)

where the star indicates that the fit is on the *restricted* reduced form.

We are now in the same position as if we had been able to complete the first stage of 2SLS in (20-2) (except that we are now using a restricted rather than a freely fitted reduced form, and we have also overcome the d.f. problem).

Step 4. This fitted $\hat{\mathbf{Y}}^*$ can now be used in the second stage of 2SLS, thus providing new estimates of **B** and **Γ**. To equivalently state this step, $\hat{\mathbf{Y}}^*$ can now be used as instrumental variables to reestimate **B** and **Γ**.

Step 5. We can iterate by returning to step 2, and repeating.

To review: This approach solves the d.f. problem in step 1 after which it is not encountered again. It is called a limited information method because it is applied to each equation one at a time, and it does not exploit an estimated covariance matrix of disturbances throughout the system [as suggested in (20-5)]. On the other hand, it is more than the classical definition of limited information might suggest, since it does exploit prior restrictions on all equations in the system[14] [as suggested in (20-4)].

The remarkably clean and simple characteristics of this approach may best be illustrated by asking: If we use inconsistent OLS rather than some consistent IV method in step 1, will the final estimates still be consistent? The answer is yes. All the fitted $\hat{\mathbf{Y}}^*$'s used in step 4 are seen in (20-40) to be linear functions of the **X**'s, that is, they lie in the subspace spanned by the original set of instrumental variables. Hence they also qualify as instrumental variables, and accordingly yield a consistent set of estimates in step 4. In fact, some authors (e.g., Brundy and Jorgenson 1974) regard OLS as the preferred estimator in step 1, because OLS estimates are simple, and have already been calculated for many economic models (hence the first step of LIVE is already complete, and need not be undertaken again). However, if OLS is to be used for step 1, then an even stronger argument can be made,

---

[14] See Fair, 1970 for an extension of this technique to allow for autoregressive error (LIVER). Another important extension of LIVE is to take account of nonlinearities in the structural equations.

Although we consider here the application of LIVE to estimate all equations in a system (one at a time), it can obviously be used to estimate only one or a few equations (in which case only the appropriate subset of $\hat{\mathbf{Y}}^*$'s need be calculated for step 4).

on efficiency grounds, for continuing LIVE through a second full iteration at least.[15]

A natural analogy suggests itself next: Why not extend LIVE into a full systems method by estimating the covariance matrix of errors in the system, and exploiting this information—just as we extended 2SLS into 3SLS?

20-6 FULL INFORMATION INSTRUMENTAL VARIABLES (FIVE[16])

Just as the final stage of 3SLS follows 2SLS, so FIVE follows LIVE. Recall that in step 4 of LIVE, the structure of the entire system ($\hat{\mathbf{B}}$ and $\hat{\mathbf{\Gamma}}$) is estimated. Each fitted equation (say the *j*th) then generates an observed error vector $\hat{\mathbf{e}}_j$. This is then used to calculate $\hat{\sigma}_{ij}$ in (20-37), and thus to estimate the full covariance matrix of errors in the system:

$$\hat{\mathbf{\Sigma}} = \begin{bmatrix} \hat{\sigma}_{11}\mathbf{I} & \hat{\sigma}_{12}\mathbf{I} & \cdots & \\ \hat{\sigma}_{21}\mathbf{I} & \cdot & & \\ \cdot & & \cdot & \\ \cdot & & & \cdot \\ \cdot & & & \\ & & & \hat{\sigma}_{QQ}\mathbf{I} \end{bmatrix} \qquad \begin{matrix}(20\text{-}41)\\ \text{like } (20\text{-}31)\end{matrix}$$

Although the final stage of FIVE is then like the final stage of 3SLS [i.e., an IV transformation and GLS using (20-41)], there are two respects in which it is different. In the first place, the d.f. problem we face prevents an application of *all* the instrumental variables in the system. What instrumental variables should we then use? The following smaller set is recommended: on each equation, use only the $\hat{\mathbf{Y}}^*$'s (calculated in step 3 of LIVE) and the

[15] It is evident, from the recommendation that OLS be used in step 1, that estimation of simultaneous equations increasingly involves a search for the best combination of various techniques. For example, if there is no d.f. problem, and the model is already estimated using OLS, then Mikhail, 1975 suggests the following procedure: If the estimated errors that fall out of the OLS fit of each equation exhibit substantial covariance, then they may be used immediately in the third stage of 3SLS.

[16] The extension of this technique to take autoregression into account is referred to as FIVER; again see Fair 1970.

X's that appear in that equation; in other words, use the following instrumental variable transformation:

$$\mathbf{W} = \begin{bmatrix} \mathbf{W}_1 & & & & \\ & \mathbf{W}_2 & & \mathbf{0} & \\ & & \cdot & & \\ & & & \cdot & \\ & & & & \cdot \\ \mathbf{0} & & & & \mathbf{W}_Q \end{bmatrix} \tag{20-42}$$

where

$$\begin{aligned} \mathbf{W}_1 &= [\hat{\mathbf{Y}}_1^*, \mathbf{X}_1] \\ \mathbf{W}_2 &= [\hat{\mathbf{Y}}_2^*, \mathbf{X}_2] \\ &\text{etc.} \end{aligned} \tag{20-43}$$

and of course $\hat{\mathbf{Y}}_1^*$ and $\mathbf{X}_1$ include only the variables that appear in the first equation.

The second difference is that the application of GLS does not follow this IV transformation, but instead occurs at the same time. Recall from Chapter 16 that GLS is equivalent to the Aitken transformation followed by OLS. Accordingly, we apply the IV transformation and the Aitken transformation at the same time; in other words transform the system with

$$\bar{\mathbf{W}} \equiv \mathbf{W}\hat{\mathbf{\Sigma}}^{-1/2}$$

where $\mathbf{W}$ is the IV transformation (20-42) and $\hat{\mathbf{\Sigma}}^{-1/2}$ is the necessary Aitken transformation (see Section 16-5). Then, as the Aitken transformation requires, we apply OLS.[17]

To sum up, 3SLS uses the error covariance matrix that falls out of a 2SLS estimation of each equation, and exploits it in applying GLS to the entire system; similarly FIVE uses the error covariance matrix that falls out of a LIVE estimation of each equation, and exploits it in an analogous way to estimate the entire system.

---

[17] The W transformation puts the system into exactly the right row dimension so that there are exactly as many equations as unknowns. Accordingly, OLS reduces to solving the system for the unique solution, as in Problem 12-14.

20-7 DISTRIBUTIONS OF ESTIMATORS: ANALYTICAL AND EMPIRICAL (MONTE CARLO) STUDIES

In the interests of brevity, in these last two chapters we have derived only the point estimator for each method; we have not derived its variance or its distribution. Of course, without this information, tests of significance and confidence intervals could not be developed. These obviously are such important issues for practical econometrics, that we now sketch them briefly.

Why can't we analytically derive the moments of any simultaneous equation estimator just like we analytically derived the mean and variance of OLS in (12-31) and (12-32)? Although it is possible to do this asymptotically, small sample properties are often exceedingly difficult to derive; successful investigations have been limited in number—and also limited to very small econometric models.

Thus, to a substantial degree, our knowledge of the exact distribution of a simultaneous equation estimator is still restricted to its large sample (asymptotic) properties and in particular its asymptotic variance.[18] Typically, when an equation is estimated with one of these methods, it is desirable to indicate the asymptotic standard error below each estimated coefficient. In small samples, such an asymptotic standard error will produce confidence intervals and tests that are not quite right, but reader will get at least a rough indication (just as statisticians got a rough indication using the normal distribution before the t-distribution was discovered).

This severely limited analytical knowledge of small sample distributions (along with the analytical conclusion that in some cases certain moments of an estimator do not even exist) has led naturally to a heavy dependence on Monte Carlo investigations.[19] Still of prime importance in this research are

---

[18] For example, under appropriate assumptions (e.g., no error correlation) 2SLS, LIVE, and LI all have the same asymptotic distribution: normal with covariance matrix that may be consistently (asymptotically) estimated by

$$\text{cov}\begin{bmatrix}\hat{\boldsymbol{\gamma}}_1\\ \hat{\boldsymbol{\beta}}_1\end{bmatrix} \approx s^2([\hat{\mathbf{Y}}_1, \mathbf{X}_1]'[\hat{\mathbf{Y}}_1, \mathbf{X}_1])^{-1} \qquad \text{like (12-32)}$$

where s^2 is the residual variance. (Note that LI includes LI/ML, LI/LVR, and LI/LGV, which are all equivalent, i.e., always yield exactly the same estimate, regardless of the sample size. Note that this is a much stronger condition than having the same asymptotic distribution.)

Similarly, 3SLS, FIVE, and FI (including FI/ML and FI/LGV as detailed in Appendix 20-A) all have the same asymptotic distribution: normal, with covariance matrix that may be consistently (asymptotically) estimated.

[19] Described in Section 6-7g.

traditional Monte Carlo questions, such as:

1. Are the small sample properties of an estimator reasonably close to its large sample (asymptotic) properties?
2. How serious are departures from the standard theoretical models?[20]

At the same time these investigations have recently been taking some new directions. Initially Monte Carlo studies were based on small simultaneous equation models. But now that estimators in some of these small models have been described analytically, Monte Carlo studies are being run on larger models—with the question being: Do the analytical results in the small models carry over to larger models? Another important new direction is in improving computer sampling designs, in order to sharpen our ability to discern differences in estimators.

20-8 A COMPARISON OF ESTIMATORS

Some of the basic methods for estimating a system of equations are compared in Table 20-1. Before discussing these, a few words are in order on the simplest method of all, namely OLS on one equation at a time. When used in this way, OLS is being asked to do more than it was designed for, and yields an estimate that is biased and inconsistent. Since it is biased in infinite samples, whereas the other (consistent) estimators are not, one might predict that OLS would have greater bias in small samples as well. By and large, Monte Carlo studies have confirmed this expectation—and in the process have also uncovered one respect in which OLS may not perform too badly: Compared to LI it may have relatively small variance[21] (indeed, in some comparisons the smaller variance of OLS more than offsets its greater bias, so that it has smaller mean squared error). In addition, OLS is familiar and simple to compute—and these considerations explain why it is still sometimes used on simultaneous equations. In short, it cannot necessarily be rejected out of hand in small samples because of its large sample weakness of inconsistency. Nevertheless, estimators can generally be found in Table 20-1 that will outperform OLS. In particular, 2SLS usually does better.

When we turn in Table 20-1 to a comparison of the consistent estimators specifically designed for simultaneous systems, certain tentative conclusions emerge. If there are no d.f. problems, the estimators in the left-hand

[20] For example, we have already noted that when the error covariance matrix is diagonal, 2SLS and 3SLS coincide. If this matrix is *almost* diagonal, would 2SLS and 3SLS *almost* coincide?
[21] For example, Goldberger 1964 (pp. 359–360) shows that OLS has a smaller variance than 2SLS.

TABLE 20-1 Comparison of Various Consistent Estimators for a System of Simultaneous Equations

Does estimator take into account: (*i*) *Prior restrictions in other equations?*	(*ii*) *Error covariance?*	*Are degrees of freedom a problem?* *No*	*Yes*
No	No	2SLS LI[a]	2SLS with PC SOIV
Yes	No		LIVE
Yes	Yes	3SLS FI[b]	FIVE

[a] Includes the equivalent LI/ML, LI/LVR, and LI/LGV.
[b] Includes the equivalent FI/ML and FI/LGV.

column may be applied; but if there are d.f. problems we are forced into the right-hand column.

As we go from top to bottom in this table, we move from limited- to full-information estimators. Thus estimators in the first row take account of neither the prior restrictions on other equations (20-4) nor the error covariance in the system (20-5); the estimator in the second row takes account only of (20-4), and the full-information estimators in the last row take account of both.

If the objective is to do as good a job as possible in a world chronically short of degrees of freedom, why not move as far as possible to the southeast in the table? On theoretical grounds, that is not a bad first recommendation: Use FIVE. More specifically, FIVE will generally be preferred to LIVE because it requires little additional computing burden, and some Monte Carlo results (Carter 1981) confirm our strong theoretical expectation that, by taking error covariance into account, FIVE can outperform LIVE.

Now compare FIVE with 3SLS and FI, the other full information estimators. Although they have the same asymptotic distribution,[22] FIVE may be preferred to 3SLS because it is simpler, and handles the d.f. problem.

[22] There is another noteworthy equivalence as well: In the limit as the number of iterations increases, FIVE approaches FI.

And even if there is no d.f. problem, FIVE (including at least one further iteration) may be preferred to 3SLS, since 3SLS estimates $\hat{\boldsymbol{\Sigma}}$ once-and-for-all, while FIVE improves its estimate on each iteration.[23]

Curiously, it is only when FIVE is compared to the more elementary estimators in the first row (in particular, 2SLS)[24] that its clear superiority can no longer be established. Unlike 2SLS, FIVE takes into account the prior restrictions on other equations in the system. As already noted, this is an advantage if the system is correctly specified. But if the system is badly misspecified, then this may become a disadvantage (in his Monte Carlo study, Cragg 1968 shows how badly misspecification can dislocate an estimator). In this case, 2SLS may be preferred, precisely because it is not burdened with the excess baggage of specification errors committed in other equations in the system.

This then leads us to a somewhat more sophisticated, though still rough-and-ready, recommendation. Use FIVE (if possible, with a second iteration) unless there is a substantial risk of specification error; if there is, then use a limited information estimator like 2SLS (with, if necessary, a device like PC for conserving d.f.). However, this advice is easier to give than to follow, since it is difficult to know how much specification error is being committed. Nonetheless, at least one tentative conclusion is possible; in an economic world in which any Y tends to depend on a large number of other variables in the economy, the more one reduces the model size in order to provide theoretical and mathematical simplicity (and perhaps conserve degrees of freedom), the greater may be the risk of misspecification; accordingly, the more one might prefer 2SLS.

20-9 CONCLUDING REMARKS

In systems of equations the selection of the best model specification remains at least as important as the selection of the best estimator. Indeed, a judgement on specification error will be an important influence in determining

---

[23] For a Monte Carlo confirmation of this advantage, see Carter 1981.

In fairness, one should perhaps compare FIVE including an additional iteration to 3SLS including an additional iteration (i.e., use the 3SLS estimates of the structure to generate a better set of observed errors, on which the third stage can be rerun). To date, we know of no such comparison.

[24] Of the limited information estimators, 2SLS is used as our point of reference because of its apparent superiority over LI. For one thing, it is easier to compute. Moreover, Monte Carlo studies confirm our earlier suspicion (in Section 19-4) that LI can be very unstable, especially in very small samples.

which estimator is best. If there is high confidence in the model specification, then a full information technique like FIVE is indicated. On the other hand, if there is little confidence in the specification, then it may be better to go back to a simple limited information estimator like 2SLS (or a variant that conserves d.f.) in order to insulate estimation of any equation from the specification errors committed in other equations.

In specifying a model, there is no substitute for good economic theory, richly laced with good judgement. Even though we have said it before, there is no better parting thought.

APPENDIX 20-A

Other Full Information Estimators

To complete this discussion, we return to the assumption that there is no d.f. problem, and ask: What other full systems methods are there that compete directly with 3SLS?

(a) Simultaneous Least Squares (SLS)

When we extend the 2SLS single-equation method into system estimation, the result is 3SLS; similarly, when LWV is extended into systems estimation, the result is Simultaneous Least Squares. This involves estimating all reduced form equations so as to minimize the weighted[25] trace of $\hat{\Omega}$ in (19-52), subject to the restrictions in all structural equations. We note that $\hat{\Omega}$ is now of dimension Q, since it is the covariance matrix of errors in all reduced form equations.

(b) Full Information/Least Generalized Variance (FI/LGV); Full Information/Maximum Likelihood (FI/ML)

The advantage of minimizing the determinant of $\hat{\Omega}$ rather than its trace, applies in systems as well as single-equation estimation; since this can be reviewed in Chapter 19-4, it is not repeated here. As expected, this procedure is called least generalized variance (FI/LGV).

---

[25] In fact SLS, as originally developed by Brown 1960, involved minimizing the trace of $\hat{\Omega}$, with all elements weighted equally. This raises difficulties, as we have seen in the single-equation case of Chapter 19-3. SLS was subsequently modified by rescaling all observed variables—a procedure that achieved some of the same objectives as weighting the trace (see Brown 1967).

It can be shown to be equivalent to maximum likelihood estimation (FI/ML), assuming the errors are multivariate normal; accordingly, either of these equivalent methods is referred to simply as FI.

FI shares with 3SLS a sensitivity to misspecification, that is, it may give wild estimates when the structural equations do not have the variables correctly specified.

A detailed comparison of LI/LGV and FI/LGV will now be given, to illustrate the similarity of a single-equation method and its systems analogue.[26]

[26] This will be our first explicit treatment of LI/LGV. Recall in Section 19-4 that, after the LI/LGV concept of minimizing $|\hat{\mathbf{\Omega}}|$ was introduced, we dropped this procedure in favor of the equivalent but simpler LI/LVR approach.

Limited Information/Least Generalized Variance (LI/LGV)

The observations on the first equation are assembled:

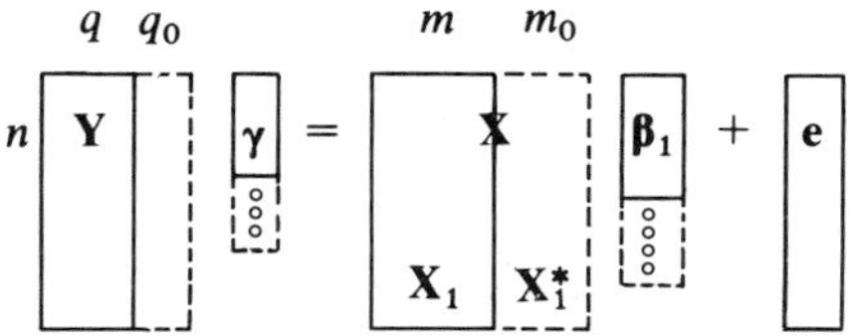

(20-44)
(19-54) repeated

where there are q endogenous and m exogenous variables included in this equation. Note how the last q_0 columns in **Y** and m_0 columns in **X** do not come into play because of the prior zero restrictions in $\boldsymbol{\gamma}$ and $\boldsymbol{\beta}_1$.

The corresponding reduced form is:

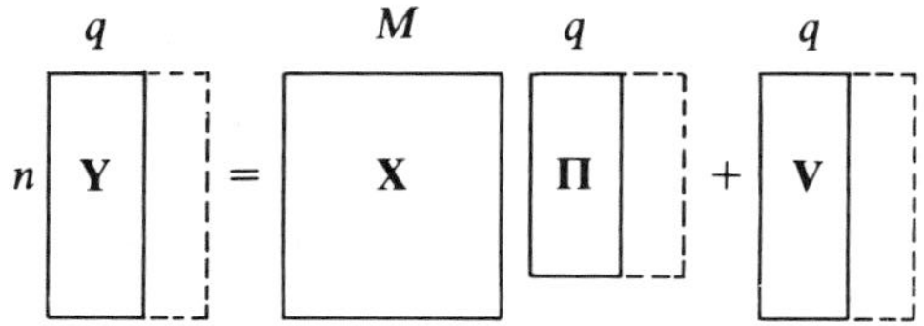

(20-46)

Note that we need concern ourselves only in the first q reduced form equations—that is, those equations corresponding to the q endogenous variables appearing in (20-44).

Full Information/Least Generalized Variance (FI/LGV)

The observations on all equations in the system are assembled:

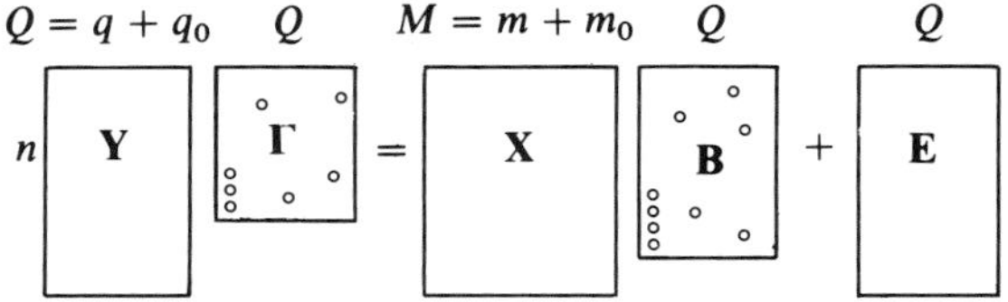

(20-45)

Note that all **Y**'s and **X**'s are included here; also note how the zero prior restrictions are scattered in **Γ** and **B**.

The corresponding reduced form is:

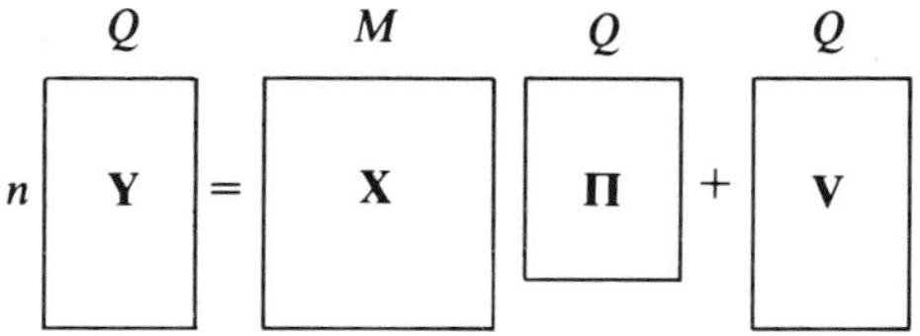

(20-47)

Here we are concerned with all reduced form equations.

LI/LGV (continued)

Postmultiplying (20-46) by $\boldsymbol{\gamma}$ yields:

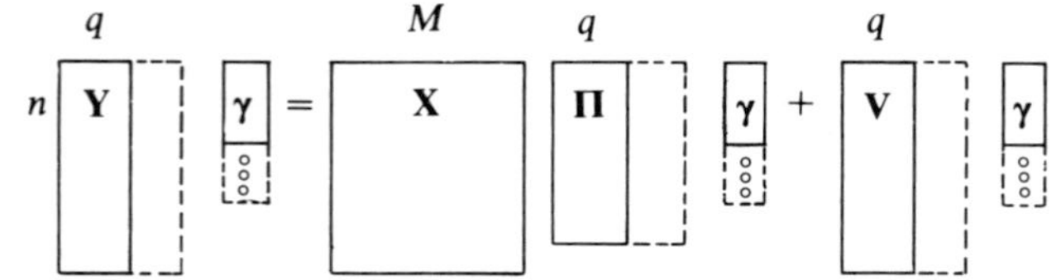

(20-48)

Comparing (20-48) with (20-44) we see that they are equivalent if:

(a) $\mathbf{V}\boldsymbol{\gamma} = \mathbf{e}$, and

(b)

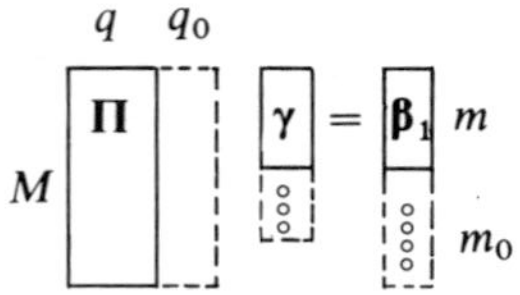

(20-50)

FI/LGV (continued)

Postmultiplying (20-47) by $\boldsymbol{\Gamma}$ yields:

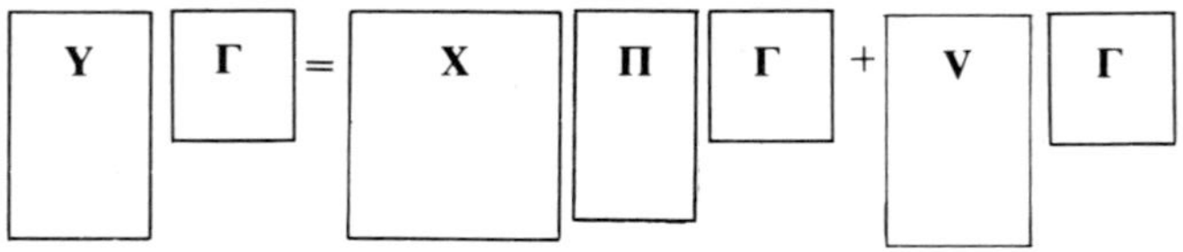

(20-49)

(20-49) and (20-45) are equivalent if:

(a) $\mathbf{V}\boldsymbol{\Gamma} = \mathbf{E}$, and

(b)

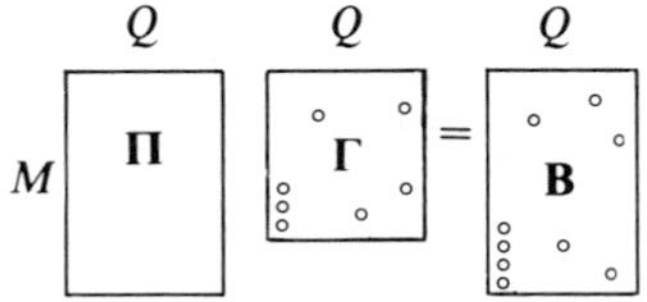

(20-51)

LI/LGV (continued)

We are not allowed a free, unrestricted fit of Π as in (20-46). Instead, we must estimate Π and γ subject to the restrictions in (20-50). But the first m equations provide no restraint on our selection of Π and γ, since the first m elements in β are unrestricted. The only restraints, therefore, are the last m_0 equations, where β is set *a priori* at zero. Thus, the restraints in (20-50) reduce to:

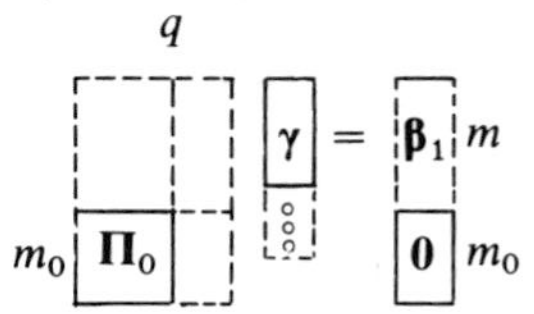

$$
\begin{array}{c}
q \\
\left[\begin{array}{c} \\ \Pi_0 \\ \end{array}\right]
\end{array}
\quad
\gamma = \left[\begin{array}{c} \beta_1 \\ \hline \mathbf{0} \end{array}\right]
\begin{array}{c} m \\ m_0 \end{array}
\qquad (20\text{-}52)
$$

or

$$\Pi_0 \gamma = 0 \qquad (20\text{-}53)$$

(18-9) repeated

where Π_0 is the lower left corner of Π.

Note how the prior restrictions on γ and β appearing in (20-52) cause restrictions on Π_0 and γ in (20-53).

FI/LGV (continued)

We must estimate Π and Γ subject to the restrictions given in (20-51). There are as many linear restrictions as there are zeros specified in $\mathbf{B}$. These restrictions reduce to:

$$\Pi^0 \Gamma^0 = 0 \qquad (20\text{-}54)$$

with these matrices being the appropriate segments of Π, Γ, and $\mathbf{B}$, as in the LI case. Again, the prior restrictions on Γ and $\mathbf{B}$ in the structure (20-45) cause restrictions on Π^0 and Γ^0 in (20-54).

LI/LGV (continued)	FI/LGV (continued)
Subject to these constraints, we wish to minimize the determinant of $\hat{\mathbf{\Omega}}$, the q-dimension covariance matrix of $\hat{\mathbf{V}}$, the estimated errors in the reduced form. Noting that our fit of (20-46) will yield:	Again, we minimize the determinant of $\hat{\mathbf{\Omega}}$, the estimated covariance matrix of errors $\hat{\mathbf{V}}$. But now $\hat{\mathbf{\Omega}}$ has dimension Q rather than q as in the LI case. We leave the rest of this argument as an exercise for the student, with these clues:
$$\hat{\mathbf{V}} = \mathbf{Y} - \mathbf{X}\hat{\mathbf{\Pi}} \qquad (20\text{-}55)$$	Same as (20-55), noting the greater dimension of $\hat{\mathbf{V}}$.
we therefore wish to minimize $$\lvert\hat{\mathbf{\Omega}}\rvert = \lvert\hat{\mathbf{V}}'\hat{\mathbf{V}}\rvert = \lvert(\mathbf{Y} - \mathbf{X}\hat{\mathbf{\Pi}})'(\mathbf{Y} - \mathbf{X}\hat{\mathbf{\Pi}})\rvert \qquad (20\text{-}56)$$	Same as (20-56), noting the greater dimension of $\hat{\mathbf{\Omega}}$.
subject to (20-53), that is, $$\hat{\mathbf{\Pi}}_0\hat{\boldsymbol{\gamma}} = \mathbf{0} \qquad (20\text{-}57)$$	
Minimization is accomplished by differentiating the Lagrange multiplier ($\boldsymbol{\gamma}$) function: $$\lvert(\hat{\mathbf{Y}} - \mathbf{X}\hat{\mathbf{\Pi}})'(\mathbf{Y} - \mathbf{X}\hat{\mathbf{\Pi}})\rvert - \boldsymbol{\lambda}'(\hat{\mathbf{\Pi}}_0\hat{\boldsymbol{\gamma}}) \qquad (20\text{-}58)$$ with respect to its arguments $\hat{\mathbf{\Pi}}$, $\hat{\gamma}$, $\boldsymbol{\lambda}$, setting these partial derivatives equal to zero, and solving for the estimates. With $\hat{\mathbf{\Pi}}$ and $\hat{\boldsymbol{\gamma}}$ thus determined, $\hat{\boldsymbol{\beta}}_1$ is found using (20-50).	Similar to LI.
To sum up: We have minimized $\lvert\hat{\mathbf{\Omega}}\rvert$, the generalized variance of the reduced form errors, subject to the zero restrictions on the first equation.	Conclusions are the same, except that we minimize the generalized variance of *all* reduced form errors (rather than some), subject to the zero restrictions on *all* structural equations (rather than just the first).

TABLES

TABLE 1

Common Logarithms,[1] Log N
(To Obtain Natural Logarithms,[2] Multiply by 2.30)

Second Decimal Place of N

$\overrightarrow{\downarrow N}$	.00	.01	.02	.03	.04	.05	.06	.07	.08	.09
1.0	.0000	.0043	.0086	.0128	.0170	.0212	.0253	.0294	.0334	.0374
1.1	.0414	.0453	.0492	.0531	.0569	.0607	.0645	.0682	.0719	.0755
1.2	.0792	.0828	.0864	.0899	.0934	.0969	.1004	.1038	.1072	.1106
1.3	.1139	.1173	.1206	.1239	.1271	.1303	.1335	.1367	.1399	.1430
1.4	.1461	.1492	.1523	.1553	.1584	.1614	.1644	.1673	.1703	.1732
1.5	.1761	.1790	.1818	.1847	.1875	.1903	.1931	.1959	.1987	.2014
1.6	.2041	.2068	.2095	.2122	.2148	.2175	.2201	.2227	.2253	.2279
1.7	.2304	.2330	.2355	.2380	.2405	.2430	.2455	.2480	.2504	.2529
1.8	.2553	.2577	.2601	.2625	.2648	.2672	.2695	.2718	.2742	.2765
1.9	.2788	.2810	.2833	.2856	.2878	.2900	.2923	.2945	.2967	.2989
2.0	.3010	.3032	.3054	.3075	.3096	.3118	.3139	.3160	.3181	.3201
2.1	.3222	.3243	.3263	.3284	.3304	.3324	.3345	.3365	.3385	.3404
2.2	.3424	.3444	.3464	.3483	.3502	.3522	.3541	.3560	.3579	.3598
2.3	.3617	.3636	.3655	.3674	.3692	.3711	.3729	.3747	.3766	.3784
2.4	.3802	.3820	.3838	.3856	.3874	.3892	.3909	.3927	.3945	.3962
2.5	.3979	.3997	.4014	.4031	.4048	.4065	.4082	.4099	.4116	.4133
2.6	.4150	.4166	.4183	.4200	.4216	.4232	.4249	.4265	.4281	.4298
2.7	.4314	.4330	.4346	.4362	.4378	.4393	.4409	.4425	.4440	.4456
2.8	.4472	.4487	.4502	.4518	.4533	.4548	.4564	.4579	.4594	.4609
2.9	.4624	.4639	.4654	.4669	.4683	.4698	.4713	.4728	.4742	.4757
3.0	.4771	.4786	.4800	.4814	.4829	.4843	.4857	.4871	.4886	.4900
3.1	.4914	.4928	.4942	.4955	.4969	.4983	.4997	.5011	.5024	.5038
3.2	.5051	.5065	.5079	.5092	.5105	.5119	.5132	.5145	.5159	.5172
3.3	.5185	.5198	.5211	.5224	.5237	.5250	.5263	.5276	.5289	.5302
3.4	.5315	.5328	.5340	.5353	.5366	.5378	.5391	.5403	.5416	.5428
3.5	.5441	.5453	.5465	.5478	.5490	.5502	.5514	.5527	.5539	.5551
3.6	.5563	.5575	.5587	.5599	.5611	.5623	.5635	.5647	.5658	.5670
3.7	.5682	.5694	.5705	.5717	.5729	.5740	.5752	.5763	.5775	.5786
3.8	.5798	.5809	.5821	.5832	.5843	.5855	.5866	.5877	.5888	.5899
3.9	.5911	.5922	.5933	.5944	.5955	.5966	.5977	.5988	.5999	.6010

[1]To find the log of a number outside the range 1 to 10, just shift its decimal place until it falls within the range 1 to 10. Then look up the log, and add 1 for each place you shifted the decimal point left. For example, log 2310 = log 2.310 + 3 = .3636 + 3 = 3.3636. Similarly, log 0.0231 = log 2.31 − 2 = .3636 − 2 = −1.6364.

[2]Common logs use base 10, while natural logs (ln) use base $e \simeq 2.718$.

To find ln 4.7 for example, first find log 4.7 = .6721, and then multiply by 2.30, obtaining $.6721 \times 2.30 = 1.546$. Thus ln 4.7 = 1.546.

TABLE 1 (Continued)

→ ↓N	.00	.01	.02	.03	.04	.05	.06	.07	.08	.09
4.0	.6021	.6031	.6042	.6053	.6064	.6075	.6085	.6096	.6107	.6117
4.1	.6128	.6138	.6149	.6160	.6170	.6180	.6191	.6201	.6212	.6222
4.2	.6232	.6243	.6253	.6263	.6274	.6284	.6294	.6304	.6314	.6325
4.3	.6335	.6345	.6355	.6365	.6375	.6385	.6395	.6405	.6415	.6425
4.4	.6435	.6444	.6454	.6464	.6474	.6484	.6493	.6503	.6513	.6522
4.5	.6532	.6542	.6551	.6561	.6571	.6580	.6590	.6599	.6609	.6618
4.6	.6628	.6637	.6646	.6656	.6665	.6675	.6684	.6693	.6702	.6712
4.7	.6721	.6730	.6739	.6749	.6758	.6767	.6776	.6785	.6794	.6803
4.8	.6812	.6821	.6830	.6839	.6848	.6857	.6866	.6875	.6884	.6893
4.9	.6902	.6911	.6920	.6928	.6937	.6946	.6955	.6964	.6972	.6981
5.0	.6990	.6998	.7007	.7016	.7024	.7033	.7042	.7050	.7059	.7067
5.1	.7076	.7084	.7093	.7101	.7110	.7118	.7126	.7135	.7143	.7152
5.2	.7160	.7168	.7177	.7185	.7193	.7202	.7210	.7218	.7226	.7235
5.3	.7243	.7251	.7259	.7267	.7275	.7284	.7292	.7300	.7308	.7316
5.4	.7324	.7332	.7340	.7348	.7356	.7364	.7372	.7380	.7388	.7396
5.5	.7404	.7412	.7419	.7427	.7435	.7443	.7451	.7459	.7466	.7474
5.6	.7482	.7490	.7497	.7505	.7513	.7520	.7528	.7536	.7543	.7551
5.7	.7559	.7566	.7574	.7582	.7589	.7597	.7604	.7612	.7619	.7627
5.8	.7634	.7642	.7649	.7657	.7664	.7672	.7679	.7686	.7694	.7701
5.9	.7709	.7716	.7723	.7731	.7738	.7745	.7752	.7760	.7767	.7774
6.0	.7782	.7789	.7796	.7803	.7810	.7818	.7825	.7832	.7839	.7846
6.1	.7853	.7860	.7868	.7875	.7882	.7889	.7896	.7903	.7910	.7917
6.2	.7924	.7931	.7938	.7945	.7952	.7959	.7966	.7973	.7980	.7987
6.3	.7993	.8000	.8007	.8014	.8021	.8028	.8035	.8041	.8048	.8055
6.4	.8062	.8069	.8075	.8082	.8089	.8096	.8102	.8109	.8116	.8122
6.5	.8129	.8136	.8142	.8149	.8156	.8162	.8169	.8176	.8182	.8189
6.6	.8195	.8202	.8209	.8215	.8222	.8228	.8235	.8241	.8248	.8254
6.7	.8261	.8267	.8274	.8280	.8287	.8293	.8299	.8306	.8312	.8319
6.8	.8325	.8331	.8338	.8344	.8351	.8357	.8363	.8370	.8376	.8382
6.9	.8388	.8395	.8401	.8407	.8414	.8420	.8426	.8432	.8439	.8445
7.0	.8451	.8457	.8463	.8470	.8476	.8482	.8488	.8494	.8500	.8506
7.1	.8513	.8519	.8525	.8531	.8537	.8543	.8549	.8555	.8561	.8567
7.2	.8573	.8579	.8585	.8591	.8597	.8603	.8609	.8615	.8621	.8627
7.3	.8633	.8639	.8645	.8651	.8657	.8663	.8669	.8675	.8681	.8686
7.4	.8692	.8698	.8704	.8710	.8716	.8722	.8727	.8733	.8739	.8745
7.5	.8751	.8756	.8762	.8768	.8774	.8779	.8785	.8791	.8797	.8802
7.6	.8808	.8814	.8820	.8825	.8831	.8837	.8842	.8848	.8854	.8859
7.7	.8865	.8871	.8876	.8882	.8887	.8893	.8899	.8904	.8910	.8915
7.8	.8921	.8927	.8932	.8938	.8943	.8949	.8954	.8960	.8965	.9971
7.9	.8976	.8982	.8987	.8993	.8998	.9004	.9009	.9015	.9020	.9025

TABLE 1 (Continued)

↓N →	.00	.01	.02	.03	.04	.05	.06	.07	.08	.09
8.0	.9031	.9036	.9042	.9047	.9053	.9058	.9063	.9069	.9074	.9079
8.1	.9085	.9090	.9096	.9101	.9106	.9112	.9117	.9122	.9128	.9133
8.2	.9138	.9143	.9149	.9154	.9159	.9165	.9170	.9175	.9180	.9186
8.3	.9191	.9196	.9201	.9206	.9212	.9217	.9222	.9227	.9232	.9238
8.4	.9243	.9248	.9253	.9258	.9263	.9269	.9274	.9279	.9284	.9289
8.5	.9294	.9299	.9304	.9309	.9315	.9320	.9325	.9330	.9335	.9340
8.6	.9345	.9350	.9355	.9360	.9365	.9370	.9375	.9380	.9385	.9390
8.7	.9395	.9400	.9405	.9410	.9415	.9420	.9425	.9430	.9435	.9440
8.8	.9445	.9450	.9455	.9460	.9465	.9469	.9474	.9479	.9484	.9489
8.9	.9494	.9499	.9504	.9509	.9513	.9518	.9523	.9528	.9533	.9538
9.0	.9542	.9547	.9552	.9557	.9562	.9566	.9571	.9576	.9581	.9586
9.1	.9590	.9595	.9600	.9605	.9609	.9614	.9619	.9624	.9628	.9633
9.2	.9638	.9643	.9647	.9652	.9657	.9661	.9666	.9671	.9675	.9680
9.3	.9685	.9689	.9694	.9699	.9703	.9708	.9713	.9717	.9722	.9727
9.4	.9731	.9736	.9741	.9745	.9750	.9754	.9759	.9763	.9768	.9773
9.5	.9777	.9782	.9786	.9791	.9795	.9800	.9805	.9809	.9814	.9818
9.6	.9823	.9827	.9832	.9836	.9841	.9845	.9850	.9854	.9859	.9863
9.7	.9868	.9872	.9877	.9881	.9886	.9890	.9894	.9899	.9903	.9908
9.8	.9912	.9917	.9921	.9926	.9930	.9934	.9939	.9943	.9948	.9952
9.9	.9956	.9961	.9965	.9969	.9974	.9978	.9983	.9987	.9991	.9996

TABLE II(a)

Random Digits

(Blocked merely for convenience)

39 65 76 45 45	19 90 69 64 61	20 26 36 31 62	58 24 97 14 97	95 06 70 99 00
73 71 23 70 90	65 97 60 12 11	31 56 34 19 19	47 83 75 51 33	30 62 38 20 46
72 20 47 33 84	51 67 47 97 19	98 40 07 17 66	23 05 09 51 80	59 78 11 52 49
75 17 25 69 17	17 95 21 78 58	24 33 45 77 48	69 81 84 09 29	93 22 70 45 80
37 48 79 88 74	63 52 06 34 30	01 31 60 10 27	35 07 79 71 53	28 99 52 01 41
02 89 08 16 94	85 53 83 29 95	56 27 09 24 43	21 78 55 09 82	72 61 88 73 61
87 18 15 70 07	37 79 49 12 38	48 13 93 55 96	41 92 45 71 51	09 18 25 58 94
98 83 71 70 15	89 09 39 59 24	00 06 41 41 20	14 36 59 25 47	54 45 17 24 89
10 08 58 07 04	76 62 16 48 68	58 76 17 14 86	59 53 11 52 21	66 04 18 72 87
47 90 56 37 31	71 82 13 50 41	27 55 10 24 92	28 04 67 53 44	95 23 00 84 47
93 05 31 03 07	34 18 04 52 35	74 13 39 35 22	68 95 23 92 35	36 63 70 35 33
21 89 11 47 99	11 20 99 45 18	76 51 94 84 86	13 79 93 37 55	98 16 04 41 67
95 18 94 06 97	27 37 83 28 71	79 57 95 13 91	09 61 87 25 21	56 20 11 32 44
97 08 31 55 73	10 65 81 92 59	77 31 61 95 46	20 44 90 32 64	26 99 76 75 63
69 26 88 86 13	59 71 74 17 32	48 38 75 93 29	73 37 32 04 05	60 82 29 20 25
41 47 10 25 03	87 63 93 95 17	81 83 83 04 49	77 45 85 50 51	79 88 01 97 30
91 94 14 63 62	08 61 74 51 69	92 79 43 89 79	29 18 94 51 23	14 85 11 47 23
80 06 54 18 47	08 52 85 08 40	48 40 35 94 22	72 65 71 08 86	50 03 42 99 36
67 72 77 63 99	89 85 84 46 06	64 71 06 21 66	89 37 20 70 01	61 65 70 22 12
59 40 24 13 75	42 29 72 23 19	06 94 76 10 08	81 30 15 39 14	81 83 17 16 33
63 62 06 34 41	79 53 36 02 95	94 61 09 43 62	20 21 14 68 86	94 95 48 46 45
78 47 23 53 90	79 93 96 38 63	34 85 52 05 09	85 43 01 72 73	14 93 87 81 40
87 68 62 15 43	97 48 72 66 48	53 16 71 13 81	59 97 50 99 52	24 62 20 42 31
47 60 92 10 77	26 97 05 73 51	88 46 38 03 58	72 68 49 29 31	75 70 16 08 24
56 88 87 59 41	06 87 37 78 48	65 88 69 58 39	88 02 84 27 83	85 81 56 39 38
22 17 68 65 84	87 02 22 57 51	68 69 80 95 44	11 29 01 95 80	49 34 35 86 47
19 36 27 59 46	39 77 32 77 09	79 57 92 36 59	89 74 39 82 15	08 58 94 34 74
16 77 23 02 77	28 06 24 25 93	22 45 44 84 11	87 80 61 65 31	09 71 91 74 25
78 43 76 71 61	97 67 63 99 61	80 45 67 93 82	59 73 19 85 23	53 33 65 97 21
03 28 28 26 08	69 30 16 09 05	53 58 47 70 93	66 56 45 65 79	45 56 20 19 47
04 31 17 21 56	33 73 99 19 87	26 72 39 27 67	53 77 57 68 93	60 61 97 22 61
61 06 98 03 91	87 14 77 43 96	43 00 65 98 50	45 60 33 01 07	98 99 46 50 47
23 68 35 26 00	99 53 93 61 28	52 70 05 48 34	56 65 05 61 86	90 92 10 70 80
15 39 25 70 99	93 86 52 77 65	15 33 59 05 28	22 87 26 07 47	86 96 98 29 06
58 71 96 30 24	18 46 23 34 27	85 13 99 24 44	49 18 09 79 49	74 16 32 23 02
93 22 53 64 39	07 10 63 76 35	87 03 04 79 88	08 13 13 85 51	55 34 57 72 69
78 76 58 54 74	92 38 70 96 92	52 06 79 79 45	82 63 18 27 44	69 66 92 19 09
61 81 31 96 82	00 57 25 60 59	46 72 60 18 77	55 66 12 62 11	08 99 55 64 57
42 88 07 10 05	24 98 65 63 21	47 21 61 88 32	27 80 30 21 60	10 92 35 36 12
77 94 30 05 39	28 10 99 00 27	12 73 73 99 12	49 99 57 94 82	96 88 57 17 91

TABLE **II(b)**

Random Normal Numbers, $\mu = 0, \sigma = 1$
(Rounded to 1 Decimal Place)

.5	.1	2.5	−.3	−.1	.3	−.3	1.3	.2	−1.0
.1	−2.5	−.5	−.2	.5	−1.6	.2	−1.2	.0	.5
1.5	−.4	−.6	.7	.9	1.4	.8	−1.0	−.9	−1.9
1.0	−.5	1.3	3.5	.6	−1.9	.2	1.2	−.5	−.3
1.4	−.6	.0	.3	2.9	2.0	−.3	.4	.4	.0
.9	−.5	−.5	.6	.9	−.9	1.6	.2	−1.9	.4
1.2	−1.1	.0	.8	1.0	.7	1.1	−.6	−.3	−.7
−1.5	−.5	−.2	−.1	1.0	.2	.4	.7	−.4	−.4
−.7	.8	−1.6	−.3	−.5	−2.1	−.5	−.2	.9	−.5
1.4	.2	.4	.8	.2	−.7	1.0	−1.5	−.3	.1
−.5	1.7	−.1	−1.2	−.5	.9	−.5	−2.0	−2.8	−.2
−1.4	−.2	1.4	−.6	−.3	−.2	.2	.8	1.0	−.9
−1.0	.6	−.9	1.6	.1	.4	−.2	.3	−1.0	−1.0
.0	−.9	.0	−.7	1.1	−.1	1.1	.5	−1.7	.4
1.4	−1.2	−.9	1.2	−.2	−.2	1.2	−2.6	−.6	.1
−1.8	−.3	1.2	1.0	−.5	−1.6	−.1	−.4	−.6	.6
−.1	−.4	−1.4	.4	−1.0	−.1	−1.7	−2.8	−1.1	−2.4
−1.3	1.8	−1.0	.4	1.0	−1.1	−1.0	.4	−1.7	2.0
1.0	.5	.7	1.4	1.0	−1.3	1.6	−1.0	.5	−.3
.3	−2.1	.7	−.9	−1.1	−1.4	1.0	.1	−.6	.9
−1.8	−2.0	−1.6	.5	.2	−.2	.0	.0	.5	−1.0
−1.2	1.2	1.1	.9	1.3	−.2	.2	−.4	−.3	.5
.7	−1.1	1.2	−1.2	−.9	.4	.3	−.9	.6	1.7
−.4	.4	−1.9	.9	−.2	.6	.9	−.4	−.2	−.1
−1.4	−.2	.4	−.6	−.6	.2	−.3	.5	.7	−.3
.2	.2	−1.1	−.2	−.3	1.2	1.1	.0	−2.0	−.6
.2	.3	−.3	.1	−2.8	−.4	−.8	−1.3	−.6	−1.0
2.3	.6	.6	−.7	.2	1.3	.1	−1.8	−.7	−1.3
.0	−.3	.1	.8	−.6	.5	.5	−1.0	.5	1.0
−1.1	−2.1	.9	.1	.4	−1.7	1.0	−1.4	−.6	−1.0
.8	.1	−1.5	.0	−2.1	.7	.1	−.9	−.6	.6
.4	−1.7	−.9	.2	−.7	.3	−.1	−.2	−.1	.4
−.5	−.3	.2	−.7	1.0	.0	.4	−.8	.2	.1
.3	−.5	1.3	−1.2	−.9	.1	−.5	−.8	.0	.5
1.0	3.0	−.6	−.5	−1.1	1.3	−1.4	−1.3	−3.0	.5
−1.3	1.3	−.6	−.1	−.5	−.6	2.9	.5	.4	.3
−.3	−.1	−.3	.6	−.5	−1.2	−1.2	−.3	−.1	1.1
.2	−.9	−.9	−.5	1.4	−.5	.2	−.4	1.5	1.1
−1.3	.2	−1.2	.4	−1.0	.8	.9	1.0	.0	.8
−1.2	−.2	−.3	1.8	1.4	.6	1.2	.7	.4	.2
.6	−.5	.8	.1	.5	−.4	1.7	1.2	.9	−.3
.4	−1.9	.2	−.5	.7	−.1	−.1	−.5	.5	1.1
−1.4	.5	−1.7	−1.2	.8	−.7	−.1	1.0	−.8	.2
−.2	−.2	−.4	−.8	.3	1.0	1.8	2.9	−.8	−.1
−.3	.5	.4	−1.5	1.5	2.0	−.1	.2	.0	−1.2
.4	−.4	.6	1.0	−.1	.1	.5	−1.3	1.1	1.1
.6	.7	−1.1	−1.4	−1.6	−1.6	1.5	1.3	.7	−.9
.9	−.9	−.1	−.5	.5	1.4	.0	−.3	−.3	1.2
.2	−.6	.0	−.5	−.9	−.4	−.5	1.7	−.2	−1.2
−.9	.4	.8	.8	.4	−.3	−1.1	.6	1.4	1.3

TABLE III(a)

Binomial Coefficients $\binom{n}{s}$

$n \backslash s$	*0*	*1*	*2*	*3*	*4*	*5*	*6*	*7*	*8*	*9*	*10*
0	1										
1	1	1									
2	1	2	1								
3	1	3	3	1							
4	1	4	6	4	1						
5	1	5	10	10	5	1					
6	1	6	15	20	15	6	1				
7	1	7	21	35	35	21	7	1			
8	1	8	28	56	70	56	28	8	1		
9	1	9	36	84	126	126	84	36	9	1	
10	1	10	45	120	210	252	210	120	45	10	1
11	1	11	55	165	330	462	462	330	165	55	11
12	1	12	66	220	495	792	924	792	495	220	66
13	1	13	78	286	715	1287	1716	1716	1287	715	286
14	1	14	91	364	1001	2002	3003	3432	3003	2002	1001
15	1	15	105	455	1365	3003	5005	6435	6435	5005	3003
16	1	16	120	560	1820	4368	8008	11440	12870	11440	8008
17	1	17	136	680	2380	6188	12376	19448	24310	24310	19448
18	1	18	153	816	3060	8568	18564	31824	43758	48620	43758
19	1	19	171	969	3876	11628	27132	50388	75582	92378	92378
20	1	20	190	1140	4845	15504	38760	77520	125970	167960	184756

Note. $\binom{n}{s} = \dfrac{n(n-1)(n-2)\cdots(n-s+1)}{s(s-1)(s-2)\cdots 3\cdot 2\cdot 1}$; $\binom{n}{0} = 1$; $\binom{n}{1} = n$.

For coefficients missing from the above table, use the relation:

$$\binom{n}{s} = \binom{n}{n-s}, \quad \text{e.g.,} \quad \binom{20}{11} = \binom{20}{9} = 167960.$$

TABLE III(b)
Individual Binomial Probabilities $p(s)$

n	s	π .10	.20	.30	.40	.50	.60	.70	.80	.90
1	0	.9000	.8000	.7000	.6000	.5000	.4000	.3000	.2000	.1000
	1	.1000	.2000	.3000	.4000	.5000	.6000	.7000	.8000	.9000
2	0	.8100	.6400	.4900	.3600	.2500	.1600	.0900	.0400	.0100
	1	.1800	.3200	.4200	.4800	.5000	.4800	.4200	.3200	.1800
	2	.0100	.0400	.0900	.1600	.2500	.3600	.4900	.6400	.8100
3	0	.7290	.5120	.3430	.2160	.1250	.0640	.0270	.0080	.0010
	1	.2430	.3840	.4410	.4320	.3750	.2880	.1890	.0960	.0270
	2	.0270	.0960	.1890	.2880	.3750	.4320	.4410	.3840	.2430
	3	.0010	.0080	.0270	.0640	.1250	.2160	.3430	.5120	.7290
4	0	.6561	.4096	.2401	.1296	.0625	.0256	.0081	.0016	.0001
	1	.2916	.4096	.4116	.3456	.2500	.1536	.0756	.0256	.0036
	2	.0486	.1536	.2646	.3456	.3750	.3456	.2646	.1536	.0486
	3	.0036	.0256	.0756	.1536	.2500	.3456	.4116	.4096	.2916
	4	.0001	.0016	.0081	.0256	.0625	.1296	.2401	.4096	.6561
5	0	.5905	.3277	.1681	.0778	.0313	.0102	.0024	.0003	.0000
	1	.3280	.4096	.3602	.2592	.1563	.0768	.0283	.0064	.0004
	2	.0729	.2048	.3087	.3456	.3125	.2304	.1323	.0512	.0081
	3	.0081	.0512	.1323	.2304	.3125	.3456	.3087	.2048	.0729
	4	.0004	.0064	.0284	.0768	.1563	.2592	.3602	.4096	.3280
	5	.0000	.0003	.0024	.0102	.0313	.0778	.1681	.3277	.5905
6	0	.5314	.2621	.1176	.0467	.0156	.0041	.0007	.0001	.0000
	1	.3543	.3932	.3025	.1866	.0938	.0369	.0102	.0015	.0001
	2	.0984	.2458	.3241	.3110	.2344	.1382	.0595	.0154	.0012
	3	.0146	.0819	.1852	.2765	.3125	.2765	.1852	.0819	.0146
	4	.0012	.0154	.0595	.1382	.2344	.3110	.3241	.2458	.0984
	5	.0001	.0015	.0102	.0369	.0938	.1866	.3025	.3932	.3543
	6	.0000	.0001	.0007	.0041	.0156	.0467	.1176	.2621	.5314
7	0	.4783	.2097	.0824	.0280	.0078	.0016	.0002	.0000	.0000
	1	.3720	.3670	.2471	.1306	.0547	.0172	.0036	.0004	.0000
	2	.1240	.2753	.3177	.2613	.1641	.0774	.0250	.0043	.0002
	3	.0230	.1147	.2269	.2903	.2734	.1935	.0972	.0287	.0026
	4	.0026	.0287	.0972	.1935	.2734	.2903	.2269	.1147	.0230
	5	.0002	.0043	.0250	.0774	.1641	.2613	.3177	.2753	.1240
	6	.0000	.0004	.0036	.0172	.0547	.1306	.2471	.3670	.3720
	7	.0000	.0000	.0002	.0016	.0078	.0280	.0824	.2097	.4783

TABLE III(b) (continued)

n	s	.10	.20	.30	.40	π .50	.60	.70	.80	.90
8	0	.4305	.1678	.0576	.0168	.0039	.0007	.0001	.0000	.0000
	1	.3826	.3355	.1977	.0896	.0313	.0079	.0012	.0001	.0000
	2	.1488	.2936	.2965	.2090	.1094	.0413	.0100	.0011	.0000
	3	.0331	.1468	.2541	.2787	.2188	.1239	.0467	.0092	.0004
	4	.0046	.0459	.1361	.2322	.2734	.2322	.1361	.0459	.0046
	5	.0004	.0092	.0467	.1239	.2188	.2787	.2541	.1468	.0331
	6	.0000	.0011	.0100	.0413	.1094	.2090	.2965	.2936	.1488
	7	.0000	.0001	.0012	.0079	.0313	.0896	.1977	.3355	.3826
	8	.0000	.0000	.0001	.0007	.0039	.0168	.0576	.1678	.4305
9	0	.3874	.1342	.0404	.0101	.0020	.0003	.0000	.0000	.0000
	1	.3874	.3020	.1556	.0605	.0176	.0035	.0004	.0000	.0000
	2	.1722	.3020	.2668	.1612	.0703	.0212	.0039	.0003	.0000
	3	.0446	.1762	.2668	.2508	.1641	.0743	.0210	.0028	.0001
	4	.0074	.0661	.1715	.2508	.2461	.1672	.0735	.0165	.0008
	5	.0008	.0165	.0735	.1672	.2461	.2508	.1715	.0661	.0074
	6	.0001	.0028	.0210	.0743	.1641	.2508	.2668	.1762	.0446
	7	.0000	.0003	.0039	.0212	.0703	.1612	.2668	.3020	.1722
	8	.0000	.0000	.0004	.0035	.0176	.0605	.1556	.3020	.3874
	9	.0000	.0000	.0000	.0003	.0020	.0101	.0404	.1342	.3874
10	0	.3487	.1074	.0282	.0060	.0010	.0001	.0000	.0000	.0000
	1	.3874	.2684	.1211	.0403	.0098	.0016	.0001	.0000	.0000
	2	.1937	.3020	.2335	.1209	.0439	.0106	.0014	.0001	.0000
	3	.0574	.2013	.2668	.2150	.1172	.0425	.0090	.0008	.0000
	4	.0112	.0881	.2001	.2508	.2051	.1115	.0368	.0055	.0001
	5	.0015	.0264	.1029	.2007	.2461	.2007	.1029	.0264	.0015
	6	.0001	.0055	.0368	.1115	.2051	.2508	.2001	.0881	.0112
	7	.0000	.0008	.0090	.0425	.1172	.2150	.2668	.2013	.0574
	8	.0000	.0001	.0014	.0106	.0439	.1209	.2335	.3020	.1937
	9	.0000	.0000	.0001	.0016	.0098	.0403	.1211	.2684	.3874
	10	.0000	.0000	.0000	.0001	.0010	.0060	.0282	.1074	.3487

TABLE III(c)
Cumulative Binomial Probability in Right-Hand Tail

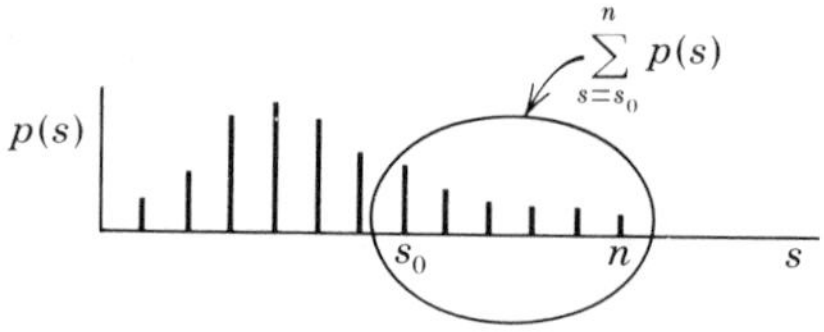

n	s_0	.10	.20	.30	.40	π .50	.60	.70	.80	.90
2	1	.1900	.3600	.5100	.6400	.7500	.8400	.9100	.9600	.9900
	2	.0100	.0400	.0900	.1600	.2500	.3600	.4900	.6400	.8100
3	1	.2710	.4880	.6570	.7840	.8750	.9360	.9730	.9920	.9990
	2	.0280	.1040	.2160	.3520	.5000	.6480	.7840	.8960	.9720
	3	.0010	.0080	.0270	.0640	.1250	.2160	.3430	.5120	.7290
4	1	.3439	.5904	.7599	.8704	.9375	.9744	.9919	.9984	.9999
	2	.0523	.1808	.3483	.5248	.6875	.8208	.9163	.9728	.9963
	3	.0037	.0272	.0837	.1792	.3125	.4752	.6517	.8192	.9477
	4	.0001	.0016	.0081	.0256	.0625	.1296	.2401	.4096	.6561
5	1	.4095	.6723	.8319	.9222	.9688	.9898	.9976	.9997	1.0000
	2	.0815	.2627	.4718	.6630	.8125	.9130	.9692	.9933	.9995
	3	.0086	.0579	.1631	.3174	.5000	.6826	.8369	.9421	.9914
	4	.0005	.0067	.0308	.0870	.1875	.3370	.5282	.7373	.9185
	5	.0000	.0003	.0024	.0102	.0313	.0778	.1681	.3277	.5905
6	1	.4686	.7379	.8824	.9533	.9844	.9959	.9993	.9999	1.0000
	2	.1143	.3446	.5798	.7667	.8906	.9590	.9891	.9984	.9999
	3	.0159	.0989	.2557	.4557	.6562	.8208	.9295	.9830	.9987
	4	.0013	.0170	.0705	.1792	.3438	.5443	.7443	.9011	.9842
	5	.0001	.0016	.0109	.0410	.1094	.2333	.4202	.6554	.8857
	6	.0000	.0001	.0007	.0041	.0156	.0467	.1176	.2621	.5314
7	1	.5217	.7903	.9176	.9720	.9922	.9984	.9998	1.0000	1.0000
	2	.1497	.4233	.6706	.8414	.9375	.9812	.9962	.9996	1.0000
	3	.0257	.1480	.3529	.5801	.7734	.9037	.9712	.9953	.9998
	4	.0027	.0333	.1260	.2898	.5000	.7102	.8740	.9667	.9973
	5	.0002	.0047	.0288	.0963	.2266	.4199	.6471	.8520	.9743
	6	.0000	.0004	.0038	.0188	.0625	.1586	.3294	.5767	.8503
	7	.0000	.0000	.0002	.0016	.0078	.0280	.0824	.2097	.4783

TABLE III(c) (continued)

n	s_0	π .10	.20	.30	.40	.50	.60	.70	.80	.90
8	1	.5695	.8322	.9424	.9832	.9961	.9993	.9999	1.0000	1.0000
	2	.1869	.4967	.7447	.8936	.9648	.9915	.9987	.9999	1.0000
	3	.0381	.2031	.4482	.6846	.8555	.9502	.9887	.9988	1.0000
	4	.0050	.0563	.1941	.4059	.6367	.8263	.9420	.9896	.9996
	5	.0004	.0104	.0580	.1737	.3633	.5941	.8059	.9437	.9950
	6	.0000	.0012	.0113	.0498	.1445	.3154	.5518	.7969	.9619
	7	.0000	.0001	.0013	.0085	.0352	.1064	.2553	.5033	.8131
	8	.0000	.0000	.0001	.0007	.0039	.0168	.0576	.1678	.4305
9	1	.6126	.8658	.9596	.9899	.9980	.9997	1.0000	1.0000	1.0000
	2	.2252	.5638	.8040	.9295	.9805	.9962	.9996	1.0000	1.0000
	3	.0530	.2618	.5372	.7682	.9102	.9750	.9957	.9997	1.0000
	4	.0083	.0856	.2703	.5174	.7461	.9006	.9747	.9969	.9999
	5	.0009	.0196	.0988	.2666	.5000	.7334	.9012	.9804	.9991
	6	.0001	.0031	.0253	.0994	.2539	.4826	.7297	.9144	.9917
	7	.0000	.0003	.0043	.0250	.0898	.2318	.4628	.7382	.9470
	8	.0000	.0000	.0004	.0038	.0195	.0705	.1960	.4362	.7748
	9	.0000	.0000	.0000	.0003	.0020	.0101	.0404	.1342	.3874
10	1	.6513	.8926	.9718	.9940	.9990	.9999	1.0000	1.0000	1.0000
	2	.2639	.6242	.8507	.9536	.9893	.9983	.9999	1.0000	1.0000
	3	.0702	.3222	.6172	.8327	.9453	.9877	.9984	.9999	1.0000
	4	.0128	.1209	.3504	.6177	.8281	.9452	.9894	.9991	1.0000
	5	.0016	.0328	.1503	.3669	.6230	.8338	.9527	.9936	.9999
	6	.0001	.0064	.0473	.1662	.3770	.6331	.8497	.9672	.9984
	7	.0000	.0009	.0106	.0548	.1719	.3823	.6496	.8791	.9872
	8	.0000	.0001	.0016	.0123	.0547	.1673	.3828	.6778	.9298
	9	.0000	.0000	.0001	.0017	.0107	.0464	.1493	.3758	.7361
	10	.0000	.0000	.0000	.0001	.0010	.0060	.0282	.1074	.3487

TABLE IV

Standard Normal, Cumulative Probability in Right-Hand Tail (For Negative Values of z, Areas are Found by Symmetry)

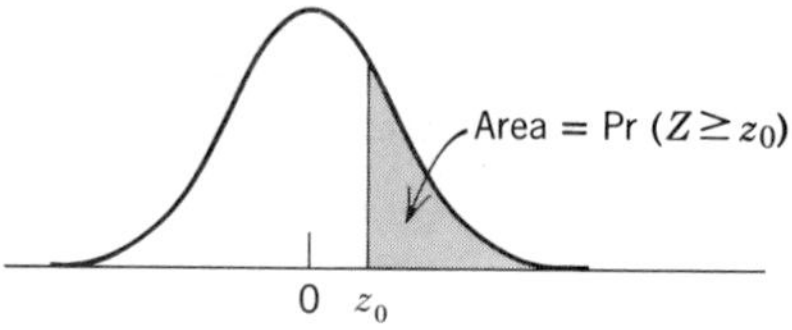

	Second Decimal Place of z_0									
$\rightarrow$ $\downarrow z_0$	*.00*	*.01*	*.02*	*.03*	*.04*	*.05*	*.06*	*.07*	*.08*	*.09*
0.0	.5000	.4960	.4920	.4880	.4840	.4801	.4761	.4721	.4681	.4641
0.1	.4602	.4562	.4522	.4483	.4443	.4404	.4364	.4325	.4286	.4247
0.2	.4207	.4168	.4129	.4090	.4052	.4013	.3974	.3936	.3897	.3859
0.3	.3821	.3783	.3745	.3707	.3669	.3632	.3594	.3557	.3520	.3483
0.4	.3446	.3409	.3372	.3336	.3300	.3264	.3228	.3192	.3156	.3121
0.5	.3085	.3050	.3015	.2981	.2946	.2912	.2877	.2843	.2810	.2776
0.6	.2743	.2709	.2676	.2643	.2611	.2578	.2546	.2514	.2483	.2451
0.7	.2420	.2389	.2358	.2327	.2296	.2266	.2236	.2206	.2177	.2148
0.8	.2119	.2090	.2061	.2033	.2005	.1977	.1949	.1922	.1894	.1867
0.9	.1841	.1814	.1788	.1762	.1736	.1711	.1685	.1660	.1635	.1611
1.0	.1587	.1562	.1539	.1515	.1492	.1469	.1446	.1423	.1401	.1379
1.1	.1357	.1335	.1314	.1292	.1271	.1251	.1230	.1210	.1190	.1170
1.2	.1151	.1131	.1112	.1093	.1075	.1056	.1038	.1020	.1003	.0985
1.3	.0968	.0951	.0934	.0918	.0901	.0885	.0869	.0853	.0838	.0823
1.4	.0808	.0793	.0778	.0764	.0749	.0735	.0722	.0708	.0694	.0681
1.5	.0668	.0655	.0643	.0630	.0618	.0606	.0594	.0582	.0571	.0559
1.6	.0548	.0537	.0526	.0516	.0505	.0495	.0485	.0475	.0465	.0455
1.7	.0446	.0436	.0427	.0418	.0409	.0401	.0392	.0384	.0375	.0367
1.8	.0359	.0352	.0344	.0336	.0329	.0322	.0314	.0307	.0301	.0294
1.9	.0287	.0281	.0274	.0268	.0262	.0256	.0250	.0244	.0239	.0233
2.0	.0228	.0222	.0217	.0212	.0207	.0202	.0197	.0192	.0188	.0183
2.1	.0179	.0174	.0170	.0166	.0162	.0158	.0154	.0150	.0146	.0143
2.2	.0139	.0136	.0132	.0129	.0125	.0122	.0119	.0116	.0113	.0110
2.3	.0107	.0104	.0102	.0099	.0096	.0094	.0091	.0089	.0087	.0084
2.4	.0082	.0080	.0078	.0075	.0073	.0071	.0069	.0068	.0066	.0064
2.5	.0062	.0060	.0059	.0057	.0055	.0054	.0052	.0051	.0049	.0048
2.6	.0047	.0045	.0044	.0043	.0041	.0040	.0039	.0038	.0037	.0036
2.7	.0035	.0034	.0033	.0032	.0031	.0030	.0029	.0028	.0027	.0026
2.8	.0026	.0025	.0024	.0023	.0023	.0022	.0021	.0021	.0020	.0019
2.9	.0019	.0018	.0017	.0017	.0016	.0016	.0015	.0015	.0014	.0014
3.0	.00135									
3.5	.000 233									
4.0	.000 031 7	To interpolate carefully, see Table X.								
4.5	.000 003 40									
5.0	.000 000 287									

TABLE V
Student's *t* Critical Points

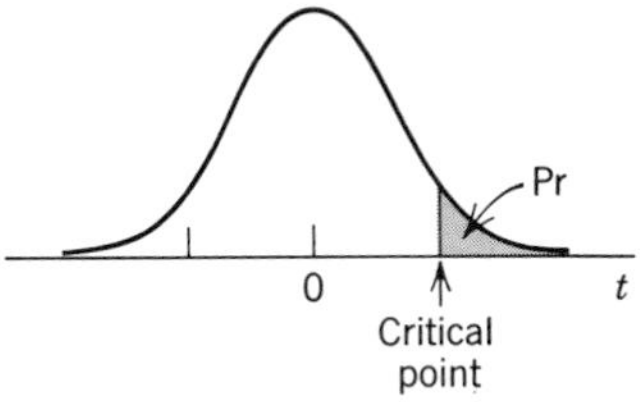

Pr / d.f.	.25	.10	.05	.025	.010	.005	.0025	.0010	.0005
1	1.000	3.078	6.314	12.706	31.821	63.637	127.32	318.31	636.62
2	.816	1.886	2.920	4.303	6.965	9.925	14.089	22.326	31.598
3	.765	1.638	2.353	3.182	4.541	5.841	7.453	10.213	12.924
4	.741	1.533	2.132	2.776	3.747	4.604	5.598	7.173	8.610
5	.727	1.476	2.015	2.571	3.365	4.032	4.773	5.893	6.869
6	.718	1.440	1.943	2.447	3.143	3.707	4.317	5.208	5.959
7	.711	1.415	1.895	2.365	2.998	3.499	4.020	4.785	5.408
8	.706	1.397	1.860	2.306	2.896	3.355	3.833	4.501	5.041
9	.703	1.383	1.833	2.262	2.821	3.250	3.690	4.297	4.781
10	.700	1.372	1.812	2.228	2.764	3.169	3.581	4.144	4.537
11	.697	1.363	1.796	2.201	2.718	3.106	3.497	4.025	4.437
12	.695	1.356	1.782	2.179	2.681	3.055	3.428	3.930	4.318
13	.694	1.350	1.771	2.160	2.650	3.012	3.372	3.852	4.221
14	.692	1.345	1.761	2.145	2.624	2.977	3.326	3.787	4.140
15	.691	1.341	1.753	2.131	2.602	2.947	3.286	3.733	4.073
16	.690	1.337	1.746	2.120	2.583	2.921	3.252	3.686	4.015
17	.689	1.333	1.740	2.110	2.567	2.898	3.222	3.646	3.965
18	.688	1.330	1.734	2.101	2.552	2.878	3.197	3.610	3.922
19	.688	1.328	1.729	2.093	2.539	2.861	3.174	3.579	3.883
20	.687	1.325	1.725	2.086	2.528	2.845	3.153	3.552	3.850
21	.686	1.323	1.721	2.080	2.518	2.831	3.135	3.257	3.189
22	.686	1.321	1.717	2.074	2.508	2.819	3.119	3.505	3.792
23	.685	1.319	1.714	2.069	2.500	2.807	3.104	3.485	3.767
24	.685	1.318	1.711	2.064	2.492	2.797	3.091	3.467	3.745
25	.684	1.316	1.708	2.060	2.485	2.787	3.078	3.450	3.725
26	.684	1.315	1.706	2.056	2.479	2.779	3.067	3.435	3.707
27	.684	1.314	1.703	2.052	2.473	2.771	3.057	3.421	3.690
28	.683	1.313	1.701	2.048	2.467	2.763	3.047	3.408	3.674
29	.683	1.311	1.699	2.045	2.462	2.756	3.038	3.396	3.659
30	.683	1.310	1.697	2.042	2.457	2.750	3.030	3.385	3.646
40	.681	1.303	1.684	2.021	2.423	2.704	2.971	3.307	3.551
60	.679	1.296	1.671	2.000	2.390	2.660	2.915	3.232	3.460
120	.677	1.289	1.658	1.980	2.358	2.617	2.860	3.160	3.373
∞	.674	1.282	1.645	1.960	2.326	2.576	2.807	3.090	3.291

To interpolate carefully, see Table *X*.

TABLE **VI(a)**

χ^2 Critical Points

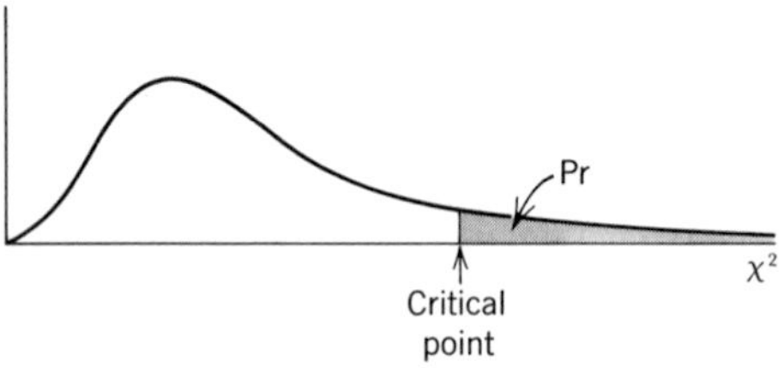

Pr / *d.f.*	*.250*	*.100*	*.050*	*.025*	*.010*	*.005*	*.001*
1	1.32	2.71	3.84	5.02	6.63	7.88	10.8
2	2.77	4.61	5.99	7.38	9.21	10.6	13.8
3	4.11	6.25	7.81	9.35	11.3	12.8	16.3
4	5.39	7.78	9.49	11.1	13.3	14.9	18.5
5	6.63	9.24	11.1	12.8	15.1	16.7	20.5
6	7.84	10.6	12.6	14.4	16.8	18.5	22.5
7	9.04	12.0	14.1	16.0	18.5	20.3	24.3
8	10.2	13.4	15.5	17.5	20.1	22.0	26.1
9	11.4	14.7	16.9	19.0	21.7	23.6	27.9
10	12.5	16.0	18.3	20.5	23.2	25.2	29.6
11	13.7	17.3	19.7	21.9	24.7	26.8	31.3
12	14.8	18.5	21.0	23.3	26.2	28.3	32.9
13	16.0	19.8	22.4	24.7	27.7	29.8	34.5
14	17.1	21.1	23.7	26.1	29.1	31.3	36.1
15	18.2	22.3	25.0	27.5	30.6	32.8	37.7
16	19.4	23.5	26.3	28.8	32.0	34.3	39.3
17	20.5	24.8	27.6	30.2	33.4	35.7	40.8
18	21.6	26.0	28.9	31.5	34.8	37.2	42.3
19	22.7	27.2	30.1	32.9	36.2	38.6	32.8
20	23.8	28.4	31.4	34.2	37.6	40.0	45.3
21	24.9	29.6	32.7	35.5	38.9	41.4	46.8
22	26.0	30.8	33.9	36.8	40.3	42.8	48.3
23	27.1	32.0	35.2	38.1	41.6	44.2	49.7
24	28.2	33.2	36.4	39.4	32.0	45.6	51.2
25	29.3	34.4	37.7	40.6	44.3	46.9	52.6
26	30.4	35.6	38.9	41.9	45.6	48.3	54.1
27	31.5	36.7	40.1	43.2	47.0	49.6	55.5
28	32.6	37.9	41.3	44.5	48.3	51.0	56.9
29	33.7	39.1	42.6	45.7	49.6	52.3	58.3
30	34.8	40.3	43.8	47.0	50.9	53.7	59.7
40	45.6	51.8	55.8	59.3	63.7	66.8	73.4
50	56.3	63.2	67.5	71.4	76.2	79.5	86.7
60	67.0	74.4	79.1	83.3	88.4	92.0	99.6
70	77.6	85.5	90.5	95.0	100	104	112
80	88.1	96.6	102	107	112	116	125
90	98.6	108	113	118	124	128	137
100	109	118	124	130	136	140	149

To interpolate carefully, see Table *X*.

TABLE VI(b)
C^2 Critical Points ($C^2 = \chi^2/\text{d.f.}$)

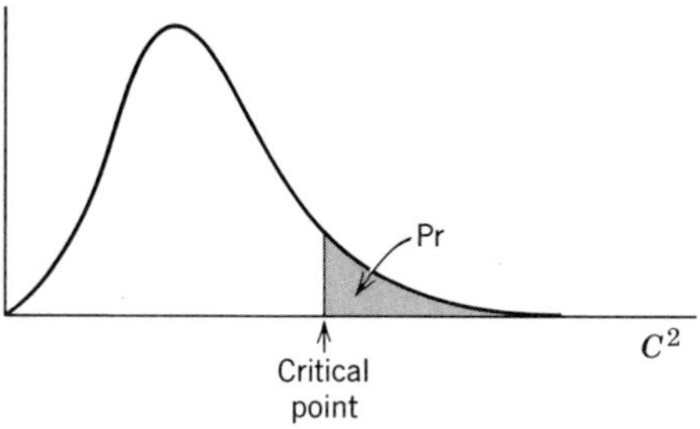

d.f. \ *Pr*	*.995*	*.990*	*.975*	*.95*	*.90*	*.10*	*.05*	*.025*	*.010*	*.005*
1	.000039	.00016	.00098	.0039	.0158	2.71	3.84	5.02	6.63	7.88
2	.00501	.0101	.0253	.0513	.1054	2.30	3.00	3.69	4.61	5.30
3	.0239	.0383	.0719	.117	.195	2.08	2.60	3.12	3.78	4.28
4	.0517	.0743	.121	.178	.266	1.94	2.37	2.79	3.32	3.72
5	.0823	.111	.166	.229	.322	1.85	2.21	2.57	3.02	3.35
6	.113	.145	.206	.273	.367	1.77	2.10	2.41	2.80	3.09
7	.141	.177	.241	.310	.405	1.72	2.01	2.29	2.64	2.90
8	.168	.206	.272	.342	.436	1.67	1.94	2.19	2.51	2.74
9	.193	.232	.300	.369	.463	1.63	1.88	2.11	2.41	2.62
10	.216	.256	.325	.394	.487	1.60	1.83	2.05	2.32	2.52
11	.237	.278	.347	.416	.507	1.57	1.79	1.99	2.25	2.43
12	.256	.298	.367	.435	.525	1.55	1.75	1.94	2.18	2.36
13	.274	.316	.385	.453	.542	1.52	1.72	1.90	2.13	2.29
14	.291	.333	.402	.469	.556	1.50	1.69	1.87	2.08	2.24
15	.307	.349	.417	.484	.570	1.49	1.67	1.83	2.04	2.19
16	.321	.363	.432	.489	.582	1.47	1.64	1.80	2.00	214
18	.348	.390	.457	.522	.604	1.44	1.60	1.75	1.93	2.06
20	.372	.413	.480	.543	.622	1.42	1.57	1.71	1.88	2.00
24	.412	.452	.517	.577	.652	1.38	1.52	1.64	1.79	1.90
30	.460	.498	.560	.616	.687	1.34	1.46	1.57	1.70	1.79
40	.518	.554	.611	.663	.726	1.30	1.39	1.48	1.59	1.67
60	.592	.625	.675	.720	.774	1.24	1.32	1.39	1.47	1.53
120	.699	.724	.763	.798	.839	1.17	1.22	1.27	1.32	1.36
∞	1.000	1.000	1.000	1.000	1.000	1.00	1.00	1.00	1.00	1.00

To interpolate carefully, see Table *X*.

TABLE VII
F Critical Points

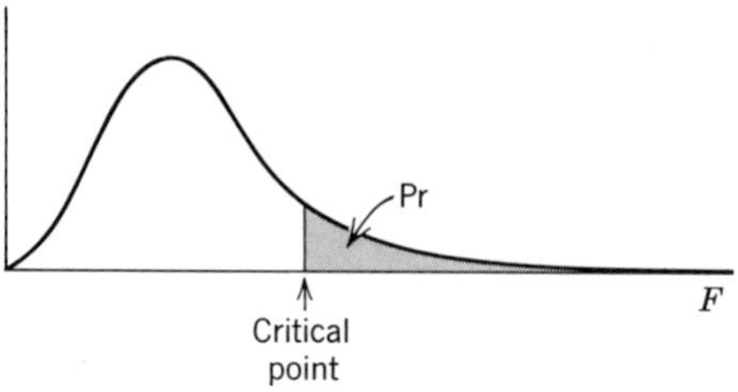

Degrees of freedom for denominator	*Pr*	Degrees of freedom for numerator: 1	2	3	4	5	6	8	10	20	40	∞
1	.25	5.83	7.50	8.20	8.58	8.82	8.98	9.19	9.32	9.58	9.71	9.85
	.10	39.9	49.5	53.6	55.8	57.2	58.2	59.4	60.2	61.7	62.5	63.3
	.05	161	200	216	225	230	234	239	242	248	251	254
2	.25	2.57	3.00	3.15	3.23	3.28	3.31	3.35	3.38	3.43	3.45	3.48
	.10	8.53	9.00	9.16	9.24	9.29	9.33	9.37	9.39	9.44	9.47	9.49
	.05	18.5	19.0	19.2	19.2	19.3	19.3	19.4	19.4	19.4	19.5	19.5
	.01	98.5	99.0	99.2	99.2	99.3	99.3	99.4	99.4	99.4	99.5	99.5
	.001	998	999	999	999	999	999	999	999	999	999	999
3	.25	2.02	2.28	2.36	2.39	2.41	2.42	2.44	2.44	2.46	2.47	2.47
	.10	5.54	5.46	5.39	5.34	5.31	5.28	5.25	5.23	5.18	5.16	5.13
	.05	10.1	9.55	9.28	9.12	9.10	8.94	8.85	8.79	8.66	8.59	8.53
	.01	34.1	30.8	29.5	28.7	28.2	27.9	27.5	27.2	26.7	26.4	26.1
	.001	167	149	141	137	135	133	131	129	126	125	124
4	.25	1.81	2.00	2.05	2.06	2.07	2.08	2.08	2.08	2.08	2.08	2.08
	.10	4.54	4.32	4.19	4.11	4.05	4.01	3.95	3.92	3.84	3.80	3.76
	.05	7.71	6.94	6.59	6.39	6.26	6.16	6.04	5.96	5.80	5.72	5.63
	.01	21.2	18.0	16.7	16.0	15.5	15.2	14.8	14.5	14.0	13.7	13.5
	.001	74.1	61.3	56.2	53.4	51.7	50.5	49.0	48.1	46.1	45.1	44.1
5	.25	1.69	1.85	1.88	1.89	1.89	1.89	1.89	1.89	1.88	1.88	1.87
	.10	4.06	3.78	3.62	3.52	3.45	3.40	3.34	3.30	3.21	3.16	3.10
	.05	6.61	5.79	5.41	5.19	5.05	4.95	4.82	4.74	4.56	4.46	4.36
	.01	16.3	13.3	12.1	11.4	11.0	10.7	10.3	10.1	9.55	9.29	9.02
	.001	47.2	37.1	33.2	31.1	29.8	28.8	27.6	26.9	25.4	24.6	23.8
6	.25	1.62	1.76	1.78	1.79	1.79	1.78	1.77	1.77	1.76	1.75	1.74
	.10	3.78	3.46	3.29	3.18	3.11	3.05	2.98	2.94	2.84	2.78	2.72
	.05	5.99	5.14	4.76	4.53	4.39	4.28	4.15	4.06	3.87	3.77	3.67
	.01	13.7	10.9	9.78	9.15	8.75	8.47	8.10	7.87	7.40	7.14	6.88
	.001	35.5	27.0	23.7	21.9	20.8	20.0	19.0	18.4	17.1	16.4	15.8
7	.25	1.57	1.70	1.72	1.72	1.71	1.71	1.70	1.69	1.67	1.66	1.65
	.10	3.59	3.26	3.07	2.96	2.88	2.83	2.75	2.70	2.59	2.54	2.47
	.05	5.59	4.74	4.35	4.12	3.97	3.87	3.73	3.64	3.44	3.34	3.23
	.01	12.2	9.55	8.45	7.85	7.46	7.19	6.84	6.62	6.16	5.91	5.65
	.001	29.3	21.7	18.8	17.2	16.2	15.5	14.6	14.1	12.9	12.3	11.7
8	.25	1.54	1.66	1.67	1.66	1.66	1.65	1.64	1.63	1.61	1.59	1.58
	.10	3.46	3.11	2.92	2.81	2.73	2.67	2.59	2.54	2.42	2.36	2.29
	.05	5.32	4.46	4.07	3.84	3.69	3.58	3.44	3.35	3.15	3.04	2.93
	.01	11.3	8.65	7.59	7.01	6.63	6.37	6.03	5.81	5.36	5.12	4.86
	.001	25.4	18.5	15.8	14.4	13.5	12.9	12.0	11.5	10.5	9.92	9.33
9	.25	1.51	1.62	1.63	1.63	1.62	1.61	1.60	1.59	1.56	1.55	1.53
	.10	3.36	3.01	2.81	2.69	2.61	2.55	2.47	2.42	2.30	2.23	2.16
	.05	5.12	4.26	3.86	3.63	3.48	3.37	3.23	3.14	2.94	2.83	2.71
	.01	10.6	8.02	6.99	6.42	6.06	5.80	5.47	5.26	4.81	4.57	4.31
	.001	22.9	16.4	13.9	12.6	11.7	11.1	10.4	9.89	8.90	8.37	7.81

To interpolate carefully, see Table X.

TABLE VII (Continued)

Degrees of freedom for denominator	Pr	Degrees of freedom for numerator										
		1	*2*	*3*	*4*	*5*	*6*	*8*	*10*	*20*	*40*	∞
10	.25	1.49	1.60	1.60	1.59	1.59	1.58	1.56	1.55	1.52	1.51	1.48
	.10	3.28	2.92	2.73	2.61	2.52	2.46	2.38	2.32	2.20	2.13	2.06
	.05	4.96	4.10	3.71	3.48	3.33	3.22	3.07	2.98	2.77	2.66	2.54
	.01	10.0	7.56	6.55	5.99	5.64	5.39	5.06	4.85	4.41	4.17	3.91
	.001	21.0	14.9	12.6	11.3	10.5	9.92	9.20	8.75	7.80	7.30	6.76
12	.25	1.56	1.56	1.56	1.55	1.54	1.53	1.51	1.50	1.47	1.45	1.42
	.10	3.18	2.81	2.61	2.48	2.39	2.33	2.24	2.19	2.06	1.99	1.90
	.05	4.75	3.89	3.49	3.26	3.11	3.00	2.85	2.75	2.54	2.43	2.30
	.01	9.33	6.93	5.95	5.41	5.06	4.82	4.50	4.30	3.86	3.62	3.36
	.001	18.6	13.0	10.8	9.63	8.89	8.38	7.71	7.29	6.40	5.93	5.42
14	.25	1.44	1.53	1.53	1.52	1.51	1.50	1.48	1.46	1.43	1.41	1.38
	.10	3.10	2.73	2.52	2.39	2.31	2.24	2.15	2.10	1.96	1.89	1.80
	.05	4.60	3.74	3.34	3.11	2.96	2.85	2.70	2.60	2.39	2.27	2.13
	.01	8.86	5.51	5.56	5.04	4.69	4.46	4.14	3.94	3.51	3.27	3.00
	.001	17.1	11.8	9.73	8.62	7.92	7.43	6.80	6.40	5.56	5.10	4.60
16	.25	1.42	1.51	1.51	1.50	1.48	1.48	1.46	1.45	1.40	1.37	1.34
	.10	3.05	2.67	2.46	2.33	2.24	2.18	2.09	2.03	1.89	1.81	1.72
	.05	4.49	3.63	3.24	3.01	2.85	2.74	2.59	2.49	2.28	2.15	2.01
	.01	8.53	6.23	5.29	4.77	4.44	4.20	3.89	3.69	3.26	3.02	2.75
	.001	16.1	11.0	9.00	7.94	7.27	6.81	6.19	5.81	4.99	4.54	4.06
18	.25	1.41	1.50	1.49	1.48	1.46	1.45	1.43	1.42	1.38	1.35	1.32
	.10	3.01	2.62	2.42	2.29	2.20	2.13	2.04	1.98	1.84	1.75	1.66
	.05	4.41	3.55	3.16	2.93	2.77	2.66	2.51	2.41	2.19	2.06	1.92
	.01	8.29	6.01	5.09	4.58	4.25	4.01	3.71	3.51	3.08	2.84	2.57
	.001	15.4	10.4	8.49	7.46	6.81	6.35	5.76	5.39	4.59	4.15	3.67
20	.25	1.40	1.49	1.48	1.46	1.45	1.44	1.42	1.40	1.36	1.33	1.29
	.10	2.97	2.59	2.38	2.25	2.16	2.09	2.00	1.94	1.79	1.71	1.61
	.05	4.35	3.49	3.10	2.87	2.71	2.60	2.45	2.35	2.12	1.99	1.84
	.01	8.10	5.85	4.94	4.43	4.10	3.87	3.56	3.37	2.94	2.69	2.42
	.001	14.8	9.95	8.10	7.10	6.46	6.02	5.44	5.08	4.29	3.86	3.38
30	.25	1.38	1.45	1.44	1.42	1.41	1.39	1.37	1.35	1.30	1.27	1.23
	.10	2.88	2.49	2.28	2.14	2.05	1.98	1.88	1.82	1.67	1.57	1.46
	.05	4.17	3.32	2.92	2.69	2.53	2.42	2.27	2.16	1.93	1.79	1.62
	.01	7.56	5.39	4.51	4.02	3.70	3.47	3.17	2.98	2.55	2.30	2.01
	.001	13.3	8.77	7.05	6.12	5.53	5.12	4.58	4.24	3.49	3.07	2.59
40	.25	1.36	1.44	1.42	1.40	1.39	1.37	1.35	1.33	1.28	1.24	1.19
	.10	2.84	2.44	2.23	2.09	2.00	1.93	1.83	1.76	1.61	1.51	1.38
	.05	4.08	3.23	2.84	2.61	2.45	2.34	2.18	2.08	1.84	1.69	1.51
	.01	7.31	5.18	4.31	3.83	3.51	3.29	2.99	2.80	2.37	2.11	1.80
	.001	12.6	8.25	6.60	5.70	5.13	4.73	4.21	3.87	3.15	2.73	2.23
60	.25	1.35	1.42	1.41	1.38	1.37	1.35	1.32	1.30	1.25	1.21	1.15
	.10	2.79	2.39	2.18	2.04	1.95	1.87	1.77	1.71	1.54	1.44	1.29
	.05	4.00	3.15	2.76	2.53	2.37	2.25	2.10	1.99	1.75	1.59	1.39
	.01	7.08	4.98	4.13	3.65	3.34	3.12	2.82	2.63	2.20	1.94	1.60
	.001	12.0	7.76	6.17	5.31	4.76	4.37	3.87	3.54	2.83	2.41	1.89
120	.25	1.34	1.40	1.39	1.37	1.35	1.33	1.30	1.28	1.22	1.18	1.10
	.10	2.75	2.35	2.13	1.99	1.90	1.82	1.72	1.65	1.48	1.37	1.19
	.05	3.92	3.07	2.68	2.45	2.29	2.17	2.02	1.91	1.66	1.50	1.25
	.01	6.85	4.79	3.95	3.48	3.17	2.96	2.66	2.47	2.03	1.76	1.38
	.001	11.4	7.32	5.79	4.95	4.42	4.04	3.55	3.24	2.53	2.11	1.54
∞	.25	1.32	1.39	1.37	1.35	1.33	1.31	1.28	1.25	1.19	1.14	1.00
	.10	2.71	2.30	2.08	1.94	1.85	1.77	1.67	1.60	1.42	1.30	1.00
	.05	3.84	3.00	2.60	2.37	2.21	2.10	1.94	1.83	1.57	1.39	1.00
	.01	6.63	4.61	3.78	3.32	3.02	2.80	2.51	2.32	1.88	1.59	1.00
	.001	10.8	6.91	5.42	4.62	4.10	3.74	3.27	2.96	2.27	1.84	1.00

TABLE VIII

Critical Points of the Durbin-Watson Test for Autocorrelation

This table gives two limiting values of critical D (D_L and D_U), corresponding to the two most extreme configurations of the regressors; thus, for every possible configuration, the critical value of D will be somewhere between D_L and D_U:

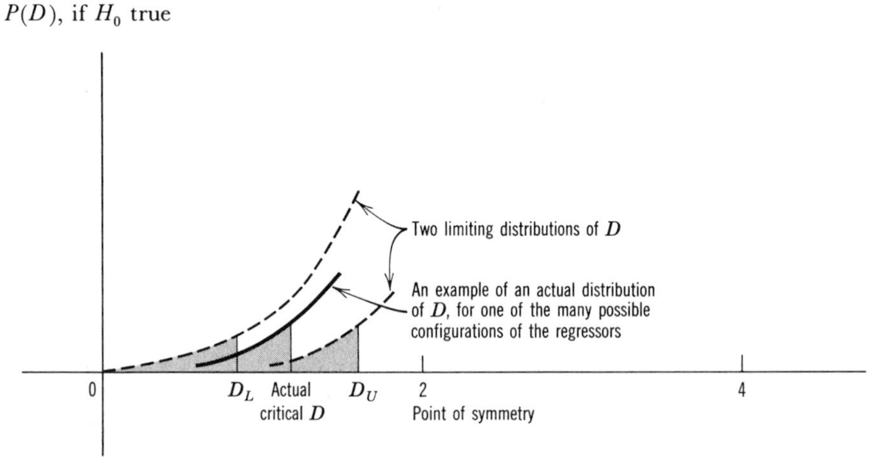

As an example of a test for positive serial correlation, suppose that there are $n = 15$ observations and $k = 3$ regressors (excluding the constant) and we wish to test $\rho = 0$ versus $\rho > 0$ at the level $\alpha = .05$. Then if D falls below $D_L = .82$, reject H_0. If D falls above $D_U = 1.75$, do not reject H_0. If D falls between D_L and D_U, this test is indecisive.

To test for negative serial correlation ($\rho = 0$ versus $\rho < 0$), the right-hand tail of the distribution defines the critical region. The symmetry of the distribution permits us to calculate these values very easily. With the same sample size, number of regressors, and level α as before, our new critical values would be $4 - D_L = 4 - .82 = 3.18$, and $4 - D_U = 4 - 1.75 = 2.25$. Accordingly, if D falls beyond 3.18, reject H_0. If D falls short of 2.25, do not reject H_0. If D falls between 2.25 and 3.18, this test is indecisive.

TABLE **VIII (Continued)**

Sample size = n	*Pr = Probability in Lower Tail (Level, α)*	*k = Number of Regressors (Excluding the Constant)* 1		2		3		4		5	
		D_L	D_U	D_L	D_U	D_L	D_U	D_L	D_U	D_L	D_U
	.01	.81	1.07	70	1.25	.59	1.46	.49	1.70	.39	1.96
15	.025	.95	1.23	.83	1.40	.71	1.61	.59	1.84	.48	2.09
	.05	1.08	1.36	.95	1.54	.82	1.75	.69	1.97	.56	2.21
	.01	.95	1.15	.86	1.27	.77	1.41	.68	1.57	.60	1.74
20	.025	1.08	1.28	.99	1.41	.89	1.55	.79	1.70	.70	1.87
	.05	1.20	1.41	1.10	1.54	1.00	1.68	.90	1.83	.79	1.99
	.01	1.05	1.21	.98	1.30	.90	1.41	.83	1.52	.75	1.65
25	.025	1.18	1.34	1.10	1.43	1.02	1.54	.94	1.65	.86	1.77
	.05	1.29	1.45	1.21	1.55	1.12	1.66	1.04	1.77	.95	1.89
	.01	1.13	1.26	1.07	1.34	1.01	1.42	.94	1.51	.88	1.61
30	.025	1.25	1.38	1.18	1.46	1.12	1.54	1.05	1.63	.98	1.73
	.05	1.35	1.49	1.28	1.57	1.21	1.65	1.14	1.74	1.07	1.83
	.01	1.25	1.34	1.20	1.40	1.15	1.46	1.10	1.52	1.05	1.58
40	.025	1.35	1.45	1.30	1.51	1.25	1.57	1.20	1.63	1.15	1.69
	.05	1.44	1.54	1.39	1.60	1.34	1.66	1.29	1.72	1.23	1.79
	.01	1.32	1.40	1.28	1.45	1.24	1.49	1.20	1.54	1.16	1.59
50	.025	1.42	1.50	1.38	1.54	1.34	1.59	1.30	1.64	1.26	1.69
	.05	1.50	1.59	1.46	1.63	1.42	1.67	1.38	1.72	1.34	1.77
	.01	1.38	1.45	1.35	1.48	1.32	1.52	1.28	1.56	1.25	1.60
60	.025	1.47	1.54	1.44	1.57	1.40	1.61	1.37	1.65	1.33	1.69
	.05	1.55	1.62	1.51	1.65	1.48	1.69	1.44	1.73	1.41	1.77
	.01	1.47	1.52	1.44	1.54	1.42	1.57	1.39	1.60	1.36	1.62
80	.025	1.54	1.59	1.52	1.62	1.49	1.65	1.47	1.67	1.44	1.70
	.05	1.61	1.66	1.59	1.69	1.56	1.72	1.53	1.74	1.51	1.77
	.01	1.52	1.56	1.50	1.58	1.48	1.60	1.46	1.63	1.44	1.65
100	.025	1.59	1.63	1.57	1.65	1.55	1.67	1.53	1.70	1.51	1.72
	.05	1.65	1.69	1.63	1.72	1.61	1.74	1.59	1.76	1.57	1.78

TABLE IX
Interpolating Tables V to VII

For all the exercises in the text, simple linear interpolation gives a good enough approximation. However, important research data may deserve more careful interpolation, as follows.

Table V (Student's t) may require interpolation in either of two directions:

(a) Down (interpolating d.f.); or

(b) Across (interplating Pr).

We give examples of both kinds of interpolation, showing the tabled values in black, and interpolation calculations in color.

(a) Interpolation of d.f.

First, calculate $r = 1/\text{d.f.}$ Then interpolate linearly with r. For example, let us find $t_{.025}$ for d.f. = 600:

d.f.	$r = \dfrac{1}{\text{d.f.}}$	$t_{.025}$
120	$\dfrac{1}{120} = .00833$	1.980
600	$\dfrac{1}{600} = .00167$	$1.960 + (1.980 - 1.960)\left(\dfrac{.00167 - 0}{.00833 - 0}\right) = 1.964$
∞	$\dfrac{1}{\infty} = 0$	1.960

(b) Interpolation of Pr

First, calculate $L = \log \text{Pr}$. Then interpolate linearly with L. For example, when d.f. = 4, let us find Pr corresponding to $t = 1.800$:

Pr	.10	.0734	.05
$L = \log \text{Pr}$	-1.00	$-1.00 + (-1.301 + 1.00)\left(\dfrac{1.800 - 1.533}{2.132 - 1.533}\right) = -1.134$	-1.301
t	1.533	1.800	2.132

Finally, we note that Tables VI(b)[1] and VII can be interpolated similarly, while Table VI(a) can be calculated from Table VI(b).

[1]The right half of Table VI(b) can be interpolated similarly; the left half requires first calculating the tail probability $(1 - \text{Pr})$ in place of Pr.

ANSWERS TO ODD-NUMBERED PROBLEMS

2-1 (a) $Y = 80 + .070x$
or $\quad = 59 + .070X$
(c) $a = 80$ is the estimated yield when the average amount (300 lb) of fertilizer is applied, while $a_0 = 59$ is the estimated yield when no fertilizer is applied.
(d) MPP = .070 bushels per lb. of fertilizer.
(e) MRP = \$.14 per lb. of fertilizer. So it is economic to apply.

2-3 $C = .396 + .856X$
Slope is .856, which equals $1 - .144$, that is, the consumption coefficient is the complement of the savings coefficient.

2-5 (c) yes, the new equation is indeed $y = bx$

2-7 (a) .067
(b) $(Y_7 - Y_1)/(X_7 - X_1)$
(c) yes
(d) yes
(e) By the Gauss-Markov theorem, var $\tilde{\beta} >$ var $\hat{\beta}$
(f) var $\tilde{\beta} = .000{,}005{,}6\ \sigma^2$
var $\hat{\beta} = .000{,}003{,}6\ \sigma^2$

2-9 (a) both unbiased and linear
(b) (i) $.50\ \sigma^2$, (ii) $.56\ \sigma^2$
(c) The *G-M* corollary (2-42) says the sample mean ($\hat{\mu}$) has least variance. (and $.50\ \sigma^2$ is indeed less than $.56\ \sigma^2$).

2-11 (a) $S = 1.20 + .142x$
or $= -.36 + .142X$
(b) $\beta = .142 \pm .169$
(d) $\alpha = 1.20 \pm .67$

2-13 (a) $.47 \pm .75$
(b) $.76 \pm .69$
(c) $1.05 \pm .75$
(d) $1.34 \pm .91$
(e) The interval (b) is most precise, because it is at the center of the data where $x = 0$. The interval (d) is least precise, because it is furthest from the center.
(f) Broader than the confidence interval for α, because it is predicting an erratic individual.

2-15 (a) It is preferable to observe *i* in a period of wide fluctuation.
(b) A more accurate prediction could be made nearer the center, at $Y = \$10{,}000$.

2-17 (b) (i) 50% as large
(ii) 25% as large
(iii) 71% as large

2-19 (a) $Y = 140 + 1.27x$
$= 0 + 1.27X$
(c) $\mu_Y = 229 \pm 44$
(d) $\mu_Y \simeq 140$
(e) *CI* in (c) is much better!

2-21 (a) ..., with *zero* means and *constant* variance.
(b) ... are *un*biased, ...
(c) true

2-23 $E(\hat{\beta}) = \beta$

$$\text{var } \hat{\beta} = \frac{\sum x_i^2 \sigma_i^2}{(\sum x_i^2)^2}$$

2-25 (a) In order, they are *A*, *C*, *B*
(b) *B* is biased
C and *B* have minimum variance
A has largest MSE
C is most efficient
A is least efficient

3-1 (a) $S = .76 + .115x - .0294w$
$= .105 + .115X - .0294W$
(b) multiple regression (.115) is better, because it shows the relation of *S* to *X if* W *were* constant.
(c) \$880
(d) \$230
(e) \$30

3-5 (a)

.80	.77	−8.3
±3.1	±2.7	±.12

(b) (1) False. ... it is reasonable to *accept* the null hypothesis $\beta_1 = 0$ as a working hypothesis
(2) True.

3-7 Suppose in Problem 13-5, *T* had a coefficient ten times as large. Then it should be kept, even with *t* as small as 1.4. The variable *A*, with $t = 2.2$, might be dropped because it is not very important.

3-9 All true

3-11 (a) Change as follows: If these regressors are regarded a priori as important, they should be kept; in spite of their large standard errors, the coefficients will at least be unbiased.
(b) Simple regression is too naive—it hopelessly mixes up direct and indirect effects.

3-13 (a) True
(b) True

3-15 (a) .025
(b) $.059 = .0381 + .025(.833)$

3-17 (a) (i) False. Other things being equal, we estimate that a professor earns \$230 more annually for *each* book he writes, on average.
(ii) False. ... of writing *each book*.
(iii) False. The average salary increase would average *much more* than \$190. There would be further increases because of increased performance (writing articles and books, etc.). There would also be important increases because of a generally rising wage level (which would increase starting salaries, too).
(b) Other things being equal, we *estimate* a professor annually earns on average:
(i) \$18 more for each ordinary article he has written
(ii) \$100 more for each excellent article he has written
(iii) \$490 more for each Ph.D. he has supervised
(iv) \$50 more for having a teaching evaluation in the top half (but \$50 is a *very* unreliable estimate)

4-1 (a) 10.1
(b) larger bias, because $\hat{\beta}_{wy}$ is larger.
(c) negative bias, because $\hat{\beta}_{wy}$ is negative

4-3 (a), (b)

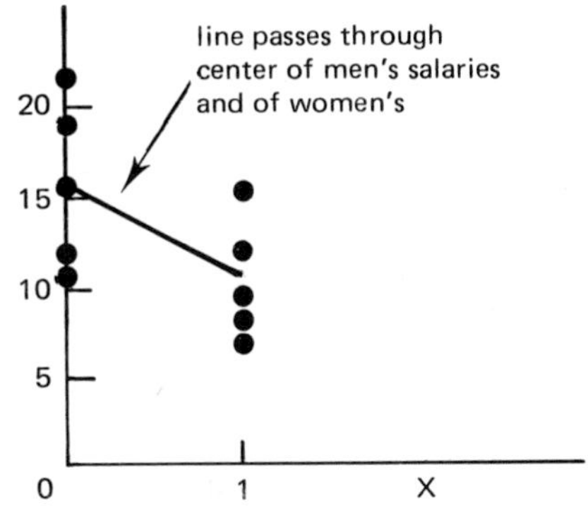

(c) $Y = 16.0 - 5.0X$

(d) $\beta = -5.0 \pm 5.8$. Women earn on average \$5,000 ($\pm$\$5,800) less than men.

(e) No. To measure discrimination, men and women *with the same qualifications* should be compared.

4-5 We disagree. The \$2400 figure may be due to discrimination, but it also may be partly due to some more subtle difference between men and women not measured in this study.

4-7

(a)

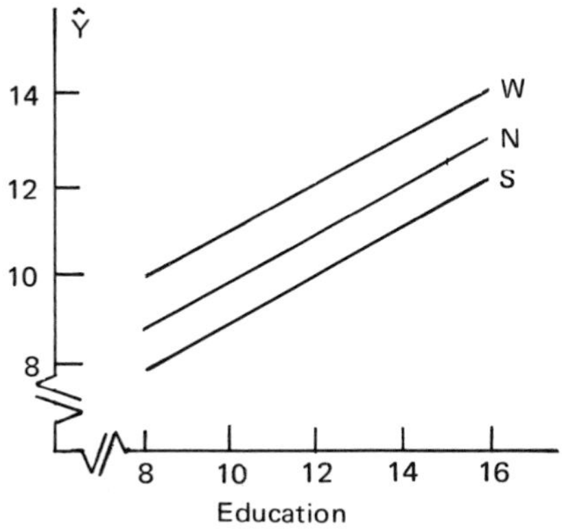

(b)

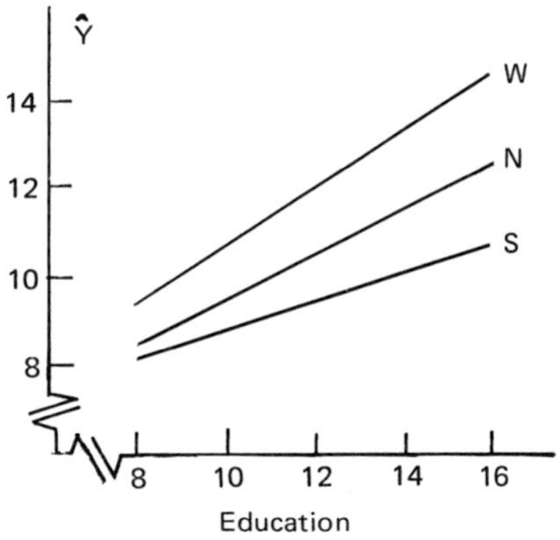

4-9 (a)

50	35
40	25
20	5

(b)

55	35
30	25
20	5

(c) additive, both sexes

4-11

(a)

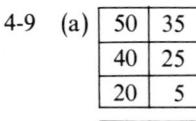

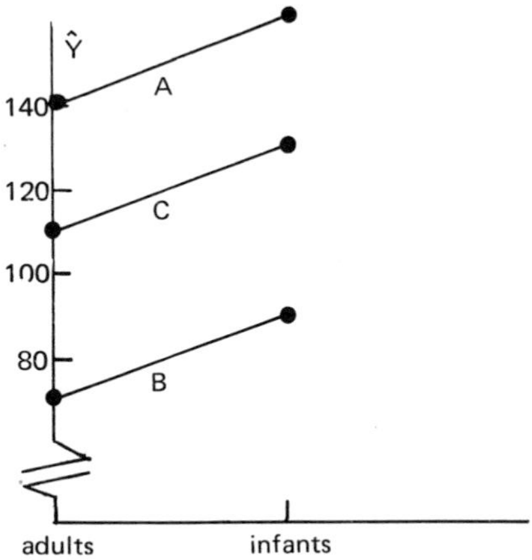

(b)

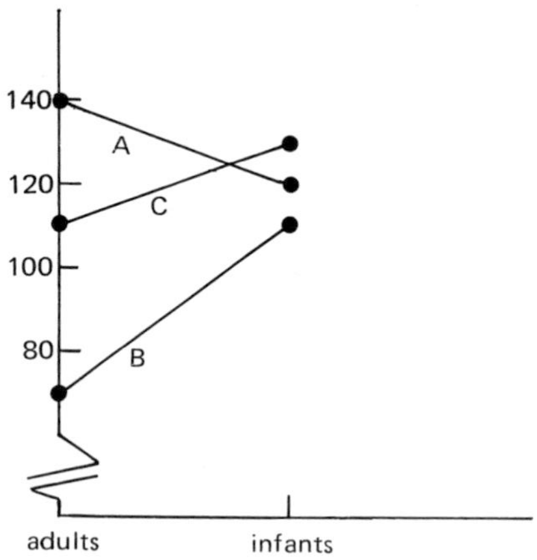

(c)

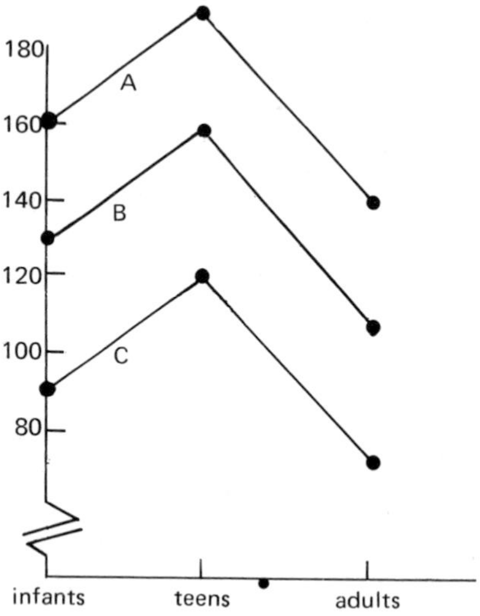

4-13 (a) Concave down, negative coefficient of X^2
(b) $\hat{Y} = 80.7 - .13X + .000333X^2$
(c) No
(d) Straight line is better. The parabola in (b) bending up would be putting far too much faith in a small unreliable sample. Or, more formally, prob-value for H_0 (no curve) is more than 50%.

4-15 (a) 3%
(b) 10%

4-17 (a) 1.30
(b) 3.9%
(c) 7.7%

4-19 (a) $B_0 = 100$, $i = 3\%$
(b) Only 2 observations are necessary

4-21 58.8%, and the drop of 1.2% is statistically indiscernible

4-23 The transformable nonlinear models (e), (f), and (h), assume a multiplicative error centered at 1. All others assume just the ordinary additive error centered at 0.

4-25 Multiple regression, with some dummies for each categorical variable such as religion.

4-27 (a) 4.6%
(b) 17%
(c) 0.1%
(d) −14% (i.e., 14% *less*)

4-29 (a) $\hat{Y} = 61 + 9D_A + 12D_B$
(b) 61, 70, 73
(c) 61, 70, 73; same as (b), of course
(d) The multiple regression in part (b) is conceptually more difficult. However, if done on a computer, it is computationally no problem, and in fact then enjoys two advantages:
(1) *CI* for β and γ would show whether the differences were discernible.

(2) Other factors such as rainfall or soil fertility could be incorporated easily, and provide a much more accurate comparison.

4-31 (a) $E = 13.625 + .000583(\text{F-8000}) - .917(\text{D-.5})$
where $D = 0$ for urban,
$D = 1$ for rural.

4-33 (a) negative (concave down)
(b) $\hat{Y} = 6.333X - .06667X^2$
(c) Straight line is probably better, because 4 points are insufficient data to support a complicated model.

4-35 (a) $P = \alpha e^{\beta T}$
(b) $\hat{P} = 2030\, e^{.0110T}$
$\tau = 63$ minutes

4-37 $\beta_1 \simeq -10.4 \pm 8.4$
$\beta_2 \simeq 1.241 \pm .176$
$\beta_3 \simeq .9539 \pm .0196$
But these *CI* are too optimistic, because observations are a time series, and therefore not independent.

5-1 (a) $r = .62$
(b) $-.47 < \rho < .95$
(c) H_0 *cannot* be rejected.

5-3 (a) $Y = 9 + .35x$
(b) $t = 2.18$, $.05 < p < .10$
(c) $t = 2.18$, $.10 < p < .20$
(d)

source	*variation*	*d.f.*
explained	12.25	1
unexplained	7.75	3
total	20.0	4

variance	*F*	*prob-value*
12.25 2.58	4.75	$.10 < p < .25$

61% explained,
39% unexplained
$.10 < p < .25$
(e) Since $r = .78$,
$-.25 < \rho < .97$
Hence $\rho = 0$ is acceptable.
(f) Yes. In every case, the null hypothesis cannot be rejected.
(g) $Y = 7.95$
$Y = 10.75$
$X = 16.75$

5-5 (a) True
(b) True
(c) True
(d) False. $\hat{\beta}_* = \dfrac{r^2}{\hat{\beta}}$

5-7 (a) $r = .56$
(b) $\hat{X}_2 = 25 + .58\, X_1$
(c) 77, 48
(d) mean = 74, about the same as 77 in (c)
(e) mean = 42.5, about the same as 48 in (c)
(f) (i) False: The pilots who scored very well or very badly on the first test X_1 *tended to be* closer to the average on the second test X_2. *Nevertheless*, the variance of X_2 is *about the same as* the variance of X_1, *as the graph in part (d) makes obvious.*
(ii) True. See part (b).

5-9 (a) The effect of criticism (or praise) cannot be distinguished from (*is confounded with*) the natural regression toward the mean.
(b) This design is still questionable, still confounded: Now the effect of criticism cannot be distinguished from the effect of practice.

5-11 (a) .404
(b) .262
(c) less. Usually true.

5-13 (a) True
(b) True
(c) True

5-15 Subject to rounding errors,
(a) $R = .9920$
(b) $r = .8737$
(c) .7633, .9841, .2208, .0159

5-17 (a) $F = 12.4, \quad p \ll .001$
(b) $F = 19.2, \quad p \ll .001$
(c) $F = 33.1, \quad p \ll .001$
(d) $F = 50.8, \quad p \ll .001$
where p is 2-sided.

5-19 (a) the same as
(b) correlated, smaller
(c) $F = t^2$
(d) $\Delta R^2 = .0076$, which confirms (b)

5-21 (a) yes, yes
(b) Introducing drugs first *or* sex first, we obtain exactly the same results:
drugs $F = 8.18, \; .001 < p < .01$
sex $F = 9.07, \; .001 < p < .01$
inter. $F = 1.24, \quad p > .25$

5-23 (b) $r = .656$
(c) $\hat{Y} = 86 + .68X$
(d) $\bar{X} = 300$, $\bar{Y} = 283$, close to regression line
(e) $\bar{X} = 243$, $\bar{Y} = 253$, close to regression line
(f) about equal:
$s_{78}^2 = 667, \quad s_{77}^2 = 622$

5-25 (a) 490
(b) requires n
(c) 77.8
(d) 67.2

5-27 (a) Yes
(b) No, $\hat{\beta}' = 100\hat{\beta}$
(c) Yes
(d) Yes

6-1 (a) $\beta = .295 \pm 2.45$
(b) $\beta = 0 \pm 2.74$
(c) *WLS* is closer to the target than is *OLS*. Only *WLS* gives a valid 90% confidence interval.

6-5 (a) True
(b) True except (iii)
(c) ... yields *approximately* the same result *in most cases.*

6-9 $D = 2$

6-11

j	0	1	2	3	4	5
β_j	.45	.27	.18	.11	.06	.03

6-13 (b)

l	0	1	2	3	...
ρ_l	1.0	−.64	.14	0	...

6-15

l	0	1	2	3	...
ρ_l	1.0	.24	.12	.06	...

7-1 (a)

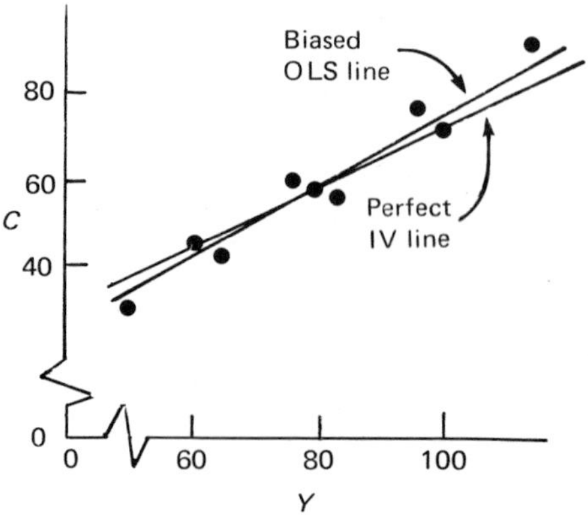

(b) $C = -1.5 + .744\,Y$
Inconsistent
(c) (i) $C = 10 + .60\,Y$,
Consistent
(ii) Exactly the same.

(d) The errors e_i exactly cancel, yielding a perfect estimate in part (c). Usually we would not be so lucky, and we would find $\hat{\beta}$ is slightly off target.

7-3 (a) .67, 3.0
(b) *OLS* yields the inconsistent estimate $\hat{\beta} = .77$
(c) (i) *OLS* estimator of β
(ii) *OLS* estimator of β of course, and *IV* estimator of β.

7-5 The weakness is in the vague phrase, "hence it has zero mean, etc." This model does not satisfy a crucial requirement for consistency: the error must be uncorrelated with the regressor.

8-1 Only equation 1 may be identified.

8-3 (a) The short equations
(b) (i) True, except for the last sentence, which should read:
"... if the number of variables on the right hand side (thus α_0 is not counted) is no more than the total number of exogenous variables in the system."
(ii) Corrected version: even though one equation in a system is identified, other equations may be unidentified as shown by Problem 8-1.

8-5 (a) The *D* and *S* bands have the same vertical spread. However, since demand has a greater slope, it has a much narrower band, and therefore has greater influence on the direction of the parallelogram.

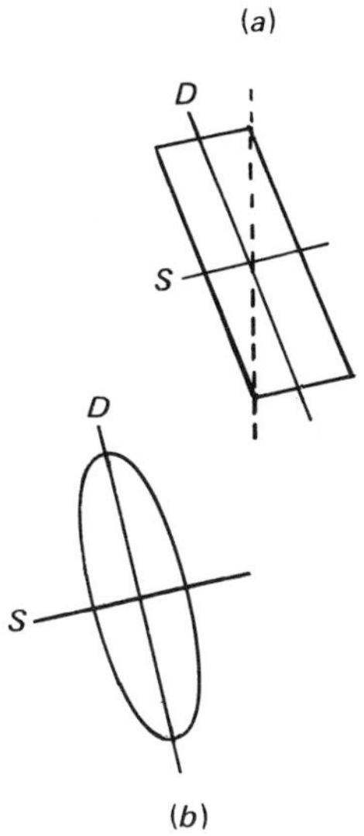

10-1 (a) .66, .34
(b) False. Since the barometer sometimes predicts "rain" when it shines, a "rain" prediction is uncertain.
(c) It is a worse predictor when it shines.

10-3 (a) .10, .40, .50
(b) .28, .44, .28

10-7 (a) $N(69.4, 5.88)$
(b) Posterior is between, but 16 times closer to the likelihood function.
(c) .0022
(d) $\mu = 69.41 \pm 4.75$ (Bayesian)
$\mu = 70.00 \pm 4.90$ (Classical)

10-9 (a) $\mu = 22.0 \pm 3.10$
(b) .0057

10-11 (a) 2.00 ± 1.26 (if $z_{.025}$ used, ± 1.05)
(b) $1.68 \pm .79$ (if $z_{.025}$ used, $\pm .70$)
(c) $1.57 \pm .60$ (if $z_{.025}$ used, $\pm .57$)

10-13 (a) $p(\pi) \propto \pi^5(1-\pi)^{30}$
(b) Approximately $\sim N(141.3, 52.2)$
$\mu = 141.3 \pm 15.0$
(if $z_{.025}$ used, ± 14.2)

(c) Approximately $\sim N(4.67, .0833)$
$\beta = 4.67 \pm .59$
(if $z_{.025}$ used, $\pm .57$)

12-5 The given hypothesis should be
(i) rejected
(ii) rejected
(iii) rejected
(iv) not rejected
(v) not rejected

12-7 (a)

	1	x_1	x_2	x_3
1	–	0	0	0
x_1	0	–	–	–
x_2	0	0	–	–
x_3	0	.048	−.076	–

(b) x_1 and x_2 are uncorrelated
x_2 and x_3 are nearly collinear ($r = -.98$)
(c) The sample size n = 37, the first element

12-9 (a)

1	8	1	0
1	11	1	0
1	9	1	0
1	12	1	0
1	5	0	1
1	3	0	1
1	6	0	1
1	10	0	1

(b) $X_1 = X_3 + X_4$ exactly

(c) $\mathbf{X'X} =$

8	64	4	4
64	580	40	24
4	40	4	0
4	24	0	4

which cannot be inverted
(d) omit X_3, X_4, or X_1

12-11 $.82 \pm .35$

12-13 (a) True (see Figure 12-2)
(b) If and only if the stochastic terms e_i are normal, *independent, and of constant variance,* the likelihood function is ...

(c) The *OLS* estimate of $\boldsymbol{\beta}$ is *always* $\hat{\boldsymbol{\beta}} = (\mathbf{X'X})^{-1}\mathbf{X'y}$

13-1 (a) 3.84
(b) 6.64

13-3 (a) $7.1 < \sigma^2 < 69$
(b) $7.8 < \sigma^2 < 104$

14-3 $C = 2/7$.

14-5 (a) $\langle 2.33, .33 \rangle$
(b) $\langle -2.1, 3.6 \rangle$
(c) $\langle -.96, -.78 \rangle$, easiest.

14-7 (a)

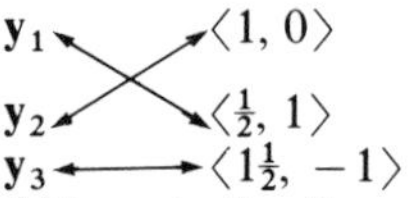

(b) Although the three points $\mathbf{y}_i$ are close, their co-ordinates are very different because the basis vectors point in nearly the same direction (are nearly collinear).

14-9 (a) True
(b) True
(c) ... the simple correlation of $\mathbf{y}$ *and* $\mathbf{x}_k$ after the influence of *all the other regressors* has been removed.

14-11 (a) True
(b) True

14-13 (b) $\hat{\beta}_2$ is unbiased
(c) 0
(d) $\hat{\beta}_1^*$ has positive bias so that we may erroneously conclude that it is significantly different from 0.
(e) $\hat{\beta}_2^*$ has negative bias, so that we may erroneously conclude that it is not significantly different from 0, i.e., reject x_2 as a regressor.
(f) it has larger $\hat{\beta}_1$ and smaller $\hat{\beta}_2$ (both are biased)
(g) residual is substantial, rather than 0 as in (c)
(h) not in this case

14-15

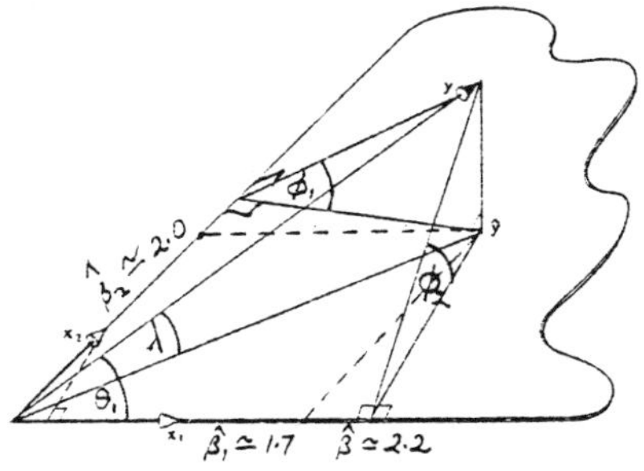

14-17 (a) $F = 2.32$, do not reject H_0
(b) $R = .77$
(c) .30

15-1

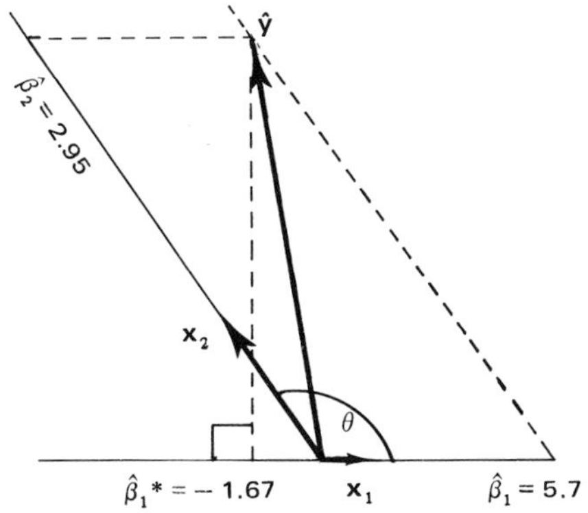

Cos θ is the correlation between $\mathbf{x}_1$ and $\mathbf{x}_2$, which is negative. Thus θ is greater than 90°.

16-3 This proof is more rigorous than in Appendix 2-C, where we neglected to check out the 2nd order conditions to ensure a minimum

16-5 (a) $e_t = .5, -.5, .5, -.5$
The serial correlation is -1 (perfectly negative).

(b) (i) .33
(ii) .92
(iii) *GLS* is much closer to β.

16-7 (b) $\hat{Y}_{n+1} = \mathbf{x}_{n+1}\hat{\boldsymbol{\beta}} + \rho\hat{e}_n$

16-9 $\text{cov}\,\hat{\boldsymbol{\beta}} = \begin{bmatrix} 4.14 & -2.53 \\ -2.53 & 1.88 \end{bmatrix}$

$\text{cov}\,\hat{\boldsymbol{\beta}}_0 = \begin{bmatrix} 6.22 & -3.67 \\ -3.67 & 2.50 \end{bmatrix}$

16-11 (a) perfect multicollinearity of **X** and **D**
(b) Impossible, because perfect multicollinearity means perfect ambiguity in the coefficients [see equation (3-10)]

17-1 (a) The distribution of errors and hence of **y**, is elliptical, rather than spherical.
(b) However, since the ellipse is still centered correctly, the *OLS* estimate is unbiased.
(c) Because of the greater variance of the *OLS* estimator, its *CI* should be wider. But instead it is narrower, because $\hat{\mathbf{e}}$ is an inappropriate $\perp$ projection, and hence understates.

18-1 Equation 1 is exactly identified,
2 is unidentified,
3 is overidentified.

19-1 *OLS* is biased (even asymptotically) because the regressors $\mathbf{Y}_1$ are correlated with **e**. Hence *OLS* is inconsistent, and should not be used for large samples.

19-3 (a) Yes
(b) Yes
(c) Yes, but the expression of $\hat{Q}$ is different.

19-5 Equivalent to 2SLS

20-1 True

BIBLIOGRAPHY

Journals are abbreviated as follows:

AER	American Economic Review
AJS	Australian Journal of Statistics
AMS	Annals of Mathematics Statistics
ECTRA	Econometrica
IER	International Economic Review
JASA	Journal of the American Statistical Association
JE	Journal of Economics
JFE	Journal of Farm Economics
JPE	Journal of Political Economy
JRSS	Journal of Royal Statistical Society
QJE	Quarterly Journal of Economics
RES	Review of Economics and Statistics

Abrahamse, A. P. J. and J. Koerts (1969), "A comparison between the power of the Durbin-Watson test and the power of the BLUS test," *JASA*, Vol. 64, pp. 938–948.

Afifi, A. and R. M. Elashoff (1966), "Missing observations in multivariate statistics," *JASA*, Vol. 61, pp. 595–604. Continued in *JASA*, Vol. 62, pp. 10–29. Also *JASA*, Vol. 64, pp. 337–365.

Aigner, D. J. (1966), "Errors of measurement and least squares estimation in a simple recursive model of dynamic equilibrium," *ECTRA*, Vol. 34, pp. 424–432.

Aigner, D. J. and G. G. Judge (1977), "Application of the Stein Rule Estimator to Economic Data," *ECTRA*, Vol. 45, pp. 1279–1288.

Aitken, A. C. (1935), "On least squares and linear combinations of observations," *Proceedings of the Royal Society*, Vol. 35, pp. 42–48.

Almon, Shirley (1965), "The distribution lag between capital appropriations and expenditures," *ECTRA*, Vol. 33, pp. 178–196.

Alt, F. (1942), Distributed lags," *ECTRA*, Vol. 10, pp. 113–158.

Amemiya, Takeshi (1966a), "On the use of principal components of independent variables in two-stage least-squares estimation," *IER*, Vol. 7, pp. 283–303.

Amemiya, Takeshi (1966b), "Specification analysis in the estimation of parameters of a simultaneous equation model with auto regressive residuals," *ECTRA*, Vol. 34, pp. 283–306.

Amemiya, Takeshi and W. A. Fuller (1967), "A comparative study of alternative estimators in a distributed lag model," *ECTRA*, Vol. 35, pp. 509–529.

Anderson, R. L. (1942), "Distribution of the serial correlation coefficients," *AMS*, Vol. 13, pp. 1–13.

Anderson, T. W. (1950), "Estimation of the parameters of a single equation by the limited information maximum likelihood method," Chapter 9 in Koopmans (1950).

Anderson, T. W. (1971), *The Statistical Analysis of Time Series*, New York; Wiley.

Anderson, T. W. and H. Rubin (1949), "Estimation of the parameters of a single equation in a complete system of stochastic equations," *AMS*, Vol. 20, pp. 46–63.

Anderson, T. W. and H. Rubin (1950), "The asymptotic properties of estimates of the parameters of a single equation in a complete system of stochastic equations," *AMS*, Vol. 21, pp. 570–582.

Arnt, S. W. (1968), "International short term capital movements: a distributed lag model of speculation in foreign exchange," *ECTRA*, Vol. 36, pp. 59–70.

Arrow, Kenneth J. (1960), in Olkin, et al, *Contributions of probability and statistics, essays in honor of Harold Hotelling*, pp. 70–78. Stanford U. Press.

Atiqullah, M. (1969), "On a restricted least squares estimator," *JASA*, Vol. 64, pp. 964–968.

Barten, A. P. (1962), "Note on unbiased estimation of the squared multiple correlation coefficient," *Statistica Neerlandica*, Vol. 16, pp. 151–163.

Basmann, R. L. (1957), "A generalized classical method of linear estimation of coefficients in a structural equation," *ECTRA*, Vol. 25, pp. 77–83.

Basmann, R. L. (1959), "The computation of coefficients in a structural equation," *ECTRA*, Vol. 27, pp. 72–81.

Basmann, R. L. (1960a), "On the asymptotic distribution of generalized linear estimators," *ECTRA*, Vol. 28, pp. 97–107.

Basmann, R. L. (1960b), "An expository note on estimation of simultaneous structural equations," Biometrics, Vol. 16, pp. 464–480.

Basmann, R. L. (1960c), "On finite sample distributions of generalized classical linear identifiability test statistics," *JASA*, Vol. 55, pp. 650–659.

Basmann, R. L. (1961), "A note on the exact finite sample frequency functions of generalized classical linear estimators in two leading overidentified cases," *JASA*, Vol. 56, pp. 619–636.

Basmann, R. L. (1963a), "The causal interpretation of nontriangular systems of economic relations," *ECTRA*, Vol. 31, pp. 439–448.

Basmann, R. L. (1963b), "Remarks concerning the application of exact finite sample distribution functions of GCL estimators in econometric statistical inference," *JASA*, Vol. 58, pp. 943–976.

Basmann, R. L. (1965a), "A Tchebychev inequality for the convergence of a generalized classical linear estimator, sample size being fixed," *ECTRA*, Vol. 33, pp. 608–618.

Basmann, R. L. (1965b), "A note on the statistical testability of 'Explicit causal chains' against the class of 'Interdependent' models," *JASA*, Vol. 60, pp. 1080–1093.

Bellman, R. and R. Roth (1969), "Curve cutting by segmented straight lines," *JASA*, Vol. 64, pp. 1079–1084.

Bennion, E. G. (1952), "The Cowles Commission's 'Simultaneous equation approach': A simplified explanation," *RES*, Vol. 34, pp. 49–56.

Bentzel, R. and B. Hansen (1955), "On recursiveness and interdependency in economic models," *RES*, Vol. 37, pp. 153–168.

Bergstrom, A. R. (1962), "The exact sampling distributions of least squares and maximum likelihood estimators of the marginal propensity to consume," *ECTRA*, Vol. 30, pp. 480–490.

Bierwag, G. O. and M. A. Grove (1966), "Aggregate Koyck functions," *ECTRA*, Vol. 34, pp. 828–832.

Bodkin, R. and L. R. Klein (1967), "Nonlinear estimation of aggregate production functions," *RES*, Vol. 49, pp. 28–44.

Box, G. E. P. and G. M. Jenkins (1970), *Time Series Analysis; Forecasting and Control*, 2nd ed., San Francisco, Holden-Day, 1970.

Box, G. E. P. and G. C. Tiao (1965), "Multiparameter problems from a Bayesian point of view," *AMS* 36, pp. 1468–1482.

Box, G. E. P. and G. C. Tiao (1973), *Bayesian Inference in Statistical Analysis*, Reading, Mass.: Addison-Wesley.

Bradu, D. and Y. Mandlak (1970), "Estimation in lognormal linear models," *JASA*, 65, pp. 198–211.

Brands, B., M. Hirst, C. W. Gowdey, J. C. Baskerville (1978), "Analgesia Duration and Physical Dependence in Mice after a Single Injection of Three Heroin Shots and Morphine Sulphate in Various Vehicles," *Archives Internationales de Pharmacodynamae et de Théraptie*, Feb. 1978, pp. 285–296.

Breusch and A. Pagan (1979), "A simple test of heteroscedasticity and random coefficient variation," *ECTRA*, Vol. 47,

Brillinger, D. R. (1975), *Time Series: Data Analysis and Theory*, New York: Holt, Rinehart and Winston.

Bronfenbrenner, J. (1953), "Sources and size of least squares bias in a two-equation model," Chapter 9 in *Studies in Econometric Methods*, W. C. Hood and T. C. Koopmans (eds.), Cowles Foundation for Research in Economics, Monograph No. 14, New York: Wiley.

Brown, T. M. (1952), "Habit persistence and lags in consumer behavior," *ECTRA*, Vol. 20, pp. 355–371.

Brown, T. M. (1954), "Standard error of forecast of a complete econometric model," *ECTRA*, Vol. 22, pp. 178–192.

Brown, T. M. (1959), "Simplified full maximum likelihood and comparative structural estimates," *ECTRA*, Vol. 27, pp. 638–653.

Brown, T. M. (1960), "Simultaneous least squares: A distribution free method of equation system structure estimation," *IER*, Vol. 1, pp. 173–191.

Brown, T. M. (1963), "Structure estimation for nonlinear systems of simultaneous equations," *IER*, Vol. 4, pp. 117–133.

Brown, T. M. (1967), "Simultaneous least squares and invariance under changes of units of measurement," *IER*, Vol. 8, pp. 97–102.

Brundy, J. M. and D. W. Jorgenson (1971), "Efficient estimation of simultaneous equations by instrumental variables," *RES*, 53, pp. 207–224.

Carter, R. A. L. (1977), "The exact distribution of an instrumental variable estimator," *IER*, Vol. 18, pp. 228–33.

Carter, R. A. L. (1981), forthcoming book on Monte Carlo.

Champernowne, D. G. (1948), "Sampling theory applied to autoregressive sequences," *JRSS, Series B*, Vol. 10, pp. 204–231.

Champernowne, D. G. (1960), "An experimental investigation of the robustness of certain procedures for estimating means and regression coefficients," *JRSS, Series A*, Vol. 123, pp. 398–412.

Chang, T. C. (1948), "A statistical note on world demand for export," *RES*, Vol. 30, pp. 106–116.

Chatfield, C. (1975), *The Analysis of Time Series: Theory and Practice*. London: Chapman and Hall.

Chernoff, H. and N. Rubin (1953), "Asymptotic properties of limited information estimates under generalized conditions," Chapter 7 in *Studies in Econometric Methods*, W. C. Hood and T. C. Koopmans (eds.). New York: Wiley.

Chetty, V. K. (1968), "Bayesian analysis of Haavelmo's models," *ECTRA*, Vol. 36, pp. 582–602.

Chow, G. C. (1960), "Tests of equality between sets of coefficients in two linear regressions," *ECTRA*, Vol. 28, pp. 591–605.

Chow, G. C. (1964), "A comparison of alternative estimators for simultaneous equations," *ECTRA*, Vol. 32, pp. 532–553.

Chow, G. C. (1968), "Two methods of computing full-information maximum likelihood estimates in simultaneous stochastic equations," *IER*, Vol. 9, pp. 100–112.

Chow, G. C. and D. K. Ray-Chandhuri (1967), "An alternative proof of Hannan's theorem on cononical correlation and multiple equation systems," *ECTRA*, Vol. 35, pp. 139–142.

Christ, Carl F. (1956), "Aggregate econometric models: A review article," *AER*, Vol. 46, pp. 385–408. Reprinted in R. A. Gordon and L. R. Klein (eds.) (1965), *Readings in Business Cycles*. Homewood, Ill: Irwin.

Christ, C. F., C. Hildreth, T. Liu, and L. R. Klein (1960), "A symposium on simultaneous equation estimation," *ECTRA*, Vol. 28, pp. 835–871.

Cochran, W. G. (1970), "Some effects of errors of measurement on multiple correlation," *JASA*, Vol. 65, pp. 22–34.

Cochrane, D. and G. H. Orcutt (1949a), "Application of least squares regression to relationships containing auto-correlated error terms," *JASA*, Vol. 44, pp. 32–61.

Cochrane, D. and G. H. Orcutt (1949b), "A sampling study of the merits of auto-regressive and reduced form transformations in regression analysis," *JASA*, Vol. 44, pp. 356–372.

Cragg, J. G. (1966), "On the sensitivity of simultaneous-equations estimators to the stochastic assumptions of the models," *JASA*, Vol. 61, pp. 136–151.

Cragg, J. G. (1967), "On the relative small sample properties of several structural equation estimators," *ECTRA*, Vol. 35, pp. 89–110.

Cragg, J. G. (1968), "Some effects of incorrect specification on the small sample properties of several simultaneous equation estimators," *IER*, Vol. 9, pp. 63–86.

Cramér, H. (1946), *Mathematical Methods of Statistics*, Princeton U. Press.

Daniel, Cuthbert, et al (1971), *Fitting Equations to Data*. New York: Wiley.

Daniels, H. E. (1956), "The approximate distribution of serial correlation coefficients," *Biometrika*, Vol. 43, pp. 169–185.

Dhrymes, Phoebus J. (1967), "Adjustment dynamics and the estimation of the CES class of production functions," *IER*, Vol. 8, pp. 209–217.

Dhrymes, Phoebus J. (1969a), "Efficient estimation of distributed lags with autocorrelated errors," *IER*, Vol. 10, pp. 47–67.

Dhrymes, Phoebus J. (1969b), "An identity between double k-class and two stage least squares estimators," *IER*, Vol. 10, pp. 114–117.

Dhrymes, Phoebus J. (1970), *Econometrics*. New York: Harper and Row, 1970.

Dhrymes, Phoebus J. (1971a), *Distributed Lags: Problems of Estimation and Formulation*. San Francisco: Holden-Day.

Dhrymes, Phoebus J. (1971b), "A simplified structural estimator for large scale econometric models," *AJS*, Vol. 23, pp. 168–175.

Dhrymes, Phoebus J. (1978), *Introductory Econometrics*. New York: Springer-Verlag.

Dhrymes, P. J., R. Berner and D. Cummins (1974), "A Comparison of Some Limited Information Estimators for Dynamic Simultaneous Equations Models with Autocorrelated Errors," *ECTRA*, Vol. 42, pp. 311–332.

Draper, N. R. and H. Smith (1966), *Applied Regression Analysis*. New York: Wiley.

Duesenberry, J., G. Fromm, E. Kuh, and L. Klein, eds. (1965), *The Brookings Quarterly Econometric Model of the United States*. Chicago: Rand McNally, and Amsterdam: North Holland Press.

Duncan, D. B. and R. H. Jones (1966), "Multiple regression with stationary errors," *JASA*, Vol. 61, pp. 917–928.

Dunn, O. J. (1959), "Confidence intervals for the means of dependent normally distributed variables," *JASA*, Vol. 54, pp. 613–621.

Durand, D. (1954), "Joint confidence regions for multiple regression coefficients," *JASA*, Vol. 49, pp. 130–146.

Durbin, J. (1953), "A note on regression when there is extraneous information about one of the coefficients," *JASA*, Vol. 48, pp. 799–808.

Durbin, J. (1957), "Testing for serial correlation in systems of simultaneous regression equations," *Biometrika*, Vol. 44, pp. 370–377.

Durbin, J. (1960), "Estimation of parameters in time-series regression models," *JRSS, Series B*, Vol. 22, pp. 139–153.

Durbin, J. (1970), "Testing for serial correlation in least squares regression when some of the regressors are lagged dependent variables," *ECTRA*, pp. 410–421.

Durbin, J. and G. S. Watson (1950), "Testing for serial correlation in least squares regression I," *Biometrika*, Vol. 37, pp. 409–428.

Durbin, J. and G. S. Watson (1951), "Testing for serial correlation in least squares regression II," *Biometrika*, Vol. 38, pp. 159–178.

Eicker, F. (1963), "Asymptotic normality and consistency of the least squares estimators for families of linear regressions," *AMS*, Vol. 34, pp. 447–456.

Eisenpress, H. (1962), "Note on the computation of full information maximum likelihood estimates of coefficients of a simultaneous system," *ECTRA*, Vol. 30, pp. 343–348.

Eisenpress, H. and R. J. Foote (1960), "Systems of simultaneous equations on the IBM 704 and 709, *JFE*, Vol. 42, pp. 1445–1449.

Eisenpress, H. and J. Greenstadt (1966), "The estimation of nonlinear econometric systems," *ECTEA*, Vol. 34, pp. 851–861.

Eisner, Robert (1960), "A distributed lag investment function," *ECTRA*, Vol. 28, pp. 1–29.

Ericson, W. A. (1970), "On the posterior mean and variance of a population mean," *JASA*, Vol. 65, pp. 649–652.

Fair, R. C. (1970), "The estimation of simultaneous equations models with lagged endogenous and first order serially correlated errors," *ECTRA*, Vol. 38, pp. 507–516.

Fair, R. C. (1972), "Efficient estimation of simultaneous equations with auto-regressive errors by instrumental variables," *RES*, Vol. 54, pp. 444–449.

Fairley, W. B. and Mosteller, F. (1977), *Statistics and Public Policy*, Reading, Mass: Addison Wesley.

Farrar, D. E. and R. R. Glauber (1967), "Multicollinearity in regression analysis: The problem revisited," *RES*, Vol. 49, pp. 92–107.

Feldstein, M. S. (1974), "Errors in variables: A consistent estimator with smaller mean square error in finite samples," *JASA*, Vol. 69, pp. 990–996.

Fisher, F. M. (1959), "Generalization of the rank and order conditions for identifiability," *ECTRA*, Vol. 27, pp. 431–447.

Fisher, F. M. (1961a), "Identifiability criteria in nonlinear systems," *ECTRA*, Vol. 29, pp. 574–590.

Fisher, F. M. (1961b), "On the cost of approximate specification in simultaneous equation estimation," *ECTRA*, Vol. 29, pp. 139–170.

Fisher, F. M. (1963), "Uncorrelated disturbances and identifiability criteria," *IER*, Vol. 4, pp. 134–152.

Fisher, F. M. (1965a), "Identifiability criteria in nonlinear systems: A further note," *ECTRA*, Vol. 33, pp. 197–205.

Fisher, F. M. (1965b), "Near-identifiability and the variances of the disturbance terms," *ECTRA*, Vol. 33, pp. 409–415.

Fisher, F. M. (1965c), "The choice of instrumental variables in the estimation of economy-wide econometric models," *IER*, Vol. 6, pp. 245–274.

Fisher, F. M. (1966a), "Restrictions on the reduced form and the rank and order conditions," *IER*, Vol. 7, pp. 77–82.

Fisher, F. M. (1966b), *The Identification Problem in Econometrics*. New York: McGraw-Hill.

Fisher, F. M. (1966c), "The relative sensitivity to specification error of different k-class estimators," *JASA*, Vol. 61, pp. 345–356.

Fisher, F. M. (1967), "Approximate specification and the choice of a k-class estimator," *JASA*, Vol. 62, pp. 1265–1276.

Fisher, Janet A. (1962), "An analysis of consumer durable goods expenditures in 1957," *RES*, Vol. 44, pp. 64–71.

Fisher, R. A. (1966), *The Design of Experiments*, 8th ed. Edinburgh: Oliver and Boyd.

Fisher, W. (1962), "Estimation in the linear-decision model," *IER*, Vol. 3, pp. 1–29.

Fox, K. A. (1954), "Structural analysis and the measurement of demand for farm products," *RES*, Vol. 36, pp. 57–66.

Fox, Karl (1956), "Econometric models on the United States," *JPE*, Vol. 64, pp. 128–142.

Friedman, Milton (1957), *A Theory of the Consumption Function.* Princeton U. Press.

Frisch, R. and F. V. Waugh (1933), "Partial time regression as compared with individual trends," *ECTRA*, Vol. 1, pp. 221–223.

Geary, R. C. (1949), "Determination of linear relations between systematic parts of variables with errors of observation, the variances of which are unknown," *ECTRA*, Vol. 17, pp. 30–58.

Giles, D. E. A. (1973), *Essays on Econometric Topics: From theory to Practice*, Research Paper No. 10, Reserve Bank of New Zealand.

Girshick, M. A. and T. Haavelmo (1947a), "Statistical analysis of the demand for food," *ECTRA*, Vol. 15, pp. 79–110. Also in Hood and Koopmans (1953).

Girshick, M. A. and T. Haavelmo (1947b), "Statistical analysis of the demand for food: Examples of simultaneous estimation of structural equations," *ECTRA*, Vol. 15, pp. 79–110.

Glahn, Harry R. (1969), "Some relationships derived from canonical correlation theory," *ECTRA*, Vol. 37, pp. 252–256.

Glejser, H. (1969), "A new test for heteroskedasticity," *JASA*, Vol. 64, pp. 316–323.

Godfrey, L. G. (1976), "Testing for serial correlation in dynamic simultaneous equation models," *ECTRA*, Vol. 44, pp. 1077–1084.

Godfrey, L. G. (1978a), "Testing against general autoregressive and moving average error models when the regressors include lagged dependent variables," *ECTRA*, Vol. 46, pp. 1293–1301.

Godfrey, L. G. (1978b), "Testing for higher order serial correlation in regression equations when the regressors include lagged dependent variables," *ECTRA*, Vol. 46, pp. 1303–1310.

Godfrey, L. G. (1978c), "Testing for Multiplicative Heteroscedasticity," *JE*, Vol. 8, pp. 227–236.

Goldberger, A. S. (1959), *Impact multipliers and dynamic properties of the Klein-Goldberger model.* Amsterdam: North-Holland Publishing Co.

Goldberger, A. S. (1961), "Stepwise least squares, residual analysis and specification errors," *JASA*, Vol. 56, pp. 998–1000.

Goldberger, A. S. (1964), *Econometric Theory*. New York: Wiley.

Goldberger, A. S. (1965), "An instrumental variable interpretation of k-class estimation," *Indian Economic Journal* (Econometric Annual), Vol. 13, pp. 424–431.

Goldberger, A. S. (1968), "The interpretation and estimation of Cobb-Douglas functions," *ECTRA*, Vol. 36, pp. 464–472.

Goldberger, A. S. and O. D. Duncan (eds.) (1973), *Structural Equation Methods in the Social Sciences*. New York: Seminar Press.

Goldberger, A. S., A. L. Nagar and H. S. Odeh (1961), "The covariance matrices of reduced-form coefficients and of forecasts for a structural econometric model," *ECTRA*, Vol. 29, pp. 556–573.

Goldfeld, S. M. and R. E. Quandt and H. F. Trotter (1966), Maximization by quadratic hill-climbing," *ECTRA*, Vol. 34, p. 541.

Goodnight, J. and T. D. Wallace (1972), "Operational techniques and tables for making weak MSE tests for restrictions in regressions," *ECTRA*, Vol. 40, pp. 699–709.

Granger, C. W. J. and P. Newbold (1973), "Some comments on the evaluation of economic forecasts," *Applied Economics*, pp. 35–47.

Granger, C. W. J. and P. Newbold (1977), *Forecasting Economic Time Series*. New York: Academic Press.

Grenander, U. (1954), "On the estimation of regression coefficients in the case of an autocorrelated disturbance," *AMS*, Vol. 25, pp. 252–272.

Grenander, U. and M. Rosenblatt (1957), *Statistical analysis of stationary time series*. New York: Wiley.

Griliches, Z. (1961), "A Note on serial correlation bias in estimates of distributed lags," *ECTRA*, Vol. 29, pp. 65–73.

Griliches, Z. (1967), "Distributed lags: A survey," *ECTRA*, Vol. 35, No. 1, pp. 16–49.

Griliches, Z. (1968), "The Brookings Model Volume: A Review Article," *RES*, Vol. 50, pp. 215–234.

Griliches, Z. and Rao, P. (1969), "Small sample properties of several two-stage regression methods in the context of autocorrelated errors," *JASA*, Vol. 64, pp. 253–272.

Gujarati, D. (1978), *Basic Econometrics*. New York: McGraw-Hill.

Gupta, Y. P. (1969), "Least squares variant of the Dhrymes two-step estimation procedure of the distributed lag model," *IER*, Vol. 10, pp. 112–113.

Haavelmo, T. (1943), "The statistical implications of a system of simultaneous equations," *ECTRA*, Vol. 11, pp. 1–12.

Haavelmo, T. (1944), "The probability approach in econometrics," *ECTRA*, Vol. 12, p. 118.

Haavelmo, T. (1950), "Remarks on Frisch's confluence analysis and its use in econometrics," Chapter 5, p. 260 in T. Koopmans (ed.), *Statistical Inference in Dynamic Economic Models*. New York: Wiley.

Haavelmo, T. (1953), "Methods of measuring the marginal propensity to consume," Chapter 4 in *Studies in Econometric Methods*, W. C. Hood and T. C. Koopmans (eds.), Cowles Foundation for Research in Economics, Monograph No. 14, New York: Wiley.

Halperin, M. (1961), "Fitting of straight lines and prediction when both variables are subject to error," *JASA*, Vol. 56, pp. 657–669.

Halperin, M. and N. Mantel (1963), "Interval estimation of non-linear parametric functions," *JASA*, Vol. 58, pp. 611–627.

Hannan, E. J. (1957), "Testing for serial correlation in least squares regression," *Biometrika*, Vol. 44, pp. 57–66.

Hannan, E. J. (1962), *Time Series Analysis*. London: Methuen.

Hannan, E. J. (1963), "The estimation of seasonal variation in economic time series," *JASA*, Vol. 58, pp. 31–44.

Hannan, E. J. (1965), "The estimation of relationships involving distributed lags," *ECTRA*, Vol. 33, pp. 206–224.

Hannan, E. J. (1967), "Canonical correlation and multiple equation systems in economics," *ECTRA*, Vol. 35, pp. 123–138.

Hannan, E. J. (1969), "A note on an exact test for trend and serial correlation," *ECTRA*, Vol. 37, pp. 485–489.

Hannan, E. J. (1970), *Multiple Time Series*. New York: Wiley.

Hannan, E. J. and R. D. Terrell (1968), "Testing for serial correlation after least squares regression," *ECTRA*, Vol. 36, pp. 133–150.

Harris, R. J. (1975), *A Primer of Multivariate Statistics*. New York: Academic Press.

Hartley, H. O. and A. Booker (1965), "Nonlinear least squares estimation," *AMS*, Vol. 36.

Harvey, A. C. (1976), "Estimating regression models with multiplicative heteroscedasticity," *ECTRA*, Vol. 44, pp. 461–466.

Hausman, J. A. (1974), "Full information instrumental variables estimation of simultaneous equations systems," *Annals of Economic and Social Measurement*, Vol. 4, pp. 641–652.

Hausman, J. A. (1978), "Specification tests in econometrics," *ECTRA*, Vol. 46, pp. 1251–1271.

Hendry, D. F. (1976), "The structure of simultaneous equations estimators," *JE*, Vol. 4, pp. 51–88.

Hendry, D. F. and R. W. Harrison (1974), "Monte Carlo methodology and the small sample behaviour of ordinary and two-stage least squares," *JE*, Vol. 2, pp. 151–174.

Henshaw, Richard C. Jr. (1966a), "Application of the general linear model to seasonal adjustment of economic time series," *ECTRA*, Vol. 34, pp. 381–395.

Henshaw, Richard C. Jr. (1966b), "Testing single-equation least-squares regression models for autocorrelated disturbances," *ECTRA*, Vol. 34, pp. 646–660.

Hildreth, C. (1960), "Simultaneous equations: Any verdict yet?" *ECTRA*, Vol. 28, pp. 846–854.

Hill, T. P. (1959), "An analysis of the distribution of wages and salaries in Great Britain," *ECTRA*, Vol. 27, pp. 355–381.

Hoadley, B. (1970), "A Bayesian look at inverse linear regression," *JASA*, Vol. 65, pp. 356–369.

Hoch, I. (1962), "Estimation of production function parameters combining time-series and cross-section data," *ECTRA*, Vol. 30, pp. 34–53.

Hoch, Irving and Y. Munlak (1965), "Consequences of alternative specifications in estimation of Cobb-Douglas production functions," *ECTRA*, Vol. 33, pp. 814–828.

Hodges, Dorothy J. (1969), "A note on estimation of Cobb-Douglas and CES production function models," *ECTRA*, Vol. 37, pp. 721–725.

Hoel, P. G. (1971), *Introduction to Mathematical Statistics*, 4th edition. New York: Wiley.

Hoerl, A. E. and R. W. Kennard (1970), "Ridge regression: Applications to nonorthogonal problems," *Technometrics*, pp. 55–82.

Hooper, J. W. (1959), "Simultaneous equations and canonical correlation theory," *ECTRA*, Vol. 27, pp. 245–256.

Hooper, J. W. and A. Zellner (1961), "The error of forecast for multivariate regression models," *ECTRA*, Vol. 29, pp. 544–555.

Hood, W. C. and T. C. Koopmans (1953), (eds.), *Studies in Econometric Method*. New York: Wiley.

Hurwicz, L. (1950), Chapters 6, 7, and 15, in T. C. Koopmans (ed.), *Statistical Inference in Dynamic Economic Models*. New York: Wiley.

Hymans, Saul H. (1968), "Simultaneous confidence intervals in econometric forecasting," *ECTRA*, Vol. 36, pp. 18–30.

Ijiri, Yuji (1968), "The linear aggregation coefficient as the dual of the linear correlation coefficient," *ECTRA*, Vol. 36, pp. 252–259.

Intriligator, M. (1978), *Econometric Models, Techniques and Applications*. Englewood Cliffs, New Jersey: Prentice Hall.

Jeffreys, H. (1961), *Theory of Probability*. Oxford University Press.

Jenkins, G. M. (1956), "Tests of hypotheses in the linear autoregressive model II," *Biometrika*, Vol. 43, pp. 186–199.

Johnston, J. (1960), *Statistical Cost Analysis*. New York: McGraw-Hill, 1960.

Johnston, J. (1972), *Econometric Methods*, 2nd ed. New York: McGraw-Hill, 1972.

Johnston, H. N., L. R. Klein and K. Shinjo (1974), "Estimation and prediction in dynamic econometric models," in *Essays in Honour of Jan Tinbergen*. Amsterdam: North-Holland, 1974.

Jorgenson, Dale W. (1963), "Capital theory and investment behavior," *AER*, Vol. 53, pp. 247–259.

Jorgenson, Dale W. (1967), "Seasonal adjustment of data for econometric analysis," *JASA*, Vol. 62, pp. 137–140.

Judge, G. G. and T. Takayama (1966), "Inequality restrictions in regression analysis," *JASA*, Vol. 61, pp. 166–181.

Kabe, D. G. (1963), "A note on the exact distributions of the GCL estimators in two leading overidentified cases," *JASA*, Vol. 58, pp. 535–537.

Kabe, D. G. (1964), "On the exact distributions of the GCL estimators in a leading three equation case," *JASA*, Vol. 59, pp. 881–894.

Kadane, J. B. (1970), "Testing overidentifying restrictions when the disturbances are small," *JASA*, Vol. 65, pp. 182–185.

Kadane, J. B. (1971), "Comparison of k-class estimators when disturbances are small," *ECTRA*, Vol. 39, pp. 723–738.

Kadiyala, K. R. (1968), "A transformation used to circumvent the problem of autocorrelation," *ECTRA*, Vol. 36, pp. 93–96.

Kakwani, N. C. (1967), "The unbiasedness of Zellner's seemingly unrelated regression equations estimators," *JASA*, Vol. 62, pp. 141–2.

Kakwani, N. C. and A. L. Nagar (1964), "The bias and moment matrix of a mixed regression estimator," *ECTRA*, Vol. 32, pp. 174–182.

Kalejian, H. H. (1969), "Missing observations in multivariate regression: efficiency of a first order method," *JASA*, Vol. 64, pp. 1609–1616.

Kane, E. J. (1968), *Economic Statistics and Econometrics*. New York: Harper and Row.

Katz, D. A. (1973), "Faculty salaries, promotions and productivity at a large university," *AER*, Vol. 63, pp. 469–477.

Kaufmann, Gordon M. (1969), "Conditional prediction and unbiasedness in structural equations," *ECTRA*, Vol. 37, pp. 44–49.

Kendall, M. G. (1961), "A theorem in trend analysis," *Biometrika*, Vol. 48, pp. 224–227.

Kendall, M. G. and C. A. O'Muircheartaigh (1977), *Path Analysis and Model Building* (Tech. Bulletin 414), World Fertility Survey.

Kendall, M. G. and A. Stuart (1963), *The Advanced Theory of Statistics*, Vol. I, II, III. New York: Hafner.

Klein, L. R. (1943), "Pitfalls in the statistical determination of the investment schedule," *ECTRA*, Vol. 11, pp. 243–258.

Klein, L. R. (1951), "Estimation patterns of savings behavior for sample survey data," *ECTRA*, Vol. 19, pp. 438–454.

Klein, L. R. (1955), "On the interpretation of Theil's method of estimating economic relationship," *Metroeconomica*, Vol. 7, pp. 147–153.

Klein, L. R. (1958), "The estimation of distributed lags," *ECTRA*, Vol. 26, pp. 553–565.

Klein, L. R. (1960), "Single equation versus equation system methods of estimation in econometrics," *ECTRA*, Vol. 28, pp. 866–871.

Klein, L. R. (1969), "Estimation of interdependent systems in macroeconometrics," *ECTRA*, Vol. 37, pp. 171–192.

Klein, L. R. and A. S. Goldberger (1955), *An Econometric Model of the United States, 1929–52*. Amsterdam: North-Holland Press.

Klein, L. R. and R. S. Preston (1969), "Stochastic nonlinear models," *ECTRA*, Vol. 37, pp. 95–106.

Kloek, T. and L. B. M. Mannes (1960), "Simultaneous equations estimation based on principal components of predetermined variables," *ECTKA*, Vol. 28, pp. 45–61.

Kmenta, J. (1964), "Some properties of alternative estimates of the Cobb-Douglas production function," *ECTRA*, Vol. 32, pp. 183–188.

Kmenta, J. (1967), "On estimation of the CES production function," *IER*, Vol. 8, pp. 180–193.

Kmenta, J. (1971), *Elements of Econometrics*. New York: Macmillan, 1971.

Kohn, M. G., C. F. Minski and D. S. Mundel (1974), "An empirical investigation of factors which influence college going behavior," Rand Corporation Report R1470-NSF.

Konijn, H. S. (1958), "A restatement of the conditions for identifiability in complete systems of linear difference equations," *Metroeconomica*, Vol. 10, pp. 182–190.

Koopmans, T. C. (1945), "Statistical estimation of simultaneous economic relations," *JASA*, Vol. 40, pp. 448–466.

Koopmans, T. C. (1949), "Identification problems in economic model construction," Chap. II in *Hood and Koopmans* (1953). Also in *ECTRA*, Vol. 17, Apr. 1949, pp. 125–144.

Koopmans, T. C. (1950), (ed.), *Statistical Inference in Dynamic Economic Models*. New York: Wiley.

Koopmans, T. C. and W. C. Hood (1953), "The estimation of simultaneous linear economic relationships," Chap. VI in Hood and Koopmans (1953).

Koopmans, T. C. and O. Reiersol (1950), "The identification of structural characteristics," *AMS*, Vol. 21, pp. 165–181.

Koopmans, T. C., H. Ruben and R. B. Leipnik (1950), "Measuring the equation systems of dynamic economics," Chap. II in Koopmans (1950).

Koyck, L. M. (1954), *Distributed Lags and Investment Analysis*. (Contributions to Economic Analysis No. 4). Amsterdam: North-Holland Press.

Krishnaiah, P. R. and V. K. Murthy (1966), "Simultaneous tests for trend and serial correlations for Gaussian Markov residuals," *ECTRA*, Vol. 34, pp. 472–480.

Kuh, E. (1959), "The validity of cross-sectionally estimated behavior equations in time series applications," *ECTRA*, Vol. 27, pp. 197–214.

Kymn, Kern O. (1968), "The distribution of the sample correlation coefficient under the null hypothesis," *ECTRA*, Vol. 36, pp. 187–189.

Ladd, G. W. (1964), "Regression analysis of seasonal data," *JASA*, Vol. 59, pp. 402–421.

Lee, Tong Hun (1963), "Demand for housing: A cross-section analysis," *RES*, Vol. 45, pp. 190–196.

Lefcoe, N. M. and T. H. Wonnacott (1974), "The prevalence of chronic respiratory disease in four occupational groups," *Archives of Environmental Health*, Vol. 29, pp. 143–146.

Leser, C. E. V. (1966), "The role of macroeconomic models in short-term forecasting," *ECTRA*, Vol. 34, pp. 862–872.

Lindgren, B. W. (1968), *Statistical Theory*, 2nd ed. New York: Macmillan.

Lindley, D. V. (1965), *Introduction to Probability* and Statistics. Cambridge, England: Cambridge University Press.

Liu, T. C. (1960), "Underidentification, structural estimation and forecasting," *ECTRA*, Vol. 28, pp. 855–865.

Liu, T. C. and W. J. Breen (1969), "The covariance matrix of the limited information estimator and the identification test," *ECTRA*, Vol. 37, pp. 222–227.

Liviatan, N. (1961), "Errors in variables and Engel curve analysis," *ECTRA*, Vol. 29, pp. 336–362.

Liviatan, N. (1963), "Consistent estimation of distributed lags," *IER*, Vol. 4, pp. 44–52.

Ljung, G. M. and G. E. P. Box (1978), "On a measure of lack of fit in time series models," *Biometrika*, Vol. 65, pp. 297–304.

Long, R. (1970), "Forecasting specific turning points," *JASA*, Vol. 65, pp. 520–531.

Lovell, M. C. (1963), "Seasonal adjustment of economic time series and multiple regression analysis," *JASA*, Vol. 58, pp. 993–1010.

Lovell, M. C. and E. Prescott (1970), "Multiple regression with inequality constraints: Pretesting bias, hypothesis testing and efficiency," *JASA*, Vol. 65, pp. 913–925.

McElroy, F. W. (1967a), "Note on the CES production function," *ECTRA*, Vol. 35, pp. 154–156.

McElroy, F. W. (1967b), "A necessary and sufficient condition that ordinary least squares estimations be best linear unbiased," *JASA*, Vol. 62, pp. 1302–1304.

Madansky, A. (1959), "The fitting of straight lines when both variables are subject to error," *JASA*, Vol. 54, pp. 173–205.

Madansky, A. (1964a), "On the efficiency of three-stage least squares estimation," *ECTRA*, Vol. 32, pp. 51–56.

Madansky, A. (1964b). "Spurious correlation due to deflating variables," *ECTRA*, Vol. 32, pp. 652–655.

Maddala, G. S. (1977), *Econometrics*. New York: McGraw-Hill.

Malinvaud, E. (1961), "The estimation of distributed lags: A comment," *ECTRA*, Vol. 29, pp. 430–433.

Malinvaud, E. (1970), *Statistical Methods of Econometrics*, 2nd ed. Amsterdam: North-Holland Press.

Mann, H. B. and A. Wald (1943), "On the statistical treatment of linear stochastic difference equations," *ECTRA*, Vol. 11, pp. 173–220.

Mariano, R. S. (1975), "Some large-concentration-parameter asymptotics for the k-class estimators," *JE*, Vol. 3, pp. 171–178.

Mariano, R. S. and T. Sawa (1972), "Exact finite sample distribution of the limited information maximum likelihood estimator in the case of two included endogenous variables," *JASA*, Vol. 67, pp. 159–163.

Meyer, J. R. and H. L. Miller, Jr. (1954), "Some comments on the simultaneous equations approach," *RES*, Vol. 36, pp. 88–92.

Mikhail, W. M. (1972), "Simulating the small sample properties of econometric estimators," *JASA*, Vol. 67, pp. 620–624.

Mikhail, W. M. (1975), "A comparative Monte Carlo study of the properties of econometric estimators," *JASA*, Vol. 70, pp. 94–104.

Mitchell, B. M. and F. M. Fisher (1970), "The choice of instrumental variables in the estimation of economy-wide econometric models: Some further thoughts," *IER*, Vol. 11, pp. 226–234.

Morrison, D. F. (1967), *Multivariate Statistical Methods*. New York: McGraw-Hill.

Mosteller, F. and J. W. Tukey (1977), *Data Analysis and Regression: A Second Course in Statistics*. Reading, Mass.: Addison-Wesley.

Mundlak, Yair (1961), "Aggregation over time in distributed lag models," *IER*, Vol. 2, pp. 154–163.

Mundlak, Yair (1967), "Long-run coefficients and distributed lag analysis: A reformulation," *ECTRA*, Vol. 35, pp. 278–293.

Nagar, A. L. (1959), "The bias and moment matrix of the general k-class estimators of the parameters in simultaneous equations," *ECTRA*, Vol. 27, pp. 575–595.

Nagar, A. L. (1960), "A Monte Carlo study of alternative simultaneous equation estimators," *ECTRA*, Vol. 28, pp. 573–590.

Nagar, A. L. (1961), "A note on the residual variance estimation in simultaneous equations," *ECTRA*, Vol. 29, pp. 238–243.

Nagar, A. L. (1962), "Double k-class estimators of parameters in simultaneous equations and their small sample properties," *IER*, Vol. 3, pp. 168–188.

Nagar, A. L. and N. C. Kakwani (1964), "The bias and moment matrix of a mixed regression estimator," *ECTRA*, Vol. 32, pp. 174–182.

Nagar, A. L. and N. C. Kakwani (1966), "Note on the bias of a mixed simultaneous equation estimator," *IER*, Vol. 7, pp. 65–71.

Nagar, A. L. and A. Ullah (1973), "Note on approximate skewness and kurtosis of the 2SLS estimator," *Indian Economic Review*, Vol. 8, pp. 69–80.

Nakamura, M. (1960), "A note on the consistency of simultaneous least squares estimation," *IER*, Vol. 1, pp. 192–197.

Narayanan, R. (1969), "Computation of Zellner-Theil's three stage least squares estimates," *ECTRA*, Vol. 37, pp. 298–306.

Nerlove, M. (1958a), "Distributed lags and demand analysis for agricultural and other commodities," *Agricultural Handbook* 141, U.S. Dept. of Agriculture.

Nerlove, M. (1958b), *The dynamics of supply: Estimation of farmers' response to price*. Baltimore: Johns Hopkins U. Press.

Nerlove, M. (1958c), "Distributed lags and estimation of long-run supply and demand elasticities: Theoretical considerations," *JFE*, Vol. 40, pp. 301–311.

Nerlove, M. (1964), "Spectral analysis of seasonal adjustment procedures," *ECTRA*, Vol. 32, pp. 241–286.

Nerlove, M. (1966), "A tabular survey of macroeconometric models," *IER* Vol. 7, pp. 127–175.

Nerlove, M. and K. F. Wallis (1966), "Use of the Durbin-Watson statistic in inappropriate situations," *ECTRA*, Vol. 34, pp. 235–238.

Nicholls, D. F., A. R. Pagan and R. D. Terrell (1975), "The estimation and use of models with moving average disturbance terms; a survey," *IER*, Vol. 16, pp. 113–134.

Novick, M. R. and P. H. Jackson (1974), *Statistical Methods for Educational and Psychological Research*. New York: McGraw-Hill.

Oi, Walter Y. (1969), "On the relationship among different members of the k-class," *IER*, Vol. 10, pp. 36–46.

Orcutt, G. H. (1950), "Measurement of price elasticities in international trade," *RES*, Vol. 32, pp. 117–132.

Orcutt, G. H. and D. Cochrane (1949), "A sampling study of the merits of autoregressive and reduced from transformations in regression analysis," *JASA*, Vol. 44, pp. 356–372.

Orcutt, G. H. and H. S. Winokur, Jr. (1969), "First order autoregression: Inference estimation, and prediction," *ECTRA*, Vol. 37, pp. 1–14.

Park, R. E. (1966), "Estimation with heteroscedastic error terms," *ECTRA*, Vol. 34, p. 888.

Park, R. W. (1967), "Efficient estimation of a system of regression equations when disturbances are both serially and contemporaneously correlated," *JASA*, Vol. 62, pp. 500–509.

Pindyck, R. S. and D. L. Rubinfeld (1976), *Econometric Models and Economic Forecasts*. New York: McGraw-Hill.

Prais, S. J. and H. S. Houthakker (1955), *The analysis of family budgets*. Cambridge, England: Cambridge U. Press.

Quandt, Richard E. (1962), *Some small sample properties of certain structural equation estimators*. (Research memorandum No. 48, Princeton University Econometric Research Program).

Quandt, R. E. (1965), "On certain small sample properties of k-class estimators," *IER*, Vol. 6, pp. 92–104.

Raiffa, H. (1968), *Decision Analysis*. Reading, Mass.: Addison-Wesley.

Rao, C. R. (1970), "Estimation of heteroscedastic variances in linear models," *JASA*, Vol. 65, pp. 161–172.

Rao, C. R. (1976), "Estimation of parameters in linear models," *The Annals of Statistics*, Vol. 4, pp. 1023–1037.

Rao, P. and Z. Griliches (1969), "Small-sample properties of several two-stage regression methods in the context of autocorrelated errors," *JASA*, Vol. 64, pp. 253–272.

Richardson, D. H. and De-Min Wu (1970), "Least squares and grouping methods estimators in the errors in variables model," *JASA*, Vol. 65, pp. 724–748.

Rosenblatt, M. (1956), "Some regression problems in time series analysis," in *Proceedings of the Third Berkeley Symposium of Mathematical Statistics and Probability*, Vol. 1.

Rosett, R. N. (1959), "A statistical model of friction in economics," *ECTRA*, Vol. 27, pp. 263–267.

Rothenberg, Thomas J. (1963), *A Bayesian analysis of simultaneous equation systems*, (Econometric Institute, Netherlands School of Economics, Rotterdam, Report 6315).

Rothenberg, T. J. and C. T. Leenders (1964), "Efficient estimation of simultaneous equation systems," *ECTRA*, Vol. 32, pp. 57–76.

Rutemiller, H. C. and D. A. Bowers (1968), "Estimation in a heteroscedastic regression model," *JASA*, Vol. 63, pp. 552–557.

Sargan, J. D. (1958), "The estimation of economic relationships using instrumental variables," *ECTRA*, Vol. 26, pp. 393–415.

Sargan, J. D. (1961), "The maximum likelihood estimation of economic relationships with autoregressive residuals," *ECTRA*, Vol. 29, pp. 414–426.

Sargan, J. D. (1964), "Three-stage least squares and full maximum likelihood estimates," *ECTRA*, Vol. 32, pp. 77–81.

Savage, L. J. (1954), *Foundations of Statistics*. New York: Wiley.

Sawa, T. (1969), "The exact sampling distribution of ordinary least squares and two-stage least squares estimators," *JASA*, Vol. 64, pp. 923–937.

Sawa, T. (1972), "Finite-sample properties of the k-class estimators," *ECTRA*, Vol. 40, pp. 653–680.

Sawa, T. (1973), "Almost unbiased estimator simultaneous equation systems," *IER*, Vol. 14, pp. 97–106.

Scheffé, H. (1959), *The Analysis of Variance*. New York: Wiley.

Shiller, R. J. (1973), "A distributed lag estimator derived from smoothness priors," *ECTRA*, Vol. 41, pp. 775–788.

Simon, H. (1953), "Causal ordering and identifiability," Chap. III in Hood and Koopmans (1953).

Sims, C. (1974), "Distributed lags," in M. D. Intriligator and D. A. Kendrick (eds.), *Frontiers of Quantitative Economics*. Amsterdam: North Holland Press.

Singh, B. and A. Ullah (1974), "Estimation of seemingly unrelated regressions with random coefficients," *JASA*, Vol. 69, pp. 191–195.

Singh, B. and A. Ullah (1976), "The consumption function: The permanent income versus the habit persistence hypothesis," *RES*, Vol. 58, pp. 96–103.

Solow, R. (1960), "On a family of lag distributions," *ECTRA*, Vol. 28, pp. 393–406.

Stedler, H. O. (1968), "Forecasting with econometric models: An evaluation," *ECTRA*, Vol. 36, pp. 437–463.

Stone, J. R. N. (1945), "The analysis of market demand," *JRSS*, Vol. 108, pp. 287–382.

Stone, J. R. N. (1949), "Prediction from autoregressive schemes and linear stochastic difference systems," *ECTRA*, Vol. 17, pp. 29–37.

Stone, J. R. N. (1954), *The measurement of consumers' expenditure and behaviour in the United Kingdom, 1920–1938*. Cambridge, England: Cambridge U. Press.

Strotz, R. H. and H. Wold (1960), "Recursive vs nonrecursive systems: An attempt at synthesis," *ECTRA*, Vol. 28, pp. 417–427.

Strotz, R. H. and H. Wold (1963), "The causal interpretability of structural parameters: A reply," *ECTRA*, Vol. 31, pp. 449–450.

Stuvel, G. (1965), "A systematic approach to macroeconomic policy design," *ECTRA*, Vol. 33, pp. 114–140.

Suits, D. B. (1957), "Use of dummy variables in regression equations," *JASA*, Vol. 52, pp. 548–551.

Suits, D. B. (1962), "Forecasting and analysis with an econometric model," *AER*, Vol. 52, pp. 104–132.

Suits, D. B. (1965), "Forecasting with an econometric model," in R. A. Gordon and L. R. Klein (eds.), in *The American Economic Association's Readings in Business Cycles*, pp. 597–625. Homewood, Ill.: Richard D. Irwin.

Summers, R. (1965), "A capital intensive approach to the small sample properties of various simultaneous equation estimators," *ECTRA*, Vol. 33, pp. 1–41.

Suzuki, Yukio (1964), "On the use of some extraneous information in the estimation of the coefficients of regression," *Annals of the Institute of Statistical Mathematics* (Tokyo), Vol. 16, pp. 161–173.

Swamy, P. A. V. B. (1971), *Statistical Inference in Random Coefficient Regression Model*. New York: Springer-Verlag.

Takeuchi, K. (1979), Exact sampling moments of ordinary least squares, instrumental variables, and two-stage least squares estimators," *IER*, Vol. 20.

Tanur, J., F. Mostelleller, *et al* (1977), *Statistics: A Guide to Political and Social Issues*. San Francisco: Holden Day.

Taylor, W. E. (1978), "The heteroscedastic linear model: Exact finite sample results," *ECTRA*, Vol. 46, pp. 663–675.

Taylor, Lester D. and T. A. Wilson (1964), "Three-pass least squares: A method for estimating models with a lagged dependent variable, *RES*, Vol. 46, pp. 329–346.

Theil, H. (1953), *Estimation and simultaneous correlation in complete equation systems*. The Hague: Central Planning Bureau.

Theil, H. (1957), "Specification errors and the estimation of economic relationships," *Review of the International Statistical Institute*, Vol. 25, pp. 41–51.

Theil, H. (1958), *Economic Forecasting and Policy* (especially Chap. 6). Amsterdam: North Holland Press.

Theil, H. (1965), "The analysis of disturbances in regression analysis," *JASA*, Vol. 60, pp. 1067–1079.

Theil, Henri (1968), "A simplification of the BLUS procedure for analyzing regression disturbances," *JASA*, Vol. 63, pp. 242–251.

Theil, H. (1971), *Principles of Econometrics*. New York: Wiley.

Theil, H. and J. C. G. Boot (1962), "The final form of econometric equations systems," Review of the International Statistical Institute, Vol. 30, pp. 41–51.

Theil, H. and A. S. Goldberger (1961), "On pure and mixed statistical estimation in economics," *IER*, Vol. 2, pp. 65–78.

Theil, H. and A. L. Nagar (1961), "Testing the independence of regression disturbances," *JASA*, Vol. 56, pp. 793–806.

Theil, H. and M. Scholes (1967), "Forecast evaluation based on a multiplicative decomposition of mean square errors," *ECTRA*, Vol. 35, pp. 70–88.

Theil, H. and R. M. Stern (1960), "A simple unimodal lag distribution," *Metroeconomica*, Vol. 12.

Thornber, H. (1967), "Finite sample Monte Carlo studies: An autoregressive illustration," *JASA*, Vol. 62, pp. 801–818.

Tintner, G. (1946), "Multiple regression for systems of equations," *ECTRA*, Vol. 14, pp. 5–36.

Tintner, G. (1952), *Econometrics*. New York: Wiley.

Tobin, J. (1950), "A statistical demand function for food in the U.S.A.," *JASA*, Vol. 113, 113–141.

Tobin, J. (1958), "Estimation of relationships for limited dependent variables," *ECTRA*, Vol. 26, pp. 24–36.

Toro-Vizcarrondo, C. and T. D. Wallace (1968), "A test of the mean square error criterion for restriction in linear regression," *JASA*, Vol. 63, pp. 558–572.

Tukey, J. W. (1977), *Exploratory Data Analysis*. Reading, Mass.: Addison-Wesley.

Ullah, A. and A. L. Nagar (1974), "The exact mean of the two-stage least squares estimator of the structural parameters in an equation having three endogenous variables," *ECTRA*, Vol. 42, pp. 749–758.

Ullah, A. and S. Ullah (1978), "Double k-class estimators of coefficients in linear regression," *ECTRA*, Vol. 46, pp. 705–722.

Van de Geer, J. P. (1971), *Introduction to Multivariate Analysis for the Social Sciences*. San Francisco: Freeman.

Vinod, H. D. (1973), "Generalization of the Durbin-Watson statistic for higher order autoregressive processes," *Communications in Statistics*, Vol. 2, pp. 115–144.

Vinod, H. D. (1978), "A Survey of Ridge Estimation," *RES*, Vol. 60, pp. 121–131.

Wagner, H. M. (1958), "A Monte Carlo study of estimates of simultaneous linear structural equations," *ECTRA*, Vol. 26, pp. 117–133.

Wahba, Grace (1969), "Estimation of the coefficients in a multidimensional distributed lag model," *ECTRA*, Vol. 37, pp. 398–407.

Wald, A. (1940), "The fitting of straight lines if both variables are subject to errors," *AMS*, Vol. 11, pp. 284–300.

Wald, A. (1950), "Note on the identification of economic relations," Chap. 3 in Koopmans (1950).

Walker, A. M. (1962), "Large sample estimation of parameters for autoregressive processes with moving average residuals," *Biometrika*, Vol. 49, pp. 117–131.

Wallace, T. D. (1964), "Efficiencies for stepwise regression," *JASA*, Vol. 59, pp. 1179–1182.

Wallace, T. D. (1972), "Weaker criteria and tests for linear restrictions in regression," *ECTRA*, Vol. 40, pp. 689–698.

Waller, R. A. and D. B. Duncan (1969), "A Bayes rule for the symmetric multiple comparison problems," *JASA*, Vol. 64, pp. 1484–1503.

Walters, A. A. (1963), "Production and cost functions: An econometric survey," *ECTRA*, Vol. 31, pp. 1–66.

Wampler, R. H. (1970), "A report of the accuracy of some widely used least squares computer programs," *JASA*, Vol. 65, pp. 549–565.

Watson, G. S. (1955), "Serial correlation in regression analysis," *Biometrika*, Vol. 42, p. 327.

Watson, G. S. (1956), "On the joint distribution of the circular serial correlation coefficients," *Biometrika*, Vol. 43, pp. 161–168.

Waugh, Frederick V. (1961), "The place of least squares in econometrics," *ECTRA*, Vol. 29, pp. 386–396.

Wickens, M. R. (1969), "The consistency and efficiency of generalized least squares in simultaneous equation systems with autocorrelated errors," *ECTRA*, Vol. 37, pp. 651–659.

Williamson, R. E., R. H. Crowell and H. F. Trotter (1972), *Calculus of Vector Functions*, 3rd ed., Englewood Cliffs, N.J.: Prentice Hall.

Wold, H. (1949), "Statistical estimation of economic relationships," *ECTRA*, Supplement, Vol. 17, pp. 1–22.

Wold, H. (1950), "On least square regressions with autocorrelated variables and residuals," *Bulletin de L'Institut International de Statistique*, Vol. 32, pp. 277–289.

Wold, H. (1954), "Causality and econometrics," *ECTRA*, Vol. 22, pp. 162–177.

Wold, H. (1956), "Causal inference from observation 1 data: A review of ends and means," *JRSS*, Series A, Vol. 119, pp. 28–61.

Wold, H. (1959), "Ends and means in econometric model building," in U. Grenander (ed.), *Probability and Statistics: The Harold Cramer Volume*. New York: Wiley.

Wold, H. (1960), "A generalization of causal chain model," *ECTRA*, Vol. 28, pp. 443–463.

Wold, H. (ed.) (1964), *Econometric Model Building; Essays on the Causal Chain Approach*. Amsterdam: North Holland Press.

Wold, H. and P. Faxer (1957), "On the specification error in regression analysis," *AMS*, Vol. 28, No. 1, Mar. 1957, pp. 265–267.

Wonnacott, T. H. (1976), *Calculus, an Applied Approach*. New York: Wiley.

Wonnacott, T. H. and R. J. Wonnacott (1977), *Introductory Statistics for Business and Economics*, 2nd. ed. New York: Wiley.

Working, E. J. (1927), "What do statistical demand curves show?" *QJE*, Vol. 41, pp. 212–235.

Yasui, T. (1965), "The CES production function: A Note," *ECTRA*, Vol. 33, pp. 646–648.

Zellner, A. (1957), "The short-run consumption function," *ECTRA*, Vol. 25, pp. 552–567.

Zellner, A. (1961), "Econometric estimation with temporally dependent disturbance terms," *IER*, Vol. 2, pp. 164–178.

Zellner, A. (1962), "An efficient method of estimating seemingly unrelated regressions and tests for aggregation bias," *JASA*, Vol. 57, pp. 348–368.

Zellner, A. (1966), "On the analysis of first order autoregressive models with incomplete data," *IER*, Vol. 7, pp. 72–76.

Zellner, A. (ed.) (1968), *Readings in Economic Statistics and Econometrics, Part II*. Boston: Little, Brown and Co.

Zellner, A. (1970), *Introduction to Bayesian Inference in Econometrics*. New York: Wiley.

Zellner, A. and V. K. Chetty (1965), "Prediction and decision problems in regression models from the Bayesian point of view," *JASA*, Vol. 60, pp. 608–616.

Zellner, A. J. and J. Dreze (1966), "Specification and estimation of Cobb-Douglas production function models," *ECTRA*, Vol. 34, pp. 784–795.

Zellner, A. and D. S. Huang (1962), "Further properties of efficient estimators for seemingly unrelated regression equations," *IER*, Vol. 3, pp. 300–313.

Zellner, A. and H. Theil (1962), "Three-stage least squares: Simultaneous estimation of simultaneous equations," *ECTRA*, Vol. 30, pp. 54–78.

Zellner, A. and H. Thornber (1960), "A symposium on simultaneous equation estimation," *ECTRA*, Vol. 28, pp. 835–871.

Zellner, A. and H. Thornber (1966), "Computational accuracy and estimation of simultaneous equation econometric models," *ECTRA*, Vol. 34, pp. 727–729.

Zellner, A. and G. C. Tiao (1964), "Bayesian analysis of the regression model with auto-correlated errors," *JASA*, Vol. 59, pp. 763–778.

INDEX

Book # 12566659